The
Truth
and the Trident

Draws the line between truth and error.

The forgotten doctrine of God

and it's significance for

the present day.

****

By
Barry Mellor

Third Edition

Published by:
Wilderness Publishing
919 Swafford Rd.
Spring City, TN 37381
Email: wildernesspublishing@outlook.com

All Scripture used in this book is from the Authorized King James Version.

All emphasis in this book is expressly the author's unless otherwise stated.

ACKNOWLEDGEMENTS:

I am totally indebted to our Heavenly Father, to Jesus our Saviour and to our other Comforter and Guide, the Holy Spirit for all the truth contained in these pages.

Also, I am deeply indebted to Patrick Jones, for His unfailing support and encouragement, for his contributions to the content of this book, especially the precious insight into how the lintel and the two side-posts, to which the Hebrews applied the blood on the night of the Exodus, constitute the true symbol of the Heavenly Trio: the Godhead.

To God be the glory!

Printed in the United States of America

Third Edition

Copyright Ⓒ 2014

Library of Congress Control Number: (Pending)

ISBN #: 978-1-4951-0873-0

Published by
Wilderness Publishing

TABLE OF CONTENTS

Chapter	Title	Page
	INTRODUCTION	V
1	THE HISTORY OF TRINITARIANISM IS CHECKERED AND TROUBLING	1
2	THE SDA PIONEERS AND THE TRINITY DOCTRINE	23
3	CATHOLIC CATECHISM AND THE 'TRINITY' VS. THE TRUTH	55
4	JOHN HARVEY KELLOGG AND THE TRINITY	63
5	FROM THE ALPHA TO THE OMEGA	74
6	THE TRINITY DOCTRINE—THE WINE OF BABYLON	91
7	M. L. ANDREASEN AND THE TRINITY	97
8	ANOTHER PERSPECTIVE OFTHE 1913 F.M. WILCOX "TRINITY" STATEMENT	101
9	THE OMEGA OF APOSTASY	110
10	MICHAEL = CHRIST: The Pre-Incarnation, Divine Second Person of the Godhead	139
11	WHO IS MICHAEL THE ARCHANGEL?	150
12	WHEN WAS JESUS BEGOTTEN?	158
13	THREE-IN-ONE OR ONE-IN-THREE?	167
14	THOUGHTS ON MELCHIZEDEK	190
15	AN INTRODUCTION TO THE DOCTRINE OF THE GODHEAD	203
16	LIVING WATER	218
17	LIVING WATER AND THE TREE OF LIFE	225
18	ALL MANNER OF … BLASPHEMY	233
19	THE ROLE OF THE HOLY SPIRIT IN THE PLAN OF SALVATION	244
20	GOD COMMUNICATES WITH MAN THROUGH CHRIST, THE HOLY SPIRIT, AND ANGELS	252
21	MEMBERS OF THE GODHEAD ARE DISTINCT PERSONS	260
22	THE MOST HIGH GOD, THE GOD OF GODS	273
23	THE SHEMMAH	294
24	THE HOLY SPIRIT AND THE TABLE OF SHOWBREAD	304

25 THE "ONE"NESS OF THE GODHEAD AND OF CHRIST'S FOLLOWERS 308

26 THE "FULLNESS OF THE GODHEAD" 322

27 THE DIVINE POWER EXERCISED BY CHRIST DURING THE INCARNATION 327

28 WHAT JESUS LAID ASIDE IN ORDER TO REACH US 330

29 THE LIFE HE LAID DOWN 364

30 WHAT POWER RAISED JESUS FROM THE DEAD AND RAISES THE REDEEMED?
    373

31 THE 'SPIRIT' OF A MAN 391

32 THE UNKNOWN GOD 399

33 WHO ARE WE PRAYING TO? 407

34 TRINITARIANISM DISTORTS THE TRUTH—PART ONE 417

35 TRINITARIANISM DISTORTS THE TRUTH—PART TWO 427

36 TRINITARIANISM DISTORTS THE TRUTH—PART THREE 436

37 TRINITARIANISM TRENDS TO BAD 'BIRDS' 445

38 EKRON'S "ELIXIR" 449

39 WHOM DO WE WORSHIP: THE GOD OF THE FIRST DAY OR THE GOD OF THE
    SABBATH? 472

40 AN EXHORTATION 500

41 A SYNOPSIS: THE TRUE GOD OF THE BIBLE 509

42 TRI-THEISM AND THE TRUTH 550

43 WORTHY, WORTHY, IS THE LAMB 554

44 A TRUE KNOWLEDGE OF GOD 560

APPENDICES 574

BIBLIOGRAPHY 610

iv

INTRODUCTION

I am a Seventh-day Adventist. I firmly believe that God has given a special 'message of mercy to a dying world', to His denominated people to disseminate throughout the world: a message that begins with the call to **"Fear God, and give glory to him**; for the hour of his judgment is come: ..." (Revelation 14:7) God's final message to the world includes a call for His earthly children to be aware of the fact that "Babylon's" final fall is heralded by her enforcing her intoxicating "wine of the wrath of her fornications" upon "all nations" (Revelation 14:8). This alert is followed by the warning **not to worship the "beast and his image"** if one desires to avoid receiving the "wine of the wrath of God." (Revelation 14:9, 10) There is awe-inspiring privilege and responsibility resting upon all who acknowledge and accept God's call to give these messages. Never, never be ashamed to be a Seventh-day Adventist. However, we need to "weep between the porch and the altar" (Joel 2:17) because of the abominations that have been insinuated in among us. It is time to cry: "Spare thy people, O LORD" (Joel 2:17). It is time to "Cry aloud, spare not" (Isaiah 58:1) and to show God's denominated people their sins and iniquities and plead with God to take care of our own personal ones.

Among us, as Seventh-day Adventists: God's "denominated people" (Counsels to Writers and Editors, 109.3), there is a fairly general consensus of opinion that "we have nothing to fear for the future..." (Counsels to the Church, 359.4) as far as the church "going through" is concerned. In our drowsy Laodicean state we recite but seem to fail to grasp the significance of the words that follow those given in the partial quote penned above; words given by God's messenger as a **warning** as well as an encouragement. She goes on to introduce the **condition** upon which God's people can base their confidence in the future; God's messenger says: "We have nothing to fear for the future, **EXCEPT** as we shall forget the way the Lord has led us, **AND His teaching in our past history.**"

As a people we seem to love to have smooth things preached to us from the pulpit. We love to hear that 'the ship is going through' (*Review & Herald* 9-20-1892, par. 13) and that "enfeebled and defective as it may appear, the church is the one object upon which God bestows in a special sense His supreme regard" (Acts of the Apostles, 12.1); the 'church' is 'the apple of God's eye' (*Signs of the Times*, 7-13-1904, par. 2), etc. We seem to forget that God's Word declares the principle that "if thine eye **offend thee,** pluck it out" (Matt. 18:9). The question can rightfully be asked: Is a major component, among God's denominated people, offending God at this time? We also tend to forget the **principle** that God operates on, as conveyed to us by His messenger in Upward Look, page 131.3: "The Lord Jesus will always have a **chosen people** to serve Him. When the Jewish people rejected Christ, the Prince of life, He took from them the kingdom of God and gave it unto the Gentiles. **God will continue to work on this principle with every branch of His work. When a church proves unfaithful to the word of the Lord, whatever their position may be, however high and sacred their calling, the Lord can no longer work with them. Others are then chosen to bear important responsibilities."** (The Jews looked for a false Christ. God's denominated people are falling into the same trap in looking for a 'Trinitarian Christ'.)

As a church we tend to ascribe the 'ship' that is "going through" to being the 'organizational structure' of the denomination. God's messenger, on the other hand makes it very clear that the 'ship' that will safely reach the 'haven of rest' is the 'vessel' of **TRUTH**! (9 Manuscript Releases, 361.1, 2). Indeed God's messenger describes **another 'vessel'** the condition of which we should pay special heed to: **"The facts concerning the real condition of the professed people of God, speak more loudly than their profession,** and make it evident that **some power has cut the cable that anchored them to the Eternal Rock, and that they are drifting away to sea, without chart or compass**. " (*Review & Herald*, July 24, 1888 par. 1)

Our **history** demonstrates, beyond dispute, that the organizational structure of the denomination is **NOT** the "church". God's **PEOPLE** acquired the name "Seventh-day Adventist" on September 29, **1860**: they were God's 'denominated' people: His "church" on earth. As God's church on earth they **adopted a system of organization** in order to facilitate Church growth, management and outreach: **Organization was to be a TOOL** in the hands of God's church: a 'vehicle' for global evangelization. **The General Conference of Seventh-day Adventists was organized in May of 1863**. God ordained that His church be established first; established before organization was adopted, as an eternal object lesson to the truth that the "church" are His **people**: those "who love God and keep His commandments" (Upward Look, 315), even if they are a "humble few". (Ibid)

The book that you hold in your hands assails the denominational departure from God's teaching in our past history, particularly with regard to the 'Doctrine of God'! For some two thousand years the church of God and the nominal church have wrestled with a true understanding of this doctrine. **The great "whore" of Revelation, the apostate church system that rides the "beast" of united "church-craft" and "state-craft" evolved, under very dubious circumstances, the doctrine of the "Trinity".** The readers of this book will discover, in the pages of this book, just why this doctrine is false, and also the ramification of error that this deadly false doctrine leads to. The reader will also discover how, gradually and insidiously, the enemy of souls has, through his witting and unwitting agents, transformed the Seventh-day Adventist **organization** from a non-Trinitarian to a fully Trinitarian **organization** that is consequently leading God's denominated people, His church, astray. Our religion has been changed!

The topic of **this** book is: The 'Doctrine of God', and is infinite in scope. Men have wrestled with this doctrine for centuries, but God's denominated people have been privileged to receive precious instruction and insight through His messenger to His people. As the pages of this book will demonstrate, beyond dispute, Ellen White and her husband James never endorsed, but actively disputed, the erroneous amalgam of paganism and misapplied Scripture which constitutes the doctrine termed 'Trinitarianism'. In putting together this book the author has, in his human frailty, attempted to look at the 'Doctrine of God' from many related angles. This approach has necessitated quite a degree of the repetitious use of certain quotations and conclusions. Should the reader be perturbed by this please blame it on the author's limitations.

The author of this book is totally convinced that most of God's denominated people have a true, but somewhat uncrystalized, concept of the Godhead: that the Godhead is comprised of three separate and distinct entities whose 'one'-ness is incomprehensible. Many sincere and devoted Seventh-day Adventists think that the terms 'Trinity' and 'Godhead' are synonymous appellations which both describe the same "mystery". There are others, however, who have drunk deeply of the 'wine' of 'Babylon' and have, and still are, entrenching a totally false perception concerning the 'Doctrine of God' among the people of God. At the highest levels they have met with singular success and the false 'Doctrine of God' is gradually percolating down through the echelons of church membership to the rank and file laity. This book will discover to the reader the source of these errors, the agencies introducing them to God's people, and the successful institutionalization of this soul jeopardizing error. This book will discover to the reader the soul destroying byways of error that this false teaching called Trinitarianism leads to. This book will discover to the reader and make plain how far a departure has been made from the truth on this topic, and the consequences of that departure from the faith of our spiritual fathers, and from the faith of God's messenger to His remnant people.

There is never any joy in bringing to the light aberrant, soul destroying errors, or in exposing to all the agents and agencies involved in the dissemination of these abominations. Nevertheless, God demands that error be met (Upward Look, 88.2; 1Selected Messages, 205.3), that wrong teaching and practice be identified (4 Bible Commentary, 1156.8) and not covered up. The correction has to be as broad as the injury given: "...

vii

When men endanger the work and cause of God by their own wrong course of action, shall they hear no voice of reproof? **If the wrongdoer only were concerned, and the work reached no farther than him, he alone should have the words of warning; but when his _[or 'their']_ course of action is doing positive harm to the cause of truth, and souls are imperiled, God requires that the warning be as broad as the injury done.** The testimonies will not be hindered. The words of rebuke and warning, the plain "Thus saith the Lord," will come from God's appointed agencies; for the words do not originate with the human instrument; they are from God, who appointed them their work...." (2 Selected Messages, 152.4) **This is not a Matthew 18:15-17 situation where one goes to one's brother in private to discuss the perceived "hurt"; this is a 1 Timothy 5:20 situation which says: "Them that sin rebuke before all, that others also may fear."** God's Word puts it this way: "Preach the word; be instant in season, out of season; reprove, rebuke, exhort with all longsuffering and doctrine." (2Tim. 4:2). Isa. 58:1 is even more explicit: "Cry aloud, spare not, lift up thy voice like a trumpet, and show my people their transgression, and the house of Jacob their sins."

God's messenger tells us in plain American English: **"If wrongs are apparent among His people, and if the servants of God pass on indifferent to them, they virtually sustain and justify the sinner, and are alike guilty and will just as surely receive the displeasure of God; for they will be made responsible for the sins of the guilty.** In vision I have been pointed to many instances where the displeasure of God has been incurred by a neglect on the part of His servants to deal with the wrongs and sins existing among them. **Those who have excused these wrongs have been thought by the people to be very amiable and lovely in disposition, simply because they shunned to discharge a plain Scriptural duty.** The task was not agreeable to their feelings; therefore they avoided it. (Testimonies Volume 3, 265.2)

"The true people of God, who have the spirit of the work of the Lord and the salvation of souls at heart, will ever view sin _[the dissemination of error is sin]_ in its real, sinful character. They will always be on the side of faithful and plain dealing with sins which easily beset the people of God. **Especially in the closing work for the church**, in the sealing time of the one hundred and forty-four thousand who are to stand without fault before the throne of God, will they feel most deeply the wrongs of God's professed people. This is forcibly set forth by the prophet's illustration of the last work under the figure of the men each having a slaughter weapon in his hand. One man among them was clothed with linen, with a writer's inkhorn by his side. "And the Lord said unto him, Go through the midst of the city, through the midst of Jerusalem, and set a mark upon the foreheads of the men that

sigh and that cry for all the abominations that be done in the midst thereof."
(Testimonies Volume 3, 266.2)

"**Who are standing in the counsel of God at this time? Is it those who virtually excuse wrongs among the professed people of God and who murmur in their hearts, if not openly, against those who would reprove sin? Is it those who take their stand against them and sympathize with those who commit wrong?** No, indeed! Unless they repent, and leave the work of Satan in oppressing those who have the burden of the work and in holding up the hands of sinners in Zion, they will never receive the mark of God's sealing approval. They will fall in the general destruction of the wicked, represented by the work of the five men bearing slaughter weapons. Mark this point with care: Those who receive **the pure mark of TRUTH, wrought in them by the power of the Holy Ghost,** represented by a mark by the man in linen, are those "that sigh and that cry for all the abominations that be done" in the church. Their love for purity and the honor and glory of God is such, and they have so clear a view of the exceeding sinfulness of sin, that they are represented as being in agony, even sighing and crying. Read the ninth chapter of Ezekiel. (Testimonies Volume 3, 267.1)

Referring specifically to "error", and its spiritually corrosive nature, God's messenger declares: "Each may have heaven's light to guide him. If we discern the truth, and obey it, our whole course of action will be in accordance with the truth; for **the truth sanctifies the receiver**. But if men refuse to search for the truth as for hidden treasure**, if the mind is pleased with the theories of error, the soul will remain in darkness. The course of the life, the development of the character, will be corrupted by false sentiments. Error never sanctifies. It can do no good. And how full of darkness is the soul that receives error as truth, and shapes his course of action in accordance with it.**" *Review & Herald*, August 23, 1898 par.2.

"**No error is of the truth, and error never sanctifies the receiver. It is by the truth that we are to be sanctified. Error possesses no sanctifying power.** It can not save the soul. **How careful, then, should the teachers of truth be that their words are true words**,--words such as fall from the lips of the great Teacher!" *Southern Watchman*, March 1, 1904 par. 6.

We are called to be "Bereans" with regard to that which we are taught: "The minds of the Bereans were not narrowed by prejudice, and **they were willing to investigate and receive the truths preached by the apostles**. If men and women would follow the example of the noble Bereans, in searching the Scriptures daily, and in **comparing the messages brought to them with what is there recorded**, there would be thousands loyal to God's law, where there is one today. **Even many who profess to love God**

have no desire to change from error to truth, but cling to the pleasing fables of Satan's creation. Error never sanctifies the receiver; but truth of heavenly origin purifies the heart." (*pamphlet 8 of 'Redemption: or the Teachings of Paul, and his Mission to the Gentiles' series,* pg. 51.1)

The Word of God in John 17:3 tells us of the salvational importance of the topic we are engaged in: **"And this is life eternal, that they might know thee the only true God, and Jesus Christ, whom thou hast sent."** God's messenger endorses the importance of this verse, and the depth of meaning it contains, and our responsibility regarding this great truth: "All to whom the heavenly inspiration has come are put in trust with the gospel. **The most solemn responsibility rests upon them to devote their powers to making known the only true God, and Jesus Christ, whom he has sent**...." (*Review and Herald*, August 23, 1898 par. 3) This is a fundamental part of the first Angel's message: "Fear God, and give glory to him; for the hour of his judgment is come: and worship him that made heaven, and earth, and the sea, and the fountains of waters." Revelation 14:7.

The enemy of souls will endeavor to interpose between God's people and the Light; especially on this salvationally significant subject which he has striven for centuries to obscure. Many will rise up in rejection of the truth about the Godhead, because they are "comfortable" with old and cherished deceptions. Nevertheless, God's messenger has left us the following clear instruction which came to her from God: **"I am instructed to say that we must do all we possibly can for these deceived ones. Their minds must be freed from the delusions of the enemy, and if we fail in our efforts to save these erring ones, we must "come out from among them" and be separate.**--*Manuscript* 106, 1905, page 8. (**"A Plea for Loyalty,"** November 20, 1905.) (7 Manuscript Releases, 190.1) We must remember that **it is 'loyalty' to God and His truth that is here being spoken of in this title given to *Manuscript* 106**.

To anyone who maintains that the quote from 7MR 190.1 is not referring to "deceived ones" in the Adventist denomination, but to "deceived ones" in Babylon, the author wishes to refer such gainsayers to the context from which this quote from 7MR 190.1 comes. The reader will not find the context on page 190 of 7MR, but must needs find it in Upward Look page 338 which quotes much more extensively from the article "A Plea for Loyalty" penned by God's messenger, November 20, 1905 and kept as *Manuscript* 106 at the E.G. White Estate. Using the CD Rom it is not possible to access this complete document (I wonder why?). However, by placing Upward Look page 338 together with 7MR 190.1 it is patently clear that the words of this last mentioned paragraph were, and are, indeed directed at God's denominated people, and not relegated to those outside Adventist ranks.

Introduction

There are some who have perceived the insidious error inherent in Trinitarianism through their reading of the writings of some of the SDA pioneers who, while opposing Trinitarianism, had injected so called "Arian" (or Semi-Arian) concepts into their speculations on the doctrine of God: Making of Christ a Being "begotten" at some point in infinite pre-history. Some of these pioneers also perceived the Holy Spirit to be an emanation of God's and Christ's power and not a Divine Being in His own right. In their opposition to the correctly perceived anti-Trinitarianism espoused by these said pioneers, these persons who have read the pioneer's works have also, mistakenly, accepted the so-called 'Arian' and 'Semi-Arian' speculations of these aforesaid pioneers. Consequently these have written copiously, and preached widely, a message that God's messenger preached and wrote against. God's messenger repeatedly wrote against the false notion that Christ was "begotten" at some point in infinity. In so doing she was refuting both the "Arian" notion and the Catholic notion that Christ was "generated" at some point in infinity, and is subsequently being continuously "generated". This book will discover to the reader the truth about the Godhead: A truth that sanctions neither the Catholic Trinity nor the "Arian" or "Semi-Arian" 'two-Person' Godhead' doctrine that is making its presence felt among God's denominated people.

The reader will discover that Trinitarianism is the glue that coheres the whole, and invidiously successful, ecumenical movement together. Trinitarianism has been the facilitator in introducing a false "New Theology" 'Christ' among God's people. Trinitarianism has been the facilitator in drawing denominational leaders into more than tentative ecumenical involvement.

May God help His people to arouse and purchase, without money and without price, the heavenly eye salve which will bring clear spiritual perception and lead them to buy of the heavenly Merchantman gold tried in the fire and white raiment that the shame of nakedness be covered.

May God save us all from the deceptions of the enemy is my sincere prayer.

Chapter 1

THE HISTORY OF TRINITARIANISM IS CHECKERED AND TROUBLING

William knocked on the door of his professor's office at the college he was attending. William was a Seventh-day Adventist student training to be a gospel minister at a small Seventh-day Adventist college. (However it could not be called by that name. We should mention to the reader that this was in a day when to put the name "Seventh-day Adventist" in the name of the college, would have meant a certain lawsuit from those who had usurped the name from God's people and trademarked it under commercial law **employing a Catholic lawyer** to get this done.) He was invited in by Professor Miller, a longtime faculty member at this small Seventh-day Adventist College, and with earnest inquiry William began to ask the question that puzzled him.

WILLIAM: Professor Miller, I have been asked by certain friends from Southern Adventist University if I believe in the Trinity. I told them I did, but I am not quite sure if I know what the Trinity doctrine really is.

(Professor Miller smiled and shook his head.)

PROFESSOR: You have brought up a doctrine that is very broad and has deep and far-reaching consequences for God's people. It is a doctrine that is built up more by pride, greed, and force than by any clear Scripture. But since most Christian church systems teach it, it is accepted as truth by the laity, who put their trust in the clergy. But frankly, William, most people don't know what the Trinity doctrine really teaches, even though the term is used ubiquitously.

WILLIAM: Yes, you hear the word all the time.

PROFESSOR: William, I believe you are an honest seeker for truth. Let me first give you a brief history of that doctrine. I think that a greater grasp of the history and the implications involved in the doctrine of the **Trinity,** will lead you to reject the doctrine—a doctrine which, we will also see, has **no foundation in Scripture.**

WILLIAM: In my mind, I see the Father, and the Son, and the Holy Spirit—three divine Persons. Isn't that the Trinity?

PROFESSOR: Many people think the same way you do. And they think that that is what the Trinity doctrine teaches, but it is not. What you have described to me, is actually the true Biblical doctrine of the Godhead, which rises as a standard against the false doctrine of the enemy. The Trinity is more complicated than that which you have described. It will take some time, but may God bless you as we prayerfully study this matter. Let us pray to the Father in Jesus's name that He would send us the Holy Spirit to guide us into the truth as we consider what follows.

(Professor Miller and William knelt down and asked for the promised Gift as they renewed the surrender of their wills to God. As they arose, Professor Miller then went to the bookshelf behind him and pulled out a volume.)

PROFESSOR: This is <u>History of Christianity</u>, written by Edward Gibbons, who was not a Christian. In the Preface, he writes this:

> "If **Paganism** was conquered by **Christianity,** it is equally true that **Christianity** was corrupted by **Paganism**. The pure Deism of the first **Christians**... was changed by the Church of Rome **into the incomprehensible dogma of the Trinity.** Many of the **Pagan** tenets, invented by the Egyptians and idealized by Plato, were retained as being worthy of belief."

Interesting comment from the historian, isn't it, William? Remember, however, that Gibbons trashed all Christianity, including the incarnation of Christ. Nevertheless, his observation on the Trinity dogma and its pagan origins is valid.

WILLIAM: Oh! So the Trinity doctrine has roots in the earlier teachings of Egypt and Greece?

PROFESSOR: If not Babylon, also. Corrupted notions on the personality of God and members of the Godhead occurred well before the third century AD when the first real application of the term "Trinity" was made by Tertullian (AD 160-225). **Tertullian** was one of the earliest **Western** churchmen to write in Latin and he is also credited with inventing the word **'persona'**. (See Appendix A) Tertullian is credited with having added 509 new nouns, 284 new adjectives, and 162 new verbs to the Latin glossary. It was Tertullian who put forward the term **'persona'** to translate the Greek

2

word '**hypostasis**': a term that could more accurately be rendered as "**mode of manifestation**". Tertullian's Latin term '**persona**' was **also used to refer to theater masks, theater figures or roles**. The early, apostatizing, Western church 'decided' (?) that God is a "person", but the conceptual connotations that they assumed into that term diverge substantially from our present application of the word. The Catholic Church employs Tertullian's 'persona' when describing the '**persons**' of the Trinity: they are but '**modes of manifestation**' and not distinct, self-existent, divine Persons.

The earliest, discovered use of the term "Trinity" among Christians appears to be where Theophilus of Antioch, used the term in his letter to the pagan Autolycus in 181 AD. (See Appendix B) However, Theophilus' use of the term did not denote the "Trinity" with the meaning as concocted at the Council of Nicea in 325 AD, or as defined in the Athanasian Creed of the **fifth** century. (See Appendix C)

Theophilus' usage deployed the term as meaning "God," His "Word," and His "Wisdom." The Athanasian Creed, on the other hand, states "We worship one God in trinity, and trinity in unity, neither confounding the persons, **nor separating the substance.**" The full horror of this Romish invention will become clear as we proceed.

(Professor Miller went to the chalkboard and wrote down the following list as he described various related theological terms):

Nestorianism: which divided Christ's manhood from His divinity.

Monophysitism-Monotheletism: which held that Christ was not truly man.

Gnosticism: Keepers of secret knowledge and secret traditions, supposedly received from Christ, but actually derived from **heathen** poets and philosophers.

Among these perversions was another called:

Monarchianism, which was divided into two schools of thought:

A) **Dynamic Monarchianism, (Adoptionism):** which held that Christ was only human, but was "adopted" and given Divine power.
B) **Modalism:** which held that there was only God, who acted out three modes of "God" portraying the Father in the role of the Creator, the Son as the Redeemer, and the Holy Spirit as the Guide for the Church. This view has adapted the **Heathen Trinity** of one god with three heads, or one head

3

with three faces, each portraying one of the three roles of the triune deity. **Modalism** is the concept which most concerns **Trinitarianism**.

(At this point, Professor Miller tapped the chalkboard for emphasis, and then he turned to William, and said):

PROFESSOR: William, as we study, I will show you that the Bible and God's messenger, Ellen White, refutes and countermands every one of these errors.

WILLIAM: Tell me more about Modalism then, Professor.

PROFESSOR: OK, William, but what happened in history gets a little complicated, so listen closely.
  In AD 264, a synod was convened at Antioch. Antioch was the place where Christ's followers were first called "Christians", and also the place that was "home" to the **Antiochian Text.** This text was used in the **Textus Receptus,** and is also the ancestor of the Waldensian Bible, and the **King James Version [KJV]** Bible.
  Anyway, they gathered there to consider the beliefs of a bishop in Antioch who believed in **Modalistic Monarchianism.** Instead of teaching that the Father and Son were two separate and distinct persons, he taught that **they were the very same Being—one God,** who became the Son at the time of the incarnation; and, at Pentecost, He became the Holy Spirit. This branch of **Monarchianism** claimed that the Father, Son and Holy Spirit were "*Homoousios*"—all three were of **one substance**; or one being only. (The English word used to denote this state is "**Consubstantiality**", meaning "the same identical, indivisible substance"!)

WILLIAM: I don't quite understand this concept of "consubstantiality." Can you explain a little more please?

PROFESSOR: In other words, the Father, Son and Holy Spirit were not of a "like substance", for that would imply three separate beings of "like substance" in the same way that three separate human beings are of like substance.
  You see, William, we are both of like substance, but we are not of the "same, identical, indivisible substance." **Consubstantiality (Homoousios)** on the other hand, implied three Emanations and actions of "one substance," that is, of a **one God-Being.** Here is a Catholic depiction of this concept.

4

WILLIAM: Yow! I don't believe that!

PROFESSOR: Unfortunately, many Seventh-day Adventists do. Here, look at this (See Appendix D to see what the Professor showed William). The **Synod at Antioch rightly condemned this teaching as heresy.** However, this heresy continued to surface, as we shall see.

A similar heresy, borrowed from **Heathenism,** came to be known as **Sabellianism.** Sabellianism taught that "God" was revealed in three ways, in the same sense as the sun is (1) bright, (2) hot and (3) round, a portrayal of a "Triune God," perceived in three different ways.

Both **Modalistic Monarchianism** and **Sabellianism** have been taught by many Roman Catholics throughout history. In countries where **Heathenism** abounded, the papal church has used pictures of exactly the same three-faced idols of the Heathen to denote their beliefs.

(Professor Miller had taken his laptop, typed in "Three-faced god," and found just such pictures.)

PROFESSOR: During the **nineteenth century** (and through the twentieth century to the present) Modalistic Monarchianism was rife among Roman Catholics, as we shall see.

Let me show you another picture. This is a picture of **a Celtic medallion that shows "Lugh"—the three faced god.**

Let me show you another one. This is a picture of **the three-faced Hindu god—Shiva.**

You see, it is a concept straight from heathenism. The Hindus called this the **"Trimurti".**

As the Scriptures state, Satan is the "god of this world." He is one individual, but manifests himself in various ways in order to deceive. He will even manifest himself as Christ. He frequently appears as the "spirit" of some departed person, as occurred when the witch of Endor brought up "Samuel."

This **"Consubstantiality"** form of the **Trinity** doctrine confronted the pioneers of the SDA Church and, as we shall see, was fully repudiated. But the way God has led the SDA church in the past has been forgotten, and the error of Trinitarianism again confronts us today. Since it is now the official doctrine of the Seventh-day Adventist church, and all the other mainline churches, we are forced to decide if this is what the Bible teaches, or not.

WILLIAM: What did the SDA pioneers think of the Trinity?

PROFESSOR: I'll answer that question more fully later, but let me show you the objection raised by John N. Loughborough. He really highlights the tremendous assault that **Trinitarianism,** as put forward by the Papal Church, poses for the Biblical Sanctuary Doctrine which is so fundamental to Adventism.

(Professor Miller went to the latest EGW CD rom which also contained all the writings of the pioneers. There he found what Loughborough had written in the):

> *Review and Herald,* No.5, 1861, Volume18, page 184, and read:
> "To believe that doctrine *[the Trinity doctrine]* when reading the Scriptures, we must believe **that God sent Himself into the world, died to recover the world to Himself, raised Himself from the dead, ascended to Himself in Heaven, <u>pleads before Himself</u> in heaven to reconcile the world to Himself, and is the only Mediator between man and Himself...**"

WILLIAM: I can see that how we view God is very important. It affects other things that we believe.

PROFESSOR: Yes, William. It should be clear as we study this topic that the doctrine of the **Trinity**—with its concomitant and innate notion of **Consubstantiation**—will inexorably destroy a Seventh-day Adventist's belief in the Sanctuary doctrine. It is nonsense to believe in a God **interceding with Himself;** whereas we know that Jesus, a distinct divine, personal Being, is interceding on our behalf before His Father, also a distinct personal Being.

The way is left open in the **Trinitarian** belief system for **other mediators** between God and man, namely Popes, and prelates, priests and "Saints," and, of course, "Mary"! As we shall continue to discover, Trinitarian doctrine is indeed the foundational doctrine of all of Rome's intoxicating wine.

WILLIAM: So you're saying that the Trinity doctrine is like the trunk of a tree that has a lot of branches.

PROFESSOR: Absolutely!

7

(Professor Miller went to his file and pulled out an issue of *The Catholic Faith*, May/June, 2001. In it was an article written by John A. Hurdon, S.J.—a Jesuit—entitled "Catholic Doctrine on the Holy Trinity.") Let's go to the horse's mouth:

> "The mystery of **the Holy Trinity is the most fundamental of our faith. On it everything else depends and from it everything else derives.** Hence the Church's constant concern to safeguard **the revealed truth that God is <u>One in Nature</u> and Three in Persons.**"

WILLIAM: No wonder the SDA Sabbath School lesson for spring of 2006, Lesson 1, on the "Triune God" asked the question, "How can a three-pronged fork illustrate the nature of God?" The three prongs all have the same identical substance.

PROFESSOR: Good memory and good point. But God's messenger disagrees and emphatically declares that the members of the **Godhead** are "**one in purpose, in mind, in character, but not in person.** It is thus that God and Christ are one." <u>Ministry of Healing</u>, page 422.

WILLIAM: Yes, a perfect harmony! Like a trio of singers. Three distinct Persons, but blending their voices so beautifully, that it sounds like one. Yet each sings a different part that the others cannot sing.

PROFESSOR: Correct, William. A+. You wonder why they didn't suggest that to illustrate the nature and the structure of the Godhead in the 2006 Sabbath School quarterly.

In fact, William, the "nature" of Jesus is **now** radically different from that of his Father since Jesus has assumed human nature with which His divine nature is **blended** forever.

WILLIAM: **Does the Catholic Church still teach the Modalistic Monarchianism form of Trinitarianism?**

To answer that question, Professor Miller went to the bookshelf and pulled out the book entitled <u>The Holy Catholic Faith, or The Lamp of Truth in the Catholic Home Containing Beautiful Gems from the Writings of the Most Eminent Authorities on the Doctrines, Practices and Virtues of the One True Church</u>, Patrick L. Baine Publisher, Chicago, IL, Volume 1. On page 311 he found the following, which he read to William:

"Though there is but one God, nevertheless there is in this one God three totally distinct and different Persons, viz: God the Father, God the Son and God the Holy Ghost. **All three possessed not a similar, but the self-same nature..,. The Divine nature is not divided between the Persons.** Each possessed it in its integrity and fullness, **yet the Divine nature is not multiplied, but one and indivisible....**" The Holy Catholic Faith, page 311.

PROFESSOR: This defines *homoousios*: **Consubstantial.** This is **Modalistic Monarchianism** plain and simple... or should I say, it is **Sabellianistic** and incomprehensible and spiritualistic. I will read on:

"The Father is omnipotent, infinite and omniscient, The Son is omnipotent, infinite, and omniscient, *[Professor Miller paused, and said, "William, We know that Jesus surrendered His omnipotence, His omnipresence, His memory, His foreknowledge – at least during the incarnation. He had to learn at His mother's knee the very things which He had inspired the prophet to write. You can read this in Desire of Ages, page 70. He, Himself also claimed that He did not know the time of His second coming—That only the Father knew: Matthew 24:36, Mark 13:32. Let me continue reading:]* and the Holy Ghost is omnipotent, infinite and omniscient; yet **there are not three omnipotents, infinites and onmiscients, but only One infinite, One omnipotent and One omniscient.** The Three Divine persons, possessing the **self-same nature,** are **inseparable,** though distinct...." Ibid, page 311.

PROFESSOR: Do you know what this means, William?

WILLIAM: What?

PROFESOR: The above declaration denies by direct implication that a divine member of the Godhead—Jesus—was "in all points tempted like as we are." (Hebrews 4:15).

WILLIAM: How is that?

PROFESSOR: Because the Bible says that "God cannot be tempted." (James 1:13). If the Divine nature is one "inseparable" unit (one nature) shared by three separate manifestations thereof, **then to tempt Christ was impossible for God cannot be tempted.**

9

Furthermore, William, it was "**separation**" from His Father that brought about Jesus' death on the cross, wasn't it?

WILLIAM: Yes, the Bible says that Jesus cried out, "My God, My God, why hast Thou **forsaken** me?"

PROFESSOR: If the Father and the Son shared one **indivisible** nature, **separation would be impossible.** This clearly demonstrates the falsehood involved in this heretical notion of **consubstantiality.**

By the way, William, apart from the Gospels, I highly recommend (and urge) that you read what actually occurred at the cross in the following references from Ellen White's compiled books: That I Might Know Him, page 218, and The Story of Jesus, pages 145, 206, 209, 214, 312.

Now, let me read on in:

> The Holy Catholic Faith, page 311:
> "In Jesus Christ, therefore, there dwelt in... **inseparable unity**, the Father and the Holy Ghost. **It was not the divine nature which became man. Had the nature of God become man, the Father and the Holy Ghost would be truly man as well as the Eternal Son.**" Ibid., page 311.

WILLIAM: Jesus was Divine though, wasn't he?

PROFESSOR: Yes. The truth is that **in** Jesus, Divinity **was blended** with humanity. He, at His incarnation, was a **union** of humanity and divinity. See 1888 Materials, page 332, and Signs of the Times, 3/8/1899.

Now, let me read on in:

> The Holy Catholic Faith, page 311:
> "But since it was not the **nature**, but the person of God, and not the three Persons, but only the Second Person of the Blessed Trinity that was made man. The Father is not the man, not the Holy Ghost, but only God the Son. But though neither Father nor Holy Ghost became man, they are both **inseparably** and eternally united with the man Jesus Christ, who, as God, is one with them, and so far as His Divine nature and **essence** are concerned, indistinguishable from them."

Truly, such contradictory theological saber-dancing is indeed **"incomprehensible dogma!"** as the historian Gibbons declared.

WILLIAM: How did the Trinity doctrine become so dominant?

10

PROFESSOR: By the fourth century a most powerful challenge confronted the ascendancy of the Church of Rome—the "heresy" of **Arianism.**
The professor pulled another book off the shelf and read:

> "It involved the question of the divinity of Christ and His relation to the Father, and indirectly the whole dogma of the **Trinity.**" (A Dictionary of Christian Biography, Sir William Smith & Henry Wace London, John Murray, 1877, Volume 1, article: *Arianism*, page 144)

PROFESSOR: Arius, a Presbyter (a priest, not a bishop) of Alexandria had views which challenged **Trinitarianism.** Arius, from whom the name "Arian" is derived, was not the first to challenge Rome on its dogma concerning God, but his challenge led to a series of violent controversies which shook the Roman Empire to its very base, especially in the East.

WILLIAM: What exactly did he teach?

PROFESSOR: There is little agreement in the various explanations as to what Arius actually taught. Various authors are dependent upon what previous writers wrote, who themselves were dependent upon what others had said, none of whom may have had the writings of Arius, but in their own words gave the supposed belief. On one hand, he is believed to have regarded Jesus as a created being, "the beginning of the creation of God" (Revelation 3:14), but bear in mind, that this actually refers to the Word who created all things. (John 1:1-3, Colossians 1:15, 17, 18). So the Word was therefore the One who **began the creation process and carried it through at God the Father's behest. God the Father created the universe through His Son (Heb. 1:2, 2:10; Eph. 3:9), therefore Jesus is "the beginning of the creation of God," and not Himself a created Being.**
On the other hand, Arius did oppose that figment of spiritism, namely "consubstantiation".
One writer, attempting to explain **Arianism**, stated that Arius taught that:

> "God cannot create the world directly, but only through an agent, the Logos (Word), who is himself created for the purpose of creating the world.... Christ is Himself a creature, the first creature of God, through whom the father created other creatures..."—A Dictionary of Christian Biography, Volume 1, article *Arianism*, pages 155-156.

WILLIAM: Do you think that is true, Professor?

PROFESSOR: As very few of the Arian manuscripts exist today, (Rome is very good at eliminating evidence she does not like) one cannot totally refute the above statement. **However, since we are seeing the very same charges made against anti-Trinitarians today, it is more likely that the accusation is indeed false.** Listen to this:

> The Concise Oxford Dictionary, (page 60) under *'Arian'* defines Arius' teachings as follows:
> "(*Holder*) of the doctrine of Arius of Alexandria (*4th century*), who denied [*the*] **consubstantiality** of Christ."

This sounds closer to the truth concerning **Arianism.** Remember, it was predicted that Rome would "wear out the **saints** of the Most High." Daniel 7:25.

It is noteworthy that those kings who subscribed to Arius' teachings were those "worn out" by the Papal forces. Indeed, Phillipus Limborch doubts that Arius himself ever held that Christ was created. –Limborch, The History of the Inquisition, London, 1731, page 95.

Some believe that Arius contended that Christ was the literal only-begotten Son of His heavenly Father. They believe he was simply taking John 3:16 as it reads: "For God so love the world, that He gave **His only-begotten Son**..." We will later investigate this view in some depth. (See pages 16, 17 and Chapter 12 in this book).

> The Century Dictionary and Cyclopedia, Volume1, Article *Arian*, page 308, states:
> "Arius... held that the Son was begotten of the Father, and therefore not **co-eternal,** nor **consubstantial with the Father,** but created by, and subordinate... to the Father, though possessing a similar nature..."

We notice that each writer explains Arius' beliefs **differently.** It is no wonder that there is confusion as to what Arius actually believed. However, **one thing is certain: Those who opposed Trinitarianism believed that the Ten Commandments—which included the Sabbath Commandment—are the moral law of God, perfect, eternal and unchangeable. They also believed in religious liberty.**

(Professor Miller turned to a well-worn volume laying on his desk and read):

12

Truth Triumphant, B. G. Wilkinson, Teach Services, c. 1994, page 94:

"All the disputants over the **Trinity** recognized that when God made man **in His image**, it was the equivalent of writing the Ten Commandments in His heart by creating man with a **flawless** moral nature.... *[After sin, man had broken the law and defaced the "image of God" in man. Trinitarianism teaches that Jesus was a "modality" of the one-god substance, and that therefore, only His human body died at Calvary, and that his "god-modality" returned to heaven; while His soul/spirit went to preach to the souls in hell. This means we have only a human sacrifice. Accordingly, the One who was equal with the law did not die. Therefore, the law is changeable, according to this doctrine]* Those who rejected the intense, exacting definition of three Divine Persons sharing One body *[common substance]* as laid down by the Council of Nicaea, **believed that Calvary had made Christ a Divine Sacrifice, the sinner's Substitute.** *[Only One equal with the law could pay the "penalty" of the law—thus establishing the law's eternally binding claims.]* The Papacy repudiated the teaching that Jesus died as man's substitute upon the cross."

WILLIAM: Why was that?

PROFESSOR: **Because, to the Papacy, the law is not binding!** It can—according to them—be changed by the Pope: hence Sunday worship. To the Papacy, Jesus' crucifixion was not substitutionary, but was **a 'sacrifice'—as in a heathen 'appeasement sacrifice.'** (That is why Catholic film-maker Mel Gibson's money-making movie, "The Passion of Christ" **focused on the physical pain** endured by Jesus Christ at His crucifixion. From this horrid misconception comes the notion of 'doing penance;' of 'self-flagellation;' 'vows of silence;' 'pilgrimages;' the continual 'sacrifice of the mass' and other rites of 'appeasement' as practiced in Romanism.)

Furthermore, the Papacy, by

"...repudiating the teaching that Jesus died as man's **Substitute** upon the cross, consequently... ignored the exalted place given to the Decalogue *[including the fourth commandment]* by the crucifixion of Christ. **Those who saw the eternal necessity of magnifying the law and making it honorable, maintained that death claimed the Son of God, but had left untouched the Father and the Holy Spirit.**" Ibid, page 94.

13

This was because they were recognized as separate and distinct Divine Persons—not emanations of One substance, as decreed by Rome.

WILLIAM: The amazing thing is that something so subtle, so seemingly true, like the Trinity doctrine, can be so diabolical.

PROFESSOR: William, can you see **that the Catholic Trinity doctrine leads inexorably to a rejection of the binding nature of God's law.** If Christ was not man's substitute, then the law is of lesser consequence and therefore subject to being changed—as attempted by the "man of sin." Such notions lead to the Sabbath being "lightly regarded." Once such a stance is consciously or unconsciously accepted, it leads the "worldly, world loving class" to "abandon their position" and "join the ranks of the opposition." (Great Controversy, Ellen G. White, page 608). Such are the invidious results of accepting **Trinitarianism.**

WILLIAM: It's the broad, popular road that leads to destruction.

PROFESSOR: But on the way, there's a lot of money to be made. Because of his belief that God the Father, God the Son and God the Holy Spirit were not **consubstantial,** but rather were separate and distinct Divine Persons, the teachings of Arius caused great concern to the Papal Church. Those princely priests, who craved the crown but shunned the cross, correctly discerned that Arius' teachings on this issue would directly undermine their **goldmine** of "pilgrimages" and their continual "sacrifices" of the mass, for which revenue was levied, to appease the "wrath of God" and get souls out of purgatory, etc.

Also, if the law of God was unchangeable (as the substitutionary death of Jesus proves) how can the Papacy justify the change that they "made" to the law?

WILLIAM: So what did they do to get rid of Arius?

PROFESSOR: A **council was called in AD 325 at Nice (Nicaea)** to which bishops of both persuasions were invited, including Arius—despite his not being a bishop. During the proceedings, one of the Trinitarian Bishops jumped up and punched Arius in the face when he was permitted to express his opinions. After much discussion, a draft creed was drawn up by Athanasius, a Deacon who had accompanied his Bishop. This creed was circulated among the Bishops, for them to read and sign if they were in agreement with the content. When it was discovered that **eighteen of the Arian Bishops had also signed the document,** the Papal opponents broke into wild uproar, and tore the document to shreds. They then expelled Arius

14

from the assembly. You can read all about it in Eusebius: Ecclesiastical History, pages 15-17. Clearly, the intention of the council of Nicea was not **only** to unite Christendom, but **also to destroy Arianism**—for reasons already discussed.

In the ensuing commotion, Eusebius of Caesarea presented an old creed before the council. When it was read, the **Arian** Bishops signified their willingness to sign acceptance of it too, the very thing the Papal party did not want! **How to come up with a creed that the Arian Bishops would not sign?**

During the ensuing discussion, the Greek word *"homoousios"* was bandied about. Here was a term, meaning "same substance" as opposed to *"homoiousios"* meaning "like substance"; to describe the "One-ness" of God. The Arians accepted the word homoiousios (**like** substance) when describing the three Persons of the Godhead. However, they rejected the word *"homoousios"* (**same identical, indivisible** substance.)

You see, William, we have no problem recognizing that we humans are all of "like substance," that is "flesh and blood," and we have no problem recognizing that we are not all of the "same substance", that is our particular flesh and blood is **not identical** to another person's flesh and blood—we do not share a "common" physical nature—we are "alike," but not "identical." We still are separate and distinct individuals.

WILLIAM: It sounds like they found their key.

PROFESSOR: Yes! When this distinction became apparent, the Papal party had found the distinguishing point of objection that they were looking for. The creed was amended to include the word *"homoousios"* (**Consubstantial**: "same identical, indivisible substance"). The Papists signed the document, but the Arians abstained. Arius and his followers were banished from church office; and every known book, paper and manuscript of Arius' were burned.

Remember that Council at Antioch that we were talking about earlier?

WILLIAM: Yes, where they made the right decision.

PROFESSOR: **It is noteworthy that the synod at Antioch, sixty years earlier, had condemned the word *"homoousios"* because it meant "one identical substance"** as believed by Modalistic Monarchians. **The Nicene council employed the very same word to exclude and condemn the Arians:** A clear demonstration of Rome's "variable appearance of the chameleon" and its "invariable venom of the serpent." (See Great Controversy, page 571).

"At the Council of Nicaea an erroneous charge was circulated that all who were called Arian believed that Christ was a created being." Truth Triumphant, page 92. To stigmatize your opponent is an old trick in the Papal repertoire.

It took until the sixth century for **Romanism** to reach full agreement on the place of the Holy Spirit in **Trinity** dogma. By AD 558, the Arian believers were in full retreat before the Catholic forces, leaving the Papacy as the sole "Corrector of Heretics". Anyone opposing the Catholic teaching of the Trinity (or Consubstantiation) was persecuted, for **"The mystery of the Trinity is the central doctrine of the Catholic Faith."** Handbook for Today's Catholic, page11

You either converted to the Trinitarian belief, or you would either be killed, or banished from the empire, which was then, the known world.

To oppose Trinitarianism is to oppose Rome.

WILLIAM: Rome does not believe in religious liberty.

PROFESSOR: No indeed. Let me tell you about three church councils that were convened during this period; and listen to their declarations.

At the **Council of Rome,** (Tome of Damascus), Canon 11, **AD 382** it was declared: "If anyone does not say that the Son was begotten of the Father, that is, of **the Divine substance of Him Himself, he is a heretic."**

It was stated in the **Athanasian Creed (ca. AD 475)** that: "The Father is not made nor created nor begotten by anyone. The Son from the Father alone, not made or created but begotten... **Let him who wishes to be saved, think thus concerning the Trinity.** But it is necessary for eternal salvation that he faithfully believe also in the incarnation of Our Lord Jesus Christ. Accordingly, it is the right faith, that we believe and confess that our Lord Jesus Christ, the Son of God, is God and man. **He is God begotten of the substance of the Father before time, and he is man born of the substance of His mother in time. This is the Catholic faith. Unless everyone believes this faithfully and firmly, he cannot be saved." This actually teaches what they accused Arius of teaching; namely that Jesus had a beginning!**

This is a little tangent, but did you notice, William, that this creed denies that Jesus is "from everlasting" (Micah 5:2). And it also contradicts what God's messenger has told us:

Signs of the Times, August 29, 1900:
"Christ is the **pre-existent, self-existent Son of God**.... In speaking of his pre-existence, Christ carries the mind back through dateless ages. He assures us that **there never was a time when He was not in close fellowship with the eternal God.** He

16

to whose voice the Jews were then listening had been with God as one brought up with Him."

Jesus assures us that "He had no existence separate from His Father." This concurs exactly with the above statement that "**there NEVER was a time when He was not in close fellowship with the eternal God.**"

Review & Herald, January 7, 1890:
"The world's Redeemer was **equal with God.** His authority was as the authority of God. He declared that he had **no existence separate from the Father.**"

Manuscript 101, 1897:
"He was equal with God, infinite and omnipotent. . . . **He is the eternal, self-existent Son.**"

Desire of Ages, page 470:
"He had announced Himself to be **the self-existent One,** He who had been promised to Israel, "whose goings forth have been from of old, **from the days of eternity.**" Micah 5:2, margin."

I bring these points up William, so that you notice that these statements we have just read destroy two false doctrines: 1) It demolishes the notion of consubstantiality, in that for Christ to be **self-existent,** precludes Him from being "generated" as a "modality" of a one-god substance. And 2) it negates the notion that Christ was "begotten" at some point prior to His incarnation. (For more on this point see Chapter 2 of this book)

Now, let's go back to our history of Trinitarianism.

Second Council of Constantinople
At the **Second Council of Constantinople** (*concerning the Three Chapters, Canon 2, AD 553*) it was recorded: **"If anyone does not confess that there are two generations of the Word of God, one from the Father before all ages,** without time and incorporeally, **the other in the last days when the same came down from heaven and was incarnate... let such a one be anathema."**

WILLIAM: "Two generations" of Christ?

PROFESSOR: As we have seen God's messenger categorically refutes the notion that Jesus was "generated" ("begotten") by the Father at some point prior to His incarnation. She categorically states that **"He is the self-existent Son of God."** Evangelism, page 615, MS 101, 1897

17

The Bible states in Psalm 2:7 - "I will *[future]* declare the decree: the LORD hath said unto me, Thou [art] my Son; **this day** have I begotten thee." This is a pre-incarnational declaration of intent. God's Word also tells us in Acts 13:33 – "God hath fulfilled the same unto us their *[the earlier Israelite's]* children, in that **he hath raised up Jesus again** *[at the resurrection]*; **as it is also written in the second psalm, Thou art my Son, this day have I begotten thee**." This Scripture clearly indicates that Jesus was **"begotten"** at his resurrection—now forever a divine/human Being—in glorified humanity; while Galatians talks about his being begotten of a woman at His incarnation (Gal. 4:4 - "But when the fulness of the time was come, God sent forth his Son, **made of a woman** *[how is a man "made of a woman"? He is begotten!]*, made under the law *[under the 'penalty', i.e. in our fallen humanity]*," see also Isaiah 7:14 – "Therefore the Lord himself shall give you a sign; Behold, a virgin shall conceive, **and bear a son** *[we all know this is 'begetting']*, and shall call his name Immanuel *["God with us"; united to our humanity; a completely new and unique Being; a union of creature, and Creator]*.", and Luke 1:35 – "And the angel answered and said unto her, The Holy Ghost shall come upon thee, and the power of the Highest shall overshadow thee: therefore also that holy thing which **shall be born** *["begotten"]* of thee **shall be** *[ever after]* **called the Son of God**." What we have just looked at is the fulfillment of John 3:16 – "For God so loved the world, that he **gave his only begotten** Son *[when Christ entered the human arena, on our behalf, for the first time in universal history, a "new Creature" was "begotten" into existence and not "spoken" into existence, nor had life "breathed" into pre-formed matter, as was the "first Adam". Jesus, the "second Adam", in His humanity, is the only "begotten" "new Creation" ever "begotten of God" into existence. Sinners have to be re-"begotten" of God, in order to, one day, receive glorified humanity.]*, that whosoever believeth in him should not perish, but have everlasting life."). These are the only "two generations" of Christ.

Christ was "the Only Begotten Son" before the foundation of the world, just as He was the "Lamb of God" before the foundation of the world. This is because when God declares something, it is as if it was already, even before it takes place. Notice what the following statement says confirming this last point:

1Bible Commentary, page 1099.5:

"**I Am** means an eternal presence**; the past, present, and future are ALIKE to God**. He sees the most remote events of past history, and the far distant future with as clear a vision as we do those things that are transpiring daily. We know not what is before us, and if we did, it would not contribute to our eternal welfare. God gives us an opportunity to exercise faith and trust in the great I AM." (Lt 119, 1895).

WILLIAM: God's word has the power in it to make it happen. He can never err.

PROFESSOR: Roman Catholic **Trinitarian** theology can never be fully understood because it is a confused and confusing synthesis of **Paganism** and Scripture, a blending of truth and error.
Notice how the Catholic Ms. Lacugna put it in:

How to Understand the Creed, page 305:
"Ultimately, the only appropriate response to the mystery of God revealed in the economy is adoration. For these reasons we might compare the doctrine of the **Trinity** to an **Icon**."

How very well put! It is upon this quicksand of man-devised confusion that all of Rome's doctrines are built.

WILLIAM: Who we worship—the doctrine of God—is very important.

PROFESSOR: Unquestionably. But not only is "Who" we worship important, but **"when"** we worship. Notice the connection between Trinitarianism and Sunday worship:

Dr. Henry Tuberville, in the Douay Catechism, stated:
"It [Sunday] is a day dedicated by the Apostles [?] to the honor of the Most Holy Trinity, and in memory that Christ our Lord arose from the Dead upon Sunday, sent down the Holy Ghost on a Sunday [?], etc., **and therefore is called the Lord's Day.** It is also called Sunday from the old Roman denomination of Dies Solis, the day of the sun, to which it was sacred."

As we have noted, to believe that only Christ's human body died on Calvary, lowers the status of the law of God to a position that sanctions its alteration by a man, who claims to be God's representative on earth.
Do you see, William? The doctrine of the **Trinity** as well as Sunday Sacredness mark mainstream **Protestantism** as still under Rome's authority in matters of doctrine.

WILLIAM: That is why Rome exalts tradition as equal to the Scriptures.

19

PROFESSOR: Right! **The Catholic Church recognizes that these doctrines are not taught in the Scriptures.** Romanism states:

> Catholic Encyclopedia, page 49:
> "Our opponents sometimes claim that no belief should be held dogmatically which is not explicitly stated in Scripture (ignoring that it is only on the authority of the Church we recognize certain Gospels and not others as true). **But the Protestant churches have themselves accepted such dogmas as the Trinity for which there is no such precise authority in the Gospels.**" (Brackets in original)
> The Encyclopedia Britannica, 1976, Volume 2, page 241, states:
> "Biblical Basis—Neither the word "Trinity" nor the explicit doctrine as such appears at any one place in the Bible…."

Even an Andrews University lecturer, Raoul Dederen, writing in:

> *Adventist Review*, August 26, 1993, page 8, stated:
> **"Some will tend to resist this doctrine** *[of the Trinity]* **because it is not found expressly stated in the Scripture."**

Now! If the Bible and the Bible only is our creed, then how can we accept Catholic Trinitarianism as a "Fundamental Belief"?

WILLIAM: As **true** Protestants, we can't.

PROFESSOR: Even Hans Kung, famous Catholic theologian, declares there is no evidence for the Trinity in the Bible. Under the title "**No Doctrine Of The Trinity In The New Testament**," Kung states:

> Christianity: Essence, History, and Future. Trans. by John Bowden. New York, 1995, page 95:
> "In short, in Judaism, indeed throughout the New Testament, while there is belief in God the Father, in Jesus the Son and in God's Holy Spirit, **there is no doctrine of one God in three persons** (modes of being), no doctrine of a 'triune God,' a 'Trinity.'" (Brackets in the original).

WILLIAM: He is a brave and honest man.

PROFESSOR: Rome claims to be the "Mother" of the Protestant Churches and is calling them to return to her. **Most mainline Protestant churches**

20

have retained Roman DNA by clinging both to Sunday sacredness and to the Nicean and Athanasian Creed of the Trinity.

Rome challenges Protestantism, maintaining that if they acknowledge Rome's authority by holding to these unbiblical doctrines, they acknowledge her authority in all matters of faith. **Gradually, through the ecumenical movement, the churches are complying.** This is observable in Ministerial Associations, prayers for Unity, combined services, using Catholic terminology such as calling **"Communion" the "Eucharist"** (as found in the book Seventh-day Adventists Believe..., page 198); singing along with Trinitarian hymns that are included in the "new" 1985 SDA Hymnal, inviting Catholic speakers to address student bodies and to General Conference gatherings, adopting priestly regalia for ministers to officiate in, and many other subtle ways.

(Professor Miller handed William a list of the hymns devoted to the Trinity in the 1985 SDA Hymnal. (This list is seen in Appendix E)   William looked at the paper closely and remarked):

WILLIAM: I didn't know the SDA church taught and believed in the Catholic Trinity. That's not what I have read in the Spirit of Prophecy.

PROFESSOR: Yes, William, the Seventh-day Adventist Church organization now professes to be **Trinitarian.** But this was not always so. Adventist pioneers rejected the **Trinity** dogma in the strongest terms, calling it "unscriptural error" and "the old **Trinitarian** absurdity." (James White, 1846 and 1852)

WILLIAM: They saw the "one substance" consubstantiality error.

PROFESSOR: One more point, William.   The Catholic view of the "Trinity"—that the One God is manifested in three different forms, as the Father; Son; and Holy Spirit is not very far distant from **Pantheism** in which God is in everything.   Both views are spiritualistic; both views etherealize and mystify the truth that God is "...not something intangible, but [*is*] a personal God...." (This Day With God, page 273)   Ms 117, September 21, 1898.

WILLIAM: What about God's messenger, Ellen White?

PROFESSOR: It is an interesting fact that God's messenger herself never employed the Catholic-coined code words "Trinity," or "Triune," or "co-eternal," or "co-equal*" in describing the Godhead. Not once!—though she was well aware of the concept, having come out of the Methodist Church –

21

a Trinitarian church. Does she (or the Bible) ever speak of a one-in-three God? Never! When God's messenger (or the Bible) uses the word "God," does that word ever direct our attention to all three Members of the Godhead at once? Never!

(*NOTE: Please see Appendix P)

WILLIAM: Could it be that God's messenger was herself anti-Trinitarian? Did she ever make anti-Trinitarian statements?

PROFESSOR: Yes, indeed. There are clear, truth-filled statements that completely contradict Trinitarian dogma and place in a clear setting the truth concerning the Godhead—as opposed to the confusing figments of consubstantiality - indeed she did - as we shall continue to see as we proceed with these lessons.

Chapter 2

THE SDA PIONEERS AND THE TRINITY DOCTRINE

WILLIAM: Professor, does the Seventh-day Adventist church really believe in the Trinity doctrine that was formulated, and expanded upon, in the Councils of Nicaea (*325 AD*) and Constantinople (*381 AD*)?

PROFESSOR: In the book <u>Issues: The Seventh-day Adventist Church and Certain Private Ministries</u>, published in 1980 under the auspices of the North American Division and Union Presidents, the following statement is found on page 39:

> "For those who would wish to define 'Historic Adventism' in terms of specific doctrinal content, the 1872 date presents a real dilemma...
> "Would one be willing to accept **all** the content from that earlier era? **Are the modern defenders of so-called Historic Adventism really prepared to return to a <u>non-Trinitarian</u> position?**"

WILLIAM: I would say, Yes!

PROFESSOR: **The answer is, of course, a resounding "Yes!"**

WILLIAM: So that means that the Seventh-day Adventist church did not originally believe in the Trinity doctrine.

PROFESSOR: The facts are clear and undeniable that the pioneers of the Seventh-day Adventist Church believed a distinctly different doctrine to the Trinitarian doctrine held by the structure and a number of independent ministries of today. Back then, statements like the following came off the denominational presses. Here is a statement from Merritt E. Cornell, an Adventist writing in 1858:

Merritt E. Cornell, <u>Facts for the Times</u>, page 76, 1858
"Protestants and Catholics are so nearly united in sentiment, that it is not difficult to conceive how Protestants may make an

image to the beast. **The mass of Protestants believe with Catholics in the Trinity**, immortality of the soul, consciousness of the dead, rewards and punishment at death, the endless torture of the wicked, inheritance of the saints beyond the skies, sprinkling for baptism, and the pagan Sunday for the Sabbath; all of which is contrary to the spirit and letter of the New Testament. **Surely there is between the mother and daughters, a striking family resemblance."**

WILLIAM: The Trinity was the first doctrine he put in his list.

PROFESSOR: More recently "certain men" (see Jude 3 and 4) have stealthfully been involved in gradually "genetically modifying" the Seventh-day Adventist denomination to make it also resemble and be more acceptable to the "family" mentioned above. The Trinity doctrine was formally approved in 1980 after many years of gradual changes.

WILLIAM: But **many** of the early SDA Pioneers believed that Jesus Christ was "begotten" of the Father at some remote point in eternity **prior** to His incarnation, didn't they? And were consequently classified as being "Arians" or "semi-Arians"?

PROFESSOR: Many did. You're right, but that concept of Christ being begotten at some point in eternity differs little to the Catholic view of Christ being "generated" by the Father at some point in eternity. However the Catholics were the ones who condemned Arias for supposedly believing that Christ was 'begotten' at some point in infinity. Look at this quotation from a Catholic Catechism that shows how, according to Rome, the "persons" of the trinity have distinct "origins."

(Professor Miller gave William the book, My Catholic Faith, and directed him to page 31):

> "1. This is the simplest way by which the **distinct origin** of each Divine Person has been explained: God is a spirit, and the first act of a Spirit is to know and understand God, **knowing Himself from all eternity** brings forth the knowledge of Himself, His own image. This was not a mere thought, as our knowledge of ourselves would be, but a Living Person, **of the same substance** and one with the Father. *This is God the Son.*

Thus the Father 'begets' the Son, the Divine Word, the Wisdom of the Father….

"2. God the Father, seeing His own Image in the Son, *loves* the Son; and God the Son loves the Father from all eternity. **Each loves the other**, because each sees in the other the Infinity of the Godhead, the beauty of Divinity, the Supreme Truth of God. The two Persons loving each other do not just have a thought, as human beings would have, but **from Their mutual love is breathed forth, as it were, a Living Person, one with Them, and of Their own substance. This is God the Holy Ghost.** Thus the Holy Ghost, the Spirit of Love, 'proceeds' from the Father and the Son….

"3. But we are *not to suppose* that once God the Father begot the Son and now no longer does so, nor that once the love of the Father and the Son for each other breathed forth the Holy Ghost, but now no longer does. These truths are eternal, everlasting.

"God the Father **eternally knows Himself, and continues to know Himself**, and thus continues to bring forth the Son. **God the Father and God the Son continue to love each other, and their delight in each other continues to bring forth the Spirit of Love, God the Holy Ghost.** In a similar way, fire has light and color. As long as there is fire, it continues to produce light. As long as there is fire with light, there is produced color. But all three exist at one and the same time."

One may ask, how does this whole Catholic concept really differ from that of "begetting"? Also, did you recognize the Sabelianism (see page 5 of this book) in that last statement?

WILLIAM: And is it any wonder that such a mental idol—the Trinity concept—would breed so much sexual misconduct within the churches that subscribe to it.

PROFESSOR: This is a **shocking** description of the "**origin**" of members of the Godhead as they supposed it to have occurred.

They condemned Arius who, according to them, postulated that Christ had an origin, but what is **this** that they say? Furthermore, to propose that the Holy Spirit "proceeds" from the Father and the Son's love for each other, differs little from the proposition that the Holy Spirit is a "power" proceeding from the Father and the Son, as those who propose a two-person Godhead say.

25

WILLIAM: Did Ellen White believe like the pioneers?

PROFESSOR: God's messenger **corrected** the first misconception very plainly by declaring that Christ is the pre-existing, "**self-existing**, Son of God" *(Youth Instructor, June 21, 1900)*; that there "**never was a time** when He was not in close fellowship with the eternal God" *(Signs, August 29, 1900)*; that "In Christ is life, **original**, unborrowed, **underived**." (Desire of Ages, page 530). One cannot be "self-existing" if One's existence is predicated on another Being's "knowing" Himself nor can one's life be "**underived**" if such life was indeed 'derived' from a preceding Being.

And the second misconception, held by many of the pioneers who did not believe that the Holy Spirit was a separate, distinct Being, but was an emanation of God and Christ's power, God's messenger also clearly and forcefully **corrected** by plainly declaring that **the Holy Spirit was "as much a person as God is a person."** (Sermons & Talks, Volume 2, 137; Evangelism, page 616)

WILLIAM: Many people think that if you believe in three Persons, that is the Trinity.

PROFESSOR: The Trinity doctrine is very deceptive. The deception is that when the word "Persons" is used, it does not mean "Persons" as you and I would understand it. In the Trinity doctrine "Persons" means an "emanation" of the one-God-substance or "essence." God's messenger, Ellen White, on the other hand, portrays God the Father, not as a mystical emanation, but as a personal Being:

> Ministry of Healing, page 413:
> "The mighty power that works through all nature and sustains all things is not, as some men of science [*e.g. John Harvey Kellogg*] represent, merely an all-pervading principle, an actuating energy. **God is a Spirit; yet He is a personal Being;** for so He has revealed Himself:
> "'The Lord is the true God, He is the living God, and an everlasting King:... The gods that have not made the heavens and the earth, Even they shall perish from the earth, and from under these heavens. The portion of Jacob is not like them: For He is the former of all things. **He hath made the earth by His power,** He hath established the world by His wisdom, And hath stretched out the heavens by His discretion.' Jeremiah 10:10, 11, 16, 12.

26

[*Far from Himself being an emanation of God's power, the Holy Spirit administers God's power to all of His vast creation.*]

Ministry of Healing, page 413 continues:
"God's handiwork in nature is not God Himself in nature. **The things of nature are an expression of God's** character and **power;** but we are not to regard nature as God."

SDA PIONEER POSITIONS:

WILLIAM: Who were the pioneer Adventists that were against the Trinity?

PROFESSOR: According to the Seventh-day Adventist Encyclopedia, pages 286, 287, "James White and Uriah Smith were 'the two leading anti-Trinitarians' though Joseph Bates, J.H. Waggoner, and E.J. Waggoner and W.W. Prescott were also so inclined." Some say that W.W. Prescott believed in the Trinity, but he might have, like many others today, really had the concept of the Heavenly Trio—3 distinct eternal Beings—but used the term "Trinity" (*not perceiving it was a term describing a 3-in-one god*)

WILLIAM: It would be interesting to hear what the prophet's husband, James White had to say.

PROFESSOR: James and Ellen White were very much in harmony in their beliefs. She wrote concerning her husband:

Testimonies to the Church, Volume 3, page 85:
"He *[God]* **has also given my husband great light upon Bible subjects, not for himself alone, but for others.** I saw that these things should be written and talked out, and **that new light would continue to shine upon the word.**"

This **"new light,"** of course, would not contradict light already given.
One of the first pronouncements on the subject of the Trinity from Elder White came in an early issue of *The Day Star*. In an exposition on Jude 3, 4, he wrote:

J.S. WHITE, *The Day Star,* January 24, 1846:
"The way that spiritualizers *[Trinitarians and Pantheists]* this way have disposed of or denied the only Lord God and our Lord Jesus Christ is first using the old unscriptural creed, viz. **that**

27

Jesus Christ is the eternal God, though they have not one passage to support it, while we have plain Scripture testimony in abundance that He is the Son of the Eternal God."

James White is here referring to such biblical statements as found in Romans 1:4 and 1 Corinthians 8:6. This does not mean that his views were "Arian" as defined by Romanists. In fact, we will see that James White wrote that "...It is not robbery for the Son to be equal with the Father ...He is equal..." Nevertheless, Scripture shows Him to be **voluntarily** subordinate to the Father.

Eight years later he wrote this:

J.S. WHITE, *Review & Herald,* September 12, 1854:
"As **fundamental errors,** we might class with this counterfeit sabbath other errors which Protestants have brought away from the Catholic church, such as sprinkling for baptism, **the trinity,** the consciousness of the dead and eternal life in misery. The mass who have held these **fundamental errors,** have doubtless done it ignorantly; **but can it be supposed that the church of Christ will carry along with her these errors till the judgment scenes burst upon the world? We think not.**"

In 1856, Elder White wrote the following statement in reply to a "communication... from an esteemed friend":

J.S. WHITE: *Review & Herald,* February 7, 1856:
"The 'mystery of iniquity' began to work in the church in Paul's day. It finally crowded out the simplicity of the gospel, and corrupted the doctrine of Christ, and the church went into the wilderness. Martin Luther, and other reformers, arose in the strength of **God,** and with the **Word and Spirit,** made mighty strides in the Reformation. [*Do we notice the Heavenly Trio in this statement? God the Father, Christ the Word, and the Holy Spirit are presented.*] The greatest fault we can find in the Reformation is, the Reformers stopped reforming. Had they gone on, and onward, till they had left the last vestige of Papacy behind, such **as natural immortality, sprinkling, the trinity, and Sunday-keeping,** the church would now be free from her **unscriptural errors.**"

28

Regrettably, the SDA church organization has apostatized and retrogressed. **What James White called a "fundamental error" and an "unscriptural error," has become a "fundamental belief!"** As we have seen, even Rome acknowledges that the Scriptures do not present Trinitarianism! Referring to John 17:20-23, James White wrote:

> J.S. WHITE, Life Incidents, 1868, page 343:
> "Jesus prayed that **his disciples might be one as he was one with his Father. This prayer did not contemplate one disciple with twelve heads, but twelve disciples, made one in object and effort in the cause of their master. Neither are the Father and the Son parts of the 'three-one God.' They are two distinct beings,** yet one in the design and accomplishment of redemption."

This view is in complete accord with that of his wife as recorded in Ministry of Healing, page 422.

(Just because James White does not refer to the Holy Spirit in this statement does not imply that he did not believe the Holy Spirit to be the mighty Third Person of the Godhead. See statements by James White at the end of this segment on his writings. This above given statement and the ones which we will see later, completely concur with those of his wife on the topic.)

> J.S. WHITE, *Review & Herald,* November 29, 1877:
> "Paul affirms of the Son of God that He was in the form of God, and that He was equal with God. 'Who being in the form of God, thought it not robbery to be equal with God.' Phil. 2:6. The reason why it is not robbery for the Son to be equal with the Father is the fact that He is equal... **The inexplicable Trinity that makes the Godhead three-in-one, and one-in-three, is bad enough; but that ultra-Unitarianism that makes Christ inferior to the Father is worse. Did God say to an inferior, 'Let us make man in our image?'"**

Notice, James White firmly believed that **Christ was not inferior** to God the Father.

WILLIAM: Undoubtedly James White believed that the Father and the Son were two distinct Eternal Beings. But did he believe that the Holy Spirit was a distinct eternal Being?

29

PROFESSOR: Let us allow James White to speak for himself! The following quotes are from the book, <u>Bible Adventism; Sermons on the Coming Kingdom of our Lord Jesus Christ</u>, by Elder James White, and published by the Seventh-day Adventist Publishing Association, Battle Creek, MI, pages 41, 48, 49:

JAMES WHITE, <u>Bible Adventism</u>, page 41:
"Jesus also assured them that the Father would give them 'another comforter,' even the Spirit of Truth, which should **dwell with** them, and be **in them**. Chapter 14:16, 17. The words, 'another comforter,' suppose two, at least. *[Two separate and distinct Beings—a distinction being made between Jesus and the Holy Spirit.]* The **one** *[Comforter]* was the person of our divine Lord. The other *[Comforter]* is the Spirit of Truth. Both were comforters of the church. Christ was such *[a Comforter]* in a special sense while with his disciples. The other *[Comforter]* was to abide with the church, to **administer** the blessings and gifts of the Holy Spirit to the church, until her **absent** Lord should return in glory to take her to himself."

JAMES WHITE, <u>Bible Adventism</u>, pages 48, 49:
"May the Lord help them to see the difference between the manifestations of the Holy Spirit, and the personal presence of Christ at his second appearing, while we appeal to the Scriptures. 'I will pray the Father,' says Jesus, 'and he shall give you **another** Comforter.' John 14:16. This language implies more than one comforter. **When Christ was with his people, he was their comforter. In his absence,** the **Father** was to send **another comforter,** even the Spirit of truth. During the **absence** of the Son, the Holy Spirit was to be his *[the Son's]* **representative,** and the comforter of his dear, sorrowing people. The **facts** in the case are distinctly stated in the following impressive words: 'But now I go my way **to Him** that **sent me;** and none of you asketh me, Whither goest thou? But because I have said these things unto you, sorrow hath filled your heart. Nevertheless I tell you the truth. It is **expedient** for you that I go away; for if I go not away, the Comforter will not come unto you; but if I depart, I will **send him** unto you. And when **he** is come, **he** will reprove the world of sin, and of righteousness, and of judgment.' John 16:5-8."

These words of James White, and the Scripture he quotes, make it clear that he did not believe the Holy Spirit was only a force, or power, or emanation proceeding from the Father and/or the Son. It is therefore, clear why the prophet, his wife, did not have to correct his views on either the beliefs he held with regard to the 'Trinity' doctrine, or his belief in the separate role and distinct, separate personhood of the Holy Spirit.

WILLIAM: But why do most Adventists believe that James White was at least semi-Arian and that he did not believe that the Holy Spirit was a person?

PROFESSOR: They believe that because that is what they are taught. They mistakenly believe and teach that the Heavenly Trio is the Trinity. And thus, they think that Ellen White, who used the term "the Heavenly Trio," was talking about the Trinity. And they believe that if you didn't believe in the Trinity, you didn't believe in the Heavenly Trio either. That is why RUSSELL HOLT in his book, The Doctrine of the Trinity in the Seventh-day Adventist Denomination: Its Rejection and Acceptance, page 7, writes concerning James White:

> "The evidence from his pen seems to indicate that from his first affiliations with the Christian Connection until his death at the age of 60, **James White opposed the Trinity,** both on the basis of logic and Scripture, while holding a definite concept of the exalted position and divinity of Jesus Christ. The conclusion reached is intriguing due to his unique and special relationship to the Lord's messenger, who happened to be his wife. She was surely aware of his thinking on the subject. Did she approve? If not, why did he continue his belief? Did she simply refrain from correcting him? Why? The questions raised are fascinating, but not easily answered *[See answer below]*. At least **James White himself can be demonstrated to have been a consistent anti-Trinitarian.**"

Why did Ellen White not say anything to her husband about his stand? **The answer is simple.** James White's views were in agreement with those truths revealed by God to his wife. They both believed in the Heavenly Trio—three distinct Eternal Beings—the Godhead; while they both did not believe in the Trinity—the one-in-three God. (If the reader thinks that this is Tri-theism, see Chapter 42).

31

In fact **James says plainly that Ellen wasn't a Trinitarian**, and that the creed of the trinity could not line up with her writings, nor with the Bible. **James White declares his wife to be anti-Trinitarian:**

> JAMES WHITE: "Mutual Obligation," *Review and Herald*, June 13, 1871:
> "**We invite all to compare the testimonies of the Holy Spirit through Mrs. W., with the word of God.** And in this we do not invite you to compare them with your creed. That is quite another thing. **The trinitarian may compare them with his creed, AND BECAUSE THEY** *[the Testimonies]* **DO NOT AGREE WITH IT,** condemn them. The observer of Sunday, or the man who holds eternal torment an important truth, and the minister that sprinkles infants, may each condemn the testimonies' of Mrs. W. because they do not agree with their peculiar views. And a hundred more, each holding different views, may come to the same conclusion. But their genuineness can never be tested in this way."

WILLIAM: It's interesting that the Holy Spirit, who is supposed to be part of the Trinity, never inspired Ellen White to use the word.

PROFESSOR: In addition, James White neither needed, nor received, any correction, on his views about Trinitarianism.

Here is another evidence that James White understood the difference between the doctrine of the 'Trinity'—a foundational doctrine of the Catholic Church—and the biblical doctrine of the 'Godhead'—as supported by the inspired writings of his wife, Ellen White: James White approved an article (see below) that clearly showed the difference between the Trinitarian view of the nature of Christ and the biblical view:

> J.M STEPHENSON—AUTHOR. (EDITOR—JAMES WHITE)
> *Review & Herald,* November 21, 1854:
> "The Trinitarian view, I think is equally exceptionable. They claim that the Son of God had **three distinct natures** at the same time; viz., a human body, a human soul, united with his Divine nature: the body being mortal, the soul immortal, **the Divinity co-equal, co-existent, and co-eternal with the everlasting Father.** Now, none of the advocates of this theory, claim that either his soul or Divinity died, [but] that the body was the only part of this triple being which actually died 'the death of the

cross;' hence, according to this view (which makes the death of Christ the grand atoning sacrifice for the sins of the world) we only have the sacrifice of the most inferior part—the human body—of the Son of God."

Stephenson recognized that the Trinitarian view of Christ's nature and the implications for the Atonement are diametrically opposed to Scripture. Isaiah 53:12 states that "He hath **poured out His soul unto death**…"

On careful analysis, we find that the Roman Church's 'Trinity' doctrine of consubstantiality **demands** a three-nature Christology (simply put: that Jesus had a human nature, an immortal soul, and a divine nature, that these three natures were separate at all times—his human nature dying on the cross, his "immortal soul" went and preached to the "souls" in "hell, and his divine nature returning to the Father from which, in "essence" it had never been separated.) In contrast to this, **the pioneers believed in a one-nature Christology, the divine and the human being 'blended' into one.**

WILLIAM: Did Ellen White support that view?

PROFESSOR: Notice again what the prophet wrote on **this** issue:

> 1888 Materials, page 332:
> "Christ could have done **nothing** during His earthly ministry in saving fallen man if the divine had not been **blended** with the human. The limited capacity of man cannot define this wonderful mystery—**the blending of the two natures, the divine and the human.** It can never be explained. Man must wonder and be silent. And yet man is privileged to be a partaker of the divine nature, **and in this way he can to some degree enter into the mystery.** This wonderful exhibition of God's love was made on the cross of Calvary. Divinity took the nature of humanity, and for what purpose?—That through the righteousness of Christ humanity might partake of the divine nature."

Again, she wrote:

> *Signs of the Times,* March 8, 1899:
> "When He came to the world the first time, divinity and humanity were **blended. This is our only hope.** The Son of man is fully qualified to be the **originator** of **a humanity that**

will blend with divinity by partaking of the divine nature."
[See Chapter 10 of this book]

The blending of Christ's human nature with divinity is akin to the blending of the redeemed sinner's human nature with divinity. Christ had laid aside His divinity, as we shall see from inspiration. Divine power was administered to Him by the indwelling divine Holy Spirit. He did not cease to be a divine Person, but One who had laid aside the panoply of divinity. When He died, a divine Person died, but Deity in the Person of the Holy Spirit, who dwelt in Him, did not die. That would have been impossible. His paying a divine price for our redemption makes it possible for fallen human beings *[us]* to receive the indwelling presence of the Holy Spirit, and so become a "union" of humanity and divinity as He was. And when a child of God dies, the Holy Spirit, to whom he was united, does not die. "Behold, what manner of love, that we should be called the sons of God." 1 John 3:1. And "He is not ashamed to call them *[us, if we are faithful]* brethren." Hebrews 2:11.

WILLIAM: What did some of the other early pioneers write on the 'trinity"?

PROFESSOR: Well, let's look at what Joseph Bates wrote:

JOSEPH BATES, Autobiography of Joseph Bates, pages 204, 205:
"Respecting the trinity, I concluded that it was an impossibility for me to believe that the Lord Jesus Christ, the Son of the Father, was also the Almighty God, the Father, one and the same being. I said to my father, 'If you can convince me that we are one in this sense, that you are my father, and I your son; and also that I am your father, and you my son, then I can believe in the trinity.'"

JOSEPH BATES in a letter to William Miller, Past and Present Experience, pages 187, 188.—1848:
"Much derision is made about those of our company that have joined the Shakers. I say it is a shame to them first, to have preached so clearly and distinctly the speedy coming of our Lord Jesus Christ **personally** to gather His saints—and then to go and join the Shakers in their faith, that He (Jesus) came spiritually in their mother, Ann Lee, more than seventy years ago. **This,**

without doubt in my mind, is owing to their previous teaching and belief in a doctrine called the Trinity. How can you find fault with their faith while you are teaching the very essence of **that never—no never to be understood—doctrine?**"

WILLIAM: I guess they believed that "Jesus", as a "spiritualistic modality", was in Ann Lee.

PROFESSOR: That, of course, is nonsense at best, and a satanic lie, at least.   Certainly "the man Christ Jesus" could not inhabit her, and be mediating in the heavenly sanctuary, at the same time.
Now let us look at what J. N. Andrews wrote:

John Nevins Andrews, *Review & Herald,* September 7, 1869:
(Speaking of Melchizedek) "Every member of the human family, except Adam and Eve, has had parents, and every one has had beginning of days; and indeed, with two exceptions, everyone has had end of life.   Even the angels of God have all had beginning of days, so that they would be as much excluded by this language as the members of the human family.   **And as to the Son of God, He would be excluded also, for He had God for His Father, and did, at some point in the eternity of the past, have beginning of days.**"

Clearly, J. N. Andrews, in 1869, held to what is today described as an Arian view, in that he believed that the Lord had "beginning of days."   **This view God's messenger totally refuted in 1897** (Manuscript 101) **and again in 1900** (*Signs of the Times,* Aug. 29).   Many of the Adventist pioneers held what is today regarded as a semi-Arian view—namely that the Son was (at some point before the Creation) 'generated' by the Father, as Catholicism also teaches.   (See pages 487-488 of this book).   All of these aberrant views were corrected by God's messenger.   Notice these statements from:

Evangelism, page 615:
"He was equal with God, infinite and omnipotent.... **He is the eternal, SELF-existent Son.**"—*Manuscript 101, 1897.*
"Christ is the **pre-existent, self-existent** Son of God....   In speaking of his pre-existence, Christ carries the mind back through dateless ages.   He assures us that there **NEVER was a**

time when He was not in close fellowship with the eternal God."—*Signs of the Times,* Aug. 29, 1900.

WILLIAM: These statements very clearly state that the Son of God, the Word, **always was and still is a separate and distinct Person of the Godhead—not an 'emanation' or 'mode' of a one 'God' substance.**

PROFESSOR: These inspired statements are both anti-Unitarian and anti-Trinitarian! Here is something that J.N. Andrews wrote that is pretty good:

> J. .N. Andrews: *Review & Herald,* January 27, 1874, page 52:
> "The doctrine of the Trinity was established in the church by the council of Nice, AD 325. **This doctrine destroys the personality of God, and His Son Jesus Christ our Lord.** <u>The infamous measures by which it was forced upon the church, which appear upon the pages of ecclesiastical history might well cause every believer in that doctrine to blush.</u>"

God's Messenger fully endorsed J.N. Andrews' above stated perception and distinctly underscored **the distinct and separate personalities** of the Heavenly Trio. She wrote:

> <u>Faith I Live By</u>, page 46:
> "The Lord Jesus Christ, the divine Son of God, existed from eternity, **a distinct person, yet one with the Father.**"

Jesus is not a modality-style "Person," as defined by Catholic Trinitarianism and also taught by some modern Adventist theologians. (See pages 487-488 and Chapter 38 of this book)
(Jesus' "one"ness with the Father is discussed in Chapter 25 of this book.)

WILLIAM: Did Uriah Smith write about the Godhead?

PROFESSOR: Yes, I have some of his statements here: Uriah Smith's views were very erroneous and were thoroughly refuted by God's messenger, as we will see:

> URIAH SMITH: <u>Thoughts on the Book of Daniel and the Revelation</u>, page 430. 1:

"The Scriptures nowhere speak of Christ as a created being, but on the contrary plainly state that he was begotten of the Father. *[See remarks on Rev.3:14, where it is shown that Christ is not a created being.]* But while as the Son he does not possess a co-eternity of past existence with the Father, the beginning of his existence, as the begotten of the Father, antedates the entire work of creation, in relation to which he stands as joint creator with God. John1:3; Heb.1:2. Could not the Father ordain that to such a being worship should be rendered equally with himself, without its being idolatry on the part of the worshiper? He has raised him to positions which make it proper that he should be worshiped, and has even commanded that worship should be rendered him, which would not have been necessary had he been equal with the Father in eternity of existence. *[What about Phil. 2:6, "Who being in the form of God **thought it not robbery to be equal with God.**"?]* Christ himself declares that 'as the Father hath life in himself, so hath he given to the Son to have life in himself.' John5:26. The Father has 'highly exalted him, and given him a name which is above every name.' Phil.2:9. And the Father himself says, 'Let all the angels of God worship him.' Heb.1:6. These testimonies show that Christ is now an object of worship equally with the Father; but they do not prove that with him he holds an eternity of past existence."

WILLIAM: Did Ellen White have anything to say about His statements.

PROFESSOR: **God's messenger clearly and plainly refuted Uriah Smith's "Arian" view that at some point in past infinity, Christ was "begotten."** As we have noted, she wrote:

The Faith I Live By, page 46:
"Christ is the pre-existent, **SELF-existent** Son of God.... In speaking of His pre-existence, Christ carries the mind back through dateless ages. He assures us that **never** was a time when He was not in close fellowship with the eternal God....
"Christ <u>was</u> God essentially, and in the HIGHEST sense. <u>He was with God from ALL eternity,</u> God over all, blessed forevermore. The Lord Jesus Christ, the divine Son of God, <u>existed from ETERNITY, a distinct person,</u> *[the statement also refutes Trinitarian consubstantiality. God the Father and God the Son are separate and distinct Persons, as is the Holy*

Spirit.] **yet one with the Father.** *["One"ness as clarified in John 17:20-22 and Ministry of Healing. page 422.]*
"...He **was** equal with God, infinite and omnipotent."

Notice how God's messenger corroborates the fact that Jesus previous "equality" with His Father was in **the past tense,** that is, prior to His voluntary subordination to the Father in the plan of salvation. This does not preclude His receiving it back. (*See Rev. 5:12, Acts 2:36, and 1 Peter 3:22.*)

On Jesus "equality" with God the Father from which He "stepped down" she says:

> Testimonies to the Church, Volume 4, pages 457-458:
> "Paul ...exhorts us to possess the mind 'which was also in Christ Jesus: who, being in the form of God, thought it not robbery to be equal with God: but **made Himself of no reputation,** and took upon Him the form of a servant, and was made in the likeness of men: and being found in fashion as a man, he humbled Himself, and became obedient unto death, even the death of the cross.' The apostle lingers over point after point, that our minds may grasp and fully comprehend the wonderful condescension of the Saviour in behalf of sinners. He *[Paul]* presents Christ before us as He *[Christ]* **was when equal with God** *[the Father]* and receiving the adoration of angels, and **then traces His descent** until He reaches the lowest depths of humiliation ...."

WILLIAM: I notice there that when Ellen White uses the word God, she is referring to God the Father, not a three-in-one God.

PROFESSOR: Good observation. She was obviously not Trinitarian in her thinking. (See Chapter 22 in this book)

Now to return to our discussion on Uriah Smith; here is another quotation to give us an idea of Uriah Smith's errant understanding: (Professor's comment in *italics*.)

> URIAH SMITH, Looking Unto Jesus, page 10.1:
> "God alone is without beginning. At the earliest epoch when a beginning could be—a period so remote that to finite minds it is essentially eternity—**appeared** the Word. 'In the beginning **was** the Word, and the Word was with God, and the Word **was**

God.' John 1:1. *[Note: Smith failed to realize that the phrase "in the beginning"... refers to when God began creating other beings, worlds, etc. and that, at that time, the 'Word' already 'was' or already existed, and 'was God.']*

SMITH (continued): "This **uncreated** Word was the Being *[Michael]*, who, in the fulness of time, was made flesh, and dwelt among us *[and was given a new name, 'Jesus' = Jehovah Saves]*. His beginning was not like that of any other being in the universe. It is set forth in the mysterious expressions, 'his *[God's]* only begotten Son' (John 3:16; 1John 4:9), 'the only begotten of the Father' (John 1:14), and, 'I proceeded forth and came from God.' John 8:42." *[Note: Smith failed to recognize that Michael was never spoken of in these terms, as 'Jesus' is. Jesus was 'made of a woman,' made under the law (Gal. 4:4) in a body that was 'prepared' for Him (Heb. 10:5). Born with the Holy Spirit as His earthly Progenitor, He was a union of humanity (in its fallen state as inherited from Mary) and divinity. A new being in whom Creator and creature are combined—not spoken into existence, but 'begotten.' Hence, the term 'only begotten of the Father.' For Jesus to "proceed" from the Father, does not mean that He "emanated" from the Father. He simply proceeded from, or left, His Father's immediate Presence.]*

SMITH (continued): "Thus it appears that by some divine impulse or process, not creation, known only to Omniscience, and possible only to Omnipotence, the Son of God appeared. And then the Holy Spirit (by an infirmity of translation called .. the 'Holy Ghost'), **the Spirit of God, the Spirit of Christ, the <u>divine afflatus</u> and medium of their power, representative of them both (Ps.139:7), was in existence also.**"

As we have already noted, God's messenger corrected the false notion that Jesus, the "Word" had beginning! However, Uriah Smith also did not regard the Holy Spirit as a "Person," but rather, as we have seen, as the **"divine afflatus"** (<u>Looking Unto Jesus</u>, page 10).

In the *Review & Herald,* October 28, 1890, a certain J.W.W. asked the following question of the Editor (U. Smith):

Question: "Are we to understand that the Holy Ghost is a person, the same as the Father and the Son? Some claim that it is, others that it is not."

Answer: "The terms 'Holy Ghost' are a harsh and repulsive translation. It should be 'Holy Spirit' (*Hagion Pneuma*) in every instance. This Spirit is the Spirit of God, and the Spirit of Christ; the Spirit being the same whether it is spoken of as pertaining to God or Christ. **But respecting this Spirit, the Bible uses expressions which cannot be harmonized with the idea that it is a person like the Father and the Son.** Rather, it is shown to be a divine influence from them both, **the medium which represents their presence and by which they have knowledge and power through all the universe, when not personally present.** Christ is a person, now officiating as priest in the sanctuary in heaven; and yet He says that wherever two or three are gathered in His name, He is there in the midst. Mt. 18:20. How? Not personally, but by His Spirit. In one of Christ's discourses (John 14-16) this Spirit is personified as 'the Comforter,' and as such has the personal and relative pronouns, 'He,' 'Him,' and 'Whom,' applied to it. But usually it is spoken of in a way to show that it cannot be a person, like the Father and the Son. For instance, it is often said to be 'poured out' and 'shed abroad.' But we never read about God or Christ being poured out or shed abroad. *[Note: Really, Uriah? Please read Isaiah 53:7, 10, 12.]* If it is a person, it would be nothing strange for it to appear in bodily shape; and yet when it has so appeared, the fact has been noted as peculiar *[unusual]*. Thus, Luke 3:22 says: 'And the Holy Ghost descended in a bodily shape like a dove upon Him.' But the shape is not always the same; for on the Day of Pentecost, it assumed the form of 'cloven tongues like as of fire.' Acts 2:3, 4. Again we read of 'the seven Spirits of God sent forth into all the earth.' Rev. 1:4; 3:1; 4:5; 5:6. This is unquestionably simply a designation of the Holy Spirit, put in this form to signify its perfection and completeness. But it could hardly be so described if it was a person. We never read of the seven Gods or the seven Christs."

Along the same vein, is this quotation:

URIAH SMITH, *Gen. Conf. Daily Bulletin, Volume 4,* March 18, 1891, pages 146, 147:

"The Holy Spirit is the Spirit of God; it is also the Spirit of Christi. **It is that divine, mysterious emanation through which they carry forward their great and infinite work.**"

Incidentally, William, here are some quotations from the cup of the 'woman' who rides the beast which clearly show the 'source' of this confusion concerning the Holy Spirit and concerning Christ:

The Catholic Encyclopedia, 1915 Edition, article: Holy Ghost:
"Every good Catholic **must** accept that the **Holy Spirit comes out of the Father and the Son, and does not have a separate existence**... He *[the Holy Spirit]* proceeds, not by way of generation, but by way of **'spiration'**, from the Father and the Son together, as from a single principle. **Such is the belief the Catholic faith demands.**"

In addition, the Catholic Church teaches that the Son has no separate existence, but flows out from the Father:

Ibid:
"**The Holy Spirit proceeds out of the Father and the Son... The Son proceeds from the Father,** the Holy Ghost proceeds from the Father and the Son."

A Practical Catholic Dictionary, page 32:
"**Whereas Christ proceeds from the mind of the Father, the Holy Spirit flows outward from His will**... St. Thomas (I. Q. xxvii) following St. Augustine (Do Trin, IV, xxvii), finds the explanation and, as it were the epitome *[best statement]* of the doctrine in principle that, **in God, the Son proceeds through the intellect and the Holy Ghost through the will.**"

WILLIAM: **But Ellen White did not agree with these views nor with Uriah Smith's views on the Holy Spirit not being a "person," but merely the "divine afflatus." Did she not state the correct view on both Christ's eternal pre-existence and that the Holy Spirit is indeed the "Third Person of the Godhead"?**

PROFESSOR: Yes. Look at this:

Manuscript Releases, Volume 2, page 34:

41

"Evil had been accumulating for centuries, and could only be restrained and resisted by **the mighty power of the Holy Spirit, the Third Person of the Godhead,** who would come with no modified energy, but in the fullness of divine power. Another spirit must be met, for the essence of evil was working in all ways, and the submission of man to this satanic captivity was amazing...."

Uriah Smith was wrong! God's messenger categorically refuted Smith's view that the Holy Spirit is only an "emanation". Her method of correcting error was to simply present the truth on a topic without entering into debate. She wrote:

Evangelism, page 617:
"The Holy Spirit always leads to the written word. **The Holy Spirit is a person,** for **He beareth witness** with our spirits that we are the children of God. When this witness is borne, it carries with it its own evidence. At such times we believe and are sure that we are the children of God.... **He must also be a divine Person, else He could not <u>search out</u> the secrets which lie hidden in the mind of God.**" *Manuscript* 20, 1906

WILLIAM: Right. An 'emanation' or "force" can't "search out" anything!

PROFESSOR: God's messenger also pointed out that, though He (the Holy Spirit) is a Person, He is not limited by the limitations of **human** personality, but is a "Personality" nevertheless! (See pages 65, 172, 182, 234, 243, and 264 of this book).

Now let's look at the understanding of S.N. Haskell:

Stephen N. Haskell: The Story of the Seer of Patmos, page 217:
"Before the creation of our world, 'there was war in heaven.' Christ and the Father covenanted together; and Lucifer, the covering cherub, grew jealous because he was not admitted into the eternal councils **of the Two who sat upon the throne.**"

Those who would teach a Two Person Godhead (Stump, Clayton, Beachy, etc.) make much of quotes like that of S. N. Haskell as given above. They completely overlook, or attempt in every way possible, to denigrate clear statements by God's messenger that the Holy Spirit, while He has personality—not human personality—is nevertheless a distinct and separate Being, Whose **nature** we cannot comprehend. (God's messenger declares that He is **"divested"** of human personality; see DA 669.) Inspiration indicates that the Holy Spirit is not normally depicted as having graspable form, but is portrayed as being like wind, breath, water, oil, or fire, etc., and that the Holy Spirit inhabits the mind of God and Christ (see FE 393) and the redeemed, despite being a distinct Entity. For instance, as the oil permeated the two stacks of shewbread on the table of showbread, so does the Holy Spirit permeate 'the Two who sat upon the throne' referred to by Haskell above.

In order to promote the notion of a two-person Godhead, Allen Stump (in his book "The Foundation of our Faith, pages 74, 75) quotes from Patriarch & Prophets, page 36: "The Son of God shared the Father's throne, and the glory of the eternal, self-existent One encircled both.... Before the assembled inhabitants of heaven the King declared that none but Christ, the Only Begotten of God, could fully enter into **His purposes,** and to Him it was committed to **execute** the mighty counsels of His will."

In one place he makes a plea to follow Sister White's counsel to go with the 'weight of evidence,' but builds his case on statements like these given above while ignoring or discounting other statements and clear Scriptural evidence, which speak plainly against his theories.

And his interpretation of the above statement is not correct. The only other Member of the Godhead who "could fully enter into His *[the Father's]* **purposes**" was Christ, as only He could lay down His divine life. The Holy Spirit's nature and function precluded His carrying out this **purpose.**

WILLIAM: That is pretty clear. What other pioneer wrote on this subject?

PROFESSOR: Let's look at the writings of J.H. Waggoner, (father of E.J. Waggoner):

> JOSEPH HARVEY WAGGONER, The Atonement in the Light of Nature and Revelation, pages 164, 165, 168, 169:
> "Many theologians really think that the Atonement, in respect to its dignity and efficacy, **rests upon the doctrine of a trinity.** But we fail to see any connection between the two. To the contrary, the advocates of **that doctrine** really fall into the difficulty which they seem anxious to avoid. Their difficulty consists in this: **They take the denial of a trinity to be equivalent to a denial of the divinity of Christ. Were that the case, we should cling to the doctrine of a trinity as tenaciously**

as any can; but it is not the case. They who have read our remarks on the death of the Son of God know that we firmly believe in the divinity of Christ; but we cannot accept the idea of **a trinity, as it is held by Trinitarians, without giving up our claim on the dignity of the sacrifice made for our redemption.**"

The reason being that Trinitarianism means that we only have the human body of Christ as our sacrifice because the consubstantial divine essence of His divine personhood—being consubstantial with God the Father and with the Holy Spirit did not—according to the innate Trinitarian concept—die. Indeed, according to Trinitarianism, Christ's <u>soul</u> lived on, and went and preached to the spirits in hell, a misapprehension of 1 Peter 3:19.

WAGGONER (Continued): "The distinction between Christ and the true God is most clearly shown by the Saviour's own words in John 17:3: 'That they might know thee, the only true God, and Jesus Christ, whom thou hast sent.'

"Much stress is laid on Isaiah 9:6, as proving a trinity, which we have before quoted, as referring to our High Priest who shed his blood for us. **The advocates of that theory will say that it refers to a trinity because Christ is called the everlasting Father.** But for this reason, with others, we affirm that it can have **no reference to a trinity.** Is Christ the Father in the trinity? If so, how is he the Son? Or if he is both Father and Son, how can there be a trinity? For a trinity is three persons *[really, "emanations." Waggoner, who believed in a two-person Godhead, was wrong. A "Trinity," in reality, comprises three emanations of an indivisible substance or essence, which are deceptively referred to as "Persons" by Trinitarians. His point about Isaiah 9:6 is, however, plain and valid.]* To recognize a trinity, the distinction between the Father and Son must be preserved. Christ is called 'the second person in the trinity;' but if this text proves a trinity, or refers to it at all, it proves that he is not the second, but the first. And if he is the first, who is the second? It is very plain that this text has no reference to such a doctrine."

What Waggoner, and most people, have failed to recognize about the reference to Christ being "the everlasting Father" in Isaiah 9:6, is

44

that as our Creator, the One **through** Whom the Most High God created all things (Col. 1:16), He (Christ) is our "everlasting Father" by creation and regeneration. However, **unregenerate** human beings, with hearts (minds) that are "desperately wicked and deceitful above all things" are of **their "father** the devil." **It is to those who are "born of God" through the Holy Spirit—made possible by redemption through Christ—that provision is made for mankind to again call the Most High God "Abba, Father."** But Christ is also their "Father" in much the same way that Paul was Timothy's "father." (1 Tim. 1:2; 2 Tim. 1:2; 2:1.)

J. H. Waggoner's' incorrect view that the Godhead was not comprised of "three collateral, coordinate, and self-originated Beings" (Waggoner, *Thoughts on Baptism*, 1878, page180) is clearly corrected by God's messenger **in** such statements as found in *Signs of the Times,* August 29, 1900 ("Christ is the pre-existent, self-existent Son of God." MS 101, 1897, already quoted before.) God's messenger emphatically stated:

> Special Testimonies, Series B, No. 7, pages 62, 63:
> "There are **three living persons of the heavenly trio;** in the name of these **three great powers**—the Father, the Son, and the Holy Spirit—those who receive Christ by living faith are baptized, and these **powers** will co-operate with the obedient subjects of heaven in their efforts to live the new life in Christ."

Notice in the statement below the distinctions of function made by God's messenger regarding status among members of the Godhead:

> ELLEN WHITE, *Signs of the Times,* July 22, 1886, par. 2:
> "**God** as the **Supreme Ruler** of the universe has ever required prompt and unquestioning obedience. **Even Christ,** in the days of His flesh, **was obedient to the law of the Father.**"

WILLIAM: A heavenly Trio with the Father being the "Most High God"!

PROFESSOR: Right. The unwarranted fear of being labeled "tri-theistic" has obscured the biblical truth which directs our worship to the Most High God—Christ and the Holy Spirit, being the most prominent Advocates of this practice. The fact that there are three separate and distinct Members of the Godhead, two of Whom have accepted subordinate roles to the Father, the Most High God, should clarify Who the "only true God" is, without denigrating the status or honor due to Christ and the Holy Spirit for their

45

selflessness in voluntarily making this infinite, sacrificial, abnegation in the "Councils of Peace". (See Chapter 43)

In his booklet, *The Spirit of God; Its Offices and Manifestations,* pages 8, 9, 1877, J.H. Waggoner disputes "the personality of the Spirit of God." Once again God's messenger clarifies the issue, plainly declaring the Holy Spirit to be a separate and distinct personality (*Evangelism, 616,617*), but unencumbered by the limitations of **human** personality. (See <u>Desire of Ages,</u> page 669 and <u>Christian Service</u>, page 255):

> J. H. WAGGONER, <u>The Atonement in the Light of Nature and Revelation</u>, pages 164, 165:
> "**Unitarians** believe that Christ was a prophet, an inspired teacher, but merely human; that his death was that of a human body only. **Trinitarians hold that the term 'Christ' comprehends two distinct and separate natures: one that was merely human; the other, the second person in the trinity, who dwelt in the flesh for a brief period, but could not possibly suffer, or die; that the Christ that died was only the human nature** in which the divinity had dwelt. **Both classes have a human offering, and nothing more.** No matter how exalted the pre-existent Son was; no matter how glorious, powerful, or even eternal; if the manhood only died, the sacrifice was only human. And so far as the vicarious death of Christ is concerned, this is Socinianism. Thus the remark is just, that **the doctrine of a trinity degrades the Atonement, resting it solely on a human offering as a basis.**"

Waggoner is absolutely correct in this assertion, despite his other misconceptions. He did not recognize, however, that to thus degrade the atonement automatically also degrades the law, and therefore, the Sabbath of the law.

WILLIAM: What pioneers are next?

PROFESSOR: We'll look at Hull and Washburn to finish up:

> D. W. HULL: *Review & Herald,* November 10, 1859:
> "The inconsistent positions held by many in regard to the Trinity, as it is termed, has, no doubt, been the prime cause of many other errors. Erroneous views of the divinity of Christ are apt to lead us into error in regard to the nature of the atonement.

Viewing the atonement as an arbitrary scheme (and all must believe it to be so, who view Christ as the only 'very and eternal God'), has led to some of the arbitrary conclusions of one or two classes of persons; such as Predestinarianism, Universalism, etc., etc.

"The doctrine which we propose to examine, was established by the Council of Nice, AD 325, and ever since that period, persons not believing this peculiar tenet, have been denounced by popes and priests, as dangerous heretics. **It was for a disbelief in this doctrine, that the Arians were anathematized in AD 513.**

"**As we can trace this doctrine no farther back than the origin of the 'Man of Sin,'** and as we find this dogma at that time **established rather by force** than otherwise, we claim the right to investigate the matter, and ascertain the bearing of Scripture on this subject.

"Just here I will meet a question which is very frequently asked, namely, **Do you believe in the divinity of Christ? Most unquestionably we do; but we don't believe, as the M. E.** [*Methodist Episcopal*] **church Discipline teaches, that Christ is the very and eternal God; and, at the same time, very man; that the human part was the Son, and the divine part was the Father.**"

(See Chapter 28 of this book for a discussion of points raised by Hull's last statement.)

WILLIAM: Hull makes a good point about the Arians and the use of force against them!

PROFESSOR: Now hear J. S. Washburn:

JUDSON SYLVANEOUS WASHBURN (1863-1955)—Letter, written in 1939:
"**The doctrine of the Trinity is a cruel heathen monstrosity, removing Jesus from His true position of divine Saviour and Mediator.** It is true we cannot measure or define divinity. It is beyond our finite understanding, yet on the subject of the personality of God, the Bible is very simple and plain. The Father, the Ancient of Days, is from eternity. Jesus was begotten of the Father. Jesus, speaking through the Psalmist

says: 'The Lord (Jehovah) has said unto me, Thou art my Son, this day have I begotten thee.' (Ps. 2:7). Again in Proverbs (where Jesus is spoken of under the title of wisdom, See 1 Cor. 1:25) we read: 'The Lord (Jehovah) possessed me in the beginning of His way.' Proverbs 8:22. 'Before the mountains were settled, before the hills, was I brought forth.' (Proverbs 8:24). The Son says He was brought forth, begotten, born of His Father (Jehovah)."

Note: **The biblical text does not say what Washburn asserts regarding Proverbs 8: 22, 24!** "Wisdom" is personified in these texts. As God's messenger has clearly stated Christ is "self-existent" and that there "**never** was a time" that He was not one with His Father, however "**wisdom**" **is an attribute** that He would have "possessed in the beginning of His way"—like His Father.

WILLIAM: Professor, I want you to look at the 9th page of this booklet The Trinity in Evangelism by Gary Hullquist and Margaretha Tierney where they disagree with you and state:

"Who says Christ did not pre-exist Bethlehem? It is certainly not those who believe Him to be the Son of the living God. What about Trinitarians – Do they believe Christ – the Son of God – pre-existed Bethlehem? The answer is NO, not as the Son of God, and this is the issue."

Hullquist and Tierney then go on and quote a passage from Signs of the Times August 29, 1900 which links the words from Proverbs 8:22 and 24 to Christ as the personification of 'Wisdom':

"Through Solomon Christ declared: "The Lord possessed Me in the beginning of His way, before His works of old. I was set up from everlasting, from the beginning, or ever the earth was. When there were no depths, I was brought forth; when there were no fountains abounding with water. Before the mountains were settled, before the hills was I brought forth. . . . When He gave to the sea His decree, that the waters should not pass His commandment; when He appointed the foundations of the earth; then I was by Him, as one brought up with Him; and I was daily His delight, rejoicing always before Him." {ST, August 29, 1900 par. 14}

PROFESSOR: I fully understand their consternation, so let us carefully and prayerfully analyze those statements as we re-examine them. Firstly, the authors of The Trinity in Evangelism state on page 9 of their book:

> The Trinity in Evangelism, page 9:
> "Who says Christ did not pre-exist Bethlehem? *[Of course Jesus pre-existed Bethlehem, but then He was known as 'Michael'.]* It is certainly not those who believe Him to be the Son of the living God. What about Trinitarians – Do they believe Christ – the Son of God – pre-existed Bethlehem? The answer is NO, not as the Son of God, and this is the issue. *[Right here one must pause for a moment and reflect whether this last statement is a true and correct observation. We have repeatedly noticed that both 'Binit-arians' and **especially** 'Trinit-arians' teach and believe that Christ was "generated", "begotten" or "brought forth" at some point in past infinity. It is only since the writings of God's messenger (eg DA page 530.3) that Adventist religionists, like M. L. Andreason, etc., came to recognize that Christ the Messiah, who was, pre-incarnation, called by the name Michael: the 'One who is like God'; who was both pre-existent and **SELF-existent**, had "**unborrowed** and **underived**" life innate within Himself: A truth which quells forever both 'Arianism' and Trinitarianism; a truth which dispels forever the notion that Christ was "generated" or "begotten" at some point in past infinity otherwise His life would have been 'derived' from the Father!]*

Tierney/Hullquist then go on to say:

> Ibid.:
> "Did God consent for His loving and willing Son to come to earth? Or did a **co-equal, co-eternal** Being volunteer to take on **the role of a Son**? Pre-existence is not in question in the current debate; it is whether God had an only-begotten Son at some time in the days of eternity."

I want you to notice, William, that God's messenger has clearly answered their perplexities in clear, unambiguous, American English. The **facts** concerning Christ's life and pre-existence and the **fact** that Christ's life was **"underived"** she made abundantly clear in:

Manuscript 101, 1897; Evangelism, page 615:
"He was equal *[not CO-equal]* with God, *[He was]*
INFINITE and omnipotent... He is the **eternal** *[not CO-
eternal]*, **SELF-existent** Son." *[Self-existent does NOT mean to
be "begotten" and then to exist as a distinct Being.* **It means
that that "self-existent" Being's life and very existence is
"UNDERIVED" from any other source.**]

Take note of the following quote:

Desire of Ages, page 530.3:
"...Jesus declared, "I am the resurrection, and the life." **In
Christ is life, original** *[self-existent]*, **unborrowed,
UNDERIVED.** "He that hath the Son hath life." 1 John 5:12.
The divinity of Christ is the believer's assurance of eternal life.
"He that believeth in Me," said Jesus, **"though he were dead, yet
shall he live: and whosoever liveth and believeth in Me shall
never die. Believest thou this?" Christ here looks forward to
the time of His second coming. Then the righteous dead shall
be raised incorruptible, and the living righteous shall be
translated to heaven without seeing death.** The miracle which
Christ was about to perform, in raising Lazarus from the dead,
would represent the resurrection of all the righteous dead. By His
word and His works He declared Himself the Author of the
resurrection. He who Himself was soon to die upon the cross
stood with the keys of death, a conqueror of the grave, and
asserted His right and power to give eternal life."

Furthermore, that very important statement by God's messenger, found
in *ST* 8/29/1900, declares some fundamentally important aspects
surrounding Christ's pre-existence and which links Proverbs 8:22 and 24 to
Christ, but does **not** make the connection between Christ and Wisdom to
mean what they or Washburn thought it did. Let's read it analytically:

Signs of the Times, August 29, 1900:
"Through Solomon, Christ declared: 'The Lord possessed
Me **in the BEGINNING of His way** *[What does this last phrase
from Solomon's writings mean? Does this phrase indicate that
"the Lord" (God), who clearly had "Wisdom"/Christ with Him
(See the words: "possessed Me"), had a "beginning of His
way", at which point He "possessed" "Wisdom"/Christ? So*

does or does not this phrase indicate that God the Father had a "__beginning__ of His way"? I believe the answer is obviously NO! This is poetic 'personification' speech concerning Christ who is being portrayed as the acme of "Wisdom": which is clearly an attribute that both He and His Father have always possessed in infinite capacity. Let us continue reading from this quote found in ST 8/29/1900:] before His works of old *[creation].* I *["Wisdom"/Christ]* was **set up** from everlasting *[comment: to be "__set up__ from EVERLASTING" does NOT imply a "beginning"! The term "everlasting" makes that plain]* from the beginning, or ever the earth was. When there were no depths, I was **brought forth**; when there were no fountains abounding with water. Before the mountains were settled, before the hills was I **brought forth**. ... When He gave to the sea His decree, that the waters should not pass His commandment; when He appointed the foundations of the earth; then I *["Wisdom"/Christ]* was **by** **Him** *[the Most High God],* **as** *[like]* one **brought up** **WITH Him** *[notice: __not__ BY Him but WITH Him];* and I was daily His delight, rejoicing always before Him."

For "Wisdom"/Christ to be "brought up" **with** God the Father would, to the surface reader, imply that Christ and the Father were **"brought up" together** ever since the "**beginning** of His (the Father's) way", that is, **if** one wants to take these terms literally. Remember one cannot select some of these terms to be literal and read the ones you don't wish to apply literally to be poetic or figurative speech. I do not believe that either Christ or the Father had "beginning" but that they both are "pre-existent" and "**self**-existent", both having "...life original, unborrowed, underived (DA p. 530.3 and Ev. p. 616)." "This life is not inherent in man. *[Obviously]* **He** *[man]* **can possess it** only through Christ.** He *[man]* cannot earn it; **it** *[life, original, unborrowed, underived]* **is given him** *[man]* **as a free gift** if he will believe in Christ as his *[man's]* personal Saviour." 1SM p. 296-7. **The reception of the "original, unborrowed, underived" life of Jesus by redeemed sinners is** *ipso facto* **the reception of Christ's immortal life which, post Calvary, Christ takes up and gives to His redeemed ones at His second coming (DA p. 786.4), so that this "mortal" can put on "immortality", which has ever been exclusively the property of Deity.** God's Word tells us that only Members of the Godhead "...hath immortality" (1 Timothy 6:15, 16). This is "I AM", "SELF-existent" life. **The redeemed receive Christ's "I AM" "SELF-existent" life which Christ never 'borrowed' and which Christ never 'derived' from any**

51

other Source: that is what "self-existent" and "underived" means! To attempt to make the inspired words of God's messenger mean that Christ 'derived' His life from the Father at some point in infinity is to attempt to wrest her plain American English to mean the opposite of what God's messenger wrote.

Let's return to the Trinity doctrine, and what Washburn goes on to say about it in his 1939 letter:

"Satan has taken some heathen conception of a three-headed monstrosity, and with deliberate intention to cast contempt upon divinity, has woven it into Romanism as our glorious God, an impossible, absurd invention. **This monstrous doctrine transplanted from heathenism into the Roman Papal Church is seeking to intrude its evil presence into the teachings of the Third Angels Message**....

"And **the fact that Christ is not the mediator in the Roman Church demonstrates that the Trinity destroys the truth that Christ is the one, the only Mediator. The so-called Christian Church, the Papacy, that originated the doctrine of the Trinity, does not recognize Him as the only mediator, but substitutes a multitude of ghosts of dead men and women as mediators. If you hold the Trinity doctrine, in reality, Christ is no longer your mediator....**

"**The whole Trinity doctrine is utterly foreign to all the Bible and the teachings of the Spirit of Prophecy.** Revelation gives not the slightest hint of it. This monstrous heathen conception finds no place in all the free universe of our blessed heavenly Father and His Son, our Lord and Saviour, Jesus Christ.... **The Catholic heathen doctrine of the Sunday Sabbath is just as sacred as the Catholic pagan doctrine of the Trinity** and more so.... **Seventh-day Adventists claim to take the Word of God as supreme authority and to have 'come out of Babylon,' to have renounced forever the vain traditions of Rome.** If we should go back to the immortality of the soul, purgatory, eternal torment and the Sunday Sabbath, would that be anything less than apostasy? **If, however, we leap over all these minor, secondary doctrines and accept and teach the very central root doctrine of Romanism, the Trinity, and teach that the Son of God did not die, even though our words seem to be spiritual, is this anything else or** anything less than apostasy, and <u>the very Omega</u> of apostasy?

"However kindly or beautiful or apparently profound his sermons or articles may be, <u>when a man has arrived at the place where he teaches the heathen Catholic doctrine of the Trinity, and denies that the Son of God died for us, is he a true Seventh-day Adventist?</u> Is he even a true preacher of the gospel? And when many regard him as a great teacher and accept his unscriptural theories, absolutely contrary to the Spirit of Prophecy, <u>it is time that the watchmen should sound a note of warning.</u>"

WILLIAM: That was a strong point: "**The fact that Christ is not the mediator in the Roman Church demonstrates that the Trinity doctrine destroys the truth that Christ is the one, the only Mediator.**"

PROFESSOR: <u>Yes, and Washburn sees this doctrine as the Omega of apostasy. I agree with him.</u>

If "Jesus" was consubstantial with the Father—as the Trinitarian doctrine teaches—then Jesus could not actually have died—unless one believes He had three natures (as already discussed) and that only His human nature died: leaving one with only a human "appeasement" sacrifice—as Romanists believe.

From what we studied previously and from what we have again looked at in this study of the pioneers, they, including **James White**, husband of the prophet, were indeed vociferously 'Anti-Trinitarian.' However, is it fair or honest to extrapolate from **that** fact that they did not believe in separate and distinct persons in the Godhead? Can we conclude, as Allen Stump has done in his book, The Foundation of our Faith, that **all** the pioneers did not believe that Holy Spirit was the Third Person of the Godhead?

Did God's messenger correct wrong views held by some of the pioneers, even though she endorsed their overall teachings that were in accord with the truth? Clearly she did, and we need not return to these errors of concept that she corrected, as Allan Stump, David Clayton, and others have done by trying to proclaim a two-person Godhead!

<u>However, the pioneer's clear-sighted view of the unscriptural nature of Trinitarian doctrine should be retained, and not discarded into the historical trash-basket as is being done within the ranks of Adventism</u>—by those who now hold to the Trinitarian view proclaimed in Statement of Belief #2 of the 1980 statement of beliefs.

53

WILLIAM: Praise the Lord for a clear presentation of what the SDA pioneers believed. Thank you for showing me from their own writings.

PROFESSOR: Yes, Praise the Lord.

Chapter 3

CATHOLIC CATECHISM AND THE 'TRINITY' VS. THE TRUTH

WILLIAM: Why did the Adventist Pioneers write so much against Trinitarian teaching?

PROFESSOR: There has to be a reason, and there is—a good one! They recognized Babylonian wine when they saw it. Rome's stand is plain:

> The Handbook for Today's Catholic, page16:
> "Unless (people) keep this Faith whole and undefiled, without doubt (they) shall perish everlastingly. And **the Catholic faith is this: we worship one God in Trinity.** The mystery of **the trinity is the central doctrine of Catholic faith.** Upon it are based all the other teachings of the church."

WILLIAM: Does that mean that the doctrines of 'original sin,' 'infant baptism,' and the 'immaculate conception,' etc. are all based on this 'central doctrine'—the doctrine of the Trinity?

PROFESSOR: Let us examine this hypothesis. If these doctrines (original sin, etc.) are false doctrines, then the foundational doctrine on which they are predicated must also be false! It must be false, for false doctrine can never be built **on** truth, while at the same time it must cling **to** 'some' truth in order to sustain itself from falling, like Dagon, flat on its face. (See 1 Samuel 5:3, 4.) Turning to the book:

> Catechism of the Catholic Church, pages 54, 55, 180 we read about the Trinity Doctrine:
> Page 54: "The Christian faith confesses that **God is one in nature, substance and essence**."
> Page 55: "We firmly believe and confess without reservation that there is only one true God, eternal, infinite (immensus) and unchangeable, incomprehensible, Almighty and ineffable, the Father and the Son and the Holy Spirit; Three Persons indeed, **but one essence, substance or nature** entirely simple."

*[As we have seen, the Catholic Church has coined a word to encapsulate this teaching: the word is **'consubstantiation'** = sharing the same indivisible substance or essence.]*

<u>Page 180</u>: "To believe in the Holy Spirit is to profess that the Holy Spirit is one of the Persons of the Holy Trinity, **consubstantial** with the Father and the Son...."

It follows logically, that if the Father, The son and the Holy Spirit co-share one substance, then they are each but different revelations of that one substance and that is indeed how they have portrayed their notion of the Trinity: **The illustration below is from an SDA Bible-Study Handbook, which is sold at ABC bookstores.**

This illustration above, however, was inspired by Catholic sources. For instance, the two illustrations below are from the Catholic catechism entitled, <u>My Catholic Faith</u>, pages 32-33:

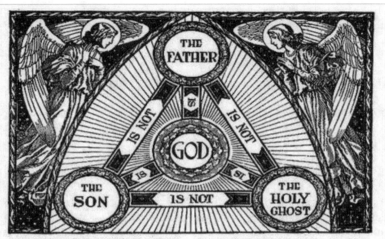

A good concrete illustration of the Blessed Trinity is an equilateral triangle. Such a triangle has three sides equal in every way, and yet distinct from each other. There are three sides, but only one triangle. As we see in this illustration, each Divine Person is different from the other two, but all three are God. Each one is God, distinct from the two others, and yet one with them. The three Persons are equal in every way, with one nature and one substance; three Divine Persons, but only one God.

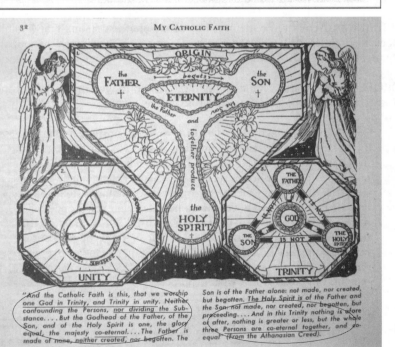

32   MY CATHOLIC FAITH

"And the Catholic Faith is this, that we worship one God in Trinity, and Trinity in unity. Neither confounding the Persons, nor dividing the Substance.... But the Godhead of the Father, of the Son, and of the Holy Spirit is one, the glory equal, the majesty co-eternal.... The Father is made of none, neither created, nor begotten. The Son is of the Father alone: not made, nor created, but begotten. The Holy Spirit is of the Father and the Son: not made, nor created, nor begotten, but proceeding.... And in this Trinity nothing is more or after, nothing is greater or less, but the whole three Persons are co-eternal together, and co-equal (from the Athanasian Creed).

57

WILLIAM: So this illustration reveals why you cannot say that each member of the Trinity is **eternal.**

PROFESSOR: Right. Instead you have to say they are **"co-eternal."**

WILLIAM: And you can't say that each "Person" is **equal** to the other.

PROFESSOR: You would have to say they are _____?

WILLIAM: "Co-equal."

PROFESSOR: Right! Let us examine where such a notion or doctrine will lead us.

As we have seen, the Roman Church's 'Trinity' doctrine, the doctrine of 'consubstantiality' demands a **two-nature** Christology at least! Simply put, it demands that Jesus had a **human** and a **divine** nature, and **that these two natures were separate at all times,** with only His human nature dying on the cross. In contrast to this, the SDA pioneers believed in a **one** nature Christology, the divine and the human 'blended' into one.

WILLIAM: Actually, I remember one of the pioneers stating that Catholic doctrine implies that Christ had **three** natures: The human nature, the divine nature, and the immortal soul.

PROFESSOR: Good point, William, but you're getting ahead of me. Remember what God's messenger wrote on **this** issue:

1888 Materials, page 332: [Doctrine of Righteousness by Faith.]
"Christ could have done **nothing** during His earthly ministry in saving fallen man if the divine had not **blended** with the human. The limited capacity of man cannot define this wonderful mystery—the **blending** the two natures, the divine and the human. It can never be explained. Man must wonder and be silent. **And yet man is privileged to be a partaker of the divine nature, and in this way he can to some degree enter into the mystery.** This wonderful exhibition of God's love was made on the cross of Calvary. Divinity took the nature of humanity, and for what purpose?—That through the righteousness of Christ humanity might partake of the divine nature."

Man's partaking of the divine nature was made possible through Christ's right-doing—His loyal obedience to His separate and distinct Father. Christ was empowered to fully obey His Father's will through the indwelling presence of the Holy Spirit. He has opened the way for fallen human beings to receive **the indwelling divinity of the Holy Spirit:**

> *Signs of the Times,* March 8, 1899:
> "When He came to the world the first time, **divinity and humanity were blended. This is our only hope.** The Son of man is fully qualified to be the **originator** *[2nd Adam: 1 Cor. 15:45, 47] of a humanity that will blend with divinity by partaking of the divine nature.*"

As we have noted the **Methodist church system** (like other daughters of Rome) have, as a denomination, accepted Rome's foundational doctrine—the 'Trinity'! Uriah Smith, writing in the **Review & Herald, March 27, 1888,** responded to an article in the "Free Methodist" a Chicago church paper, in which the article writer C.E. Harrow Jr., put forward the idea that Jesus was not possessed of a dual (blended) nature while here upon the earth. Smith responded:

> *Review & Herald,* March 27, 1888:
> "At the same time he *[C.E. Harrow Jr.]* fails to answer the point made by S.D. Adventists that if His *[Christ's]* nature can be separated into human and divine, and only the human part died, then the world is furnished with only a **human sacrifice, not a divine sacrifice,** as we contend." *[Smith had this last perception right, at least!]*

WILLIAM: That would not be right. A divine sacrifice, one equal with the law, was necessary to pay the penalty of the law for our sins.

PROFESSOR: Correct. And now we come to what you mentioned earlier—a statement made by J.M. Stevenson, who recognized that **Trinitarianism actually implies that Christ had three separate natures,** taking Papal falsehood to its natural conclusion:

> *Review & Herald,* November 21, 1854. Author: J.M. Stephenson. Editor, James White:
> "The 'Trinitarian' view is that the Son of God had three distinct natures at the same time *[during the*

59

incarnation]; viz. *1]* **A human body,** *2]* **a human soul, united with** *3]* **His divine nature: The body being mortal, the soul immortal, the divinity co-equal, co-existent, and co-eternal with the everlasting Father** *[so where did Jesus "empty Himself and be so that, of His own self, He "could do nothing"?]* Now none of the advocates of this Trinitarian theory claim that either His soul or Divinity died, *[but]* that the body was the only part of this **triple** being which actually died the death of the cross;" *[that is why, if you believe Catholic doctrine, His soul could go to 'hell' and preach to the 'souls' there!]* "Hence, according to this view we only have the sacrifice of the most inferior part—the human body—of the Son of God."

Stephenson recognized that the Trinitarian view of Christ's nature and the implications for the Atonement are diametrically opposed to Scripture. See **Isa. 53:12:** **"...He hath poured out His soul unto death...."**

WILLIAM: If that is true, Professor—If, according to Trinitarian doctrine, Jesus' mortal human nature died, and after his resurrection, His divinity and 'soul' have ascended to heaven; what kind of **"High Priest"** would be currently interceding on our behalf?

PROFESSOR: Certainly not the **"man"** Christ Jesus! However, the Bible assures us:

1 Timothy 2:5:
"For there is <u>one</u> God, and <u>one</u> mediator <u>between</u> God and men, **the man** Christ Jesus."

WILLIAM: Also, if as 'Trinitarians' teach, Jesus was "consubstantial" with the Father while He was here on earth, then clearly He could not be "tempted in all points like as we are" for it is not possible to tempt God ("...for God cannot be tempted with evil..." James 1:13)

PROFESSOR: Another good observation. Let's read now, what J.N. Loughborough wrote about the Trinity:

Review & Herald, November 5, 1861:

60

"Its origin is pagan and fabulous. Instead of pointing us to Scripture for proof of the Trinity, we are pointed to **the Trident of the Persians,** with the assertion that 'by this they design to teach the idea of a Trinity, and if they had the doctrine of the Trinity, they must have received it by tradition from the people of God."

What Loughborough is here describing is typical papal sleight of hand: putting evil for good, and good for evil: The pagan trident is presented to represent the Godhead which they equate with the Trinity.

WILLIAM: **That is just what the General Conference of SDA teaches in their Sabbath School Quarterly.** Look here:

Spring, 2006 *Sabbath School Quarterly*, Lesson #1, under the title:
"The Triune God," which states:
"'There is one God: Father, Son, and Holy Spirit, a unity of three co-eternal Persons.'
"In other words, Adventists—along with millions of other Christians—believe in the triune nature of God; that is, there is <u>one God who exists as three Persons</u>."
"...What analogies—such as ...a <u>three-pronged</u> fork— can help someone understand the idea of how one God can be composed of three equal Persons?"

PROFESSOR: Here we find the resurgence of the Persian trident referred to by Loughborough. Look at the source of this brand of "inspiration," as shown in these two pictures.

The satanic notion of the members of the Godhead being consubstantial, as taught in the Catholic Catechism, **and now found in the official Seventh-day Adventist Sabbath School Quarterly**, is a fundamental heresy straight from hell. **It is "Dragon-speak"!**

Chapter 4

JOHN HARVEY KELLOGG AND THE TRINITY

PROFESSOR: The unseen winds of false doctrine swirled through the mind of John Harvey Kellogg in the early 1900's and whipped through the denomination. The Bible warns:

Ephesians 4:14:
"That we henceforth be no more children, tossed to and fro, and carried about with every wind of doctrine, by the sleight of men, and cunning craftiness, whereby they lie in wait to deceive;"

Back then, mixed in with the true understanding of the Godhead held by James and Ellen White, were the erroneous, so-called "Semi-Arian" and "Arian" views held by many of the early Adventist Pioneers. As if these erroneous views did not cause enough confusion, there was another erroneous view held—the equally egregious and confusing notion that the Holy Spirit was not a distinct "Person" of the Godhead, but was simply an emanation of God's and Christ's power.

The following correspondence between Dr. John Harvey Kellogg and Elder George I. Butler classically **highlights how both of these errors played into confirming Kellogg in his pantheistic views.**

WILLIAM: A perfect storm.

PROFESSOR: One of those that come every 100 years or so. It could have been prevented had Kellogg and others listened to the "storm warnings" being given him from God's messenger. Listen as Kellogg describes this turbulent issue with Elder Butler.

(Letter from J. H. Kellogg to G.I. Butler, October 28, 1903):
"As far as I can fathom, the difficulty which is found in <u>The Living Temple</u>, the whole thing may be simmered down to the question: Is the Holy Ghost a person? You say no. *[Kellogg knew that Butler was clearly of Uriah Smith's persuasion—that the Holy Spirit is not a person. God's messenger clearly*

countermanded this error of Smith and others, as we have noted. (See pages 38-43 of this book)]. I had supposed the Bible said this *[that the Holy Spirit is a Person.]* for the reason that the personal pronoun 'he' is used in speaking of the Holy Ghost. **Sister White uses the pronoun 'he' and has said in so many words that the Holy Ghost is the third person of the Godhead** *[which she did, thus refuting the erroneous views of Smith, Butler, and many others.]* How the Holy Ghost can be the third person and not be a person at all is difficult for me to see."

WILLIAM: I guess it was like two weather fronts colliding here. No wonder there was a major storm brewing. Kellogg had some truth on one front—at least on this aspect of the issue—it seems to me.

PROFESSOR: Yes, he did. Listen as he repeats the partial truth that he had.

(Letter from J. H. Kellogg to G. I. Butler, February 21, 1904)
"I believe this Spirit of God to be a personality you don't. But this is purely a question of definition. I believe the Spirit of God is a personality; you say, No, it is not a personality. Now the only reason why we differ is because we differ in our ideas as to what a personality is. Your idea of personality is perhaps that of semblance to a person or a human being."

It is abundantly clear from the writings of God's messenger that these observations by Dr. Kellogg concerning the personhood and personality of the Holy Spirit were correct: (See Evangelism, pages 614-617). However, Kellogg's understanding of the Holy Spirit's personality was clouded, as we shall see.

WILLIAM: It seems that Butler did not perceive the truth on **this** issue, because he also had a wrong understanding of the Holy Spirit.

PROFESSOR: Exactly. He did not understand the truth on the Holy Spirit's personality, his Personhood, so he continued to hold on to the false notion that the Holy Spirit was not a person at all, but just a power. God's messenger qualified our normally homocentric view of personality (the one rejected by Butler), by clearly stating:

Evangelism, page 617:
"The Holy Spirit has a personality, else He could not bear witness to our spirits and with our spirits that we are the children of God. **He must also be a divine person,** else He could not search out the secrets which lie hidden in the mind of God. "For what man knoweth the things of a man, save the spirit of man which is in him? even so the things of God knoweth no man, but the Spirit of God."—Manuscript 20, 1906. *[See Chapter 31: "The 'Spirit' of a Man."]*

However, God's messenger clarified that the "personality" of the Holy Spirit is unlike our usual homocentric perception of the term:

Desire of Ages, page 669:
"The Holy Spirit is Christ's representative, but **divested** of the **personality of humanity,** and independent thereof."

(Incidentally, for the Holy Spirit to be "**divested** of the personality of humanity," clearly implies that at some point the Holy Spirit did indeed assume the "personality of humanity" and later "divested" Himself thereof. See pages 184-186 of this book)

WILLIAM: It sounds as if Kellogg was on the right track in **this** regard, but Butler thought he was wrong.

PROFESSOR: Those who today still cling to the views of Uriah Smith, Butler, J.H. Waggoner, etc. attempt to strain the above quoted letters by Dr. Kellogg as proving that Kellogg was in error for believing that the Holy Spirit is a "Person" and has "personality." To justify their claim they quote from God's messenger:

Special Testimonies, Series B, No. 2, pages 53, 54:
"I am compelled to speak in denial of the claim that the teachings of Living Temple can be sustained by statements from my writings. There may be in this book expressions and sentiments that are in harmony with my writings. And there may be in my writings many statements which, taken from their connection, and interpreted according to the mind of the writer of Living Temple, would seem to be in harmony with the teachings of this book. This may give apparent support to the assertion that

the sentiments in <u>Living Temple</u> are in harmony with my writings. But God forbid that this sentiment should prevail."

The reason they misconstrue the above inspired statement by God's messenger is to sustain their argument that Uriah Smith, J.H. Waggoner, Butler, etc. were correct in their view that the Holy Spirit was an emanation of God's power, and not a "Person," and then they go on in their attempt to prove a "two-Person" Godhead, with the Holy Spirit being only an emanation of God and Christ's power.

WILLIAM: Well, where **did** Kellogg go wrong?

PROFESSOR: **The truth is that Kellogg's view of the Godhead had become beclouded with Trinitarianism.** While he, correctly, asserted that the Holy Spirit was a "Person," having "Personality," with regards to the interrelationship of the "Heavenly Trio," his view was that of them being "consubstantial" Persons *[?]*; with "God the Holy Spirit" being that member of the "Trinity" who was present "in" all things. **It was this pantheistic, spiritualistic, salvation-destroying error that God's messenger most strongly objected to—the notion that "God" was <u>in</u> all created things.**

Kellogg's apparent acceptance of the "Person"hood and "personality" of the Holy Spirit were actually obfuscating his really more Catholic concept of the application of these terms 'person,' 'personality,' when referring to 'members' of the Trinity. He apparently subscribed to the Trinitarian view of three modalities (or hypostases) of the One God "essence" or "substance", (See Chapter 1 of this book) with one of these modalities, or 'persons,' being present **in all** nature. Hence 'God' was, according to Kellogg, **in** all created things.

Kellogg's acknowledgement of his having accepted Trinitarian concepts is recorded in the following correspondence between two church officials engaged in the <u>Living Temple</u> controversy:

(Letter: A. G. Daniels to W. C. White, Oct. 29, 1903; pages 1, 2.):

"Ever since the council closed I have felt that I should write you confidentially regarding Dr. Kellogg's plans for revising and republishing 'The Living Temple'.... He (Kellogg) said that some days before coming to the council, he had been thinking the matter over, and began to see that he had made a slight mistake in expressing his views. He said that all the way along he had been troubled to know how to state the character of God and his relation to his creation works... **He then stated that his former views regarding the trinity had stood in his way of making a clear and absolutely correct statement; but that within a short time <u>he had come to believe in the trinity</u> and** could now see pretty clearly where all the difficulty was, and believed that he could clear the matter up satisfactorily.

"He told me that he now believed in God the Father, God the Son, and God the Holy Ghost; and his view was that it was God the Holy Ghost, and not God the Father, that filled all space, and every living thing. *[Note: Did or does the Holy Spirit fill Satan? His demons? Hitler? A mad dog? A rattlesnake? A leech? A willful sinner? The demon possessed? Clearly, Kellogg was confused between God's power on the one hand, and the Holy Spirit on the other. God's power **sustains all created things** and is administered by the Holy Spirit, without the Holy Spirit being **in** them.]*

(A.G. DANIELS continues):
"He said if he had believed this before writing the book, he could have expressed his views without giving the wrong impression the book now gives. I placed before him the objections I found in the teaching, and tried to show him that the teaching was so utterly contrary to the gospel that I did not see how it could be revised by changing a few expressions.

"We argued the matter at some length in a friendly way; but I felt sure that when we parted, the doctor did not understand himself, nor the character of his teaching. And I could not see how it would be possible for him to flop over, and in the course of a few days fix the books up so that it would be all right."

With reference to the Kellogg Pantheistic heresy, God's messenger gave counsel:

<u>Manuscript Releases</u>, Volume 11, page 211. (Diary, #48, pages 153, 163, August 25 and 28, 1904):
"We are now to be on guard, and not drawn away from the all-important message given of God for this time. **Satan is not ignorant of the result of trying to define God and Jesus Christ in a spiritualistic way that sets God and Christ as a nonentity.** *[That is, not as personal, distinct Beings—but as*

67

modalities of a "God" essence.] The movements occupied in this kind of science are, in the place of preparing the way of the Lord, making a way for Satan to come in and confuse the minds with mysticisms of his own devising. Although they are dressed up in angel robes they have made our God and our Christ a nonentity *[an "essence" or "substance"].* Why?—because Satan sees the minds are all fitted for his working. **Men have lost track of Christ and the Lord God,** and have been obtaining an experience that is Omega to one of the most subtle delusions that will ever captivate the minds of men."

Did you notice that God's messenger just declared the making of God to be a "non-entity"—not a distinct Person—this is "Omega" "...one of the most subtle delusions that will ever captivate the minds of men." This is EXACTLY what Trinitarianism is and does!
Trinitarianism, and the deadly doctrine that Christ only partook of unfallen humanity at His incarnation, both destroy the biblical teaching on 'One'ness that has to exist between God and the redeemed (as described in John 17: 21-23.) Both destroy the idea that **God is a personal Being, and that we have a personal God and a personal Saviour,** who is "touched with the feeling of **our** infirmities." Hebrews 4:15.

WILLIAM: Professor, Do you have a copy of Kellogg's Living Temple?

PROFESSOR: Yes, it is over there on the bookshelf, in the "K's."

WILLIAM: Hold it, a minute. (William ran to get a book off the book shelf.) You have it! A copy of Kellogg's book The Living Temple!

PROFESSOR: Open it. Read the first pages. (William opened the book and began to examine the first chapter.)

WILLIAM: He is talking in just the manner that Ellen White warned about, Professor! Listen to this! (William began to read the very first words of Kellogg's book):

The Mystery of Life

"FOR ages men have sought to solve the mystery of life. Philosophers have speculated, chemists and naturalists have delved deep into the secrets of matter, living and inert; but they have brought back only a report of fathomless depths of mystery, of unknown and incomprehensible energies, too subtle for the most delicate balance, too vast for apprehension or expression, intangible, yet mighty in overcoming the forces of the inanimate world, and able to build up immense structures, such as the giants of the forests and the monarchs of the animal world, and equally active in the tearing asunder of mountain peaks, which crumble beneath the dissolving action of lichens and mosses, and are split and pulverized by the wedge-like action of the roots of pines and other mountain trees."

The Brotherhood of Being

"This wonderful life is active all about us in an infinite variety of forms; in bird, insect, fish, reptile, and all the million creatures which people the earth and sea, we recognize **one common Life—a kindred force** which springs in every limb that leaps and moves, which throbs in every beating heart, thrills through every nerve, and quivers in every brain. We behold also a like evident brotherhood or sisterhood of life in vegetable forms, joining in one common family the stately cedars of Lebanon's rugged sides with the grasses of the plain, and the molds and mosses of the ancient wall.

"While human knowledge stands mute respecting the origin of life, investigation has gone far enough to show that **life is one—that animal life and vegetable life are not merely kindred lives, but are really one and the same.**

"The manifestations of life are as varied as the different individual animals and plants, and parts of animated things. Every leaf, every blade of grass, every flower, every bird, even every insect, as well as every beast or every tree, bears witness to the infinite versatility and inexhaustible resources of the **one all-pervading, all-creating, all-sustaining Life.**

"As we go about plucking flowers and leaves, trampling upon the grass, perhaps crushing under our feet a score of ants, beetles, worms, or other humble creatures, we seldom stop to think of the vast extent of the abounding life above and all about us. Think, for a moment, of the grass, that commonest of all plants. It is more interesting than it appears to be, for the botanists have sorted out five thousand different species or more. What a magnificent carpet the green grass spreads over all the fertile earth in every clime where an unencumbered soil is found, and every blade witnesses to active life, shaping and forming it down in the darkness of the soil, and pushing it up to the air and the sunlight. And then the leaves, so many that were they stripped from all the trees, and spread out upon the earth, a surface of more than forty-two million square miles would be covered; and yet no two leaves and no two blades of grass have ever been found exactly alike.1 Calculate the number of blades of grass in an acre, and in a square mile, and remember that every one is a witness to the active presence of **the one infinite, abounding Life."**

He is talking about Life with a capital "L." That is pantheism.

PROFESSOR: Plain as day. I'm going to read from:

Ministry of Healing, page 413:
"The mighty power that works <u>through</u> all nature and <u>sustains</u> all things is not, as some men of science represent, merely an all-pervading principle, an actuating energy. **God is a Spirit; yet He is a personal Being;** for so He has revealed Himself:
"'The Lord is the true God, He is the living God, and an everlasting King: ...The gods that have not made the heavens and the earth, Even they shall perish from the earth, and from under these heavens.'
"'The portion of Jacob is not like them: For He is the former of all things.'
"'He hath made the earth by His power, He hath established the world by His wisdom, And hath stretched out the heavens by His discretion.' Jeremiah 10:10, 11, 16, 12: *[Note: Read Hebrews 1:3.]*
"God's handiwork in nature **is not God Himself <u>in</u> nature. The things of nature are an expression of God's character and power; but we are not to regard nature as God."**

For God is not **'in'** His creation, not even by His Representative, the Holy Spirit. The Holy Spirit is present, but not **in** His created works, **except for the holy angels and those who have accepted redemption.** Kellogg's spiritualistic views finally took him clear out of God's truth as he stubbornly clung to His errors.

WILLIAM: Did God's messenger correct these wrong views held by Kellogg and some of the pioneers, even though she endorsed their overall teachings that were in accord with the truth?

PROFESSOR: Clearly she did, and we need not return to these errors of concept that she corrected, as others have done! Nor need we return to the corrupt wine of Babylon proffered in Trinitarianism as the General Conference leaders have done.

In 1904, God's messenger warned against the false, spiritualistic notions of Kellogg concerning the nature of God—that: 1) God is an "essence", and 2) that He pervades all nature:

Testimonies to the Church, Volume 8, pages 291, 292:
"Already there are coming in among our people spiritualistic teachings that will undermine the faith of those who give heed to them. **The theory that God is an <u>essence</u> pervading all nature is one of Satan's most subtle devices.** It misrepresents God and is a dishonor to His greatness and majesty.

"Pantheistic theories are not sustained by the word of God. **The light of His truth shows that these theories** *[1—that God is an essence, and 2—that the God "essence" pervades all nature.]* **are soul-destroying agencies.**   Darkness is their element, sensuality their sphere *[since, if "God" is in us, redeemed or not, then all that we do is **holy!** This perception was demonstrated in the "holy flesh" movement described in Evangelism, page 600 (Review & Herald, Jan. 21, 1904).]* They gratify the natural heart and give license to inclination. **Separation from God is the result of accepting them.** *[Did you get that?   To believe that God is an essence, and not a Personal God, separates you from Him!]*

"Our condition through sin has become preternatural, and the power that restores us must be supernatural, else it has no value. There is but one **power** that can break the hold of evil from the hearts of men, and that is the **power of God** *[administered through His representative, the Holy Spirit]* in Jesus Christ. Only through the blood of the Crucified One is there cleansing from sin. His grace alone can enable us to resist and subdue the tendencies of our fallen nature. This power the spiritualistic theories concerning God make of no effect. **If God is an essence pervading all nature, then He dwells in all men; and in order** to attain holiness, man has only to develop the power that is within him. "These theories, followed to their logical conclusion, sweep away the whole Christian economy. They do away with the necessity for the atonement and make man his own savior. These theories regarding God make His word of no effect, and those who accept them are in great danger of being led finally to look upon the whole Bible as a fiction. **They may regard virtue as better than vice; but God being removed from His position of sovereignty, they place their dependence upon human power, which, without God, is worthless.** *[Reader, please remember to note: Selected Messages Book 1, pages 204-206 quoted on page 74 of this book].* The unaided human will has no real power to resist and overcome evil. The defenses of the soul are broken down. Man has no barrier against sin. When once the restraints of God's word and His Spirit are rejected, we know not to what depths one may sink.

"Those who continue to hold these spiritualistic theories will surely spoil their Christian experience, **sever their connection with God, and lose eternal life."**

According to what God's messenger penned above, **it is spiritually fatal to regard God as an "essence"** and/or to regard God, in whatever "modality," as pervading all nature. **Pantheism and Trinitarianism are closely related aberrations.**

WILLIAM: I see. One is the "Alpha," and the other is the "Omega" of apostasy—**and we are definitely in the Omega right now. No wonder God's messenger 'trembled for our people'.**

PROFESSOR: It is also amazing that but few of the "brethren" recognized the apostasy in Kellogg's book until God's messenger pointed it out to them.

Review & Herald, October 22, 1903:
"I have some things to say to our teachers in reference to the new book, 'The Living Temple.' **Be careful how you sustain the sentiments of this book regarding the personality of God.** As the Lord represents matters to me, these sentiments do not bear the endorsement of God. They are a snare that the enemy has prepared for these last days. **I thought that this would**

surely be discerned, and that it would not be necessary for me to say anything about it. But since the claim has been made that the teachings of this book can be sustained by statements from my writings, I am compelled to speak in denial of this claim. There may be in this book expressions and sentiments that are in harmony with my writings. And there may be in my writings many statements which, when taken from their connection, and interpreted according to the mind of the writer of 'The Living Temple,' would seem to be in harmony with the teachings of this book. This may give apparent support to the assertion that the sentiments in 'The Living Temple' are in harmony with my writings. But God forbid that this opinion should prevail.

"We need not the mysticism that is in this book. "

WILLIAM: The same in our day. No one sees that they are worshipping a false god—a spiritualistic, "consubstantial" "essence," instead of a personal God, Whom to know is "life eternal." (John 17:3). God's word warns: "My people are destroyed for lack of knowledge...." Hosea 4:6.

PROFESSOR: It is by following the world that we will wind up 'wondering after the beast'. We have been warned by God's messenger:

Manuscript Releases, Volume 8, page 304.1-3:
"**The world is full of speculation and false theories regarding the nature and character of God. The enemy of our souls is earnestly at work to introduce among the Lord's people pleasing speculation, and incorrect views regarding the personality of God** ....

"I have seen the results of these fanciful views of God, in apostasy, spiritualism, freelovism. The free love tendencies of these teachings were so concealed that it was difficult to present them in their real character. . . .

"**There is a strain of spiritualism coming in among our people, and it will undermine the faith of those who give place to it, leading them to give heed to seducing spirits, and doctrines of devils**.--Letter 230, 1903, pages 1, 3, 5. (To Dr. E. J. Waggoner, October 2, 1903.)"

Chapter 5

FROM THE ALPHA TO THE OMEGA

PROFESSOR: During the upsurge of Dr. John Harvey Kellogg's pantheistic theories and His publication of the book <u>The Living Temple</u>, God's messenger was called of God to "meet" the looming threat to the spiritual life of God's people.

> <u>Selected Messages Book 1</u>, page 200:
> "I am instructed to speak plainly. 'Meet it,' is the word spoken to me. 'Meet it firmly, and without delay.' But it is not to be met by our taking our working forces from the field to investigate doctrines and points of difference. We have no such investigation to make. **In the book Living Temple there is presented the alpha of deadly heresies. The omega will follow, and <u>will be received by those who are not willing to heed the warning God has given</u>.**"

What was the "warning God has given"? Remember, the warning given was to not make of God an "essence" (the term by which God is described in Trinitarianism), a "non-entity," an ectoplasmic blob manifesting itself in different hypostases, thereby demeaning and confusing the "Personhood" of God—as the Omega does.

WILLIAM: And also confusing the mind of the Trinitarian believer.

PROFESSOR: Absolutely!

WILLIAM: What did Sister White mean by "Meet it"?

PROFESSOR: The answer to that question was given to Ellen White in a dream and it is very interesting:

> <u>Selected Messages Book 1</u>, pages 204-206:
> "In a vision of the night I was shown distinctly that these sentiments have been looked upon by some as the grand truths that are to be brought in and made prominent at the present time.

I was shown a platform, braced by solid timbers--the truths of the Word of God. Someone high in responsibility in the medical work was directing this man and that man to loosen the timbers supporting this platform. Then I heard a voice saying, "**Where are the watchmen that ought to be standing on the walls of Zion? Are they asleep?** This foundation was built by the Master Worker, and will stand storm and tempest. Will they permit this man to present doctrines that deny the past experience of the people of God? The time has come to take decided action.

"The enemy of souls has sought to bring in the supposition that a great reformation was to take place among Seventh-day Adventists, and that this reformation would consist in giving up the doctrines which stand as the pillars of our faith, **and engaging in a process of reorganization.** Were this reformation to take place, what would result? The principles of truth that God in His wisdom has given to the remnant church, would be discarded. **Our religion would be changed.** The fundamental principles that have sustained the work for the last fifty years would be accounted as error. **A new organization would be established. Books of a new order would be written.** A system of intellectual philosophy would be introduced. The founders of this system would go into the cities, and do a wonderful work. The Sabbath of course, would be lightly regarded, as also the God who created it. Nothing would be allowed to stand in the way of the new movement. The leaders would teach that virtue is better than vice, **but God being removed,** they would place their dependence on human power, which, **without God,** is worthless. Their foundation would be built on the sand, and storm and tempest would sweep away the structure.

"Who has authority to begin **such a movement?** We have our Bibles. We have our experience, attested to by the miraculous working of the Holy Spirit. We have a truth that admits of no compromise. **Shall we not repudiate everything that is not in harmony with this truth?**

"I hesitated and delayed about the sending out of that which the Spirit of the Lord impelled me to write. I did not want to be compelled to present the misleading influence of these sophistries. **But in the providence of God, the errors that have been coming in must be met.**

"Shortly before I sent out the testimonies regarding the efforts of the enemy to **undermine the foundation of our faith**

through the dissemination of seductive theories, I had read an incident about a ship in a fog meeting an iceberg. For several nights I slept but little. I seemed to be bowed down as a cart beneath sheaves.

"One night a scene was clearly presented before me. A vessel was upon the waters, in a heavy fog. Suddenly the lookout cried, 'Iceberg just ahead!' There, towering high above the ship, was a gigantic iceberg. An authoritative voice cried out, **'Meet it!'** There was not a moment's hesitation. It was a time for instant action. The engineer put on full steam, and the man at the wheel steered the ship straight into the iceberg. With a crash she struck the ice. There was a fearful shock, and the iceberg broke into many pieces, falling with a noise like thunder to the deck. The passengers were violently shaken by the force of the collisions, but no lives were lost. The vessel was injured, but not beyond repair. She rebounded from the contact, trembling from stem to stern, like a living creature. Then she moved forward on her way.

"Well I knew the meaning of this representation. I had my orders. I had heard the words, like a voice from our Captain, "Meet it!" I knew what my duty was, and that there was not a moment to lose. **The time for decided action had come. I must without delay obey the command, 'Meet it!'.**

"That night I was up at one o'clock, writing as fast as my hand could pass over the paper. For the next few days I worked early and late, **preparing for our people the instruction given me regarding the errors that were coming in among us.**"

This is the **vessel of Truth** meeting the iceberg of error head on!

It is noteworthy that Kellogg's view of the nature of God [*and of God in nature*] drifted far from the Scriptural views of God's messenger, or, for that matter, of her husband James White and other pioneers and members. **Kellogg no longer saw God as a personal divine Being.** He espoused the Trinitarian view that depicted God as an "essence" pervading everything in the universe—an all pervading "Life." This pantheistic view, you remember, we clearly saw in the beginning words of his book, The Living Temple:

The Living Temple, pages 17, 18:
"For ages men have sought to solve the mystery of life. ...This wonderful life is active all about us in an infinite variety of forms; in bird, insect, fish, reptile, and all the million creatures

which people the earth and sea, we recognize **one common Life—a kindred force** which springs in every limb that leaps and moves, which throbs in every beating heart, thrills through every nerve, and quivers in every brain....

"While human knowledge stands mute respecting the origin of life, investigation has gone far enough to show that life is one—that animal life and vegetable life are not merely kindred lives, but are really **one and the same.**

"...Every leaf, every blade of grass, every flower, every bird, even every insect, as well as every beast or every tree, bears witness to the infinite versatility and inexhaustible resources of **the one all-pervading, all-creating, all-sustaining Life.**"

WILLIAM: So beautifully written.

PROFESSOR: Satan attracts us with things that tantalize the senses—make-up and tinsel, perfume, music—the glories of this world. But he also uses flattering theories that appeal to the carnal heart. All these are used to mask the unseen danger below the surface.

Dr. Kellogg's beautifully written pantheistic teachings that "made of God a non-entity;" his lust for power; his selfishness; his attempt to centralize all church administrative influence in Battle Creek; his domineering administrative style; his control of minds by hypnotic practices and power; his dissemination of "books of a new order;" and his refusal (and the refusal of those church leaders which were under his influence) to rely on and follow the counsels of God's messengers—all constituted and contributed to what Sister White identified as the "alpha of a train of heresies." She declared that "the omega would follow."

Selected Messages Book 1, page 203:
"Living Temple contains the alpha of these theories. **I knew that the omega would follow** in a little while; and **I trembled for our people.**"

And, as we have seen:

Selected Messages Book 1, page 200:
"The omega will follow, and **will be received** *[future tense, starting in her time]* **by those who are not willing to heed the warning God has given.**"

So God's warnings, through His servant, were to be discounted by some at a future time, and the "Omega" heresy would be received by these insubordinate ones.

WILLIAM: Reminds me of her warning:

Last Day Events, page 72:
"We have nothing to fear for the future, **except as we shall forget the way the Lord has led us, and His teaching in our past history.**"—LS 196 (1902).

PROFESSOR: Yes, because if we do forget, the result is horrifyingly tragic:

Selected Messages Book 1, pages 203-204:
"**Few can discern** the result of entertaining the sophistries advocated by **some** *[this word "some" indicates that more than just Kellogg were involved]* at this time. But the Lord has lifted the curtain, and has shown me the result that would follow. **The spiritualistic theories regarding the personality of God,** followed to their logical conclusion, **sweep away the whole Christian economy.**"

Special Testimonies, Series B, No. 7, page 38:
"We are not to allow atheistic *[atheistic in the sense that God is made a "non-entity"]*, spiritualistic sentiments to be brought before our youth. **God has led us in the past, giving us truth, eternal truth. By this truth we are to stand.** Some of the leaders in the medical work have been deceived, and if they continue to hold fanciful, spiritualistic ideas, **they will make many believe that the platform upon which we have been standing for the past fifty years has been torn away.** These men need now to see with anointed eyes, with clear spiritual vision, that in spite of all men can do, 'the foundation of God standeth sure,' and 'the Lord knoweth them that are His.'

"The message to the Laodicean church comes to us at this time with special meaning. Read it, and ask God to show you its import. Thank God that He is still sending us messages of mercy. Those accepting the theories regarding God that are introduced in 'Living Temple' are in great danger of being led **finally to look**

78

upon the whole Bible as a fiction; for these theories make of no effect the plain word of God."

Clearly, an impersonal god-"essence" cannot be related to as a personal heavenly Father. That is why Catholics readily relate to the pope, saints, "Mary," etc. and not to the God of the Bible.

WILLIAM: Such teachings would have done away with the Three Angel's messages!—the whole Protestant Bible!!

PROFESSOR: Yes, remember the first angel's message is to "Fear God and give glory to Him, for the hour of His judgment is come." Rev. 14:7. And it goes on to refer to God as the Creator. The second and third angel's messages are predicated upon the first. The Everlasting Gospel, Creation, the Judgment, the Sanctuary Message, the Last Warning to a dying world— indeed the whole Bible are all predicated on God's Creatorship. The attack by Satan is against "the remnant of her seed" that gives this final warning. The prophet Daniel points us to the fountainhead of these aberrations that undermine these precious gospel truths:

Daniel 11:30:
"For the ships of Chittim shall come against him: therefore he shall be grieved, and return, and have indignation against the holy covenant: so shall he do; he shall even return, **and have intelligence with them that forsake the holy covenant.**"

Commenting on this verse, God's messenger declares:

Manuscript Releases, Volume 13, page 394:
"Much of the history that has taken place in fulfillment of this prophecy will be repeated. In the thirtieth verse a power is spoken of that 'shall be grieved, and return, and **have indignation against the holy covenant** [*the Ten Commandments*]: so shall he do; **he shall even return, and have intelligence** [*ecumenical engagement*] **with them that forsake the holy covenant.**' [*Verses 31-36, quoted.*] Scenes similar to those described in these words will take place. We see evidence that Satan is fast obtaining the control of human minds that have not the fear of God before them."

WILLIAM: She is saying that there will be a repeat of forsaking God's holy covenant, which is the Ten Commandments—the transcript of God's character.

PROFESSOR: Yes! Remember, we covenant with God at baptism.

It is reasonable to conclude that those with whom the "king of the north" (the papacy) has "intelligence," are those among God's denominated people who have **"forsaken the holy covenant,"** that is, quit demonstrating allegiance to God and Him only, by their disregard of His counsels, His will, His Person, and finally, His law! Already, within Adventism, the "new theology" teaches that men cannot keep His law this side of the Second Coming.

Daniel's prophecy suggests that this is a two-fold attack against God's denominated people—from without and from within. The "King of the north" (the Papacy) having "intelligence" with those who forsake the Holy covenant, and then these in turn "employ their powers to deceive" others among God's people.

According to inspiration, God's people should **not have "intelligence"** with Rome or her daughters. Regrettably, there are "forsakers of the holy covenant" who go ahead and encourage this "intelligence." This is seen in the various ecumenical dialogues that the General Conference has held, and continues to hold, with the Catholic Church system and other fallen Protestant church systems. (For example, the SDA—Mennonite World Communion dialogue in 2010-2012 Source: http://mwc-cmm.org/joomla/index.php/news-releases/104-seventh-day-adventists-and-mennonite-world-conference-begin-conversation.)

WILLIAM: That is exactly what is happening! In 1998 the General Conference leaders made an agreement on Justification by Faith after four years of dialogue with the Lutheran church system (which has rejected obedience to the 4th commandment). (Source:http://www.lutheranworld.org/What_We_Do/OEA/Bilateral_Relations/OEA-Lutheran-Seventh_day_Adventist.html).

PROFESSOR; Yes, that's right. Representing the SDA church system was Bert Beach (*co-chair of the meetings*), Neils-Erik Andreasen, John Graz, Johan Heinz, William Johnsson, Pardon Mwansa, Aulikki Nabkola, Jan Paulsen, Jonathan Pauline, George Reid, Angel Rodriguez, and William Shea. (See Appendix F)

The next year (1999) the Lutheran Church made a similar agreement on Justification by Faith with Roman Catholic Church system (the Mother of harlots, Rev. 17:5).

(Source: http://www.lutheranworld.org/Special_Events/LWF-Special_Events-Justification.html).

From left: Bishop Dr. Christian Krause and Edward Idris Cardinal Cassidy sign the Joint Declaration on the Doctrine of Justification by Faith. (See Appendix G)

The rule in algebra is: If A = B and B = C, then A = C.

81

A = SDA church. B = Lutheran Church. C = Roman Catholic Church. For the Seventh-day Adventist church to make such an agreement with the Lutheran church system on Justification by Faith, and therefore indirectly with Roman Catholicism, who signed a similar agreement with the Lutheran Church, is horrifying. **They have agreed to a false brand of "Justification by Faith" with systems that have rejected obedience to all the commandments of God.** Such agreements with fallen church systems imply that you don't have to keep God's commandments to demonstrate God's sanctifying Spirit working in one's life, thereby showing, by obedience to God's law, the fruit of being justified by Christ's faith; whereas, it is by faith, Jesus' faith, and the faith He nurtures in us, that we can receive Holy Spirit power, enabling us sinners to walk in obedience:

> Selected Messages Book 1, pages 396, 397:
> "No one can believe with the heart unto righteousness, and obtain **justification by faith, while continuing the practice of those things which the Word of God forbids, or while neglecting any known duty."**

> Counsels for the Church, page 268:
> "This is what will distinguish between those who honor God and those who dishonor him. Here is where we are to prove our loyalty. The history of God's dealings with his people in all ages shows that **He demands exact obedience."**

WILLIAM: By the way, Professor, all three, A, B, and C already had agreement on the Trinity doctrine.

PROFESSOR: Right, they have been in agreement on that since 1980.
  And this ecumenical "intelligence" with those who forsake the Holy Covenant is being received, and the false teaching gets passed on to our children and youth, by "Adventist" teachers and ministers teaching Catholic doctrine and Catholic **spiritual formation**.
  More horrifying than the agreement with the Lutheran Church, is the fact that **the "Superior Authority of the Seventh-day Adventist Church in Poland", on the 14th of December 1999, signed an agreement directly with the Roman Catholic Church.** The Commission of the Episcopate for Ecumenical Matters of the Catholic Church in Poland and the Adventist leaders got together and signed the agreement on that day **in celebration of 15 years of dialogue between the two parties.** (See Appendix H)

82

I want you to pay special heed, William, to what foundation undergirded those years of dialogue and the agreement reached:

Point No. 5 of the actual agreement 'Statement':
"5. It is neither possible to treat the Seventh-day Adventist Church like a "new religious movement" because it has been in existence in Polish Lands for over 110 years, nor like a "sect", because firstly–it has a specific doctrine, organization and cultic rites, **secondly–in its teaching and service it cultivates the most important principles of Catholic faith, especially the belief in the Blessed Trinity,** ..."

Ibid, Point No.7:
"7. Taking into consideration all positive achievements of **the past fifteen years of our Roman Catholic - Adventist inter-denominational dialogue**, we would like to thank the Superior Authorities of both Churches for all examples of benevolence and ask for further support for the Christian dialogue in the name of love and truth. **We are also especially grateful to the Only One God in the BLESSED TRINITY for the privilege of a brotherly dialogue and common Christian prayer for the gift of unity in Christ.**"

You can see where Trinitarianism has led, and is still leading, the leadership of the organization. **Trinitarianism is the fundamental DNA of Babylon and her daughters – and now of her "Sister"???** God's messenger, in warning against encroaching immorality into the church, wrote:

Manuscript Releases, Volume 21, page 380.1:
"**We are in danger of becoming a sister to fallen Babylon**, of allowing our churches to become corrupted, and filled with every foul spirit, a cage for every unclean and hateful bird; and will we be clear unless we make decided movements to cure the existing evil?"

Because her warning was against physical immorality, does that justify us in assuming that forbidden spiritual fraternizing exempts us from the principle presented in her words? I don't think so. Those who lead out in reaching the denominational **hand across the gulf** have assumed a fearful responsibility:

2 Corinthians 11:13-15:
13) "For such are false apostles, deceitful workers, transforming themselves into the apostles of Christ.
14) And no marvel; for Satan himself is transformed into an angel of light.
15) Therefore it is no great thing if his *[Satan's]* ministers also be transformed as the ministers of righteousness; whose end shall be according to their works."

WILLIAM: The people are taught that this is true Adventism!

PROFESSOR: For that very reason, God has warned:

Selected Messages Book 2, page 371:
"There is to be **no compromise** with those who make void the law of God. **It is not safe to rely upon them as counselors.**" *[But we study in their universities and go to Willow Creek and the Shalem Institute, etc., for "guidance." The people are encouraged to read and teach their written works on spiritual formation, and practice its spiritualistic exercises, etc.]*

Early Writings, pages 124, 125:
"I was shown the necessity of those who believe that we are having the last message of mercy, **being separate from those who are daily imbibing new errors.** I saw that neither young nor old should attend their meetings; for it is wrong to thus encourage them while they teach error that is a deadly poison to the soul and teach for doctrines the commandments of men. The influence of such gatherings is not good. If God has delivered us from such darkness and error, **we should stand fast in the liberty wherewith He has set us free and rejoice in the truth.** God is displeased with us when we go to listen to error, without being obliged to go."

Men from denominational, ministerial ranks and some lay persons are sent to "Willow Creek;" the "Shalem Institute," etc., to learn "**spiritual formation.**" "**Spiritual Formation**" has become a prerequisite attainment for those involved in the preparation of church material for the spiritual education of church youth. All training in spiritual formation is centered in the spiritual exercises of Ignatius Loyola. Central to its teachings are "centering" and "contemplative" prayer—exercises that bring on a mindless state in which demons have direct access to the initiate—a state where the initiate becomes "one" with the god "essence" (of Trinitarianism and Pantheism) and experiences the "god" within.

WILLIAM: Like the temptation in the Garden of Eden, the fruit looks so temptingly delicious, so attractive, so harmless looking, so 'wise' in the eyes of the world.

PROFESSOR: That is why Eve was warned not even to go near the Tree of Knowledge of Good and Evil. And we too are warned:

> Manuscript Releases, Volume 10, page 163:
> "Just as long as men consent to listen to these sophistries, a subtle influence will weave the fine threads of these seductive theories into their minds, and men who should turn away from the first sound of such teaching will learn to love it. As loyal *[not Loyola's]* subjects we must refuse even to listen to these sophistries. Their influence is something like a deadly viper, poisoning the minds of all who listen. **It is a branch of hypnotism, deadening the sensibilities of the soul.**"

God's messenger wrote the statement above about Kellogg's **Trinitarian-centered** Pantheism. Today the great originator of Trinitarian falsehood and the great source of Jesuit Spiritual Formation, Rome, is, through the Spiritual Formation seminars and agents, having "intelligence" with those of God's denominated people who "forsake the holy covenant" they made at their baptism with the "Only True God." Andrews' University offers a doctoral program in Spiritual Formation under Jon Dybdahl. At least one course in spiritual formation is now mandatory for all SDA ministerial students. Derek Morris introduced it to Southern Adventist University (from 1987, when his doctoral theses, "Nurturing the Pastor's Spiritual Discipline of Prayer through the Dynamic of Spiritual Direction," came out and onward to 2008-2009 when he was a professor at Southern Adventist University). Denominational minsters and others are being initiated into its "mysteries." **Since the minds of those who have disobeyed** and have gone to listen to, and learn how to engage in, these spiritualistic Spiritual Formation classes and exercises, **have now been "enlightened" by darkness and error** and demon possession, **can anyone safely go and listen to them?** Or would you even know who they are?

Early Writings, page 124:

"If God has any new light to communicate, He will let His chosen and beloved understand it, **without their going to have their minds enlightened by hearing those who are in darkness and error.**"

WILLIAM: They think the awesome Word of God is dullsville. It is as Jeremiah said:

Jeremiah 2:13:
For my people have committed two evils; they have forsaken me the fountain of living waters, and hewed them out cisterns, broken cisterns, that can hold no water.

PROFESSOR: Rather than having communion with God through His Word—the fountain of living water—they hew them out broken cisterns that can hold no water, by having "intelligence with them that have forsaken the holy covenant."

The word **"intelligence"** regarding the "King of the North's" intercourse with those who have "forsaken the holy covenant" found in Daniel 11:30, comes from a unique Hebrew word used nowhere else in the Bible. This fascinating word means to "**cunningly observe, choose, and separate out in order to instruct.**"

Spiritual Formation is a teaching originating with the King of the North (the Papacy) and **rooted in Rome's spiritualistic Trinitarian theology** which makes of God a "non-entity," an "essence" that is manifested in different "modes." Spiritual Formation is, together with Trinitarianism which preceded it, becoming established in the S.D.A. denomination. Both of these gulps from Rome's goblet are the result of some Seventh-day Adventist leaders succumbing to the "intelligence" with Rome and/or her daughters.

WILLIAM: When a person, or nation (or denomination) "separates from" or forsakes the pure Source of Truth, they want to have intelligence with those that forsake the Holy Covenant. That "intelligence" is actually communication with another "source."

It reminds me of King Saul, who cut himself off from every avenue by which God could communicate with him (Samuel, David, Jonathan, Ahimelech, the priests). It left him with only one source to go to—to the witch of Endor—to Spiritualism.

PROFESSOR: To Satan.

86

Selected Messages Book 2, page 60:
"But ministers who bear the last message of mercy to fallen men **must utter no random words** *[like 'Trinity' for Godhead, or 'Eucharist' for communion, etc.]*; **they must not open doors whereby Satan shall find access to human minds.** It is not our work to experiment, to study out something new and startling that will create excitement. **Satan is watching his chance** to take advantage of anything of this order that he may bring in his deceiving elements."

Instead of a God who is an **actual personal Being,** the "god" of Trinitarianism and of Spiritual Formation is indeed a kind of "essence" claimed to be located in the hearts of all men. Trinitarianism contradicts the certainty that the Father and the Son have an **actual personal presence** in heaven. This falsehood endeavors to sweep away the personality of God and the daily mediatorial work of Christ in the heavenly sanctuary and to relocate **their** presence to the hearts of **all** human beings, renewed or not. This is "universalism." However, God's messenger declares:

Sermons and Talks, Volume 1, page 34:
"In Living Temple the assertion is made that God is in the flower, in the leaf, in the sinner. **But God does not live in the sinner.** The Word declares that He *[through the indwelling Holy Spirit]* abides only in the hearts of those who love Him and do righteousness *[John 14:15-17]*. God does not abide **in** the heart of the sinner; it is **the enemy** who abides there."

WILLIAM: It is communing with Satan, when we think we are communing with God. We certainly must try the "spirits." We need the true Holy Spirit.

As John 14 points out, it is the mighty Third Person of the Godhead— God and Christ's representative—the "Other Comforter"—who abides in the heart of the redeemed and through whom "oneness with God is achieved and maintained."

PROFESSOR: But the General Conference is going a different direction.

ATN News announced [Feb. 3, 2004]:
http://news.adventist.org/ 2004/02/a-feature-church- cogregatios
-icrease-focus-o- spiritual-formatio.html:

"The Adventist world church created the International Board of Ministerial and Theological Education (IBMTE) in September, 2001, designed to provide overall guidance and standards to the professional training of pastors, evangelist, theologians, teachers, chaplains and other denominational employees involved in ministerial and **religious formation, or spiritual formation,** in each of the church's 13 regions around the world."

WILLIAM: **And Ted Wilson, now President, was a member of that Board (IBMTE).**

PROFESSOR: Not only was he a member, he was the vice-chair, but if he was against spiritual formation, as he claims to be, he did not speak up at that critical time. Isaiah warns:

> **Isaiah 56:10:**
> "His watchmen are blind: they are all ignorant, they are all **dumb dogs, they cannot bark;** sleeping, lying down, loving to slumber."

Still today, Richard Foster, George Barna, and Leonard Sweet, and other "Emerging church" leaders (who all teach Spiritual Formation) are often invited to speak at Adventist seminars and universities.

Those determined to spread Spiritual Formation in the Seventh-day Adventist denomination are clearly deceived and taken in by Satan's spiritualistic "omega" deception in which Trinitarianism and Spiritual Formation walk in lockstep.

God says:

> Selected Messages Book 2, page 350:
> "To study this science is to pluck the fruit from the tree of knowledge of good and evil. God forbids you or any other mortal to learn or to teach such a science.   ...**Cut away from yourselves** *["hand," "eye," etc.]* everything that savors of hypnotism, the science by which satanic agencies work."

Mark 9: 43-45:
43) "And if thy **hand** offend thee, cut it off: it is better for thee to enter into life maimed, than having two hands to go into hell, into the fire that never shall be quenched:

44) "Where their worm dieth not, and the fire is not quenched.

45) "And if thy foot offend thee, cut it off: it is better for thee to enter halt into life, than having two feet to be cast into hell, into the fire that never shall be quenched."

2 Corinthians 6:15:

"And what concord hath Christ with Belial? Or what part hath he that believeth with an infidel? *["Infidel": Someone who demonstrates their "infidelity" to God and to His holy covenant.]*

Amos 3:3:

"Can two walk together, except they be agreed?"

2 Corinthians 6:14:

"Be ye not unequally yoked together with unbelievers *[those who don't believe the plain Word and Counsels of God]*: for what fellowship hath righteousness *[right doing]* with unrighteousness? *[Should be none!]* And what communion *[fellowship and communication]* hath light with darkness?"

2 Corinthians 6:16-18:

16) "And what agreement hath the temple of God *[you?]* with idols? *[e.g., one's own ego: thinking it can conjure up God like a genie by engaging in certain "exercises"?]* For **ye** are the temple of the living *[personal]* God; as God hath said, I will dwell in them *[by the Holy Spirit]*, and walk in *them;* and I will be their God *[the Only True God]*, and they shall be my people.

17) "Wherefore come out from among them, and be ye separate, saith the Lord, *[stop fraternizing]* and touch not the unclean *thing;* and I will receive you,

18) "And will be a Father *[personal, loving, caring Individual]* unto you, and ye shall be my sons and daughters, saith the Lord Almighty."

Amos 3:7:

"Surely the Lord GOD will do nothing, but he **revealeth his secret** unto his servants the prophets."

2 Chronicles 20:20:

"...Believe in the LORD your God *[not the Trinity]*, so shall ye be established; **believe his prophets,** so shall ye prosper."

William, I want you to read what the great Adventist pioneer, J. N. Andrews, after whom Andrews University is named had to say about Trinitarianism. Consider it your assignment.

Chapter 6

THE TRINITY DOCTINE—THE WINE OF BABYLON

By J.N. Andrews, The Three Angels' Messages, pages 53-60.

We understand that the fall of Babylon is her rejection by God. That the Holy Spirit leaves her in consequence of her alienation from God and union with the world, and that thus she is left to the spirit of Devils. As an illustration we will refer to the fall of the Jewish church, the harlot of Eze. xvi. This fall is distinctly stated in Rom xi. Its particulars may be gathered from Matt. xxi, 43; xxiii; xii, 43-45. **That fall was her rejection by God;** her destruction was deferred for a considerable period.

1. The nature of the reasons assigned for the fall of Babylon proves that it is a moral fall. For it is because she has made the nations drunk with her wine. In other words, it is her wickedness that has caused God to reject her.

2. The consequences of her fall, testify that **that fall is her rejection by God,** and not her destruction. For her fall causes her to become the hold of foul spirits, and the cage of unclean and hateful birds. This shows that God has given her up to strong delusions. For this reason it is that the voice from heaven cries, "Come out of her my people."

The cause of the fall of Babylon is thus stated: **"she made all nations drink of the <u>wine</u> of the wrath of her fornication."** Her fornication was her unlawful union with the kings of the earth. The wine of this, is that with which the church has intoxicated the nations of the earth. **There is but one thing that this can refer to, viz., <u>false doctrine</u>.** This harlot, in consequence of her unlawful union with the powers of earth, has corrupted the pure truths of the Bible, and with **the wine of her false doctrine, has intoxicated the nations.** A few instances of her corruption of the truths of the Bible must suffice:

1. The doctrine of the natural immortality of the soul. This was derived from the Pagan mythology, and was introduced into the church by means of distinguished converts from Paganism, who became "fathers of the church." This doctrine makes man's last foe, death, the gate to endless joy, and leaves the resurrection as a thing of minor importance. It is the foundation of modern spiritualism.

2. The <u>DOCTRINE OF THE TRINITY</u> which was established in the church by the council of Nice, a. d. 325. This doctrine destroys the

personality of God, and his Son Jesus Christ our Lord. The infamous measures by which it was forced upon the church, which appear upon the pages of ecclesiastical history might well cause every believer in that doctrine to blush.

3. The corruption of the ordinance of baptism. Burial in baptism is the divinely authorized memorial of our Lord's burial and resurrection. This has been changed to sprinkling, or pouring, the fitting memorial of but one thing, viz., the folly and presumption of man.

4. The change of the fourth commandment. The pagan festival of Sunday has been substituted by the church for the Rest day of the Lord. The Bible plainly teaches that the sanctified Rest day of the Lord, is the divinely authorized memorial of the rest of Jehovah from the work of creation. But the church has changed this to the first day of the week, to make it a memorial of our Lord's resurrection, in the place of baptism, which has been changed to sprinkling.

5. The doctrine of a thousand years of peace and prosperity before the coming of the Lord. This doctrine will probably prove the ruin of as many souls as any heresy that ever cursed the church.

6. The doctrine of the saint's inheritance beyond the bounds of time and space. For this fable, multitudes have turned from the scriptural view of the everlasting kingdom in the new earth.

7. The spiritual Second Advent. It is well known that the great majority of religious teachers and commentators of the present time openly advocate the view that Christ's second advent, as brought to view in Matt. xxiv, took place at the destruction of Jerusalem; and also that he comes the second time whenever any person dies.

8 The right to hold human beings in bondage and to buy and sell them, is now made out in the most confident manner from the Old and New Testaments, by the leading doctors of divinity of most denominations; and some of the most distinguished and skillful are able to make out this from the golden rule. The professed church to a fearful extent, is the right arm of the slave power, and our own nation is a perfect illustration on the subject of slavery, of a nation drunken with the wine of Babylon. That most infamous law, "the fugitive slave bill," was vindicated by our most distinguished doctors of divinity as a righteous measure.

9. Finally, the lowering of the standard of godliness to the dust. This has been carried so far that the multitudes are made to believe that "every one that saith, Lord, Lord, shall enter into the kingdom of heaven." In proof of this I might appeal to almost every tomb stone or funeral discourse.

God appointed the church to be the light of the world, and at the same time ordained that his Word should be the light of the church. But **when the**

church becomes unfaithful to her trust, and corrupts the pure doctrines of the gospel, as a natural consequence the world becomes intoxicated with her false doctrine. That the nations of the earth are in such a condition at the present time is too obvious to be denied. The world is intoxicated in the pursuit of riches and honor, but the sin lies at the door of the church; for the church sanctions what the Lord strictly forbade, and she sets the example to the world. If the church had not intoxicated the world with the wine of her false doctrines, the plain truths of the Bible would powerfully move the public mind. But the world seems hopelessly drunken with the wine of Babylon.

At the time of the first angel's message, the people of God were in Babylon; for the announcement of the fall of Babylon, and the cry "Come out of her my people," is made after the first proclamation has been heard. Here also we have a most decisive testimony that Babylon includes Protestant as well as Catholic churches. It is certain that the people of God at the time of the preaching of the hour of his judgment were in all the popular churches. And this fact is a most striking testimony as to what constitutes the great city of confusion. In a word, Paul has well described the Babylon of the Apocalypse, and the duty of the people of God with reference to it, in 2 Tim. iii, 1-5. "This know also, that in the last days perilous times shall come; for men shall be lovers of their own selves, covetous, boasters, proud, blasphemers, disobedient to parents, unthankful, unholy, without natural affection, trucebreakers, false accusers, incontinent, fierce, despisers of those that are good, traitors, heady, high-minded, lovers of pleasure more than lovers of God; having a form of godliness, but denying the power thereof: from such turn away." **Who would dare to limit this description to the Catholic church?**

The preaching of the hour of God's judgment, and the immediate coming of the Lord, was at once the test of the church, and the means by which she might have been healed. It was the test of the church in that it showed that her heart was with the world, and not with her Lord. For when the evidences of his immediate Advent were set before her, she rejected the tidings with scorn, and cleaved still closer unto the world. But it might have been the means of healing her. Had she received it, what a work would it have wrought for her! Her unscriptural hope of a temporal reign, her false view of the Second Advent, her unrighteous justification of oppression and wickedness, her pride and conformity to the world, would all have been swept away. Alas that this warning from heaven was rejected! To use the language of the parable, [Luke xiv,] none that in their heart rejected that first call to the marriage supper shall ever appear as guests at that table.

93

The last means that heaven had in store to heal Babylon having failed, God gave her up to her own heart's desire.

It is well known that in immediate connection with the proclamation of the hour of God's judgment, the announcement of the fall of Babylon was everywhere made throughout our land. Its connection with the Advent message is well expressed by the following from Elder Himes, dated McConnellsville, O., Aug. 29, 1844:

"When we commenced the work of giving the 'Midnight cry' with Bro. Miller in 1840, he had been lecturing nine years. During that time he stood almost alone. But his labors had been incessant and effectual in awakening professors of religion to the true hope of God's people, and the necessary preparation for the Advent of the Lord: as also the awakening of all classes of the unconverted to a sense of their lost condition, and the duty of immediate repentance and conversion to God as a preparation to meet the Bridegroom in peace at his coming.

These were the great objects of his labor. **He made no attempt to convert men to a sect, or party, in religion. Hence he labored among all parties and sects, without interfering with their organization or discipline:** believing that the members of the different communions could retain their standing, and at the same time prepare for the Advent of their King, and labor for the salvation of men in these relations until the consummation of their hope. **When we were persuaded of the truth of the Advent at hand, and embraced the doctrine publicly, we entertained the same views and pursued the same course among the different sects, where we were called in the providence of God to labor. We told the ministers and churches that it was no part of our business to break them up, or to divide and to distract them. We had one distinct object, and that was to give the 'cry,' the warning of the '<u>judgment at the door</u>,' and to persuade our fellow men to get ready for the event. Most of the ministers and churches that opened their doors to us, and our brethren who were proclaiming the Advent doctrine, co-operated with us till the last year.** The ministry and membership who availed themselves of our labors, but had not sincerely embraced the doctrine, saw that they must either go with the doctrine, and preach and maintain it, or in the crisis which was right upon them they would have difficulty with the decided and determined believers. They therefore decided against the doctrine, and determined, some by one policy and some by another, to suppress the subject. This placed our brethren and sisters among them in a most trying position. Most of them loved their churches and could not think of leaving. But **when they were ridiculed, oppressed, and in various ways cut off from their former privileges and enjoyments, and when the 'meat in**

94

due season' was withheld from them, and the syren song of 'peace and safety' was resounded in their ears from Sabbath to Sabbath, they were soon weaned from their party predilections, and arose in the majesty of their strength, shook off the yoke, and raised the cry, 'Come out of her, my people.' This state of things placed us in a trying position.

1. Because we were near the end of our prophetic time, in which we expected the Lord would gather all his people in one.

2. We had always preached a different doctrine, and now that the circumstances had changed, it would be regarded as dishonest in us, if we should unite in the cry of separation and breaking up of churches that had received us and our message. We therefore hesitated, and continued to act on our first position until the church and ministry carried the matter so far, that we were obliged in the fear of God to take a position in defense of the truth, and the down-trodden children of God.

Apostolic example for our course. 'And he went into the synagogue, and spake boldly for the space of three months concerning the kingdom of God. But when divers were hardened, and believed not, but spake evil of that way before the multitude; he departed from them, and separated the disciples, disputing daily in the school of one Tyrannus.' Acts xix, 8, 9. It was not until divers were hardened, and spoke evil of that way (the Lord's coming) before the multitude, that the brethren were moved to come out, and separate from the churches. They could not endure this 'evil speaking' of the 'evil servants.' And the churches that could pursue the course of opposition and 'evil speaking' towards those who were looking for the 'blessed hope,' were to them none other than the daughters of the mystic Babylon. They so proclaimed them and came into the liberty of the gospel. And though we may not be all agreed as to what constitutes Babylon, we are agreed in the instant and final separation from all who oppose the coming and kingdom of God at hand. We believe it to be a case of life and death. It is death to remain connected with those bodies that speak lightly of, or oppose the coming of, the Lord. It is life to come out of all human tradition, and stand upon the word of God and look daily for the appearance of the Lord. We therefore now say to all who are in any way entangled in the yoke of bondage, 'Come out from among them, and be ye separate, saith the Lord, and touch not the unclean thing, and I will receive you, and will be a Father unto you, and ye shall be my sons and daughters, saith the Lord Almighty.' 2 Cor. vi, 17, 18."-Advent Herald.

PROFESSOR: And now they teach a doctoral course in **Spiritual Formation** at the University named after this man of God. (See Appendix I) It is noteworthy that the man who was at the head of the doctoral course in Spiritual Formation was also engaged in denominational involvement with the ecumenical movement as a representative of the planning committee for the World Council of Churches. (See Appendix J)

Chapter 7

M. L. ANDREASEN AND THE TRINITY

PROFESSOR: As we have already noted, despite her Trinitarian background in the Methodist Church, **Ellen White never used the terms 'Trinity,' 'Triune,' 'Triune God,' 'co-equal,' or 'co-eternal'**—all words that clearly or subtly connote the Trinitarian concept of God.

However, with the publication of <u>The Desire of Ages</u> in 1898, some thought that the following statement found on page 530, advocated Trinitarian theology. This was because the statement positively contradicts any "Arian" notion of Jesus being "begotten" or "generated" (*as the Catholic church teaches*), at some point in eternity.   The following statement underscores Christ's eternal divinity—His being the Eternal, Mighty, Second-Person of the Godhead:

> <u>Desire of Ages</u>, page 530:
> **"In Christ is life original, unborrowed, underived. 'He that hath the Son hath life' (1 John 5:12). The divinity of Christ is the believer's assurance of eternal life."**

The significance of the declaration was noted by Elder M.L. Andreasen, who commented about the above statement, in his biography (written by Virginia Steinweg):

> <u>Without Fear or Favor</u>, page 76:
> "This statement at that time was revolutionary and compelled a complete revision of my former view—and that of the denomination—on the deity of Christ."

While clearly speaking of the divinity of Christ, what did Ellen White mean by Christ's life being "original, unborrowed, underived"?   **To Andreasen and to others her statement exploded the Arian notion of Christ being "begotten" or "generated" at some point in eternity.** They interpreted her statement correctly as being "anti-Arian," but some wrongly surmised that therefore her statement might be pro-Trinitarian since the historical struggle was between these two parties.

WILLIAM: Like some people, he may have mistaken James and Ellen White's "Heavenly Trio" concept of three distinct eternal Beings, for the Trinity concept of one God who is composed of Three Persons.

PROFESSOR: You might have a point there. But first, let's look at Ellen White's statement. Following the rule that "the testimonies themselves will be the key that will explain the messages given," we look to an article published one year prior to the publication of The Desire of Ages, which clarifies the prophetess' understanding of the concept:

> Signs of the Times, April 8, 1897; Selected Messages Book 1, pages 296, 297:
> "In him was life; and the life was the light of men (John 1:4). **It is not physical life that is here specified, but immortality, the life which is exclusively the property of God.** The Word, who was with God, and who was God, had this life. Physical life is something which each individual receives. It is not eternal or immortal; for God, the life-giver, takes it again. Man has no control over his life. **But the life of Christ was unborrowed.** No one can take this life from Him. 'I lay it down of Myself' (John 10:18), He said. In Him was life, original, unborrowed, underived. **This life is not inherent in man.** He [man] can possess it only through Christ. He cannot earn it; it is given him as a free gift if he will believe in Christ as His personal Saviour."

This "original, unborrowed, underived" life that man may also "possess" is Christ's immortal life that was administered by the Holy Spirit. The Holy Spirit administers this life—Christ's immortal 'life'—to the redeemed:

> Desire of Ages, page 805:
> "The Holy Spirit is the breath of life in the soul. **The impartation of the Spirit is the impartation of the life of Christ."**

Christ's 'unborrowed' and **'underived'** life that He gives to the redeemed through His Holy Spirit is the life that He "laid down." Having paid the "penalty" and having conquered the adversary, He again takes up that life, "unborrowed: and "underived" and gives it to His purchased possession. (See Chapter 29 in this book on this topic.)

Clearly Andreasen's former views had been influenced by the so-called 'Arian' concepts of Uriah Smith, etc. Andreasen, however, clearly saw that the above given statement, and others like it in Sister White's writings, all convincingly countermanded the view that Christ was 'generated' or 'begotten' at some point in past time.

Those who know that **Trinitarian theology poses that Christ is 'eternally generated' by the Father, and that the Holy Spirit 'eternally proceeds' from them both,** can clearly see that the communications from God through His messenger on this topic totally overthrows such spiritualistic speculation.

Now, to answer your question, William: Andreasen had also previously subscribed to the "two Person Godhead" notion were the Holy Spirit is but an emanation from the Father and the Son. **The transparent statements by God's messenger clarifying the 'personhood' and 'personality' of the Holy Spirit emphasized that the Godhead were a 'Heavenly Trio.' Many have confused this concept with the term "Trinity"! However the term Trinity connotes three "tri-une" modalities of an indivisible god "essence," whilst the God-given term "Godhead" connotes three separate and distinct Beings, acting and thinking in perfect harmony— one Spirit *[the Holy Spirit]* filling all.** (See Chapters 21, 21, and 23 for an expanded discussion on this point.)

WILLIAM: In the Trinity concept, Christ could not have had "**life original, unborrowed, underived.**" For the "Christ modality" would have "life" derived from the One God "substance" or "essence." Ellen White's statement could only be true if He was a distinct eternal (not "co-eternal") Being—a member of the Heavenly Trio—the second Person of the Godhead.

PROFESSOR: Right. And Ellen White says this very thing in the same book, Desire of Ages:

> Desire of Ages, page 469:
> "He had announced Himself to be **the self-existent One,** He who had been promised to Israel, "whose goings forth have been from of old, **from the days of eternity**." Micah 5:2, margin.

But, William, we must now look at a statement made by F.M. Wilcox in 1913, which is used to justify and confirm the notion that by that time Trinitarianism was already accepted in the SDA denomination.

Pro Trinitarians in the denomination point to F.M. Wilcox's 1913 statement in which he used the term "Trinity" to denote the Godhead. They imply that Wilcox's use of the Catholic term demonstrates that Adventism was, at that early date, already adopting Trinitarianism as a true doctrine. What follows will demonstrate the error in their assertions. It does however, highlight the inherent danger involved in using terminology that carries connotations that are inherently antithetical to truth—the very reason that God's messenger never used the word "Trinity" or any of its associated terms. (Please read the following material carefully.)

Chapter 8

ANOTHER PERSPECTIVE OF THE 1913
F.M. WILCOX "TRINITY" STATEMENT
Saturday, 12 June 2010 10:42
Written by bobbyb

Is there something in common with Samuel Spear's (1892) article, and F. M. Wilcox's (1913) "Trinity" statement? Similar to **Samuel Spear's apparent "Trinitarian" endorsement of Adventist belief in 1892** (as reprinted by M. C. Wilcox), is the 1913 "Trinity" statement from his brother F. M. Wilcox in the Review and Herald. **Nearly every church historian and scholar who has written on the subject, grasp this statement as undeniable proof that Adventism had fully accepted the Trinity doctrine as early as 1913.** (see <u>Pfandl, footnote #64</u>)

Whidden, Moon, and Reeve say this about the Wilcox statement: "Her *[E.G.W.'s]* support for a biblical view of the Trinity became so explicit during the years between 1902 and 1907 that by 1913, **F. M. Wilcox, editor of the denomination's most influential periodical...could write in the Review and Herald without fear of contradiction by her, that 'Seventh-day Adventists believe, --1. In the divine Trinity. This Trinity consists of the eternal Father,...the Lord Jesus Christ,...{and} the Holy Spirit, the third person of the Godhead'** (Wilcox, 'The Message for Today,' Review and Herald, Oct. 9, 1913)." (See <u>Google Books</u>)

WHY NOT QUOTE THE ENTIRE STATEMENT?
Yet, Pfandl, Whidden, Moon, and Reeve don't quote the entire "Trinity" statement for several specific reasons. **Firstly, Wilcox's 1913 statement is not much different from the 1872, and 1889 statement. The following is the 1889 statement regarding God:**

"**I. That there is one God, a personal, spiritual being, the creator of all things, omnipotent, omniscient, and eternal, infinite in wisdom, holiness, justice, goodness, truth, and mercy; unchangeable, and everywhere present by his <u>representative</u>, the Holy Spirit. Ps. 139:7.**

II. That there is one Lord Jesus Christ, the Son of the Eternal Father, the one by whom God created all things, and by whom they do consist;..."

NOTICE THE DIFFERENCES YET MANY SIMILARITIES WITH WILCOX'S 1913 STATEMENT:

"For the benefit of those who may desire to know more particularly the cardinal features of the faith held by this denomination, we shall state that Seventh-day Adventists believe,—
1. In the divine Trinity. This Trinity consists of the eternal Father, a personal, spiritual being, omnipotent, omniscient, infinite in power, wisdom, and love; of the Lord Jesus Christ, the Son of the eternal Father, through whom all things were created, and through whom the salvation of the redeemed hosts will be accomplished; the Holy Spirit, the third person of the Godhead, the one regenerating agency in the work of redemption." (F. M. Wilcox, The Message for Today, RH Oct. 9, 1913, page 21)

1913 STATEMENT AVOIDS DISCUSSION OF INNER-TRINITARIAN RELATIONS.

We have already mentioned that **Wilcox's statement is not much different from the 1872, and 1889 statements** excepting in the "term" Trinity, and the Holy Spirit as "the third person of the Godhead." The second reason why Pfandl, Whidden, Moon, and Reeve don't quote Wilcox's entire statement is because it does not explain or detail Trinitarian theology and could be accepted by non-trinitarians just like Samuel Spears' "Bible Doctrine of the Trinity" article. Modern Adventist church leader Gilbert M. Valentine has researched and written upon this subject. The following are his observations about the 1913 Wilcox statement:

"Even though F. M. Wilcox had published in the Review in 1913 that Adventists believed in the divine Trinity, the **statement avoids discussion of inner-trinitarian relations, stating that Jesus is 'the Son of the eternal Father' rather than the eternal Son.** RH, Oct. 9, 1913, page 21. **Semi-arians such as Washburn could live with it.**" (Gilbert M. Valentine, W.W. Prescott, page 285)

"Although Review editor F. M. Wilcox was able to say in a doctrinal summary in the Review in 1913 that Adventists believed "in the divine Trinity," **his language sidestepped the issue of the eternal self-existent deity of Christ** and was still **sufficiently vague as to be able to include both the traditional semi-Arians and the Trinitarians.** Jesus was simply "the son of the Eternal Father." But the Holy Spirit was the third "person" of the Godhead. "The Message for Today" RH October 9, 1913,21."(Gilbert M. Valentine, How clear views of Jesus developed in the Adventist Church)

MOTIVATION FOR MAKING THE 1913 STATEMENT.

At this point, the question could be asked, if Wilcox's statement "was still sufficiently vague as to be able to include both the traditional semi-Arians and the Trinitarians," what motivated him to make this statement? While there is only circumstantial evidences at best for any answer, Adventist Trinitarian author Glyn Parfitt gives us his opinion:

"This is a decidedly Trinitarian statement, and Wilcox states it in a matter of fact way, clearly saying that this is what Seventh-day Adventists believe. It is not just his own opinion. Unless there is an earlier statement, not yet discovered, this is the first Trinitarian statement of Seventh-day Adventist beliefs....The **motivation of Wilcox in publishing his statement** may well have been the fact that just two years earlier, the 1872 statement was republished for the ninth and last time in a denominational periodical. **Wilcox must have come to the conclusion that it was time for an update, in a number of key doctrinal areas."** (The Trinity: what has God revealed?: objections answered, 2008, Glyn Parfitt)

Well, if Mr. Parfitt can speculate about Wilcox's "motivation" for including the term Trinity in his 1913 statement, then so can we. Let's assume Wilcox did "come to the conclusion that it was time for an update, in a number of key doctrinal areas." Let's assume he did update the 1872 statement from non-trinitarian, to a fully Trinitarian theology. Who gave F. M. Wilcox the authority to speak for the entire denomination?

There is no recorded discussion about the trinity during the 1913 G.C. session which had convened just six months prior to Wilcox's statement. Does Mr. Parfitt really believe that one man, without the support or authorization of the leadership, and general church membership, can change "key doctrinal areas" of foundational beliefs? In other words, there is no record of ANYONE authorizing, or even wanting an updated, "Trinitarian," statement of beliefs.

At this point Parfitt along with Moon would argue that because Mrs. White's "support for a biblical view of the Trinity became so explicit during the years between 1902 and 1907 that by 1913" the Trinity doctrine was generally accepted by "common consent." This argument holds no weight however because of the following evidences:

1) (1919) The opposition to Trinitarian concepts being introduced during the 1919 Bible Conference. (Merlin Bert)

2) (1928) The opposition to Trinitarian concepts being introduced through Froom's book "The Coming of the Comforter" (1928).

"May I state that my book, The Coming of the Comforter was the result of a series of studies that I gave in 1927-28 to ministerial institutes throughout North America. **You cannot imagine how I was pummeled by some of the old timers because I pressed on the personality of the Holy Spirit as the Third Person of the Godhead. Some men denied that--still deny it.** But the book **has come to be generally accepted** as standard..." (LeRoy Froom to Dr. Otto H. Christenson, Oct 27,1960.)

3) (1931) Even Froom admits there was still no denominational unity regarding the Trinity by 1931. Also, that the 1931 statement including the "term" Trinity could not have been issued prior to 1921 without "strong protest."

"After carefully reading Wilcox's [1931] "Fundamental Beliefs" statement, Nichol expressed appreciation and approval of its scope and balance. He noted that it was conservatively stated—doubtless framed that way in the hope that it might be **acceptable to those** [non-trinitarians] **who had held divergent views, especially over the Godhead.** Yes, **that was true,** Wilcox assented." (Froom, MOD, page 414; emphasis supplied)

"His *[F. M. Wilcox's]* consistent life and teachings had won for him the deepest respect of **both parties** *[non vs. pro-trinitarian]* in the old controversies **over the Godhead.**...He was doubtless the one personality who could formulate a basic statement of Adventist faith, so carefully yet faithfully phrased that it would have **general acceptance by all.** Such was the setting for his draft of the 'Fundamental Beliefs of the Seventh-day Adventists,' quietly framed by him in 1931 in the midst of his life of earnest service. It would have been well-nigh impossible for a statement of "Fundamental Beliefs," such as was drafted by Wilcox in 1931...to have been issued a score of years, or **even a decade prior to 1931, without strong protest by some.**"

"...Watson stated to me, that in the thinking of the **small committee, no formal or official approval should be sought** for the **unofficial** Wilcox statement of 1931. It was therefore not brought before the General Conference Committee. It had not been prepared as a creed, but as a summary of our fundamental beliefs, **to see how it** *[the "Trinity" term]* **would be received.** To this end the committee of four had been given power to act." (Froom, MOD, page 418, 419, emphasis supplied)

4) (1942) The committee to "revise" Daniel and Revelation by Uriah Smith, admitted that there were still "some differences of view among us" regarding the Sonship of Christ in eternity.

"But later he *[Uriah Smith]* revised his belief and teaching to the effect that Christ was begotten sometime back in eternity before the creation of the world....Since there is some **difference of view among us on this point,** it seemed to the committee wise to omit this teaching without comment."

"Again on Oct. 28, 1942 Howell told the assembled council: **'Our committee had not thought of making a pronouncement on the doctrine for the denomination.** But knowing there are some **differences of view among us,** it was our judgment that it would be better to omit the subject altogether from the book, without comment, and leave the matter **open for all to study** without let or hindrance.'" (The Ministry, May, 1945, page 4; Froom, MOD, page 427, emphasis supplied)

WHY DOESN'T FROOM MENTION THE 1913 WILCOX STATEMENT?

Having briefly examined some of the evidences that Trinitarianism was not generally accepted until much, much, later than 1913; Glyn Parfitt raises some interesting questions about the F. M. Wilcox statement.

"Froom does not mention that Wilcox, the one who drafted the 1931 statement, had much earlier published a Trinitarian statement of beliefs in the Review & Herald. This happened in 1913, the same year in which Froom began his work as a minister, so **he may not have been aware of it."** "The S.D.A. Encyclopedia, although detailing the various times when the 1872 Statement was published, **omitted all mention of this 1913 Statement."** (The Trinity: what has God revealed?: objections answered, 2008, Glyn Parfitt)

WHY DID FROOM CHOOSE NOT TO TELL.

It's highly unlikely Froom was unaware of the 1913 statement. Think about it, **LeRoy Froom spent his entire career championing Adventist Trinitarianism while simultaneously apologizing for Adventism's non-trinitarian roots.** Froom worked closely with F. M. Wilcox for many years. Wilcox's 1913 statement was not "forgotten" in some dusty archives. Froom and everyone else "omitted all mention of this 1913 statement" not because they were not "aware of it," but rather as a deliberate, calculated choice.

'FISHING' FOR PROTESTERS.

Watson admitted they were stepping on eggshells with **the 1931 "Trinity" statement.** That's why it **was just published with "no formal or official approval"** in order to **"see how it would be received."** In other words how many leaders and members would PROTEST the Trinity term. Like the 1931 statement, the 1913 statement could have been the "Trinity" bait, while "fishing" for protesters. However many protested we don't know, yet the line wasn't cast out again until 1931.

ADVENTIST DOCTRINE ESTABLISHED BY DICTUM?

If Pfandl, Whidden, Moon, Reeve, and Parfitt are interpreting the significance of the 1913 statement incorrectly (i.e. there was not a general or majority acceptance of the Trinity in Adventism as early as 1913); then the reason why Froom and others **feared** to mention this statement becomes painfully obvious. **Maybe Adventist doctrine is established by dictum: That one, or a few key leaders can, and do change doctrinal beliefs behind closed doors, and all the peon church members must follow in blind obedience.**

If F. M. Wilcox was nefariously trying to change the denominational belief about the Trinity in 1913, it didn't work. No one referenced his 1913 statement as the denominational belief regarding the Trinity. This leads to a more plausible rationale for His Motive. What was so significant and important about the year 1913? Had denominational leaders been studying the Trinity so hard and long that now we are ready to publish an official change of beliefs to the world? There is another reason that is much more probable.

EVANGELICAL CONFERENCES WITH CANRIGHT?

It is possible that F. M. Wilcox was chosen, or voluntarily chose to directly counter D. M. Canright's accusation: "They [Adventists] reject the Trinity." Canright personally knew F. M. Wilcox, and regularly met with SDA ministers and church leaders between 1910 and 1916. Canright also spent two weeks meeting with church leaders at Battle Creek during the year 1913. "D. M. Canright seemed to have no hesitation about visiting freely with the Adventist Church leaders. Elder **F. M. Wilcox,** for thirty-three years editor in chief of the Review and Herald, relates one such incident:

"I recall an interesting conversation which I had with D. M. Canright some time before his death. I was attending a general meeting held in Battle Creek, Michigan. Elder Canright was at the sanitarium taking treatment. He attended some of our meetings.'" (I Was Canright's Secretary, page 102).

"Elder Lee remembers seeing Canright only once, when he walked quietly into a 'workers' meeting at Grand Rapids. Whenever possible, this seemed to be Canright's custom during the years **1910-1916.** He especially enjoyed **attending meetings of Seventh-day Adventist ministers....**

Canright's visit to Battle Creek about the time this incident took place is attested to in a letter he wrote to Elder J. H. Morrison, dated **June 25, 1913.** Speaking of his former brethren he says: **'I have just spent two weeks in Battle Creek, attending all their meetings and having long visits with ministers,** brethren and sisters.' " (I was Canright's secretary page 104).

WHAT DID THEY TALK ABOUT?

Although admitting to: "attending all their meetings and having long visits with ministers," Canright doesn't say what they talked about. Ever since his book "Adventism Renounced" was published in 1889: "Nearly every religious paper in Christendom has heralded his apostasy, and become, to some extent, the medium through which he has vented his feelings..." So what did Canright and the Adventist church leaders talk about in 1913? **Whatever they talked about in 1913, Canright removed his accusation: "They [Adventists]reject the trinity" when he reprinted his book the following year (1914).** Was this just a coincidence? It's highly unlikely.

Although this new edition of "Adventism Renounced" continued to charge Adventist's with believing "in the Sonship of Christ," all references to the trinity were completely removed. My guess is that a church leader, or leaders convinced Canright that they now believed in the separate personality of the Holy Spirit; while failing to convince him that they now denied Christ's "begotten" origin from the Father in eternity. He must have had some motivation to edit his book.

Based only on circumstantial evidence, it's highly likely that one or more Adventist leaders protested to Canright about the church's fundamental belief about God. Canright might have conceded and said, "If you can show me an official church statement about the Trinity, I'll remove that accusation from my book." Then someone probably pulled out "The Desire of Ages" and quoted something about "life original, unborrowed, underived," and the "third person of the Godhead" etc. etc. Then Canright might have said, "Mrs. White isn't even directly talking about the Trinity in any of these quotes, I want an official 'statement of belief,' then I will retract." Obviously, this is all hypothetical. However, F. M. Wilcox's "Trinity" statement in the Review apparently was sufficient enough evidence for Canright to re-edit his book and remove the non-Trinity accusation.

PACIFY THE CRITICS.

D. M. Canright was not the only one accusing Adventists of rejecting the Trinity in 1913. A highly respected Protestant author had this to say about Adventists in his new book:

"The Seventh-day Adventists...reject the doctrine of the Trinity, which involves the Deity of Christ, though this is not stated....We would recommend you to read Seventh-Day Adventism Renounced, by Elder Canright..." (Bible Problems Explained, James Martin Gray, 1913)

Not only was the 1913 statement an answer to Canright, it was intended to counteract the negative influence of Gray's book as well. F. M. Wilcox did (in The Review) almost exactly what his non-trinitarian brother had done back in 1892 when reprinting Samuel Spears' article (in Signs of the Times). **They both sought to relieve pressure from Adventist critics who were accusing Adventists of rejecting the trinity, while at the same time trying to uphold the previous non-trinitarian foundational beliefs.**

USING THE "TERM" WITHOUT THE BAGGAGE OF THE INFERRED CONCEPT, IS A DECEPTION.

If the "term" Trinity means a simple belief in the Father, his Son, and Holy Spirit, then Adventists have always been "Trinitarian." Yet, if "Trinity" includes non-biblical extreme human speculations, then Adventists have always been non-trinitarian. F.M. Wilcox appears to use the "Term" (like Samuel Spear) while seeking to avoid affirmations of the "baggage" associated with the term. This is another classic example of "When trinity doesn't really mean Trinity." (See Brendan Knudson's paper here) While conceding to use the "term" trinity without believing the "concept" as defined by the creeds, is in reality a deception. It's like making a promise with your fingers crossed behind your back. The following is an illustration of this kind of deception:

Adventists believe in the **eternal torment** of the wicked in hell fire; (in the context of annihilationism).

Adventists believe in the **immortality of the soul**; (in the context of soul-sleep and the final judgment).

Adventists believe in **keeping the "Lords day" sacred**; (if the Lords day is defined as the seventh-day sabbath).

Adventists **believe in the Trinity**; (if it's according to our own interpretation and definition; and NOT according to Catholic or Protestant creeds).

NOT INTENDED TO UNIFY BUT TO REPUDIATE.

Wilcox's 1913 statement was probably never intended to UNIFY denominational Adventism into accepting Trinitarianism. Rather, it **was intended to specifically remove Adventism from the Protestants' non-trinitarian / non-christian, cult, watch-list.** Similarly, the book **"Adventists Answer Questions on Doctrine" was never intended to as a "profession of faith" for Adventists, but rather a public "repudiation" of early Adventism's non-trinitarian faith for the benefit of non-Adventists.** (Froom, MOD, page 483)

The simple irony is that ever since Canright's Trinity accusation, Adventist leaders have held closed door sessions with Protestant leaders at least several different times in order to answer the exact same questions. Even in 2010, questions regarding the orthodoxy of SDA's "version" of the Trinity are as controversial as they were in the day of Canright, and Walter Martin.

Chapter 9

The Omega of Apostasy
INTRODUCTION OF TRINITARIANISM INTO THE SDA CHURCH

PROFESSOR: The Bible teaches us that there would be a strong tendency among God's people to fall away from truth following the death of God's chosen leaders and servants. Notice the following verses:

Deuteronomy 31:16-18:
16) "And the LORD said unto Moses, Behold, **thou shalt sleep with thy fathers; and this people will rise up, and go a whoring after the gods of the strangers of the land,** whither they go to be among them, and will forsake me, and break my covenant which I have made with them.

17) Then my anger shall be kindled against them in that day, and I will forsake them, and I will hide my face from them, and they shall be devoured, and many evils and troubles shall befall them; so that they will say in that day, Are not these evils come upon us, because our God is not among us?

18) And I will surely hide my face in that day for all the evils which they shall have wrought, in that **they are turned unto other gods.**"

These words were spoken to Moses by the LORD Himself. The history of Israel proves the truthfulness of God's prediction. God gave Israel a good leader in Joshua following the death of Moses and his influence lasted another generation. The sacred record continues in the book of Judges:

Judges 2:7, 10-13:
7) "**And the people served the LORD all the days of Joshua, and all the days of the elders that outlived Joshua,** who had seen all the great works of the LORD, that he did for Israel.

10) ... and there arose another generation after them, which knew not the LORD, nor yet the works which he had done for Israel.

11) And the children of Israel did evil in the sight of the LORD, and served Baalim:

12) And they forsook the LORD God of their fathers, which brought them out of the land of Egypt, <u>and followed other gods, of the gods of the people that were round about them,</u> and bowed themselves unto them, and provoked the LORD to anger.

13) And they forsook the LORD, and served Baal and Ashtaroth."

The Apostle Paul in New Testament times also predicted a **"falling away" from the truth in:**

2 Thessalonians 2:3-5:

3) "Let no man deceive you by any means: for that day shall not come, except there come **a falling away** first, and that man of sin be revealed, the son of perdition;

4) Who opposeth and exalteth himself above all that is called God, or that is worshipped; so that he as God sitteth in the temple of God, shewing himself that he is God.

5) Remember ye not, that, when I was yet with you, I told you these things?"

One of the first principal doctrines corrupted by the "man of sin" was the doctrine of God! Paul went on to declare:

1 Timothy 4:1:

"Now the Spirit speaketh expressly, that **in the latter times some shall depart from the faith,** giving heed to seducing spirits, and doctrines of devils."

<u>AND IT WAS PREDICTED THAT APOSTASY WOULD BLAZE FORTH AMONG SDA's DURING THE END TIMES:</u>

Ellen G. White wrote about an "alpha" and an "omega" apostasy among God's people. She declared that the book written in her day, *The Living Temple*, a book on health, by John Harvey Kellogg, contained the theories that comprised the "alpha" of apostasy. The portions of the book that dealt

111

strictly with health were good and could be recommended, but Dr. Kellogg had woven false concepts about God into the book that were a type of pantheism, dealing with the nature, presence, and personality of God. Ellen White noted:

> Manuscript Releases, Volume 4, page 248:
> "Those who have been feeding their minds on the supposedly excellent but spiritualistic theories of *Living Temple* are in a very dangerous place. For the past fifty years I have been receiving intelligence regarding heavenly things. But the instruction given me has now been used by others to justify and endorse theories in *Living Temple* that are of a character to mislead." (*Manuscript Releases*, Volume 4, page 248)

Ellen White used the term "omega" in reference to a great apostasy that was to follow the "alpha." Notice the following:

> Special Testimonies, Series B, No. 2, page 16:
> "Be not deceived; many will depart from the faith, giving heed to seducing spirits and doctrines of devils. We have now before us the alpha of this danger. **The omega will be of a most startling nature."** (Also found in Selected Messages Book 1, page 197)
> "I am instructed to speak plainly. "Meet it," is the word spoken to me. "Meet it firmly, and without delay." But it is not to be met by our taking our working forces from the field to investigate doctrines and points of difference. We have no such investigation to make. In the book "Living Temple" there is presented the alpha of deadly heresies. **The omega will follow, and will be received by those who are not willing to heed the warning God has given."** *Ibid.*, page 50. (Also found in Selected Messages Book 1, page 200)
> **"I knew that the omega would follow in a little while; and I trembled for our people.** I knew that I must warn our brethren and sisters not to enter into controversy over **the presence and personality of God**. The statements made in "Living Temple" in regard to this point are incorrect. The scripture used to substantiate the doctrine there set forth, is scripture misapplied." *Ibid.*, page 53. (Also found in Selected Messages Book 1, page 203)

From this statement one can plainly see that the **omega** issue would revolve around "the presence and personality of God."

Further Statements on Apostasy

Complementary statements to those above are found in *Special Testimonies*. While they do not mention the term "omega," they deal with the same apostasy.

> Special Testimonies, Series B, No. 7, page 57:
> "One thing it is certain is soon to be realized—the great apostasy, which is developing and increasing and waxing stronger, and will continue to do so until the Lord shall descend from heaven with a shout. **We are to hold fast the first principles of our denominated faith, and go forward from strength to increased faith. Ever we are to keep the faith that has been substantiated by the Holy Spirit of God from the earlier events of our experience until the present time.** [i.e. *Those points of faith in the experience of God's people that the Holy Spirit clarified through God's messenger to His people.]* **We need now larger breadth, and deeper, more earnest, unwavering faith in the leadings of the Holy Spirit.** If we needed the manifest proof of the Holy Spirit's power to confirm truth in the beginning, after the passing of the time, **we need today all the evidence in the confirmation of the truth, when souls are departing from the faith and giving heed to seducing spirits and doctrines of devils.** There must not be any languishing of soul now."

With regards to this topic, the following statement that we have already looked at bears further scrutiny:

> Selected Messages Book 1, pages 204, 205:
> "The enemy of souls has sought to bring in the supposition that a great reformation was to take place among Seventh-day Adventists, and that this reformation would consist in giving up the doctrines which stand as the pillars of our faith, and engaging in a process of reorganization. Were this reformation to take place, what would result? **The principles of truth that God in His wisdom has given to the remnant church, would be discarded. Our religion would be changed. The fundamental**

principles that have sustained the work for the last fifty years would be accounted as error. A new organization would be established. Books of a new order would be written. A system of intellectual philosophy would be introduced. The founders of this system would go into the cities, and do a wonderful work. The Sabbath, of course, would be lightly regarded, as also the God who created it. **Nothing would be allowed to stand in the way of the new movement.** The leaders would teach that virtue is better than vice, **but God being removed** *[replaced by the Roman "Trinity"]***,** they would place their dependence on human power *[just as Catholicism does in employing the state to enforce her dogmas]*, which, without God, is worthless. Their foundation would be built on the sand, and storm and tempest would sweep away the structure.

"Who has authority to begin such a movement? We have our Bibles. We have our experience, attested to by the miraculous working of the Holy Spirit. **We have a truth that admits of no compromise. Shall we not repudiate everything that is not in harmony with this truth?**" (Special Testimonies, Series B, No.2, pages 54, 55)

It should be clear that all of Sister White's statements (quoted above) refer to only one issue: the nature of God's presence and personality as revealed in Pantheism, and also found in the false, pagan/papal Trinity doctrine. Some writers have attempted to connect the omega with the collapse of the medical work as it was first established. While it is true that the alpha began within the ranks of the medical work, the medical teachings of Dr. Kellogg were never brought into question by the brethren. Others have sought to connect the omega to the Seventh-day Adventist/Evangelical conferences of 1955-1956. While these conferences were a *fruit* of the omega, they were not the beginning of the omega. **It was the acceptance of the Trinity doctrine that made these conferences possible.** (See pages 124-128 of this book)

The Alpha of Apostasy

To better understand the whole issue, we need to go back to Dr. Kellogg and look at his understanding of the Holy Spirit. As we have noted before, the problem with *The Living Temple* was not physiology, but rather theology. Writing to George I. Butler, Kellogg noted:

Letter from J. H. Kellogg to G. I. Butler, October 28, 1903:

As far as I can fathom, the difficulty which is found in <u>The Living Temple</u>, the whole thing may be simmered down to the question: Is the Holy Ghost a person? You say no. I had supposed the Bible said this for the reason that the personal pronoun "he" is used in speaking of the Holy Ghost. Sister White uses the pronoun "he" and has said in so many words that the Holy Ghost is the third person of the Godhead. How the Holy Ghost can be the third person and not be a person at all is difficult for me to see."

"I believe this Spirit of God to be a personality you don't. But this is purely a question of definition. I believe the Spirit of God is a personality; you say, No, it is not a personality. Now the only reason why we differ is because we differ in our ideas as to what a personality is. Your idea of personality is perhaps that of semblance to a person or a human being.

While Kellogg appealed to Sister White's writings for support of his theories, **Ellen White declared that Kellogg's thoughts did not have a foundation in her writings:**

<u>Special Testimonies, Series B</u>, No. 2, pages 53, 54:

"I am compelled to speak in denial of the claim that the teachings of <u>Living Temple</u>" can be sustained by statements from my writings. There may be in this book expressions and sentiments that are in harmony with my writings. And there may be in my writings many statements which, taken from their connection, and interpreted according to the mind of the writer of <u>Living Temple</u>, would seem to be in harmony with the teachings of this book. This may give apparent support to the assertion that the sentiments in <u>Living Temple</u> are in harmony with my writings. But God forbid that this sentiment should prevail."

Neither did Elder Butler agree that Kellogg properly represented Sister White's thoughts in <u>The Living Temple</u>. Replying to Dr. Kellogg he wrote:

Letter from G. I. Butler to J. H. Kellogg, April 5, 1904:

"God dwells in us by His Holy Spirit, as a Comforter, as a Reprover, especially the former. When we come to Him we partake of Him in that sense, because the Spirit comes forth from him; it comes forth from the Father and the Son. It is not a person walking around on foot, or flying as a literal being, in any such sense as Christ and the Father are—at least, if it is, it is utterly beyond my comprehension of the meaning of language or words."

While Dr. Kellogg did not appear to fully understand the Trinitarian position at the time of his writing The Living Temple, the concepts in Trinitarianism paved the way for him to later fully accept and promote the doctrine of Pantheism.

The Omega of Apostasy

False concepts about God constituted both the "alpha" and the "omega" of apostasy. As we examine Ellen White's statements concerning the "omega" we will see that the Trinity doctrine and its acceptance within the larger body of Adventism perfectly fits her predictions.

First, she stated that "The Omega will be of a most startling nature." (*Series B, no. 2, page 16*) Let us consider this statement in the light of the following candid acknowledgment by Elder William Johnsson, editor of the *Adventist Review*:

> *Adventist Review*, January 6, 1994, pages 10, 11:
> William Johnsson: "Adventist beliefs have changed over the years under the impact of 'present truth.' ...**The Trinitarian understanding of God, *now* part of our fundamental beliefs, *was not* generally held by the early Adventists.** Even today a few do not subscribe to it."

Johnsson candidly admits that our teachings have <u>changed</u> and that the "Trinitarian understanding of God" is "*now* part of our fundamental beliefs." That is a startling 180° turn-around.

Ellen White wrote that the omega would come and it would be of such a nature that she trembled "for our people" indicating that it would attack the **entire denomination.** (Series B, no. 2, pages 50, 53). **Today, acceptance of the 28 Fundamentals, which includes the Trinity doctrine [#2], is necessary to be part of the corporate S. D. A. Church (and also part of the World Council of Churches!)**

Ellen White also predicted the time frame within which the Omega would exist. She stated in 1904 "that the omega would follow **in a little while**." She also indicated that it would arise primarily after her death. "Great things shall come to pass **after I am gone; Satan will work as**

116

never before. All that can be shaken will be shaken out. We must draw near to God, for **we cannot lean upon man or the crowd. We must know the Lord deeply as never before.**" (*Asiatic Division News*, May 1-15, 1915, page 43, quoted from *The Alpha and the Omega of Apostasy* by Julius Gilbert White.)

She also stated: "One thing it is certain is soon to be realized—**the great apostasy, which is developing and increasing and waxing stronger, and will continue to do so until the Lord shall descend from heaven with a shout.**" (Series B, no. 7, page 57) The omega apostasy would breach the church ranks *shortly* after the death of Ellen White and would continue until Jesus comes in the clouds of heaven.

Let us now look at the chronological development of the Omega of apostasy:

THE 1913 F. M. WILCOX "TRINITY" STATEMENT

The first semi-official statement by an Adventist that uses the word "Trinity" was made by F.M. Wilcox and is found in the Review and Herald in 1913.

F. M. Wilcox, "The Message for Today," *Review &Herald,* Oct. 9, 1913, page 21:
"For the benefit of those who may desire to know more particularly the cardinal features of the faith held by this denomination, we shall state that Seventh-day Adventists believe,—1. In the divine Trinity. This **Trinity consists of** the eternal Father, a personal, spiritual being, omnipotent, omniscient, infinite in power, wisdom, and love; of the Lord Jesus Christ, the **Son of the eternal Father**, through whom all things were created, and through whom the salvation of the redeemed hosts will be accomplished; the Holy Spirit, the third person of the Godhead, the **one regenerating agency** in the work of redemption."

Nearly every modern church historian and scholar *[Pfandl, Whidden, Moon, and Reeve, etc.]* who has written on the Trinity, point to this statement as undeniable proof that Adventism had fully accepted the Trinity doctrine as early as 1913. Yet, Pfandl, Whidden, Moon, and Reeve don't quote the entire "Trinity" statement for several specific reasons. **Firstly, Wilcox's 1913 statement is not much different from the 1872, and 1889 statements.** The following is the 1889 statement regarding God:

117

1889 Statement of Belief (as found in the 1889 SDA Yearbook):
"I. That there is **one God**, a personal, spiritual **being**, the creator of all things, omnipotent, omniscient, and eternal, infinite in wisdom, holiness, justice, goodness, truth, and mercy; unchangeable, and **everywhere present by** his representative, the Holy Spirit. Ps. 139:7.

"II. That there is one Lord Jesus Christ, the **Son of the Eternal Father**, the one by whom God created all things, and by whom they do consist;..."

Both the statement by Wilcox, and the 1889 Statement of Beliefs, actually describe the **Heavenly Trio concept—three distinct eternal Beings.** The only new phrasing that Wilcox used was that Jesus was "the son of the Eternal Father," and the Holy Spirit was "the third person of the Godhead." But unfortunately Wilcox used one word that was new to the vocabulary of Adventist-written literature—the Catholic word, "Trinity." This brought confusion. This confusion is still in many Adventist minds.

For many years no one referenced Wilcox's 1913 statement as the denominational belief regarding the Trinity. **So why did he make the statement and use the word, "Trinity"?** What was so significant and important about the year 1913? It is interesting that after many years of charging Adventists that they do not believe in the Trinity, arch-accuser, ex-Adventist D.M. Canright removed the words— "They *[Adventists]* reject the trinity"—when he reprinted his book in 1914—the year following the Wilcox statement. Was this just a coincidence? It's highly unlikely.

F. M. Wilcox did (*in The Review*) almost exactly what his non-trinitarian brother had done back in 1892 when reprinting Samuel Spears' article on the "Trinity" (in *Signs of the Times*). They both sought to relieve pressure from Adventist critics who were accusing Adventists of rejecting the trinity, while at the same time trying to uphold the previous non-trinitarian foundational beliefs.

To use the "term" trinity without believing the "concept" as defined by the creeds, is in reality a deception. If the "term" Trinity means a simple belief in the Father, his Son, and Holy Spirit (which it does not), then Adventists have always been "Trinitarian." But if "Trinity" includes non-biblical extreme human speculations as defined by the Catholic church for centuries, then Adventists have always been non-Trinitarian. **Using the "term" without the baggage of the inferred concept, is a deception.**

1919—SDA Bible Conference

118

In the 1919 Bible Conference, W. W. Prescott gave a series of studies entitled, "The Person of Christ." These studies, promoting the Heavenly Trio concept—Three, distinct, eternal Beings (*again using the term "Trinity"*)—were not unanimously received by the delegates. The discussion following his presentations became quite intense. G. C. President A. G. Daniells, attempted to calm the discussions down by stating: "We are not going to take a vote on Trinitarianism or arianism, but we can think." (*Transcript from the 1919 Bible Conference*).

1919—Bible Handbook, by Stephen Haskell

This is a handy little book containing proof texts from the Bible to support various doctrines of the SDA church. Beside each text are a few words just to describe what the verse is saying. Under the doctrine of "Baptism," 16 verses are listed. The 14th verse uses the term, "Trinity" without explanation: "**Matt. 28:19. In the name of the Trinity.**"

Again, Haskell is using this false term in the same way as Wilcox—to please Babylon while staying with the truth of the Heavenly Trio.

1928—The Coming of the Comforter

The movement to adopt Trinitarianism and to become like the rest of the world was on. Ellen White predicted that "books of a new order would be written." In 1928 LeRoy Froom's book, The Coming of the Comforter was published. In this book, Froom teaches the false doctrine of the Trinity and, as Kellogg did before him, he uses Ellen White quotes to substantiate his position. This book was the result of studies that Froom had given during the 1928 North American union ministerial institutes. At the time of the writing, **Froom did not mention that he received help from Babylon in producing his book. It was over forty years later that he would confess the sources for this book as we see in his subsequent book:**

Movement of Destiny, page 322:
"May I here make a frank personal confession? When, back between 1926 and 1928, I was asked by our leaders to give a series of studies on the Holy Spirit, covering the North American union ministerial institutes of 1928, I found that, aside from priceless leads found in the Spirit of Prophecy, there was practically nothing in our literature setting forth a sound Biblical exposition in this tremendous field of study. There were no previous pathfinding books on the question in our literature.

119

"I was compelled to search out a score of valuable books written by **men outside our faith**—those previously noted—for initial clues and suggestions, and to open up beckoning vistas to intensive personal study. Having these, I went on from there. But they were decided early helps. And scores, if not hundreds, could confirm the same sobering conviction that **some of these other men frequently had a deeper insight into the spiritual things of God than many of our own men then had on the Holy Spirit and the triumphant life.** It was still a largely obscure theme."

Please carefully note what Elder Froom was saying. Why was there nothing in our literature? Because pioneer Adventists were not Trinitarians. But he went to Trinitarians for "enlightenment" and then read the Spirit of Prophecy through these new spectacles. We must remember that God's messenger has told us that those who pray to the false 'Christ' in the first apartment of the heavenly sanctuary receive from him "**light** and much power". Satan's object is "to keep them deceived and to draw back and deceive God's children." Here is what God's messenger wrote:

Early Writings, page 56.1:
"I turned to look **at the company who were still bowed before the throne** *[in the first apartment of the sanctuary]*; **they did not know that Jesus had left it.** Satan appeared to be by the throne, trying to carry on the work of God. I saw them look up to the throne, and pray, "Father, give us Thy Spirit." **Satan would then breathe upon them an unholy influence; in it there was light and much power,** but no sweet love, joy, and peace. **Satan's object was to keep them deceived and to draw back and deceive God's children."**

1931—Statement of Beliefs

1931 is a pivotal date in Adventist history. The 1931 SDA Yearbook – forerunner to the Church Manual – which was a precursor to the now creedal "27/28 Fundamental Beliefs," was published.

Sister White warned that our whole religious structure—the structure of truth—would be changed:

Selected Messages Book 1, page 204:

120

"**The principles of truth** that God in His wisdom has given to the remnant church, **would be discarded. Our religion would be changed.** The fundamental principles that have sustained the work for the last fifty years would be accounted as error. A new organization would be established. Books of a new order would be written. A system of intellectual philosophy would be introduced." (Series B, no. 2, page 55)

When the theology of any religious organization is altered, that system is changed at its very foundation. For nearly a century, the church had professed an anti-Trinitarian position. In 1931 a new Statement of Beliefs was introduced, which for the first time, officially **promoted** the Trinity.

With the urging of the General Conference Statistical Secretary, Edson Rogers, along with certain requests for a clarified statement from the field, a committee of four was appointed to oversee the preparation of a new Statement of Beliefs. The four chosen were Milton E. Kern, Francis M. Wilcox, Edwin R. Palmer, and Charles H. Watson. **Wilcox, the man who, in 1913, had first employed the term "Trinity" to describe the Godhead, was chosen by the other three to prepare the main draft.** With the full knowledge and approval of the others, **Wilcox reiterated his 1913 view in the statement he gave to Rogers, who placed it in the 1931 SDA Yearbook.** It appeared in the *Church Manual* in 1933. **This statement was not voted on by the General Conference.** Did someone fear a possible backlash? The first and second statements read:

1931 SDA YEARBOOK:
"1) That the Holy Scriptures of the Old and New Testaments were given by inspiration of God, contain an all-sufficient revelation of His will to men, and are the only unerring rule of faith and practice. 2 Timothy 3:15-17.

"2) That the **Godhead**, or **Trinity**, consists of the Eternal Father, a personal, spiritual Being, omnipotent, omnipresent, omniscient, infinite in wisdom and love; the Lord Jesus Christ, the Son of the Eternal Father, through whom all things were created and through whom the salvation of the redeemed hosts will be accomplished; the Holy Spirit, the Third Person of the Godhead, the great regenerating power in the work of redemption. Matt. 28:19. *[Here the terms Godhead and Trinity are officially employed as synonyms for the first time.]*

"3) That Jesus Christ is very God, **being of the same nature and essence as the Eternal Father.** While retaining His divine nature He took upon Himself the nature of the human family, lived on the earth as a man..." *[Here the Catholic notion of consubstantiality is now fully deployed on the Adventist people.]*

Concerning this statement of belief, Froom wrote:

Movement of Destiny, pages 418, 419, emphasis supplied
"It would have been well-nigh impossible for a statement of "Fundamental Beliefs," such as was drafted by Wilcox in 1931...to have been issued a score of years, or **even a decade prior to 1931, without strong protest by some.**
"...Watson stated to me, that in the thinking of the **small committee, no formal or official approval should be sought** for the **unofficial** Wilcox statement of 1931 *[yet it was published abroad in an official publication]*. It was therefore not brought before the General Conference Committee. It had not been prepared as a creed, but as a summary of our fundamental beliefs, **to see how it** *[the "Trinity" term]* **would be received.** To this end the committee of four had been given power to act."

This is typical, sneaky, political style maneuvering and manipulating!

1941—Baptismal Vow and New Hymnal

A new baptismal vow was introduced in 1941 which included an affirmative statement of the candidates' belief in the Trinity.

Holdouts

By the early 1940's, there were still some holdouts who resisted the new theology. One was a minister by the name of Elder J. S. Washburn, who in 1940 wrote a blistering attack against the Trinity. Washburn's paper was liked so well by one conference president that he asked for thirty-two copies to distribute to all the ministers in his conference. **The significance of this is that in 1940 there was still an anti-Trinitarian faction in the church.**
Another long holdout was Elder Charles S. Longacre. Like Washburn, Longacre was an older minister who personally knew and had talked with Ellen White. He was no "off-shoot" individual. His list of positions of responsibility in the church was long and weighted with important posts.

Elder Longacre was still alive when *Questions on Doctrine* was being prepared. **The original draft sent out contained the following question and response:**

> Question #34, *Questions on Doctrine* file:
> "Is it possible for an individual to remain in good and regular standing in the Seventh-day Adventist Church if he consistently refuses to submit to church authority regarding the historic doctrine of the deity of Jesus Christ?
> The answer to this question is an unequivocal No."

(Satan's successful snare has been to equate denying the Trinity to denying the divinity or deity of Christ—just as he successfully did at the Council of Nicea in 325 AD.) Of the copies sent to the field for consideration, one copy was returned with the following question handwritten in beside the answer mentioned above: "Would we disfellowship Elder Longacre?" Here, just months before his death in 1958, Elder Longacre was still a known anti-Trinitarian.

Leroy Edwin Froom, in his treatise on Adventist history, describes some of the machinations used to deploy Trinitarianism within the denomination:

> Movement of Destiny, page 419:
> "On January 14, 1942, the General Conference Committee voted that the (*Wilcox*) statement of "Fundamental Beliefs" be made available in leaflet form. It had appeared in our **official** *Church Manual* of 1933—similarly **without formal adoption**—and has been in each succeeding edition. **It was therefore by common consent and not by formal voted acceptance** that Wilcox's suggested "Fundamental Beliefs," ... became our accepted Statement of Faith." (emphasis in the original)

Here we have an unequivocal revelation, by an 'insider', on how the General Conference Committee 'inserts' belief concepts that they want to have accepted by the denominational psyche. Is this how things should be done?

1946—The Publication of Evangelism

The book *Evangelism* was published in 1946 to help continue the progress of Trinitarianism within Adventism by attaching the authoritativeness of inspiration to the "new theology." Editors LeRoy Edwin Froom and Roy Allen Anderson compiled E.G. White's statements and inserted the word "Trinity" in subtitles to advance the Trinity doctrine, even though she and all the pioneers were anti-Trinitarian.

1950—A Call for Repentance

In 1950, two young missionaries from Africa attended the General Conference Session at Cleveland, Ohio. Elders **Robert Wieland and Donald K. Short** expressed concern to the brethren that the church had veered off the course given by the Lord in 1888. They were asked to write out their thoughts with the result being the manuscript, *1888 Re-Examined.* While not seeing the Trinitarian issue, they did an excellent work, in a short period of time, discussing the situation of the church at that time. They believed that the church was "ripe for disillusionment:"

A careful reading of *1888 Re-Examined* reveals that while Wieland and Short mostly discussed the importance of the incarnation and the high priestly ministry of Christ, there were touches of Christology that ran against the normal Trinitarian thinking. For example, they stated clearly that Christ had accepted the "likeness of sinful flesh" that it "was not mere *appearance*, but reality." (*Ibid.*, page 156 - emphasis in original) This led them to believe that Jesus "emptied Himself of all divine power to work a miracle, except through faith in the Father." (*Ibid.*, page 156, 157) Further, **they taught that Christ really died at Calvary.**

God was using Wieland and Short in an attempt to rescue His people. While they did not understand all the issues involved at the time, it was more than a modest start. The General Conference, however, officially rejected the message and began at once to counter the work that Wieland and Short began.

1955, 1956—The SDA/Evangelical Conferences

These landmark conferences were held between prominent Evangelicals (Walter Martin, George E. Cannon, Donald Barnhouse) and leaders of the Adventist Church (LeRoy Froom, Roy A. Anderson, Walter E. Read, and T. E. Unruh). **The main focal point of these conferences was: 1) the Trinitarian doctrine, 2) the nature of Christ, and 3) the importance of His ministry in the Most Holy Place of the heavenly sanctuary.** Roy A. Anderson later wrote about his experience of first coming in contact with the Evangelicals, Martin and Barnhouse. Note the significance of his statement and the question they asked:

Adventist Review, September 8, 1983, page 4l:
"'**What do you folks believe about the Trinity?**' was a question put to me some years ago by two gracious Christian gentlemen who came unannounced to the General Conference headquarters in Washington D. C. ...
"Both men were Christian college professors who had read much about Adventists, but all from detractors, and one of them was commissioned to write a new book about Adventist beliefs. However, they felt they should contact the headquarters to discover what we *actually* believe on points of vital interest rather than just quoting from others.
"The answers to their earnest questions lengthened into days of prayerful discussions. **Our answer concerning the Godhead and the Trinity was crucial,** for in some of the books they had read that Adventists were classed as Arians; that is, those who claim Christ was not one with the Father from all eternity, but was a created being. We reassured the visitors when we turned first to the Scriptures, then to the "Fundamental Beliefs" of Adventism. They discovered that we were in harmony with sound Biblical scholarship, **not only on the Trinity,** but on every other cardinal doctrine of Christianity...."

As Martin had noted to Anderson, some books had classed Adventists as Arians because of their anti-Trinitarian belief. In fact, Martin had failed to classify Seventh-day Adventists as "Christians" in the first printing of his book, *The Rise of the Cults*. **The emphasis at the beginning of the conferences was on past anti-Trinitarian statements made by the pioneers of Adventism including Ellen White!** In 1989 Martin gave a brief history of how it occurred to a group of ministers:

Walter Martin—Taped conference, Loma Linda, CA, January, 1989:
"The climate at that time [*1955, 1956*], Adventism was considered like Jehovah's Witnesses, like Mormonism, like most of the major cultic structures of the day. ...
"When I first met with L. E. Froom, he took me to task for about fifteen minutes on how I could ever possibly think that Adventism was a cult. 'Adventism rings as true as steel." I said

'do you think Arius was a Christian?' And he was an excellent church historian and he said, 'Of course he wasn't a Christian, he denied the deity of Jesus Christ.' I said, 'So did Ellen White.' Dr. Froom replied, 'What!' I said, 'yes' and opened up a suitcase and produced at least twelve feet of Adventist publications stacked up and marked for Dr. Froom's perusal. And for the perusal of the committee to check the sources in there. And they were in mortal shock I might add, to think that it was as pervasive as it was. Mrs. White reversed herself later on very quickly, and affirmed the doctrine of the Trinity very strongly and taught it. But she was influenced by Uriah Smith. She did deny the eternal deity of Christ at one time and relegated Him to the place of a second deity. That's why you were classified with the Jehovah's Witnesses early on, because of the Arian emphasis in Adventism. **And because of the fact that you affirmed Michael the Archangel to be Christ.**

"Dr. Froom and the committee decided that they would peruse this material immediately. So we adjourned the meeting and they took all the materials with them and I guess others, and went through the materials. *They came back and said,* **'Well, a great deal of these things you're calling attention to are there, we agree, and we don't agree with these statements. They do not reflect orthodox Adventist theology, and we reject it.'**

"I said, 'Good, happy to hear that, now can you fault us , because we read this material, and it's not peripheral issues we are talking about.' ...

"We went through all kinds of materials and then the idea came for a book where **WE would question** and the Adventist **denomination would respond**. ... Out of that came the book Questions on Doctrine. Contrary to some of the fantasies and myths which I hear today from Adventists who ought to know better, **the book had the approval of the General Conference**." *[The General Conference still approves of Questions on Doctrine and it has recently not disapproved or opposed it being republished, which has happened.]*

Elder Froom and those who met with Martin "accounted as error" the foundation that had sustained the work since its early times. Dr. Barnhouse, writing in *Eternity* magazine, noted:

Eternity, September, 1956:

"Immediately it was perceived that the Adventists were strenuously denying certain doctrinal positions which had been previously attributed to them.

"The Adventists specifically repudiate any teachings by ministers or members of their faith who have believed, proclaimed, and written any matter which would classify them among Arians."

Elder Froom, in *Questions on Doctrine* and later in *Movement of Destiny*, blatantly lied concerning our history. He attempted to show that anti-Trinitarianism was "an encapsulated cancer, gross but confined." Both Martin and Barnhouse, on the one hand, and Froom and the group that met with the Evangelicals, failed to distinguish between the "arianism" of Uriah Smith and others, as well as the anti-two-person Godhead concepts held by them, all of which God's messenger refuted and corrected. **To accept that in her early ministry God's messenger was influenced to promote the views of Uriah Smith and others, and then later changed her view, is to deny that she was inspired by God, and would bring into question her validity as God's messenger to His denominated people.** Froom noted that some of the answers given to the Evangelicals were made as a public disavowal of statements made by the early pioneers, "the early erroneous concepts of a *[so-called]* minority clearly needed *[to be]* repudiated. So the appointed framers of the answers to their questions prepared a simple statement disavowing these personal, individual, *[so-called]* minority positions, for inclusion in the forthcoming book, to be called *Seventh-day Adventists Answer Questions on Doctrine.*" (*Movement of Destiny*, pages 483, 484) These statements were necessary to clear up the misconceptions from prior statements. The disavowal read in part:

Questions on Doctrine, pages 31, 32:
"The belief of Seventh-day Adventists on these great truths *[including Trinitarianism]* is clear and emphatic. And we feel that we should not be identified with, or stigmatized for, certain limited and faulty concepts held by some, particularly in our formative years.

"This statement should therefore nullify the stock "quotations" that have been circulated against us. **We are one with our fellow Christians** *[Are Adventists of "one spirit" with them?]* **of denominational groups** *[fallen Babylon]* **in the great fundamentals of the faith once delivered to the** *[Roman Catholic?]* **saints.**"

127

What a shame to say that we are "one with our fellow Christians of denominational groups." Froom and his colleagues can call the fallen Protestant church systems "Christian," but God calls them "the daughters of BABYLON" (Rev. 17:5). What authority do we have to call "Christian" that which God pronounces "Babylon?" How can Adventism be "one" with Babylon?

1971—Movement of Destiny

LeRoy Froom writes Movement of Destiny—a clear attempt to rewrite SDA history and present the growth of the Advent movement as being of an "evangelical" character from its roots. It fully supported the Trinity doctrine and the continued compromises made in the 1950's.

In Movement of Destiny, Froom claims that in 1888, God was trying to bring the Trinity doctrine into the Seventh-day Adventist Church through E.J. Wagonner and A.T. Jones, but that the church could not go forward because we did not believe in the Trinity! Froom writes:

> Movement of Destiny, page 279:
> "Wagonner spoke with studied care. He phrased his thoughts with exactness, and in full understanding of their import. He clearly believed in the Trinity of Persons comprising the Godhead. And in such a frame of reference he thus recognized **the component** First, Second, and Third Persons as **coequal and consubstantial**...." *[See the whole chapter, pages 269-280 in his book.]*

In other words, Froom claims that part of the latter rain that God wants to give to the SDA church is a belief in the Trinity doctrine!

Reader, please note that Froom fully subscribed to the papal doctrine of "consubstantiality"! This is not merely an issue of confusing or blurring the distinctions between the terms "Trinity" and "Godhead"! This is way past mere "semantics." This is manipulating a paradigm shift in Adventist theology to make us 'acceptable' to the Evangelicals. This is a Trojan deployment of "dark sentences". (*Daniel 8:23.*)

1980—Statement of Fundamental Beliefs of the SDA Church

The General Conference at Dallas in 1980 provided the laity a final opportunity to "meet" the omega of apostasy. The main focus of the session was the development of a new Statement of Beliefs to replace the 1931 statement which had only undergone minor revisions. **The final product was an officially voted statement that affirmed the Trinitarian teaching.** (Appalling apostasy has exponentially accelerated in the denomination since then. Is that what Froom meant about the church going "forward"?) This statement has since taken on the lion-like jaws of a creed. Those who are found not lining up are disfellowshipped! The following statement, made in the summer of 1980, was first printed in the 1981 SDA Yearbook.

But first a question: Why Were 27 Statements of Faith Made and Not Another Number? It is disconcerting to note how the number of "Fundamental Beliefs" was arrived at. (Subsequently a 28ᵗʰ has been added):

"**The number twenty-seven was a fairly arbitrary initiative of mine.** As secretary of the group, I was given the task of recording and organizing the results of our deliberations. Since there was no predetermined number of sections, **we could have come out with twenty-six or twenty-eight; but I preferred twenty-seven.** Twenty-six seemed (to me) to be a dull, uninteresting number; twenty-eight seemed better because it was four times seven, the arithmetical product of two numbers prominent in the Book of Revelation. **But twenty-seven seemed more interesting still: it was three to the third power, three times three times three. Given the importance of the Trinity** (Matt. 28:19; 2 Cor. 13:13 [14]), and the threefold praise of the angels, 'Holy, Holy, Holy' (Isa. 6:3), **the other numbers didn't have a chance: twenty-seven it would be.**" *[Fritz Guy, "Uncovering the Origins of the Statement of Twenty-seven Fundamental Beliefs," published in September, 2002.]*

Let us look at what was said in the yearbook:

1981 SDA YEARBOOK Fundamental Principles of SDA's No. 3, page 5:

"**2) The Trinity:**
"**There is one God: Father, Son and Holy Spirit, a unity of three co-eternal Persons....**"

129

Notice that, here, the term "Godhead" has been totally dropped in favor of the Catholic term "Trinity." In 1931 the correct term "Godhead" was placed alongside the false term "Trinity" as though the two terms are synonymous, which they absolutely are not! By 1981 the false term had supplanted the true. It is via this gradual "drip" system that the enemy engineers the various paradigm shifts from truth to error that he designs for God's people and drowsy Laodicea sleep-walks into his traps.

Notice, also, the word *"co-eternal"*, Why was not the word "eternal" used, which would be the normal word to use? It is because *"co-eternal"* is a code word for the Trinity doctrine as we have seen in the Catholic Catechism. [See illustrations on page 57.] It means that they are all eternal together with the **same substance.** Also, the word *"persons"* when employed to describe the Trinity, means **"mode of manifestation."**

The following "correct" [?] definition for Trinity comes from My Catholic Faith, by Bishop Louis Laravoire Morrow, S.T.D., pages 30-33. (Notice to the reader. The Trinity doctrine uses deceptive wording: the word **"Persons" does** not mean what we think it means. See point "c." below):

> My Catholic Faith, by Bishop Louis Laravoire Morrow, S.T.D., pages 30-33.
>
> "(a) God is **One** yet at the same time **He is three Persons.**
>
> "(b) **One** means one identical nature, essence, or being, which or who **is essentially the Father.** The Oneness is not generic based on likeness, but rather is numeric based on sameness.
>
> "(c) **"Three persons" does not mean "persons" as we normally understand the word**, but rather, three **expressions**, **extensions**, **manifestations**, or **modes** *[otherwise theologically called 'hypostases.']*"

Does this look like solid theological reasoning? Does this represent Holy Spirit guidance?

1984—New Pro-Trinitarian Baptismal Vow

1985—New SDA Church HYMNAL

1985 ushered in the new Seventh-day Adventist Hymnal with its strong pro-Trinitarian position. (See Appendix E) For the first time, in the Table of Contents, a category of hymns is labeled, *TRINITY*, pages 70-73.

One of these hymns, *Holy, Holy, Holy,* was originally written in 1826 by Reginald Heber. In its original form it was a Trinitarian song, which read at the end of the first and fourth stanzas as follows: *"God in three persons, blessed Trinity!"* This song was put into the 1909 and 1941 Seventh-day Adventist Hymnals, but the trinity part was changed to: *"God over all who rules eternity!"* and *"Perfect in power, in love and purity."* This song was purposely changed into a non-trinitarian song by Seventh-day Adventists, reflecting their views on the *Trinity* at the time of the change.

In the new 1985 Adventist Hymnal this song was changed back to its original, pro-Trinitarian posture, reflecting the current views of the Adventist Church at this time. Once it was *Non-Trinitarian*, but now has changed into a *Trinitarian* church.

Not only that, but another hymn, was deliberately changed in the new hymnal. More new wording appeared. In the hymn *Come, Thou Almighty King,* SDA worshippers are led to sing: *"To Thee, **great One in Three**, eternal praises be."*

At least **fifteen hymns to the trinity were added that did not appear in the old hymnal.** In *Creator of the Stars of Night*, Adventists are led to sing to a false God with these words: *"To God the Father, God the Son, and God the Spirit, **Three in one.**"*

Another new hymn, *"Of the Father's Love Begotten"* teaches Adventists that Christ was **begotten** *"Ere the worlds began to be."*

(**Yet they profess to shy away from "Arianism"**! **Have they now accepted Catholicism?**)

Bible Version	# Times Used	%
New International Version	69	31
Jerusalem Bible (Catholic)	38	17
New King James Version	33	14
Revised Standard Version	28	12
New English Bible	22	10
The Good New Bible	15	7
King James Version	15	7
New American Standard	4	2
Adapted	1	<<1

If that were not enough, there is a responsive reading in the back of the hymnal devoted to God under the title, *"TRINITY."* (**Astoundingly**, of the 225 places where Scripture is used in the new SDA Hymnal, **the pro-**

131

Catholic Bible versions predominate. For example, the Jerusalem Bible is used 38 times, the NIV 69 times and the RSV 28 times, while the Protestant King James Version is used just 15 times.)

Thus, since 1985, the SDA church has an officially selected and approved hymnal from which Adventists worship the god of the beast system. It is a Catholic hymnal.

1988—Book of a New Order (Subsequent to 'Questions on Doctrine' and 'Movement of Destiny', etc.):

Seventh-day Adventists Believe... was published, in which the Trinity doctrine is firmly established and taught. Again it is equated as a synonym for the Godhead (pages 22 and 15), as was done in the 1931 yearbook, which brings confusion, and allows itself to be perceived by trusting members as a biblical belief.

1993—The Book 'Issues' was published by the North American Division of the SDA Church, which challenged "independent" ministries who claim to be "Historic Adventist" to return to an anti-Trinitarian position (page 39).

1993—SDA Pioneers Not Allowed to be "SDA" members?

George Knight, without contradiction from anyone in "church" leadership position, makes the following public statement:

> *Ministry,* October 1993, page 10:
> **"Most of the founders of Seventh-day Adventism would not be able to join the church TODAY** if they had to subscribe to the denomination's *["new"]* Fundamental Beliefs. More specifically, **most would not be able to agree to belief number 2, which deals with the doctrine of the trinity.**"

Question to reader: Since the SDA pioneers would not be able to join the modern G.C.-sponsored church system, would they continue to worship the true God, in Spirit and in Truth, separately—apart from the present apostasy where error is forced home by the power of the will? God's messenger warned:

Early Writings, page 124.3, 4:

"I was shown the necessity of those who believe that we are having the last message of mercy, being separate from those who are daily imbibing new errors. I saw that neither young nor old should attend their meetings; for it is wrong to thus encourage them while they teach error that is a deadly poison to the soul and teach for doctrines the commandments of men. The influence of such gatherings is not good. If God has delivered us from such darkness and error, **we should stand fast in the liberty wherewith He has set us free and rejoice in the truth**. God is displeased with us when we go to listen to error, without being obliged to go; for unless He sends us to those meetings where error is forced home to the people by the power of the will, He will not keep us. The angels cease their watchful care over us, and we are left to the buffetings of the enemy, to be darkened and weakened by him and the power of his evil angels; and the light around us becomes contaminated with the darkness.

"I saw that we have no time to throw away in listening to fables. Our minds should not be thus diverted, but should be occupied with the present truth, and seeking wisdom that we may obtain a more thorough knowledge of our position, that with meekness we may be able to give a reason of our hope from the Scriptures. **While false doctrines and dangerous errors are pressed upon the mind, it cannot be dwelling upon the truth which is to fit and prepare the house of Israel to stand in the day of the Lord."**

That which God's messenger enunciated in the above quotation is a principle, and cannot, justifiably, only be applied to the assemblies of the fallen churches.

1994—WILLIAM JOHNSSON STATEMENT:

Adventist Review, January 6, 1994, pages 10, 11:
William G. Johnsson: "Likewise the Trinitarian understanding of God, **now part of our fundamental beliefs,** was not generally held by the early Adventists. Even today **a few do not subscribe to it."**

1999—SDA/ROMAN CATHOLIC AGREEMENT

The SDA church in Poland signs an agreement statement with the Roman Catholic Church after 15 years of dialogue, in which it says that the SDA church should not be considered a "sect" because "in its teaching and service **it cultivates the most important principles of Catholic faith, especially the belief in the Blessed Trinity**." *[See Appendix G for complete document and comments.]*

2000—OUR AWESOME GOD

Reinder Bruinsma, author of *Our Awesome God*, published by Pacific Press, in the seventh chapter, teaches God's people all about the 'God' they worship: the Trinity concept. After explaining the history of the Trinity doctrine in the fourth century AD and how "person" means "a mode of manifestation," he writes:

> Reinder Bruinsma, <u>Our Awesome God</u>, page 91 (all emphasis is as found in book):
> "It is a basic Christian doctrine that God is a Trinity of three persons **('modes of eternal manifestation') having one substance (essence or being)."**
> "…It took the Adventist Church until far into the nineteenth century to agree that **the doctrine of the Trinity was indeed biblical** and **belonged among the fundamental Adventist beliefs**."

2002—The Trinity, written by Woodrow Whidden, Jerry Moon, John W. Reeve, publish by Review & Herald.

2004—ROMAN CATHOLIC STATEMENT ABOUT SDA CHURCH

"Seventh-Day Adventists agree with many Catholic doctrines, including the Trinity." From Catholic Answers, article "Seventh-Day Adventism."

2006—SABBATH SCHOOL QUARTERLY

The Adult Sabbath School Quarterly Lesson for **Sunday**, March 26, is entitled, **"The Triune God."** After quoting the second fundamental belief of the Seventh-day Adventist church, it then states:

<u>SDA Sabbath School Quarterly</u>, Sunday, March 26:

"In other words, Adventism **along with millions of other Christians**—believe in the **triune** nature of God; that is, there is one God (Dt. 6:4) who exists as three Persons."

What god is worshipped by millions of other 'Christians'? Answer: **The Trinity.**

Who is breathing an unholy influence upon them as their prayers do not ascend to the second apartment of the sanctuary? Answer: **Satan.**

What term describes the church systems that the millions of other Christians worship in? Answer: **Babylon.** The "king of the north" has invaded the "glorious land"! Daniel 11:41. He has planted his standards well within the boundaries of the "territory of truth" that God's people should occupy!

How can we worship the same 'God' as Babylon, when the worship of the false 'God' of Babylon leads to worship on a pseudo sabbath? Answer: "As for me and my house, we will serve the LORD." Joshua 24:15.

Let's hear again James White's counsel to the church on this topic:

James White: *Review & Herald,* September 12, 1854:
"As fundamental errors, we might class with this counterfeit Sabbath **other errors which Protestants have brought away from the Catholic Church**, such as sprinkling for baptism, **THE TRINITY**, the consciousness of the dead and eternal life in misery. The **mass** who have held these fundamental errors, have doubtless done it ignorantly, **BUT CAN IT BE SUPPOSED THAT THE CHURCH OF CHRIST WILL CARRY ALONG WITH HER THESE ERRORS TILL THE JUDGMENT SCENES BURST UPON THE WORLD? We think not.**"

James White: *Review & Herald,* February 7, 1856:
"**The greatest fault** we can find in the Reformation **is, the Reformers stopped reforming.** Had they gone on, and onward, till they had left the last vestige of Papacy behind, such as natural immortality, sprinkling, **the trinity**, and Sunday keeping, the church would now be **free from her unscriptural errors.**"

Again, the **2006 Sabbath School Quarterly** cites two Ellen White quotations where she calls the Father, Son, and Holy Spirit **"the heavenly trio"** and **"these three great powers"** as a support for the trinity doctrine. This is misleading and untrue, and this false perception is derived from the

misconceptions of those pioneers who did not believe that the Holy Spirit
was a person, and therefore only believed in a two-person Godhead. **These
phrases from Ellen White quoted in the 2006 Sabbath School quarterly
are clearly _against_ both the Trinity doctrine and the two-person-
Godhead notion, as they positively describe three separate and distinct
Individuals.** Finally, the 2006 quarterly asks:

> SDA Sabbath School Quarterly, Sunday, March 26:
> "What analogies—such as **a triangle or a three-pronged
> fork**—can help someone understand the idea of how **one God
> can be composed of three equal Persons?**"

We answer: The pagan god Neptune (really Satan) holds a 3-pronged
spear—**a trident**. Analogies, like that just quoted from the Sabbath School
Quarterly, mix pagan symbols with Scripture which results in a papal
amalgam. Why not use the analogy that was given by Ellen White—the
heavenly trio—three separate individuals in perfect harmony with one
Spirit in all? [See Chapter 24]

2006—Adventist Theological Society National Conference meets March
30 to April 1. Eighteen SDA theologians present topics on the Trinity. The
final meeting topic? "The Trinity: **A Mark** of Seventh-day Adventist
Identity." **(Since Trinitarianism and Sunday worship are closely linked,
is Trinitarianism a facet of the "Mark of the Beast"?)**

2006—SDA/PRESBYTERIAN CHURCH DIALOGUES

**William Johnsson gives a presentation to the Presbyterian Church in
Ecumenical Dialogue #1 in Nov., 2006**, in which he says, (See Appendix
K):

> William Johnsson:
> "As we look over the 28 statements of Adventist doctrine, we
> are led to three conclusions: (1) The articles that are first and
> form the basis for the remainder, **namely** articles dealing <u>with</u>
> **the Trinity**, the person of Christ, and salvation, **conform to**
> <u>orthodox</u> **Christian understanding.**"

And which church system has determined this "orthodoxy"? The
Council of Nicea, as upheld by the Church of Rome! **This statement**

**above is an unequivocal acknowledgement by a highly placed church
official that the Adventist denomination's concept of the 'Trinity' is
essentially identical to that of Rome and her daughters.** The change,
within the denomination, from being an anti-Trinitarian to a fully
Trinitarian structure has been made without any official vote being taken at
any General Conference Session. As we have seen, the new belief in the
'Trinity' has been insinuated into the church psyche by a few key
individuals.

2010—*Adventist World,* **February issue, "1+1+1=One – The keystone of
biblical theology," by Norman R. Gulley.**

2011—*Adventist World,* **March issue, "God in Three Persons, Blessed
Trinity," by Jo Ann Davidson.**

The title says it all.

2012—Spring Quarter, SDA Sabbath School Quarterly:

The Sabbath School Quarterly asks the question on page 7: **"How does
the New Testament talk about the oneness of God?"** The question is
designed to teach you that there **is one God who is composed of three
Persons.** They give you two texts to look up, but each is employed
deceptively.

DECEPTION #1: Students are first directed to go to James 2:19—
"Thou believest that there is **one God**; thou doest well: the devils also
believe, and tremble."
Comment: In this verse, where it speaks of "one God," the Quarterly is
trying to teach you that that means Father, Son, and Holy Spirit. But they
don't tell you to go to **James 3:9 which tells us who the "one god" spoken
of in James 2:19 is.** James 3:9 declares: "Therewith bless we **God, even
the Father."**

DECEPTION #2: Students are directed to go to 1 Corinthians 8:4—"As
concerning therefore the eating of those things that are offered in sacrifice
unto idols, we know that an idol is nothing in the world, and that there is
none other God but one."
Comment: Again, the Quarterly is trying to teach that the Father, Son,
and the Holy Spirit are this "one God." **But they don't tell you to read
verse 6 which tells who this "one God" is.**

1 Corinthians 8:6: "But to us there is but **one God, the Father,** of whom are all things, and we in him; and one Lord Jesus Christ, by whom are all things, and we by him."

This quarterly is deceptive and teaching a false god. This quarterly is not scholarly nor honest.

2012— *Adventist World,* June issue, "Distinct, But Indivisible," by Daniel K. Bediako, who writes:

"We worship one God who reveals Himself in and **consists of three, distinct persons who participate in one substance and coexist in unity.**"

2012—Fall Quarter, SDA Sabbath School Quarterly:

The Sabbath School Quarterly teaches "The Mystery of the Triune God" on page 17—**"There is only one God…" And this god has a "three-part nature."**

SUMMARY: Trinitarianism has percolated down from the effort of a few key men in high positions. God's sheep are being led astray by "certain men" which have "crept in unawares." Jude 4.

"While men slept, his enemy came and sowed tares among the wheat." (Matthew 13:25.)

Chapter 10

MICHAEL = CHRIST:
The Pre-Incarnation, Divine Second Person of the Godhead

PROFESSOR: As we consider the true concept of the Godhead, it is essential that we establish Christ's identity before the incarnation. What name do you think Jesus was known by before sin?

WILLIAM: Michael?

PROFESSOR: Spot on, William! Michael is mentioned several times in the Scriptures.

Revelation 12:7:
"And there was war in heaven: **Michael** and his angels fought against the dragon; and the dragon fought and his angels...."

Jude 9:
"Yet **Michael the archangel,** when contending with the devil he disputed about the body of Moses, durst not bring against him a railing accusation, but said, The Lord rebuke thee."

Daniel 10:13:
"But the prince of the kingdom of Persia withstood me one and twenty days: but, lo, **Michael,** one of the **chief princes,** came to help me; and I remained there with the kings of Persia."

Daniel 10:21:
"But I will show thee that which is noted in the scripture of truth: and [there is] none that holdeth with me in these things, but **Michael your prince.**"

Daniel 12:1:
"And at that time shall **Michael** stand up, **the great prince** which standeth for the children of thy people: and there shall be a

time of trouble, such as never was since there was a nation [even] to that same time: and at that time thy people shall be delivered, every one that shall be found written in the book."

WILLIAM: These Scriptures do not tell us Who Michael is.

PROFESSOR: No, but notice in Jude 9 that Michael is called the "archangel." The word *Angel, from the greek word 'Angelos',* means "Messenger"; the word "Archangel" means "The Chief of the Angels." (Just as the **arch**bishop is over the bishops in the Catholic Church system). You will remember the taped conversation at Loma Linda, CA in 1989 (see page 125 of this book) where Walter Martin spoke disparagingly of Adventism believing that Michael, the Archangel is Christ. Well look at these scriptures:

1 Thessalonians 4:16:
"**The Lord Himself** shall descend from Heaven with a shout, **with the voice of the archangel,** and with the trump of God and the dead in Christ shall rise first."

And John 5:25, proves that **it is the voice of the Son of God that wakes the dead to life:**

John 5:25:
"**The dead shall hear the voice of the Son of God; and they that hear shall live.**"

These texts prove that **Michael is the Son of God.**

WILLIAM: Was this Jesus' name in the Old Testament before His incarnation?

PROFESSOR: Yes. The Hebrew word for Michael is *Miykkael,* which means, "Who is Like God." That is why Jesus could say to Philip:

John 14:9, 10:
9) "He that hath seen me hath seen the Father; and how sayest thou [then], Show us the Father?
10) Believest thou not that I am in the Father, and the Father in me? the words that I speak unto you I speak not of myself: but the Father that dwelleth in me, he doeth the works."

140

Remember, the Father dwells in Jesus through the Holy Spirit, which Spirit they share, just as Jesus "dwells in" believers by the same Holy Spirit. (See John 14:10, 16-18.) The Spirit of Prophecy clearly supports the view that Jesus is Michael in Early Writings, page 36; and Spirit of Prophecy, Volume 2, page 330. Also, in:

Patriarchs & Prophets , page 366:
"Christ was not only the leader of the Hebrews in the wilderness—the **Angel** in whom was the name of Jehovah [Michael—One Who is Like God], and who, veiled in the cloudy pillar, went before the host—but it was He who gave the law to Israel." [Who shared the name 'Yahweh' or 'self-existent' with His Father because they are both 'self-existent'.]

WILLIAM: When did Christ get the name "Jesus"?

PROFESSOR: **Jesus is the name given by the angel to Mary before His incarnation. Jesus is His name as the "Son of Man" which He had to become to implement His salvational role for the lost race!**

Matthew 1:21:
And she shall bring forth a son, and thou shalt call his name JESUS: for he shall save his people from their sins. [Yasua = "JEHOVAH Saves."]

Jesus was sent into this world by the Father (John 17:3). The Father 'gave His only-begotten Son (John 3:16). The Father was "in" Christ reconciling the world to Himself. (2 Corinthians 15:19). The Father was "in" Christ in the same way that Christ, and the Father are "in" faithful disciples, (See 2 Corinthians 5:19 and John 14:10, 17, 18, 23): by the Holy Spirit!

WILLIAM: Jesus and the Father can be "in" us through the Holy Spirit?

PROFESSOR: Yes, William. The Scriptures show that the Holy Spirit represents Jesus now on earth, but we will study that topic more in depth later. (See Chapter 14)

WILLIAM: What does it mean that Jesus was "the only-begotten Son"?

PROFESSOR: When Jesus came to this earth "made of a woman, made under the law…" (Gal. 4:4), **Jesus was "begotten."** **For the first time in universal History a new type of being came into existence who was both Creator and creature—a union of Divinity and humanity**—a unique Being. Definitely **not** "altogether such an one as ourselves." This new Being, Jesus, was not spoken into existence; nor was He formed of the dust, to then have the breath of life breathed into Him; He was "begotten" ("made of a woman") into existence—the **"only-begotten of the Father."** God's messenger, referring to Christ's, incarnation, warns us:

> *Manuscript Releases*, Volume 13, page 19:   (Known as the "Baker Letter").
>
> "Never, in any way, leave the slightest impression upon human minds that a taint of, or inclination to corruption rested upon Christ, or that He in any way yielded to corruption. He was tempted in all points like as man is tempted, yet He is called that holy thing. It is a mystery that is left unexplained to mortals that Christ could be tempted in all points like as we are, and yet be without sin. The incarnation of Christ has ever been, and will ever remain a mystery. That which is revealed, is for us and for our children, but let every human being be warned from the ground of **making Christ altogether human, such an one as ourselves: for it cannot be."**

Jesus had only God as His Father. He was not "begotten" by the "will of the flesh." Jesus was a Being born—post Adam—after the entrance of sin—with a "sanctified human will," a will at enmity against the serpent— not possessing the same "sinful, corrupt, fallen disloyalty we possess" when we are born into this world. The Bible calls this fallen mindset, that we come into the world with the "carnal heart."   This "carnal heart" Jesus never had:

> *Signs of the Times,* October 29, 1894:
> "Jesus Christ is our example in all things. **He began life, passed through its experiences, and ended its record, with a sanctified human will.** He was tempted in all points like as we are, and yet because **he kept his will surrendered** and sanctified, he never bent in the slightest degree toward the doing of evil, or toward manifesting rebellion against God."

142

Having "free will," Jesus "kept" (maintained) the sanctified mindset by constant surrender of His human will to that of His Father. Notice also the strong admonition given by God's messenger concerning Christ's will and mindset from birth. He was not born with a "carnal heart" (mind). He was the "Seed" promised to Eve that would have "enmity" against the "serpent." We, on the other hand, who are born by the "will of the flesh" and have earthly fathers, we are born with a "carnal heart" which is "enmity against God," which is "not subject to the law, neither indeed can be." To receive the "mind of Christ" we have to be "born again," also of the Holy Spirit whereby we are "sealed unto the day of redemption" and become "new creatures"—"all things" becoming new.

Jesus is, therefore, the **"second Adam"**:

1 Corinthians 15:45-47:

45) "And so it is written, **The first man Adam** was made a living soul; **the last Adam was made a quickening spirit.**

46) Howbeit that was not first which is spiritual, but that which is natural; and afterward that which is spiritual.

47) The first man is of the earth, earthy: **the second <u>man</u>** *[second Adam]* **is the Lord from heaven.**"

Jesus is **set to be the head of an entirely new line of "born-again" beings,** whom He would not be ashamed to call brethren.

2 Corinthians 5:17:

"Therefore if any man be in Christ, **he is a new creature:** old things are passed away; behold, all things are become new."

Galatians 6:15:

"For in Christ Jesus neither circumcision availeth any thing, nor uncircumcision, **but a new creature.**"

Hebrews 1:11-13:

11) "For both he that sanctifieth and they who are sanctified [are] all of one: for which cause he is not ashamed to call them brethren,

12) Saying, I will declare thy name unto my brethren, in the midst of the church will I sing praise unto thee.

13) And again, I will put my trust in him. And again, Behold I and **the children which God hath given me.**"

143

Through the redemption accomplished at Calvary, Jesus can send the Holy Spirit to be a **permanent** indwelling entity in the redeemed (John 14:16-18) if they choose to not grieve Him away. As the second Adam, He is, in a sense, their spiritual "Father"—their "Everlasting Father" (Isaiah 9:6). Furthermore, in the same way that Adam is the 'Father' of the human race, so also is the Second Adam, the Father of 'born again', 'new creature' beings. Having been born of a woman (as we all are) He is also our "Brother" if we have been "born again" of the Holy Spirit, as He was born of the "Holy Ghost." Jesus' Father is then also "Our Father." Having been "born again" of the Holy Spirit, the Redeemed would then have the same earthly progenitor (the Holy Spirit) as Jesus had. All of this is only possible because of Jesus sacrificial life and death:

Matthew 1:18:
"Now the birth of Jesus Christ was on this wise: When as his mother Mary was espoused to Joseph, before they came together, **she was found with child of the Holy Ghost."**

Luke 1:35:
"And the angel answered and said unto her, **The Holy Ghost shall come upon thee, and the power of the Highest shall overshadow thee: therefore also that holy thing which shall be born of thee** shall be called **the Son of God."**

God's messenger tells us plainly:

Signs of the Times, May 30, 1895:
[When Jesus came into this world He came as the 'only-begotten Son;' the "Firstborn of a new line of Beings. He was] **"...not a son by creation,** as were the angels, **nor a son by adoption,** as is the forgiven sinner, **but a Son begotten in the express image of the Father's person,** and in all the brightness of His majesty and glory *[character]*, one equal with God in authority and dignity, and Divine perfection. **In Him dwelt all the fullness of the Godhead bodily"** *[by the Holy Spirit.]*

Isaiah 9:6:
"For **unto us a child is born**, unto us a Son is given: and the government shall be upon His shoulder and His name shall be called Wonderful, Counsellor, the Mighty God, the Everlasting Father, The Prince of Peace."

Jesus was made a priest "after the order of Melchizedek," **Prince of Salem** (*Peace*).

Psalm 110:4:
   "The LORD hath sworn, and will not repent, **Thou art a priest for ever after the order of Melchizedek.**"

WILLIAM: Once again, how can Jesus be the everlasting Father?

PROFESSOR: In Isaiah 9:6 Jesus is called the "Everlasting Father." He is to us a "Father" by recreation. After creation Adam was called "the son of God." In the same way that Adam is the father of the human race; just so the "Second Adam" (*Jesus*) is the Father of the "new creation."
   Some use that verse to say Jesus is "**the** Father." However, since Jesus is the "Son of God," as Isaiah 9:6 says "unto us a Son is given" and He "shall be called... the everlasting Father." How can we understand this? Isaiah clarifies:

Isaiah 8:18
   "Behold, **I and the children whom the LORD hath given me**"

Jesus is the spiritual Father of the children which Jehovah has given Him, in the same sense that Adam is the father of humanity; Jesus is Father of those who have accepted and received His Spirit. Divinity and humanity are mysteriously blended in those who have the "Spirit of Christ." Jesus is the spiritual "Father" of the redeemed in the same way that Paul claimed Timothy and Onesimus (*2* Timothy 2:1; Philemon 10) as his sons, and that Peter claimed Marcus as his son (1 Peter 5:13).
   The members of the Godhead, are "one" in character, **purpose and intent** (MH 422); they are "the same yesterday, and today, and for ever" (Heb. 13:8); and they are those "Who change not" (Mal. 3:6). Thus, when the members of the Godhead make a decision, **that which they have decided is already a fact; even before the decision is carried out.** Should sin enter Creation it had been determined in the secret councils of the Godhead that Christ would pay the ransom. **He was the Lamb slain from the foundation of the world—even before He was slain,** de facto. This is corroborated by Scripture:

Romans 4:17:

"Even God, who quickeneth the dead, and <u>calleth those things which be not as though they were</u>."

1Bible Commentary, page 1099.5:
"<u>I Am</u> means an eternal presence; the past, present, and future are ALIKE to God." (Lt 119, 1895).

Notice also that Jesus was the "Mediator of the Everlasting Covenant" eons before taking up that role:

Selected Messages Book 1, page 247:
"While God's Word speaks of the humanity of Christ when upon this earth, it also speaks decidedly regarding His pre-existence. The Word existed as a divine being, even as the eternal Son of God, in union and oneness with His Father. **From everlasting He was the Mediator of the covenant**, the one in whom all nations of the earth, both Jews and Gentiles, if they accepted Him, were to be blessed. 'The Word was with God, and the Word was God' (John 1:1). Before men or angels were created, the Word was with God, and was God.

"The world was made by Him, 'and without him was not any thing made that was made' (John 1:3). If Christ made all things, He existed before all things. The words spoken in regard to this are so decisive that no one need be left in doubt. Christ was God essentially, and in the highest sense. He was with God from **ALL** eternity, God over all, blessed forevermore. *[See Chapter 22 on this point.]*

"The Lord Jesus Christ, the divine Son of God, existed from eternity, a distinct person, yet one with the Father. He was the surpassing glory of heaven. He was the commander of the heavenly intelligences, and the adoring homage of the angels was received by Him as His right. This was no robbery of God."

It is no marvel then that inspiration refers to Jesus as the "only-begotten of the Father," even before Mary gave birth to the Messiah in Bethlehem. **Nowhere in inspiration is it recorded that 'Michael' is referred to as the "only-begotten Son of God." Jesus is the name employed in these inspired statements.** Jesus is the "new name" that was given at the incarnation. (Matt. 1:20-23; Luke 1:31, 32; John 1:12-14). (Jesus is also referred to as Emmanuel [Matt. 1:23] and "the Branch" [Zech. 6:12; 3:8]).

146

**Jesus was "begotten" <u>again</u> into "glorified humanity" at the
resurrection.** The fallen humanity which He inherited from Mary died
eternally. Fallen humanity never came out of the grave. Fallen humanity
cannot "inherit the kingdom of God (1 Cor. 15:50), His humanity is
"changed" just as ours must be in order to go to heaven. **Christ came forth
from the tomb in glorified humanity.**

Acts 13:33:
"God hath fulfilled the same unto us their children, in that he
hath **raised up Jesus again; as it is also written in the second
psalm, Thou art my Son, this day have I begotten thee.**"

When Jesus was resurrected, He ascended to heavenly mount Zion to sit
at the right hand of God.

Psalm 2:6, 7:
6) **"Yet have I set my king upon my holy hill of Zion.**
7) I will declare the decree: the LORD hath said unto me,
Thou [*art*] my Son; **this day have I begotten thee.**"

WILLIAM: **Inspiration is clear that Jesus was not "begotten"** (or
"generated" as taught in the Trinity doctrine) **at some point in antiquity.
It also clearly indicates the exalted position that He stepped down from
in order to reach and save us and be the Mediator between us and God
the Father.**

PROFESSOR: The following compilation of statements confirms your
statements:

Faith I Live By, page 46 (EV 615; 5BC 1127):
"**Christ was one with the Father** before the foundation of
the world was laid. **This is the light shining in a dark place,
making it resplendent with divine, original glory.** *[See
Chapter 25 on this "one"ness to see why the truth on Christ's
"one"ness with His Father is "the light shining in a dark
place".]*
"**Christ is the pre-existent, self-existent Son of God....** In
speaking of His pre-existence, Christ carries the mind back
through dateless ages. **He assures us that there NEVER was a
time** *[never previously "begotten"]* **when He was not in close**

147

fellowship with the eternal God *[known to us as God the Father]*....

"His divine life could not be reckoned by human computation. The existence of Christ before His incarnation is not measured by figures.

"Christ was God essentially, and in the highest sense. *[There are lesser "gods"—God is a "God of gods." See Ps. 82:6.]* **He was with God from all eternity, God over all, blessed forevermore.** The Lord Jesus Christ, *[prior to His incarnation He was known as Michael (the One who is like God) the Archangel, the Captain of the armies of Heaven]* **the divine Son of God, existed from eternity, a distinct person** *[not an inseparable emanation of some primal "God" substance]*, **yet one with the Father** *["one" in purpose, in mind, in character, and in spirit]*. **He was the surpassing glory of heaven. He was the commander of the heavenly intelligences, and the adoring homage of the angels was received by Him as His right.**

"He <u>was</u> *[past tense]* **equal with God, infinite and omnipotent.**

"But He humbled Himself *["made Himself of no reputation;" Philippians 2:7]*, **and took mortality upon Him.** As a member of the human family, He was mortal; but as **a God** *[notice "a" God]*, **He was the fountain of life to the world. He could, in His divine person, ever have withstood the advances of death, and refused to come under its dominion** *[however He laid down His divine power—His Divinity (See Ser. B. No. 9, page 3; LHU, 233)—and took upon Himself our humanity in order to be able to die (7 BC page 925.6)]*; **but He voluntarily laid down His life, that in so doing He might give life and bring immortality to light** *[He laid down His immortal life that He might give it to us who deserve eternal death]*. **He bore the sins of the world, and endured the penalty** *[eternal death]*, **which rolled like a mountain upon His divine soul.** *[Just because Jesus had laid down the panoply of Divinity does not mean that He lost His identity as a Divine member of the Godhead.]* **He yielded up His life** *[the life of a Divine Person who had laid aside His Divine powers and abilities: a Divine Person now made human through being "made of a woman, made under the law:" yet still "that holy thing" (Lk. 1:35)]* **a sacrifice,** that man should not **eternally die.** He died, not

148

through being compelled to die, but by His own free will *[by laying down His immortal life]*.

"And *[God's messenger says]* this wonderful mystery, the incarnation of Christ and the atonement that He made, must be declared to every son and daughter of Adam."

Here follows a good exposition on Michael's identity for you to read, William: (See next chapter.)

Chapter 11

WHO IS MICHAEL THE ARCHANGEL?

by Doug Batchelor and David Boatwright
[http://www.amazingfacts.org/media-library/book/e/85/t/who-is-michael-the-archangel.aspx]

The Michael Enigma

Questions frequently arise in Christian circles about the true identity of the biblical Michael, sometimes called "Michael the great Prince" or "Michael the archangel." Some claim that Michael is the highest of the heavenly angels, one of the covering cherubs, or a special messenger like Gabriel, and as such is a created being. Others, such as the Bible commentator Matthew Henry, assert that Michael is simply another name for Jesus Himself. Can we know the real identity of this mysterious individual? The key to this puzzling question is found in the Scriptures.

A quick look in a Bible concordance reveals that there are 15 references to the name Michael. The first 10 of them are found in Old Testament chronologies and obviously refer to real people named Michael. In fact, the entry for "Michael" in the lexicon (a Greek and/or Hebrew dictionary) states: "The name of an archangel and nine Israelites." It is the identity of Michael, the archangel and prince, mentioned in the last five references that we are seeking.

The first three of these references are in the apocalyptic Old Testament book of Daniel. The last two are in the New Testament books of Jude and Revelation. During an honest study and comparison of these verses and others, clues emerge that lead us to an inescapable conclusion that the identity of Michael is none other than Jesus, God the Son, and that He is not a created angel, but God's eternal Son!

At first glance it appears that the Old Testament portrays Michael as a prince and the New Testament as an angel. But by looking at other related scriptures where similar language and wording are used, we will see a different pattern emerge.

It's in the Name

First, let's consider the meaning of some words and names. In the Greek New Testament, as compared to the Old Testament, the word "angel" means "messenger," and "arch" means "chief, principle, greatest, or highest." So "archangel" simply means "highest or greatest messenger." The Hebrew name "Michael" means "who is like God" or "Who is like God?" Whether this name is a question, statement, or a challenge will be clear by further study. One angel did profess to be like God. That fallen being is Lucifer, the covering cherub in the heavenly courts who became the devil, Satan, by claiming to "be like the most High" (Isaiah 14:14). In Revelation 12:7 Satan is opposed by "Michael and his angels" and is cast out of heaven.

It is not implausible to assume that if Christ came to earth and became a man in His battle against Satan to save human beings, He might also have identified with the angels to protect them from Satan's evil influence in heaven. In fact, there are several references in Scripture to a mysterious being identified as "the angel of the Lord" before Christ's earthly incarnation. Yet each time He is mentioned there are clues to His identity. Let's review them briefly.

Hagar

After Hagar bore Ishmael to Abraham, she and the barren Sarah could no longer coexist peacefully. Sarah mistreated her now haughty handmaid until Hagar fled into the desert. "And the angel of the Lord found her by a fountain of water in the wilderness" (Genesis 16:7). The angel told Hagar to go back and submit to Sarah, and promised that her son, Ishmael, would be the father of a great nation. When the "angel" disappeared, Hagar, "called the name of the Lord that spake unto her, Thou God seest me" (verse 13). It appears Hagar recognized that the "angel" who had spoken to her was really God.

Abraham

God told Abraham to sacrifice his son, Isaac, on mount Moriah. Just as he was about to plunge the dagger into his son of promise, the angel of the Lord stopped him. "And the angel of the Lord called unto him out of heaven, and said, Abraham, Abraham: and he said, Here am I. And he said, Lay not thine hand upon the lad, neither do thou any thing unto him: for now I know that thou fearest God, seeing thou hast not withheld thy son, thine only son from me" (Genesis 22:11, 12).

It is clear that Abraham was offering his son to God and not to a mere angel. "And the angel of the Lord called unto Abraham out of heaven the second time, And said, By myself have I sworn, saith the Lord, for because thou hast done this thing, and hast not withheld thy son, thine only son: That in blessing I will bless thee, ... because thou hast obeyed my voice"

151

(Genesis 22:15-18). In recounting this experience of Abraham in Acts 3:25, Peter also identifies this "angel of the Lord" as God.

Jacob

While fleeing from his angry brother Esau, Jacob had a dream in which God confirmed the covenant of Abraham to him. After receiving assurance that God would be with him and bring him back safely to his home in Canaan, Jacob vowed to return to God a tithe of all his increase. He set up the stone he had been using for a pillow and anointed it with oil to solemnize his vow. Then he named the place Beth-el, or house of God, since God had appeared to him there.

Twenty years later Jacob was on his way back home, not a penniless fugitive, but a wealthy man. God reminded Jacob who had really brought him success. Here's how Jacob recounted the story: "And the angel of God spake unto me in a dream, saying, Jacob: And I said, Here am I" (Genesis 31:11). In verse 13 this "angel of God" identifies Himself: "I am the God of Beth-el, where thou anointedst the pillar, and where thou vowedst a vow unto me."

Then, when Jacob wrestled with a heavenly being (Genesis 32:22-32), he was given a new name and blessed. Jacob called the name of the place Peniel, "For I have seen God face to face, and my life is preserved" (verse 30). In the New Testament, Jesus is the one who blesses His people and gives them a new name (Matthew 5:3-12; Revelation 2:17). Clearly, the angel of the Lord is Jesus Himself.

When Jacob was on his death bed blessing Joseph's two sons, Ephraim and Manasseh, he used the terms "angel" and "God" interchangeably. "God, before whom my fathers Abraham and Isaac did walk, the God which fed me all my life long unto this day, The Angel which redeemed me from all evil, bless the lads" (Genesis 48:15, 16). Once again we see that the angel who redeemed Jacob is another name for our Redeemer, Jesus!

Moses

Moses saw a burning bush that was not consumed. "And the angel of the Lord appeared unto him in a flame of fire out of the midst of a bush" (Exodus 3:2). Verse four identifies this angel: "God called unto him out of the midst of the bush." And in verse six He identifies Himself. "I am the God of thy father, the God of Abraham, the God of Isaac, and the God of Jacob." The angel of the Lord identifies Himself as God!

In his last sermon before he was stoned to death, Stephen agrees with the Exodus account. "And when forty years were expired, there appeared to him in the wilderness of mount Sinai an angel of the Lord in a flame of fire

152

in a bush. When Moses saw it, he wondered at the sight: and as he drew near to behold it, the voice of the Lord came unto him, Saying, I am the God of thy fathers, the God of Abraham, and the God of Isaac, and the God of Jacob" (Acts 7:30-32).

In another instance, the children of Israel were led through the wilderness by God, "And the Lord went before them by day in a pillar of a cloud, to lead them the way; and by night in a pillar of fire, to give them light; to go by day and night" (Exodus 13:21). Moses describes it this way: "And the angel of God, which went before the camp of Israel, removed and went behind them; and the pillar of the cloud went from before their face, and stood behind them" (Exodus 14:19). Again, "the angel of God" is identified as God.

Balaam

In the story of Balaam and his talking donkey, the angel of the Lord again figures prominently. It is this angel who nearly kills the covetous prophet, who is on his way to curse God's people, and saves the donkey from her merciless master (Numbers 22:21-35). After Balaam's close brush with death, "the angel of the Lord said unto Balaam, Go with the men: but only the word that I shall speak unto thee, that thou shall speak" (verse 35). The next chapter reveals who put the words in the prophet's mouth: "And God met Balaam: ... And the Lord put a word in Balaam's mouth, and said, Return unto Balak, and thus shalt thou speak" (Numbers 23:4, 5). Here again, "the angel of the Lord" turns out to be God Himself.

Gideon

Gideon had an encounter with the angel of the Lord in the book of Judges. The angel told Gideon that the Lord was with him. Gideon pointed to the oppression of Israel by the Midianites as evidence to the contrary. "And the Lord looked upon him, and said, Go in this thy might, and thou shalt save Israel from the hand of the Midianites: have not I sent thee?" (Judges 6:14). Throughout the rest of the narrative, the person speaking to Gideon is identified interchangeably as the Lord, the angel of the Lord, and the angel of God.

Manoah

Samson's mother, the wife of Manoah, was barren. "And the angel of the Lord appeared unto the woman" (Judges 13:3). This angel told her she would bear a son who would deliver the apostate Israelites from their heathen oppressors. She quickly called Manoah, who prayed for another visit from the "man of God." When the angel came the second time,

Manoah asked him his name. The King James Version of the Bible says that the angel told Manoah that his name was "Secret," with a margin notation that translates it as "Wonderful." This immediately makes us think of Isaiah's familiar prophecy that the name of the coming Messiah would be "Wonderful, Counselor, The mighty God, The everlasting Father, The Prince of Peace" (Isaiah 9:6). The name "Wonderful" for the angel of the Lord who appeared to Manoah connects this "angel" with the coming Messiah who was to be called "Wonderful."

No One Has Seen the Father

Suddenly we have more leads than we can follow at once. The "angel of the Lord" is clearly shown to be God. But the Bible states, "No man hath seen God at any time; the only begotten Son, which is in the bosom of the Father, he hath declared him" (John 1:18). John 6:46 tells us, "Not that any man hath seen the Father, save he which is of God, he hath seen the Father." Obviously, since no man has seen God the Father, all of these Old Testament sightings of God as the "angel of the Lord" must have been Jesus, God the Son, veiling His glory so they could endure His presence without being consumed.

Rebuking the Accuser

There is one more important reference where the angel of the Lord appears in the Old Testament. The prophet Zechariah was given a vision of Joshua the high priest standing before the angel of the Lord. Satan is standing at his right hand to resist him. Here we see two adversaries contending over a sinful human being. In this case the sin is represented by Joshua's filthy garments (Zechariah 3:3).

In this narrative the name changes quickly from "the angel of the Lord" (verse 1) to "the Lord" (verse 2), indicating again that they are one and the same. Then the Lord makes an interesting statement. "And the Lord said unto Satan, The Lord rebuke thee, O Satan" (Zechariah 3:2) There is only one other place in Scripture, Jude verse nine, where this sentence is found, and it is spoken by Michael the archangel!

In the small New Testament epistle of Jude we see a vignette similar to Joshua and the angel in the book of Zechariah. "Yet Michael the archangel, when contending with the devil he disputed about the body of Moses, durst not bring against him a railing accusation, but said, The Lord rebuke thee" (Jude 1:9). The situations are amazingly parallel. Christ and Satan are contending over a sinner. A live one in the case of Joshua, and a dead one in the case of Moses. The debate is ended abruptly when Jesus says, "The Lord rebuke thee." Jesus also rebuked the devil when He was tempted in the wilderness. "And Jesus answered and said unto him, Get thee behind me, Satan" (Luke 4:8).

Michael the Prince

Isaiah's prophecy about the Messiah (Isaiah 9:6) reveals a key word that bears investigating. One of the names he says that would apply to the Messiah is "Prince of Peace." This immediately reminds us of the three verses in Daniel in which Michael is called a "prince."

There is another verse in Daniel where the "Prince of princes" is mentioned. Again the cosmic conflict is being played out with Christ on one side and the devil on the other, with humanity serving as the battlefield. Symbolic names identify the two arch foes. Both struggle to gain control, Satan against our will and Christ only with our willingness.

"Prince of princes" is actually the same term that is translated "prince of the host" in verse 11. This is similar to "Lord of lords" (Psalm 136:3), "God of gods" (Deuteronomy 10:17), and "King of kings" (Revelation 19:16). All these are titles of deity. He is even referred to as "Messiah the Prince" (Daniel 9:25).

One, or First?

Daniel 10:13 is probably the most difficult verse regarding Michael: "But the prince of the kingdom of Persia withstood me one and twenty days: but, lo, Michael, one of the chief princes, came to help me." It appears at first glance that Michael is only "one of" the chief princes. This is an unfortunate translation in the King James Version. The word "one" comes from the Hebrew word "echad" which also means "first," as in "first day" (Genesis 1:5). This changes the whole meaning of the verse to Michael being first of, or highest of, the chief princes. Again, a reference to Jesus.

The Voice of Michael

If we take the term "Michael the archangel" and examine the word "archangel," we see another interesting match. The only other passage in the Bible that uses the word "archangel" is 1 Thessalonians 4:16. But look at its context. "For the Lord himself shall descend from heaven with a shout, with the voice of the archangel, and with the trump of God: and the dead in Christ shall rise first." It is the voice of the archangel that raises the dead in Christ, and the Lord Himself who shouts it. This indicates that they are one and the same. Jesus is the one who shouts with the voice of the archangel, or "greatest Messenger," to raise the dead!

Obviously, angels don't have the power to resurrect the dead. Only God who gives life has the power to restore it. "For as the Father hath life in himself; so hath he given to the Son to have life in himself. ... Marvel not at this: for the hour is coming, in the which all that are in the graves shall hear his voice, And shall come forth" (John 5:26, 28, 29).

In Jude we see the archangel contending with the devil for the body of Moses, who, incidentally, was resurrected and taken to heaven from whence he appeared on the mount of transfiguration to encourage Christ (Mark 9). In 1 Thessalonians, the apostle Paul describes the resurrection as happening in response to the voice of the archangel. Again we see the parallel between these two verses; both describe the archangel in the act of resurrecting.

When Michael stands up in Daniel chapter 12, there also follows a resurrection, and he is described as the one who, "standeth for the children of thy people" (verse 1). Commenting on this verse, Matthew Henry states: "Michael signifies, 'Who is like God,' and his name, with the title of 'the great Prince,' points out the Divine Savior. Christ stood for the children of our people in their stead as a sacrifice, bore the curse for them, to bear it from them. He stands for them in pleading for them at the throne of grace." Jesus is clearly the one who always stands in our place and for our defense.

Worshiping the Commander

In Revelation, Michael is portrayed as leading the heavenly hosts, or armies, in the war against the rebellious Lucifer that took place there. "And there was war in heaven: Michael and his angels fought against the dragon; and the dragon fought and his angels" (Revelation 12:7). Here the term "dragon" is a symbolic name for Satan, the leader of evil (verse 9), so it is very safe to assume that Michael is another name for Jesus, the embodiment and leader of good. But there is more evidence.

Just as Israel was preparing for its first battle after crossing into the Promised Land, Joshua had an encounter with an unusual warrior. "And it came to pass, when Joshua was by Jericho, that he lifted up his eyes and looked, and, behold, there stood a man over against him with his sword drawn in his hand: and Joshua went unto him, and said unto him, Art thou for us, or for our adversaries? And he said, Nay; but as captain of the host of the Lord am I now come. And Joshua fell on his face to the earth, and did worship, and said unto him, What saith my lord unto his servant? And the captain of the Lord's host said unto Joshua, Loose thy shoe from off thy foot; for the place whereon thou standest is holy. And Joshua did so" (Joshua 5:13-15).

Not only did Joshua worship this being, but the heavenly captain received his worship. If he had been a mere angel, he would have rebuked Joshua just like the angel rebuked John for trying to worship him (see Revelation 19:10; 22:8, 9).

In all the cases where the angel of the Lord accepts worship, it is clearly the Son of God. But where regular created angels are worshiped, they refuse it. Even Jesus reminded Satan in the wilderness, "For it is written, Thou shalt worship the Lord thy God, and him only shalt thou serve" (Luke 4:8).

In fact, all the created angels are commanded to worship Jesus as they did during His first advent. "And again, when he bringeth in the first begotten into the world, he saith, And let all the angels of God worship him" (Hebrews 1:6). The devil is infuriated because he knows that someday even he will be compelled to acknowledge Jesus as king and worship Him. "That at the name of Jesus every knee should bow, of things in heaven, and things in earth, and things under the earth; And that every tongue should confess that Jesus Christ is Lord, to the glory of God the Father" (Philippians 2:10, 11).

The phrase "Lord of hosts" is found 245 times in the Bible and refers to the "commander of God's angelic army." So the "captain of the Lord's host" that Joshua saw was not an angel, but Jesus Himself. That explains why He demanded that Joshua remove his shoes. The place was holy because Jesus was there, just as Jesus' presence at the burning bush made that ground holy for Moses. So Michael, the captain of the Lord's host, or army, is another title for Jesus.

Who Is as God!

When Phillip asked Jesus to show the disciples the Father, Christ responded: "Have I been so long time with you, and yet hast thou not known me, Philip? he that hath seen me hath seen the Father" (John 14:9).

Some think that God's Son waited 4,000 years to personally intervene in the affairs of man. Not so! Though it is true that the incarnation occurred 4,000 years after man's fall, God the Son has been personally involved in the history and affairs of His people.

What a wonderful truth that Jesus, God's eternal Son, has ever been actively occupied in watching over, providing for, and protecting His children! He spoke face to face with Abraham and Moses and wrestled with Jacob. He led the Israelites through the wilderness, providing food and water and victory against their enemies.

Remember that the title "Michael the archangel" means "The greatest messenger who is as God." It was Jesus, "the image of the invisible God" (Colossians 1:15), who brought the greatest message of hope, the gospel, to our perishing world!

157

Chapter 12

WHEN WAS JESUS BEGOTTEN?

WILLIAM: Professor, in the Catholic Catechism concerning the Trinity, it says that Christ was begotten (or "generated") by God from all eternity, and that it is an eternal begetting. How does Inspiration describe **when** Christ was begotten?

PROFESSOR: The Bible is actually pretty clear on the subject. There should be no confusion. First we need to see that Christ is an eternal member of the Godhead with no beginning.

Micah 5:2:
"But thou, Bethlehem Ephratah, though thou be little among the thousands of Judah, yet out of thee shall he come forth unto me that is to be ruler in Israel; **whose goings forth have been from of old, from everlasting.**"

John 5:58:
"Jesus said unto them, Verily, verily, I say unto you, Before Abraham was, **I am.**"

"**I AM**" is a name that only belongs to the "**SELF**-existent"!

Selected Messages Book 1, page 247:
"The Word existed as a divine being, even as the **eternal** Son of God, in union and oneness with His Father. **From EVERLASTING He was the Mediator of the covenant,** the one in whom all nations of the earth, both Jews and Gentiles, if they accepted Him, were to be blessed. 'The Word was with God, **and the Word was God'** (John 1:1). Before men or angels were created, the Word was with God, and was God.

"The world was made by Him, 'and without him was not any thing made that was made' (John 1:3). If Christ made all things, He existed before all things. The words spoken in regard to this are so decisive that no one need be left in doubt. Christ was God essentially, and in the highest sense. **He was with God from ALL eternity,** God over all, blessed forevermore.

"The Lord Jesus Christ, the divine Son of God, **existed from eternity, a <u>distinct person</u>,** yet one with the Father."

This statement aggressively refutes any notion of 'consubstantiality' and is consequently an anti-Trinitarian statement. God's messenger says above, that Christ **'was with God from ALL eternity'! To have existed from ALL 'eternity, a distinct Person' denies any scope to the notion of Him being 'begotten' or 'generated' at some point in the past ages before Creation.**

This statement also indicates that a station, title, or office is eternally recognized by the Godhead, even before a particular role is actively commenced. Notice! 'From everlasting, He was the Mediator of the Covenant.' <u>Jesus only became the active Mediator once sin entered.</u> Is it possible that His Sonship, His being the "only begotten" Son of God the Father, rests on the same criteria?

WILLIAM: Yes, I think so. Just as Jesus is described as "the Lamb slain from the foundation of the world" (Rev. 13:8), but only died at 31 AD on Calvary. Did Ellen White ever refute the idea that Christ was a Being "begotten" or created at some point in incomprehensible antiquity?

PROFESSOR: As we have noted, indeed she did! She declared:

The Faith I Live By, page 46:
"**Christ is the pre-existent, <u>SELF-existent</u> Son of God** *[SELF-existence precludes being "generated" by another]*… In speaking of His pre-existence, Christ carries the mind back through dateless ages. **He assures us that there NEVER was a time when He was not in close fellowship with the eternal God….** *["Fellowship" necessitates two individuals at least.]*
"His divine life could not be reckoned by human computation. The existence of Christ before His incarnation is not measured by figures.
"**Christ was God essentially, and in the highest sense. He was with God from <u>ALL</u> eternity,** God over all, blessed forevermore. The Lord Jesus Christ, the divine Son of God, **existed FROM *[ALL]* ETERNITY, a distinct person,** yet one with the Father. *[with the 'one'ness described in John ch.17 and <u>Ministry of Healing</u>, page 422]*
"**He was equal with God, infinite and omnipotent. [See** *Phil. 2:6-8. Christ voluntarily stepped down from that exalted*

159

position, in order to reach us where we are. He "...made Himself of no reputation..." Strong's-#2758: to make empty, that is, to neutralize. Greek Lexicon.] "**But He humbled Himself**, and took **mortality upon Him.** *[In order to be able to die. Deity cannot die.]* As a member of the human family, He was mortal; but as **a God**, He was the fountain of life to the world. *[He offers us His life, which is immortality, the life that only God has. 1 Tim. 6:16; 2 Tim. 1:10; 1 Cor. 15:53, 54.]* **He could, in His divine person,** ever have withstood the advances of death, and refused to come under its dominion; but **He voluntarily laid down His life,** that **in so doing He might give life and bring immortality to light.** *[Before coming to this earth He had laid aside His divinity (divine attributes), had emptied Himself. See Series B, No. 9, page 3 (page 278 in collection), and Lift Him Up, page 233 (Signs, 3/17/1887).]* He bore the sins of the world, **and endured the penalty, which rolled like a mountain upon His divine soul. He yielded up His life a sacrifice, that man should not eternally die** *[the 'penalty']*. He died, not through being compelled to die, but by His own free will" *[because He laid down His immortal life voluntarily.]*

Signs of the Times, May 30, 1895, par. 3:
"A complete offering has been made; for "God so loved the world, that he gave his only-begotten Son"—**not a son by creation,** as were the angels, **nor a son by adoption,** as is the forgiven sinner, **but a Son begotten in the express image of the Father's person,** and in all the brightness of his majesty and glory, one equal with God in authority, dignity, and divine perfection. In him dwelt all the fullness of the Godhead bodily."

<u>Desire of Ages</u>, page 51:
"**The dedication of the first-born had its origin in the earliest times. God had promised to give the First-born of heaven to save the sinner.**"
[The 'dedication of the first-born' was a practice on this planet, after the entrance of sin—not in infinity. To implement the plan of salvation our Saviour had to become the "only begotten" Son of God: the 'First Born' of many 'born again' sons and daughters of the living God.]

God's Amazing Grace, page 282:

"Through the Holy Spirit she *[Mary]* received wisdom to co-operate with the heavenly agencies in the development of **this child** *[Jesus]*, **who could claim only God as His Father**.... From her lips and from the scrolls of the prophets, He learned of heavenly things. The very words which He Himself had spoken to Moses for Israel He was now taught at His mother's knee.... And spread out before Him was the great library of God's created works. He who had made all things studied the lessons which His own hand had written in earth and sea and sky...."

God's message to King David concerning the 'Son of David' was:

2 Samuel 7:12-16:

12) "And when thy days be fulfilled, and thou shalt **sleep** with thy fathers, I will set up **thy seed** after thee, which shall proceed out of thy bowels, and I will establish his kingdom.

13) He shall build an house for my name, and I will stablish the throne of his kingdom **for ever.**

14) **I will be his father, and he shall be my son. If he commit iniquity, I will chasten him with the rod of men, and with the stripes of the children of men:** *[This statement—("If he commit iniquity....") applied to Solomon! Satan instigated the Jews to apply it to Christ—to discourage Him!]*

15) But my mercy shall not depart away from him, as I took it from Saul, whom I put away before thee.

16) And thine house and thy kingdom shall be established for ever before thee: **thy throne shall be established for ever.**"

These texts clearly state that Jesus would be (future tense) the Son! Not Solomon, who soon apostatized. **Jesus is the "seed" referred to, whose "throne would be established forever"!** (Verse 14 clearly includes Solomon, who did fall into deep apostasy.)

Peter, on the day of Pentecost, applies this prophecy (*2 Sam 7: 12-16*) to Jesus Christ—See:

Acts 2:29, 30:

29) "Men and brethren, let me freely speak unto you of **the patriarch David,** that he is both dead and buried, and his sepulchre is with us unto this day.

30) **Therefore being a prophet, and knowing that God had sworn with an oath to him, that of the fruit of his loins, according to the flesh, he would raise up Christ to sit on his** *[David's]* **throne.**"

God's messenger tells us:

Selected Messages Book 1, pages 226, 227:
"In His humanity He was a **partaker** of the divine nature. **In His incarnation He gained in a new sense the title of the Son of God.** Said the angel to Mary, 'The power of the Highest shall overshadow thee: therefore also that holy thing which shall be born of thee **shall be called the Son of God**' (Luke 1:35). While the Son of a human being, **He became the Son of God in a new sense.** *[In the sense that what had been planned, was now actuality. Jesus was now, literally, "begotten of God."]* Thus He stood in our world—the Son of God, yet allied **by birth** *[by being "begotten"]* **to the human race.**"

Luke 1:35:
"And the angel answered and said unto her, The Holy Ghost shall come upon thee, and the power of the Highest shall overshadow thee: therefore also **that holy thing which shall be born** of thee **SHALL BE** called the Son of God.**"

Strong's #40, "thing": *hagios* = Sacred ... (most) holy (one, thing), saint. An indicator of when Jesus became (was "born" as) the "Son of God" in a literal, physical sense.

Hebrews 1: 5, 6:
5) "For unto which of the angels said he at any time, **Thou art my Son, this day** *[a fixed point in history]* **have I begotten thee?** And again, **I WILL BE** to him a Father, and he **SHALL BE** to me a Son?
6) And *[in another place]* again, when he bringeth in the firstbegotten **into the world,** he saith, And let all the angels of God worship him."

Then finally, William, is this wonderful verse:

Acts 13: 32, 33:
32) "And we declare unto you glad tidings, how that the promise which was made unto the fathers,
33) God hath fulfilled the same unto us their children, **in that he hath raised up Jesus again; as it is also written in the second psalm, Thou art my Son, this day have I begotten thee."**

WILLIAM: I ran up against an objection to Christ's eternal self-existence in a booklet entitled The Trinity in Evangelism by Margaretha Tierney and Gary Hullquist, which quotes from Signs of the Times, August 29, 1900 and from Volume 8 of the Testimonies, page 268, on the 8th page of their booklet, **in which they try to show that the words of God's messenger do not declare that Christ had no beginning**. From this they attempt to draw the conclusion that at some point in infinity Christ was exalted to equal status with the Father after His being "begotten".

PROFESSOR: God's messenger does not employ those exact words, namely 'that Christ had no beginning', but, in her own words, she makes it abundantly clear that Christ indeed 'had no beginning'. When we read Testimonies, Volume 8, page 268.2, 3 (and not just an excerpt from paragraph 3, as is quoted out of context, on the 8th page of their book), we discover that the context of the statement revolves around the incarnation and post incarnational events concerning Christ, Who, according to:

Testimonies Volume 8, page 268.3:
"...has been **given** an exalted position. He has been **made equal** with the Father. All the counsels of God are opened to His Son."

But we see that this **'exaltation'** and **'equalization'** occurs **post ascension** as we now read from the previous paragraph:

Testimonies Volume 8, page 268.2:
""...**when He had by Himself purged our sins, sat down on the right hand of the Majesty on high;** being **made** *[post incarnation]* so much better than the angels *[despite His now being eternally united to humanity which was initially made a 'little lower than the angels']*, as He hath by **inheritance** *[having*

been born/begotten as God's Son in human form] obtained a more excellent name than they *[the angels].* For unto which of the angels said He **at any time,** Thou art My Son, **THIS** day *[fixed point in time and history]* **have I begotten Thee?** And again, I **will be** *[predictive statement concerning Christ's Sonship]* to Him a Father, and He **shall be** *[predictive statement]* to Me a Son?' **Hebrews 1:1-5.**"

In Hebrews 1:1-5 Paul was clearly and unambiguously establishing that the **divine Christ,** by whom God created all things, was our divine sin purging Saviour who has risen and has been enthroned alongside His Father and has, in His humanity united to divinity, obtained high status by His victory. His Father has, post ascension, reversed Christ's making of Himself "of none effect" as seen in Hebrews l:1-5. **Paul then points the reader back to those predictive, pre-Advent, statements of God announcing His INTENTIONS to 'beget' Jesus** as the Messiah at a specific point in prophetic time, which clearly occurred at Bethlehem and **again** at the resurrection.

The Bible clearly states in:

Luke 1:30-35:
    30   "And the angel said unto her, Fear not, Mary: for thou hast found favour with God.
    31   And, behold, **thou shalt conceive in thy womb, and bring forth a son,** and shalt call his name JESUS.
    32   He shall be great, **and shall be called the Son of the Highest:** and the Lord God shall give unto him the throne of his father David:
    33   And he shall reign over the house of Jacob for ever; and of his kingdom there shall be no end.
    34   Then said Mary unto the angel, How shall this be, seeing I know not a man?
    35   And the angel answered and said unto her, The Holy Ghost shall come upon thee, and **the power of the Highest shall overshadow thee: therefore also that holy thing which shall be born of thee shall be called the Son of God.**"

It was also predicted in Scripture that at His resurrection Jesus would also be **'begotten' again**; a second 'birth' as it were. This is found in:

Psalms 2:7:

164

"**I will** declare the decree: the LORD hath said unto me,
Thou [art] my Son; this day have I begotten thee."

Verse 35 of Luke Chapter 1 is referring to the **first** 'begetting' of Christ
whilst Acts 13:33 clearly declares Christ's resurrection to be the **second**
fulfillment of Psalms 2:7. Notice the word **"again"**:

Acts 13:33:
"**God hath fulfilled the same** unto us their children, **in that
he hath raised up Jesus AGAIN; as it is also written in the
second psalm, Thou art my Son, this day have I begotten
thee.**"

Without question, as God's messenger is expressing what happened to
Christ, **post incarnation**, in:

Testimonies, Volume 8, page 268.3:
"God is the Father of *[the]* Christ *[Messiah]*; *[the]* Christ
[Messiah] is the Son of God. To Christ has been given an exalted
position. He has been made equal with the Father. All the
counsels of God are opened to His Son."

'Messiahship' is an incarnational relationship: the word 'Christ' means
'Messiah'. It was Christ Who, prior to His death, "could not see through
the portals of the tomb" (see DA p. 753.2). Who, prior to His birth, had laid
aside His memory and had to learn at His mother's knee the things that He
(as Michael) had revealed to the prophets (see DA 70.1). This whole
concept is endorsed by John and God's messenger as we see in:

Testimonies, Volume 8, page 268.4:
"Jesus said to the Jews: 'My Father worketh hitherto, and I
work. . . . The Son can do nothing of Himself, but what He seeth
the Father do: for what things soever He doeth, these also doeth
the Son likewise. For the Father loveth the Son, and showeth
Him all things that Himself doeth.'   John 5:17-20."

That Michael/Jesus eternally pre-existed His Messiahship is also cogently
and clearly expressed by God's messenger, in the:

Review and Herald, April 5, 1906 (quoted in Evangelism, pages 615-
616), and that the:

165

"...Word **EXISTED** as a divine being, even as the **ETERNAL Son of God**, in union and oneness with His Father. From **EVERLASTING** He was the Mediator of the covenant *[despite the FACT that He only took up His mediatorial role at the inception of sin, which role is only now, since 1844, in the final phase]*, the one in whom all nations of the earth, both Jews and Gentiles, if they accepted Him, were to be blessed...." *[As we can see, the notion of Christ having a 'beginning' has no 'firm foundation'!]*

Also, from the above, and from a multitude of other inspired statements, it is plain that a divine designation or role can be, and often is, employed and/or referred to eons before the actual implementation of such a role; as is the case with Christ being the "Messiah" and consequently the "Mediator". **For the Godhead, what is foreseen is as real and actual as present reality.** Notice how God's messenger expresses it:

Bible Commentary Volume 1, page 1099.5:
"**I AM** means an eternal presence; **the past, present, and future are alike to God. ...**" (Lt 119, 1895)

It is not surprising, therefore, that the Archangel *[which means 'Chief of the angels']*, Michael *[which means the 'One who is like God']* should also have inherent in Himself the eternal truth designated by the name Yashua/Jesus *[which means Yahweh/Jehovah saves.]* **Yahweh means "self-existent". <u>That name is applied to Christ and the Father.</u> Either they are both "self-existent" and therefore both "eternal" or inspiration is slipping and I do not give credence to that thought for a moment. The Father and Christ are both "I AM"; both are "ETERNAL"; One is not more "eternal" than the other.**

WILLIAM: So Jesus was begotten first at his birth, and again at his resurrection.

PROFESSOR: Yes. Firstly, Jesus came as the first being begotten as a union of our fallen humanity and divinity and secondly, at the time of His resurrection, **He became the first and only <u>Divine</u> Being to be, forever, in glorified human flesh.** Jesus had passed from "death to life" (John 5:24; 1 John 3:14) as our Elder Brother in the faith.

Chapter 13

THREE-IN-ONE OR ONE-IN-THREE?

WILLIAM: Should we, as a people, even use the term 'Trinity' to describe the Godhead?

PROFESSOR: William, my answer is in love, but firm as a rock: No! We should not! Nowhere in Scripture or in the inspired writings of God's last day messenger to the church will one ever find the term 'Trinity' used, because of what the term connotes.

WILLIAM: She never used the term "triune" (which means "three in one") either.

PROFESSOR: Yes, for the very reasons we have already noted. Throughout the inspired writings the **God-given** term used is the term 'Godhead.'

Acts 17:29:
"Forasmuch then as we are the offspring of God, we ought not to think that the **Godhead** is like unto gold, or silver, or stone, **graven by art and man's device.**" [*i.e.: Cannot be comprehended or conceived of by man and so rendered, physically, in human philosophical terms or speculative representations. **Can we, by searching find out God? "Canst thou find out the Almighty unto perfection?** Job 11:7, See the Persian Trident and all the other grotesque three-headed representations of Paganism. These are grotesque disparagements of God! They are "devices" of men!]*

However Scripture gives us a clue on how to, at least partially, grasp the truth concerning the Godhead:

Romans 1:20 says:
"For the **invisible things of him from the creation of the world are clearly seen, being understood by the things that**

are made, even his eternal power and Godhead; so that they are without excuse."

WILLIAM: Fascinating, that the seen illustrates the unseen.

PROFESSOR: The Godhead **is always revealing the character or "glory" of God, even through the Creation.** God's 'glory' or character, is intangible and therefore 'invisible' as an object, but his character can be 'seen' through Jesus' life, which was a perfect revelation of God's character, and through the Spirit-inspired Word, and, to an important, but imperfect, degree, through His creation.

When men refuse to "glorify" God by reflecting His character, this refusal is tantamount to base ingratitude for all the goodness of God that has been revealed to them through Creation, Christ, and the inspired Word. When men refuse to be transformed in character to reflect God's goodness, they end up belittling God and misrepresenting Him:

Romans 1:21-23:
    21) "Because that, when they knew God, they **glorified** him not as God, neither were thankful; but became vain in their imaginations, and their foolish heart was darkened.
    22) Professing themselves to be wise, they became fools,
    23) And changed the glory [*character*] of the uncorruptible God into an image made like to corruptible man, and to birds, and fourfooted beasts, and creeping things."

Romans 1:25 says:
    They "...changed the **truth** of God into a lie, and **worshipped** and **served** the creature *[other men and demons and animals and figments of their vain imaginations]* **more than** the Creator, who is blessed for ever. Amen."

Colossians 2:6-9:
    6) "As ye have therefore **received** Christ Jesus the Lord, [*so*] walk ye in him:
    7) Rooted and built up in him, and **stablished in the faith**, as ye have been taught, abounding therein with thanksgiving.
    8) Beware lest **any man spoil** you through **philosophy** and **vain deceit**, after the **tradition of men**, after the rudiments of the world, and not after Christ.

9) **For in him dwelleth all the fulness of the Godhead bodily.**" [See Chapter 26]

John 1:14:
"And the Word was **made** flesh, and dwelt among us, (and we beheld his glory, the glory as of the **only begotten of the Father,) full of grace and truth.**"

WILLIAM: Jesus is the clearest, brightest revelation of the character of God.

PROFESSOR: The "Godhead" spoken of in Scripture is composed of 3 distinct Persons: 1) The first is God the Father, who is the "**Sender**"—Who **sent** His Son that we might be saved.

1) GOD THE FATHER—THE SENDER

When Jesus sent His disciples to evangelize and do missionary work, He said:

Luke 10:16:
"…and he that despiseth you despiseth me; and he that despiseth me despiseth **him that sent** me."

Conversely, if Christ's representatives, His "sent" ones, are accepted, then He, Christ, is accepted. And to accept Christ is to accept the One whom He represents—His Father, the One who "sent" Him!

Romans 8:3:
"…**God sending his own Son** in the likeness of sinful flesh, and for sin, condemned sin in the flesh."

2) AS THE "SENT" ONE, JESUS IS THE RECONCILER AND SAVIOUR:

Romans 5:10:
"For if, when we were enemies, we were reconciled to God by the death of his Son, much more, being reconciled, we shall be saved by his life.

169

3) THE OMNIPRESENT HOLY SPIRIT IS THE REGENERATOR AND GUIDE.

John 3:5:
"Jesus answered, Verily, verily, I say unto thee, Except a man be born of water and of the Spirit, he cannot enter into the kingdom of God."

John 16:13-15:
13) "Howbeit **when he,** the Spirit of truth, is come, **he** will **guide** you into all truth: for he shall **not speak of himself;** but whatsoever he shall **hear,** that shall he **speak:** and he will show you things to come.
14) He shall **glorify** me: for he shall receive of mine, and shall show it unto you.
15) All things that the **Father** hath are mine: therefore said I, that **he** shall take of **mine,** and shall show it unto you."

WILLIAM: So three distinct Persons comprise the Godhead, while two members of which direct our worship to the "Most High God"—the Father?

PROFESSOR: Absolutely! I want you to consider again the illustration drawn from the pages of Holy Writ. It will help you to grasp the truth about the Godhead as we go forward with this discussion.

171

William, you will notice that the Lintel of the doorway represents God the Father who does not come into direct contact with the dust of the earth, while the Side posts do, yet they are in direct contact with the Lintel and are stationed beneath it to collectively form the doorway.

You will also recall that the actual Door – the wooden door – represents Christ's humanity. In John the 10th chapter Jesus claimed that He is the 'Door' (John. 10: 7, 9). He also claimed that of His own self He could do nothing (John. 5:19, 30). In His humanity He was dependent upon Holy Spirit power to live victoriously and perform miracles of healing, etc. His humanity was supported and sustained by the Holy Spirit. That is why, in the illustration, the "Door" is hinged on the Side Post representing the Holy Spirit – our **other** "Comforter" (John. 14:16).

You will also notice that the blood was applied to the Lintel and the Side Posts: All three members of the Godhead suffered in the plan to rescue us from "Egypt". God's messenger clearly enunciates the Father's experience of the sufferings of His Son in the following statement, which also, so emphatically, stresses the distinction of Being of these two divine Persons, and that the Holy Spirit dwells in and is common to them both; just as He can dwell in and be common to you and I:

> *The Youth's Instructor*, December 16, 1897 par. 5:
> "As the disciples comprehended it, as their perception took hold of God's divine compassion, they realized that there is a sense in **which the sufferings of the Son were the sufferings of the Father.** From eternity there was a complete unity between the Father and the Son. **They were two, yet little short of being identical; two in individuality, yet one in SPIRIT, and heart, and character.**"

We can only imagine the sufferings of the Holy Spirit when Christ became 'sin' for us and then paid sin's penalty for us when we consider that our individual sins 'grieve' Him.

Yes, we worship a Three Person Godhead, two members of which direct our worship to the Father – the "Most High God." The doctrine of the Trinity, on the other hand, maintains that there are 3 members of the Trinity and that the three are **one**, not only in purpose, but also one in **substance.*** (* "Consubstantial" is the term used in the Nicene Creed.) **That is an error!** We do not worship a "One-in three" God.

Concerning the station and function of the Holy Spirit, God's messenger tells us:

Evangelism, page 615:
"The Comforter that Christ promised to send after He ascended to heaven, is **the Spirit in all the fullness of the Godhead,** making manifest the power of divine grace to all who receive and believe in Christ as a PERSONAL Saviour. **There are three living persons of the heavenly trio**; in the name of **these three great powers—the Father, the Son, and the Holy Spirit**—those who receive Christ by living faith are baptized, and **these powers** will co-operate with the obedient subjects of heaven in their efforts to live the new life in Christ. Special Testimonies, Series B, No. 7, pages 62, 63. (1905)."

Does the Holy Spirit also have the fullness of Divine Power? Does He administer the power of God to His creation? Does He administer saving grace purchased for us by Jesus? God's messenger answers:

Desire of Ages, page 671:
"The Spirit was to be given as a **regenerating AGENT** *[rebirth]*, and **without this the sacrifice of Christ would have been of no avail.** The power of evil had been strengthening for centuries, and the submission of men to this satanic captivity was amazing. Sin could be resisted and overcome only through the mighty agency of the **Third PERSON** of the Godhead, who would come with no modified energy, but **in the fullness of divine power.** It is the Spirit that makes effectual what has been wrought out by the world's Redeemer."

WILLIAM: **Is the Holy Spirit God?**

PROFESSOR: Let us see what God's messenger tells us:

Signs of the Times, October 3, 1892:
"The Holy Spirit indites all genuine prayer. I have learned to know that in all my intercessions the Spirit intercedes for me and for all saints; but his intercessions are according to the will of God, never contrary to his will. 'The Spirit also helpeth our infirmities;' **and the Spirit, being God, knoweth the mind of God;** therefore in every prayer of ours for the sick, or for other needs, the will of God is to be regarded."

Please note that an "emanation," an "afflatus" of divine power cannot "**know** the mind of God," neither can such a hypothetical projection be called "God." This statement above utterly overturns the posturings of those who deny that the Holy Spirit is a divine Person.

WILLIAM: **So the Holy Spirit is also a distinct Divine Person, who is also entitled to the title "God"!**

PROFESSOR: Absolutely.

Evangelism, page 616:
"**We need to realize that the Holy Spirit, who is as much a person as God is a person,** is walking through these grounds.— Manuscript 66, 1899. (From a talk to the students at the Avondale School.)"

Notice also that the Holy Spirit actually inhabits the mind of God and knows the innermost secrets of God. Only a "Person" can intelligently "search out" anything.

Evangelism, page 617:
"The Holy Spirit has a personality, else He could not bear witness to our spirits and with our spirits that we are the children of God. **He must also be a divine person, else He could not search out the secrets which lie hidden in the mind of God.**"

Manuscript Releases, Volume 20, page 68:
"The Holy Spirit always leads to the written word. **The Holy Spirit is a person; for He beareth witness with our spirits that we are the children of God.**"

My Life Today, page 36:
"Christ determined that when He ascended from this earth He would bestow a gift on those who had believed on Him and those who should believe on Him. What gift could He bestow rich enough to signalize and grace His ascension to the mediatorial throne? It must be worthy of His greatness and His royalty. He determined to give **His representative, the third person of the Godhead.**"

Upward Look, page 51:

"Evil had been accumulating for centuries, and could only be restrained and resisted by the mighty power of **the Holy Spirit, the third person of the Godhead,** who would come with no modified energy, but **in the fullness of divine power** *["In all the fullness of the Godhead," Evangelism, page 615].*"

SDA Bible Commentary, Volume 6, page 1074:
"The work is laid out before every soul that has acknowledged his faith in Jesus Christ by baptism, and has become a receiver of the pledge from **the three persons--the Father, the Son, and the Holy Spirit** (MS 57, 1900)."

Counsels on Health, page 222:
"**The Godhead** was stirred with pity for the race, **and the Father, the Son, and the Holy Spirit gave Themselves to the working out of the plan of redemption.**"

SDA Bible Commentary, Volume 6, page 1075:
"When we have accepted Christ, **and in the name of the Father, and of the Son, and of the Holy Spirit have pledged ourselves to serve God, the Father, Christ, and the Holy Spirit—the three dignitaries and powers of heaven—pledge themselves** that every facility shall be given to us if we carry out our baptismal vows to 'come out from among them, and be . . . separate,... and touch not the unclean thing.' When we are true to our vows, He says, 'I will receive you' (MS 85, 1901)."

SDA Bible Commentary, Volume 6, page 1075:
"Those who are baptized in the **threefold name** *['Beware of Him, and obey His voice, provoke Him not; for He will not pardon your transgressions: **for My Name is in Him.** Ex. 23:21.]* of the Father, the Son, and the Holy Ghost, at the very entrance of their Christian life declare publicly that they have accepted the invitation, 'Come out from among them, and be ye separate, saith the Lord, and touch not the unclean thing; and I will receive you, and will be a Father unto you, and ye shall be my sons and daughters, saith the Lord Almighty.' 'Having therefore these promises, dearly beloved, let us cleanse ourselves from all filthiness of the flesh and spirit, perfecting holiness in the fear of God.' 'If ye then be risen with Christ, seek those

175

things which are above, where Christ sitteth on the right hand of God.'

"Let those who received the imprint of God by baptism heed these words, remembering that upon them the Lord has placed His signature, declaring them to be His sons and daughters.

"The Father, the Son, and the Holy Ghost, **powers** [*not a power!*] infinite and omniscient, receive those who truly enter into covenant relation with God...."

Evangelism, page 615:

"The Comforter that Christ promised to send after He ascended to heaven, is **the Spirit in all the fullness of the Godhead** [*The Holy Spirit inhabits both the Father and the Son (See 1 Cor. 2:10-12; Romans 8:9). He also inhabits the "born again" children of God (1 Cor. 6:19), and is come:*], **making manifest the power of divine grace** to all who receive and believe in Christ as a personal Saviour. **There are three living persons of the heavenly trio; in the name of these three great powers—the Father, the Son, and the Holy Spirit** [*The name 'Yahweh' a.k.a. 'Jehovah', or 'Self-existent One', applies to all three members of the Godhead, and that name's meaning completely overthrows any notion of any of them being 'begotten' or 'generated' at some point in antiquity. It is into the 'name' of these three great Powers that:*] – those who receive Christ by living faith are baptized, and **these powers** will co-operate with the **obedient** subjects of heaven in their efforts to live the new life in Christ.—Special Testimonies, Series B, No. 7, page 62, 63. (1905)."

WILLIAM: Clearly the Godhead, which is the term denoting these great powers (plural term), is comprised of Three, with the Holy Spirit a bonafide individual with a "personality".

PROFESSOR: That is right, William. Firstly, however, I want you to notice what God's messenger stated in the reference we just looked at, about the "**name** of these three great powers"! God's messenger refers to one "name" that applies to all three. How can that be? We find that "Jehovah" (*Yahweh*) is the name employed in Scripture to refer to the Father and to Christ, who share the Holy Spirit's indwelling presence.

Concerning the Father we read:

Psalms 83:18:
"That [men] may know that thou, whose name alone [is] JEHOVAH, [art] **the most high** over all the earth."

Concerning Christ we read:

Exodus 6:3:
"And **I appeared** unto Abraham, unto Isaac, and unto Jacob, by [the name of] God Almighty [*El Shadday-Strong's #7706 = Almighty*], but by my name JEHOVAH [*Strong's #3068 = self-existent*] was I not known to them."

Remember **it was Christ who appeared unto the patriarchs.**

Isaiah 12:2:
"Behold, God [is] my salvation; I will trust, and not be afraid: for the LORD JEHOVAH [is] my strength and [my] song; he also is become my salvation."

Christ "is become *[our]* salvation."
In the next text we find God the Father (*Yahweh*) addressing Christ, David's "Lord":

Psalms 110:1:
"A Psalm of David. The LORD said unto my *[David's]* Lord, Sit thou at my right hand, until I make thine enemies thy footstool. "

Jesus refers to this statement in Matthew:

Matthew 22:41:
41) "While the Pharisees were gathered together, Jesus asked them,
42) Saying, What think ye of Christ? whose son is he? They say unto him, [The son] of David.
43) He saith unto them, How then doth David in spirit call him Lord, saying,
44) The Lord said unto my Lord, Sit thou on my right hand, till I make thine enemies thy footstool?

45)   If David then call him Lord, how is he his *[David's]* son?"

And in Acts it is clarified that this is a member of the Godhead speaking of One who would sit at His right hand:

Acts 2:34:
"For David is not ascended into the heavens: but he saith himself, The Lord said unto my Lord, Sit thou on my right hand,"

God the Father Himself tells us that His name (Yahweh = the **self-existent** One) is **in** Christ:

Exodus 23:20:
"Behold, I send an Angel *[Michael = Christ]* before thee, to keep thee in the way, and to bring thee into the place which I have prepared. 21)   Beware of him, and obey his voice, provoke him not; for he will not pardon your transgressions: **for my name [is] in him**."

God's messenger makes it plain that the "name" Jehovah (Yahweh) is applied to Christ also:

Patriarchs and Prophets, page 366.2:
"Christ was not only the leader of the Hebrews in the wilderness--**the Angel in whom was the name of Jehovah**, and who, veiled in the cloudy pillar, went before the host--but it was He who gave the law to Israel. [SEE APPENDIX, NOTE 7.] Amid the awful glory of Sinai, Christ declared in the hearing of all the people the ten precepts of His Father's law."

Patriarchs and Prophets page 761 APPENDIX NOTE 7:
"NOTE 7. PAGE 366. THAT THE ONE WHO SPOKE THE LAW, WHO CALLED MOSES INTO THE MOUNT AND TALKED WITH HIM, WAS OUR LORD JESUS CHRIST, IS EVIDENT FROM THE FOLLOWING CONSIDERATIONS: {PP 761.3}
"CHRIST IS THE ONE THROUGH WHOM GOD HAS AT ALL TIMES REVEALED HIMSELF TO MAN. "BUT TO US THERE IS BUT ONE GOD, THE FATHER, OF WHOM ARE

ALL THINGS, AND WE IN HIM; AND ONE LORD JESUS
CHRIST, BY WHOM ARE ALL THINGS, AND WE BY
HIM." 1 CORINTHIANS 8:6. "THIS IS HE [MOSES], THAT
WAS IN THE CHURCH IN THE WILDERNESS WITH THE
ANGEL WHICH SPAKE TO HIM IN THE MOUNT SINAI,
AND WITH OUR FATHERS: WHO RECEIVED THE LIVELY
ORACLES TO GIVE UNTO US." ACTS 7:38. THIS ANGEL
WAS THE ANGEL OF GOD'S PRESENCE (ISAIAH 63:9),
THE ANGEL IN WHOM WAS THE NAME OF THE GREAT
JEHOVAH (EXODUS 23:20-23). THE EXPRESSION CAN
REFER TO NO OTHER THAN THE SON OF GOD. {PP
761.4}
   "AGAIN: CHRIST IS CALLED THE WORD OF GOD.
JOHN 1:1-3. HE IS SO CALLED BECAUSE GOD GAVE HIS
REVELATIONS TO MAN IN ALL AGES THROUGH
CHRIST. IT WAS HIS SPIRIT THAT INSPIRED THE
PROPHETS. 1 PETER 1:10, 11. HE WAS REVEALED TO
THEM AS THE ANGEL OF JEHOVAH, THE CAPTAIN OF
THE LORD'S HOST, MICHAEL THE ARCHANGEL."

**The "name" (Jehovah = self-existent) of these three great Powers is
clearly the name referring to their collective yet distinct and personal
self-existence** and applies to each member of the Godhead; two Members of
which defer to, and refer our attention to, the Most High God, our Heavenly
Father.
   So Christ is called the "self-existent" One, a concept confounding
Trinitarianism in which all "hypostases" or "modalities" **co-exist**. As God's
messenger states:

Evangelism, page 615.1:
   "Christ is the pre-existent, **self-existent** Son of God."

And He is also known as the "I AM", which also emphasizes His self-
existence:

Exodus 3:14:
   "And God said unto Moses, I AM THAT I AM: and he said,
   Thus shalt thou say unto the children of Israel, I AM hath sent
   me unto you."

John 8:58:

179

"Jesus said unto them, Verily, verily, I say unto you, Before Abraham was, I am."

This concept is repeated by God's messenger in:

Desire of Ages, page 469:
"With solemn dignity Jesus answered, 'Verily, verily, I say unto you, Before Abraham was, I AM,'"

But William, I want you to now pay very close attention as we examine one of the most subtly deceptive examples of word-craft ever foisted upon God's trusting and unsuspecting denominated people:

In Volume 7A of the Bible Commentary, page 439, the compiler (Leroy Edwin Froom) juxtaposes a series of quotations from God's messenger demonstrating that Christ is also called Jehovah. This is all well and good. However, a quote is sandwiched in between two that obviously refer to Christ, whereas the quote in question, from Patriarchs and Prophets page 305.4 has no bearing on Christ personally but is a plain statement referring to the Father: however, Froom, a Trinitarian, would have us believe that this particular statement refers to Christ because it makes a declaration on Who is entitled to "supreme reverence and worship", a clear reference to the "Most High God".   Here is the reference as Froom presents it:

Bible Commentary 7A, page 439.1-3 (Questions on Doctrine):
"The world's Redeemer was equal with God. His authority was as the authority of God. He declared that he had no existence separate from the Father. The authority by which he spoke, and wrought miracles, was expressly his own, yet he assures us that he and the Father are one.--The Review and Herald, January 7, 1890, page 1.
"**Jehovah, the eternal, self-existent, uncreated One, Himself the source and sustainer of all, is alone entitled to supreme reverence and worship.--Patriarchs and Prophets, page 305.**
"Jehovah is the name given to Christ. "Behold, God is my salvation," writes the prophet Isaiah; "I will trust, and not be afraid; for the Lord Jehovah is my strength and my song; He also is become my salvation. Therefore with joy shall ye draw water out of the wells of salvation. And in that day ye shall say, Praise the Lord, call upon His name, declare His doings among the people, make mention that His name is exalted." "In that day

shall this song be sung in the land of Judah: We have a strong city; salvation will God appoint for walls and bulwarks. Open ye the gates, that the righteous nation which keepeth the truth may enter in. Thou wilt keep him in perfect peace whose mind is stayed on Thee, because he trusteth in Thee. Trust ye in the Lord forever; for in the Lord Jehovah is everlasting strength."--*The Signs of the Times*, May 3, 1899, page 2.

When we reference this quote in Patriarchs and Prophets, page 305.4, in its correct setting and context, we find that God's messenger is delineating the ten precepts of the law, beginning with the first Commandment, and I quote:

Patriarchs and Prophets, page 305.2-4:
"The law was not spoken at this time exclusively for the benefit of the Hebrews. God honored them by making them the guardians and keepers of His law, but it was to be held as a sacred trust for the whole world. The precepts of the Decalogue are adapted to all mankind, and they were given for the instruction and government of all. Ten precepts, brief, comprehensive, and authoritative, cover the duty of man to God and to his fellow man; and all based upon the great fundamental principle of love. "Thou shalt love the Lord thy God with all thy heart, and with all thy soul, and with all thy strength, and with all thy mind; and thy neighbor as thyself." Luke 10:27. See also Deuteronomy 6:4, 5; Leviticus 19:18. In the Ten Commandments these principles are carried out in detail, and made applicable to the condition and circumstances of man.
"'Thou shalt have no other gods before Me.'
"Jehovah, the eternal, self-existent, uncreated One, Himself the Source and Sustainer of all, is alone entitled to supreme reverence and worship."

As God the Father's **Representative** to fallen man, Christ, the Word, spoke the Commandments to all Israel; and the One before whom we may "have no other gods" is, according to the context of this declaration, none other than the One who is the "Source and sustainer of **all**". **Even Christ, during the incarnation, was sustained by Him.**
Jesus said:

John 6:57:

"As the living Father hath sent me, and **I live by the Father**: so he that eateth me, even he shall live by me."

And:

John 5:30:
"**I can of mine own self do nothing**: as I hear, I judge: and my judgment is just; because I seek not mine own will, but the will of the Father which hath sent me."

It is the Father to whom our "**supreme reverence and worship**" is directed. We come to Him through Jesus by the inner working, on our hearts, of the Holy Spirit. The Supreme Ruler of the universe has **given** His **name**, "Jehovah", to His **self-existent** Son. The name describes the truth of Christ's self-existence.

The compiler of 7ABC page 439 has striven to imply that Christ and the One entitled to "supreme reverence and worship" are of one and the same "essence" in order to bolster the Trinitarian perception.

Froom has been the most vociferous promoter of Trinitarianism in the Adventist denomination (See pages 104, 118, 489-490 of this book). Since this piece of word-craft is found in Q.O.D., which is filled with aberrant misrepresentations on the Nature of Christ, and attempts to align Adventism with the Babylonian wine of Rome and her daughters, these forms of deception should come as no surprise to godly seekers after God's truth. Notice the name "Jehovah" is **given** to Christ:

Signs of the Times May 3, 1899 par. 18:
"Jehovah is the name **given** to Christ. *[Who **gave** Christ that name? Clearly the Father.]* 'Behold, God is my salvation,' writes the prophet Isaiah; 'I will trust, and not be afraid; for the Lord JEHOVAH is my strength and my song; He also is become my salvation. Therefore with joy shall ye draw water out of the wells of salvation. And in that day ye shall say, Praise the Lord, call upon His name, declare His doings among the people, make mention that His name is exalted.' 'In that day shall this song be sung in the land of Judah: We have a strong city; salvation will God appoint for walls and bulwarks. Open ye the gates, that the righteous nation which keepeth the truth may enter in. Thou wilt keep him in perfect peace whose mind is stayed on Thee, because he trusteth in Thee. Trust ye in the Lord forever; for in the Lord JEHOVAH is everlasting strength.'"

William, take careful note of the following Scriptures which demonstrate the Father's paramount position in the Godhead, as necessitated by the inception of sin:

1 Corinthians 15:23-28:
23)   But every man in his own order: Christ the firstfruits; afterward they that are Christ's at his coming.

24)   Then [cometh] the end, when he *[Christ]* shall **have delivered up the kingdom to God, even the Father;** when he *[the Father]* shall have put down all rule and all authority and power.

25)   For he *[the Father]* must reign, till he *[the Father]* hath put all enemies under his *[Christ's]* feet.

26)   The last enemy [that] shall be destroyed [is] death.

27)   For he *[the Father]* hath put all things under his *[Christ's]* feet. **But when he *[the Father]* saith all things are put under [him, it is] manifest that he *[the Father]* is excepted, which did put all things under him *[Christ]*.**

28)   **And when all things shall be subdued unto him *[the Father]*, then shall the Son also himself be subject unto him *[the Father]* that put all things under him *[Christ]*, that God may be all in all *[by His Spirit]*.**

Jesus will be "King of Kings and Lord of Lords"; His Father will always be the "Most High God" and "God of gods":

Thoughts From the Mount of Blessing, page 108.2:
    "The heavenly gates are again to be lifted up, and with ten thousand times ten thousand and thousands of thousands of holy ones, our Saviour will come forth as King of kings and Lord of lords. Jehovah Immanuel "shall be king over all the earth: in that day shall there be one Lord, and His name one."

The question arises: **How does the truth concerning the name "Jehovah" apply to the Holy Spirit?** Well, consider this: The Holy Spirit **represents** both the Father and the Son, as we see in the following inspired statements:

Ministry of Healing, page 417.2:

183

"The Bible shows us God in His high and holy place, not in a state of inactivity, not in silence and solitude, but surrounded by ten thousand times ten thousand and thousands of thousands of holy beings, all waiting to do His will. Through these messengers He is in active communication with every part of His dominion. By His Spirit He is everywhere present. Through the agency of His Spirit and His angels He ministers to the children of men."

The Home Missionary, December 1, 1894 par. 11:
"The Holy Spirit, **Christ's representative**, is to teach the soul."

We come to Christ through the action of the Holy Spirit upon the heart of man; we come to the Father through Jesus the Son.

The Scriptures refer to the Holy Spirit as the "Spirit of God" and the "Spirit of Christ":

Romans 8:9:
"But ye are not in the flesh, but in the Spirit, if so be that the **Spirit of God** dwell in you. Now if any man have not the **Spirit of Christ**, he is none of his."

The Holy Spirit inhabits both the Father and the Son and is, as their Representative, involved in the "name" by which they are called: the "name" which the Father Himself, through the Holy Spirit, declares to man to be IN His Son (Exodus 23:20).

Also, with regards to "personality", God's messenger has the following to say:

Evangelism, page 613; (9T 68):
"The Father and the Son each have a personality."

As does the Holy Spirit:

Evangelism, page 617:
"The Holy Spirit has a personality, else He could not bear witness to our spirits and with our spirits that we are the children of God. **He must also be a divine person, else He could not search out the secrets which lie hidden in the mind of God."**

However God's messenger does caution our limited grasp of the Holy Spirit's personality:

Manuscript Releases, Volume 20, page 324:
"**The Holy Spirit is the Comforter,** in Christ's name. **He personifies Christ, yet is a distinct PERSONALITY.**"

God's messenger makes a distinction between our usual concept of the term "personality" and the "personality" of the Holy Spirit:

Desire of Ages, page 669:
"The Holy Spirit is Christ's representative, but **divested of the personality of humanity, and independent thereof.** *[Jesus has now, and forever, the personality of humanity, which imposes eternal restriction on Him. The Holy Spirit is a distinct person with a distinct personality but a personality that imposes no restrictions on His omnipresence.]* Cumbered with humanity, Christ could not be in every place personally. Therefore it was for their *[the disciples and believers generally]* interest that He should go to the Father, and send the Spirit to be His successor on earth." *[Because the Holy Spirit is everywhere present, but not **in** everything. Post Calvary and redemption the Holy Spirit can now dwell permanently **in** 'born again' believers.]*

The **"nature"** of the Holy Spirit is beyond our comprehension. There are aspects of the Holy Spirit that have never been revealed to us:

Acts of the Apostles, page 52:
"**The nature of the Holy Spirit is a mystery. Men cannot explain it, because the Lord has not revealed it to them.** Men having fanciful views may bring together passages of Scripture and put a human construction on them, but the acceptance of these views will not strengthen the church. Regarding such mysteries, which are too deep for human understanding, silence is golden."

We cannot adequately conceive of a personal Being who, by nature, is everywhere:

Manuscript Releases, Volume 14, pages 23, 24:

185

"Cumbered with humanity, Christ could not be in every place personally; therefore it was altogether for their advantage that He should leave them, go to His father, **and send the Holy Spirit to be His successor on earth. The Holy Spirit is Himself divested of the personality of humanity** and independent thereof. He [Jesus] would **represent** Himself as present in all places **by His Holy Spirit, as the Omnipresent.**"

The above statement does not say that the Holy Spirit is divested of personality, **but divested of the personality of humanity.** Allen Stump makes the case that "if the Holy Spirit is a Third Being as the Father and Son are, **it is certain that he never was a human,** and therefore it would be impossible for him to strip or rid *[divest]* himself of humanity." (The Foundations of Our Faith, page 102)

WILLIAM: But as we saw, the Holy Spirit does have personality!

PROFESSOR: Yes. However He is "divested" of the "personality **of humanity.**" One can only "divest" oneself of something one once had or once put on.

WILLIAM: That makes me wonder, Who was Melchizedek?

PROFESSOR: Good question. Let's look at what the Scriptures say about Him:

> **Hebrews 7:3:**
> "**Without father, without mother** *[Jesus had both at the incarnation]*, **without descent, having neither beginning of days, nor end of life;** *[according to Scripture, who alone has immortality? The answer is: God! See 1 Timothy 6:16: "Who only hath immortality, dwelling in the light which no man can approach unto; whom no man hath seen, nor can see: to whom [be] honour and power everlasting. Amen."]* **but made** *[not born or 'begotten']* **like unto the Son of God** *[capable of contact with sinners]*; **abideth a priest continually.**"

This description of Melchizedek, priest of the Most High God and after whose order Christ was to become a High Priest forever, describes a Divine Being: one having no "beginning" and no "end of life"! Remember, according to Scripture, only God has immortality! Could it be, that, since

186

Melchizedek was not Christ (Heb. 7:3), and not the Father (Gen. 14:18, even Abraham would have been destroyed by the Father's presence); could it be, that the Holy Spirit assumed the "personality of humanity" as Melchizedek?—the "personality of humanity" that He prior to this appearance had not assumed, and afterward **divested** Himself thereof? However, as Divine Persons it was both the Holy Spirit and The Most High God who "sent" Jesus into the world, as we read in:

Isaiah 6:8:
"Also I heard the voice of the Lord, saying, Whom shall I send, and **who will go for us**? Then said I, Here am I; send me."

This was the Father talking to the Holy Spirit, while Jesus responds, "Send me." Notice:

Isaiah 48:16:
"Come ye near unto me, hear ye this; I have not spoken in secret from the beginning; from the time that it was, there am I: and **now the Lord GOD, and his Spirit, hath sent me.**"

God's messenger applies Isaiah 6:8 to Jesus who responds "...send me," as we see in:

Youth Instructor, June 21, 1900:
"**But Christ is equal with God, infinite and omnipotent.** He could pay the ransom for man's freedom. He is the eternal, self-existing Son, on whom no yoke had come; **and when God asked, 'Whom shall I send?'** he [Christ] could reply, 'Here am I; send me.'"

And:

Manuscript Releases, Volume 12, page 395:
"No one of the angels could become **a substitute** and surety for the human race, for **their life is God's;** they could not surrender it. **On Christ alone the human family depended for their existence.** *[He had bought them a probationary life by being willing to take the penalty of the law upon Himself.]* **He is the eternal, self-existent Son,** on whom no yoke had come. **When God asked, 'whom shall I send, and who will go for Us?'** *["Us" referring to the remaining members of the Godhead!*

187

Notice: upper case "U" in the quote.] **Christ alone of the angelic host could reply, 'Here am I; send Me.'** He alone had covenanted before the foundation of the world to become a surety for man. He could say that which not the highest angel could say—"I have power over My own life. I have power to lay it down, and I have power to take it again." *[see the full Biblical statement in John 10:18 which goes on to say: "...This commandment (authority to do so)* **have I received of My Father***." (See John 10:18, last part of verse.) Jesus had said, "I ...came not to do Mine own will, but the will of Him who* **sent** *Me." (John 6:38.) He also said: "I can of Mine own self, do nothing." (John 5:30). "I live by the Father." (John 6:57). Etc. The 'taking up' of Christ's life was under the auspices of His Father. See Romans 8:9-11: 9)But ye are not in the flesh, but in the Spirit, if so be that the Spirit of God dwell in you. Now if any man have not the Spirit of Christ, he is none of his. 10) And if Christ [be] in you, the body [is] dead because of sin; but the Spirit [is] life because of righteousness. 11) But if the Spirit of him that raised up Jesus from the dead dwell in you, he that raised up Christ from the dead shall also quicken your mortal bodies by his Spirit that dwelleth in you.]*

Ponder these questions: Just as the **sons** of Aaron held the office of High Priest **by inheritance**, is that not a **'type'** of Christ's Melchizedekian priesthood? **For was not the Holy Spirit Christ's earthly progenitor at the incarnation?**

If the Scripture references regarding Melchizedek are indeed descriptions of the Holy Spirit, having, for a period, adopted the "personality of humanity", which He afterward "divested" Himself of, then the Holy Spirit must indeed be "self-existent" since Melchizedek is described as being **"without beginning and without end"** and therefore fully eligible for the "name" or title that denotes that status.

What have we discovered from inspiration? We find three distinct Persons in one harmonious Unit known as the Godhead, two of Whom are inhabited by the Third Person Who also condescends to dwell in our surrendered hearts. The plan of salvation necessitates that one Member of the Godhead maintains the integrity of the Godhead. This is the Father, the "Most High God." The remaining two Members have voluntarily subordinated Themselves to the Father in order to reach fallen man, without Their presence destroying man. Christ and the Holy Spirit's self-abnegation automatically elevates the Father's position to "God of gods" and "Most

High God". This in **NO WAY** denigrates or detracts from the greatness, majesty, or love of Christ or the Holy Spirit, but actually serves to emphasize these qualities and Their selflessness. What we have studied does **NOT** present an "essence" manifested in three different "hypostases" or "modalities": **It does not present a trinity** but, rather, a "HEAVENLY TRIO"!

PROFESSOR: William, here is something for you to read on the topic of Melchizedek:

Chapter 14

THOUGHTS ON MELCHIZEDEK
By G.B. Starr

http://sabbathsermons.com/2009/10/21/who-is-melchizedek/

PROFESSOR: William, here is a statement on Melchizedek by G. B. Starr, who lived back when God's messenger was still alive. Many regard this statement as apocryphal, but I want you to see how authentic in tenor this brief statement is:

"At a council meeting at Avondale School, about the year 1893, there were present Elders Haskell, F.L.H. Baker, G.B. Starr, and their wives, and Sister E.G. White, also W.A. Colcord, who was the editor of the Australian Signs of the Times. Elder Colcord requested the privilege of reading some articles regarding the personality of Melchisedec. We all listened as he read and were surprised that Sister White listened also, with seeming interest, as she was not accustomed to listening to any argumentative writings.

" As Elder Colcord was reading, Sister White interrupted him, saying: "Elder Colcord, I would not publish these articles, if I were you." "Why not?" He inquired.

"'Because they are not correct.'" She answered.

"He then asked, "Who then was Melchisedec?"

"She replied, "**I will tell you who Melchisedec was. He was the Holy Spirit, the third person of the Godhead, who took the form of humanity and represented the Lord Jesus Christ to that generation.**"

"That ended the council on that subject. Elder Colcord offered no argument to refute her position, and we all seemed perfectly satisfied with the statement; in fact, I had never heard an explanation that was satisfactory before.

"After the meeting, Elder S.N. Haskell said to me, "Elder Starr, when the Spirit of Prophecy speaks so plainly as that about a matter, it can be proved by the Bible, so let's look it up."

"We found that description of Melchisedec in *Hebrews* 7:3 was fully met by the Holy Spirit. "**Without father, without**

mother, without descent, having neither beginning of days, nor end of life; but made like unto the Son of God; abideth a high priest continually."

"We found that in *Hebrews* 9:14 that statement, "The Eternal Spirit." That would meet, also, "Without beginning of days, nor end of life."

"Then in *Romans* 8:26, **"likewise the Spirit also helpeth our infirmities: for we know not what we should pray for as we ought: but the Spirit itself maketh intercession for us with groanings which cannot be uttered"** (By man). Thus - These statements make the Holy Spirit a high priest forever. Every specification was met by the Holy Spirit, A HIGH PRIEST FOREVER, but cannot be met by any angel or human being.

"Elder Haskell published this matter as reported above in his paper at South Lancaster, Mass. Thus we have TWO witnesses of the truthfulness of Sister White's statement regarding (the person) Melchisedec."　　Signed - G.B. Starr

WILLIAM:　The statement by Starr certainly sounds very reasonable and plausible to me.

PROFESSOR:　Let us now look at some powerful, inspired evidence that tends to strongly support what Starr recounts:

Hebrews 7:1-4:

1)　"For this Melchisedec, king of Salem, priest of the most high God, who met Abraham returning from the slaughter of the kings, and blessed him;

2)　To whom also Abraham gave a tenth part of all; first being by interpretation King of righteousness, and after that also King of Salem, which is, King of peace;

3)　Without father, without mother, without descent, having neither beginning of days, nor end of life; but made like unto the Son of God; abideth a priest continually.

4)　Now consider how great this man [was], unto whom even the patriarch Abraham gave the tenth of the spoils."

Now let's consider Melchizedek and make a list of his characteristics that we find here. What strikes you?

WILLIAM: I see the following characteristics of Melchizedek. He is:

1. <u>King of Righteousness.</u>
2. <u>King of Peace.</u>
3. **Without father.**
4. **Without mother.**
5. **Without descent.**
6. **Having neither beginning of days.**
7. **Having no end of life.**
8. Made Like unto the Son of God.
9. A continual priest.

PROFESSOR: **Those are attributes of a divine Person!** Now pay close attention to Melchizedek's actions as recorded in:

Genesis 14:18:
"And Melchizedek king of Salem **brought forth bread and wine**: and he [was] the priest of the most high God."

Bread and wine are "New Testament" symbols of the broken body and spilt blood of Jesus, the Lamb of God. Also, notice that Melchizedek is the priest of "the most high God". We see here a 'priest' who looks beyond the patriarchal priesthood, beyond the Levitical and Aaronic priesthood into the era of Christ's high Priesthood and the priesthood of believers. This implies thorough foreknowledge of intimate, then future, details in the plan of salvation. Christ introduced the symbolic use of the "bread and wine" at the last supper.

WILLIAM: Look at his name. His name means "King of Righteousness". And he is King of Peace (Salem).

PROFESSOR: Jesus is the **Prince** of Peace. Here Melchizedek is described as the **King** of Peace. King of Peace! And he is King of Righteousness. Does that mean that he was a peaceful and righteous King? No, it means he was KING <u>of</u> righteousness and peace. He controls righteousness and peace. It means that 'righteousness' and 'peace' have a king, whose name is Melchizedek. Only a divine member of the Godhead can be King <u>of Righteousness</u> and King <u>of Peace</u>. Look at the following verses and see how righteousness and peace relate to the Holy Spirit:

Romans 14:17:
"For the kingdom of God is not meat and drink; but **righteousness, and peace, and joy in the Holy Ghost.**"

Isaiah 32:17:
"And the work of **righteousness** shall be **peace**; and the effect of **righteousness** quietness and assurance for ever."

Isaiah 48:18:
"O that thou hadst hearkened to my commandments! then had thy **peace** been as a river, and thy **righteousness** as the waves of the sea:"

WILLIAM: So, when the Holy Spirit, who is King of Righteousness and King of Peace dwells in our heart and writes God's law on our hearts and minds according to the New Covenant, He brings righteousness and resulting peace with God.

PROFESSOR: Remember we listed 9 characteristics for Melchizedek; do they all apply to the Holy Spirit?

WILLIAM: Yes, I believe He is the only one that fits all those nine points.

PROFESSOR: There is another Scripture that lists nine things regarding the Holy Spirit. Let me put them next to the list we have already looked at:

Melchizedek is:	The fruit of the Spirit is:
1. King of Righteousness	1. Love,
2. King of Peace.	2. Joy,
3. Without father.	3. Peace,
4. Without mother.	4. Longsuffering,
5. Without descent.	5. Gentleness,
6. Having neither beginning of days.	6. Goodness,
7. Having no end of life.	7. Faith,
8. Made Like unto the Son of God	8. Meekness,
9. A continual priest.	9. Temperance: against
Hebrews 7:1-3.	such there is no law.
	Galatians 5:22, 23

These further nine attributes; can only result through a divine Person. **Furthermore for Him to have no father and no mother and to be 'without descent' means to be "self-existent".** Reason allows no other 'reasonable' view. **The <u>Fruit</u> of the Spirit is peace, and Melchizedek was King of Salem – King of Peace.** Is Salem the same as Jeru-salem? Was he the king of Jerusalem? At that time Jerusalem could not have typified

193

godly 'peace'. Jerusalem later came to be built on Mount Moriah. Mount Moriaht is where God had told Abraham to go to offer Isaac. Notice:

Genesis 22:2:
"And he said, Take now thy son, thine only [son] Isaac, whom thou lovest, and get thee into the land of Moriah; and offer him there for a burnt offering upon one of the mountains which I will tell thee of."

What was also later built on Mount Moriah? Turn to:

2 Chronicles 3:1:
"Then Solomon began to build the house of the LORD at Jerusalem in mount Moriah, where [the Lord] appeared unto David his father, in the place that David had prepared in the threshingfloor of Ornan the Jebusite."

The messenger of the Lord confirms this:

Prophets and Kings, page 37:
"At last the temple planned by King David, and built by Solomon his son, was completed. 'All that came into Solomon's heart to make in the house of the Lord,' he had 'prosperously effected.' 2 Chronicles 7:11. **And now, in order that the palace crowning the heights of Mount Moriah might indeed be, as David had so much desired, a dwelling place 'not for man, but for the Lord God'** (1 Chronicles 29:1), there remained the solemn ceremony of formally dedicating it to Jehovah and His worship."

Abraham was going to the future temple site. Isaac was a symbol of the **future Lamb of God** – Emmanuel – God with us. **The peace of reconciliation with God, from whom sin has estranged us; that 'peace' is what Melchizedek was king of.**

WILLIAM: But when Abraham bound his son Isaac, the only priest present was Abraham for it was the time of the patriarchal priesthood and Abraham was the priest of his family. On the other hand, the temple at Jerusalem was to be located at the very spot where Abraham was to sacrifice his son Isaac. Mount Moriah, where Jerusalem became established, was held at one time by the Jebusites. I am sure that godly peace did not reign at **that** time in Jerusalem.

PROFESSOR: **God intended that Jerusalem become the abode of 'peace', but, instead, Jerusalem slew the "Prince of Peace".** Melchizedek is a priest of the heavenly Salem. He belongs to the heavenly sanctuary. **He is a priest of the overarching 'Everlasting Covenant'** that oversees the Old and New Covenants which have the Cross as their watershed. Remember that Melchizedek was made like unto the Son of God. They have similarities, not only in the office of priest, but also in appearance and character. Notice these interesting statements from God's messenger:

> *Youth Instructor,* November 1, 1904:
> "As the king gazed upon that lofty tree, he beheld 'a Watcher,' even 'an Holy One'—**a divine Messenger, similar in appearance to the One who walked with the Hebrews in the fiery furnace. This heavenly Being** approached the tree ..."

> SDA Bible Commentary, Volume 1, pages 1092, 1093:
> "At one time **Melchisedek represented the Lord Jesus Christ in person,** to reveal the truth of heaven, and perpetuate the law of God. (Letter 190, 1905).

> *Review & Herald,* February 18, 1890:
> "It was Christ that spoke through Melchisedek, the priest of the most high God. **Melchisedek was not Christ, but he was the voice of God in the world, the representative of the Father.**

We should recall that, the Holy Spirit has always been the representative of both the Father and the Son:

> The Desire of Ages, page 669:
> **"The Holy Spirit is Christ's representative**..."

Since Christ represents the Father and the Holy Spirit represents Jesus, so the Holy Spirit automatically represents both.

WILLIAM: The Bible says that Melchizedek "abideth a priest continually." Is He still a priest today? Is the Holy Spirit a priest?

PROFESSOR: The Word of God says:

Romans 8:26
"Likewise the Spirit also helpeth our infirmities: for we know not what we should pray for as we ought: but **the Spirit itself maketh intercession for us with groanings which cannot be uttered.** ...because **he maketh intercession for the saints** according to the will of God."

WILLIAM: The Holy Spirit then, is a priest **in the "courtyard"** of the heavenly temple and ministers in the temple of our bodies, a priest-king ruling on the throne of our minds and hearts and bringing us peace with God.

PROFESSOR: And the Holy Spirit is a priest in another way:

Hebrews 9:14:
"How much more shall the blood of Christ, **who through the eternal Spirit offered himself without spot to God**, purge your conscience from dead works to serve the living God?"

It was by the power of the Spirit that Jesus overcame in Gethsemane and was empowered to go on to Calvary.
Interceding and bringing sacrifices are the duties of a priest. This is the work Melchizedek still does today. Every godly self-sacrifice that we make is made under the Holy Spirit's direction and empowerment. All this brings us to another very interesting point, William. Look at Melchizedek's behavior. When Melchizedek met Abraham, what did he bring? And what did He do?

Genesis 14:18:
"And Melchizedek king of Salem **brought forth bread and wine**: and he *was* the priest of the most high God. And he blessed him."

If Melchizedek was a typical priest, as in the Levitical priesthood, he would have offered a sacrifice. But **Melchizedek showed that He had nothing to do with sacrificial animals**. Notice these special verses in:

Hebrews 7:4-11:

196

4) **"Now consider how great this man was,** unto whom even the patriarch Abraham gave the tenth of the spoils.

5) And verily they that are of the sons of Levi, who receive the office of the priesthood, have a commandment to take tithes of the people according to the law, that is, of their brethren, though they come out of the loins of Abraham:

6) **But he whose descent is not counted from them received tithes of Abraham, and blessed him that had the promises.**

7) And without all contradiction the less is blessed of the better.

8) And **here men that die receive tithes;** but there **he receiveth them, of whom it is witnessed that he liveth**.

9) **And as I may so say, Levi also, who receiveth tithes, payed tithes in Abraham.**

10) For he was yet in the loins of his father, when Melchisedec met him.

11) If therefore perfection were by the Levitical priesthood, (for under it the people received the law,) what further need was there that **another** priest should rise after the order of Melchisedec, and not be called after the order of Aaron?"

Melchizedek was greater than Levi, because Levi (in the loins of Abraham) paid tithes to Melchizedek.

Melchizedek showed that he had nothing to do with sacrifical animals, **because he was a priest after an antitypical order.** He had nothing to do with shadows; **he as the priest of the Everlasting Covenant and as such presents to Abraham the 'New Covenant' symbols "bread and wine."** Later he was involved in the anti-typical sacrifice of Christ on the cross. (Heb. 9:14.) His priesthood spans the Old and New Covenants.

WILLIAM: And the "bread and the wine" were symbols pointing to Christ, and that is exactly what the Holy Spirit does—He points us (not to Himself, but) to Jesus Christ. Amazing.

PROFESSOR: That's not all, William. Paul asks:

Hebrews 7:11:
"What further need was there that **another priest** should rise after the order of Melchisedec, and not be called after the order of Aaron?"

He is talking about Jesus. Jesus would be "another priest" like Melchizedek.

Likewise, Jesus said that He would send "another Comforter." That other "Comforter" was the Holy Spirit. The Holy Spirit is a divine "Comforter" as Jesus was.

WILLIAM: So Jesus would be **"another priest" after the order of Melchizedek, and Melchizedek, the Holy Spirit, was the first priest of that order.**

PROFESSOR: Right, William. But this means something that is very important and very interesting. Watch; God the Father told Jesus what kind of priest He would be:

Psalm 110:4:
"The LORD hath sworn, and will not repent, Thou *art* a priest for ever **after the order of Melchizedek.**"

How could Jesus be a Heavenly High Priest after an order pertaining to a mere earthly man? Melchizedek had to be a heavenly, divine Being for Christ to be a Priest after His 'order'! Christ is our Heavenly High Priest, remember?

As we saw, Paul asks:

Hebrews 7:11:
"What further need was there that another priest should rise after the order of Melchisedec, and not be called after the order of Aaron?"

His answer is given in:

Hebrews 7:12-28:
12)   "For the priesthood being changed, there is made of necessity a change also of the law.

13)   For he of whom these things are spoken pertaineth to another tribe, of which no man gave attendance at the altar.

14)   For *it is* evident that our Lord sprang out of Juda; of which tribe Moses spake nothing concerning priesthood.

15)   And it is yet far more evident: for that **after the similitude of Melchisedec there ariseth another priest,**

198

16)   Who is made, not after the law of a carnal commandment, but after **the power of an endless life.**

17)   For he testifieth, Thou *art* a priest for ever after the order of Melchisedec. *[Who must also have had "the power of an endless life"]*

18)   For there is verily a disannulling of the commandment going before for the weakness and unprofitableness thereof.

19)   For the law made nothing perfect, **but the bringing in of a better hope** *did*; by the which we draw nigh unto God.

20)   And inasmuch as not without an oath *he was made priest*:

21)   (For those priests were made without an oath; but this with an oath by him that said unto him, **The Lord sware and will not repent, Thou** *art* **a priest for ever** <u>after the order of Melchisedec:</u>)

22)   By so much was Jesus made a surety of a better testament.

23)   And they truly were many priests, because they were not suffered to continue by reason of death:

24)   But this *man*, because he continueth ever, hath an unchangeable priesthood.

25)   Wherefore he is able also to save them to the uttermost that come unto God by him, seeing he ever liveth to make intercession for them.

26)   For such an high priest became us, *who is* holy, harmless, undefiled, separate from sinners, and made higher than the heavens;

27)   Who needeth not daily, as those high priests, to offer up sacrifice, first for his own sins, and then for the people's: for this he did once, when he offered up himself.

28)   For the law *[of sin and sacrifice (Leviticus 7:37): of a forward pointing, typical, animal sacrifice as mandated up until Calvary]* maketh men high priests **which have infirmity**; but the word of the oath, which was since the law, *maketh* the Son, who is consecrated for evermore."

(Professor Miller went again to the chalkboard and made two lists comparing the Order of Aaron with the Order of Melchizedek. The numbers in parentheses are the verse numbers of Hebrews 7.)

Order of Aaron (11)	Order of Melchizedek (11)
Tribe of Levi (11)	Tribe of Judah (14)
Law (power) of a carnal Commandment (16)	Power (law) of an Endless Life (16)
Weak unprofitable command (20)	Powerful Divine oath (21)
Law made nothing perfect (19)	Better hope makes perfect (19)
Priest made without oath (21)	Made with Divine oath (21)
Chosen From Among Men (5:1)	Chosen from Godhead (7:2, 3)
Priests died (23)	Ever liveth to make intercession (25)
Many priests (23)	Another priest after order of Melchizedek (17)
Priests needed sacrifice for themselves (27)	Needed No Sacrifice for Himself. (27)
Had Infirmities (28)	He Sacrificed Himself (27)
Law of priesthood changed (12)	Holy, Harmless, Undefiled (26)
	Unchangeable priesthood (24)

Old Covenant	New better Covenant (22)
Sanctuary pitched by man	True Temple pitched by the Lord
Pattern of heavenly things	Heavenly realities
Promises based on the Lamb to be slain	Better Promises based on Christ's victory
Provisional clean heart	Secured new heart, new spirit
Law written on stone	Law written on fleshy tables of heart
Outward ceremony	Inward reality
Blood of bulls & goats	His own blood
Testament made by blood of animals	Testament made by blood of the Lamb of God
Death of animals	Death of Christ
Sacrifices often	One Sacrifice.
Sins remembered every year	Sins blotted out (forgotten - 10:17)

WILLIAM: That comparison really shows the difference between the two orders of priesthoods. **It shows that only divine Beings could be priests after the order of Melchizedek.** By the way, what does "order" mean?

PROFESSOR: I am glad you asked that question, William. Order = descent. The "order of Aaron" means those who are descended from Aaron (Exodus 40:13-15). There had to be a proper descent. If a person was not descended from Aaron, he could not be the high priest (2 Chronicles 13:9, 10). Is the same true with the Order of Melchizedek? **Jesus was a priest after the <u>order</u> of Melchizedek!**

WILLIAM: You mean Jesus would have to be a descendent of Melchizedek? Was he?

PROFESSOR: Yes. Gabriel told Mary:

Luke 1:35:
"**The Holy Ghost** shall come upon thee, and the power of the Highest shall overshadow thee:** therefore also that holy thing which shall be born of thee shall be called the Son of God."

The same angel told Joseph:

Matthew 1:20, 21:
"Joseph, thou son of David, fear not to take unto thee Mary thy wife: **for that which is conceived in her is of the Holy Ghost.** And she shall bring forth a son, and thou shalt call his name JESUS: for he shall save his people from their sins."

WILLIAM: Amazing! Jesus really was a priest after the <u>order</u> of Melchizedek.

PROFESSOR: One last point, William, before we go. It was through the Holy Spirit that God gave Abraham power to subdue his enemies when he rescued Lot. It will be by the power of the Holy Spirit that God's last day people will rescue "Lot" again. Look at these Bible verses and then Ellen White's comment.

Psalm 110:1-4:
    1) **"The LORD said unto my Lord, Sit thou at my right hand, until I make thine enemies thy footstool.**
    2)   The LORD shall send the rod of thy strength out of Zion: rule thou in the midst of thine enemies.
    3)   Thy people *shall be* willing in the day of thy power, in the beauties of holiness from the womb of the morning: thou hast the dew of thy youth.
    4)   The LORD hath sworn, and will not repent; **Thou *art* a priest for ever after the order of Melchizedek."**

Hebrews 10:12-17:
    12) "But this man, after he had offered one sacrifice for sins for ever, **sat down on the right hand of God;**

201

13)   **From henceforth expecting till his enemies be made his footstool.**

14)   For by one offering he hath perfected for ever them that are sanctified.

15)   *Whereof* **the Holy Ghost also is a witness** to us: for after that he had said before,

16)   This *is* the covenant that I will make with them after those days, saith the Lord, I will put my laws into their hearts, and in their minds will I write them;

17)   And their sins and iniquities will I remember no more."

Early Writings, pages 278, 279:
"Servants of God, endowed with *[Holy Spirit]* power from on high with their faces lighted up, and shining with holy consecration, went forth to proclaim the message from heaven. **Souls that were scattered all through the religious bodies answered to the call, and the precious were hurried out of the doomed churches, as Lot was hurried out of Sodom before her destruction.** God's people were strengthened by the excellent glory which rested upon them in rich abundance and prepared them to endure the hour of temptation.   I heard everywhere a multitude of voices saying, 'Here is the patience of the saints: here are they that keep the commandments of God, and the faith of Jesus.'"

Chapter 15

AN INTRODUCTION TO THE DOCTRINE OF
THE GODHEAD

PROFESSOR: This is not a topic of minor importance. "...**THIS is life eternal**..." John 17:3. According to John 5:39, we must "Search the scriptures; for in them ye think ye have eternal life: and they are they which testify of me." And Jesus came to reveal the Father (John 6:46; 14:8, 9). Jesus came to "show us the Father" because of the profound truth found in John 17:3:

> **John 17:3:**
> "And **this is life eternal**, that they might **know thee the only true God,** and **Jesus Christ, whom thou hast sent.**"

WILLIAM: This only speaks of two Members of the Godhead, where is the Holy Spirit if He is the 3rd Person of the Godhead?

PROFESSOR: He is making it all happen. It is **not possible to 'know' 'the only true God, and Jesus Christ, whom He "hast sent"** except **through the spiritual discernment imparted by the Holy Spirit.** For:

> **1 Corinthians 2:14:**
> **"The natural man receiveth not the things of the Spirit of God: for they are foolishness unto Him: neither can he know them, because they are spiritually discerned."**

> Testimonies to the Church, Volume 5, page 737:
> "No man, **without divine aid,** can attain to this knowledge of God."

Furthermore, while "the secret things belong unto the Lord our God," nevertheless "**those things which are revealed belong unto us and to our children for ever (Deut. 29:29).**
God's messenger comments on this verse in:

> Ministry of Healing, page 429.1:

"'The secret things belong unto the Lord our God: but those things which are revealed belong unto us and to our children forever.' Deuteronomy 29:29. **The revelation of Himself that God has given in His word is for our study. This we may seek to understand. But beyond this we are not to penetrate.**"

WILLIAM: I don't remember seeing any verse in the Bible where the word God means "three Persons." The word "God" always refers to one Member of the Godhead. (See Chapter 23 on the Shemmah.)

PROFESSOR: But Rome and others have speculated "beyond this"— beyond what is revealed—as in deciding that God is a essence or substance manifested in three different modes, or an "essence" in all creation. John H. Kellogg did this as well, as we saw. (See Chapter 4 of this book)
  Job poses the question:

Job 11:7-9:
  7) "Canst thou by searching find out God? canst thou find out the Almighty unto perfection?
  8) It is as high as heaven; what canst thou do? deeper than hell; what canst thou know?
  9) The measure thereof is longer than the earth, and broader than the sea."

All we can know is that which is revealed to us by His Holy Spirit and His Son.

WILLIAM: What do we know of God? What has been revealed to us?

PROFESSOR: That is a good question. All that we know of God has been revealed to us through His prophets in the written Word. Jesus, the living Word, came to reveal God the Father to us. To know God, we must believe and understand the Word, and this we cannot do on our own—we need the Holy Spirit. The Word tells us:

John 16:3:
  "When He, the Spirit of truth is come, He will guide you into all truth."

God's messenger tells us:

(Ye Shall Receive Power, 107); *Sabbath School Worker*, Dec. 1, 1909:

"It is through the impartation of the Holy Spirit that we are made to understand the Word of God."

She warns:

Sermons and Talks Volume 1, page 343:

"There are some things upon which we must reason, and there are other things that we must not discuss. In regard to God—what He is and where He is—silence is eloquence. **When you are tempted to speak of what God is, keep silence, because as surely as you begin to speak of this, you will disparage Him.** *[Declaring God to be an "essence" or "substance"manifested as "hypostases" or "modalities" disparages Him. Also, declaring God to be "in" rocks and bugs, etc.—as Kellogg did—disparages Him.]*

"**Our ministers must be very careful not to enter into controversy in regard to the personality of God** *[as in portraying God as 'an essence pervading all nature,' etc.]* This is a subject that they are not to touch. It is a mystery, and the enemy will surely lead astray those who enter into it. **We know that Christ came in person to reveal God to the world. God is a person** and **Christ is a person**. Christ is spoken of in the Word as "the brightness of His Father's glory, and **the express image of His person**.""

On **what** God **is**, the Bible has this to say:

John 4:24:
"**God is a Spirit:** and they that worship Him must worship Him in spirit and **in truth**."

WILLIAM: I perceive God the Father to be a Personal Being.

PROFESSOR: You're right; however, He is a personal, spirit Being. We are told in:

Education, page 132:
"God is a spirit; yet He is a personal being, for man was made in His image. As a personal being, God has revealed Himself in

His Son. The greatness of God is to us incomprehensible. **'The Lord's throne is in heaven' (Psalm 11:4); yet by His Spirit** *[the Holy Spirit who searches out the deep things of God.]* **He is everywhere present.** He has an intimate knowledge of, and a personal interest in, all the works of His hand."

So we see that God is a Spirit, and He has a Spirit: the Holy Spirit. However, unlike the Holy Spirit's usual manifestation, He also has a localized Presence and an Appearance.

Education, page 15:
"When Adam came from the Creator's hand, he bore, **in his physical,** mental, and spiritual nature, **a likeness to his Maker**."

Faith I Live By, page 40:
"**God is a Spirit; yet He is a personal being; for so He has revealed Himself** *[not as a 'modality.']***.**

"**As a personal being, God has revealed Himself in His Son. The outshining of the Father's glory, 'and the express image of his person,'** *[Heb. 1:3.]* **Jesus, as a personal Saviour, came to the world. As a personal Saviour He ascended on high. As a personal Saviour He intercedes in the heavenly courts.** *[A modality cannot intercede with another modality of its own substance! That is preposterous!]*

"I saw a throne, and on it sat the Father and the Son. I gazed on Jesus' countenance and **admired His lovely person. The Father's person I could not behold,** for a cloud of glorious light covered Him. **I asked Jesus if His Father had a form like Himself. He said He had,** but I could not behold it, for said He, **'If you should once behold the glory of His person, you would cease to exist.'**"

On where God is, inspiration informs us in Desire of Ages, page 356: that God is in His high and holy place. Paul tells us of a "third heaven." 2 Cor. 12:2. That is all that is revealed as to God's whereabouts. Solomon advises that God dwells "in thick darkness." (1 Kings 8:12; 2 Chron. 6:1). That is, that God is obscured from human prying.

WILLIAM: I know three Scriptures that tell us a little more about where God is.

PROFESSOR: What are they?

WILLIAM: God is in the heavenly sanctuary:

Psalm 11:4:
"The LORD *is* **in his holy temple, the LORD'S throne** *is*
in heaven: his eyes behold, his eyelids try, the children of men."

Jeremiah 17:12:
"A glorious high **throne** from the beginning *is* the **place of
our sanctuary.**"

Isaiah 6:1:
"In the year that king Uzziah died I saw also **the Lord sitting
upon a throne, high and lifted up, and his train filled the
temple."**

PROFESSOR: Excellent. But William, please note in Isaiah 6:1 that Isaiah
was in vision when he saw the Lord and not in His immediate presence.

WILLIAM: Is that because the Father cannot communicate with us
directly?

PROFESSOR: Exactly! God the Father cannot come into direct contact
with sinners. They would be destroyed. **In the plan of salvation two
members of the Godhead have undertaken subordinate roles to thereby
come into direct communication with mankind and this sin-filled
planet.** The structure of the Godhead, as set up in order to save sinners, is
graphically depicted in the instruction given to Israel to apply the blood of
the Lamb to **the lintel and the two door posts.**
Notice how specific the wording is. It is powerful:

Exodus 12:22, 23:
22) "And ye shall take a bunch of hyssop, and dip it in the
blood that is in the bason, **and strike the lintel and the two side
posts with the blood** that is in the bason; and none of you shall
go out at the door of his house until the morning.
23) For the LORD will pass through to smite the Egyptians;
and when he seeth the blood upon the lintel, and on the two

side posts, the LORD will pass over the door, and will not suffer the destroyer to come in unto your houses to smite you."

Here we see the "Lintel" symbolizing the One who is high and lifted up, separate from sin and sinners, maintaining the integrity of the Godhead as the "Most High God." The side posts symbolize Michael/Christ (the Second Person of the Godhead) and the Holy Spirit (the Third Person of the Godhead) who have subordinated themselves to the Most High God in order to reach man, (symbolized by the dust from which he is made), without man being consumed. The Three Mighty Powers of heaven!—all working, Their suffering symbolized by the blood applied to save fallen man! They form the doorway to eternal life, the "fold" for God's children. Jesus' humanity, represented by the wooden door (John 10:7), is the only "way" into the fold. He is "the Way, the Truth, and the Life, no man cometh unto the Father but by *[Him]*" (John 14:6).

WILLIAM: Three distinct symbolic entities: The lamb, the blood, and the doorway; and the doorway itself is also a symbol of three distinct Entities operating as a unit.

PROFESSOR: The "Lintel" remains above the earth—in "heaven." The two Side Posts while they have access to heaven, also come in touch with the sinful earth.

But notice the next Catholic style representation of the Trinity—a "device" of man's devising; a "vain" imagining:

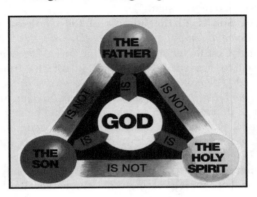

The Catholic depiction of the Trinity, **found in an SDA Bible Study Handbook is a clear illustration of God being "one substance" revealed as three "manifestations."** This plainly illustrates "consubstantiation." **This is a spiritualistic representation, making of God a non-entity.**

WILLIAM: Right. This misleading illustration tells me that God is "Someone" who is composed of the "Father," the "Son," and the "Holy Spirit": three modalities of a consubstantial 'God' essence. The Biblical "Godhead" refers to distinct divine Persons.

PROFESSOR: In the Bible the word "God" usually refers to the Father, symbolized by the lintel, because He is the Most High God. (See Chapter 22) In order for there to be a doorway, a "way of escape" (1 Cor. 10:13; AA, page316) from temptation and sin—a way of entrance into the "fold" (John 10), there has to be a "Lintel," which does not come into contact with the "dust." Notice how God's messenger speaks of the Godhead:

Counsels on Health, page 222:
    "The Godhead [every one of the Members of this Body] was stirred with pity for the race, and the Father, the Son,

and the Holy Spirit gave themselves to the working out of the plan of redemption."

Evangelism, pages 614, 615:
"**The Father is all the fullness of the Godhead bodily,** and is invisible to mortal sight.
"**The Son is all the fullness of the Godhead manifested.** *[Jesus came to "manifest" or reveal the Father.]*
"**The Comforter** that Christ promised to send after He ascended to heaven, **is the Spirit in all the fullness of the Godhead [***Because the Holy Spirit also dwells **in** the Father and administers His power to the universe.***]**, making **manifest** the **power** of divine grace to all who receive and believe in Christ as a personal Saviour. *[The Holy Spirit administers and reveals the grace and power of God to men and acquaints them with the Word.]*
"**There are three living persons of the heavenly trio;** in the name of these three great powers—the Father, the Son, and the Holy Spirit—those who receive Christ by living faith are baptized..."

The word "Godhead" is used in the Bible in three passages, Romans 1:20; Colossians 2:9; and Acts 17:29. In these 3 passages the word "Godhead" is translated from one of three Greek words: *Theotes, Theios,* and *Theiotes.* All of these words have the same basic meaning.

Strong's gives the following definitions:
Theotes: #2320—Divinity, Godhead. **Colossians 2:9**
Theios: #2304—Divine, Godhead. **Acts 17:29**
Theiotes: #2305—Divinity, Godhead. **Romans 1:20**

Let us read these verses:

Colossians 2:9:
"For in him *[Jesus]* **dwelleth** all the fulness of the Godhead bodily."

The Holy Spirit, who comes "**in** all the fullness of the Godhead," **dwelt** in Christ, and Christ "**manifested**" all the fullness of the Godhead, which His Father **"is."**

The Godhead is **not** some philosophical, spiritualistic, platonic concept conjured by the vain imaginings of men!

Acts 17:29:
"Forasmuch then as we are the offspring of God, **we ought not to think that the Godhead is like unto gold, or silver, or stone, graven by art and man's device.**" *[The "trinity" concept is "man's device".]*

Romans 1:20:
"For the invisible things of him from the creation of the world **are clearly seen, being understood by the things that are made, even his** *[the Father's]* **eternal power and Godhead; so that they are without excuse.**"

WILLIAM: I know of one other Scripture that uses the Greek word for Godhead, but translates it another way.

PROFESSOR: Share it, please!

WILLIAM: It is:

2 Peter 1:4:
"Whereby are given unto us exceeding great and precious promises: that by these ye might be partakers of **the divine** *[Theios: #2304]* **nature**, having escaped the corruption that is in the world through lust."

PROFESSOR: William, do you see that 2 Peter 1:4 could also be translated; "that by these ye might be partakers of **the Godhead nature?**" And how are we "partakers of the divine nature?"

WILLIAM: Through the indwelling presence of the Holy Spirit!

PROFESSOR: Right! And He "is the Spirit **in** all the fullness of the Godhead." **Now we have all three of the Heavenly Trio connected in the term "the Godhead."** And they work together that men might also be **"partakers of the divine** *[Godhead]* **nature"** (2 Peter 1:4).

WILLIAM: What does this term 'Godhead' describe? What is the 'fullness of the Godhead'?

211

PROFESSOR: According to God's messenger, it means the "THE ABSOLUTE GODHEAD!"

<u>SDA Bible Commentary</u>, Volume 7, page 914:
   "'It is written in the prophets, And they shall be all taught of God. **Every man therefore that hath heard, and hath learned of the Father** *[through the Holy Spirit]*, **cometh unto me'—not through confessionals or priests or popes, but through Me, your Saviour.** 'Not that any man hath seen the Father, **save he** *[Christ]* **which is of God, he hath seen the Father.** *[The only Man ever 'begotten of God', the Father, through the agency of the Holy Spirit].* Verily, verily, I say unto you, **He that believeth on me** *[Christ]* **hath everlasting life** *[through the indwelling presence of the Divine Mighty Third Person of the Godhead].'* **This is the absolute Godhead.** *[This is receiving, from Christ, "self-existent", "Godhead"- type life. That is why the Scripture says: "This is life eternal, that they might know thee the only true God, and Jesus Christ, whom thou hast sent" (John. 17:3). Jesus said, "No man cometh unto the Father but by Me." (John 14:6). We "come" to the Father, and come to "know" the Father, through Jesus the Son, by the power and guidance and regeneration administered to us by the Holy Spirit, who is our "seal" unto "everlasting life".]* The mightiest created intellect cannot comprehend Him; words from the most eloquent tongue fail to describe Him. Silence is eloquence.
   "Christ represented His Father to the world, and He represents before God the chosen ones in whom He has restored the moral image of God. They are His heritage. To them He says, 'He that hath seen me hath seen the Father.' 'No man knoweth... the Father, save the Son, and he to whomsoever the Son will reveal him.' No priest, no religionist, can reveal the Father to any son or daughter of Adam *[who are all born of the 'will of the flesh.' Jesus, however was 'begotten' of Mary by God. He has come down from Heaven. He **alone** can cause us to 'know the only true God." To have the Holy Spirit dwell in the body temple is to partake of the "divine" or "Godhead" nature: bringing man into "one"ness with God through the same mighty and divine agency—the Holy Spirit—who dwells in Christ and His Father. This constitutes them "one" in purpose,*

in character, and in Spirit, so that we can worship Him "in spirit and in truth."]

"Men have only one Advocate, one Intercessor, who is able to pardon transgression. Shall not our hearts swell with gratitude **to Him** *[the* Father*]* who gave Jesus to be the propitiation for our sins? Think deeply upon the love **the Father** has manifested in our behalf, the love that He has expressed for us. We cannot measure this love. Measurement there is none. We can only point to Calvary, to the Lamb slain from the foundation of the world. It is an infinite sacrifice. Can we comprehend and measure infinity? . . .

"John 17:19-21, 24-26: 'And for their sakes I sanctify myself, that they also might be sanctified through the truth. 20) Neither pray I for these alone, but for them also which shall believe on me through their word; 21) That they all may be one; as [*in the same way that*] thou, Father, [art] **in** me, and I **in** thee, that they also may be ONE **in** us: that the world may believe that thou hast sent me. 24) Father, I will that they also, whom thou hast given me, be with me where I am; that they may behold my glory, which thou hast given me: for thou lovedst me before the foundation of the world. 25) O righteous Father, the world hath not known thee: but I have known thee, and these have known that thou hast sent me. 26) And I have declared unto them thy name, and will declare [it]: that the love wherewith thou hast loved me may be in them, and I in them.'

"Here we see the great Intercessor presenting His petition **to His Father. No middle man comes between the sinner and Christ. No dead prophet, no buried saint is seen.** Christ Himself is our Advocate. **All that the Father is to His Son, He is to those whom His Son in His humanity represented.** In every line of His work **Christ acted as a representative of the Father.** He lived as our substitute and surety. He labored as He would have His followers labor, unselfishly appreciating the value of every human being for whom He suffered and died." (MS 128, 1897).

WILLIAM: Jesus was "sent" to represent God the Father to us.

PROFESSOR: Yes, He is **TWICE A REPRESENTATIVE!**

SDA Bible Commentary, Volume 7, page 914:

"**Christ is the representative of God to man and the representative of man to God.**" (MS 29, 1899).

WILLIAM: **Why only One Mediator?**

PROFESSOR: This is the great wonder of the plan of salvation.

SDA Bible Commentary, Volume 7, page 914:
> "**Jesus alone could give security to God; for He was equal to God. He alone could be a mediator between God and Man; for He possessed divinity and humanity.**" *[He is our Door into the fold of God.]*

Michael did not possess humanity, but had voluntarily accepted a role subordinate to the Father in order to come in contact with sinful mankind prior to the incarnation. Michael had to become the divine "Seed" to be born of Mary, and assume our fallen humanity, and was henceforth known to men as "Jesus." (See Chapters 10 and 11)

The "one"ness and unity and at-one-ment with God and our fellow pilgrims, that Jesus prayed for in John 17:17-21, commences and is maintained through God's people all having one "Spirit"—even the "Holy Spirit of truth":

Ephesians 4:4-6:
4) "**There is one body** *[God's people, the church]*, **and one Spirit, even as ye are called in one hope of your calling;** *[Notice the true church is "one body" because "one Spirit" is in each member of the "body." The Spirit is "in" the body "temple!" Similarly, the Spirit dwelt "in" Christ and also searches out the deep things in the "mind of God" (Evangelism page 617) and so is in God the Father and thus "in" the Godhead, and is a member of the Godhead."]*

5) "**One Lord** *[Jesus]*, **one faith, one baptism,**

6) "**One God and Father of all, who is above all** *[including above Jesus, because Jesus chose to come down to reach us in our sinful condition]*, **and through all, and in you all** *[through His Holy Spirit]*."

Remember also that Jesus said, "My Father is greater than I." John 14:28. Hence, the Father is "above all." This is a situation that

Christ voluntarily accepted when He undertook His role in the plan of redemption.

WILLIAM: Was Jesus just like us then?

PROFESSOR: Although Jesus "Christ took upon Him the infirmities of degenerate humanity" (See Desire of Ages, page 117), having the Holy Spirit as His earthly progenitor, Christ's "head," His **mind** was untouched by Satan. **The spirit of Satan never occupied Him.** He never had a "carnal heart." His mind was sensitive and responsive to the promptings of the Holy Spirit from conception and birth. We are to let such a mindset be in us. As we have seen:

Signs of the Times, October 29, 1894:
"He began life, passed through its experiences, and ended its record, with a sanctified human will."

SDA Bible Commentary, Volume 5, page1117:
"No one, looking upon the childlike countenance, shining with animation, could say that Christ was just like other children. *[There had never been a child born like Christ. Never.]* **He was God in human flesh.** When urged by His companions to do wrong, divinity flashed through humanity, and He refused decidedly. In a moment He distinguished between right and wrong, and placed sin in the light of God's commands, holding up the law as a mirror which reflected light upon wrong. It was this keen discrimination between right and wrong that often provoked Christ's brothers to anger. Yet His appeals and entreaties, and the sorrow expressed in His countenance, revealed such a tender, earnest love for them that they were ashamed of having tempted Him to deviate from His strict sense of justice and loyalty. (*Youth Instructor,* September 8, 1898.)"

The power and discernment of God **dwelt** in Christ's human body **by the agency of the indwelling mighty Third member of the Godhead.** We, too, can be partakers of the fulness of the Godhead through the indwelling of the same Holy Spirit.

Selected Messages Book 3, page 131:
"Through being **partakers of the divine nature** we may stand pure and holy and undefiled. **The Godhead was not made**

215

human, and the human was not deified by the blending together of the two natures. Christ did not possess the same sinful, corrupt, fallen <u>disloyalty</u> we possess, for then He could not be a perfect offering.—(Manuscript 94, 1893.)"

He maintained His loyalty to His Father by continually **choosing** the path of obedience to His Father's will. Christ came as God the Father's representative to man. When Jesus ascended, He sent the Holy Spirit as His and the Father's representative.

<u>Christ Triumphant</u>, page 301:
"Christ determined to bestow **a gift** on those who had been with Him and on those who should believe on Him, because this was the occasion of His ascension and inauguration, a jubilee in heaven. **What gift could Christ bestow** rich enough to signalize and grace His ascension to the mediatorial throne? It must be worthy of His greatness and His royalty. **Christ gave His representative, the third person of the Godhead, the Holy Spirit. This Gift could not be excelled....**"

So we see that all three Members of the Godhead each play distinctive roles in the plan of salvation:

<u>Counsels on Health</u>, page 222:
"**The Godhead** *[every one of the Members of this Body]* **was stirred with pity for the race, and the Father, the Son, and the Holy Spirit gave <u>themselves</u> to the working out of the plan of redemption.**"

All three Members of the Godhead have, and still do, suffer in the plan of salvation. Every lost sinner who rejects the redemption paid causes sorrow in heaven to this day.

WILLIAM: Yes, because when we sin **we sin against God the Father,** we demonstrate the willingness to crucify Christ afresh, and we cause grief to the Holy Spirit, Who could have helped us to overcome. All heaven mourns.

But on the other hand when we repent it causes all heaven to rejoice! **"Joy shall be in heaven over one sinner that repenteth."** Luke 15:7.

PROFESSOR: A frequently misunderstood verse in Scripture regarding knowing God is found in 1 John. However, when we compare Scripture with Scripture, we get clarity. The Word of God tells us in:

1 John 5:20:
"And we know that the Son of God is come, and hath given us an **understanding**, that we may **know Him that is true** *[the only true God (John 17:3), the Father, whom we can only know by spiritual revelation through the Holy Spirit, for "God is a spirit (John 4:24), and spiritual things are "spiritually discerned" (1 Cor. 2:14). This discernment is given us by the Holy Spirit whom Christ has given us (John 14:26). And in that way we obtain "an understanding" of the "true God" of Whom Christ is the "express image (Heb. 1:3)]* and we are **in** Him that is true *[in the same way that the Father and the Son can be "in" us—by the Holy Spirit (John 14:23; John 17:21)]* even **in** His *[the Father's]* Son Jesus Christ. *[By sharing Jesus' Spirit we can be "in" Him; and by the Spirit Jesus came to make known the Father to us (Matt. 11:27; Luke 10:22)]* This is the true God, and eternal life." *[As is also clearly stated in John 17:3. And if we are "in" Christ, by sharing His Spirit, we are then also "in" the Father whose Spirit is also Christ's Spirit.]*

Romans 8:9:
"But ye are not in the flesh, but **in** the Spirit, if so be that the Spirit of God dwell **in** you. Now if any man have not the Spirit of Christ, he is none of his.

Chapter 16

LIVING WATER

PROFESSOR: William, I want you to notice what God's word says regarding how we can gain an insight into the makeup of the Godhead. Look at this passage in Romans:

Romans 1:20:
> **"For the invisible things of him** from the creation of the world are clearly seen, **being understood by the things that are made, [even] his eternal power and Godhead; so that they are without excuse:"**

WILLIAM: How can we see the "invisible things" of God and His position in the Godhead; in "the things that are made"?

PROFESSOR: All the physical things that God has made are comprised of atoms—'individual atoms' which come together with other atoms to form another **unit** called **molecules.** There is one molecule without which **life cannot exist: Water!** H_2O: two atoms of Hydrogen combined with one atom of oxygen—to form one molecule of water. **Hydrogen can be a 'consuming fire.' Oxygen enables combustion and oxygen sustains life. But together, they form water, which sustains all life and extinguishes fire.** All living things are comprised largely of water, and all living cellular activity takes place in a medium of water.
   A water molecule is composed of three separate and distinct atoms, but together they form a unity. H_2O as a molecule gives us a clue as to the composition of the Godhead—**Three distinct Persons operating in a unity** (*or unit*). Two Hydrogen atoms, each combined with one oxygen atom = a unity of distinct atoms working to sustain life. However, this molecule can be split or "separated." This **unit** is not "indivisible"! Jesus offers us **the water of life** freely (*Rev. 21:6 and Rev. 22:17*). Through the Holy Spirit, whom He sends us, we can come to know the "only true God, and Jesus Christ whom He has sent," and **"this is** life eternal" (John 17:3).
   The Holy Spirit is referred to in the Word as the "living water" and as "water of life" (John 4:10, 11; 7:38, 39 and Revelation 21:6; 22:1, 17). It is He who reveals to us the "Most High God", the Father, and administers temporal life that comes from the Father to us and returns to Him at our

death; it is He who represents both the Father and the Son to us, and administers Christ's immortality to the redeemed sealed ones (Ephesians 4:30) at Christ's second coming when "this mortal [shall] put on immortality" (1 Corinthians 15:53); which is the life of Christ that He takes up and gives to His redeemed ones (DA 767.4)

Selected Messages, Book 1, pages 296, 297:
  "'In Him was **life; and the life was the light of men'** *(John 1:4).* **It is not physical life that is here specified, but immortality, the life which is exclusively the property of God. The Word** *[One of Christ's titles, or names which extend both before and after His incarnation],* who was with God, **and who was God** *["God" is a title denoting a station of being],* **had this life.** *[But notice John 5:26 which says, "For as the Father hath life in Himself; so hath He given to the Son to have life in Himself" because Jesus laid down His immortality and had taken mortality upon Himself in order to be able to die.]* Physical life is something which each individual receives. It is not eternal or immortal; for God, the Life-giver, takes it again. Man has no control over his life. But the *[immortal]* life of Christ was unborrowed. No one can take this life from Him. "I lay it down of myself" (John 10:18). *["...I have power to lay it down and I have power to take it again.* **This commandment** *(or authority)* **have I received of My Father."** *As we were reading:]* "I lay it down of myself" (John 10:18), He said. **In Him was life, original, unborrowed, underived.** *[What original, unborrowed, underived life was* **in** *Christ that was* **'given'** *Him by the Father (John 5:26)? And which is not inherent in man?* **Notice John 6:57:** *"As the living Father hath sent Me, and* **I live by the Father; so he that eateth Me, even he shall live by Me."** *What "immortality" or immortal life can we receive that is exclusively the property of God? This "immortality" can only be the life that Jesus laid down and takes up again and gives to His redeemed ones,]* **This life is not inherent in man. He can possess it...** *[What is "it"?* **"It" is "life, original, unborrowed, underived," i.e. immortal life—which man can possess].** **He** *[man]* **can possess it only through Christ.** *[Man cannot receive the permanent indwelling presence of the Holy Spirit—becoming a union of humanity and divinity as Christ was – except through the reconciliation effected by Christ. The Holy Spirit is immortal and He administers the*

219

*immortal life that Jesus laid down, to the redeemed. Thus, to be united to the Godhead through the indwelling Spirit is **to have life everlasting**;* held in guarantee until the resurrection of the just.] **He *[man]* cannot earn it."**

But Jesus the spotless One could! As we see in the next statement, Jesus "earned" it for us:

> Upward Look, page 263:
> "Then the mighty angel, with a voice that caused the earth to quake, was heard to say, "Jesus, Thou Son of God, Thy Father calls Thee." Then **He who had _earned_ the power to conquer death** and the grave came forth, and proclaimed over the rent sepulcher of Joseph, "I am the resurrection and the life."

Having laid down His immortal life and having taken mortality in order to be able to die as man's divine substitute, Christ had to 'earn the power to conquer death' by perfect obedience to God's Holy Law. The Scriptures tell us plainly that:

> **Deuteronomy 8:3:**
> "…but by every [word] that proceedeth out of the mouth of the LORD **doth man _live_**."

ANYONE not living by every word that proceeds out of the Lord's mouth is "dead in trespass and sins" and in need of salvation. Perfect obedience brings a perfect reward. Only Jesus has rendered that perfect obedience, by faithful trust in His Father, so that we can receive the 'robe' of His righteousness; **the reward of His faith** (we are saved **by the faith of Jesus**), and **He took and bore our sinfulness to eternal death in His humanity.** What a wonderful, risk fraught, glorious transaction. Only the Godhead could have conceived of such a plan!

Fallen man **cannot "earn"** it: **"the power to conquer death"!** Speaking of fallen man, God's messenger says:

> Selected Messages Book 1, page 297:
> "He cannot earn it *[through works, etc.]*; it is **given** him as a free gift if he will believe in Christ as His personal Saviour. **'This is life eternal, that they might know thee the only true God, and Jesus Christ, whom thou hast sent'** (John 17:3). **This is the open fountain of life for the world."**

220

WE NEED TO GRASP THE IMPORT OF WHAT GOD'S MESSENGER JUST STATED, for it opens new vistas of meaning to the following verses of Scripture:

John 1:12-14:
12) "But as many as received Him *[Christ]*, to them gave He **power** *[by the Spirit of God]* to become the sons of God," (See John 3:3, 5, 6.) **even to them that believe on His name;** *[His name, Jesus (Yeshua) means "Jehovah saves" (from sin).]*
13) Which were born, **not of blood,** *[human or animal life]* ***nor of the will of the flesh*** *[desire, or lust, or human love—the flesh profiteth nothing]*, **nor of the will of man** *[whose will is corrupted]*, but of God *[just as Jesus was]*.
14) And the **Word** *[Michael's other name or title]* was made flesh *["made of a woman; made under the law" Gal. 4:4]*, and dwelt among us *[being ... "in all points tempted like as we are, yet without sin. Heb. 4:15]*, (and we beheld his glory, the glory as of **the only begotten of the Father,) full of grace and truth."**

Mankind can relate to a personal God who "gave His only begotten Son;" a personal God who ran the risk of being eternally separated from His "fellow" (Zechariah 13:7); a personal God who loves beings other than Himself and who is willing to make infinite personal sacrifices on their behalf: sacrifices which could never be made by an indivisible "essence" who could never "give" an **indivisible** portion of Himself. **Trinitarians, on the other hand, tend to relate to <u>human</u> "leadership" figures rather than to the "only true God".**

William, you will remember that, while on earth, Jesus said, "I live by the Father" (John 6:57).

WILLIAM: Why did He say that?

PROFESSOR: He had laid aside the panoply of Divinity and laid down His immortality, His own life, in order to be able to die.

<u>Desire of Ages</u>, page 21:
"**<u>All</u> things Christ received from God,** *[Christ, on earth, was constantly praying to His Heavenly father for daily strength and power. He said, 'I can of Mine own Self do nothing.' John 5:30.]* **but He took to give. So in the heavenly courts, in His ministry for all created beings: <u>through the beloved Son</u>, the**

221

Father's life flows out to all; *[The life that is sustaining us right now, is through Christ's mediation. Adam would have died the day he sinned, but through Christ a probationary life was granted to fallen man.]* through the Son it returns, in praise and joyous service, a tide of love, to **the great Source of all.** And thus through Christ the circuit of beneficence is complete, representing the character of the great Giver, the law of life."

WILLIAM: The Father's life through Christ sustains the universe!

PROFESSOR: Yes, through Christ, He is the fountain of life!

> *Review & Herald,* April 5, 1906:
> "'I am the Way, the Truth, and the Life,' Christ declares; 'no one cometh unto the Father, but by me.' **Christ is <u>invested</u> with power to give life to all creatures**."

The life that Christ finally gives the redeemed at His return is the life that He laid down—His own immortal life—a life that "measures with the life of God" (<u>Gospel Workers</u>, page 349).

> **John 17:2:**
> "As thou hast **given him power** over all flesh, that he should **give eternal life** to as many as thou hast given him."

> <u>Desire of Ages</u>, page 786:
> "To the believer, Christ is the resurrection and the life. In our Saviour **the life that was lost through sin is restored;** for He has life in Himself to quicken whom He will. **He is invested with the right to** *[finally]* **give immortality. The life that He laid down in humanity, He takes up again, and gives to humanity.** 'I am come,' He said, 'that they might have life, and that they might have it more abundantly.' **'Whosoever drinketh of the water that I shall give him shall never thirst; but the water that I shall give him shall be in him <u>a well of water</u> springing up into everlasting life.' (John 5:14)."** See and read:

> **John 7:37-39:**
> 37) "If any man thirst, let him come unto Me, and drink.
> 38) He that believeth on me, as the scripture hath said, **out of his belly shall flow rivers of <u>living water</u>.**

39) (But this spake he of the Spirit, which they that believe on him should receive: for the Holy Ghost was not yet *given;* because that Jesus was not yet glorified.)"

It is through the redemption effected by Jesus that Man can receive the indwelling of the Holy Spirit, who is their obedience-empowering, overcoming-power-bringing "**seal** unto the day of redemption." The Holy Spirit, by whom the redeemed are sealed, and who is forever united to their glorified humanity, will be the Agent in administering Christ's immortality which He then gives to His redeemed. It is through Christ that we can receive His life-administering Agent: the Holy Spirit: the 'Living Water':

Patriarchs & Prophets, pages 412, 413:
"[John 7:37-39 quoted.] **The refreshing water,** welling up in a parched and barren land, causing the desert place to blossom, and flowing out to give life to the perishing, **is an emblem of the divine grace which Christ alone can bestow, and which is as the living water, purifying, refreshing, and invigorating the soul....**

"**The same figure Christ had employed in His conversation with the woman of Samaria at Jacob's well: 'Whosoever drinketh of the water that I shall give him shall never thirst; but the water that I shall give him shall be in him a well of water springing up into everlasting life.'** John 4:14. Christ combines the two types. He is the rock, He is the living water. *[See John 14:15-18 where Jesus plainly declared that the **other** "Comforter", the Holy Spirit's presence with His followers, was tantamount to He Himself being present.]*

"The invitation is given, '**Ho, every one that thirsteth, come ye to the waters.' Isaiah 41:17; 44:3; Isaiah 35:6; 55:1. And in the closing pages of the Sacred Word this invitation is echoed. The river of the water of life, 'clear as crystal,' proceeds from the throne of God and the Lamb;** and the gracious call is ringing down through the ages, 'Whosoever will, let him take the water of life freely.' Revelation 22:17. (See John 7:37-39.)"

Because the Holy Spirit is the "Spirit of God" and the "Spirit of Christ," His indwelling Presence includes the mind of God and the mind of Christ. That is why Jesus said in John 14:23:

John 14:23:

"If a man love me, He will keep my words: and my Father will love him, and **we** will come to him, and make **our** abode with him."

And we know that it is by the Holy Spirit that this is effected. **To have the Holy Spirit is to have the Godhead's Presence dwell within**. Through the Holy Spirit, we fulfill Jesus' prayer in John 17, and we are "one" with all Spirit-filled children of God and with the Godhead. **The Holy Spirit has the outworking of "Living Water." He brings the presence of the Father and the Son with Him, placing the Spirit-filled children of God in contact with the mind of Christ and, thereby, of His Father.**

As we have seen, "Water" is another fitting symbol of the Godhead. To have this "living water" is to have the indwelling Presence of the Holy Spirit who reveals to us, and causes us to know, the "only true God and Jesus Christ Whom He has sent," Whom to "know" is "life eternal." (John 17:3)

WILLIAM: I would like to conclude this wonderful study, Professor, with these two verses:

1 John 4:7:

"Beloved, let us love one another: for love is of God;

and every one that loveth is born of God, and knoweth God."

Psalm 36:8, 9:

8) "...Thou shalt make them drink of the river of thy pleasures.

9) For with thee is the fountain of life...:"

Chapter 17

LIVING WATER AND THE TREE OF LIFE

WILLIAM: What are we going to study today?

PROFESSOR: Remembering what we have just studied, we are going to look at the work of the Holy Spirit—the One who is represented by "living water" (John 4:10, 14; John 7:38, 39). Let us open our Bibles to the book of John. Here, in the 14th chapter we find Jesus speaking about the inner union that exists between Himself and His Father:

> **John 14:10-12:**
>   10) "Believest thou not that **I am in the Father, and the Father in me?** The words that I speak unto you I speak not of myself: but **the Father that dwelleth in me** [*by His Holy Spirit, in the same way that Christ dwells in His disciples, by His Holy Spirit*]**, he doeth the works.**
>   11) "**Believe me that I am in the Father, and the Father in me:** or else believe me for the very works' sake.
>   12) "Verily, verily, I say unto you, He that believeth on me, the works that I do shall he do also; **and greater works than these shall he do;** because I go unto my Father."

As we have noted, it is by the Holy Spirit that Christ and the Father are "in" each other. God's Spirit seeks to dwell **in** us as a fountain of "living water" imparting new spiritual life to the believer; ultimately imparting immortality at the second coming.

Review & Herald, June 13, 1899:
> "**The impartation of the Spirit was the impartation of the very life of Christ.**"

For a human being to receive the indwelling presence of the Holy Spirit is to receive of Jesus' saving life: Jesus is the "light of life" (John 8:12); the "Minorah" of the Sanctuary through which flows the 'Holy Oil', bringing light to the "Seven Churches".

<u>SDA Bible Commentary</u>, Volume 6, page 1118 (MS 1a, 1890):

"No candlestick, no church, shines of itself. From Christ emanates all its light"

Divine, overcoming Power is imparted to the human agent through the Holy Spirit.

General Conference Bulletin, May 17, 1909:
"To abide **in Christ** means that **you shall be a partaker of the divine nature.** Humanity lays hold upon divinity, and **you have divine power.**"

WILLIAM: Jesus was "a root out of dry ground" (Isaiah 53:2). Dry ground is dust. Dust is what humanity is made of (Genesis 2:7; Psalms 103:14). The Divine Seed that was implanted into humanity took root in that "dust". Thus Jesus was human as we are, but also "that Holy Thing" (Luke 1:35; Selected Messages Book 1 page 227), a union of **our** humanity and Divinity, into whom we have to be "grafted" by the Holy Spirit and become **"one"** with Him, which, by implication, also makes us **"one"** with the Father.

PROFESSOR: Yes, William, Jesus took our nature. Our nature does not naturally have the "living water," but is "dry." Jesus was able to grow "out of dry ground" because He was filled with the Holy Spirit, the "Living Water". Yes, Jesus showed how we may live—through the power of the Holy Spirit.

Reflecting Christ, page 130 (Letter 352, 1908):
"**Christ is our pattern,** our example in all things. **He was filled with the Spirit, and the Spirit's power was manifested through Him,** not by bodily movements *[as in celebration style Pentecostalism, or Catholic genuflections]*, but by a zeal for good works."

Incidentally, when we are told in Scripture, and by God's messenger, that Christ "was filled with the Spirit", are we to understand that He was filled with Himself? Or was He filled with His Father? If the Holy Spirit is 'Christ's own Person' and 'the Father's own Person', who filled Christ if the Holy Spirit is not a distinct divine Person in His own right?

While Jesus was on earth His Father was in Heaven, administering the affairs of men and the universe by His Holy spirit and His angels. We have repeatedly noted the following statement by God's messenger:

226

Ministry of Healing, page 417:
"The Bible shows us God in His high and holy place, not in a state of inactivity, not in silence and solitude, but surrounded by ten thousand times ten thousand and thousands of thousands of holy beings, all waiting to do His will. Through these messengers He is in active communication with every part of His dominion. **By His Spirit He is everywhere present. Through the agency of His Spirit and His angels He ministers to the children of men.**"

Does this mean that the Father ministers to men through the agency of 'Himself' and His holy angels?

You will also see in the next statement that the Holy Spirit is also referred to by the title "God" (see Chapter 22, "God of gods"). He is, after all, the "mighty Third Person" of the Godhead. Nevertheless, one of His roles is to indite prayer to God the Father, and to intercede for us "with groanings that cannot be uttered" (Romans 8:26). It is He who makes efficacious the work of the human instrumentality. **If the Holy Spirit 'God's own Person' He would not have to intercede with Himself!**

Testimonies to Ministers, page 404:
"All should bear in mind that Satan's special efforts are directed against the ministry. **He knows that it is but a human instrumentality, possessing no grace or holiness of its own.** He knows that it is an agent that God has ordained to be a powerful means for the salvation of souls **and is efficacious only as God, the eternal Spirit, makes it so.**"

God is referred to as "the eternal Spirit" in this quote. It is **through His representative, the Holy Spirit**, that God makes "the human instrumentality" "efficacious". **However, the following Scripture makes it abundantly clear that the Holy Spirit is also referred to as "eternal Spirit".** The Holy Spirit was intimately involved in Calvary and Christ's suffering:

Hebrews 9:14:
"How much more shall the blood of Christ, **who through the eternal Spirit** offered himself without spot **TO God**, purge your conscience from dead works to serve the living God?"

We see all three separate and distinct Persons of the Godhead referred to in this last verse!

Testimonies to the Church, Volume 4, page 123:
"A solemn statement was made to ancient Israel that the man who should remain unclean and refuse to purify himself should be cut off from among the congregation. This has a special meaning for us. If it was necessary in ancient times for the unclean to be purified by the blood of sprinkling, how essential for those living in the perils of the last days, and exposed to the temptations of Satan, **to have the blood** *[The "life" of Jesus: "The blood thereof is the life thereof" Gen. 9:4; Lev. 17:14. "We shall be saved by His life" (Rom. 5:10). The forfeiture of His blood—His life—takes away our sin and guilt]* **of Christ applied to their hearts daily.** 'For if the blood of bulls and of goats, and the ashes of an heifer sprinkling the unclean, sanctifieth to the purifying of the flesh: how much more shall the blood of Christ, **who through the eternal Spirit** offered Himself without spot **TO God**, purge your conscience from dead works to serve the living God?'"

Did Jesus offer Himself "through" Himself "to God"? Or "through" His Father TO His Father?
What God said through Paul to the church, He repeated, through His messenger to the ministers, while repeating that **it was "through the eternal Spirit"** that Christ, our Example, was able to offer "Himself without spot to God"**:

Testimonies to Ministers, page 98:
"I entreat you now to **humble yourselves and cease your stubborn resistance of light and evidence.** Say unto the Lord, Mine iniquities have separated between me and my God. O Lord, pardon my transgressions. Blot out my sins from the book of Thy remembrance. Praise His holy name, there is forgiveness with Him, and you can be converted, transformed.

"'For if the blood of bulls and of goats, and the ashes of an heifer sprinkling the unclean, sanctifieth to the purifying of the flesh: how much more shall the blood of Christ, who **through the eternal Spirit** offered Himself without spot **to God**, purge your conscience from dead works to serve the living God?'"

The work of the Holy Spirit is **symbolized** in different ways:

Revelation 22:2:
"In the midst of the street of it, and on either side of the river, *was there* the tree of life, which bare twelve *manner of* fruits, *and* yielded her fruit every month: and the leaves of the tree *were* for the healing of the nations."

The Greek word for "tree" (in this case, the "tree of life") is *xulon,* meaning "wood." This is same word used in the NT for "cross", which is also called a "tree." **Jesus' cross is become a tree of life** to those who accept His sacrifice for them.

The Tree of Life in heaven has two trunks, co-joined above the river of Life, symbolizing the Son—His human and Divine nature which are 'blended' into one, and it yields leaves which are for the 'healing of the nations' (Revelation 22:2). The Word of God are those leaves (Evangelism, page 138). The 'blended' Tree yields the fruit of a righteous, everlasting life. **The River of the water of life, a symbol of the Holy Spirit flowing from the Father's throne, runs between the trunks of the tree of life and on outward to all creation and especially to fallen man. It is the Father who sends the 'other Comforter' whom we can receive only through Jesus.**

The Holy Spirit is available to us "without money and without price" on our part; but it cost an infinite price for the Holy Spirit to become **united** with repentant sinners.

The Scriptures tell us:

John 7:37-39:
37) "In the last day, that great [day] of the feast, Jesus stood and cried, saying, **If any man thirst, let him come unto me, and drink.**

38) "He that believeth on me, as the scripture hath said, out of his belly shall flow rivers of living water.

39) **(But this spake he of the Spirit, which they that believe on him should receive.)**"

Now focus on Jesus' words to the woman at the well:

John 4:10, 14:
10) "Jesus answered and said unto her, If thou knewest the gift of God, and who it is that saith to thee, Give me to drink;

229

thou wouldest have asked of him, and he would have given thee living water.

14) "But whosoever drinketh of **the water that I shall give him shall never thirst; but the water that I shall give him shall be in him** *[see John 14:17 on the promise of the Spirit]* **a well of water springing up into everlasting life."** *[See Romans 8:9-11.]*

Read also John 14:23-26. The Father sends the Holy Spirit, represented by the "River of Life" proceeding from the Father's throne.

Isaiah 41:17, 18:

17) "When the poor and needy **seek water,** and there is none, and their tongue faileth for thirst, I the LORD will hear them, I the God of Israel will not forsake them.

18) "**I will open rivers in high places,** and fountains in the midst of the valleys: I will make the wilderness a pool of water, and the dry land springs of water."

Isaiah 44:3:

"For I will pour water upon him that is thirsty, and floods upon the dry ground: **I will pour my Spirit** upon thy seed, and my blessing upon thine offspring."

Psalm 36:7-9:

7) "How excellent is thy lovingkindness, O God! Therefore the children of men put their trust under the shadow of thy wings.

8) They shall be abundantly satisfied with the fatness of thy house; **and thou shalt make them drink of the river of thy pleasures.**

9) **For with thee [is] the fountain of life...."**

Isaiah 55:1:

"Ho, every one that thirsteth, **come ye to the waters,** and he that hath no money; come ye, buy, and eat; yea, come, buy wine and milk without money and without price."

Revelation 22:17:

"And the Spirit and the bride say, Come. And let him that heareth say, Come. And let him that is athirst come. And whosoever will, **let him take the water of life freely."**

Psalm 1:1-3:
1) "Blessed is the man that walketh not in the counsel of the ungodly, nor standeth in the way of sinners, nor sitteth in the seat of the scornful.

2) But his delight is in the law of the LORD; and in his law doth he meditate day and night.

3) **And he shall be like a tree planted by the rivers of water** *[just like Jesus]*, **that bringeth forth his fruit in his season; his leaf also shall not wither;** and whatsoever he doeth shall prosper...."

Jesus was like that. The Tree of Life represents Him. He wants us to be like Him.

SDA Bible Commentary, Volume 7, pages 988 (R&H, 1/26/1897)
"The Tree of life is a representation of the preserving care of Christ for His children."

As He was spiritually nourished and sustained by the Holy Spirit here on earth, so through Jesus, the Holy Spirit is given to fallen man to nourish, sustain, and empower him, uniting humanity with Holy Spirit divinity. Men become like Jesus and become "Trees in the garden of God" (Great Controversy page 601.2) who through the "Living Water" are enabled to bear good fruit.

Selected Messages Book 2, page 187:
"God accepts the services of those only who are **partakers of the divine nature.** Without Christ man can do nothing. Love for God and man alone places human beings on vantage ground with God. Obedience to the divine command enables us to become laborers together with God. Love is the fruit that is borne on the Christian tree, the fruit that is as the leaves of **the tree of life** for the healing of the nations."

'Love' was the 'Fruit' borne by the cross. Loving, Christ-like 'fruit', borne by a disciple, influences others to examine the Word: the pages of Scripture are the leaves of that Tree. The leaves of the tree of life, nourished by the Living Waters, are the words of Jesus, by which men may live:

John 6:63:
"It is the spirit that quickeneth; the flesh profiteth nothing: **the words that I speak unto you, they are spirit, and they are life.**"

The Life of the Tree of Life is in its fruit: (the righteousness of Christ), the fruit that the redeemed will eat and which will cause them to live forever. Jesus gives us His righteous Life.

Revelation 2:7:
"He that hath an ear, let him hear what the Spirit saith unto the churches; To him that overcometh **will I give to eat of the tree of life,** which is in the midst of the paradise of God."

Even now we may eat of the leaves. They are for the "healing of the nations" (Rev. 22:2). They are for the healing of our spiritual backslidings:

SDA Bible Commentary, Volume 7, page 957:
"[Revelation 2:7 quoted.] Must we wait until we are translated before we eat of **the leaves of the tree of life**? He who receives into his heart **the words of Christ** knows what it means to eat the **leaves** of the tree of life. [John 6:33-63 quoted.]"

Evangelism, page 138 (Letter 17, 1902):
"The Word of God is our sanctification and righteousness, because it is spiritual food. **To study it is to eat the leaves of the tree of life.**"

The "Word of God" is turgid with the presence of the Holy Spirit: the "Living Water," found in every "leaf" and 'fruit' borne by that precious "tree".

Chapter 18

All Manner of … Blasphemy

PROFESSOR: William, let us read the following Scripture:

Matthew 12: 22-32:
22) "Then was brought unto him one possessed with a devil, blind, and dumb: and he healed him, insomuch that the blind and dumb both spake and saw.

23) And all the people were amazed, and said, Is not this the son of David?

24) But when the Pharisees heard [it], they said, This [fellow] doth not cast out devils, but by Beelzebub the prince of the devils.

25) And Jesus knew their thoughts, and said unto them, Every kingdom divided against itself is brought to desolation; and every city or house divided against itself shall not stand:

26) And if Satan cast out Satan, he is divided against himself; how shall then his kingdom stand?

27) And if I by Beelzebub cast out devils, by whom do your children cast [them] out? therefore they shall be your judges.

28) **But if I cast out devils by the Spirit of God, then the kingdom of God is come unto you.**

29) Or else how can one enter into a strong man's house, and spoil his goods, except he first bind the strong man? and then he will spoil his house.

30) He that is not with me is against me; and he that gathereth not with me scattereth abroad.

31) Wherefore I say unto you, **All manner of sin and blasphemy shall be forgiven unto men: but <u>the blasphemy [against] the [Holy] Ghost shall not be forgiven unto men.</u>**

32) **And whosoever speaketh a word against the Son of man, it shall be forgiven him: but <u>whosoever speaketh against the Holy Ghost, it shall not be forgiven him, neither in this world, neither in the [world] to come.</u>**"

Since it is not possible to blaspheme an abstraction; a power; an 'emanation', the above statement by Jesus unequivocally endorses the

Deity and Personhood of the Holy Spirit, whilst at the same time underscoring the essential uniqueness of the Holy Spirit's function within the Godhead. He is that Member of the Godhead who convicts us both of our sin and of our need. He is the One who guides us into 'all truth' and who acquaints us with our Saviour and our Heavenly Father. Drive Him from us and we can never know our true condition or 'the Way, the Truth and the Life'. **To relegate the Holy Spirit to being a mere perceptual abstraction is a serious denigration of His Being.** Such an approach is to skate on the thinnest theological ice.

WILLIAM: Why is the Holy Spirit sometimes referred to, in Scripture, by the pronoun "it"?

PROFESSOR: Much 'ado about nothing' is made of the use of pronouns found in both the Biblical and Spirit of Prophecy references to the Holy Spirit. It is spiritual myopia that fosters a failure to recognize the Holy Spirit's Personhood simply because the Holy Spirit is sometimes referred to by the pronoun 'it' instead of the pronoun "He". That does NOT negate His 'Personhood'! The deployment of the pronoun 'it' simply reflects the fact that, in the English language, the term 'Spirit' connotes an intangible, unmeasurable, sexless though not necessarily genderless state of being that is essentially beyond the scope of our comprehension. Have you not noticed that the term 'evil spirit' engenders the same response when deploying pronouns? In speaking or writing of an 'evil spirit' we would readily say or write that: "It plagued it's victims", yet never even begin to consider 'it' to be an **'emanation'** of Satan's power, a demonic "afflatus", but would unambiguously understand 'it' to be an 'evil spirit' in its own right. The whole argument surrounding the intermittent use in Scripture of the pronoun 'it', when referencing the Holy Spirit, and the attempt to extrapolate from such usage that this signifies the Holy Spirit is simply an 'emanation' of God's and Christ's power, is patently ludicrous and totally unwarranted, not to mention spiritually dangerous.

You will recall that in 1888 it was men like Uriah Smith (who described the Holy Spirit as the "divine afflatus") who did not acknowledge the Personhood of the Holy Spirit and rejected the light He brought at that time. They were foremost in rejecting the message of "Righteousness by Faith" presented by brethren Waggoner and Jones and, in consequence; God's people have had to remain in this sinful world "many more years". Could there be a link between their spiritual myopia (their inability to apprehend the truths presented at the Minneapolis meeting—truths resoundingly endorsed by God's messenger) and their relegation of the Holy Spirit to being a mere 'emanation'? The precipitous landslide into Laodiceanism, the 'creeping compromise', the encroaching corruption and the drowsy indifference to truth and righteousness current among God's professed people are all largely attributable to what occurred at that fulcrum-point of faith. We must never forget that God has told us through His messenger that **"error NEVER sanctifies"**:

> *Review and Herald, August 23, 1898 par. 2:*
> "Each may have heaven's light to guide him. If we discern the truth, and obey it, our whole course of action will be in accordance with the truth; **for the truth sanctifies** the receiver. But if men refuse to search for the truth as for hidden treasure, **if the mind is pleased with the theories of error, the soul will remain in darkness.** The course of the life, the development of the character, will be corrupted by false sentiments. **Error never sanctifies. It can do no good. And how full of darkness is the soul that receives error as truth, and shapes his course of action in accordance with it.**"

I believe that what has transpired among God's denominated people is a sad confirmation of this **invariable truth** about 'error'.

Those who would revive the 'Arianism' and those faulty perceptions (about the Godhead) held by Uriah Smith and some other early Adventist leaders, and who maintain that the declarations about the presence of the Holy Spirit are simply an alternative way of stating that it is God the Father who is personally present, fail to recognize the Biblical truth that God the Father **CANNOT**, personally, come and be present with sinners without destroying them by His presence.

From the following statement by God's messenger, who was in vision at the time, we find that Christ warned her that for her to even see the glory of God's person, in vision let alone in person, would cause her to cease to be:

> Early Writings, page 54.2:
> "I saw a throne, and on it sat the Father and the Son. I gazed on Jesus' countenance and admired His lovely person. The Father's person I could not behold, for a cloud of glorious light covered Him. I asked Jesus if His Father had a form like Himself. He said He had, but I could not behold it, for said He, 'If you should once behold the glory of His person, you would cease to exist.'"

In their booklet <u>Putting the Pieces Together</u> Coming Home Publishers of Alabama strive to present and uphold the 'two Person Godhead' position, as well as the notion that the Holy Spirit is not a separate and distinct Being in His own right.

After quoting what God's messenger presented as found in:

<u>Evangelism</u>, pages 616-617:
"The Holy Spirit is a person, for He beareth witness with our spirits that we are the children of God. When this witness is borne, it carries with it its own evidence. At such times we believe and are sure that we are the children of God. . .

The Holy Spirit has a personality, else He could not bear witness to our spirits and with our spirits that we are the children of God. He must also be a divine person, else He could not search out the secrets which lie hidden in the mind of God. "For what man knoweth the things of a man, save the spirit of man which is in him? even so the things of God knoweth no man, but the Spirit of God." *[1 Corinthians 2:11]*--Manuscript 20, 1906.

They then go on to say:

<u>Putting the Pieces Together</u>, page 18:
"The quoted verse (1 Corinthians 2:11) is the key to understanding the statement. According to Paul man and his spirit is comparable to God and His Spirit. **Just as man's spirit is not a different person to man, even so God's Holy Spirit is not a different person to God. <u>Just as man's spirit is his very own person, even so God's Spirit is His very own person.</u>**"
[Emphasis: mine]

(They clearly have a very weird concept concerning man's "spirit". See Chapter 32 on "The Spirit of a Man" in <u>The Truth and the Trident</u>)

What the writer/s of <u>Putting the Pieces Together</u> do not quote from Evangelism page 616 is the statement which immediately precedes the statement which they do quote:

<u>Evangelism</u>, page 616.5:
"We need to realize that **the Holy Spirit, who is as much a person as God is a person,** is walking through these grounds."--

236

Manuscript 66, 1899. (From a talk to the students at the Avondale School.)

This statement unassailably declares God and the Holy Spirit to each be a Person in their own right. This overthrows the notion that the Holy Spirit is God's "very own person".

The writer/s of <u>Putting the Pieces Together</u> quote from <u>7T</u> page 273.1:

"In giving us **His Spirit**, God gives us **Himself**, making **Himself** a fountain of **divine influences**, to give health and life to the world." (Emphasis theirs)

Clearly the compiler/s//writer/s of <u>Putting the Pieces Together</u> fail to grasp the significance of those other inspired statements by God's messenger which state:

<u>Christian Service</u>, page 255.3:
"Cumbered with humanity, **Christ could not be in every place <u>personally</u>. Therefore it was for their interest that He should go to the Father, and <u>send</u> the Spirit to be His successor on earth.** No one could then have any advantage because of his location or his personal contact with Christ. By the Spirit the Saviour would be accessible to all. In this sense He would be nearer to them than if He had not ascended on high."-- The Desire of Ages, p. 669.

<u>Life Sketches</u>, page 472.3:
"**The Holy Spirit, Christ's <u>representative</u> on earth**, is set forth and exalted as **the heavenly teacher and guide <u>sent</u> to this world <u>by</u> our Lord** at His ascension,…"
With regards to the Father, we read:

<u>Ministry of Healing</u>, page 417.2, 3:
"<u>**The Bible shows us God in His high and holy place**</u>, not in a state of inactivity, not in silence and solitude, but surrounded by ten thousand times ten thousand and thousands of thousands of holy beings, all waiting to do His will. Through these messengers He is in active communication with every part of His dominion. By His Spirit He is everywhere present. **Through the**

agency of **His Spirit** and **His angels** He ministers to the children of men.

"**Above the distractions of the earth He sits enthroned**; all things are open to His divine survey; and from His great and calm eternity He orders that which His providence sees best."

If the angels of God, as separate and distinct beings, minister to His creation alongside and in conjunction with the Holy Spirit, while God is in His "high and holy place"; this fact TOTALLY REFUTES the notion that the Holy Spirit's presence is God the Father's personal presence.

To postulate that the 'Holy Spirit' is but an extension of God's own Being, as a proposition, differs not a 'jot' or a 'tittle' from the equally egregious notion put forward by Trinitarian doctrine that 'God' oozes forth in different manifestations or "modalities" of 'Himself': each "modality" having a different name, in this case the name being the 'Holy Spirit'.

To postulate that the 'Christ', at some point in infinity, was, by the 'Father' Himself, 'torn from the bosom of the Father' to become the Second 'Person' of the Godhead, as a notion, differs not a wit from the speculations of Trinitarianism which mandate that, in order to be saved, one must believe that the 'Son' was "begotten" of the 'Father's' own substance at some point in infinity.

At the **Council of Rome,** (Tome of Damasus), Canon 11, **AD 382** it was declared: "If anyone does not say that the Son was begotten of the Father, that is, of **the Divine substance of Him Himself, he is a heretic.**"

It was stated in the **Athanasian Creed (ca. AD 475)** that: "The Father is not made nor created nor begotten by anyone. The Son from the Father alone, not made or created but begotten... **Let him who wishes to be saved, think thus concerning the Trinity.** But it is necessary for eternal salvation that he faithfully believe also in the incarnation of Our Lord Jesus Christ. Accordingly, it is the right faith, that we believe and confess that our Lord Jesus Christ, the Son of God, is God and man. **He is God begotten of the substance of the Father before time, and he is man born of the substance of His mother in time. This is the Catholic faith. Unless everyone believes this faithfully and firmly, he cannot be saved." This actually teaches what they accused Arius of teaching; namely that Jesus had a beginning!**

My Catholic Faith, page 31:
    "2. God the Father, seeing His own Image in the Son, *loves* the Son; and God the Son loves the Father from all eternity.

Each loves the other, because each sees in the other the Infinity of the Godhead, the beauty of Divinity, the Supreme Truth of God. The two Persons loving each other do not just have a thought, as human beings would have, but **from Their mutual love is breathed forth, as it were, a Living Person, one with Them, and of Their own substance. This is God the Holy Ghost.** Thus the Holy Ghost, the Spirit of Love, 'proceeds' from the Father and the Son....

"3. But we are *not to suppose* that once God the Father begot the Son and now no longer does so, nor that once the love of the Father and the Son for each other breathed forth the Holy Ghost, but now no longer does. These truths are eternal, everlasting".

"God the Father **eternally knows Himself, and continues to know Himself,** and thus continues to bring forth the Son. **God the Father and God the Son continue to love each other, and their delight in each other continues to bring forth the Spirit of Love, God the Holy Ghost.**

The weird thing about these 'theses' is that they both demonstrate that neither Trinitarianism nor so called 'Arianism' differ by a whisker from each other in making the 'members' of their concept of 'God' to be "consubstantial": i.e. of not being distinct "SELF-EXISTENT" Beings, each in their own right.

Through His messenger, **God has given us clear and distinct instruction as to how we should approach an understanding of His written word:**

Bible Training School, December 1, 1905 par. 3:
    "**Let us receive the precious words of God just as they read. Let us not cover them up with human suppositions.** The Word is ours to comprehend. Let us have faith in God."

Following this counsel, let us now read the following Scriptures concerning the Holy Spirit:

Luke 12:12:
    "For **the Holy Ghost shall teach you** in the same hour what ye ought to say." *[He teaches]*

Acts 1:16:

"Men [and] brethren, this scripture must needs have been fulfilled, **which the Holy Ghost by the mouth of David <u>spake</u>** before concerning Judas, which was guide to them that took Jesus." *[He communicates through agencies]*

Acts 5:3, 32:

3) "But Peter said, Ananias, **why hath Satan filled thine heart to <u>lie to the Holy Ghost</u>**, and to keep back [part] of the price of the land?

32) And **we are his witnesses** of these things; and **<u>[so is]</u> <u>also</u> the Holy Ghost, whom <u>God hath given</u>** to them that obey him." *[He can be lied to and He Himself is "given" just as Jesus was "given" by the Father]*

Acts 13:1, 2, 4:

1) "Now there were in the church that was at Antioch certain prophets and teachers; as Barnabas, and Simeon that was called Niger, and Lucius of Cyrene, and Manaen, which had been brought up with Herod the tetrarch, and Saul.

2) As they ministered to the Lord, and fasted, **the Holy Ghost <u>said</u>**, Separate me Barnabas and Saul for the work whereunto I have called them.

4) So they, being <u>**sent** </u>**forth by the Holy Ghost**, departed unto Seleucia; and from thence they sailed to Cyprus." *[He speaks to God's people and sends them on missions]*

Acts 15:28:

"For it <u>**seemed good to the Holy Ghost**</u>, and to us, to lay upon you no greater burden than these necessary things;" *[He has an opinion]*

Acts 16:6:

"Now when they had gone throughout Phrygia and the region of Galatia, and **were <u>forbidden</u> of the Holy Ghost to preach** the word in Asia," *[He forbids]*

Acts 21:11:

"And when he was come unto us, he took Paul's girdle, and bound his own hands and feet, and said, **Thus <u>saith</u> the Holy Ghost**, So shall the Jews at Jerusalem bind the man that owneth

240

this girdle, and shall deliver [him] into the hands of the Gentiles." *[He declares the future]*

Acts 28:25:
"And when they agreed not among themselves, they departed, after that Paul had spoken one word, **Well spake the Holy Ghost by Esaias** the prophet unto our fathers," *[He speaks]*

1 Corinthians 2:13:
"Which things also we speak, not in the words which man's wisdom teacheth, but which **the Holy Ghost teacheth**; comparing spiritual things with spiritual." *[He teaches]*

Hebrews 3:7:
"Wherefore (**as the Holy Ghost saith**, To day if ye will hear his voice," *[He admonishes]*

Hebrews 10:15:
"[Whereof] the Holy Ghost also is a **witness** to us: for after that he had said before," *[He is a witness]*

As we can clearly see, **when applying the principle given in *Bible Training School*, December 1, 1905 par. 3 to receive "The precious words of God just as they read", the attributes of the Holy Spirit displayed in the aforegoing Scriptures clearly depict a separate and distinct Entity whom God and Christ "send" and who displays the attributes of separate and distinct Personhood. If Paul meant to say 'God' or 'Christ' there is no earthly reason why he should not have done so UNLESS he perceived and understood the Holy Spirit to be, as God's servant expressed it, the mighty third Person of the Godhead; which Paul clearly did.**

God's messenger is clear and unambiguous also:

Desire of Ages, page 671.2-4:
"**In describing to His disciples the office work of the Holy Spirit**, Jesus sought to inspire them with the joy and hope that inspired His own heart. He rejoiced because of the abundant help He had provided for His church. **The Holy Spirit was the highest of all gifts that He could solicit from His Father for the exaltation of His people.** The Spirit was to be **given as a regenerating agent**, and without this the sacrifice of Christ

241

would have been of no avail. The power of evil had been strengthening for centuries, and the submission of men to this satanic captivity was amazing. **Sin could be resisted and overcome only through the <u>mighty agency of the THIRD PERSON of the Godhead</u>**, who would come with no modified energy, but in the fullness of divine power. It is the Spirit that makes effectual what has been wrought out by the world's Redeemer. It is by the Spirit that the heart is made pure. Through the Spirit the believer becomes a partaker of the divine nature. Christ has given His Spirit as a divine power to overcome all hereditary and cultivated tendencies to evil, and to impress His own character upon His church.

"**Of the <u>Spirit</u> Jesus said, "<u>HE</u> shall glorify Me.**" The Saviour came to glorify the Father by the demonstration of His love; so the Spirit was to glorify Christ by revealing His grace to the world. The very image of God is to be reproduced in humanity. The honor of God, the honor of Christ, is involved in the perfection of the character of His people.

"**When HE [the Spirit of truth] is come, HE will reprove the world of sin, and of righteousness, and of judgment.**" The preaching of the word will be of **no avail without the continual presence and aid of the Holy Spirit.** This is the only effectual teacher of divine truth. **Only when the truth is accompanied to the heart by the Spirit will it quicken the conscience or transform the life.** One might be able to present the letter of the word of God, he might be familiar with all its commands and promises; but **unless the <u>Holy Spirit sets home the truth</u>, no souls will fall on the Rock and be broken. No amount of education, no advantages, however great, can make one a channel of light without the <u>co-operation of the Spirit of God.</u> …**"

This is plain speech about a PERSON, not personification of an 'IT'!

Finally, Paul warns us in:

Ephesians 4:29, 30:

29) "Let no corrupt communication proceed out of your mouth, but that which is good to the use of edifying, that it may minister grace unto the hearers.

242

30)   And <u>grieve not the holy Spirit of God</u>, whereby ye are sealed unto the day of redemption."

Chapter 19

THE ROLE OF THE HOLY SPIRIT IN THE PLAN OF SALVATION

PROFESSOR: Today I would like to talk about the role of the Holy Spirit in the plan of salvation.

WILLIAM: I notice that there are over 30 pages of references to the Holy Spirit in the Index to the Writings of E.G. White!

PROFESSOR: In the Bible, too, we find that Jesus spoke more of the Holy Spirit than any other topic. Let's look at some of these references in the Spirit of Prophecy:

> Acts of the Apostles, pages 51, 52:
> **"It is not essential for us to be able to define just what the Holy Spirit is.** Christ tells us that the Spirit is the Comforter, 'the Spirit of truth, which proceedeth **from** the Father.' It is plainly declared regarding the Holy Spirit that, in His work of guiding men into all truth, **'He shall not speak of Himself.'** **John 15:26; 16:13**
> "The <u>nature</u> of the Holy Spirit is a mystery. Men cannot explain it *[the 'nature' of the Holy Spirit]*, because the Lord has not revealed it to them. Men having fanciful views may bring together passages of Scripture and put a human construction on them, but the acceptance of these views will not strengthen the church. **Regarding such mysteries, which are too deep for human understanding, silence is golden."**

WILLIAM: I noticed that she used the term "nature" indicating that the Holy Spirit is a living Being.

PROFESSOR: Energy, or power, as an entity, has "properties," not a "nature." Only living beings have a "nature" in the way described by God's messenger, and she confirms this:

> Evangelism, page 616 (MS66, 1899):

"We need to realize that **the Holy Spirit, who is as much a person** as God is a person, is walking through these grounds.-- Manuscript 66, 1899. (From a talk to the students at the Avondale School.)

"**The Holy Spirit is a person,** for He beareth witness with our spirits that we are the children of God. When this witness is borne, it carries with it its own evidence. At such times we believe and are sure that we are the children of God...."

Faith I Live By, page 52:

"**The Holy Spirit has a personality, else He could not bear witness to our spirits and with our spirits that we are the children of God. He must also be a divine person, else He could not search out the secrets which lie hidden in the mind of God.**

"**The Holy Spirit is a free, working, independent agency.** The God of heaven uses His Spirit as it pleases Him; and human minds, human judgment, and human methods can no more set boundaries to its working, or prescribe the channel through which it shall operate, than they can say to the wind, 'I bid you to blow in a certain direction, and to conduct yourself in such and such a manner.'

"From the beginning God has been working by His Holy Spirit through human instrumentalities for the accomplishment of His purpose in behalf of the fallen race.... The same power that sustained the patriarchs, that gave Caleb and Joshua faith and courage, and that made the work of the apostolic church effective, has upheld God's faithful children in every succeeding age. *[Notice next the Holy Spirit's essential role in the plan of salvation:]*

"The Holy Spirit was the highest of all gifts that He *[Jesus]* could solicit from His Father for the exaltation of His people. **The Spirit was to be given as a regenerating agent, and without this the sacrifice of Christ would have been of no avail.** The power of evil had been strengthening for centuries, and the submission of men to this satanic captivity was amazing. **Sin could be resisted and overcome only through the mighty agency of the third person of the Godhead,** who would come with no modified energy, **but in the fullness of divine power.**"

Is it not an anomaly that we believe that a man can be demon possessed, that is, controlled by a distinct, personal demonic spirit-being, and yet some refuse to acknowledge the Holy Spirit—who should dwell in them—as a distinct, personal Spirit-Being?

1 Corinthians 6:19:

"What? know ye not that your body is the **temple** of the Holy Ghost [which is] in you, which ye have of God, and ye are not your own?"

Notice the things that He does for us:

Desire of Age, pages 671, 672:

"**The Comforter** is called "the Spirit of truth." **His work** is to define and maintain the truth. **He** first dwells in the heart as the Spirit of truth, **and thus He becomes the Comforter.** There is comfort and peace in the truth, but no real peace or comfort can be found in falsehood. It is through false theories and traditions that Satan gains his power over the mind *[false theories like the trinity]*. By directing men to false standards, he misshapes the character. **Through the Scriptures the Holy Spirit speaks to the mind, and impresses truth upon the heart. Thus He exposes error, and expels it from the soul.** It is by *[through the agency of]* the Spirit of truth, working through the word of God, that Christ subdues His chosen people to Himself.

"In describing to His disciples **the office work of the Holy Spirit**, Jesus sought to inspire them with the joy and hope that inspired His own heart. He rejoiced because of the abundant help He had provided for His church. **The Holy Spirit was the highest of all gifts that He could solicit from His Father** for the exaltation of His people. **The Spirit was to be given as a regenerating agent, and without this the sacrifice of Christ would have been of no avail.** The power of evil had been strengthening for centuries, and the submission of men to this satanic captivity was amazing. **Sin could be resisted and overcome only through the mighty agency of the Third Person** of the Godhead, who would come with no modified energy, but in the fullness of divine power *["in the fullness of the Godhead" (Acts of the Apostles pg. 49.3; Evangelism pg. 615.1)]*. **It is the Spirit that makes effectual what has been**

wrought out by the world's Redeemer. It is by the Spirit that the heart is made pure. Through the Spirit the believer becomes a partaker of the divine nature. Christ has given His Spirit as a divine power to overcome all hereditary and cultivated tendencies to evil, and to impress His own character upon His church.

"Of the Spirit Jesus said, **"He shall glorify Me."** The Saviour came to glorify the Father by the demonstration of His love; so the Spirit was to glorify Christ by revealing His grace to the world.** The very image of God is to be reproduced in humanity. The honor of God, the honor of Christ, is involved in the perfection of the character of His people.

"When He /the Spirit of truth/ is come, **He will reprove the world of sin, and of righteousness, and of judgment."** The preaching of the word will be of no avail without the continual presence and aid of the Holy Spirit. This is the only effectual teacher of divine truth. Only when the truth is accompanied to the heart by the Spirit will it quicken the conscience or transform the life.** One might be able to present the letter of the word of God, he might be familiar with all its commands and promises; but **unless the Holy Spirit sets home the truth, no souls will fall on the Rock and be broken."**

WILLIAM: I like that thought: **"It is the Spirit that makes effectual what has been wrought out by the world's Redeemer."** It shows that we need both Jesus and the Holy Spirit, and that we need the Holy Spirit in order to be like Jesus.

PROFESSOR: In fact, William, Jesus, as a man here on Earth, needed the Holy Spirit to empower Him to be like His Father.

Desire of Ages, page 675:
"So Christ **in His humanity was dependent upon divine power.** 'I can of Mine own self do nothing,' He declared. John 5:30."

Now that Jesus is ascended, He sends the Holy Spirit to us to empower us to be like Him:

Desire of Ages, page 668:

"The Holy Spirit is Christ's **representative,** but **divested** *[As we have noted, this is an interesting term!]* of the personality of humanity, and independent thereof. *[On the other hand]* Cumbered with humanity, **Christ could not be in every place PERSONALLY.** *[This statement clearly and unequivocally distinguishes between Christ and the Holy Spirit as two and distinctly separate Beings.]* Therefore it was for their *[the disciples']* interest that He should go to the Father, and **send the Spirit to be His SUCCESSOR** on earth. No one could then have any advantage because of his location or his **personal** contact with Christ. By the Spirit the Saviour would be **accessible** to all. *[Because the Spirit inhabits both Christ and His faithful people, the contact with Jesus is through the Holy Spirit who is the denominator common to Christ, His true followers, and to the Father—making all "one" in character, mind, and purpose.]* In this sense He would be nearer to them than if He had not ascended on high."

WILLIAM: Tell again why do you think that the word "divested" is interesting?

PROFESSOR: Because that means that the Holy Spirit once employed, or bore, that which he was "divested" of.

Jesus, on the other hand, bears humanity forever:

Lift Him Up, page 243:
"Jesus is 'not ashamed to call them brethren' (Hebrews 2:11); He is our Sacrifice, our Advocate, our Brother, **bearing our human form before the Father's throne, and through eternal ages ONE with the race He has redeemed--the Son of man.**"

He shares one humanity with us so that we can share one Spirit with Him. Jesus' humanity now is that which the redeemed will one day receive—glorified humanity. His transformation from the last images of Him seen at the crucifixion, by His disciples, was so marked that:

Desire of Ages, page 829:
"After His resurrection He tarried on earth for a season**, that His disciples might become familiar with Him in His risen and glorified body.**"

And while the Father administers the universe and Jesus is interceding in the Most Holy Place, the Holy Spirit is their agent. Concerning the Father, we have already noted:

Ministry of Healing, p 417:
"**The Bible shows us God in His high and holy place,** not in a state of inactivity, not in silence and solitude, but surrounded by ten thousand times ten thousand and thousands of thousands of holy beings, all waiting to do His will. Through these messengers He is in active communication with every part of His dominion. **By His Spirit He is everywhere present. Through the agency of His Spirit and His angels He ministers to the children of men.**"

Concerning Christ, we also note:

Desire of Ages, page 668:
"Cumbered with humanity, Christ could not be in every place personally. Therefore it was for their interest that He should go to the Father, and **send the Spirit to be His successor** on earth *[not the pope]*. No one could then have any advantage because of his location or his **personal** contact with Christ. **By the Spirit the Saviour would be accessible to all.** In this sense He would be nearer to them than if He had not ascended on high."

So near in fact, that repentant sinners who choose the path of obedience, thereby demonstrating their love for Jesus and the Father, could actually receive the indwelling Presence of the Comforter, making them **"one Spirit"** with Christ and the Father:

1 Corinthians 6:17:
"But he that is joined unto the Lord is **one spirit.**"

1 Corinthians 12:13:
"For by **one Spirit** are we all baptized into one body, whether we be Jews or Gentiles, whether we be bond or free; **and have been all made to drink into <u>one Spirit</u>.**"

Ephesians 2:18:

"For through him we both have access **by one Spirit** UNTO the Father."

Ephesians 4:4:
"There is one body, and **one Spirit,** even as ye are called in one hope of your calling;"

Philippians 1:27:
"Only let your conversation be as it becometh the gospel of Christ: that whether I come and see you, or else be absent, I may hear of your affairs, that ye stand fast **in one spirit,** with one mind striving together for the faith of the gospel."

I want you to pay close attention to what God's messenger tells us in:

Manuscript Releases, Volume 8, page 292.1-2:
"**The prayer of Christ is for all who acknowledge that they are His people, <u>denominated to be loyal and true to all the light that Christ has given them</u>.** He FIRST prays for **their purity**, and NEXT He prays for **their unity**. The wisdom from above is first pure, then peaceable, then easy to be entreated by the invitation of the Holy Spirit, which Christ's true disciples shall receive in large measure, because they are assimilated to His image--partakers of the divine nature. . . .

"But **shall not this prayer be answered by those who claim to believe the truth? <u>Those who are truly joined to the Lord are controlled by ONE SPIRIT.</u> They are stamped with the same image and superscription, and they give evidence that they are influenced by the same power,** because they are joined to the Lord by the infinite Sacrifice made by Christ, that they might be **knit together through the sanctification of the truth**, in the bonds of love, perfect, heavenborn love. They have exchanged the heart of selfishness and sin for the heart that God gives. They are partakers of the divine nature. They may differ in speech and attitude, but **they are guided <u>by the same Spirit</u>**. No vainglory, no independent "I" *[independent of God's Spirit]* comes in to take possession. **The quarrelsome** *[satanic, carnal]* **spirit ceases**, and the world is given evidence of the power of true conversion.--Ms 29, 1906, page 5, 8. ("That They All May Be One," March 8, 1906.)"

In the times that we live in the following statement by God's messenger holds special significance:

Evangelism, page 617:
"**The prince of the power of evil can only be held in check by the power of God in the third PERSON of the Godhead, the Holy Spirit.--Special Testimonies, Series A, No. 10, page 37. (1897)**"

Chapter 20

GOD COMMUNICATES WITH MAN THROUGH CHRIST, THE HOLY SPIRIT, AND ANGELS

WILLIAM: Professor, we know that we do not communicate directly with God the Father, but our prayers, indited by the Holy Spirit, are offered up to the Father through Christ, our Mediator.

PROFESSOR: Remember the words of the hymn, *To God be the Glory,* which says, "Oh come to the Father **through** Jesus the Son"? Inspiration is clear on how we get access to God:

GOD COMMUNICATES WITH US THROUGH JESUS

John 14:6:
"No man cometh unto the Father, but by me."

John 1:50, 51:
50) "Jesus answered and said unto him, Because I said unto thee, I saw thee under the fig tree, believest thou? thou shalt see greater things than these.
51)   And he saith unto him, Verily, verily, I say unto you, Hereafter ye shall see heaven open, and **the angels of God ascending and descending upon the Son of man.**"

Jesus is the ladder Jacob saw in his dream, linking the throne of God with the dust that we are made from (Genesis 28:12). Jesus is the divine intermediary:

1 Timothy 2:5:
"For there is **one God**, and **one mediator between God and men**, the man Christ Jesus."

Hebrews 1:1-3:
1) "**God,** who at sundry times and in divers manners spake in time past unto the fathers by the prophets,

2) **Hath in these last days spoken unto us by his Son,** whom he hath appointed heir of all things, by whom also he made the worlds;

3) Who being the brightness of his glory, and the express image of his person, and upholding all things by the word of his power, when he had by himself purged our sins, sat down **on the right hand of the Majesty on high**."

Jesus enlightens us and dispels the moral darkness:

John 1:9, 10:
9) "That was **the true Light, which lighteth every man that cometh into the world.**

10) He was in the world, and the world was made by him, and the world knew him not."

Jesus communicated the thought and will, and words of God to us:

John 14:10:
"Believest thou not that I am **in** the Father, and the Father **in** me? **the words that I speak unto you I speak not of myself: but the Father that dwelleth in me, he doeth the works.** *[How does the Father dwell in Jesus? By the same "spirit of God" and "Spirit of Christ," (Romans 8:9)—the Holy Spirit—Who can also dwell in us.]*"

John 14:24:
"He that loveth me not keepeth not **my sayings**: and **the word which ye hear is not mine, but the Father's which sent me.**"

In this verse we see that Jesus spoke God's own words; the Holy Spirit inspires men with God's own thoughts.

GOD COMMUNICATES WITH MAN THROUGH THE HOLY SPIRIT

Isaiah 30:21:
"**And thine ears shall hear a word behind thee,** saying, This is the way, walk ye in it, when ye turn to the right hand, and when ye turn to the left."

253

This is not audible. This is thought communication!

God's Amazing Grace, page 190:
"**Before the entrance of sin, Adam enjoyed open communion with his Maker; but since man separated himself from God by transgression, the human race has been cut off from this high privilege.** By the plan of redemption, however, a way has been opened whereby the inhabitants of the earth may still have connection with heaven. **God has communicated with men by His Spirit, and divine light has been imparted to the world by revelations to His chosen servants.**"

Desire of Ages, page 322:
"**It is by the Spirit that God works upon the heart**; when men willfully reject the Spirit, and declare It to be from Satan, **they cut off the channel by which God can communicate with them.**"

The Holy Spirit infused Christ with Divine Power because Jesus had laid His aside when He took humanity upon Himself. Jesus Himself makes that plain:

Matthew 12:28:
"**But if I cast out devils by the Spirit of God, then the kingdom of God is come unto you.**"

Matthew 9:34:
"But the Pharisees said, **He casteth out devils through the prince of the devils.**"

They did not "know" the only true God or Jesus Christ Whom He had sent. They were grieving away His Spirit, who alone could make them "one" with God.

Desire of Ages, pages 321,322:
"Christ told them plainly that in attributing **the work of the Holy Spirit** to Satan, they were cutting themselves off from the fountain of blessing *[living water = Holy Spirit]*."

Jesus still acts through the Holy Spirit:

God's Amazing Grace, page 196:
  "**The Lord Jesus acts through the Holy Spirit; for it is His representative.**"

God and Christ acted through the Holy Spirit, even before the incarnation:

2 Peter 1:21:
  "For the prophecy came not in old time by the will of man: but **holy men of God spake as they were moved by the Holy Ghost.**"

All gifts of the Spirit prior to Christ's victory on the cross were conditional; conditional on Christ's paying the penalty for sin after having triumphed over sin. Post cavalry, mankind now lives under the "new covenant" which is based on "better promises" (Hebrews 8:6). The promise of salvation is now secured, the penalty has been met, Satan is vanquished, the only imponderable left is how we decide and choose. God's covenant is founded on the Rock, Christ Jesus: our mighty and victorious Saviour.

THE HEAVENLY ANGELS WORK WITH THE HOLY SPIRIT

Revelation 1:1, 2:
  1) "The Revelation of Jesus Christ, which God gave unto him, to shew unto his servants things which must shortly come to pass; and **he sent and signified it by his angel unto his servant John:**
  2)   Who bare record of the word of God, and of the testimony of Jesus Christ, and of all things that he saw."

Hebrews 1:13, 14:
  13) "But to which of **the angels** said he at any time, Sit on my right hand, until I make thine enemies thy footstool?
  14)   Are they not all **ministering spirits, sent forth to minister for them who shall be heirs of salvation?**"

Acts 7:53:
  "Who have received the law by the **disposition of angels,** and have not kept *it*".

255

Selected Messages Book 1, page 96:

"We have an Advocate pleading in our behalf. **The Holy Ghost is continually engaged in beholding our course of action.** We need now keen perception, that by our own practical godliness the truth may be made to appear truth as it is in Jesus. **The angelic agencies are messengers from heaven, actually ascending and descending, keeping earth in constant connection with the heaven above.** These angel messengers are observing all our course of action. They are ready to help all in their weakness, guarding all from moral and physical danger according to the providence of God. **And whenever souls yield to the softening, subduing influence of the Spirit of God under these angel ministrations, there is joy in heaven;** the Lord Himself rejoices with singing."

GOD COMMUNICATES WITH US THROUGH HEAVENLY ANGELS

We have already looked at Ministry of Healing, page 417 about how God ministers to man by His Holy Spirit and His holy angels (see pages 183, 223, 237, 256, 322, 338, 417 in this book):

Luke 1:11-13:

11)   "**And there appeared unto him** *[Zacharias]* **an angel of the Lord** standing on the right side of the altar of incense.

12)   And when Zacharias saw him, he was troubled, and fear fell upon him.

13)   **But the angel said unto him,** Fear not, Zacharias: for thy prayer is heard; and thy wife Elisabeth shall bear thee a son, and thou shalt call his name John."

Luke 1:18, 19:

18)   "And **Zacharias said unto the angel,** Whereby shall I know this? for I am an old man, and my wife well stricken in years.

19)   And **the angel answering** said unto him, **I am Gabriel, that stand in the presence of God; and am <u>sent</u> to speak unto thee,** and to shew thee these glad tidings."

Luke 1:26-28:

256

26) "And in the sixth month **the angel Gabriel was** <u>sent</u> **from God** unto a city of Galilee, named Nazareth,

27) **To a virgin** espoused to a man whose name was Joseph, of the house of David; and the virgin's name was Mary.

28) **And the angel came in unto her, and said,** Hail, thou that art highly favoured, the Lord is with thee: blessed art thou among women." *[Notice: Gabriel was "**sent**", just as the Holy Spirit is "**sent**"].*

Luke 1:34, 35:

34) "Then said Mary unto the angel, How shall this be, seeing I know not a man?

35) And the angel answered and said unto her, The Holy Ghost shall come upon thee, and the power of the Highest shall overshadow thee: therefore also that holy thing which shall be born of thee shall be called the Son of God."

Luke 2:10:

"And **the angel said unto them,** Fear not: for, behold, I bring you good tidings of great joy, which shall be to all people."

Revelation 22:6:

"And **he *[the angel]* said unto me,** These sayings are faithful and true: and the Lord God of the holy prophets **sent his angel to shew unto his servants the things which must shortly be done."**

<u>In Heavenly Places</u>, page 80:

"Angels with wings outspread wait to bear their contrite prayers to God, and to register them in the books of heaven."

Review & Herald, February 1, 1912, par. 6:

"**Angels** hear the offering of praise and the prayer of faith, **and they bear the petitions to him who ministers in the sanctuary for his people,** and pleads his merits in their behalf."

<u>Christ's Object Lessons</u>, page 341, 342.

"We know not what results a day, an hour, or a moment may determine, and never should we begin the day without committing our ways to our heavenly Father. **His angels** are appointed to watch over us, and if we put ourselves under their guardianship, then in every time of danger they will be at our right hand. When unconsciously we are in danger of exerting a wrong influence, **the angels will be by our side, prompting us to a better course, choosing our words for us, and influencing our actions.**"

GOD COMMUNICATES TO OTHERS THROUGH US, IN PARTNERSHIP WITH HEAVENLY ANGELS

Desire of Ages, page 291:
"**We are to be laborers together with the heavenly angels in presenting Jesus to the world.** With almost impatient eagerness the angels wait for our co-operation; for man must be the channel to communicate with man. **And when we give ourselves to Christ in wholehearted devotion, angels rejoice that they may speak through our voices to reveal God's love.**"

JESUS CHRIST, THE HOLY SPIRIT, AND HEAVENLY ANGELS WORK TOGETHER FOR US

All that we have just looked at serves to demonstrate the lengths that God the Father, acting through His Son's mediation, has gone to in order to re-establish communication with fallen man, estranged, by sin, from direct contact with the Father. To effect this both Christ and the Holy Spirit have had to take roles and states of being that would not instantly destroy sinners. All of this communication is totally predicated upon Jesus having paid the penalty on behalf of fallen man.

The "battle" referred to by God's messenger on Selected Messages Book 3, page 426, is a battle that God's denominated people are facing. This battle has been prefigured in the history of Ancient Israel:

Selected Messages Book 3, page 426:
"All the world will be on one side or the other of the question. The battle of Armageddon will be fought. And that day must find none of us sleeping. Wide awake we must be, as wise virgins having oil in our vessels with our lamps. **The power of the Holy Ghost must be upon us and the Captain of the Lord's host will stand at the head of the angels of heaven to direct the battle.**"

We willingly accept that the angels are separate and distinct heavenly beings, yet some decide not to acknowledge that the Holy Spirit and Jesus, who work with the angels on our behalf, are separate and distinct heavenly Beings. Trinitarians definitely don't make that acknowledgement.

****

Nestled in the valley of Esdraelon, down which the river Kishon flows into the Great Sea, lies a none-too-large "tell" (mound): the site of ancient Megiddo. Indeed, the surrounding flat land along the Kishon's banks is known as the "Plain of Megiddo." Towering to the north northwest of the "tell" stands Har-Megeddon: the "Mountain of Megiddo." We know this mountain by another name. We know it as Mount Carmel! It is the mountain of decision. Here God's prophet Elijah called ancient Israel to make a decision: "How long halt ye between two opinions? If the LORD (Jehovah) be God, follow Him: but if Baal, then follow him...." (1 Kings 18:21). That day there followed a battle: a battle preceded by the devilish, dervish, foaming, slashing, prancing gesticulations of Baal's loudly vocal priests; followed, in turn, by the purposeful, focused, solemn preparations and prayers of God's prophet; followed in turn by God's fiery response, **and then came the physical slaughter**. This slaughter prefigures the destruction of all "Baal" worshippers by Christ at His second coming. The thing to note is that the **people** were confronted with a mental struggle: either to follow the false teachings of a false priesthood and worship a false god (Baal, a god of man's devising), or worship Jehovah the self-existent One. This is the battle of Har-megeddon. We know it as "Armageddon." Take note that it will be the "priests" of the Trinity: the Papacy and **all** who are in accord with this diabolical doctrine, and the Sunday Law that is predicated upon it, who will be arraigned against those who worship the Most High God of the Godhead—the CREATOR GOD of the **First, Second, and Third Angels' Messages of Rev. 14**—the God of the Sabbath—the same God worshiped by Ellen White and her husband—the God revealed in Scripture and the writings of His messenger: not the modern 'Baal'—the 'god' of Sunday worship—that has evolved out of the convoluted councils of an apostate church system.

Chapter 21

MEMBERS OF THE GODHEAD ARE DISTINCT PERSONS

PROFESSOR: We must never lose sight of the fact that, according to Catholic Trinitarian doctrine, the Father, Son, and Holy Spirit are just emanations of one 'indivisible' substance.

WILLIAM: That is why Catholicism describes them as "co-eternal" and not eternal—because they are, according to Trinitarianism, all of one identical substance; and are, therefore, **co**(llectively) **eternal** and cannot be eternal all by themselves.

PROFESSOR: Right. Romanism defines the three emanations as "co-eternal" because their substance (or essence) is identical and cannot be divided. Thus, the need for one 'emanation' to mediate with another 'emanation,' on behalf of another entity (fallen man) is preposterous. Accordingly, since all of Rome's doctrines are predicated upon the doctrine of the Trinity, Rome has therefore substituted the mediation of priests, prelates, popes and "saints" in place of the true, mediatorial role of Christ.

WILLIAM: They are putting themselves into the place of Christ.

PROFESSOR: They are truly 'anti-Christ'—in the place of Christ. They have cast Christ's continual "daily" ministration on man's behalf "down to the ground"—down to the level "of a man." Daniel 8:11-13.

During the years that span from 1898—when God's messenger wrote the 'Desire of Ages'—to 1915—when she died—she made many statements referring to the "Heavenly Trio;" the "Three Powers;" and declared that there are "Three" Persons in the Godhead, which we have looked at and discussed.

WILLIAM: And never did Ellen White ever use the word, "Trinity," to refer to God!

PROFESSOR: Never. Or to put it more strongly, **the Holy Spirit never inspired her to use the uninspired term, "Trinity."** If the Trinity was true, the Holy Spirit (a theoretical member of the so-called Trinity) would certainly have led her to use the term that would describe the "truth" accurately.

WILLIAM: Neither did she ever use the terms: "Triune", "co-equal"*, "co-eternal", "three-in-one", or "one-in-three".

PROFESSOR: Not once*.

(*NOTE: See Appendix P)

WILLIAM: She also never hinted at correcting her husband, James White's strong anti-Trinitarian stance.

PROFESSOR: Good, William, you remembered that lesson.

WILLIAM: But Professor, many think that Ellen White taught the Trinity.

PROFESSOR: **Those who claim that such terms as "Heavenly Trio" prove that she taught the "Trinity" doctrine, fail to realize that Ellen White fully understood what "Trinity" meant: One 'substance' manifested and functioning as three distinct Persons, whose 'substance' was indivisible.** During her lifetime there were those who believed in a two-Person Godhead. God's messenger corrected that aberration by proclaiming the Holy Spirit as the Third Person of the Godhead. Mistakenly, some thought that her statements supported the notion of the "Trinity" when actually she was simply declaring a Three-Person Godhead.

WILLIAM: The word, "Trio", connotes three separate and distinct Persons (with personalities) functioning harmoniously to effect one common goal. Like a trio of singers, bringing forth a message in perfect harmony.

PROFESSOR: Excellent! In this case, the heavenly Trio are singing the message of salvation of man from sin; each divine Singer has his own part, that the others cannot sing. God's messenger was clearly aware that the term "Trinity" would have misrepresented the truth.

The doctrine of consubstantiation, and of eternal generation or "spiration", which predicates Trinitarianism, in effect teaches that the Son and the Holy Spirit are not separate from the Father, but are intrinsically a part of the Being called 'God'—the 'Son' being eternally generated, and the 'Spirit' continuously proceeding from both.

As we noted in the book <u>The Holy Catholic Faith</u>, Catholic scholars declare:

<u>The Holy Catholic Faith</u>, Volume 1, page 311:
"All three possess not a similar, but the **self-same** nature.... **The Divine nature is not divided between the Persons.... The Divine nature is not multiplied, but one and indivisible.... There are not three omnipotents, infinites, and omnisicients, but only One infinite, One omnipotent, and One omniscient.** The three Divine Persons, possessing the self-same nature, are **inseparable** though distinct."

Clearly, such teaching strikes at the heart of the plan of salvation—.

WILLIAM: Right, because it was **separation** from His Father that brought about Jesus' death.

PROFESSOR: Yes, it was **separation** from His Father—not the cross that caused His death. (See <u>Story of Jesus</u>, page 145; <u>That I May Know Him</u>, page 18; <u>Testimonies For the Church</u>, Volume 2, pages 206, 209, 214; etc.) **How could Jesus cry out, "Why hast thou forsaken Me"—if the Persons of the Godhead are <u>inseparable</u> in "essence"?**
Furthermore, if 'God' is one "indivisible" substance, manifested in three different modes; 'persons'; hypostases; representations; etc. as taught by Trinitarian doctrine—then, when Jesus came to earth, yet "indivisible" from the 'God' substance, sinners would have been instantly destroyed by being confronted by 'God'!

WILLIAM: Also, as you showed me, Christ could not have been our Example, because being "indivisible" from the "God substance," he could not be "in all points tempted like as we are," since "God cannot be tempted." Heb. 4:15; James 1:13.

PROFESSOR: Good point. All of the assertions by God's messenger that the members of the Godhead are separate and distinct individual persons clearly correct the false teachings of Trinitarianism and the gross errors that such a false doctrine lead to. Look at this one:

<u>Upward Look</u>, page 367:
"The Lord Jesus Christ, the only begotten Son of the Father, **is truly God in infinity** [*eternal, self-existent, the Alpha and*

Omega, etc.], **but not in personality."** *[not homoousios, of 'one substance' or 'essence;' not consubstantial.]*

The fact that God's messenger, under Divine guidance, never employed Trinitarian terminology should also be significant to us; especially so, when we consider the vociferously anti-Trinitarian stand adopted by James White—whose work she endorsed, and who, on this issue, she never opposed. On the other hand, as we have noted, Ellen White wrote strongly opposing statements countermanding the false notion that Christ was "begotten" at some prior point in eternity as proposed by Uriah Smith, J.H. Waggoner and many others, by clearly stating that Christ was "pre-existent" and "self-existent" and that there "never was a time" in which He was "not in close fellowship with the eternal God."

And it is noteworthy that for Christ to have been "self-existent," that fact, alone, precludes Him from being of the Father's own substance. A careful study of the issues debated at the council of Antioch 264 AD and the Council of Nicea 325 AD reveal that **this issue was "hot" then and still is today. Rome openly declares that all of her doctrines are predicated on the doctrine of the Trinity.** After years of study, I find this to be true: The authority to change "times and laws" and therefore, the Sabbath; the doctrine of Original Sin; the false Christ of the Immaculate Conception; the mediation of popes, priests, saints, and "Mary"; as well as her being "Co-Redemptrix;" the Transubstantiation of the Mass; and the continual, perpetual, sacrificing of "Jesus" in the Mass; and other "appeasements" such as pilgrimages, penances, self-flagellation, etc.; and on and on—all of Rome's stupefying potion—is predicated on their doctrine of the Trinity. Here is a schematic depicting these points: (See next page)

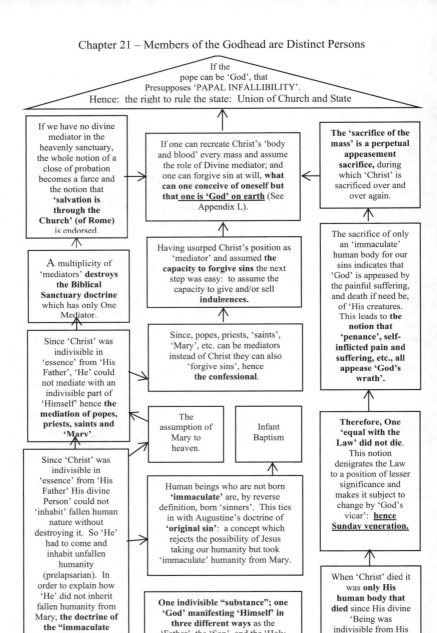

If the pope can be 'God', that Presupposes 'PAPAL INFALLIBILITY'. Hence: the right to rule the state: Union of Church and State

If we have no divine mediator in the heavenly sanctuary, the whole notion of a close of probation becomes a farce and the notion that **'salvation is through the Church' (of Rome)** is endorsed.

If one can recreate Christ's 'body and blood' every mass and assume the role of Divine mediator; and one can forgive sin at will, **what can one conceive of oneself but that one is 'God' on earth** (See Appendix L).

The 'sacrifice of the mass' is a perpetual appeasement sacrifice, during which 'Christ' is sacrificed over and over again.

A multiplicity of 'mediators' **destroys the Biblical Sanctuary doctrine** which has only One Mediator.

Having usurped Christ's position as 'mediator' and assumed **the capacity to forgive sins** the next step was easy: to assume the capacity to give and/or sell **indulgences.**

The sacrifice of only an 'immaculate' human body for our sins indicates that 'God' is appeased by the painful suffering, and death if need be, of 'His creatures'. This leads to **the notion that 'penance', self-inflicted pain and suffering, etc., all appease 'God's wrath'.**

Since 'Christ' was indivisible in 'essence' from 'His Father', 'He' could not mediate with an indivisible part of 'Himself' hence the **mediation of popes, priests, saints and 'Mary'.**

Since, popes, priests, 'saints', 'Mary', etc. can be mediators instead of Christ they can also 'forgive sins', hence **the confessional.**

Since 'Christ' was indivisible in 'essence' from 'His Father' His divine Person' could not 'inhabit' fallen human nature without destroying it. So 'He' had to come and inhabit unfallen humanity (prelapsarian). In order to explain how 'He' did not inherit fallen humanity from Mary, **the doctrine of the "immaculate conception"** of Mary was devised.

The assumption of Mary to heaven.

Infant Baptism

Therefore, One 'equal with the Law' did not die. This notion denigrates the Law to a position of lesser significance and makes it subject to change by 'God's vicar': **hence Sunday veneration.**

Human beings who are not born **'immaculate'** are, by reverse definition, born 'sinners'. This ties in with Augustine's doctrine of **'original sin'**: a concept which rejects the possibility of Jesus taking our humanity but took 'immaculate' humanity from Mary.

When 'Christ' died it was **only His human body that died** since His divine 'Being was indivisible from His Father in essence, hence could not die.

One indivisible "substance"; one 'God' manifesting 'Himself' in three different ways as the 'Father', the 'Son', and the 'Holy Spirit'.

THE TRINITY DOCTRINE

WILLIAM: Whew! That would be a study all by itself.

PROFESSOR: I prefer to stand with James White and his wife; with Joseph Bates; with B.G. Wilkinson; with the Waldenses, who were anti-Trinitarian, and of whom Great Controversy, page 65, says that they had the truth "unadulterated." I will stand with the Word of God in denouncing this confusing soul destroying error that has invaded God's denominated people.

Once again, notice how God's messenger describes the Heavenly Trio as separate distinct eternal Beings:

> Testimonies, Volume 8, page 263:
> "**The mighty power that works through all nature and sustains all things is not**, as some men of science represent, merely **an all-pervading principle, an actuating energy. God is a spirit; yet He is a personal being**, **for man was made in His image**." *[Made with a resemblance of God's form whilst needing to develop a character that reflects God's character.]* (Counsels for the Church, page74; Education, pages 131, 132.)

> Evangelism, page 615:
> "The Comforter that Christ promised to send after He ascended to heaven, is the Spirit in all the fullness of the Godhead, making manifest the power of divine grace to all who receive and believe in Christ as a personal Saviour. **There are three living persons of the heavenly trio**; in the name of these **three great powers** –the Father, the Son, and the Holy Spirit— those who receive Christ by living faith are baptized, **and these powers** will co-operate with the obedient subjects of heaven in their efforts to live the new life in Christ." (Special Testimonies, Series B, No. 7, pages 62, 63, 1905)

> Evangelism, page 616:
> "We need to realize that **the Holy Spirit, who is as much a person as God is a person**, is walking through these grounds." (*Manuscript 66, 1899.*) (From a talk to the students at the Avondale School)

> Evangelism, pages 616, 617:
> "**The Holy Spirit is a person**, for He beareth witness with our spirits that we are the children of God. When this witness is borne, it carries with it its own evidence.

"**The Holy Spirit has a personality**, else He could not bear witness to our spirits and with our spirits that we are the children of God. **He must also be a divine person,** else He could not search out the secrets which lie hidden in the mind of God. 'For what man knoweth the things of a man, save the spirit of man which is in him? even so the things of God knoweth no man, but the Spirit of God.'" *(Manuscript 20, 1906.)*

Evangelism, page 617:
"The prince of the power of evil can only be held in check by **the power of God in the third person of the Godhead, the Holy Spirit.**" *(Special Testimonies, Series A, No. 10, page 37, 1897.)*

Evangelism, page 617:
"We are to co-operate with the **three highest powers in heaven—the Father, the Son, and the Holy Ghost**—and these powers will work through us, making us workers together with God." *(Special Testimonies, Series B, No. 7, page 51, 1905.)*

Evangelism, page 614: *[Here, Sister White describes a spiritualistic depiction of god—as in Trinitarian doctrine.]*
"'The Father is like the invisible vapor; the Son is like the leaden cloud; the Spirit is rain fallen and working in refreshing power.' [—all these representations are manifestations of a shared substance = consubstantiality. God's messenger goes on to say:] **"All these spiritualistic representations are simply nothingness. They are imperfect, untrue. They weaken and diminish the Majesty which no earthly likeness can be compared to."**

What we are not told by the compilers of the book Evangelism, is that the above statement, together with others, which come from Special Testimonies Series B No. 7 page 62 1906, <u>was a refutation of the following pro-Trinitarian writings by a Rev. Boardman:</u>

The Higher Christian Life, by Rev. William E. Boardman, Part II, Chapter I:

http://www.swartzentrover.com/cotor/E-Books/holiness/Boardman/Higher/HCL_201.htm

"A glance at the official and essential relations of the persons of **the Holy Trinity** to each other and to us, may throw additional light upon our pathway. Upon this subject flippancy would border upon blasphemy. It is holy ground. He who ventures upon it may well tread with unshod foot, and uncovered head bowed low.

"Speculation here, too, is entirely out of place, unsafe, not worth the ink used in the writing. The lamp of human reason is a light too dim to guide us through the profound mysteries of the mode of the divine existence and the methods of the divine manifestation and working. God alone knows what God is. And God only can communicate to man what man can be made to know of God, especially of the personalities of the Godhead, and of their relations to each other and to us."Revelation must be our guide. Beyond what God has revealed, we know nothing. The sacred Word is all the light we have in this matter. In a sense scriptural, and true Christ is "all the fulness of the Godhead bodily."

"The express image of the invisible God." "The fulness of Him who filleth all in all." The fulness of the Father and of the Spirit. In a sense equally scriptural and true, the Father is all the fulness of the Godhead; and so also is the Spirit.

"The Father is the fulness of the Godhead in invisibility, without form, whom no creature hath seen or can see.

"The Son is the fulness of the Godhead embodied, that his creatures may see him, and know him, and trust him.

"The Spirit is the fulness of the Godhead in all the active workings, whether of creation, providence, revelation, or salvation, by which God manifests himself to and through the universe.

"The counsels of eternity are therefore all hidden in the Father, all manifested by the Son, and all wrought by the Spirit. Let us glance first at the official relations of the persons of the Godhead. To gain something like distinct ideas of these divine relations we need to be lifted up in thought, as the eyes of the patriarch Jacob were at Bethel, by a ladder with its foot on the earth but its top in heaven. Such a ladder the Bible sets up before us in the names and similies of the persons and work, especially of the Son and the Spirit. The Son is called the Word, the Logos. Now a word before it has taken on articulate form is thought. The word is the express image of the thought, the fulness of the thought made manifest. So the Son is the fulness of the Godhead made manifest. The thought is the fulness of the word not yet made manifest. So the Father is the fulness of the Godhead invisible. Again the Spirit is like the thought expressed and gone forth to do its work of enlightening, convincing, changing. When a thought has been formed into words, risen to the tongue, fallen from the lips upon other ears, into other hearts, it works there its own full work. So the Holy Spirit is the fulness of the Godhead at work fulfilling the designs of God.

THE FATHER IS LIKE THE THOUGHT
UNEXPRESSED.
THE SON IS LIKE THE THOUGHT EXPRESSED IN
WORDS.
THE SPIRIT IS LIKE THE WORD WORKING IN
OTHER MINDS.

"Another of the names of Jesus will give the same analogies in a light not less striking — The Sun of Righteousness.

"All the light of the sun in the heavens was once hidden in the invisibility of primal darkness; and after this, the light now blazing in the orb of day was, when first the command when forth, Let light be! and light was, at most only the diffused haze of the gray dawn of the morn of creation out of the darkness of chaotic night, without form, or body, or centre, or radiance, or glory. But when separated from the darkness and centered in the sun, then in its glorious glitter it became so resplendent that none but the eagle eye could bear to look it in the face.

"But then again its rays falling aslant through earth's atmosphere and vapors, gladdens all the world with the same light, dispelling the winter, and the cold, and the darkness; starting Spring forth in floral beauty, and Summer in vernal luxuriance, and Autumn laden with golden treasures for the garner.

THE FATHER IS AS THE LIGHT INVISIBLE.
THE SON IS AS THE LIGHT EMBODIED.
THE SPIRIT IS AS THE LIGHT SHED DOWN.

[This is a good example of Sabellianistic, Trinitarian expression.]

"One of the similies for the blessed influences of the SPIRIT while giving the self-same official relations of the persons of the Godhead, to each other and to us, may illustrate them still further — The Dew — The dew of Hermon — the dew on the mown meadow. Before the dew gathers at all in drops, it hangs over all the landscape in invisible vapor, omnipresent but unseen. By and by as the night wanes into morning, and as the temperature sinks and touches the dew point the invisible becomes the visible, the embodied; and, as the sun rises, it stands in diamond drops trembling and glittering in the sun's young beams in pearly beauty upon leaf and flower, over all the face of nature.But now again, a breeze springs up, the breath of heaven is wafted gently along, shaking leaf and flower, and in a moment the pearly drops are invisible again. But where now? Fallen at the root of herb and flower to impart new life, freshness, vigor to all it touches.

THE FATHER IS LIKE THE DEW IN INVISIBLE
VAPOR.
THE SON IS LIKE THE DEW GATHERED IN
BEAUTEOUS FORM.
THE SPIRIT IS LIKE THE DEW FALLEN TO THE
SEAT OF LIFE.

"Yet one more of these Bible likenings — by no means exhausting them — will not be unwelcome or useless — the Rain.

"Rain, like the dew, floats in invisibility, and omnipresence at the first, over all, around all. Seen by none. While it remains in its invisibility, the earth parches, clods cleave together, the ground cracks open, the sun pours down his burning heat, the winds lift up the dust in circling whirls, and rolling clouds, and famine gaunt and greedy stalks through the land, followed by pestilence and death. By and by, the eager watcher sees the little hand-like cloud rising far out over the sea. It gathers, gathers, gathers; comes and spreads as it comes, in majesty over the whole heavens: — But all is parched and dry and dead yet, upon earth.

"But now comes a drop, and drop after drop, quicker, faster — the shower, the rain — sweeping on, and giving to earth all the treasures .of the clouds — clods open, furrows soften, springs, rivulets, rivers, swell and fill, and all the land is gladdened again with restored abundance.

THE FATHER IS LIKE TO THE INVISIBLE VAPOR.
THE SON IS AS THE LADEN CLOUD AND PALLING RAIN.
THE SPIRIT IS THE RAIN — FALLEN AND WORKING IN REFRESHING POWER.

"These likenings are all imperfect. They rather hide than illustrate **the tri-personality of the one God**, for they are not persons but things, poor and earthly at best, to represent **the living personalities of the living God**. So much they may do, however, as to illustrate the official relations of each to the others and of each and all to us. And more. They may also illustrate the truth that all the fulness of Him who filleth all in all, dwells in each person of **the Triune God**."

Let us bear in mind that by this time her husband, James, was already dead and <u>yet God's messenger was still refuting Trinitarianism,</u> which is what Reverend Boardman's book presents.
The following statement distinctly illustrates the emphasis placed by God's messenger on the distinctiveness and individuality of the Persons of the Godhead, as opposed to Boardman's above speculations:

Testimonies, Volume 8, page 268:
"The Scriptures clearly indicate the relation between God and Christ, and they bring to view as **clearly the personality and individuality of each.**"

We have seen how God's messenger clarifies and sums up the "one"ness of the Godhead:

Ministry of Healing, pages 421, 422:
"**The personality of the Father and the Son, also the unity that exists between Them, are presented in the seventeenth chapter of John,** in the prayer of Christ for His disciples:
"'Neither pray I for these alone, but for them also which shall believe on Me through their word; **that they all may be one; as Thou, Father, art in Me, and I in Thee, that they also may be**

one in Us: that the world may believe that Thou hast sent Me.'
John 17:20, 21.
**"The unity that exists between Christ and His disciples
does not destroy the personality of either. They are <u>one in
purpose, in mind, in character, but not in person</u>. It is <u>thus</u>
that God and Christ are one."**

The inspired statements clearly describe totally **distinct** personhood for
each member of the Godhead. When God's messenger employs the term
"person" she is not deploying that term as a "smoke screen" to obscure an
esoteric "modality" or "hypostasis". In <u>Evangelism</u>, page 260.3 we are
told: "**<u>God Speaks Through Testimonies</u>.**--We must follow the directions
given through the Spirit of prophecy. We must love and obey the truth for
this time. This will save us from accepting strong delusions. **God has
spoken to us through His Word. He has <u>spoken to us through the
Testimonies</u>** to the church, **and through the books that have helped to
make plain our present duty and the position that we should now
occupy.**" Furthermore, God's messenger admonishes us to understand
God's 'words' to us at face value. In *Review and Herald*, May 1, 1900 par.
4 we read: "For a man to be effectually saved, the truth of the Word must
be inwrought in the soul. It is a power that works inwardly to bless the soul
of the receiver, and outwardly to bless the souls of others. **Take the Word
<u>just as it reads</u>, and be a doer of it.**" **From this I gather, that when God's
messenger speaks of a "person" she means just that, for it is God
communicating to us by His "Spirit of Prophecy" via His messenger.**

<u>Spiritual Gifts</u>, Volume 2, page 74:
**"I have often seen the lovely Jesus, that he is a <u>person</u>. I
asked him if his Father was a <u>person</u>, and had a form like
himself. Said Jesus, 'I am in the express image of my
Father's Person.' <u>I have often seen that the spiritual view
took away the glory of heaven,....</u>"**

Adam and Eve were totally distinct persons yet, according to Scripture,
they became "<u>one</u> flesh" (See Gen.2:24). <u>They</u> "bore" resemblance to
"their Maker":

<u>Education</u>, page 20, (1903):
"Created to be 'the image and glory of God' (1 Corinthians
11:7), Adam and Eve had received endowments not unworthy of
their **high destiny**. *[which is 'Infinite development,' Education,*

271

page 172.] Graceful and symmetrical in form, regular and beautiful in feature, their countenances glowing with the tint of health and the light of joy and hope, **they bore in outward resemblance the likeness of their Maker. <u>Nor was this likeness manifest in the physical nature only</u>. Every faculty of mind and soul reflected the Creator's glory."**

Now men want Adventism to incorporate Catholic error: They are removing the **established landmarks** of Adventism.

<u>Manuscript Release</u>, *No. 760,* page 9, (1905):
"**<u>Those who seek to remove the old landmarks are not holding fast; they are not remembering how they have received and heard</u>. Those who try to bring in theories that would remove the pillars of our faith concerning the sanctuary <u>or concerning the personality of God or of Christ</u>, are working as blind men. They are seeking to bring in uncertainties and to set the people of God adrift without an anchor."**

WILLIAM: You have clearly shown me how Trinitarianism strikes at the heart of the sanctuary message which is a pillar of our faith.

PROFESSOR: Good observation. Here, you can have these quotes for your notes. I have to go now. We'll see you tomorrow.

Chapter 22

THE MOST HIGH GOD, THE GOD OF GODS

PROFESSOR: William, today we are going to look at some startling quotations from the Bible and the Spirit of Prophecy. Take careful notes. I will merely read these quotations with a few comments to join them together, and some comments as I read them, to clarify. (These will be seen in *italics*.)

THE FATHER IS JESUS' GOD

John 14:28:
"Ye have heard how I said unto you, I go away, and come again unto you. If ye loved me, ye would rejoice, because I said, I go unto the Father: for **my Father is greater than I.**"

Notice how the above declaration by Jesus clearly indicates the subordinate role that Jesus **assumed** in the plan of salvation.

John 17:3:
"And this is life eternal that they might know thee, **the only true God; and Jesus Christ, whom thou hast sent.**"

The above pivotal verse highlights the supreme station of the Father, who maintains the integrity of the Godhead.

John 20:17:
"Jesus saith unto her *[Mary Magdalene]*, Touch me not; for I am not yet ascended to my Father: but go to my brethren, and say unto them, **I ascend unto my Father, and your Father; and [to] my God, and your God.**"

The Father is Jesus' God, and, if we are Christ's, He is our God!

WILLIAM: I read that verse I don't know how many times, and never saw that Jesus was saying that the Father was His God! It is almost unbelievable, that I never saw that before.

PROFESSOR: It speaks of the awesome sacrifice made by Jesus Christ, who "thought it not robbery to be equal with God, but made Himself of no reputation." He voluntarily subordinated Himself—a part of His "infinite sacrifice." Let's go on:

1 Corinthians 3:23:
"And ye are Christ's, and **Christ is God's.**"

1 Corinthians 11:3:
"But I would have you know, that **the head of every man is Christ;** and the head of the woman is the man; **and the head of Christ is God.**"

WILLIAM: I also found this one in:

Revelation 3:12:
Him that overcometh will I *[Jesus]* make a pillar in the temple of **my God**, and he shall go no more out: and I will write upon him the name of **my God**, and the name of the city of **my God,** which is new Jerusalem, which cometh down out of heaven from **my God:** and I will write upon him my new name.

PROFESSOR: And that was Jesus talking there in that verse. Wonderful!
Now let's look at some Scriptures that show that the apostles recognized Jesus' God as the "one God" that the Scriptures speak of:

THE "ONE GOD" OF THE BIBLE

1 Timothy 2:5:
"For there is **one God**, and one mediator between God and men, the man Christ Jesus;"

Ephesians 4:4-6:
4) "There is one body, and **one Spirit** *[the Holy Spirit]*, even as ye are called in one hope of your calling;
5) **One Lord** *[Jesus]*, one faith, one baptism,
6) **One God and Father** of all, <u>who is above all</u>, and through all, and **in** you all.

Romans 1:7:

"To all that be in Rome, beloved of **God,** called to be saints: Grace to you and peace from **God our Father**, and the Lord Jesus Christ."

Romans 3:30:
"Seeing it is **one God,** which shall justify the circumcision by faith, and uncircumcision through faith."

1Corinthians 1:3:
"Grace be unto you, and peace, from **God our Father**, and from the Lord Jesus Christ."

1 Corinthians 8:6:
"But to us there is but **one God, the Father,** of Whom are all things, and we in Him; and **one Lord** Jesus Christ, by whom are all things, and we by Him."

Galatians 1:3:
"Grace be to you and peace from **God the Father**, and from our Lord Jesus Christ,"

1 Peter 1:2:
"Elect according to the foreknowledge of **God the Father**, through sanctification of the Spirit, unto obedience and sprinkling of the blood of Jesus Christ: Grace unto you, and peace, be multiplied."

2 John 1:3:
"Grace be with you, mercy, and peace, from **God the Father**, and from the Lord Jesus Christ, the Son of the Father, in truth and love."

Jude 1:1:
"Jude, the servant of Jesus Christ, and brother of James, to them that are sanctified by **God the Father,** and preserved in Jesus Christ, and called:"

WILLIAM: It is plain that the "one God" presented in these verses of the NT is the Father.

PROFESSOR: And it is also plain that the term "God" in the NT normally refers to the Father. That is not to say that Jesus and the Holy Spirit are not called God; but that the Father maintains supreme station.

WILLIAM: The same is true in the Spirit of Prophecy writings.

PROFESSOR: Yes. But now I want to show you two Scripture verses that are deceptively deployed to teach the false Trinitarian concept. Before we do, I want you to notice what Paul says we should do when handling the Word of God:

2 Corinthians 4:2:
"But [we] have renounced the hidden things of dishonesty, not walking in craftiness, **nor handling the word of God deceitfully**; but by manifestation of the truth commending ourselves to every man's conscience in the sight of God."

The first misapplied verse we will look at was deployed in the **First Quarter, 2012, General Conference-sponsored SDA Sabbath School Quarterly, in an attempt to prove that the "one God" referred to in this text was none other than the Trinity—the 'one God manifested as three Persons'**:

1 Corinthians 8:4:
"As concerning therefore the eating of those things that are offered in sacrifice unto idols, we know that an idol *is* nothing in the world, and that *there is* **none other God but one.**"

But the notion that this verse is referring to a trinity is categorically refuted in verse 6, **which they did not show:**

1 Corinthians 8:6:
"But to us there is but **one God, the Father,** of Whom are all things, and we in Him; and **one Lord Jesus Christ,** by whom are all things, and we by Him."

This verse completely overturns the misuse of 1 Corinthians 8:4.

Again, in the same Sabbath School lesson, this deceptive practice was deployed when the lesson compiler, a doctor of theology, presented the following verse for the same purpose of confirming the "one God" to be the Trinity:

James 2:19:
"Thou believest that there is **one God;** thou doest well: the devils also believe, and tremble."

If only the Sabbath School students had read a little further...

WILLIAM: I did, Professor, and I found this verse:

James 3:9:
"Therewith bless we **God, even the Father;** and therewith curse we men, which are made after the similitude of God."

PROFESSOR: And you don't even have a degree! Your discovery of that verse reminds me of this verse:

Luke 10:21:
"In that hour Jesus rejoiced in spirit, and said, I thank thee, **O Father, Lord of heaven and earth, that thou hast hid these things from the wise and prudent, and hast revealed them unto babes:** even so, Father; for so it seemed good in thy sight."

GOD THE FATHER

Jesus was praying to His Father. Now let's see how God's messenger comments on the term "Father," showing His headship. She writes:

The Faith I Live By, page 38:
"God is our tender, pitiful **Father**... He [Jesus] pointed ...**to the Ruler** *[No. 1 spot]* **of the universe,** under the NEW name, **'Our Father.'**"

WILLIAM: Jesus taught us to pray to "Our Father, which art in heaven...." In the gospel of John, God is called **the Father** 117 times!

PROFESSOR: And remember, William, as we looked at earlier, Jesus, who is a divine Being himself, said this also in the gospel of John:

John 20:17:
"Jesus saith to her *[Mary Magdalene]*, Touch me not; for I am not yet ascended to my Father: But go to my brethren, and

277

say to them, I ascend to **My Father, and your Father; and to My God, and your God.**"

Consequently, the Father is accurately classified as the "God of gods" as He is called in the following verses:

GOD OF GODS

Deuteronomy 10:17:
"For the Lord your God is **God of gods**, and Lord of Lords, a great God, a mighty, and a terrible, which regardeth not persons, nor taketh reward."

Joshua 22:22:
"**The Lord God of gods, the Lord God of gods,** He knoweth, and Israel He shall know...."

Psalm 136:2:
"O give thanks unto **the God of gods:** for His mercy endureth for ever."

WILLIAM: If God the Father is the "God of gods," who are the gods?

YE ARE GODS

PROFESSOR: First, in the Bible, God the Father declares that He is Jesus' God.

Hebrews 1:8, 9:
8) "But unto the Son he saith, Thy throne, O God, is for ever and ever: a sceptre of righteousness is the sceptre of thy kingdom.
9)   Thou hast loved righteousness, and hated iniquity; **therefore God, even thy God,** hath anointed thee with the oil of gladness above thy fellows."

God the Father has also declared that His people are gods (lower case). Thus, it is written:

Psalms 82:6

278

"I have said, Ye are gods; and all of you are children of the most High."

Our identity as "children of the Most High" or "sons of God," is applicable if we have received the Holy Spirit: the divine nature in us. And for this reason He has communicated to His people that, "Ye are gods."

Also, William, I want you to remember that the deployment of upper and lower case "g" in the word "God," is a human tradition intended to show respect and distinction:

Psalm 82:1, 6:
1) **"God standeth in the congregation of the mighty; He judgeth among the gods."**
6) "I have said, **Ye are gods;** and all of you are **children of the Most High."**

Jesus quoted Psalm 82:6 in his own defense when set upon by the Jews for His calling Himself the Son of God:

John 10:34:
"Jesus answered them, Is it not written in your law, I said, **Ye are gods**?"

WILLIAM: Could the term "God of gods" mean that God the Father is God over the false gods—the heathen idols?

PROFESSOR: Good question. Let's see what the Bible says about

IDOLS VS. GOD

1 Corinthians 8:4-6:
4) "As concerning therefore the eating of those things that are offered in sacrifice unto idols, **we know that an idol is nothing in the world,** and there is **none other God, but one** *[the Most High God.]*"
5) **For though there be that are called gods, whether in heaven or in earth, (as there be gods many, and Lords many),**
6) **But to us there is but one God, the Father,** of whom are all things, and we in Him; and **one Lord Jesus Christ**, by whom are all things, and we by Him."

279

The Bible also tells us that:

IDOLS ARE NOT GODS

Jeremiah 16:20:
"Shall **a man make gods unto himself, and they are not gods?**

Galatians 4:8:
"Howbeit then, when ye knew not God, ye did service to them which by nature **are no gods."**

(See also Jeremiah 5:7 and 2 Chronicles 13:9).

So the term "God of gods" is not referring to the Father as being God over idols. The Bible says that the idols are not "gods." The Father is the **God of the living and not of the dead** (Mark 12:27). **He is Jesus' God. He is our God** (See Psalm 86). **He is the "God of gods."**
But the anti-Christ treads in Lucifer's steps and attempts to exalt his throne above that of the true God. Notice that Daniel also uses the term "God of gods."

Daniel 11:36:
"And the king *[Papacy]* shall do according to his will; and he shall exalt himself, and **magnify himself** above every god *[above Jesus Christ and the Father: by changing the law]*, **and shall speak marvelous** *[#6381 'hard, hidden, things too high...']* **things against the God of gods,** and shall prosper till the indignation be accomplished: for that that is determined shall be done."

Thus the Scriptures reveal one Supreme God, which clarifies the Biblical appellation "God of gods." These verses point us to the "only true God" of John 17:3.
The Bible also underscores this appellation by calling God the Father by another special term:

"MOST HIGH GOD"

Mark 5:7:

280

"And *[a demon]* cried with a loud voice, and said, What have I to do with thee, Jesus, thou **Son of the Most High God**? I adjure thee by God, that thou torment me not."

WILLIAM: That verse clearly identifies the Father as the Most High God. It endorses what you have just discussed, as do these verses I found:

Genesis 14:18:
"And **Melchizedek, King of Salem** *[Peace]*, brought forth bread and wine: and He was the priest of the **Most High God.** 19 And He blessed him, and said, Blessed be Abram of the **Most High God,** possessor of heaven and earth: 20 And blessed be the **Most High God**.... 22 And Abram said to the king of Sodom, I have lift up mine hand unto the LORD *[Jehovah]*, the **Most High God**, the possessor of heaven and earth,..."

Psalm 78:56:
"Yet they tempted and provoked the **Most High God**, and kept not his testimonies."

Acts 16:17:
"The same followed Paul and us and cried, saying, These men are the servants of **the Most High God**, which show to us **the way of salvation.**" *[The 'way' of salvation is Jesus, who is the Way, the Truth, and the Life, leading men back into harmony with the Most High God from Whom man is alienated by sin.]*

Professor, did you know that even Nebuchadnezzar identified the Father as the Most High God? Look at Daniel 3:25, 26:

Daniel 3:25, 26:
25) "He answered and said, Lo, I see four men loose, walking in the midst of the fire, and they have no hurt; and the form of **the fourth is like the Son of God.**
26) Then Nebuchadnezzar came near to the mouth of the burning fiery furnace, and spake, and said, Shadrach, Meshach, and Abednego, **ye servants of the most high God,** come forth, and come hither. Then Shadrach, Meshach, and Abednego, came forth of the midst of the fire."

PROFESSOR: And, by the way, in Daniel 4:8 Nebuchadnezzar also perceives that Daniel is filled with the Holy Spirit. The Holy Spirit was really working on the mind of the Babylonian king.

WILLIAM: I found one other place in the Bible where the Most High God is also seen. It is in Genesis

Genesis 28:12, 13:
12) "And he dreamed, and behold **a ladder set up on the earth, and the top of it reached to heaven:** and behold the angels **of God** ascending and descending on it.
13) And, behold, **the LORD stood above it,** and said, **I am the LORD God of Abraham thy father, and the God of Isaac:** the land whereon thou liest, to thee will I give it, and to thy seed."

In those verses, Jesus is symbolized by the ladder (see John 1:52) and the LORD (the Father), it says, stands above it. The word "LORD" in verse 13 is the Hebrew word "JEHOVAH" and refers here to the Father.

PROFESSOR: Very good. Now we want to see that in the plan of salvation Jesus subordinates Himself to the Father:

CHRIST, ONE EQUAL WITH THE FATHER, VOLUNTARILY TAKES A SUBORDINATE ROLE

John 5:18:
"Therefore the Jews sought the more to kill him, because he not only had broken the Sabbath *[in their eyes]*, but said also that God was His Father, **making Himself equal with God.**" *[Notice: Equal in divinity, but not equal in station!]*

Philippians 2:6, 7:
6) "Who, being in the form of God, thought it not robbery to be **equal** with God:
7) But **made Himself** of no reputation, and took upon him the form of a servant, and was made in the likeness of men." *[This is **voluntary subordination.**]*

Clearly, from the information revealed to us in the Word of God, it can be seen that **prior to the implementation of the plan of salvation and the**

282

incarnation, Christ and the Father operated on a level of complete and de facto equality ('Let us make man in our image.' Gen. 1:26.) However, when the plan of salvation was formulated, Michael/Christ voluntarily accepted (should it become necessary) to step down into **a subordinate role** in order to reach sinful man **where he is** in his lost condition—and provide a way of escape. Hence Jesus referred to the Father as His God; (See John 20:17), the "Most High God," the "God of gods."

The Youth's Instructor, April 25, 1901:
"The enemy was overcome by Christ in his human nature. **The power of the Saviour's Godhead was hidden. He overcame in human nature, relying upon God for power.**"

In the plan of salvation, Jesus had to lay aside His own divine power and set aside His exalted station. During the incarnation He became a suppliant, depending upon His Father for overcoming power.

Spirit of Prophecy, Volume 3, page 192:
"Then the mighty angel, with a voice that caused the earth to quake, was heard: Jesus, thou Son of God, thy Father calls thee! Then he who had **earned the power** to conquer death and the grave came forth, with the tread of a conqueror... and proclaimed over the rent sepulcher of Joseph, 'I am the resurrection and the life.'" [Letter 195, 9/6/1903 to W.C.White].

Question: Who determined that Christ had "earned" that power? Clearly that had to be the 'Most High God': the Father. **Would He have determined that a part of 'Himself' had "earned the power"?**

Desire of Ages, page 785:
"Over the rent sepulcher of Joseph, Christ had proclaimed in triumph, **'I am the resurrection, and the life.' These words could be spoken only by the Deity.** *[Which Jesus could have lost! See 7BC 1129]* All created beings *[Remember, Jesus, into his humanity, was 'begotten' of a created being—Mary]* live by the will and power of God. **They are dependent recipients of the life of God.** *[Jesus laid down His life that He might take it up again.]* **From the highest seraph to the humblest animate being, all are replenished from the Source of life. Only He who is one with God** *[One in 'mind, purpose and character.'* Ministry of Healing, *page 421,422.]* **could say, I have power** to

283

lay down My life, and I have power to take it again. *[The rest of this verse says: "This commandment (authority) have I received of my Father" John 10:18; "I can of mine own self do nothing" John 5:19, 30; "I live by the Father, John 6:57; etc.]* In **His divinity, Christ possessed the power to break the bonds of death."** *[But He had laid His personal divinity aside; see Series B, No. 9, page3; and* Lift Him Up, *page 233. That is why Romans 8:11 depicts the divine Holy Spirit raising Jesus to life.]*

Clearly, the divinity *[divine power]* that **Jesus was exercising was** the Father's **power administered through the Holy Spirit.** That is why He said:

Desire of Ages, page 21:
"'I do nothing of Myself,' said Christ; 'the living Father hath sent Me, and **I live by the Father.'** ...All things Christ received from God, but He took to give."

Notice what else the Bible says on this issue:

Ephesians 1:19, 20:
"And what is the exceeding greatness of His power to usward who believe, according to the working of His mighty power, 20 **which He** *[the Father]* **wrought in Christ when He** *[the Father]* **raised Him** *[Christ]* **from the dead, and set Him at His own right hand in the heavenly places** *[sanctuary?]*"

When Jesus came out of the grave His resurrection was **evidence** of His complete victory. Divine life is restored in Jesus who said:

Revelation 1:18:
"I am He that liveth, and **was dead**; and, behold, I am alive for evermore...."

Revelation 2:8:
"...These things saith the first and the last *[alpha and Omega]*, which **was dead**, and is alive."

These statements clearly show that Jesus could not have gone and preached to souls in hell as Rome and her daughters claim: He "was **dead**".

WILLIAM: **They also clearly teach that a member of the Godhead "was <u>dead</u>": separated from the Father.**

PROFESSOR: We will see now how Jesus was resurrected from the dead:

Hebrews 9:14:
"*[Christ]* who **through the eternal Spirit** offered Himself without spot to God,…"

Acts 10:38:
"How God anointed Jesus of Nazareth **with the Holy Ghost and with power.**"

Galatians 1:1:
"Paul, an apostle (not of men, neither by man, but by Jesus Christ, and God **the Father, who raised Him from the dead**)…."

(See 1 Peter 3:18 and Romans 1:4; 8:11, etc.)

2 Peter 1:19-21:
19) "But with the precious blood of Christ, as of a lamb without blemish and without spot:

20) Who verily was **foreordained before the foundation of the world, but was manifest in these last times for you,**

21) **Who by Him do <u>believe in God, that raised Him up from the dead</u>** *[also from fallen human nature]*, **and gave Him glory** *[glorified humanity]*; **that your faith and hope might be in God** *[whom we can only approach through Jesus Christ our divine Lord]*."

1 Peter 3:18:
"For Christ also hath once suffered for sins, **the just** for the **unjust** *[us]*, that He might bring us to God, being put to death in the flesh *[Greek: sarx = fallen human nature]*, **but quickened** *[made alive]* **by the Spirit.**"

Romans 8:9-11:
9) "But ye are not in the flesh *[Greek: sarx = fallen nature condition]*, but in the Spirit, if so be that the **Spirit of God** dwell

in you. Now if any man have not the **Spirit of Christ** *[see John 14:16, 17]*, he is none of His.

10) And if Christ be in you *[John 14:18]*, **the body** *[of death—Romans 7:24]* is dead because of sin *[dead in trespass and sin = under the penalty of the law]*; but the spirit is life because of righteousness. *[Because the Spirit enables fallen humanity to do the deeds of righteousness and is the seal of eternal life to those to whom the Spirit is united.]*

11) **But if <u>the Spirit of Him that raised up Jesus from the dead</u> dwell <u>in</u> you, He that raised up Christ from the dead shall quicken your mortal bodies by His Spirit that dwelleth <u>in</u> you.**"

WILLIAM: So it was the Father who raised up Jesus from the dead by His power through the Holy Spirit.

PROFESSOR: Yes. This also shows that **the Holy Spirit has similarly accepted a subordinate role in order to come into direct contact with sinners,** and even dwell "in" those who accept Jesus and seek to keep God's commandments. (See John 14:15-24.) The Bible teaches that:

THE MIGHTY THIRD PERSON OF THE GODHEAD, THE HOLY SPIRIT, SUBORDINATES HIMSELF TO THE FATHER AND THE SON.

John 16:13:
"Howbeit when he, the Spirit of truth, is come, **He will guide you into all truth: for He shall not speak of Himself; but whatsoever He shall hear, that shall He speak:** And he will show you things to come."

This verse clearly illustrates the subordinate position in the Godhead taken by the Holy Spirit. **The disciples, however, recognized the elevated role of the Father:**

John 14:8, 9:
8) "Philip saith to him, **Lord <u>show us the Father</u>**, and it sufficeth us.

9) Jesus saith to him, Have I been so long time with you, and yet has thou not known Me *[understood My role]*, Philip?

286

He that hath seen Me hath seen the Father; and how sayest thou then, Show us the Father."

In these verses Jesus made it plain that He was showing them what the Father is like. To look at Jesus' character was to see God's character and a reflection of His Personhood. Similarly, **we are called upon to let people see Jesus in us**—as we reflect His character; and **we are clearly separate and distinct individuals from Jesus. Just so Jesus, a separate and distinct Member of the Godhead, showed to mankind the Father.**

Hebrews 1:3:
"Who being the brightness of His glory *[character]*, and **the express image of His person**, and upholding all things by the word of His power, when he had by Himself purged our sins, sat down **on the right hand of the Majesty on High**."

Jesus continually sends His followers life and power, by the Spirit, so that, to those who overcome in His strength, He can grant to sit (with Him) on (His) throne, even as (He) overcame, and am set down with (His) Father on His throne. (**Revelation 3:21).**

Desire of Ages, page 827:
"**Christ gives them the breath of His own spirit, the life of His own life.** The Holy Spirit puts forth its highest energies to work in heart and mind."

The life that Jesus gives is more abundant life that seals the future of the faithful and finally infuses them with "a life that measures with the life of God"—immortal life—Jesus' life that He laid down and takes up again and gives to His redeemed, notably at His second coming.

Desire of Ages, page 805:
"Before the disciples could fulfill their official duties in connection with the church, **Christ breathed His Spirit upon them.**"

The immortal life of the ransomed is secure if thy continue to be filled with the Holy Spirit—their "seal to the day of redemption" (Eph. 4:30). Jesus tells of His power sourced to Him through the Holy Spirit.

Micah 3:8:

"But truly I am full of power by the Spirit of the Lord...."

John 6:57:

"As the living Father hath sent me, **and I live by the Father**: so he that eateth me, even he shall live by me."

His Father's "commandment" freed Jesus from the "gates of hell"— from the "prison house" of the grave.

Desire of Ages, page 780:

"The decree of heaven had loosed the captive."

At His Father's decree Jesus came forth from the grave by the life that **was** in Himself—the immortal life He had laid down when He became a man—His divine life as administered by the Holy Spirit:

Desire of Ages, page 785:

"When the voice of the mighty angel was heard at Christ's tomb, saying, Thy Father calls Thee, **the Saviour came forth from the grave by the life that was** *[previously]* **in Himself.** Now was proved the truth of His words, 'I lay down My life, that I might take it again.... I have power to lay it down, and I have power to take it again.' Now was fulfilled the prophecy He had spoken to the priests and rulers, 'Destroy this temple, and in three days I will raise it up' John 10:17, 18; 2:19.

"...Only He who is one with God could say, I have power to lay down My life, and I have power to take it again. In His divinity *[as administered by the indwelling Holy Spirit. See Romans 8:11.]*, Christ possessed the power to break the bonds of death."

The redeemed will come forth from the grave to the "Life" that was in them while on earth—the immortal life of Christ administered by the Holy Spirit and bestowed at the resurrection of the just. Having the indwelling Holy Spirit was and is the "seal unto the day of redemption" when the "bought back" faithful, who have become "one with God" through the indwelling Spirit, go home with glorified humanity and immortality (1 Cor. 15:51, 52).

Of Christ it is written:

Colossians 2:9:

288

"For **in Him dwelleth** *[by the Holy Spirit]* all the fullness of the Godhead bodily."

And that "fullness" must dwell in us that we can be "one" with the Father and the Son, and truly "know" them and have our immortal life secure in the administration of the Holy Spirit.

2 Peter 1:4:
Whereby are given unto us exceeding great and precious promises: that by these **ye might be partakers of the divine nature**, having escaped the corruption that is in the world through lust.

And having escaped, attain to that unity—that Godhead "one"ness that Jesus prayed His followers would attain to:

John 17:22:
And the glory which thou gavest me I have given them; **that they may be one, <u>even as we are one</u>**:

By the Father's express will and decision Christ was, as a man, filled with the fullness of the Godhead, through the Holy Spirit; His life manifesting the fullness of the Godhead epitomized in the Father.

Colossians 1:19:
"For **it pleased the Father that in Him should all fullness dwell**."

This verse amplifies the truth that **the Father is in charge as the Most High God**, as does the next verse:

1 Corinthians 15:27, 28:
27) "For He hath put all things under His feet. But when He saith all things are put under Him, it is manifested that He is excepted, which did put all things under Him.
28) **And when all things shall be subdued unto Him, then shall <u>the Son also Himself be subject unto Him</u> that put all things under Him, that <u>God may be all in all</u>.**"

God is "in" Christ; and the Son is "in" the Father, and they are "in" the faithful by the Holy Spirit. God is not "in" rocks, trees, stars and planets, scorpions, serpents, or demons, or the wicked, etc.

WILLIAM: It is plain why the Father is referred to as the "Most High God;" as a "God of Gods" (Deut. 10:17); a "God of the living and not of the dead;" "the only true God" (John 17:3). We know what would happen to any sinner who should happen to come into the presence of the "One true God"

PROFESSOR: That person would immediately cease to exist. Clearly, Christ and the Holy Spirit are manifested in roles that enable them to fraternize with sinful man without consuming him. The respective roles of the members of the Godhead are graphically depicted in the illustration, shown below, that we are already acquainted with.

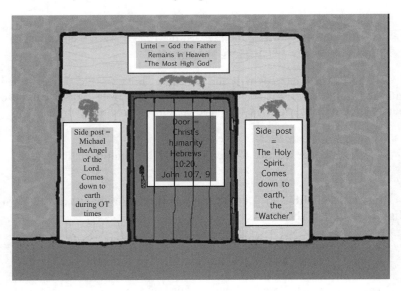

God's people, children of the "Most High God" who are also referred to as "god's" lower case (See John 10:34 and Psalm 82:1, 6) become "a royal priesthood, a holy nation, a peculiar people…" (1 Peter 2:9).

THE DOCTRINE OF THE TRINITY IS OPPOSED TO THE TRUTH OF "THE MOST HIGH GOD."

PROFESSOR: The Papal doctrine of the Trinity teaches that there is one 'God', yet through its concomitant doctrines of 'Consubstantiality' and 'Eternal Generation', **it in effect teaches that the Son and the Holy Spirit are not separate from the Father, but that all three are intrinsically parts of the Being called "God."**

WILLIAM: That would agree with the verse in Daniel that we saw:

Daniel 11:36:
"And the king *[Papacy]* shall do according to his will; and he shall exalt himself, and **magnify himself** above every god *[above Jesus Christ and the Father: by changing the law]*, **and shall speak marvelous** *[#6381 'hard, hidden, things too high...']* **things against the God of Gods,** and shall prosper till the indignation be accomplished: for that that is determined shall be done."

PROFESSOR: Yes, we saw that the sophistry of the man of sin would produce convoluted philosophies that denigrate God and attempt to make Him a non-entity by disparaging the Father's true position in the scheme of things. **By attempting to define God the papacy sets itself up above God.**

WILLIAM: How is that?

PROFESSOR: By the papacy God is **defined** as a "substance." **To define God in a "definition" and in unscriptural words of man's devising, is to set oneself above God**. Man cannot define God. Man can only find what God has seen fit to reveal. **The Bible predicted that the Papacy would "speak great words against the Most High God" "marvellous things against the God of gods"** (Daniel 11:36).

On the other hand the Scriptures teach that the expression 'one God' is exclusively applicable to one single personal Being, Who is called the Father, not an "essence" or "substance" manifested in various forms.

John 17:3:
"And this is life eternal, that they might know thee **the only true God, and Jesus Christ,** whom Thou hast sent."

Ephesians 4:6:

291

"**One God and Father of all,** who is above all, and through all, and in you all. *[Remember He is Jesus' 'Father' also. See also vs. 4: "There is one body and **one Spirit**..."].*

1 Corinthians 8:6:
"But to us **there is but one God, the Father,** of whom are all things, and we in Him; **and one Lord Jesus Christ,** by whom are all things, and we by Him."

Deuteronomy 6:4:
"Hear, O Israel: The Lord our God is one Lord." *[See the next chapter on the 'Shemmah'].*

WILLIAM: I remember that Jesus, acknowledging His subordination to His Father, said:

John 14:28:
"...For My Father is **greater than I**."

PROFESSOR: In Scripture, Jesus, the Son of God, is portrayed as a single independent entity with His own will and self-consciousness. **Is it not strange that the foremost doctrine of Catholicism, the Trinity, is so blatantly contrary to Scripture?**
The Trinity doctrine is accepted primarily on the basis of ignorance, not only of what it really teaches, but also of where that teaching leads. On the other hand, after knowledge is gained of what the Trinity doctrine really teaches, the honest will reject it. You will recall that we saw in the:

Handbook for Today's Catholic, page 16, declares:
"**The mystery of the Trinity is the central doctrine of Catholic faith. Upon it are based all other teachings of the Church.**"

WILLIAM: **And we saw that means that the doctrines of "Original Sin;" "Infant Baptism;" "The Immaculate Conception;" the "Pope's Authority to Change times and Laws;" etc. are all based on this "central doctrine:' the Doctrine of the Trinity.** (See page 263 in this book at the "Trinity Doctrine" Chart)

PROFESSOR: Let me illustrate—the Doctrine of the Immaculate Conception.

292

Simply put, **if God is represented in three distinct modes of one indivisible "essence" or "substance," then it is not possible to separate them.** Since it is not possible to tempt God (James 1:13) and since according to the Trinity doctrine, Christ is indivisible from God. He could not be "tempted in all points like as we are." His nature, therefore, was "Immaculate." However, since Mary was His human mother, **she had to be immaculate, too, else she would have passed on to Him our fallen human nature—which cannot co-inhabit with "the only true God", or it would be destroyed.** Furthermore, therefore, all human beings who are not born "immaculate" are, by reverse definition, **born** "sinners" (the doctrine of **original sin**), in need of baptism, as soon as possible, to preclude them from the awful prospect of dying before baptism and therefore dying in a "lost" condition; hence the practice of **'infant baptism'**.

Also, if Christ is "indivisible" from the Father, that is, simply one of the three "modalities" or "manifestations" of One God "essence" or "substance;" then He cannot mediate between God and man, since He would be mediating with Himself. Therefore **other mediators become necessary** and this lack is supplied by **popes, priests, saints**, etc.

If these doctrines (Original Sin, etc.) are false, then the foundational doctrine on which they are predicated must also be false, for one does not "pick figs from thistles" (Matt. 7:16) or vice versa.

To accept the Trinity doctrine is, in reality, an acceptance of the Papacy since the formation of the Papacy is predicated on the development of Trinitarian doctrine (see the Chapter 1 of this book)

WILLIAM: That's because the Trinity doctrine is based on Tradition and human councils, not on the Bible.

PROFESSOR: To accept the Trinity is to denigrate the authenticity of the SDA pioneers and is a virtual rejection of those points of truth which they made which are totally incompatible with Trinitarianism. On the other hand, to accept Trinitarianism results in exalting Papal tradition and the "patristic fathers."

The doctrine of the Trinity contradicts the clear Biblical definition of the term "One God," which in all cases refers to the Father exclusively. The term "One God" is not intended to teach that there is one Divine Being only, but rather the emphasis is on the presence of "The Most High God": a Supreme Being who is the God and Father of all, including Jesus Christ. (John 20:17; John 14:28; 1 Corinthians 15:27, 28)

293

Chapter 23

THE SHEMMAH

WILLIAM: Professor, two of the main verses that Trinitarians use to support their doctrine are Deuteronomy 6:4, 5. Can we talk about these verses please?

PROFESSOR: Those verses that you have just referred to, the Jewish people refer to as the "Shemmah" or "Shema". Let's look at the Hebrew words involved. *[Professor Miller pointed out the key words and their meaning, which are in italics within the verse.]*

> **Deuteronomy 6:4, 5:**
> 4) "Hear, O Israel: The LORD *[Yahweh]* our God *[El oheem, a plural term]* is one *[echad: see page 299, 302-303 in this book on this word]* LORD *[Jehovah]*:
> 5) And thou shalt love the LORD thy God with all thine heart, and with all thy soul, and with all thy might."

Employing the dictum that the Scriptures are their own expositor, we note that Jesus Himself quoted the Shema in:

> **Mark 12:29:**
> "And Jesus answered him, The first of all the commandments *[is]*, Hear, O Israel; The Lord *[Kurios = **Supreme Authority**]* our God *[Theos = **Supreme Divinity**]* is one Lord *[Supreme Authority]*."

Jesus words are recorded in Koine Greek—the language of the New Testament. The Shema of Deuteronomy 6:4 is, naturally, recorded in Hebrew. Trinitarians (and others) have made much of the fact that in Deuteronomy 6:4 the word "God" is translated from the Hebrew *eloheem*— a plural word which could be translated "Gods." So they postulate that, since the *"Eloheem"* are "one LORD" ("Jehovah", that is "Yahweh" in the Hebrew), this indicates a "Three-in-one" God, that is a "Trinity." Those who argue thus, fail to recognize that the word *Eloheem* is the self-same word used in Genesis 1:26: "And God (*Eloheem*) said, Let **us** make man in **our** image...." Which member of the Godhead is speaking here and referring to "us" and "our"? **Are they all speaking to themselves? No!** This is the Father speaking to His Son. God's messenger confirms this:

Early Writings, page 145:
"But when God said to His Son, "Let us make man in our image," Satan was jealous of Jesus."

The word *Eloheem* in both Genesis 1:26 and Deuteronomy 6:4 is #430 in Strong's Concordance Hebrew Dictionary, and the meaning is given: "Gods in the ordinary sense, **but specifically used of the Supreme God**;..." This special usage concurs exactly with the Greek rendition of Mark 12:29 where Mark recorded Jesus' words:

Mark 12:29:
"And Jesus answered him, The first of all the commandments *[is]*, Hear, O Israel; The Lord *[Strong's #2962 - Kurios = **Supreme in Authority**]* our God *[Strong's #2316 - Theos = **Supreme Divinity**]* is one Lord *[Kurios = Supreme in Authority]*."

No plurality is to be found. This does not support Trinitarianism, but does, however, concur with the Scriptures that call God the Father "the Most High God" (i.e. the "Supreme Divinity")—the God who is "the head of Christ" (1 Cor. 11:3)—of whom Jesus said, "My Father is greater than I"—and of whom Jesus said, "I live by the Father" while He was here on earth. (See John 14:28 and John 6:57.)

And now that He is ascended, Scripture declares:

Romans 6:9-10:
9) "Knowing that Christ being raised from the dead dieth no more; death hath no more dominion over him.
10) For in that he died, he died unto sin once: but in that he liveth, **he liveth unto God.**"

Unto Who? Unto the Father. We are "reconciled **to God** *[the Father]* by the death of His Son...." Romans 5:10. Therefore the reference to "the only true God" of John 17:3 is referring to the Father whom we cannot know except through "Jesus Christ, whom He hast sent" for God so loved the world that He gave His only begotten Son. His Son who subordinated Himself from being equal to His Father and "made Himself of none effect" in order to buy us back (redeem us), who officiates as our Mediator in the heavenly sanctuary presenting our prayers to our Father and His Father: to our God and Jesus' God. (See John 20:17). He is the only "Way" by which we can come to God. Jesus Himself said:

John 14:6:
"No man cometh unto **the Father**, but by Me."

WILLIAM: The Catholic Church system has always interpreted the word "one" in the Shema to mean a one-ness of substance or essence.

PROFESSOR: This is because they perceive the word *Elohim* in the Shema to mean a plurality. And we have noted God's messenger describes the "Oneness" in a way that negates any notion of "consubstantiality." Remember we read in:

Ministry of Healing, page 422:
"The unity that exists between Christ and His disciples does not destroy the personality of either. They are **one in purpose, in mind, in character, but not in person.** It is thus that God and Christ are one."

Now let us look again at the use of the Plural Term—Elohim— translated as "God."

Genesis 1:26:
"And God said, Let **us** make man in our image, after our likeness: and let **them** *[mankind]* have dominion over the fish of the sea, and over the fowl of the air, and over the cattle, and over all the earth, and over every creeping thing that creepeth upon the earth."

WILLIAM: Who is the "Supreme God" talking to in Genesis 1:26?

PROFESSOR: As we noted a moment ago, certainly not to Himself! Although the word "God" is *Elohim* (plural), it does not refer to all three Members of the Godhead speaking at once, and certainly not to a (one-in-three) Trinity God speaking. Rather, one Member of the Godhead is talking—the Father. God's messenger to the remnant elaborates on this conversation and tells us who the Father was speaking to. We saw:

Early Writings, page 145:

"But when **God said** to His Son, **"Let us make man in our image,"** Satan was jealous of Jesus. He wished to be consulted concerning the formation of man, and because he was not, he was filled with envy, jealousy, and hatred. He desired to receive the highest honors in heaven next to God *[Satan himself recognized the separate and distinct Personhood of Christ and was jealous of Him.]*."

The same understanding would be true of the following verses:

Genesis 3:22:
"And the LORD God said, Behold, **the man is become as one of us**, to know good and evil: and now, lest he put forth his hand, and take also of the tree of life, and eat, and live for ever."

Genesis 11:7:
"Go to, let **us** go down, and there confound their language, that they may not understand one another's speech."

Isaiah 6:8:
"Also I heard the voice of the Lord, saying, Whom shall **I** send, and who will go for **us**? Then said I, Here am I; send me."

Notice again, in the last verse, that it is the Father talking to the Holy Spirit this time, and Jesus volunteers to be sent by the Father. This is confirmed by the Bible and Spirit of Prophecy:

Isaiah 48:16:
"Come ye near unto me, hear ye this; I have not spoken in secret from the beginning; from the time that it was, there am I: **and now the Lord GOD, and his Spirit, hath sent me.**

Youth Instructor, June 21, 1900:
"Christ is equal with God *[in divinity, but not in station]*, infinite and omnipotent. He could pay the ransom for man's freedom. He is the eternal, self-existing Son, on whom no yoke had come; and **when God asked, 'Whom shall I send?' he could reply, 'Here am I; send me.'** He could pledge himself to become man's surety; for he could say that which the highest angel could not say—I have power over my own life, 'power to lay it down, and ...power to take it again.'"

297

The "us" of Isaiah 6:8 has to be the Father and the Holy Spirit since it is Christ who responds "send me." This is in perfect harmony with Isaiah 48:16. ("… and now the Lord GOD, and his Spirit, hath sent me.")

John 1:1-3:
1) "In the beginning was the Word, and **the Word was with God, and the Word was God.**
2) The same was in the beginning **with God.**
3) All things were made by him; and without him was not any thing made that was made."

The Father and the Son working in close harmony in Creation—both bearing the title "God."

WILLIAM: So we perceive three distinct eternal Beings, but each has their own role to play in the plan of salvation that the other cannot perform, and each having the title "God."

PROFESSOR: Yes, the Father is eternal. Jesus is eternal. The Holy Spirit is eternal. They are not "co-eternal. Each has a distinct and separate existence. However, as distinct and separate individuals, they are united as one in purpose, intent and character. Jesus and His Father worked in united, harmonious co-operation in the creation of the heavens, the earth, and "all that in them is".

You see, God likes UNITY IN DIVERSITY. This is how the Godhead operates, as opposed to the consubstantial Trinitarian concept of modular manifestations of a common substance. Unity in diversity is the Godhead pattern. We read in:

Mind, Character, and Personality, Volume 1, page 53:
"Like the branches of the True Vine, **the Word of God presents unity in diversity.**
There is in it a perfect, superhuman, mysterious unity."

This is because **One Spirit** is the inspiration behind each author, bringing the individual minds of the various authors into harmony with the mind of God.

Mind, Character, and Personality, Volume 2, page 423:
"It is the Lord's plan that there shall be **unity in diversity**."

298

Ibid, page 426:

"A life consecrated to the service of God will be developed and beautified in its individuality. **No person can sink his individuality in that of another,** but we are all, as individuals, to be grafted into the one parent stock, **and there is to be unity in diversity.** The great Master Artist has not made two leaves of the same tree precisely alike; so His creative power does not give to all minds the same likeness. They are created to live through ceaseless ages, and there is to be complete unity, mind blending with mind; but no two are to be of the same mold--MS 116, 1898.

God made us to live life as no one else could live it for us. We cannot live the life of another. God's example of unity in diversity as it relates to man is consummately exemplified in the Biblical description of marriage:

Genesis 2:24:

"Therefore shall a man leave his father and his mother, and shall cleave unto his wife: and they shall be one *[echad]* flesh."

Notice that the Hebrew word for "one" in this verse is _echad._ This is the same word for "one" as found in Deuteronomy 6:4. God is a Person; Jesus is a Person; The Holy Spirit is a Person; a husband is a person; a wife is a person. They can all be "echad", although they are separate and distinct persons.

Mind, Character, and Personality, page 426:
"No person can sink his individuality in that of another, ..."

But we can all come into godly harmony. This concept is in harmony with the next statement:

Mind, Character, and Personality, Volume 2, page 800:
"Unity in diversity is God's plan. Among the followers of Christ there is to be the **blending of diverse elements**, one adapted to the other, and each to do its special work for God. **Every individual has his place in the filling up of one great plan bearing the stamp of Christ's image....** One is fitted to do a certain work, another has a different work for which he is

adapted, another has a still different line; but each is to be the complement of the others. ... **The Spirit of God, working in and through the diverse elements, will produce harmony of action.... There is to be only one master spirit** *[See Chapter 31 of this book]*—**the Spirit of Him who is infinite in wisdom, and in whom all the diverse elements meet in beautiful, matchless unity.**--Lt 78, 1894.

This is the unity Christ prayed for in the 17th chapter of John!

SDA Bible Commentary, Volume 5, page 1143:

"**Unity in diversity** is a principle that pervades the whole creation. While there is an individuality and variety in nature, there is a oneness in their diversity; for all things receive their usefulness and beauty from the same Source. **The great Master Artist writes His name on all His created works**, from the loftiest cedar of Lebanon to the hyssop upon the wall. They all declare His handiwork, from the lofty mountain and the grand ocean to the tiniest shell upon the seashore.

"The branches of the vine cannot blend into each other; they are individually separate; yet every branch must be in fellowship with every other if they are united in the same parent stock. They all draw nourishment from the same source; they drink in the same life-giving properties. So each branch of the True Vine is separate and distinct, yet all are bound together in the parent stock. There can be no division. They are all linked together by His will to bear fruit wherever they can find place and opportunity. But in order to do this, the worker must hide self. He must not give expression to his own mind and will. He is to express the mind and will of Christ. The human family are dependent upon God for life and breath and sustenance. God has designed the web, and all are individual threads to compose the pattern. **The Creator is one,** and He reveals Himself as the great Reservoir of all that is essential for each separate life."

John 17:20, 21:

20) "Neither pray I for these alone, but for them also which shall believe on me through their word;

21) That they all may be one; as thou, Father, *art* in me, and I in thee, that they also may be one in us: that the world may believe that thou hast sent me."

SDA Bible Commentary, Volume 5: page 1148:

"[John 17:20, 21 quoted.] **What kind of unity is spoken of in these words?—Unity in diversity.** *[Notice! God's messenger makes the connection between this principle, "Unity in Diversity," and the Godhead!]* Our minds do not all run in the same channel, and we have not all been given the same work. God has given to every man his work according to his several ability. There are different kinds of work to be done, and workers of varied capabilities are needed. If our hearts are humble, if we have learned in the school of Christ to be meek and lowly, we may all press together in the narrow path marked out for us (MS 52, 1904).

We are all "diverse" one from another. We are diverse from God. Nevertheless, Inspiration and Scripture tell us that these separate and distinct "diverse" beings can be "one." Notice the following powerful refutation of Trinitarian consubstantiality and the concurrently powerful endorsement of true Godhead doctrine:

SDA Bible Commentary, Volume 5, page 1148:

"**Christ is one with the Father, but Christ and God are two distinct personages. Read the prayer of Christ in the seventeenth chapter of John**, and you will find this point clearly brought out. **How earnestly the Saviour prayed that His disciples might be one with Him as He is one with the Father.** But the unity that is to exist between Christ and His followers does not destroy the personality of either. They are to be one with Him as *["as"= in the same way]* **He is one with the Father**. (RH June 1, 1905)

Christ and His Father share one Spirit. The redeemed can share the same Holy Spirit. One pulse of harmony can again be present in these diverse and distinct beings; all because Jesus paid our redemption, making it possible for fallen man to be again "one spirit" with God through the indwelling Holy Spirit.

SDA Bible Commentary, Volume 5, page 1148:

"[**John 17:20-23 quoted**.] **What a wonderful statement!** The unity that exists between Christ and His disciples does not destroy the personality of either. **In mind, in purpose, in**

character, they are one, but not in person. By partaking of the Spirit of God, conforming to the law of God, **man becomes a partaker of the divine nature.** Christ brings His disciples into **a living union** with Himself and with the Father. *["This is life eternal that they might know thee, the only true god and Jesus Christ whom thou has sent.' John 17:3. A 'living union' (intimate interaction) through the same Agency: The Holy Spirit.]* **Through the working of the Holy Spirit upon the human mind, man is made complete in Christ Jesus.** Unity with Christ establishes a bond of unity with one another. This unity is the most convincing proof to the world of the majesty and virtue of Christ, and of His power to take away sin (MS 111, 1903).

WILLIAM: **The unity of the Godhead and their work in an individual's life to save from sin, paves the way for unity among Christ's followers.**

PROFESSOR: **Holy Spirit power!—through Whom we may "have this mind which was also in Christ Jesus."** The Holy Spirit who searches out the deep things of the mind of God, reveals them to us, and brings us into harmony with Him.

However, William I want you to also see that even if we take the word *"Eloheem"* in the Shema, Deut. 6:4, to actually indicate plurality; such an understanding will still **not** support "consubstantial Trinitarianism", but will support the inspired concept of the "Heavenly Trio"—the Godhead. Let us look at the verse again from this "plurality" perspective.

Deuteronomy 6:4:
"Hear, O Israel: The LORD *[Jehovah]* our God *[El oheem, plural]* is one *[echad]* LORD *[Jehovah]*."

Such an understanding of the Shema still fully supports a three-Person Godhead operating as one Supreme Authority—a unit of Authority. However, in this instance, the use of **the plural term for God's militates against the Trinitarian notion of "one God"** operating as different modalities, or whatever you care to call these 'manifestations'. Furthermore, the word for "one" as found in the verse is #254 in Strong's Concordance, and is the word *"echad"*: A primitive root meaning "to unify." As we saw *"Echad"* is the same word for **"one"** that is employed in:

Genesis 2:24:

"Therefore shall a man leave his father and his mother, and shall cleave unto his wife: and they shall be **one** *[echad]* flesh."

Just as surely as man and wife are separate and distinct individuals, who become "one" (*echad*) in that they become "unified," just so surely do the Scriptures describe the "oneness" (*echad*) of the Godhead. This is **not** consubstantial (*homousios*) **one**ness as postulated by Trinitarianism, but a description of separate and distinct individuals acting in united harmony.

So, whether one subscribes to the concept of the Hebrew word "Eloheem" being a reference to a plurality of divine Persons, or whether one accepts the point made at the beginning of this discussion on the Shema, that "Eloheem" is simply employed to describe "Supreme Divinity" (Strongs #430), either way, neither concept supports a consubstantial trinity. Whichever way you look at the Shema of Deuteronomy 6:4, it does not sustain this misbegotten medieval fable.

Chapter 24

THE HOLY SPIRIT AND THE TABLE OF SHOWBREAD

PROFESSOR: The Sanctuary message is a hallmark of Adventist biblical truth. The Psalmist says:

Psalm 77:13:
"Thy way, O God, is in the Sanctuary: Who is so great a God as our God?"

It is, therefore, no wonder that the sanctuary will reveal to us aspects of the Godhead. In the first apartment of the earthly sanctuary, to the right, stood the **golden table of 'showbread.' The Hebrew name for this bread means 'bread of the Presence.'** The showbread consisted of twelve loaves placed in two piles on the table every Sabbath.

WILLIAM: Why was the showbread placed in two piles of six? Why not three piles of four?

PROFESSOR: **It is not a long step from the table of showbread in the Old Testament to the table of the Lord in the New Testament (Luke 22:30; 1 Cor. 10:21.)** The parallel is close. The bread is His body, finally broken for us. **Who did He come to 'reveal' or 'show' to us? He came to reveal to us the Father** (of whose person He was the express image), and the Father was '**in** Christ, by His Spirit, reconciling the world to Himself.' Jesus is the 'living bread which came down from heaven' John 6:51.

I believe that the table of Showbread is a symbol of God's throne in the first apartment of the sanctuary; **the throne on which Jesus is 'set down' with His Father. (See Mark 16:19; Acts 2:33; Acts 7:55; Col. 3:1; and Heb. 10:12.)** The two piles of the 'bread of the Presence' symbolizing the true 'Presence'! The Father and the Son!

So complete will true "one"ness one day be between Christ and His people that He stated the following astounding words:

Revelation 3:21:

"To him that overcometh will I grant to sit with me in my throne, **even as I also overcame, and am set down with my Father in his throne.**"

WILLIAM: **But why only two depicted in the sanctuary? What about the "Mighty _Third_ Person of the Godhead"?**

PROFESSOR: We now come to a topic that boggles the mind. What has been revealed to us about the Holy Spirit's role in the Godhead? How has the Holy Spirit been symbolized?

God the Father and the Son are depicted as having form ("Let us make man **in our image" (Gen. 1:16)**; "If you have seen me you have **seen the Father**" (John 14:9); "He is the **express image of His (Father's) Person** (Heb. 1:3); etc.)

However, **the Holy Spirit is hardly ever described as having graspable form.** The Holy Spirit is likened to the "wind" (Acts 2:2), to "breath" (John 20:22), to "water" (John 4:10, 14; 7:38,39), to "oil" (Zech. 4:1-14; COL 408), and to "fire" (Acts 2:3), and to "leaven" (Luke 13:20,21); most frequently to oil. The mysterious Third Person of the Godhead is everywhere **present!** His **nature**—an unrevealed mystery, but some mysteries concerning the Godhead are revealed.

Notice:

1 Corinthians 2:10, 11, 13:
10) "But God hath revealed them to us by His Spirit: for **the Spirit searcheth all things, yea, the deep things of God.**

11) For what man knoweth the things of a man, save **the spirit of man which is in him?**

13) Which things also we speak, not in the words which man's wisdom teacheth, but which the Holy Ghost teacheth; comparing spiritual things with spiritual."

Remember, man is controlled/possessed by one of two spirits: either the Spirit of God or the spirit of a demon (See Chapter 31). Even a man's self-perception is flawed and frequently inaccurate. The Holy Spirit, and even Satan, knows us better than we know ourselves. As we have seen, the Holy Spirit even "searches out the deep things of the mind of God" (See Evangelism, page 617; 1 Corinthians 2:10-12).

Manuscript Releases, Volume 2, page 36:
"…And the Spirit, being God knoweth the mind of God…"

305

And He knows our mind. Read:

Manuscript Releases, Volume 4, page 379:
"If man is to become immortal, his mind must be in harmony with God's mind"!

Only through the agency of the Holy Spirit, and by beholding Christ and His example, in the mind's eye of faith, is this possible. Man may receive the same harmony that exists between the mind of Christ and the mind of His Father!

Acts of the Apostles, page 126:
"When the mind of man is brought into communion with the mind of God, the finite with the Infinite, the effect on body, mind, and soul is beyond estimate."
[Through what agency is the mind of man brought into communion with the Mind of God? Through the Holy Spirit.]

From these and similar statements, it becomes apparent that the Holy Spirit inhabits the mind of God—can discern God's very thoughts and can cause us to think God's thoughts.

WILLIAM: Now what about Jesus?

PROFESSOR: OK, let's look at:

Lift Him Up, page 301:
"In the lives of those who are partakers of the divine nature there is a crucifixion of the haughty, self-sufficient spirit that leads to self-exaltation. **In its place the Spirit of Christ abides,** and in the life the fruits of the Spirit appear. **Having the mind of Christ,** His followers reveal the graces of His character."

Rightly understood, the above, and numerous other passages, clearly indicate that the Holy Spirit inhabits the mind of God and of Christ, and can, if we so choose, inhabit our mind—bringing all things into "one"-ness, a perfect harmony with God's will.

WILLIAM: **What has this all to do with the Showbread?**—The Bread of the Presence?

PROFESSOR: I believe the following: The two piles of Showbread represent the Father and the Son; the bread is made of **flour** and <u>**oil**</u>! I conclude that **all three of the Heavenly Trio are represented at the table of Showbread.** The two members of the Godhead that have form—after whose image man was made—**and then there is the formless, all pervasive Person of the Holy Spirit, who fills both the Father and the Son. Their Presence automatically includes the Holy Spirit's presence.** The presence of a God-fearing servant of God, because of Christ's sacrifice, now automatically also includes the Holy Spirit's presence.

Similarly, the Menorah or golden candlestick, which stood across the room from the table of showbread, represents Christ who supplies the golden oil, the Holy Spirit, through the branches of the Menorah, to the "seven churches". Here again we see the Holy Spirit <u>in</u> the representation of Christ, the second Person of the Godhead.

The "Two-Person-Godhead" school of thought has tried to make much of there being only two stacks of showbread. Their postulations are invalidated by the truth. God's way of truth is perfectly demonstrated in the sanctuary, just as the Psalmist said!

Chapter 25

THE "ONE"NESS OF THE GODHEAD AND OF CHRIST'S FOLLOWERS

WILLIAM: Good morning, Professor. I would like to ask about the "oneness" of the Godhead. Look at this Scripture:

John 17:21, 22:
21) "**That they all may be one; as thou, Father, *art* in me,** and **I in thee**, that they also may be one **in** us: that the world may believe that thou hast sent me.

22) And the glory which thou gavest me I have given them; **that they may be one, even as we are one:**"

What is this "one-ness"?

PROFESSOR: **The issue of the "one-ness"** of the members of the Godhead has caused perplexity and debate over the centuries and Rome's resolution to the question is encapsulated in the doctrine of **consubstantiation** as expressed in the declaration emanating from the Council of Nicea (AD 325), and the Athanasian Creed of the fifth century. The best thing I can do is to first show you what the Bible and Spirit of Prophecy says on this subject. Let me show you these quotations below:

Selected Messages Book 1, pages 247, 248:
"**There are light and glory in the truth that Christ was one with the Father before the foundation of the world was laid.** This is the light shining in a dark place, making it *[the dark place]* resplendent with divine, original glory. **This truth, infinitely mysterious in itself, explains other mysterious and otherwise unexplainable truths, while it is enshrined in light, unapproachable and incomprehensible.**"

What is this inexplicable mystery that is "enshrined in light, unapproachable and incomprehensible"? It is totally beyond our finite comprehension how a distinct divine Person, the Holy Spirit, can actually dwell **in** another distinct divine Person—in Christ and in the Father—and can also dwell **in** us, making all "one."

Selected Messages Book 1, pages 250, 251:
"To bring humanity into Christ, **to bring the fallen race into oneness with divinity**, is the work of redemption. Christ took human nature **that men might be <u>one</u> with Him <u>as</u>** *["as" i.e. in the same way]* **He is <u>one</u> with the Father,** that God may love man **as** He loves His only-begotten Son, *[Can you imagine being loved by God in the same way that He loves His Son?]* that men may be partakers of the divine nature, and be complete in Him.

"The Holy Spirit, which proceeds from the only-begotten Son of God, binds the human agent, body, soul, and spirit, to the perfect, divine-human nature of Christ. This union is represented by the union of the vine and the branches. **Finite man is united to the manhood of Christ. Through faith human nature is assimilated with Christ's nature. <u>We are made one with God in Christ</u>."**

We are made <u>**one with God**</u> in Christ! Do we grasp that thought?

Desire of Ages, page 19:
"From the days of eternity **the Lord Jesus Christ was one with the Father.**"

John 10:30:
"**I and my Father are one.**"

2 Corinthians 5:19:
"To wit, that **God was in Christ,** reconciling the world unto Himself, not imputing their trespasses unto them; and hath committed unto us the Word of reconciliation."

The Father is **in** Christ by the Holy Spirit, and vice versa, in the same way that Christ can be **in** His disciples by the same Spirit.

John 14:10:
"Believest thou not that I am **in** the Father, and the Father **in** Me? The words that I speak unto you I speak not of myself; but **the Father that dwelleth in Me,** He doeth the works." *[See the chapter: "The Holy Spirit and the Table of Showbread" where, in*

> *the sanctuary,   the Holy Spirit is symbolized by the Oil **in**   the flour—thus contributing to the constitution of " the bread of life."]*

The **"one"ness** that exists between the Father and the Son, is the same "one"ness that Jesus prayed for in the seventeenth chapter of John, when He prayed that His disciples might be "one."

John 17:11:
"**Holy Father,** keep through thine own name those whom thou hast given me, **that they may be <u>one</u>, <u>as we are</u>"** *[i.e. in the same way that we are one].*

And see how Jesus describes that "one"ness:

John 17:21-23:
"**That they all may be <u>one</u>; as thou, Father, art <u>in</u> me and I <u>in</u> thee, that they also may be <u>one</u> <u>in</u> us** *[See John 14:16-1]*: that the world may believe that thou hast sent me."

22) "And the glory which thou gavest me, I have given them; that **they may be <u>one</u>, even as <u>we</u> <u>are one</u>:**

23)   **I <u>in</u> them, and thou <u>in</u> me, that they may be made perfect in one...."**

God's messenger tells us the following regarding Jesus' prayer for oneness in the 17th Chapter of John:

<u>Manuscript Releases</u>, Volume 5, page 365:
"Let them study the seventeenth of John, and learn how to pray and how to live the prayer of Christ. . . .

<u>Perfect oneness--a union as close as the union existing between the Father and the Son</u>--<u>this is what will give success to the efforts of God's workers</u>.--Manuscript 1, 1903, p. 6. ("An Appeal," January 7, 1903.)"

This "one"ness is not consubstantial, Trinitarian "one"ness. The "one"ness is effected in the redeemed by their being inhabited by the same Holy Spirit that inhabits the Father and the Son. **The Holy Spirit, the mighty Third Person of the Godhead, by inhabiting the minds of the Father and the Son and all the redeemed, brings about the "one-ness**

prayed for by Christ, making them all "one" in purpose, mind, and character. (See <u>Ministry of Healing</u>, page 422 below).

The Scriptures tell us of our sharing the Spirit of God with Him and His Son:

1 Corinthians 6:17:
"But he that is joined to the Lord is **one spirit**."

1 Corinthians 12:13:
"For by **one Spirit** are we all baptized into one body, whether we be Jews or Gentiles, whether we be bond or free; **and have been all made to drink into <u>one Spirit</u>**."

Ephesians 2:18:
"For through Him *[Jesus]* we both *[Jews and Gentiles]* have access **by <u>one Spirit</u>** to the Father."

Ephesians 4:4:
"There is one body *[of true believers:* the church*]* and **<u>one Spirit</u>,** even as ye are called in one hope of your calling."

Philippians 1:27:
"Only let your conversation be as it becometh the gospel of Christ: that whether I come to see you, or else be absent, I may hear of your affairs, **that ye stand fast in <u>one Spirit</u>, with one mind striving together for the faith of the gospel."**

The significance of the next inspired, and often repeated, statement cannot be overestimated:

<u>Ministry of Healing</u>, page 422:
"The unity that exists between Christ and His disciples does not destroy the personality of either. **They are one in purpose, in mind, in character, but not in person. <u>It is thus that God and Christ are one.</u>"**

This is a powerful anti-Trinitarian, anti-Consubstantiality statement, which is in full accord with the "Oneness" described in the book of John. Having **one** Spirit with God the Father and with the Son and with His children constitutes Biblical "one"-ness: not   the   figment   called

311

"consubstantiality" denoting some spiritualistic indivisible "substance"! (
concept that attempts to negate all the precious truth we have just looked at.

SDA Bible Commentary, Volume 5: page 1148:

"[John 17:20, 21 quoted.] **What kind of unity is spoken of in these words?--Unity in diversity.** Our minds do not all run in the same channel, and we have not all been given the same work. God has given to every man his work according to his several ability. There are different kinds of work to be done, and workers of varied capabilities are needed. If our hearts are humble, if we have learned in the school of Christ to be meek and lowly, we may all press together in the narrow path marked out for us." (MS 52, 1904)

As we have already seen from the pen of God's messenger:

Review and Herald, June 1, 1905:

"**Christ is <u>one</u> with the Father, but Christ and God are two distinct personages.** Read the prayer of Christ in the seventeenth chapter of John, and you will find this point clearly brought out. How earnestly the Saviour prayed that His disciples might be one with Him as He is one with the Father. **But the unity that is to exist between Christ and His followers does not destroy the personality of either. <u>They are to be one with Him as He is one with the Father</u>.**" (5BC 1148)

And God's messenger expounds on this 'one'ness in a way that total negates the 'consubstantial' Trinitarian view in the following statement th we looked at previously:

SDA Bible Commentary, Volume 5, page 1148:

"[John 17:20-23 quoted.] What a wonderful statement! The unity that exists between Christ and His disciples does not destroy the personality of either. **In mind, in purpose, in character, they are <u>one, but not in person</u>. <u>By partaking of the Spirit of God</u>, conforming to the law of God, man becomes a partaker of the divine nature. Christ brings His disciples into a living union with Himself and with the Father.** Through the working of the Holy Spirit upon the human mind, man is made complete **<u>in</u>** Christ Jesus. Unity with Christ establishes a bond of unity with one another. **This unity is the most convincing proof to the world of** the majesty and virtue of Christ, <u>and of His power to take away sin</u>." (MS 111, 1903).

<u>Patriarchs & Prophets</u>, page 34 and <u>Great Controversy</u>, page 493:
"Christ the Word, the Only Begotten of God, was **one with the eternal Father—<u>one in nature, in character, and in purpose</u>—the only being in all the universe that could enter into all the counsels and purposes of God.**"

WILLIAM: **I see that the oneness is a harmony of thought, purpose, and character and that this unity of the Father, Son, and which should be reflected in the brethren, is a result of the indwelling presence of the Holy Spirit. It has nothing to do with a oneness derived from an identical, indivisible substance, or essence.**

PROFESSOR: Amen! **God's messenger to His end-time church totally countermanded the spiritualistic notions encapsulated in these false trinitarian creeds.** Her depictions of the Godhead are clear and reasonable. Clearly sinful man cannot come into the presence of God the Father or he, sinful man, would be consumed (1 Tim. 6:16).

As we have noted, in the plan of salvation formulated by the Godhead, **it was decided that God the Father would maintain the integrity of the Godhead whilst two members of the Godhead would come into direct contact with sin and sinners. This they could not do whilst retaining all the attributes of Godhood.** Notice the following statement:

<u>Manuscript Releases</u>, Volume 9, page 122:
"**As Jehovah, the <u>supreme Ruler</u>, God <u>could not PERSONALLY communicate with sinful men</u>,** but He so loved the world that **He sent Jesus to our world as a revelation of Himself**." "I and My Father are one," Christ declared. No man knoweth "the Father, save the Son, and he to whomsoever the Son will reveal Him" (Matthew 11:27)....

"Taking humanity upon Him, Christ came to be one with humanity, and at the same time **to reveal our heavenly Father to sinful human beings.** He was in all things made like unto His brethren. He became flesh, even as we are."

(Incidentally, this last statement overturns the binit-arian assertion that the Holy Spirit "is God's own Person", since He cannot "**personally** communicate with sinful man".)

God the Father also sent The Holy Spirit as His and Christ representative: the Omnipresent One, who communicates directly wit men's minds. The One through Whom men are "born again" and throug Whom they may become a "union of humanity and divinity."

The voluntary self-abnegation of Christ in becoming a man in order t reach us where we are is aptly described in:

The Faith I Live By, page 48:
"The incarnation of Christ is the mystery of all mysteries."
(6BC 1082.)

Sign of the Times, July 4, 1895:
"Christ was one with the Father, yet ...He was willing to **step down** from the exaltation of One who **was** equal with God."

WILLIAM: But some people have showed me this reference where **God messenger has declared that Christ and the Father are of "on substance."** She stated in:

SDA Bible Commentary, Volume 7A, page 437:
"'I and my Father are one.' It seemed that divinity flashed through humanity as Jesus said, 'I and my Father are one.' The words of Christ were full of deep meaning as **He put forth the claim that he and the Father were of one substance, possessing the same attributes.** (Signs of the Times, Nov. 27, 1893).

Does this statement validate the doctrine of consubstantiality: th Trinitarian teaching?

PROFESSOR: William, as we have discussed before, you and I are of on substance! Flesh, blood, bone, sinew, etc! But are we of identical indivisib substance? Or did God's messenger mean one "common" substance? Th answer is simple.

If the very "essence" of the Father were present in Christ, then even sinner in Christ's presence would have been instantly consumed.

Furthermore, the concept of the one "essence" having to intercede wi itself and be a mediator between man and itself poses immense hurdles credulity. And how could Jesus be "tempted in all points like as we ar since it is not possible to tempt God? (James 1:13).

Also, since God alone has immortality (1 Timothy 6:16), then if He we of "one common substance" with the Father, Jesus did not really die on th cross. This notion provides Catholics with an excuse for thinking that He could go and preach to the souls in hell after the crucifixion, and prior to the resurrection—and so what then was the crucifixion, or the resurrection?

ON UNITY IN THE GODHEAD AND IN THE CHURCH

WILLIAM: How did Jesus describe the Father to His disciples?

PROFESSOR: He simply said that if you have seen Me (Jesus), you have seen the Father. Notice:

Upward Look, page 148:
"The great Teacher *[Jesus]* held in His hand the entire map of truth. In simple language He made plain to His disciples the way to heaven, and the endless subjects of divine power. **The question of the essence of God** was a subject on which He maintained a wise reserve, for **their** entanglements and specifications would bring in science *[falsely so called]* which could not be dwelt upon by unsanctified minds without confusion. *[Question: Who was it that brought in the "question of the essence of God"? Who were "they" whose "entanglements and specifications would bring in science which could not be dwelt upon by unsanctified minds without confusion"? I believe we see, as we study, that "they" fall under the headings: Paganism, Spiritualism, Trinitarianism, Pantheism, and Romanism.]* In regard to God and **in regard to His personality** *[not His being a mode of some "God essence"]*, the Lord Jesus said, "...he that hath seen me hath seen the Father" (John 14:9). *[That is, the Father is a distinct individual of whom I am the express image.]* Christ was the express image of His Father's person.
"...**In the place of devoting your powers to theorizing,** Christ has given you a work to do. His commission is, Go throughout the world and make disciples of all nations, baptizing them in **the name of the Father,** and *[the name]* of the Son, and *[the name]* of the Holy Ghost (Matt. 28:19)."

The name of the Godhead is **JEHOVAH (YAWEH) the SELF-EXISTENT.** Notice the following concerning God the Father:

Evangelism, page 614:
"The Father is all the fullness of the Godhead bodily."

315

Deuteronomy 6:4:
"Hear, O Israel: The LORD *[JEHOVAH]* our God *is* one LORD *[JEHOVAH]*:"

Psalm 83:18:
"That *men* may know that thou, whose name alone *is* JEHOVAH, *art* the **most high** over all the earth."

Christ also employed the name JEHOVAH Himself:

Exodus 6:3:
"And I appeared unto Abraham, unto Isaac, and unto Jacob, by *the name of* God Almighty *[El Shadai]*, but by **my name** JEHOVAH was I not known to them."

Isaiah 12:2:
"Behold, God *is* my salvation; I will trust, and not be afraid: for the LORD JEHOVAH *is* my strength and *my* song; he also is become my salvation."

Isaiah 26:4:
"Trust ye in the LORD for ever: for in the LORD JEHOVAH *is* everlasting strength:"

WILLIAM: Tell me again, what does JEHOVAH mean?

PROFESSOR: JEHOVAH means (Strong's #3068) Self-Existent or Eternal. **And JEHOVAH'S name is in Jesus.** See Exodus 23:21: "...**For My name is in Him.**" For the Spirit of the Father is **in** Christ: They are, all three, self-existent. See also:

Evangelism, page 614:
"The Son is all the fullness of the Godhead **manifested**. *[He came to "show us the Father" John 14:8, 9.]* The Word of God declares Him to be 'the express image of His *[the Father's]* person.'" *[So clearly did He "show us the Father."]*

Gideon spoke to Christ and addressed Him as Jehovah:

Judges 6:22-24:

316

22) "And when Gideon perceived that he *was* an angel of the LORD *["Jehovah" in the original]*, Gideon said, Alas, O Lord GOD! for because I have seen an angel of the LORD face to face.

23) And the LORD said unto him, Peace *be* unto thee; fear not: thou shalt not die.

24) Then Gideon built an altar there unto the LORD *[the self-existent divine LORD "Jehovah" with Whom Gideon was conversing, was none other than Christ]* and called it **Jehovahshalom**: unto this day it *is* yet in Ophrah of the Abiezrites."

And in:

Upward Look, page 144:
"To Moses, Jehovah declared, "I AM THAT I AM" (Exodus 3:14). **Christ** declared, "**Before Abraham was, I am**" (John 8:58). By this declaration He laid open the resources of His infinite nature...." *[See also Mount of Blessing, page34, 128.]*

Of the Holy Spirit we read in:

Evangelism, page 614:
"The Comforter that Christ promised to send after He ascended to heaven, is the Spirit **in all** the **fullness of the Godhead**, making **manifest** the power of divine grace to all who receive and believe in Christ as a personal Saviour."

That is making God's grace and power known to us! Let's continue in Upward Look:

Upward Look, page 148:
"Before the disciples shall compass the threshold *[into the heavenly sanctuary with Christ, into God's kingdom of church membership]*, **there is to be the imprint of the sacred name,** baptizing the believers **in the name** *[singular]* **of the threefold powers** *[plural]* **in the heavenly world.** The human mind is impressed in this ceremony, the beginning of the Christian life. It means very much. The work of salvation is not a small matter, but so vast that the **highest authorities** *[plural]* are taken hold of by the expressed faith of the human agent. **The eternal Godhead** *[a unit]*—**the Father, the Son, and the Holy Ghost—is involved** in

317

the action required to make assurance to the human agent, . . . confederating the heavenly powers with the human that man may become, through heavenly efficiency, partakers of the divine nature and workers together with Christ."

Counsels on Health, 1899, page 222:
   "The **Godhead** [*notice the statement is referring to all of the members of this unity*] **was stirred with pity for the race, and the Father, the Son, and the Holy Spirit gave Themselves to the working out of the plan of redemption.** In order fully to carry out this plan, **it was decided that Christ**, the only-begotten Son of God, **should give Himself an offering for sin.**"

WILLIAM: Those last two statements clearly demonstrate that **the term 'Godhead' and 'God' are two different concepts. 'Godhead' describes unity comprised of three separate and distinct individuals. 'God' is term to describe a single member of the Godhead—a distinct eterna Being.**

PROFESSOR: It also demonstrates the pending change that Chris **voluntarily accepted in order to reach fallen man where he is,** in order t carry out the plan of salvation.

WILLIAM: How important is this one-ness of unity in the Spirit?

PROFESSOR: This statement from God's messenger will help to answe your question.

Our High Calling, page 169:
   "**Unity in diversity is God's plan.** Among the followers of Christ there is to be the **blending of diverse** [*separate and distinct*] **elements,** one adapted to the other, and **each to do its special work for God.** Every individual has his place in the filling up of one great plan bearing the stamp of Christ's image.... One is fitted to do a certain work, another has a different work for which he is adapted, another has a still different line; but each is to be the complement of the others.... **The Spirit of God, working in and through the diverse elements, will produce harmony of action.... There is to be only one master spirit—the Spirit of Him who is infinite in wisdom, and in whom all the diverse elements meet in beautiful, matchless unity....**

318

"Differences of character exist by nature, **but our unity depends upon the degree in which we yield to the transforming influence of the Spirit of God.** Through the grace of Christ, some persons possess precious traits of character, a kindly and genial disposition; their very rebukes are imbued with tenderness, **for the Spirit of Christ** seems manifest in them.... The power of His grace will mold and fashion character according to the divine Model, renewing it in softness and beauty, in conformity to His own blessed image....

"How great the diversity manifested in the natural world! Every object has its peculiar sphere of action; yet all are found to be linked together in the great whole. **Christ Jesus is in union with the Father, and from the great center** *[the Godhead]* **this wonderful unity is to extend**... through all classes and diversities of talents. We are all to respect one another's talent; we are to harmonize in goodness, in unselfish thoughts and actions, **because the Spirit of Christ, as the living, working agency, is circulating through the whole.**... It is not striking actions that produce unity; **it is the mold of the Holy Spirit upon the character.**"

The unity is in diversity.

Mind, Character, and Personality, Volume 1, page 53:
"Like the branches of the True Vine, **the Word of God presents unity in diversity. There is in it a perfect, superhuman, mysterious unity.**" *[Because **One Spirit** is the inspiration behind each author.]*

Mind, Character, and Personality, Volume 2, page 423:
"It is the Lord's plan that there shall be **unity in diversity.**"

WILLIAM: That is the same thing that the book of nature beautifully teaches!

PROFESSOR: Yes! This lesson is taught so profoundly in nature.

Mind, Character, and Personality, Volume 2, page 426:
"A life consecrated to the service of God will be developed and beautified in its individuality. **No person can sink his individuality in that of another,** but we are all, as individuals, to

319

be grafted into the one parent stock, and there is to be unity in diversity. **The great Master Artist has not made two leaves of the same tree precisely alike; so His creative power does not give to all minds the same likeness.** They are created to live through ceaseless ages, and there is to be complete unity, mind blending with mind; but no two are to be of the same mold."--MS 116, 1898.

Notice, William, that God is a Person; Jesus is a Person; The Holy Spirit is a Person, and that **"No person can sink his individuality in that of another."** It is the same in nature:

> SDA Bible Commentary, Volume 5, page 1143:
> "Unity in diversity is a principle that pervades the whole creation. While there is an individuality and variety in nature, **there is a oneness in their diversity;** for all things receive their usefulness and beauty from the same Source. The great Master Artist writes His name on all His created works, from the loftiest cedar of Lebanon to the hyssop upon the wall. They all declare His handiwork, from the lofty mountain and the grand ocean to the tiniest shell upon the seashore.
> The branches of the vine cannot blend into each other; they are individually separate; **yet every branch must be in fellowship with every other if they are united in the same parent stock.** They all draw nourishment from the same source; they drink in the same life-giving properties. **So each branch of the True Vine is separate and distinct, yet all are bound together in the parent stock.** There can be no division. They are all linked together by His will to bear fruit wherever they can find place and opportunity. But in order to do this, the worker must hide self. **He must not give expression to his own mind and will. He is to express the mind and will of Christ.** The human family are dependent upon God for life and breath and sustenance. God has designed the web, and all are individual threads to compose the pattern. The Creator is one, and He reveals Himself as the great Reservoir of all that is essential for each separate life."

A graphic illustration of the "representative" nature of one member of the Godhead deferring to, and yet being equally accepted as though actually being the Most High Member, is strikingly depicted in Christ's own correction of His disciples ambitious aspirations for top honors in Christ's kingdom

Mark 9:35-37:

35 "And he sat down, and called the twelve, and saith unto them, If any man desire to be first, [the same] shall be last of all, and servant of all.

36 And he took a child *[a little human being]*, and set him in the midst of them: and when he had taken him in his arms, he said unto them,

37 Whosoever shall receive one of such children *[the children of men]* **in my name** *[Jesus=Jehovah saves from sin and its penalty]*, **receiveth me** *[although we are separate and distinct individuals]*: **and whosoever shall receive me, receiveth not me, but him** *[Christ's 'Father': the Most High God]* **that sent me."**

God's Word is so plain, so uncomplicated by human philosophical speculations and God denigrating perversion. Clearly, according to Scripture, separate and distinct individuals, who bring truth, love and life from the One who sent them, stand in the stead of such One, and the One who sent is accepted as though personally present. The Father sent Jesus, Jesus sends us. When the truth is accepted, the Father is accepted. This illustrates Biblical "one"ness. **When we are baptized into 'the name (Jehovah = Yaweh) of the Father, and of the Son, and of the Holy Spirit' we are baptized into the <u>fact</u> that they are all "self-existent"; whether we acknowledge that truth or not.**

Chapter 26

THE "FULLNESS OF THE GODHEAD"

WILLIAM: Professor, I have another question. The Bible says in Colossians 2:9: "For in him dwelleth all the fulness of the Godhead bodily." What is "the fulness of the Godhead?

PROFESSOR: Regarding the "Fullness of the Godhead," God's messenger has declared something about each member of the Godhead: first, regarding:

THE FATHER

Evangelism, pages 614, 615:
"**The Father is all the fullness of the Godhead bodily**, and is invisible to mortal sight."

The Father retains all the power and attributes of heavenly rulership and maintains the integrity of the Godhead—having no direct contact with sin or sinners directly, for such would destroy them.

Exodus 33:20:
"For there shall no man see Me, and live."

As we have repeatedly noted, God's messenger tells us:

Ministry of Healing, page 417:
"The Bible shows us **God in His high and holy place,** not in a state of inactivity, not in silence and solitude, but surrounded by ten thousand times ten thousand and thousands of thousands of holy beings, all waiting to do His will. Through these messengers He is in active communication with every part of His dominion. **By His Spirit He is everywhere present.** Through the agency of His Spirit and His angels He ministers to the children of men."

So, in the Father, every aspect of godliness, of the Godhead's qualities, is preserved, maintained, protected, and personified in Him.   Now with regard to:

THE SON

Evangelism, pages 614, 615:
"**The Son is all the fullness of the Godhead MANIFESTED.** *[He shows to men what the Father is like—at least as much as men can bear.]* The Word of God declares Him to be 'the **express image** of His person.' 'God so loved the world, that He gave His only-begotten Son, that whosoever believeth in Him should not perish, but have everlasting life' *['immortality' which belongs to God alone (1 Tim. 6:16)].* **Here is shown the personality of the Father.**"

Upward Look, page 191:
"He came and dwelt among us, **FILLED with all the fullness of the Godhead, to be one with us.**"

How did Christ come to be "filled" with all the fullness of the Godhead? God's messenger answers:

SDA Bible Commentary, Volume 7, page 907:
"**In Christ dwelt** *[through the indwelling Holy Spirit]* **all the fullness of the God-head bodily.** This is why, although He was tempted in all points like as we are, He stood before the world, from His first entrance into it, untainted by corruption, though surrounded by it. **Are we not also to become partakers of that fullness** *[through the same indwelling Holy Spirit]*, **and is it not thus, and thus only, that we can overcome as He overcame?**"

Desire of Ages, page 663:
"Though He had humbled Himself to humanity, the Godhead was still His own." (See DA 671). *[Despite being willingly subordinate, **Christ remained a member of the Divine Godhead**, receiving Divine power from His Father through the indwelling Holy Spirit.]*

And thirdly, let us look at statements concerning:

323

THE HOLY SPIRIT

Evangelism, pages 614, 615:

"**The Comforter** that Christ promised to send after He ascended to heaven, **is the Spirit IN all the fullness of the Godhead, <u>making manifest</u>** *[making known, demonstrating, showing]* <u>**the power of divine grace**</u> **to all who receive and believe in Christ as a personal** *[not as a manifestation of an essence]* **Saviour. There are three living persons of the heavenly trio;** in the name *[The" name" being Jehovah: <u>To Be Like Jesus</u>, page13, 33, 68]* of these three great powers—the Father, the Son, and the Holy Spirit—those who receive Christ by living faith are baptized, and these powers will co-operate with the obedient subjects of heaven in their efforts to live the new life in Christ." (Special Testimonies, Series B, No. 7, pages 62, 63 (1905).

The Holy Spirit administers the Divine power and grace of God to fallen man, and rebirths man of the Divine Seed, Jesus (See Galatians 3:16 and Colossians 1:27).

Desire of Ages, page 671:

"**The Spirit was to be given as a <u>regenerating</u>** *[rebirthing]* **agent,** and without this the sacrifice of Christ would have been of no avail. The power of evil had been strengthening for centuries, and the submission of men to this satanic captivity was amazing. Sin could be resisted and overcome only through **the mighty agency of the Third Person of the Godhead, who would come** with no modified energy, but **in the <u>fullness of divine POWER</u>**. It is the Spirit that makes effectual what has been wrought out by the world's Redeemer. It is by the Spirit that the heart is made pure. <u>**Through the Spirit the believer becomes a partaker of the divine nature.**</u>"

[Recreative 'Godhead' power is involved in making a sinner into a 'new creature' who partakes of divinity—the divinity of the Holy Spirit dwelling in him—the carnal spirit of demons having been evicted by the choice of the individual in choosing God's way as the right way—by choosing the "Way, the Truth, and the Life."]

The Holy Spirit conveys the divine power, love, and perspectives of God the Father to those whom the Holy Spirit inhabits. Now let us look again at:

Upward Look, page 191:
"He [Christ] came and dwelt among us, **filled** with all the fullness of the Godhead, **to be one with us**, that through His grace we might attain to perfection."

Jesus came to earth and was "filled with the Holy Spirit, who was "in the fullness of divine power." As we have seen, Jesus had laid aside his divinity. He came as a union of humanity and Holy Spirit-administered divine power, and paid the penalty that we deserve, opening the way for us to become united to Holy Spirit-divinity. Thus, we can partake of that fullness and, in that way, we can become "one" with the Father and the Son and one another.

And now let us consider statements concerning:

US

God's people—those who choose to have Jesus' loyal, obedient, and faithful mindset can and will receive the fullness of the Godhead! Look at what the Scripture says:

Colossians 2:9, 10:
9) "For in him [in Christ] dwelleth **all the fullness of the Godhead bodily,**
10) **And ye are complete in Him...**"

Ephesians 3:19:
"And to know the love of Christ which passeth knowledge, that **ye might be filled with all the fullness of God**."

Ephesians 4:4-6:
4) "There is **one body, and one Spirit,** even as ye are called in one hope of your calling;
5) One Lord, one faith, one baptism,
6) **One God and Father of all, who is above all, and through all, and in you all.**" [By His Spirit]

325

God's messenger plainly states that even the weakest can receive of the fullness of the Godhead—God's very own Spirit:

Acts of the Apostles, pages 49, 50:
"**Under the Holy Spirit's working** even the weakest, by exercising faith in God, learned to improve their entrusted powers and to become sanctified, refined, and ennobled. **As in humility they submitted to the molding influence of the Holy Spirit, <u>they received of the fullness of the Godhead</u> and were fashioned in the likeness of the divine.**"

Of Jesus, of His having the fullness of the Godhead <u>dwell</u> in Him, and how that relates to us, she wrote:

SDA Bible Commentary, Volume 7, pages 906, 907:
"**In Christ <u>dwelt</u> the fullness of the Godhead bodily.** This is why, although He was tempted in all points like as we are, He stood before the world, from His first entrance into it, untainted by corruption, though surrounded by it. **<u>Are we not also to become partakers of that fullness</u>, and is it not thus, and thus only, that we can overcome as He overcame?**"

WILLIAM: Do I understand correctly, that **we** can receive of the fullness of the Godhead?

PROFESSOR: Yes! Through the indwelling presence of the Holy Spirit!—the same Holy Spirit who filled Christ's humanity with divine power and who searches out the deep things of the mind of God. The Holy Spirit dwelt in Christ, and filled Him with the fullness of the Godhead, so that Jesus could manifest the Father to mankind. The same Holy Spirit enables us to receive of the "fulness of the Godhead" by dwelling in us. Thus, He enables us to manifest Christ to our fellows. And to manifest Christ is to manifest the Father who is abundant in "merciful and gracious, longsuffering, and abundant in goodness and truth." (Exodus 34:6) This is what the Godhead is full of. We are to be filled with all the fullness of the Godhead.

WILLIAM: What a wonderful call for us to come up higher!

326

Chapter 27

THE DIVINE POWER EXERCISED BY CHRIST DURING THE INCARNATION

WILLIAM: Since Jesus had laid aside His divinity, by what power did He perform miracles as He walked among men?

PROFESSOR: Both the Scriptures and the Spirit of Prophecy are consistent and clear on this point. Remember these verses that we noted previously:

Micah 3:8:
"But truly **I am full of power <u>by the spirit</u> of the LORD,** and of judgment, and of might, to declare unto Jacob his transgression, and to Israel his sin."

Acts 10:38:
"**How God anointed Jesus of Nazareth with the Holy Ghost and with power:** who went about doing good, and healing all that were oppressed of the devil; **for God was with him.**"

Luke 4:18, 19:
18) "**The Spirit of the Lord** *is* **upon me,** because he hath anointed me to preach the gospel to the poor; he hath sent me to heal the brokenhearted, to preach deliverance to the captives, and recovering of sight to the blind, to set at liberty them that are bruised,
19) To preach the acceptable year of the Lord."

Matthew 4:1:
"Then was Jesus **led up of the Spirit** into the wilderness to be tempted of the devil."

Luke 4:1:
"And **Jesus being full of the Holy Ghost** returned from Jordan, and was **led by the Spirit** into the wilderness...."
Jesus plainly stated:

John 5:30:
"I can of mine own self **do nothing.**"

And Jesus identified the source of His power:

Matthew 12:28:
"But if **I cast out devils by the Spirit of God,** then the kingdom of God is come unto you."

God's messenger is equally clear on this issue:

Desire of Ages, page 336:
"When Jesus was awakened to meet the storm, He was in perfect peace. There was no trace of fear in word or look, for no fear was in His heart. **But He rested not in the possession of almighty power.** It was not as the 'Master of earth and sea and sky' that He reposed in quiet. **That power He had laid down,** and He says, 'I can of Mine own self do nothing.' John 5:30. **He trusted in the Father's might.** It was in faith—faith in God's love and care—that Jesus rested, and **the power of that word which stilled the storm was the power of God.**"

Reflecting Christ, page 130:
"Christ is our pattern, our example in all things. **He was filled with the Spirit, and the Spirit's power was manifested through Him....**" Letter 352, 1908.

And, through Jesus, we can receive of the divine nature and power:

General Conference Bulletin, May 17, 1909:
"To abide in Christ means that you shall be a partaker of the divine nature. **Humanity lays hold upon divinity, and you have divine power.**"

And the Scriptures tell us of His resurrection:

1 Peter 3:18:
"For Christ also hath once suffered for sins, the just for the unjust, that he might bring us to God, being put to death in the flesh, **but quickened** *[made alive]* **by the Spirit.**"

And don't forget the powerful statements, on this topic, penned by Paul in:

Romans 8:9-11:
9) "But ye are not in the flesh, but **in the Spirit, if so be that the Spirit of God dwell in you.** Now if any man have not the Spirit of Christ, he is none of his.

10) **And if Christ be in you,** the body is dead because of sin; but **the Spirit is life** because of righteousness.

11) But if the Spirit of him that raised up Jesus from the dead **dwell in YOU,** he that raised up Christ from the dead shall also quicken your mortal bodies **by his Spirit that dwelleth in YOU."**

In John 5:13, John wrote:

John 5:13:
"These things have I written to you that believe on the name of the Son of God; that ye may know that ye have eternal life...."

That eternal life that Christ's followers may have in them is none other than the Holy Spirit who administers Christ's life to them. He is their "seal unto the day of redemption." (Eph. 4:30).

Review & Herald, June 13, 1899:
"The impartation of the Spirit was the impartation of the very life of Christ, which was to qualify the disciples for their mission."

WILLIAM: It is seems very clear that **Jesus was our Example,** in ALL things, and that He did not use His own power to perform any miracles, but relied on the Holy Spirit just as we should.

PROFESSOR: That is why Jesus could say:

Revelation 3:21:
"To him that overcometh will I grant to sit with me in my throne, **even as I also overcame** *[overcame in the same "way"],* and am set down with my Father in his throne."

Chapter 28

WHAT JESUS LAID ASIDE IN ORDER TO REACH US

WILLIAM: Do we know what Jesus Christ laid aside in order to be born into the world and reach us?

PROFESSOR: Firstly, we have to recall what status Jesus had originally so that we can know something of the qualities and capacities that He had, and which He laid aside in order to reach us in our fallen state. His previous, de facto, equality of station, is without question and is corroborated by Scripture and inspiration:

> **Philippians 2:5, 6:**
> **5) "Let this mind be in you, which was also in Christ Jesus:**
> **6) Who, being in the form of God, thought it not robbery to be equal with God."**

Despite all that He laid aside, Jesus' "**AUTHORITY**" remained constant:

> SDA Bible Commentary, Volume5, page 1142:
> "**The world's Redeemer was equal with God. His authority was as the authority of God. He declared that He had no existence separate from the Father** *[there had never, before the crucifixion, been a time of separation from His Father]*. The **authority** by which He spoke, and wrought miracles, was expressly His own, yet He assures us that He and the Father are one...."

WILLIAM: Jesus clearly was equal to the Father.

PROFESSOR: Yes, Jesus originally was equal with God the Father in every respect. His self-abnegation was voluntary. But please note, that while on earth as a man, the **authority** by which He spoke while on earth was expressly His own, but not the **power** that He exercised. The power

He exercised on earth was the "power" of God administered by the Holy Spirit. See Desire of Ages, page 335,336.

WILLIAM: So then Jesus did not stay on the same status level with His Father?

PROFESSOR: **HE DID NOT CLING TO HIS EQUALITY WITH HIS FATHER:**

The Faith I Live By, page 48:
"The incarnation of Christ is the mystery of all mysteries.
"Christ was one with the Father, yet ... **He was willing to step down from the exaltation of one who <u>was</u> [past tense] equal with God."** (*Signs of the Times,* July 4, 1895.)

Testimonies to the Church, Volume 4, pages 457, 458:
"Paul …exhorts us to possess the mind 'which was also in Christ Jesus: who, being in the form of God, thought it not robbery to be equal with God: but **made Himself of no reputation,** and **took** upon Him the form of a servant.... He [Paul] presents Christ before us **as He** [Christ] <u>was</u> **when** [past tense] equal with God [the Father] and receiving the adoration of angels, and **then traces His descent** until He reaches the lowest depths of humiliation…."

Lift Him Up, page 345:
"Jesus Christ **laid off His royal robe, His kingly crown, and clothed His divinity** [His Being a divine Person, a Member of the Godhead] **with humanity, in order to become a substitute** and surety for humanity, **that dying in humanity He might by his death destroy him who had the power of death. <u>He could not have done this as God</u>,** but **BY COMING AS MAN CHRIST COULD DIE**. By <u>death</u> He overcame death. **The DEATH of Christ bore to the death him who had the power of death, and opened the gates of the tomb** [the "gates of hell;" Gehenna; the grave] for all who receive Him as their personal Saviour."

Clearly Jesus had laid down His immortal life and taken mortality so that He, a divine member of the Godhead, one equal to the Law, could **<u>die</u>**

331

to pay man's penalty for sin. Notice what God's messenger clearly says on this topic:

> *Signs of the Times*, June 17, 1897 par. 8:
> "...**while bearing human nature, he *[Christ]* was dependent upon the Omnipotent for his life.** In his humanity, he laid hold of the divinity of God; and this every member of the human family has the privilege of doing. Christ did nothing that human nature may not do if it partakes of the divine nature."

> Selected Messages Book 3, page 131:
> "Through being partakers of the divine nature **we** may stand pure and holy and undefiled. **The Godhead was not made human *[the "Most High God", the Father, and the mighty third Person of the Godhead were separate and distinct]*, and the human was not deified by the blending together of the two natures *[just as our humanity is not deified when our humanity becomes blended with divinity by the infilling of the Holy Spirit]*.** Christ did not possess the same sinful, corrupt, fallen **disloyalty** *[the carnal heart' which is 'enmity against God'...]* we possess, for then He could not be a perfect offering."—Manuscript 94, 1893.

The Father, who "is all the fullness of the Godhead bodily," maintains the integrity of the Godhead "invisible to mortal sight;" while Jesus came to "manifest that "fullness," to show us the Father (Evangelism, page 614). So, no, **the "Godhead was not made human," nor was the human "deified."**

WILLIAM: So then Jesus was not born exactly like us?

PROFESSOR: We have "fallen disloyalty" when we are born. We are born with "carnal hearts" *[minds]* that are at "enmity against God," that are "not subject to His law, neither indeed can be." (Romans 8:7). We have to be "born again" of the same Holy Spirit, who was Jesus' earthly progenitor, and become, through the Spirit, a union of humanity and divinity as He was; receiving "clean hearts" *[minds]*: the "mind" that was in Christ Jesus, renewed in us. We are warned against making Jesus out to be "altogether human, such an one as ourselves" (5 BC page 1128.6).

Jesus was not born with a "carnal" mind. He was not 'altogether such a one as we are,' as we see in the next familiar statement:

Signs of the Times, October 29, 1894:
"Jesus Christ is our example in all things. **He began life, passed through its experiences, and ended its record, with a sanctified human will**."

(Satan never touched His 'head'; he only 'bruised His heel'.)

The height, the depth, the length, the breadth of this topic is stressed by God's messenger in the following statement:

Lift Him Up, page 40:
"The mysteries of redemption, **the blending of the divine and the human in Christ, His incarnation,** sacrifice, mediation will be sufficient to supply minds, hearts, tongues, and pens with themes for thought and expression for **all** time."

WILLIAM: Was it His divinity that was blended with his humanity?

PROFESSOR: Jesus laid aside the panoply, the power, the immortal life of divinity, and had power and life administered to Him by the Holy Spirit. In fact,

HE GAVE ALL

In fact, He Himself said:

John 6:57:
"I live by the Father..."

John 5:30:
"I can of mine own self do nothing."

And the Scriptures tell us the source of His power:

Micah 6:8:
"But truly **I am full of power by the spirit of the LORD**..."

Note that the following statements do **not** say that Jesus ceased to be a divine Person, but that He laid aside those aspects of being a divine Person that precluded Him from direct contact with fallen mankind, and from being able to pay man's penalty for sin:

333

Special Testimonies: Series B, No. 9, page 3:
"By His life of sacrifice, Christ has made it possible for man to become a partaker of the divine nature, having escaped the corruption that is in the world through lust. **The salvation of souls was the great object for which Christ sacrificed His royal robe and kingly crown, the glory of heaven and the homage of the angels, and, <u>LAYING ASIDE HIS DIVINITY</u>,** came to earth to labor and suffer with humanity upon Him."

Lift Him Up, page 233:
"He turned from His royal throne, His high command, and, **<u>LAYING ASIDE HIS DIVINITY</u>,** clothed Himself with humanity."

Bible Echo, October 12, 1896:
"At the time when He was most needed, Jesus, the Son of God, the world's Redeemer, **<u>LAID ASIDE HIS DIVINITY</u>,** and came to earth in the garb of humanity." (*Sign of the Times,* March 17, 1887).

WILLIAM: Jesus truly "emptied Himself" and "made Himself of no reputation."

PROFESSOR: Absolutely! God's messenger records this tremendous truth:

Desire of Ages, page 22.3:
"Lucifer had said, "I will exalt my throne above the stars of God; . . . I will be like the Most High." Isa. 14:13, 14. But Christ, "being in the form of God, counted it not a thing to be grasped to be on an equality with God, but **emptied Himself**, taking the form of a servant, being made in the likeness of men." Phil. 2:6, 7, R. V., margin. {DA 22.3}

Desire of Ages, page 436.1:
"While Lucifer counted it a thing to be grasped to be equal with God, Christ, the Exalted One, "**made Himself of no reputation**, and took upon Him the form of a servant, and was made in the likeness of men: and being found in fashion as a

334

man, He humbled Himself, and became obedient unto death, even the death of the cross." Phil. 2:7, 8

Now, let's look more closely at:

CHRIST'S HUMILIATION IN BECOMING A MAN—IN ORDER TO SAVE US

Review & Herald, June 15, 1905:

"**Christ could not have come to this earth with the glory that he had in the heavenly courts. <u>Sinful human beings could not have borne the sight.</u>** He veiled his divinity with the garb of humanity, but **he did not <u>part</u> with his divinity.** *[But He did lay it aside! (See Series B, no. 9, page3; <u>Lift Him</u> Up, page 233; Bible Echo, 10/2/1896 above). This statement simply means that **He did not cease to be a divine Person**—a member of the Godhead. If one lays aside one's coat, that does not mean one has "parted" with it. It is still your coat.]* **A divine-human Saviour,** he came to stand at the head of the fallen race, to share in their experience from childhood to manhood."

The Youth's Instructor, November 21, 1895:

"How can it be that the helpless babe in Bethlehem's manger **is still the divine Son of God**? Though we cannot understand it, **we can believe that He who made the worlds became, for our sakes, a helpless babe.** Though higher than any of the angels, **though as great as the Father** on the throne of heaven *[and fully "equal" to the Law of God]*, He became one with us. **In Him God and humanity became one** *[at-one-ment = atonement]*, **and it is in this fact that we find the hope of our fallen race.**"

PROFESSOR: Jesus became "one *[echad]* flesh" with us so that we can become "one *[echad]* spirit" with Him, and, through Him, with the Father.

Please notice that God remains God, and humanity remains humanity, yet they become "one". They are separate and distinct, yet "one". Just as the redeemed sinner and the Holy Spirit are separate and distinct, yet become "one" in a union of humanity and divinity. The following analogy from English literature, (the allegory entitled: 'The Prince and the Pauper') may help to clarify the issue of Christ laying aside His divinity while not parting with it.

335

The prince who decided to change places with a pauper, wearing his clothes and living his life in order to have a better knowledge of the life and struggles of the lowest of his people, **did not cease to be the prince**. But **the panoply and the power associated with being the prince, was** <u>laid</u> <u>aside</u>:

> *Signs of the Times*, May 10, 1899:
>
> "But although Christ's divine glory was for a time veiled and eclipsed by His assuming humanity, **yet He did not cease to be God when He became man. The human did not take the place of the divine, nor the divine of the human. This is the mystery of godliness.** The two expressions **<u>human and divine were, in Christ, closely and inseparably one</u>**, and <u>yet they had a distinct individuality</u>. **Though Christ humbled Himself to become man, the Godhead was still His own.** *[Because He and His Father were one!—not in essence, but in purpose, mind and character (<u>Ministry of Healing</u>, 421,422), and because Christ still remained the second Person of the Godhead, still fully divine, despite having "laid aside His divinity"].* **His Deity could not be lost while He stood faithful and true to His loyalty** *[Incidentally, how could God's messenger say that, if 'Christ' was an indivisible projection of 'God'?]."*

Notice—He <u>could lose His deity</u> if He had failed! Such were the risks involved in the plan of salvation! Truly, we are saved by the "**<u>faith</u>** of Jesus." William, I want you to see that, at times, Christ being divine, could be perceived by those around Him:

> *Signs of the Times*, May 10, 1899 par. 12 and 13:
>
> "There were occasions when Jesus stood forth while in human flesh as the Son of God. **Divinity flashed through humanity,** and was seen by the scoffing priests and rulers. Was it acknowledged? Some acknowledged that He was the Christ, but the larger portion of those who upon these special occasions were forced to see that He was the Son of God, refused to receive Him. Their blindness corresponded to their determined resistance of conviction.
>
> "When Christ's indwelling glory flashed forth, it was too intense for His pure and perfect humanity *[that was how He conducted Himself just as He asks us to do (see "...be ye therefore perfect..." Matthew 5:48), see also below in <u>Desire of</u>*

336

Ages page 664] entirely to conceal. The scribes and Pharisees did not speak in acknowledgment of Him, but their enmity and hatred were baffled as His majesty shone forth. The truth, obscured as it was by a vail of humiliation, spoke to every heart with unmistakable evidence. This led to the words of Christ, 'Ye know who I am.' Men and devils were compelled, by **the shining forth of His glory,** to confess, 'Truly, this is the Son of God.' **Thus God was revealed:** thus Christ was glorified."

WILLIAM: What "divinity" flashed through humanity, **if** Jesus had **laid aside "His divinity"**?

PROFESSOR: The following statement from inspiration gives us a clue:

Desire of Ages, page 664:
> "Jesus **revealed <u>no</u> qualities, and exercised <u>no</u> powers, that men may not have through faith in Him. His perfect humanity is that which all His followers may possess,** if they will be in subjection to God as He was."

The power and gifts that men may have are given to them by the Holy Spirit. Moses' face shone when he descended the mountain of God; Steven's face shone at his martyrdom; Elijah and Elisha, and Peter and Paul raised the dead; etc.—All these are evidences of the same divine indwelling presence and power of the Holy Spirit.

SDA Bible Commentary, Volume 5, page 1129:
> "There is no one who can explain the mystery of the incarnation of Christ. Yet we know that He came to this earth and lived as a man among men. **The man Christ Jesus was not the Lord God Almighty, yet Christ and the Father are one.**"

In this statement, the "Lord God Almighty" refers to God the Father, the "only true God" *[John 17:3].* The "one"ness we have already discussed. This statement is at odds with the notion of consubstantiation as found in Trinitarianism. We have already noted the inspired Biblical and Spirit of Prophecy descriptions of the "one"ness of the Father and the Son.

Jesus lived on earth as a divine/human Being, but, having laid aside His own divinity, the divinity of the Holy Spirit filled his humanity from the time of His birth. That is why he said, **"I can of Mine own self do nothing."** John 5:30.

337

You can see that it was Jesus and the Holy Spirit working out the Father's will together, as one. Let's look more closely at how:

GOD THE FATHER MAINTAINS THE INTEGRITY OF THE GODHEAD, WHILE CHRIST AND THE HOLY SPIRIT COME INTO DIRECT CONTACT WITH SIN AND SINNERS.

Manuscript Releases, Volume 9, page 122:
"As **Jehovah, the supreme Ruler, God could not personally communicate with sinful men,** but He so loved the world that He sent Jesus to our world as a revelation of Himself."

As we have already noted, God the Father has to communicate with this sinful world through intermediaries.

Ministry of Healing, page 417:
"The Bible shows us God in His high and holy place.... **Through the agency of His Spirit and His angels He ministers to the children of men.** Above the distractions of the earth He sits enthroned; all things are open to His divine survey; and from His great and calm eternity He *[the "Most High God"]* orders that which His providence sees best."

And we find that, after the fall, Christ immediately became the 'contact Person' of the Godhead with fallen man:

Manuscript Releases, Volume 9, page 237:
"**After the Fall Christ became Adam's instructor. He acted in God's stead** toward humanity, saving the race from immediate death. **He took upon Him the office of mediator.** Adam and Eve were given a probation in which to return to their allegiance, and in this plan all their posterity were embraced. **"In the fullness of time Christ was to be revealed in human form"** *[as the Messiah: the "Anointed One."]*

Acts 10:38:
"How **God anointed Jesus of Nazareth with the Holy Ghost and with power**: who went about doing good, and healing all that were oppressed of the devil; **for God was with him"** *[through the Holy Spirit.]*

338

Jesus said:

Matthew 12:28:
"But if I cast out devils by **the Spirit of God**, then the kingdom of God is come unto you."

Jesus, our divine/human Mediator, is the only "Way" back to the "Most High God," our Heavenly Father.

John 14:6:
"**I am the way**, the truth, and the life: **no man cometh unto the Father, but by me.**"

WILLIAM: We get back to God through Jesus:

PROFESSOR: Yes, Jesus is our vital Mediator, not any pope, priest, or saint:

Selected Messages Book 1, page 238:
"The pardon of sin, justification by faith in Jesus Christ, **access to God only through a mediator because of their lost condition, their guilt and sin—of these truths the people** *[the Israelites who had come out of Egypt]* **had little conception. In a great measure they had lost a knowledge of God and of the only way to approach Him**" *[which is through Christ].*

Paul spells it out succinctly:

1 Timothy 2:5:
"For there is **one God** *[the Father]* and **one Mediator** between **God** and men, **the man Christ Jesus**."

WILLIAM: As mediator, He directs our petitions to the Father.

PROFESSOR: **Did you notice who the One God of the Bible is**; the One to Whom Jesus taught us to pray, "**Our Father** which art in heaven…"—in His High holy place? See how Jesus emphasizes the difference in station between His Father and Himself, resulting from Jesus' own self-abnegation.

John 14:28:

"Ye have heard how I said unto you, I go away, and come again unto you. If ye loved Me, ye would rejoice, because I said, I go **unto the Father: for my Father is greater than I**."

This is a clear declaration by Jesus on the distinction between the role o the Most High God (His Father) and His own **mediatorial** role.

JESUS ASCENDED TO HEAVEN AS OUR HIGH PRIEST AN MEDIATOR IN THE HEAVENLY SANCTUARY.

Hebrews 4:14-16:

14) "Seeing then that **we have a great high priest, that is passed into the heavens, Jesus the Son of God,** let us hold fast our profession.

15) For we have not an high priest which cannot be touched with the feeling of our infirmities; but was in all points tempted like as we are, yet without sin.

16) **Let us therefore come boldly unto the throne of grace** *[God the Father's throne],* that we may obtain mercy, and find grace to help in time of need."

The high priest officiates **before God** on men's behalf. Lik Melchizedek, Jesus is also a High Priest of "the Most High God", a Hig Priest "after the order of Melchizedek" (Hebrews 5:6, 10; 6:20; 7:11, 1 21) officiating **before the Father** on our behalf.

WILLIAM: So then, did a divine Person , One equal with the Law, di when Jesus died?

PROFESSOR: That is a good recurring question. Let us first look at:

THE DEATH THAT JESUS WAS WILLING TO DIE FOR YO AND ME

Spirit of Prophecy, Volume 3, page 231:

"When Jesus had opened before his disciples the fact that he must go to Jerusalem to suffer and die at the hands of the chief priests and scribes, Peter had presumptuously contradicted his Master, saying, 'Be it far from thee, Lord; this shall not be unto thee.' He could not conceive it possible that the Son of God

340

should be put to death. **Satan suggested to his** *[Peter's]* **mind that if Jesus was the Son of God he could not die."**

This lie Satan is repeating to disciples of today. It is the same lie taught by Trinitarianism: that as an indivisible modality of the one-god substance Jesus did not die, but went and preached to the souls in hell, since, as an indivisible modality of "God", He could not die!

However, as we have noted, Jesus became a man in order for it to be possible for Him to die *(Lift Him Up page 345 "...that dying in humanity He might by his death destroy him who had the power of death. He could not have done this as God, but by coming as man Christ could die.")*. As Deity, if He had retained His divine attributes and divine immortality, that would have been impossible. It was imperative that He lay aside His divinity and also lay down his divine, immortal life, to make it possible for the divine Second Person of the Godhead to die. Just how this can be we may never fully know, and right now no one but the Godhead does. *(Nevertheless, Special Testimonies, Series B, No. 9, page 3; Signs of the Times, January 16, 1896; Bible Echo, October 12, 1896 declare that, it is so)*.

As we saw in:

SDA Bible Commentary, Volume 5, page 1129:
"There is no one who can explain the mystery of the incarnation of Christ. Yet we know that He came to this earth and lived as a man among men. **The man Christ Jesus was not the Lord God Almighty,** yet Christ and the Father are **one**." *["one"ness as described in John 17:21; Ministry of Healing page 422.]*

We have noted over and over how Christ and His Father are one! Notice, however, how God's messenger describes the incredible transaction that Christ entered into for you and I:

Review & Herald, July 5, 1887:
"The apostle would call our attention from ourselves to the Author of our salvation. He presents before us his two natures, divine and human. Here is the description of the divine: 'Who, being in the form of God, thought it not robbery **to be equal with God.**" He was "the brightness of his glory, and the express image of his person.'

"Now, of the human: 'He was made in the likeness of man: and being found in fashion as a man, he humbled himself, and became obedient unto death.' He voluntarily assumed human nature. It was his own act, and by his own consent. He clothed his divinity with humanity. **He was all the while as God, but he did not appear as God.** He veiled the demonstrations of Deity which had commanded the homage, and called forth the admiration, of the universe of God. *["Veiled" in the flesh and blood body that was prepared for Him. Hebrews 10:5]* **He was God while upon earth, but he divested himself of the form of God** *[which is spiritual form, John 4:24]*, and in its stead took the form and fashion of a man. **He walked the earth as a man. For our sakes he became poor,** that we through his poverty might be made rich. **He laid aside his glory and his majesty. He was God,** but the glories of the form of God he for a while relinquished. *[It would have been forever had He failed. See Signs of the Times, May 10, 1899, quoted on page 319 and Manuscript Release, Volume 10 - If one sin had tainted Christ's character see page 420 of this book].*

"…But he humbled himself, and **took mortality upon him.** As a member of the human family he was mortal, but **as a God** he was the fountain of life to the world. He could, in his divine person, ever have withstood the advances of death, and refused to come under its dominion; **but he voluntarily laid down his** *[immortal]* **life, that in so doing he might give life and bring immortality to light.** He bore the sins of the world, **and endured the penalty which rolled like a mountain upon his divine soul.** He yielded up his **life** a sacrifice, that man should not **eternally** die."

WILLIAM: "The wages of sin is death…."

PROFESSOR: "…But the gift of God is eternal life through Jesus Chris our Lord." Romans 6:23. So we see Christ's immortal life balanced again its opposite—the **"second death," a Bible term describing eternal death That is the "penalty" death. Eternal death is the penalty—the "wage of sin"**—not eternal burning in "hell." There are two "deaths" spoken of, the Bible. Let us see which one is meant.

THE "PENALTY" DEATH

Spirit of Prophecy, Volume 4, page 364:

"**The penalty threatened** *[for transgression of the* law*]* **is not merely temporal death**, for all must suffer this. **It is the second death, the opposite of everlasting life.**"

Testimonies to the Church, Volume 2, pages 213, 214:

"Some have limited views of the atonement. **They think that Christ suffered only a small portion of the penalty of the law of God;** they suppose that, while the wrath of God was felt by His dear Son, he had, through all His painful sufferings, the evidence of His Father's love and acceptance; that the portals of the tomb before Him were illuminated with bright hope, and that He had the abiding evidence of His future glory. **Here is a great mistake.** Christ's keenest anguish was a sense of His Father's displeasure. His mental agony because of this was of such intensity that man can have but faint conception of it....

"But bodily pain was but a small part of the agony of God's dear Son. The sins of the world were upon Him, also the sense of His Father's wrath **as** **He suffered the penalty** of **the law transgressed.** It was these that **crushed His divine soul.** It was the hiding of His Father's face—a sense that His own dear Father had forsaken Him--which brought despair. **The separation that sin makes between God and man was fully realized** *[the separation between God and man was between separate and distinct individuals: it was **this** separation that Christ "**fully realized**". The lost only 'fully realize' it at the end of the millennium (second death)]* and keenly felt by the innocent, suffering Man of Calvary. He was oppressed by the powers of darkness. He had not one ray of light to brighten the future. And He was struggling with the power of Satan, who was declaring that he had Christ in his power, that he was superior in strength to the Son of God, that the Father had disowned His Son, and that He was no longer in the favor of God any more than himself. If He was indeed still in favor with God, why need He die? God could save Him from death.

"Christ yielded not in the least degree to the torturing foe, even in His bitterest anguish. Legions of evil angels were all about the Son of God, yet the holy angels were bidden not to break their ranks and engage in conflict with the taunting, reviling foe. Heavenly angels were not permitted to minister unto the anguished spirit of the Son of God. It was in this terrible hour

343

of darkness, the face of His Father hidden, legions of evil angels enshrouding Him, the sins of the world upon Him, that the words were wrenched from His lips: 'My God, My God, why hast Thou forsaken Me?'

"The death of the martyrs can bear no comparison with the agony endured by the Son of God. **We should take broader and deeper views of the life, sufferings, and <u>death</u> of God's dear Son.**"

God's messenger makes it clear just to what extent Jesus "paid the penalty":

<u>Selected Messages Book 1</u>, page 340:
"**Justice demands that** sin be not merely pardoned, **but the death penalty must be executed.** God, in the gift of His only-begotten Son, met both these requirements. **By dying in man's stead, Christ <u>exhausted the penalty</u> and provided a pardon.**" *[Do we fully comprehend what it means for Jesus to have "exhausted the penalty"?]*

<u>Testimonies to the Church</u>, Volume 2, page 215:
"**When the atonement is viewed correctly,** the salvation of souls will be felt **to be of infinite value**" *[because an **infinite** sacrifice has been made. <u>That I May Know Him</u>, pages 73, 77, 294, 341; <u>You Shall Receive Power</u>, page 371; <u>Christ Triumphant</u>, page 31; <u>Confrontation</u>, page 92; <u>Desire of Ages</u>, page 774; <u>Heavenly Places</u>, page 14; <u>Lift Him Up</u>, page 24; <u>Mind, Character, and Personality</u>, page 94. These references all refer to Christ's **infinite sacrifice**. He 'laid down' and 'laid aside' infinite attributes and risked everything for you and me!]*

He became our Substitute, (contrary to what Rome asserts):

<u>Our Father Cares</u>, page 122:
"The sin of the whole world was laid upon Jesus, and divinity gave its highest value to the suffering of humanity in Jesus that **the whole world might be pardoned through faith in the Substitute.**"

PROFESSOR: **Roman Trinitarianism denies the <u>substitutionary</u> death of Christ, because as an indivisible manifestation of the "God" essence**

He could not actually die; only the human body that He inhabited died. That theology requires that merit be earned through penance or be purchased through indulgences. According to that theology, Christ's death—the death of His human body—was an **appeasement** sacrifice that buys us 'merit', but that 'merit' is administered by the Church of Rome. **The truth is that a divine Member of the Godhead, one equal with the law, died the "penalty death" for us on Calvary**.

WILLIAM: He died our "penalty death" that we may live His "eternal life."

PROFESSOR: **His was a divine sacrifice indeed.** Look at this statement:

Desire of Ages, page 786:
"The life that He laid down in humanity, He takes up again, and gives to humanity."

This "mortal" will be able, at Christ's second coming, to "put on immortality", a life equal with the life of God, because of Jesus' divine, infinite sacrifice. **"Immortality" put on mortality in order to be able to die. And He died the penalty death so that mortals may put on immortality**.

The Faith I Live By, page 104:
"The most guilty need have no fear that God will not pardon, for because of the efficacy of the **divine sacrifice** the penalty of the law will be remitted."

A divine life was laid down. Divine life is eternal life—immortality. The life that He laid down Jesus takes up—on His Father's authority (John 10:18) and gives to the redeemed ones, who receive immortality, "a life that measures with the life of God." (Christ's Object Lessons, page 373).

Peter's Counsel to Parents, page 10:
"In our behalf **Christ has made a tremendous sacrifice.** He laid aside His royal crown, He laid aside His royal robe, and came to this world, born of humble parentage. Many were not attracted by the humility of His life, and He was despised and rejected of men. He suffered persecution, until at length He was crucified and died a shameful death. What does this mean to us? He came as the Saviour of every sinner that will accept of the **divine sacrifice**."

345

WILLIAM: I see that clearly Jesus' death was a divine sacrifice, and not merely the sacrifice of His human body. But I find it hard to see how "deity" could die?

PROFESSOR: Deity, a member of the Godhead retaining all the attributes of Deity, cannot die, but a divine Person, who has laid down and laid aside the attributes of divinity can and did, in the Person of our Saviour, die! Jesus was equal to the Law, the transcript of His Father's character. He sanctified the humanity that He adopted and dying in humanity, becomes a divine sacrifice because He was still a divine Person despite having voluntarily divested Himself of the attributes of Deity.

However, the question is, when Christ died, what "Deity" did not sink and die? Notice the following statements:

Lift Him Up, page 76:

"Was the human nature of the Son of Mary changed into the divine nature of the Son of God? **No; the two natures were mysteriously blended in one person**—the man Christ Jesus. In Him **dwelt** *[like the Holy Spirit dwelling in the believer?]* **all the fullness of the Godhead bodily. When Christ was crucified, it was His human nature** *[fallen human nature sanctified and made Holy by the indwelling presence of the divine "Seed"]* **that died. Deity did not sink and die; that would have been impossible….** *[God the Father, by whom Jesus lived on earth (John 6:57), did not die. Also the divine mighty Third Person of the Godhead, who filled Jesus, and Whose power—from God— was employed by Jesus, did not die. Jesus cried out, Father, into thy hands, I commend my Spirit—Christ's Spirit was the Holy Spirit (John 8:9). Jesus was a union of humanity and Holy Spirit administered divinity. Also, Jesus' divine Presence made the humanity that he was blended with "Holy Ground" (Ex. 3:5; Joshua 5:15; Acts 7:33). Furthermore, His being the divine Second Person of the Godhead, despite having laid aside the panoply of that position, nevertheless sanctified His humanity, in which He could die, and, dying in humanity, he became the divine Sacrifice: the sacrifice of One equal with the Divine Law. Rightly understood, this entire statement negates consubstantiality. Because a modality cannot "blend" with humanity, but has to have a distinct identity at all times.]* Christ, the sinless One, will save every son and daughter of Adam who*

346

accepts the salvation proffered them, consenting to become the children of God. The Saviour has purchased the fallen race with His own blood.

"This is **a great mystery**, a mystery that will not be **fully, completely** understood in all its greatness until the translation of the redeemed shall take place. Then the power and greatness and efficacy of the gift of God to man will be understood. **But the enemy is determined that this gift shall be so mystified that it will become as nothingness.**" (The SDA Bible Commentary, Ellen G. White Comments, Volume 5, page 1113).

Please note that the **"great mystery"** referred to in this statement is the blending of "the two natures." However, **man can "to some degree enter into that mystery."** (See Letter 5, 1889 in SDA Bible Commentary, Volume 7A, page 904.)

Lift Him Up, page 235:
"There is no one who can explain the mystery of the incarnation of Christ. Yet we know that He came to this earth and lived as a man among men. **The man Christ Jesus was not the Lord God Almighty,** *[He was God in human flesh. However He was not the 'Most High God.' His Father is. And Jesus laid aside His own power]* **yet Christ and the Father are one** *[in purpose, etc. See Ministry of Healing, page 422]*. **The Deity** *[The Lord God Almighty; He who is all the fullness of the Godhead bodily (Evangelism, 614); He who is a separate and distinct Person of the Godhead, maintaining the integrity of the Godhead.]* **did not sink under the agonizing torture of Calvary,** yet it is nonetheless true that "God *[the Father: the Deity]* so loved the world, that he **gave** *[to pay the penalty for man's sin—God **gave** Him to the human race.]* his only begotten Son *[born of a woman—made under the law]*, that whosoever believeth in him should not perish, but have everlasting life.'"

This last sentence makes it abundantly clear that "the Deity", spoken of in the above quote, is the Father who gave "His only begotten Son".

Manuscript Releases, Volume 4, page 7:

"Jesus Christ, who has **purchased man at an infinite price, even His own life.**" *[He laid down his life. His life was immortal life—the life of God.]*

Desire of Ages, page 530:
"In Christ is life, original, unborrowed, underived. 'He that hath the Son hath life.' 1 John 5:12. The divinity of Christ is the believer's assurance of eternal life."

(See also the first page of "M. L. Andreasen and the Trinity"—Chapter 7.)

PROFESSOR: This "life" Christ laid down:

WILLIAM: Was that the "divine life" of the Holy Spirit?

PROFESSOR: Let's see. Jesus could, at any time during His earthly sojourn, have "taken up" the life of Deity again. But then He could not have saved sinners. Instead, He chose, daily, to die to self-interest. The life that Jesus lived on earth was probationary life. (RH, April 1, 1875 par. 1: "If Christ had been deceived by Satan's temptations, and had exercised his miraculous power to relieve himself from difficulty, he would have broken the contract made with his Father, to be **a probationer** in behalf of the race.") He Himself said "I live by the Father", (Christ's Object Lessons page 130.3: "Christ said, "Whoso eateth My flesh, and drinketh My blood, hath eternal life. . . . As the living Father hath sent Me, and **I live by the Father**; so he that eateth Me, even he shall live by Me. . . . It is the Spirit that quickeneth *[makes alive]*; . . . the words that I speak unto you, they are spirit, and they are life." John 6:54-63.")

Desire of Ages, page 787:
"The life that He laid down in humanity *[in taking humanity upon Him]*, He takes up again, and gives to humanity."

Which means He gives to the redeemed "immortal life," not temporal life! But while He was a man among men, He "lived by the Father" (John 6:57) as we do (Acts 17:28): He wrought by the Father as we can, if faithful. His immortal life, that He had to lay down when He became the Son of Man in order to be able to die, is the Life He now takes up and offers to His people through the Holy Spirit.

SDA Bible Commentary, Volume 7A, page 460

"Christ has purchased the world by making a ransom for it, by taking human nature. He was not only the offering, but He Himself was the Offerer. He clothed His divinity with humanity, and **voluntarily took upon Him human nature, <u>making it possible to offer Himself as a ransom</u>**.--Manuscript 92, 1899."

Jesus took upon Himself <u>mortality</u>, making it possible for Him to die and pay the penalty for sin, so that He might be able to give redeemed man <u>immortality</u>: Jesus' own Life:

Review & Herald, April 4, 1899:
"'In him dwelleth all the fulness of **the Godhead** bodily.' **Men need to understand that the Deity** *[the Godhead]* **suffered** *[but did not "sink"]* **under the agonies of Calvary.** Yet Jesus Christ whom God gave for the ransom of the world purchased the church with His own blood *[life]*. The Majesty of heaven was made to suffer at the hands of religious zealots, who claimed to be the most enlightened people upon the face of the earth."

WILLIAM: Can you summarize this for me?

PROFESSOR: The Father and the Holy Spirit did "not sink" under the agonizing torture of Calvary—only Jesus the Divine/human Person did. He "laid **down** His life" so that in humanity He could die. The **life** of One equal with His divine Father, He laid down, just as He laid down His personal divine power, so that He, our Saviour, could die—a divine Person equal with the law—yet in our humanity: thereby condemning "sin in the flesh". **This life—His immortal life**—Jesus takes up again on His Father's authority, and gives it to His redeemed.

WILLIAM: So Jesus, a divine/human Being, after living a sinless life in our fallen humanity, bore our sins on the cross, and died the penalty death, as the unrepentant sinner will do, so that the redeemed, in our fallen humanity, may become partakers of divine nature, by faith in Him, and finally receive eternal life—"immortality"—His immortal life!

PROFESSOR: Yes, as administered by the Holy Spirit to whom the redeemed become united. Jesus died that men might receive divine, overcoming power; and He lived victoriously, employing no advantages that we may not receive.

Desire of Ages, page 664:

"'He that believeth on Me, the works that I do shall he do also.' The Saviour was deeply anxious for His disciples to understand for what purpose His divinity was united to humanity. **He came to the world to display the glory** *[character]* **of God,** that man might be uplifted by its restoring power. **God was manifested in Him that He might be manifested in them** *[that is, "in" His followers].* <u>**Jesus revealed no qualities, and exercised no powers, that men may not have through faith in Him.**</u> His perfect humanity is that which all His followers may possess, if they will be **in subjection to God** as He was."

The power exercised by Jesus was divine Holy Spirit power. By Holy Spirit power Jesus manifested His Father. By **Holy Spirit** power Jesus' followers may manifest **Jesus,** which is to manifest **the Father.** We may have that power through submission to our heavenly Father.

WILLIAM: It is as Jesus said:

Revelation 3:21:
"To him that overcometh will I grant to sit with me in my throne, **even as** *[in the same way as]* **I also overcame,** and am set down with my Father in his throne."

PROFESSOR: Jesus total dependence on power from on high is clearly stated by God's messenger in the following statements:

Desire of Ages, pages 674,675:
"'I am the true Vine,' He says. Instead of choosing the graceful palm, the lofty cedar, or the strong oak, Jesus takes the vine with its clinging tendrils to represent Himself. **The palm tree, the cedar, and the oak stand alone.** They require no support. But **the vine** entwines about the trellis, and thus climbs heavenward. So Christ **in His humanity was dependent upon divine power. 'I can of Mine own self do nothing,'** He declared. **John 5:30.**"

SDA Bible Commentary, Volume 5, page 1105:
"**When Christ bowed His head and died, He bore the pillars of Satan's kingdom with Him to the earth** *[like Samson].* He vanquished Satan in the same nature over which in

350

Eden Satan obtained the victory. **The enemy was overcome by Christ in His human nature** *[weakened by four thousand years of sin. See Desire of Ages, page 48, 49.]* **The power of the Saviour's Godhead was hidden** *[because He had laid it aside: He could, by choice, have taken it up again and have left us without a Saviour].* **He overcame in human nature, relying upon God for power. This is the privilege of all.**"

Desire of Ages, page 623:
"The grain of wheat that preserves its own life can produce no fruit. It abides alone. **Christ could, if He chose, save Himself from death.** *[By taking up His life again]* **But should He do this, He must abide alone.** He could bring no sons and daughters to God *[for the penalty would not have been paid]*."

Having paid the penalty in full, Jesus is justified in giving sinners, who repent, His Holy Spirit by whom He lived and overcame all evil:
Desire of Ages, page 805:
"The Holy Spirit is the breath of spiritual life in the soul. **The impartation of the Spirit is the impartation of the life of Christ.**"

When a person is "born again" of the Spirit, He is a "new creature"—a union of humanity and divinity, receiving the seal of eternal life through the indwelling mighty Third Person of the Godhead, who imparts to that person overcoming power.

2 Corinthians 5:17:
"Therefore if any man be **in** Christ, **he is a new creature**: old things are passed away; behold, all things are become new."

When man becomes a union of humanity and divinity, as Christ was, by the indwelling Spirit, he joins the ranks of a new line of beings, with Christ, the "Firstborn", of this new line; Jesus being the "second Adam":

Galatians 6:15:
"For in Christ Jesus neither circumcision availeth any thing, nor uncircumcision, but **a new creature.**"

Through the Spirit, the "carnal heart" is subdued; a "clean heart" is created:

351

<u>God's Amazing Grace</u>, page 196:
"Through the influence of the Spirit enmity against God is changed into faith and love, and pride into humility."

WILLIAM: That is wonder working power—the power of Creation.

PROFESSOR: A new heart is given; a right spirit is renewed in man. Man receives peace with God, and enmity against the serpent, as promised to Eve in Eden after the fall (Genesis 3:15).

WILLIAM: So what then is the length, breadth, and height of the sacrifice of Christ?

PROFESSOR: Let us look at:

WHAT JESUS SACRIFICED FOR US.

As we have seen in Philippians 2:6 and <u>Special Testimonies, Series B</u>, No. 9, page 3, etc., Jesus laid aside His equality with His Father; laid aside His divinity and divine power and confronted the enemy of souls from the same position that He asks us to engage the enemy from:

Signs of the Times, January 16, 1896:
"**<u>By faith he laid hold upon divinity</u>**, even as humanity may lay hold upon infinite power through him."

Philippians 2:7:
"But made Himself of not reputation *[the Greek says He 'emptied Himself]* and took upon Him the form *[His human body = the "door" (John 10:7)]* of a servant; and was made in the **likeness** of men *[today, too often, men try to make 'likeness' mean 'unlikeness']*

<u>SDA Bible Commentary</u>, Volume 5, pages 1129, 1130:
"There is no one who can explain the mystery of the incarnation of Christ. Yet we know that He came to this earth and lived as a man among men. **The man Christ Jesus was not the Lord God Almighty,** yet Christ and the Father are one. The Deity *[Godhead—the Father is the "fullness of the Godhead bodily."]* did not **sink** under the agonizing torture of Calvary, yet

352

it is nonetheless true that 'God so loved the world, that he gave his only begotten Son *[and in so doing, suffered with His Son, but did not "sink under the agonizing torture of Calvary."]* that whosoever believeth in him should not perish, but have everlasting life.'

"In every possible way Satan sought to prevent Jesus from **developing** a perfect childhood, **a faultless manhood,** a holy ministry, and an unblemished sacrifice. But he was defeated. He could not lead Jesus into sin. He could not discourage Him, or drive Him from the work He had come to this earth to do. From the desert to Calvary the storm of Satan's wrath beat upon Him, **but the more mercilessly it fell, the more firmly did the Son of God cling to the hand of His Father,** and press on in the blood-stained path. (MS 140, 1903).

"When Jesus took human nature, and became in fashion as a man, He possessed all the human organism. His necessities were the necessities of a man. He had bodily wants to be supplied, bodily weariness to be relieved. **By prayer to the Father** He was braced for duty and for trial." (Letter 32, 1899).

WILLIAM: **In what ways did Jesus "empty" himself?**

PROFESSOR: **1) HE LAID ASIDE HIS POWER.**

John 5:30:
"I can of mine own self do nothing...."

What does "nothing" mean? It means "no single thing."

WILLIAM: Did not Jesus say in John 10:18 that He had the **power** to lay down His life and the **power** to take it up again?

PROFESSOR: Yes, Jesus said that, but remember, I told you previously, to read the whole verse:

John 10:18:
"No man taketh it from me, but I lay it down of myself *[willingly]*. I **have power** to lay it down, and I **have power** to take it again. **This commandment have I received of my Father**."

Clearly Jesus received the authority and capacity (commandment) to lay down and take up His life from His Father! This concurs with John 5:30 above, and with Romans 8:11; 1 Peter 1:20, 21; and Acts 13:30. God's messenger endorses this truth:

> Desire of Ages, page 21:
> "Looking unto Jesus we see that it is the glory of our God to give. "I do nothing of Myself," said Christ; "the living Father hath sent Me, and I live by the Father." "I seek not Mine own glory," but the glory of Him that sent Me. John 8:28; 6:57; 8:50; 7:18. In these words is set forth the great principle which is the law of life for the universe. **All things Christ received from God, but He took to give.** So in the heavenly courts, in His ministry for all created beings: **through the beloved Son, the Father's life** *[God's life giving power, bought for us by Jesus that we might have a probation—a second chance to get it right.]* **flows out to all; through the Son it returns, in praise and joyous service, a tide of love,** to the great Source of all. And thus through Christ the circuit of beneficence is complete, representing the character of the great Giver, the law of life."

We must never forget that Christ Himself became a probationer, as we have already noted, and as such "live*[d]* by the Father". (John 6:57)

WILLIAM: Did he not have power to command the wind and the waves?

PROFESSOR: Jesus had to live by faith, just as we do.

> Desire of Ages, pages 335, 336:
> "When Jesus was awakened to meet the storm, He was in perfect peace. There was no trace of fear in word or look, for no fear was in His heart. **But He rested not in the possession of almighty power.** It was not as the 'Master of earth and sea and sky' that He reposed in quiet. That power He had laid down, and He says, 'I can of Mine own self do nothing.' John 5:30. He trusted in the Father's might. **It was in faith—faith in God's love and care—that Jesus rested, and the power of that word which stilled the storm was the power of God."**

> Desire of Ages, pages 674, 675:

"The Saviour had been explaining to His disciples His mission to the world, and the spiritual relation to Him which they were to sustain. Now He illustrates the lesson. The moon is shining bright, and reveals to Him a flourishing grapevine. Drawing the attention of the disciples to it, He employs it as a symbol.

"'I am the true Vine,' He says. Instead of choosing the graceful palm, the lofty cedar, or the strong oak, Jesus takes the vine with its clinging tendrils to represent Himself. The palm tree, the cedar, and the oak stand alone. They require no support. But the vine entwines about the trellis, and thus climbs heavenward. **So Christ in His humanity was dependent upon divine power. 'I can of Mine own self do nothing,'** He declared. John 5:30."

Scripture tells us that **"the just shall live by faith."** (Hab. 2:4; Rom. 1:17; Gal. 3:11; Heb. 10:38.) **Jesus is the "Just One"** (Psalm 37:12; Zeph. 3:5; Acts 3:14; 7:52.)

WILLIAM: So Jesus, as our perfect Example, had to live by faith also!

PROFESSOR: Yes! **By Jesus' faith we are raised up from the deadness of sin. Thus, we truly live by His faith.** See Romans 3:22; Galatians 2:16; 3:22; and Revelation 14:12. By faith, Jesus laid so much aside in order to reach us where we are and save us. **The faith we receive through the Holy Spirit is made possible because of Jesus' faith and sacrificial steadfastness.**

Through faith Jesus endured the penalty for us, despite not being able to see beyond the "portals of the tomb" (Desire of Ages, page 753.2). Having triumphed through faith He has opened the way for us to receive Divine overcoming power through the indwelling other "Comforter" (John 14:16), His Holy Spirit, who enables His people to "keep the commandments of God" and to have "the faith of Jesus" (Revelation 14:12) by the indwelling "Spirit of Prophecy": the Holy Spirit (1888 Materials, page 808.4) who inspired and upheld "holy men of God" (2 Peter 1:21) and empowered them to live for God, and who did the same for God's messenger to His last-day denominated people so that they might be filled with, and empowered by, the same "Spirit of Prophecy", God's Holy Spirit: all this because of Jesus' faith.

355

2) JESUS LAID ASIDE HIS KNOWLEDGE AND WISDOM AND HIS MEMORY!

Luke 2:52:
"And Jesus **increased** in **wisdom and stature, and in favour with God and man.**"

Desire of Ages, page 70:
"His mother was His first human teacher. From her lips and from the scrolls of the prophets, He learned of heavenly things. **The very words which He Himself had spoken to Moses for Israel He was now taught at His mother's knee.**"

WILLIAM: Unbelievable sacrifice!

PROFESSOR: And not only that, but:

3) JESUS LAID ASIDE HIS FOREKNOWLEDGE!

Mark 23:32:
"But of that day and *[that]* hour knoweth **no man**, no, not the angels which are in heaven, **neither the Son**, but the Father."

Desire of Ages, page 147:
"Before He came to earth, the plan lay out before Him, perfect in all its details. **But as He walked among men, He was guided, step by step, by the Father's will.**"

Ministry of Healing, page 479:
"Christ in His life on earth made no plans for Himself. **He accepted God's plans for Him, and day by day the Father unfolded His plans.**"

Desire of Ages, page 753:
"The Saviour could not see through the portals of the tomb."
[See also "fear" and "despair" on this page of Desire of Ages.]

WILLIAM: The Word of God was: "a lamp unto *[His]* feet, and a light unto *[His]* path," just as it is to ours.

PROFESSOR: Not only that, but when He became the divine 'Seed':

4) JESUS LAID ASIDE HIS OMNIPRESENCE

Desire of Ages, page 669:
"The Holy Spirit is Christ's representative, but divested of the personality of humanity, and independent thereof. **Cumbered with humanity, Christ could not be in every place personally.** Therefore it was for their interest that He should go to the Father, and send the Spirit to be His successor on earth. No one could then have any advantage because of his location or his personal contact with Christ. By the Spirit the Saviour would be accessible to all."

WILLIAM: If Jesus could no longer be everywhere at once as a man, how could He see Nathaniel praying under the fig tree?

PROFESSOR: Just in the same manner as Peter could know about the previous agreement that Ananias made with his wife, Saphira (Acts 5:1-5)—it was revealed to them both by the Holy Spirit.
    Not only that, but when He came as a baby in Bethlehem and lived as a man:

5) JESUS LAID ASIDE HIS GLORY (CHARACTER)

John 17:5:
"And now, O Father, glorify thou me with thine own self with the glory **which I had** with thee **before the world was.**"

PROFESSOR: As a child and as a man, He had to form **'character.'**

WILLIAM: What a responsibility that was for his earthly parents!

PROFESSOR: And for Himself. Probation is given for the perfecting of character. Read what God's servant says about Jesus' being on probation:

The Youth's Instructor, July 20, 1899:
"Unless there is a possibility of yielding, temptation is no temptation. Temptation is resisted when man is powerfully influenced to do a wrong action; and, knowing that he can do it, resists, by faith, with a firm hold upon divine power. **This was the ordeal through which Christ passed.** He could not have been tempted in all points as man is tempted, had there been no

357

possibility of his failing. He was a free agent, **placed on probation**, as was Adam, and as is every man."

A manifestation of an indivisible "God" essence could never be placed on probation. Such a concept is ludicrous. But, as we see, Christ was placed on probation, which demonstrates that He was **not** consubstantial with His Father.

The Youth's Instructor, October 26, 1899:
"The temptations to which Christ was subjected were a terrible reality. As a free agent, **he was placed on probation, with liberty to yield to Satan's temptations and work at cross-purposes with God** *[How could an indivisible "modality" or "hypostasis" of "God" work at cross-purposes with Itself?].* If this were not so, if it had not been possible for him to fall, he could not have been tempted in all points as the human family is tempted."

Signs of the Times, May 10, 1899
"For a period of time **Christ was on probation.** He took humanity on Himself, to stand the test and trial which the first Adam failed to endure. Had He failed in His test and trial, He would have been disobedient to the voice of God, and the world would have been lost."

A manifestation of an indivisible "God" essence could never be placed on probation: such a concept is ludicrous. Furthermore, the Scriptures record:

Hebrews 5:8, 9:
8) "Though He were a Son, yet **learned** He obedience by the things which He suffered.
9) And being made perfect, He **became** the Author of eternal salvation unto all them that obey Him."

WILLIAM: So Jesus laid aside His omnipotent power, His memory and wisdom; He laid aside His foreknowledge; His omnipresence and His glory Truly awesome!

PROFESSOR: **He laid these aside because we do not have them.**

Micah 3:8 tells us how Jesus was able; how He was enabled, to do, to live victoriously, **to have power:** power to still the wind and waves; power to raise the dead; power to tell the future, power to read men's thoughts; power to be full of wisdom and knowledge, power to lay down his life and take it up again:

Micah 3:8:
"**But truly I am full of power by the spirit of the LORD,** and of judgment, and of might, to declare unto Jacob his transgression, and to Israel his sin." (See Isaiah 58:1).

When He returned to heaven He sent the Holy Spirit to His people to supply them with "power" to be over-comers!

Acts 1:8:
"**But ye shall receive power, after that the Holy Ghost is come upon you:** and ye shall be witnesses unto Me both in Jerusalem, and in Judea, and in Samaria, and unto the uttermost part of the earth."

John 1:12:
"But as many as received Him, to them **gave He power** to become the sons of God, even to them that believe on His name."

WILLIAM: By receiving Jesus into our hearts by faith, we can overcome as He overcame.

PROFESSOR: Much of what Jesus laid down He now has back by receiving—by it being given Him.

Revelation 5:11-13:
11) "And I beheld and I heard the voice of many angels round about the throne and the beasts and the elders: ...
12) Saying with a loud voice, Worthy is the Lamb that was slain **to receive power, and riches, and wisdom, and strength, and honour, and glory, and blessing.**
13) And every creature which is in heaven, and on the earth, and under the earth, and such as are in the sea, and all that are in them, heard I saying, **Blessing, and honour, and glory, and power, be unto him** *[the Father]* that sitteth upon the throne, **and unto the Lamb** *[the Son]* for ever and ever."

Matthew 28:18:
"**All power is given unto me** in heaven and in earth."

Acts 2:32, 33:
32) "This Jesus hath God raised up, whereof we are all witnesses.

33) Therefore being **by the right hand of God exalted, and having received of the Father the promise of the Holy Spirit**, he hath shed forth this, which ye now see and hear."

WILLIAM: Jesus truly gave all for us.

PROFESSOR: Jesus had laid aside His divinity. **The seven horns (all-power) and seven eyes (all-wisdom) were received by Jesus through the Holy Spirit.**

Revelation 5:6:
"And I beheld, and, lo, in the midst of the throne and of the four beasts, and in the midst of the elders, stood a Lamb as it had been slain, **having seven horns and seven eyes, which are the seven Spirits of God** sent forth into all the earth."

Acts 2:36:
"Therefore let all the house of Israel know assuredly, that **God hath made** that same Jesus, whom ye have **crucified** [Lamb Slain], both **Lord** and **Christ**."

ONLY A DIVINE SACRIFICE WOULD SUFFICE

Spirit of Prophecy, Volume2, pages 9, 10:
"**Man could not atone for man.** His sinful, fallen condition would constitute him an imperfect offering, an atoning sacrifice of less value than Adam before his fall. God made man perfect and upright, and after his transgression there could be no sacrifice acceptable to God for him, **unless the offering made should in value be superior to man as he was in his state of perfection and innocency.**

"**The divine Son of God was the only sacrifice** of sufficient value to fully satisfy the claims of God's perfect law. **The angels were sinless, but of less value than the law of God.** They were amenable to law. They were messengers to do the will of Christ, and before him to bow. They were created beings, and probationers. Upon Christ no requirements were laid. He had power to lay down his life, and to take it again. <u>No obligation was laid upon him to undertake the work of atonement. It was a voluntary sacrifice that he made.</u> **His life** *[divine life—the life of a divine Member of the Godhead—One equal with the Law— Who had taken mortality, making it possible for Him to die.]* was of sufficient value to rescue man from his fallen condition."

<u>SDA Bible Commentary</u>, Volume 7A, page 462:
"As the sinbearer, and priest and representative of man before God, He *[Christ]* entered into the life of humanity, bearing our flesh and blood. The life is in the living, vital current of blood, which blood was given for the life of the world. Christ made a full atonement, giving His life as a ransom for us. He was born without a taint of sin, but came into the world in like manner as the human family. He did not have a mere semblance of a body, but He took human nature, participating in the life of humanity. **According to the law** *[which]* **Christ Himself gave**, the forfeited inheritance was ransomed by the nearest of kin. Jesus Christ laid off His royal robe, His kingly crown, and clothed His divinity with humanity, in order to become a substitute and surety for humanity, **that dying in humanity** He might **by His death** destroy him who had the power of death. **He could not have done this as God** *[Why? Because Deity cannot die! See 5BC 1113]*, **but by coming as man Christ could die. By death He overcame death. The death of Christ bore to the death him who had the power of death,** and opened the gates of the tomb for all who receive Him as their personal Saviour."—*Letter 97, 1898.*

By accepting the "penalty" death in innocence, and having laid down His immortal life, and being separated from it by dying in mortality, yet still a divine Person, Jesus secured the verdict of eternal death for Satan; who had the "power of sin and death. That power is now broken, and Jesus has secured pardon and immortal life, His life, that He takes up and gives to all who come to Him in faith and remain faithful.

<u>Selected Messages Book 1</u>, page 341:

"The victory gained at **His death** on Calvary broke forever the accusing power of Satan over the universe and silenced his charges that **self-denial was impossible with God** and therefore not essential in the human family."—*Manuscript 50, 1900.*

WILLIAM: How did Jesus take up His life again?

PROFESSOR: How Jesus took up His life again is recorded by God's messenger:

The Youth's Instructor, May 2, 1901:
"He who died for the sins of the world was to remain in the tomb for the allotted time. **He was in that stony prison house as a prisoner of divine justice, and he was responsible to the Judge of the universe.** He was bearing the sins of the world, and **his FATHER ONLY could release him**. *[Because Jesus had laid aside His Divinity, as we have seen, but did not cease to be a divine member of the Godhead.]*

'Christ had declared that he would be raised from the dead on the third day; and at the appointed time a mighty angel descended from heaven, parting the darkness from his track, and resting before the Saviour's tomb. …The earth trembled at his approach, and as he rolled away the stone from Christ's grave, heaven seemed to come down to earth. The soldiers saw him removing the stone as he would a pebble, and heard him call, **Son of God, thy Father saith, Come forth.** They saw Jesus come from the grave as a mighty conqueror, and heard him proclaim, "I am the resurrection, and the life.'"—Ms 94, 1897.

Manuscript Releases, Volume 4, page 243:
"Who can approach unto a conception of what Christ has endured when standing in the place of surety for His church in the solemn hour of atonement, when Christ yielded up His life as a sacrificial offering. . . . **the only One who could bear the strokes in behalf of the sinner, and because of His innocence not be consumed.** How did the glory of God magnify itself in glorious perfection on that day when Christ's life was yielded up as a sacrifice for the world!"

Did you get that, William? **Because of His personal innocence, Christ could come back from eternal death: the penalty of the Law!**

Upward Look, page 260:

"**This is a great mystery, a mystery that will not be fully, completely understood in its greatness until the translation of the redeemed shall take place.** Then the power and greatness and efficacy of the gift of God to man will be understood. **But the enemy is determined that this gift shall be so mystified that it will become as nothingness....**" (5BC 1113)

WILLIAM: It is really unbelievable what Jesus had to "lay aside" in order for us to be with Him. Not only that, but to be willing to do it! In fact, He delighted to do it! I cannot fathom it.

Chapter 29

THE LIFE HE LAID DOWN

WILLIAM: Professor, Jesus said, "Therefore doth my Father love me, because I lay down my life, that I might take it again. No man taketh it from me, but I lay it down of myself. I have power to lay it down, and I have power to take it again." John 10:17, 18.   But many other places in the Bible tell us that the Father raised up Jesus Christ by the Holy Spirit. How can this be? **Did Jesus raise Himself, or did the Father?**

PROFESSOR: I think both perspectives are right. Listen to this quotation:

> SDA Bible Commentary, Volume 5, page 1113:
> "When the voice of the angel was heard saying, 'Thy Father calls thee,' He who had said, 'I lay down my life, that I might take it again,' 'Destroy this temple, and in three days **I will raise it up,**' came forth from the grave **to life that was in Himself. Deity did not die.**"

WILLIAM: I still don't understand.

PROFESSOR: Let me explain. On whose authority could Jesus say that He had 'power to lay it *[His life]* down, and I have power to take it again.'? **John 10:18**. We have seen repeatedly that the answer is found in the last sentence of the same verse that you did not read: "This **commandment** have I **received** of my Father." In Strong's Concordance, the word "commandment" is #1785, meaning **"an authoritative prescription":--** *[translated as]* commandment, **precept.**

When one recognizes the truth that Jesus **"received" from His Father** the authorization to lay down His life and to take it up again, one then finds **harmony** between John 10:18 and John 5:30 where Jesus states: "I can **of mine own self do nothing.**" Jesus, in John 6:57, declares: "As the living Father hath sent me, and **I live by the Father:** so he that eateth me even he shall live by me."

Jesus, during the incarnation could, clearly **of His 'own self do nothing' except to choose whom He would obey.** His very life was, according to His own words, directed and sustained by the Father. It is in accordance with the above truth that God's messenger makes the following statement about Jesus:

SDA Bible Commentary, Volume 5, page 1114:
"He was in that stony prison house as a prisoner of divine justice. ...He was bearing the sins of the world *[He was preparing to pay the 'penalty' for sin, which is eternal separation from God]*, and **His Father only could release Him.**"

In justice, His Father could release Him because "He *[personally]* knew no sin." 2 Cor. 5:21.

While on earth, and still today in the Most Holy Place of the heavenly Sanctuary, and indeed for all eternity from His incarnation onwards, **Jesus is a union of humanity and Divinity.** As we saw:

SDA Bible Commentary, Volume 5, page 1113:
"**The two natures** *[human and divine]* were **mysteriously blended** in one person—the man Christ Jesus."

SDA Bible Commentary, Volume 7, page 926:
"In Christ were **united the divine and the human**—the Creator *[The Word, John 1:1]* and the creature *[man]*. **The nature of God,** whose law had been transgressed, and **the nature of Adam, the transgressor, meet** in Jesus—the Son of God, and the Son of man."

SDA Bible Commentary, Volume 7, page 925:
"Jesus Christ laid off His royal robe, His kingly crown, **and clothed His divinity with humanity**...." (Letter 97, 1898)

WILLIAM: If Jesus could of His "own self do nothing", then how could Jesus take up His life again?

PROFESSOR: Because of Jesus' complete victory over sin, and its author, Jesus had thus "earned" the right to life:

Upward Look, page 263.2:
"Then the mighty angel, with a voice that caused the earth to quake, was heard to say, "Jesus, Thou Son of God, Thy Father calls Thee." **Then He who had earned the power to conquer**

365

death and the grave came forth, and proclaimed over the rent sepulcher of Joseph, "I am the resurrection and the life."

Through His perfect obedience Jesus participated in His own resurrection. His Father's justice mandated that Jesus be raised. When His Father raised Him, love, mercy and justice were fully satisfied. **Jesus could then take up His immortal life again, on the authority of His Father**, so that His immortal life could be administered (given) to the redeemed. It was through the agency of the Holy Spirit that this occurred, as is plainly revealed in:

Romans 8:11:
"But if **the Spirit of him that raised up Jesus from the dead** dwell in you, he that raised up Christ from the dead shall also quicken your mortal bodies **by his Spirit** that dwelleth in you."

Now, in the light of inspired quotations from God's messenger that now follow, there arises an interesting question.

First, listen carefully to the following:

Special Testimonies, Series B, No. 9, page 3:
"By His life of sacrifice, **Christ has made it possible for man to become a partaker of the divine nature,** having escaped the corruption that is in the world through lust. The salvation of souls was the great object for which Christ sacrificed His royal robe and kingly crown, the glory of heaven and the homage of the angels, and, **laying aside His divinity,** came to earth to labor and suffer with humanity upon Him."

Lift Him Up, page 233:
"...Look on Jesus, the author and finisher of your faith. He turned from His royal throne, His high command, and, **laying aside His divinity,** clothed Himself with humanity." (*Signs of the Times*, March 17, 1887.)

Bible Echo, October 12, 1896:
"At the time when He was most needed, Jesus, the Son of God, the world's Redeemer, **laid aside His divinity,** and came to earth in the garb of humanity."

366

Clearly Jesus had laid aside the **power** *[He said, "I can of mine own self do nothing." John 5:30.]* **and the immortal life of Deity. He had taken mortality and was subject to death.** Notice how God's messenger clarifies this:

Lift Him Up, page 345:
"**...By coming as man Christ could die.** By death *[dying the "second death"]* He overcame death *[the "second death": this is not speaking of the probationary death which Jesus called a "sleep"(John 11:11; see also Daniel 12:2), that all men are subject to at the end of their allotted span, but is speaking of the "penalty death"]*. The death of Christ bore to the death him who had the power of death, and opened the gates of the tomb *[2 Timothy 1:10: "But is now made manifest by the appearing of our Saviour Jesus Christ, who hath abolished death, and hath brought life and immortality to light through the gospel:"]* for all who receive Him as their personal Saviour."

Thus, the question that arises is this: "Whose 'Divinity' did Jesus clothe with humanity?" Whose "Divinity" flashed forth through Jesus on occasions during the incarnation? (See 8T 202; COL 295; DA 130, 162, 590; PK 712; 1SM 97; etc.)

If, as we have seen from inspiration, Jesus has "laid aside **His** Divinity," this does not mean that He had ceased to be a Divine member of the Godhead! It means, simply, that He had laid aside the **powers** of Divinity.

"He made Himself of none effect." (Phil. 2:7. See Strong's #2758 = **to make empty;** make of none effect). He was still the **Divine** Son of God, but had laid aside His Divine power and was dependent upon the Divine power of God the Father, whose power is transmitted through the mighty Third Person of the Godhead—the Holy Spirit—whose divine indwelling presence filled Christ's life and humanity. How do we know that? We have repeatedly seen the Scriptures that tell us the following:

Micah 3:8 tells us (speaking of the Messiah):
"But truly **I am full of power by the Spirit of the Lord....**"

Acts 10:38 tells us further:
"How **God anointed Jesus of Nazareth with the Holy Ghost and with power:** who went about doing good, and healing all that were oppressed of the devil; for God was with Him."

WILLIAM: We have also learned that Jesus did <u>all</u> His miracles through the power of the Holy Spirit. Jesus lived as our example, and demonstrated how we can both follow Him, and find access to divine power.

PROFESSOR: That's right, William. Like us, Jesus was also born "of a woman" and is called the "Son of man." He was also ministered to by the agency of the Spirit. Hence we read in:

> <u>Reflecting Christ</u>, page 130:
> "Christ is our pattern, our example in all things. **He was filled with the Spirit, and the Spirit's power was manifested through Him….**"

So we see that the divine Spirit that Christ shared with His Father, and that He shares with His faithful, Spirit-filled followers, was the divinity that flashed through Him, that empowered Him, and that raised Him from the dead. And the same Holy Spirit will also do the same for the faithful. God's people, like Jesus, can also receive Holy Spirit power. It brings one to one's knees, when one ponders, the absolute selflessness and sacrificial mindset of Christ.

WILLIAM: Christ's life and example is a call to us to come up higher in our experience, and be filled with the Holy Spirit, and receive from Him power to correct our ways.

PROFESSOR: God's messenger expressed this truth clearly in her inspired words found in the

> *General Conference Bulletin*, May 17, 1909:
> "To abide in Christ means that **you shall be a partaker of the divine nature.** Humanity lays hold upon divinity, **and you have divine power.**" *[To do God's will.]*

> *Review &Herald,* June 13, 1899:
> "**The impartation of the Spirit was the impartation of the very life of Christ,** which was to qualify the disciples for their mission." *[His "very life" on earth was imparted by the Holy Spirit during Christ's "probation", while He "live(d) by the Father" John 6:5. The power to live like Christ is inherent in "the impartation of the Spirit", who also seals us "unto the day of redemption." Ephesians 4:30.]*

The Holy Spirit's power—the impartation of Christ's life—can be ours.

WILLIAM: So even though Jesus laid aside His divinity, His death was not just a human sacrifice.

PROFESSOR: No, William. We have repeatedly seen that, **when Jesus died, a Divine/human being died.** Jesus was still the Second Person of the Godhead. God's messenger stated in:

> *Review & Herald,* June 15, 1905:
> "Christ could not have come to this earth with the glory that he had in the heavenly courts. Sinful human beings could not have borne the sight. He veiled his divinity with the garb of humanity, **but he did not part with his divinity** *[He did not part with His being a divine Person, but He did lay the panoply and power of divinity aside! See Special Testimonies, Series B, No. 9, page 3; Lift Him Up, page 233; and* **Bible Echo**, *October 12, 1896. In laying aside His divine power, Jesus did not cease to be a divine Person. He also never parted from the indwelling Holy Spirit—not for a moment—until He died and gave up the Spirit.]* A **divine-human Saviour,** he came to stand at the head of the fallen race, to share in their experience from childhood to manhood."

A divine member of the Godhead died on Calvary to save the lost race: a divine Sacrifice was made on our behalf. Having said that, I nevertheless, already hear the cries of "heresy" because the prophet has made the following statement:

> <u>Upward Look</u>, page 260:
> "In Him *[Jesus]* dwelt all the fullness of the Godhead bodily. **When Christ was crucified, it was His human nature that died. <u>Deity did not sink and die;</u> that would have been impossible.**"

Well, of course, the Mighty Third Person of the Godhead—the Holy Spirit, who filled Christ's being—the Divinity to which His humanity was united—did not die. That would have been impossible. On the cross Jesus said to his Father, the "Supreme Diety", who clearly did not die:

Luke 23:46:

369

Father into thy hands I commend my Spirit. And having said thus He gave up the ghost.

Now think on this: A "born again" man, who is united to divinity by the indwelling Holy Spirit, will, at the end of his probationary life, also die. The Holy Spirit, who dwelt in him does not die. By the agency of the Holy Spirit that man's eternal life is secure. That man has died—gone to "sleep". But **his "eternal life" is "hid with Christ in God"** (Colossians 3:3): that man has been "sealed unto the day of redemption" by God's and Christ's Holy Spirit (Ephesians 4:30).

WILLIAM: **So Christ in His experience as the "Son of Man" died the "penalty" death that the unrepentant human sinner will experience. And it was because He had never sinned, that His Father could, in justice, unlock the gates of the second death.**

PROFESSOR: What life "was in Himself" to which He "came forth from the grave"? (5BC, page 1113) What was the life which "He declares that He had …in Himself to quicken whom He will."? (Ibid)
We find God's answer in:

Romans 8:9-11:
9) But ye are not in the flesh, but in the Spirit, if so be that the Spirit of God *[Deity]* dwell in you. Now if any man have not the Spirit of Christ, he is none of his.
10) And if Christ *[through His Spirit (see John 14:15-18]* be in you, the body is dead *[subject to death]* because of sin; but the Spirit is life *[to us]* because of *[Christ's]* righteousness.
11) **But if the Spirit of him that raised up Jesus from the dead dwell in you, he that raised up Christ from the dead shall also quicken your mortal bodies by his Spirit that dwelleth in you.**

WILLIAM: That is a wonderful promise!

PROFESSOR: When a repentant sinner is "born again" of the Holy Spirit (John 3:3), "behold, a new creature…" (2 Cor. 5:17; Gal. 6:15). The "born again" Christian receives the implanting of the Divine nature by the indwelling of the Holy Spirit in the body temple. The Christian can retain the indwelling Spirit by not grieving away He who, if retained, is their seal "unto the day of redemption" (Ephesians 4:30). So long as the "born again"

Christian retains, by submission, the indwelling Holy Spirit, he or she is a union of (fallen) humanity and Divinity (the Divine Holy Spirit). He, or she, has then "passed from death to life" (John 5:24). "And if Christ *[through the indwelling presence of His Holy Spirit]* be in you, **the body** *[fallen humanity]* **is dead** because of sin; **but the Spirit is life** because of *[Christ's]* righteousness." (Romans 8:10).

The believer is buried with Christ in baptism and rises to "**walk in newness of life.**" **Romans 6:4.** "And whoever liveth *[by the Spirit]* and believeth in Me **shall never die** *[the 'penalty death']*. Believeth thou this?" **John 11:26.** "For ye *[the "body," that is, fallen humanity. (See Romans 8:10 above)]* are dead *[because of sin: we have the "body of this death" Romans 7:24]* and your **life** *[Holy Spirit administered eternal life]* is hid with Christ in God" **Colossians 3:3.**

When man becomes a union of humanity and divinity, by virtue of Jesus having paid the redemption price as our near kinsman (Numbers 5:8; Ruth 3:9, 12), the indwelling Holy Spirit: the other "Comforter", promised them by Jesus (John 14: 15-18; 16:7) **is their assurance of eternal life** (See John 4:14 and John 7:38, 39).

Should this 'body of death' die, Deity (the Holy Spirit, to whom the believer's humanity was united, does not die—that is not possible—and the believer's eternal "life is hid with Christ in God." (Col. 3:3) *[To be imparted to the believer at the resurrection]*.

Their immortal life is secure for they are recipients of the life of Christ. God alone has immortality (1 Timothy 6:16). And Christ, being God, a divine member of the Godhead, takes up the life that He laid down and gives that life to the redeemed. Then this corruption shall have put on incorruption, and this mortal shall have put on immortality. **1 Corinthians 15:54.** The redeemed put on Jesus' immortal life through the ministration of the Holy Spirit.

WILLIAM: That is the blessed hope! **Proverbs 14:32** says: "The wicked is driven away in his wickedness: but **the righteous hath hope in his death**."

THE LIFE JESUS CHRIST LAID DOWN AND TOOK AGAIN

Laid Down

1. Deity/immortality cannot die. Christ laid down His own divine immortal life at His incarnation, making it possible for him to die, to be made of a woman, made under the law, that is, subject to the penalty of the law, which is the second death. The humanity inherited from Mary, which He sanctified by taking, died forever. Fallen human nature never came out of the tomb; glorified human nature did. He was "begotten again" by the Father (Acts 13:33) by being raised in glorified humanity and immortality—the immortal life He had laid down.

2. Christ lived his human life sustained by His Father ("I live by the Father." John 6:57), and filled with the divine life of the Holy Spirit, which He commended to His Father at His death on the cross ("Father, into Thy hands I commend My Spirit." Luke 23:46.)

Took Up Again

1. The Father raises Jesus from the dead by the Holy Spirit (Romans 8:11) who administers to Christ His (Christ's) own immortal life to Him at the resurrection.

2. In this sense Jesus takes up again His own divine life, which He administers to the redeemed through the Holy Spirit, Who is His Representative and Who carries out His (Christ's) will. "The life that He laid down in humanity, He takes up again, and gives to humanity." Desire of Ages, page 786.

See John 10:10; 4:14; 6:54; and Romans 8:9-11.

Chapter 30

WHAT POWER RAISED JESUS FROM THE DEAD AND RAISES THE REDEEMED?

PROFESSOR: That is the question we will tackle today. Some think that the following inspired statement indicates that Christ raised Himself from the grave:

Faith I Live By, page 51:
"He who had said, I lay down my life, that I might take it again,' came forth from the grave **to life that was in Himself.**"

In the light of the inspired statements which follow, it is incumbent that one understands what "life" was in Jesus. **Did Jesus really die? Or was it only His human body that died, while His divine Personhood lived on to later raise His body in glorified humanity?**
During His earthly sojourn Jesus had emphatically stated:

John 6:57:
"As the living Father hath sent me, and I **live by the Father:** so he that eateth me, even He shall live by me."

It is abundantly clear in Scripture that the redeemed are raised from death and live eternal life through the power administered by the Holy Spirit that dwelt/dwells in them here on earth. Immortality depends on their humanity having become united to divinity by the indwelling presence of the Holy Spirit, who seals the faithful unto the day of redemption. (Rom. 8:9-11; Eph. 4:30). It is Jesus' redemptive life and death that enables converted sinners to receive the divine, life-imparting, indwelling presence of the Holy Spirit (John 14:15-18; John 4:10,14; John 7:38,39). It is Jesus immortal life that is administered to the redeemed at His Second Coming.
When Michael left the heavenly courts to become incarnate as 'Jesus of Nazareth,' He laid aside His divinity; His divine power, omnipotence, omnipresence, memory, character, omniscience, and came to this earth—through the ministration of the Holy Spirit—exercising no power that is not freely available to us, through grace and God's Spirit.

WILLIAM: He gave up everything!

PROFESSOR: Yes! We have seen that Jesus did not only lay His divinity and the attributes of divinity aside; but that He also laid down His life, the fountain of living water administered by the Holy Spirit. We are conventionally inclined to think of this as **only** happening on the cross where His laying down His sinless life, the life of a divine member of the Godhead, occurred. This became the final capstone to His victory over him 'who has the power of sin and death,' (namely Satan—the Adversary).

WILLIAM: So, just when did Jesus begin laying down His life—immortal life—the life of God!

PROFESSOR: This act became certain when in response to the Father's question, "Who will go for us?" Jesus voluntarily responded, "Here am I, send Me." (See Isaiah 6:8; 48:16). **From that point forward it was a certainty that Michael/Jesus would become a man in order to be able to die.** At His conception Jesus' **immortal** life was laid down.

> SDA Bible Commentary, Volume 7, page 460:
> "He clothed His divinity with humanity, and voluntarily took upon Him human nature, **making it possible to offer Himself as a ransom.**" (Manuscript 92, 1899)

> SDA Bible Commentary, Volume 7, pages 925, 926:
> "He did not have a mere semblance of a body, but He took human nature, participating in the **life of humanity** *[which is mortal]*. According to the law Christ Himself gave, the forfeited inheritance was ransomed by the nearest of kin. Jesus Christ laid off His royal robe, His kingly crown, and clothed His divinity with humanity, in order to become a substitute and surety for humanity, that **dying in humanity** He might by His death destroy him who had the power of death. **He could not have done this as God, but by coming as man Christ could die.** By death He overcame death. The death of Christ bore to the death him who had the power of death, and opened the gates of the tomb for all who receive Him as their personal Saviour." (Letter 97, 1898)

PROFESSOR: Let me repeat that quotation with some explanation:

374

"He did not have a mere semblance of a body, *[Hebrews 10:5: "Wherefore when He cometh into the world, He saith, Sacrifice and offering Thou wouldest not, but a body hast Thou prepared Me."]*, but He took human nature, **participating in the life of humanity.** *[This "life of humanity" is 'probationary life'—'mortal life'—life that is subject to death.]* …Jesus Christ laid off His royal robe, His kingly crown, and clothed His divinity with humanity *[He was still the divine second Person of the Godhead, but had laid aside and laid down the whole panoply of divinity and had to be sustained by His Father, through the agency of the Holy Spirit]*, in order to become a substitute and surety for humanity, **that dying in humanity** *[a Divine member of the Godhead dying because of the <u>separation</u> from His Father that He experienced in becoming 'sin' for us]* **He might by His death destroy him who had the power of death. He could not have done this as God, but by coming as man Christ could die.** *[But what of His immortal life? He had laid that down when He became a manchild: born of Mary, with only God as His Father. The life—immortal life—the life of Diety that Jesus laid down, He now—having effected the reconciliation—He now takes up and gives to His redeemed ones, through the agency of the mighty Third Person of the Godhead: the Holy Spirit.]* By death *[the death of a Divine member of the Godhead]* He overcame death. The *[reconciling]* death of Christ bore to the death him who had the power of death, and opened the gates of the tomb for all who receive Him as their personal Saviour."

As we saw, **Christ was "…the only One who could bare the strokes in behalf of the sinner, and because of His innocence not be consumed"** (4MR page 243.2). "The gates of hell"—the grave—could not triumph over Christ because of His loyal, spotlessly obedient faith. These same "gates" can never triumph over those who are His. They will exclaim, "O grave, where is thy victory?" 1 Cor. 15:55.

SDA Bible Commentary, Volume 7, page 463:
"Christ was suffering **the death that was pronounced upon the transgressors of God's law.**" (Manuscript 35, 1895)

WILLIAM: We have seen what death that was!

PROFESSOR: "Eternal death!" The "penalty death!" **Jesus bore fallen humanity, the condition that has devolved upon us all through Adam's fall, to eternal death**. He came forth from the grave in glorified humanity—akin to that which the redeemed receive at Jesus' Second Coming. Having laid down His "eternal life" He can, because of His sinless loyalty to His Father during His earthly sojourn, take up His divine life and give it—the **"life that measures with the life of God"** *[6T 253, 297; 7T 228; 8T 44; 9T 114]* to His redeemed ones that they might **"put on immortality"**! *[Romans 2:7; 1 Cor. 15:53, 54; 1 Tim. 6:16; 2 Tim. 1:10]*.

> The Faith I Live By, page 46:
>
> "Christ was God essentially, and in the highest sense. He was with God from all eternity, God over all, blessed forevermore. The Lord Jesus Christ, the divine Son of God, existed from eternity, **a distinct person,** yet one *[that "one"ness we have discussed]* with the Father. He was the surpassing glory of heaven. He was the commander of the heavenly intelligences, and the adoring homage of the angels was received by Him as His right.
>
> "He was equal with God, infinite and omnipotent.
>
> "But He humbled Himself, and took mortality upon Him. **As a member of the human family, He was mortal;** but as a God, He was the fountain of life to the world. *[He was that member of the Godhead, the Word, through whom the Father created the world: He was thus the "fountain of life to the world". He had immortal life, that "life" He laid down in becoming a man so that He could die.]* He could, in His divine person *[as He was before becoming mortal]*, ever have withstood the advances of death, and refused to come under its dominion; but **He voluntarily laid down His life, that in so doing He might give life and bring immortality to light** *[for redeemed sinners].* "

Remember what we read in Volume 7 of the Seventh-Day Adventist Bible Commentary, pages 925, 926, where we find God's messenger declaring categorically that Christ could not die "...as God, but by coming as man Christ could die." As God, Christ, as we know, had eternal life; as Deity Christ could not possibly die (5BC page 1113.2, see also 7BC page 926.1). It is for this reason that He had to lay down His immortal life and accept to become the Divine "Seed" without the attributes of Deity; to pass through the processes of fertilization, gestation, birth and human growth and development, accepting the mortality of a probationer, which "dust" He anctified, being still the Second Person of the Godhead in whom "all the ullness of the Godhead" dwelt through the agency of the Mighty Third 'erson of the Godhead.

He retained no power that we cannot have, and exercised no power that s not available to us.

SDA Bible Commentary, Volume 7, page 930:

"If Christ *[on earth]* **had a special power which it is not the privilege of man to have, Satan would have made capital of this matter.** The work of Christ was to take from the claims of Satan his control of man, and He could do this **only** in the way that He came—a man, tempted as a man**, rendering the obedience of a** **man**." (Manuscript 1, 1892)

Jesus, the Son of man, became a union of humanity and divinity through he ministration of the Holy Spirit, who was Jesus' earthly progenitor (Luke :35.) Galatians 4:4 tells us that He was "made of a woman, made under he law" (i.e. subject to its penalty). He voluntarily laid down His divine fe and became a man in order for it to be possible for Him to die (See etter 97, 1898 quoted above).

We have determined that as **man** Jesus never ceased to be the divine econd Person of the Godhead, but He had laid aside the panoply of power nd immortality that went with the position. Divine power (See Micah 3:8) nd divine life were administered to Jesus through the Holy Spirit—the Iighty third Person of the Godhead (See Desire of Ages, page 671). **When esus died, a divine member of the Godhead died—one equal with the aw! We cannot stress enough that we have a divine Sacrifice,** who paid he price of our salvation, once and for all. No need for ongoing sacrifices" of 'transubstantiated' wafers at ongoing "masses".

Upward Look, page 49:
"A divine life is given as humanity's ransom…"

Christ's human nature—our fallen human nature, which He had ssumed—died. **He had sanctified our nature unto Himself.** Just as His resence sanctified the very ground where Moses stood at the burning bush, o Christ's presence sanctifies! Also remember! He was a "union of umanity and divinity" (1 SM 254, 340) through the agency of the Holy pirit, and the divine power He exercised on earth was Holy Spirit power.

His life on earth was characterized by demonstrations of divine power. 'I am full of power by the Spirit." Micah 3:8.) But of His "own Self" He

377

could "do nothing." (John 5:30). When Jesus died, He commended His 'Spirit" into His Father's hands (Luke 23:46). The Holy Spirit who filled Jesus' life on earth, the mighty third Person of the Godhead, and through Whom the Father was "in Christ, reconciling the world unto Himself" (2 Cor. 5:19), being Deity, did not die, "that would have been impossible." (SDA Bible Commentary, Volume 5, page1113.)

Jesus commended His Spirit, the Holy Spirit, who administered His life into His Father's hands—His Father's oversight—trusting in His Father's love and justice—trusting by pure and naked faith alone. It is this faith, His faith that saves us.

How do we know that the Holy Spirit administered Christ's divine immortal life, and administers the same life to those who accept Jesus as their Saviour from sin? God's messenger tells us plainly:

Review & Herald, June 13, 1899:
"The impartation of the Spirit was the impartation **of the very life of Christ**."

Conflict and Courage, page 229 (2 SM 271):
"**The <u>vitalizing power of the Spirit of Christ</u> dwelling in the mortal body binds every believing soul to Jesus Christ.** Those who believe in Jesus are sacred to His heart; for **their** *[immortal]* **life is hid with Christ in God…**" *[In the same way that Jesus' immortal life was "hid" in God by the Holy Spirit. They have passed from death to life (John 5:24). They have everlasting life (John 3:16; 3:36; 4:14; 5:24; 6:40; etc.) and shall not experience the "penalty" death (John 11:26).]*

Of Jesus, we have seen that:

Acts 13:30:
"But **God raised Him from the dead**."

1 Peter 1:21:
"Who by him *[Jesus]* do believe in **God, that raised him** *[Jesus]* up from the dead, and gave him glory; that your faith and hope might be in God."

By what agency?

Romans 8:11:

378

"But if the **Spirit of him** *[the Father]* **that raised up Jesus from the dead** dwell in you, **he** *[the Father]* **that raised up Christ from the dead shall also quicken your mortal bodies by his** *the Father's]* **Spirit that dwelleth in you.**"

Selected Messages Book 2, page 270:
" 'He that raised up Christ from the dead shall also quicken your mortal bodies by His Spirit that dwelleth **in** you.' (Rom. 8:11) ...**By the power of the Saviour** *[Holy Spirit administered power]* **that dwelt in them while living and because they are partakers of the divine nature, they are brought forth from the dead.**"

1 John 3:24:
"And he that keepeth His commandments dwelleth **in** Him, and He **in** him. And hereby we know that He abideth **in** us, **by the Spirit which He hath given us.**"

Ephesians 1:19, 20, 22-23:
19) "And what is the exceeding greatness of **his power** to us-ward **who believe, according to the working of his mighty power,**
20) "**Which he** *[the Father]* **wrought in Christ, when he** *[the Father]* **raised him from the dead, and set him at his own right hand** in the heavenly places,
22) And hath put all things under his feet, and gave him to be the head over all things to the church,
23) Which is his body, **the fulness of him that filleth all in all.**" *[by His Spirit!]*

Now see:

Colossians 1:15, 18, 19 *[speaking of Jesus]*:
15) "Who is the image of the invisible God, the firstborn of every creature:
18) And he is the head of the body, the church: who is the beginning, **the firstborn from the dead;** that in all things he might have the preeminence.
19) For it pleased the Father **that in him should all fulness** *[of the Godhead]* **dwell** *[by His Spirit!]."*

Lift Him Up, page 102 (ST 5/10/1899):

"By raising Christ from the dead, **the Father glorified His Son... The voice of God was heard calling Christ from His prison house.... He came to our world as a man; He ascended to His heavenly home as God** *[as a full Member of the Godhead; though still subject to His Father, the "Most High God"]*."

Faith I Live By, page 183:

"To the believer, Christ is the resurrection and the life. In our Saviour the *[endless]* life that was lost through sin is restored; for He has life **in** Himself to quicken whom He will. **He is invested with the right** to give immortality. The life that He laid down in humanity *[divine life, which equals eternal life, that is, immortality, which He laid down in taking mortality upon Himself]*, **He takes up again,** and gives to humanity."

1 Corinthians 15:53:

"For the corruptible must put on incorruption, and this mortal must put on **immortality**." *[That is, "the life of God." See Eph. 4:18.]*

Lift Him Up, page 261 (5BC, page 1130):

"'**In** him was life; and the life was the light of men.' It is not physical life that is here specified, but eternal *[spirit imparted]* life, the life which is exclusively the property of God.

Lift Him Up, page 230 (MS 56, 1899):

"Christ was **empowered** to breathe into fallen humanity the breath of life. ...The Father **committed** the riches of heaven to Him, ..."

As a "manifestation" of the "one God" of Trinitarianism, why would Christ have to be "empowered" to do anything; or to have heavens riches "committed" to Him?

Reflecting Christ, page 45:

"Christ was treated as we deserve, that we might be treated as He deserves. He was condemned for our sins, in which He had no share, that we might be justified by His righteousness, in which we had no share. **He suffered the death which was ours, that we might receive the life which was His.**"

The death, eternal death that we deserve, is balanced against eternal life, which was Christ's. This mortal shall "put on immortality" (1 Cor. 15:53, 54), but God alone is immortal See 1 Tim. 6:16. See 2 Timothy 1:10; and Lift Him Up, page 261. So this "immortality" has to be Jesus' life that He gives to His own.

Compare the following statements:

Faith I Live By, page 50 (5 BC 1114):
"He who died for the sins of the world was to remain in the tomb the allotted time. He was in that stony prison house as **a prisoner of divine justice.** He was responsible to the Judge of the universe. He was bearing the sins of the world, and **His Father only could release Him.**"

Faith I Live By, page 51:
"He who had said, 'I lay down my life, that I might take it again,' **came forth from the grave to life that was in Himself.** *[Divine life administered through the Holy Spirit—the Deity that did not die when humanity, Christ's humanity, died.]* Humanity died: divinity *[the Holy Spirit]* did not die. In His divinity, Christ possessed the power to break the bonds of death. *[He could, at any time, have chosen to take back His divine prerogatives.]* He declares that He has life in Himself to quicken whom He will....

"He is the spring, the fountain, of life. Only He who alone hath immortality, *[1 Timothy 6:16, "Who only hath immortality...,"an aspect of the Godhead, but Who voluntarily accepting to be of "none effect", in the form of a servant, able to do nothing of Himself]* dwelling in light and life *[as He had before the incarnation]*, could say, 'I have power to lay down my life, and I have power to take it again.'...."

Selected Messages Book 1, page 302:
"Christ was **invested with the right to give immortality.** The life which He had laid down in humanity, He again took up and gave to humanity. 'I am come,' He says, 'that they might have life, and that they might have it more abundantly.'"

381

Once again we note what "life" did Jesus come to give the redeemed:

1 Corinthians 15:53:
"For this corruptible must put on incorruption, and this **mortal** [must] put on **immortality**."

Signs of the Times, June 17, 1897, par. 14:
"If we repent of our transgression, and receive Christ as the Life-giver, our personal Saviour, we become one with him, and our will is brought into harmony with the divine will. **We become partakers of the life of Christ, which is eternal. We derive immortality from God by receiving the life of Christ** for in Christ dwells all the fulness of the Godhead bodily. This life is the mystical union and cooperation of the divine with the human."

Immortality is the life of God (1 Tim. 6:16), Jesus' life that He gives to us, the life that the Father had given Him to have in Himself (John. 5:26) the life that He **fully laid down,** through the consistent exercise of free will when He said, "Father, into thy hands I commend My Spirit." (Luke 23:46). "Fully laid down," in the sense that had Jesus failed in the least particular He would have lost His Deity (*Signs of the Times*, May 10, 1899); He would have never seen His Father again (Desire of Ages, page 686); and He would have been without hope in the same way that the human race would have been without hope (Desire of Ages, page 49; SDA Bible Commentary Volume 5, page 1131).

2 Timothy 1:10:
"But is now made manifest by the appearing of our Saviour Jesus Christ, who hath abolished *[the second]* death *[for those who accept salvation]*, and hath brought life **and** immortality *[balanced against eternal death]* to light through the gospel."

Faith I Live By, page 187 (Desire of Ages, page 388):
"**It is through the Spirit that Christ dwells in us; and the Spirit of God, received into the heart by faith, is the beginning of the life eternal.**" *[See chapter 31 on "The Spirit of a Man."]*

In Heavenly Places, page 175 (Desire of Ages, page 388):

"**Christ became one flesh with us, in order that we might become one spirit with Him.** **It is by virtue of this union that we are to come forth from the grave**—not merely as a manifestation of the power of Christ, **but because, through faith, His life has become ours.**"

Review & Herald, May 19, 1904:

"**The Spirit was given as a regenerating agency** [*carnal man is 'dead in trespasses and sins' and has to be 'born again'— regenerated*], **and without this the sacrifice of Christ would have been of no avail.** The power of evil had been strengthening for centuries, and the submission of man to this satanic captivity was amazing. Sin could be resisted and overcome **only** through the mighty agency of the **third person of the Godhead,** who would come with no modified energy, but **in the fulness of divine power.** It is the Spirit that makes effectual what has been wrought out by the world's Redeemer. It is by the Spirit that the heart is made pure. Through the Spirit the believer becomes a partaker of the divine nature. **Christ has given his Spirit as a divine power to overcome all hereditary and cultivated tendencies to evil,** and to impress his own character upon the church."

Desire of Ages, page 805:

"**The impartation of the Spirit is the impartation of the life of Christ.**"

Desire of Ages, page 827:

"**Christ gives them the breath of His own Spirit, the life of His own life. The Holy Spirit puts forth its highest energies to work in hearts and mind.**"

John 5:26:

"For as the Father hath life in himself; so hath he **given to the Son to have life in himself.**"

This verse is referring, not only to Christ's birth in Bethlehem, but also to Christ's resurrection by the Father. (See Acts 13:30; Romans 8:11; 1 Peter 1:21, etc.).

Desire of Ages, page 388:

"'Verily, verily, I say unto you, **He that believeth on Me hath everlasting life.**' Through the beloved John, who listened to these words, the Holy Spirit declared to the churches, 'This is the record, that **God hath given to us eternal life, and this life is in His Son.** He that hath the Son hath life.' **1 John 5:11, 12.** And Jesus said, 'I will raise him up at the last day.' **Christ became one flesh with us, in order that we might become <u>one spirit with Him</u>.** *[If we have the Holy Spirit, we have "one Spirit with Him." See Chapter 31 on "The Spirit of a Man."]* **It is by virtue of this union that we are to come forth from the grave**—not merely as a manifestation of the power of Christ, but because, **through faith, <u>His life has become ours</u>.** Those who see Christ in His true character, and **receive Him into the heart** *[Behold I stand at the door and knock. Rev. 3:20]*, have everlasting life. **It is through the Spirit that Christ dwells in us; and <u>the Spirit of God, received into the heart by faith, is the beginning of the life eternal</u>.**"

Now, again, with regards to the "One"ness of the Godhead and of the church:

Ephesians 5:30-32:
30) "For we are members of his body, **of his flesh, and of his bones.**
31)   For this cause shall a man leave his father and mother, and shall be joined unto his wife, **and they two shall be one flesh.**
32)   **This is a great mystery: but I speak concerning Christ and the church.**"

A man and a woman are of the same 'substance'—flesh and blood and bone—each have similar, but **not** identical substance.   They are two separate and distinct entities. However, these **two** become **one** (flesh) at marriage. Paul says this is a great mystery and He is clearly also referring to Jesus becoming one flesh with fallen humanity.

Please note that Eph. 5:30 clearly teaches that Jesus partook of **our human nature** and not that of unfallen man.   **"We** are members of his body, of **his flesh,** and of **his bones.**"

Desire of Ages, page 388 says that:

"Christ became <u>one flesh with us</u>, in order that we might become <u>one spirit with Him</u>."

When a man and woman are joined together as 'one flesh' and they are or become converted and accept Jesus as Lord and Saviour and receive **the indwelling presence of the Holy Spirit**; becoming a union of humanity and divinity (as Jesus was, and is), <u>**can you see that "they twain" are now three?**</u>—**three separate and distinct Persons? They are "one" in flesh and "one" in Spirit: <u>one husband and one wife and one Holy Spirit</u>, who, in turn, makes them "one" with Jesus, and "one" with the Father. That is At-one-ment!** This At-one-ment is only eternally secure when we pass our probation on God's side of the equation; just as Jesus had to do when He took humanity upon Himself and became the "Elder Brother" of the redeemed.

John 5:24:
"And he that keepeth his commandments **dwelleth in him, and he in him. <u>And hereby we know that he abideth in us, by the Spirit which he hath given us.</u>**"

So! How are we "in Him" and "He ...in us"? By the Holy Spirit who is "in Jesus;" and by His grace "in us." The Holy Spirit is a separate and distinct "Person" inhabiting God and humanity—the redeemed. Humanity, united to divinity by the indwelling presence of the Holy Spirit, whose temple we are, finally attains to a higher plane than that attainable had they never fallen. (Desire of Ages, page 25; Lift Him Up, page 230). All this because of Jesus' **"infinite** sacrifice" making it possible for redeemed man to be set down with Him on His throne, even as He is set down with His Father on His throne.

What Oneness existed between Jesus, the Son of man, and His heavenly Father? And between Him and His disciples? God replies though His messenger.

Ministry of Healing, pages 421, 422:
"The personality of the Father and the Son, <u>also the unity that exists between</u> Them, are presented in the seventeenth chapter of John, in the prayer of Christ for His disciples:
"'Neither pray I for these alone, **but for them also which shall believe on Me through their word** *[that's us]*; that **they**

all may be one; as Thou, Father, art in Me, and I in Thee *[clearly through the Holy Spirit who searches and interprets the mind of the Father, to whose will Christ was submitted, and who renews our minds and guides God's children into all truth]*, **that they also may be one in Us** *[by the Spirit]*: that the world may believe that Thou hast sent Me.' John 17:20, 21.

The unity that exists between Christ and His disciples does not destroy the personality of either. They are one in purpose, in mind *[renewed by the Holy Spirit]*, in character, **but NOT in person. IT IS THUS THAT GOD AND CHRIST ARE ONE."** *[The Holy Spirit's indwelling presence being the unifying factor. This whole inspired statement from <u>Ministry of Healing</u> clearly indicates how separate and distinct beings may be "one", despite being distinct.]*

Christ's "one-ness" with his Father, His being "in" His Father and His Father "in" Him is a clear reference to a shared representative presence: the indwelling Holy Spirit. By the same agency of the Mighty Third Person of the Godhead, Christ dwells "in" the redeemed and they are thus also "one" with Christ and the Father.

N. B. **The unity of the Godhead is to be duplicated among Christ's followers <u>and is achieved only through truth, and the Spirit of Truth!</u> (John 14:17; 15:26; 16:13; and 1 John 4:6)**

The papacy, and other church organizations controlled by her spirit, attempt to achieve a unity by obliging everyone to believe in the 'Trinity' concept of God. We saw how they "demand" belief in their description of how the Trinity functions and exists. (See page 41 of this book, citing: <u>The Catholic Encyclopedia</u>, 1915 Edition, article: Holy Ghost)

George Knight, a leading Seventh-day Adventist theologian, has published that many of the founders of this denomination would not be able to join the present, organizationally led, Adventist movement because they did not believe in the Trinity (See pages 495-496 of this book); a belief which 'demands' acceptance if one is to become a member in 'good regular standing' with the Conference structure of today.

Does the Seventh-day Adventist structure leadership actually teach Catholic style, consubstantial Trinitarianism? Let us see by turning to:

<u>Seventh-day Adventists Believe... A Biblical Exposition of 27 Fundamental Doctrines,</u> page 152:

Belief #12 which states: "The universal *[the word Catholic means universal]* church is composed of **all** who truly believe in

386

Christ ... *[Please note that the devils truly "believe" and tremble James 2:19; the Catholic Church 'truly believes in Christ'. The question is: Which Christ?]."*

Furthermore, in <u>Seventh-day Adventists Believe</u>... the 'unity' of believers **is declared, in belief #13, to be based on the Trinity or <u>"triune God"</u>**:

Ibid, page 170:
Belief #13 which states: "…. This unity has its source in the oneness of the **triune God** ... *[We have already seen that the term "<u>triune God</u>" is a code term for the 'Trinity'.]"*

So we see that Belief #13 points one back to belief #2 (ibid. page 16) which, while employing the heading "The Godhead", goes on to define the Godhead in Trinitarianism terms:

Ibid, page 16:
Belief #2 which states: "There is **one God: Father, Son, and Holy Spirit**, a unity of three **co-eternal Persons**." *[See pages 21, 50, 56-58, 99, 129-130, 260, and others of this book, for a discussion on the term "co-eternal". The sort of "Persons" here being referred to are discussed on pages 24-25, 44, 130 and others.]*

However, Belief # 2 goes on to describe this 'Godhead'; this "one God", as though 'He' is only one (consubstantial) 'Being':

Ibid:
"**God** is immortal, ... **He** is infinite and beyond human comprehension, ... **He** is forever worthy …"

These statements are all referring back to the **"<u>one God</u>: Father, Son, and Holy Spirit"**. Such a "God" manifest in three different "Persons", **is exactly akin to the 'God' of the papacy** that we have been discussing all along. This is the same 'God' referred to by Pope Paul VI at the 1962-65 21st Ecumenical Council when he delivered the **decree on <u>ecumenism</u>** titled "Unitatis Redintegratio" in 1964 in which he stated:

"1. The restoration of unity among all Christians is one of the principal concerns of the Second Vatican Council. Christ the

Lord founded **one** *[Roman Catholic]* **Church and one** *[Roman Catholic]* **Church only….**

"**This movement toward unity is called "ecumenical." Those belong to it who invoke THE TRIUNE GOD and confess Jesus as Lord and Savior, doing this not merely as individuals but also as corporate bodies….**

"**Chapter One: Catholic Principles on Ecumenism**
"…This is the sacred **mystery of the unity of the** *[Roman Catholic]* **Church,** in Christ and through Christ, the Holy Spirit energizing its various functions. It is **a mystery that finds its highest exemplar and source in the unity of the Persons of the Trinity: the Father and the Son in the Holy Spirit, one God….**" *[See: http://www.vatican.va/archive/hist_councils/ii_ vatican_council/documents/vat-ii_decree_19641121_unitatis-redintegratio_en.html]*

This is the same 'God' referred to by Pope John Paul II in his encyclical "Ut Unum Sint" of 1995 in which he calls for **ecumenical unity based on the Trinity**:

Ut Unum Sint, # 8.3:
"The Catholic Church embraces with hope the commitment to ecumenism as a duty of the Christian conscience enlightened by faith and guided by love. Here too we can apply the words of Saint Paul to the first Christians of Rome: "God's love has been poured into our hearts through the Holy Spirit"; thus our "hope does not disappoint us" (*Rom* 5:5). **This is the hope of Christian unity, which has its divine** *[?]* **source in the Trinitarian unity** *[?]* **of the Father, the Son and the Holy Spirit.**"

Given in Rome, at Saint Peter's, on 25 May, the Solemnity of the Ascension of the Lord, in the year 1995, the seventeenth of my Pontificate. JOHN PAUL II

On page 22.6 of <u>Seventh-day Adventists Believe… A Biblical Exposition of 27 Fundamental Doctrines</u>, where Belief #2 is being clarified and explained, **the Godhead is now actually called the "Trinity"**:

"**… the Christian *[?]* concept of the triune God or Trinity – Father, Son, and Holy Spirit; …**"

388

For the Father, Son, and Holy Spirit to be a "triune God" (singular) is a depiction of none other than the Trinity of the Athanasian Creed. Clearly, the decision to adopt this view point on behalf of the entire church had to be taken at the highest level, as this book that we are now discussing, was printed by All-Africa Publications **for the Ministerial Association of the General Conference of Seventh-day Adventists**, and so bears the 'imprimatur' of denominational leadership.

As we have seen, Belief **#13: "UNITY In The Body of Christ" (the Church), declares that the unity of Christians is based on belief in the "Triune God."** Belief in the Trinity is the 'glue' that is being employed to cohere all the various daughters of Babylon, and now, it seems, the Adventist Conference structure, into one ecumenical body (See Appendices H and K). **But for God's people, unity is to be based only on TRUTH**, to which the Holy Spirit guides us as He administers enlightenment to God's faithful followers.

God's people are to be **separate** from the fallen churches **and from the false doctrines of the fallen church's "mother"**. God's true people will only come to true unity based on truth, not on error.

> Testimonies to the Church, Volume 5, page 101; (Faith I Live By, page 343):
> "Those who are drinking from the **same** fountain of blessing **will draw nearer together. Truth** dwelling in the hearts of believers will lead to **blessed and happy assimilation. Thus will be answered the prayer of Christ that His disciples might be one even as He is one with the Father. For this oneness every truly converted heart will be striving**.
>
> "With the ungodly there will be a deceptive harmony that but partially conceals a perpetual discord. **In their opposition to the will and the truth of God they are united**, while on every other point they are rent with hatred, emulation, jealousy, and deadly strife."

It is the Holy Spirit, the Spirit of **truth**, who guides into all **truth**. (John 16:13.)

In Christ the "seed of Abraham" (Heb. 2:16), the humanity of "Adam the transgressor" (7BC 926) and the divinity of the Godhead are **united.** When Jesus paid the redemption price the at-one-ment of these two separated natures was established and made secure. From the cross onwards, Jesus could impart the indwelling power and presence of the Holy

389

Spirit to His followers on an eternally secured and permanent basis (See John 14:15-18; 16:7). To those who, by steadfastness and faith, maintain victory by the power of the Spirit, He can proclaim, "Let Him who is holy be holy still," and finally and eternally confer on them "immortality," the life of God! When Jesus proclaims, "Let Him who is holy be holy still," then will the at-one-ment be permanent for, from that point onwards, the union of humanity and divinity, the indwelling presence of the Holy Spirit in the redeemed, will be "forever" (John 14:16).

Chapter 31

THE 'SPIRIT' OF A MAN

WILLIAM: Professor, I have a question. If man is filled with either God's Holy Spirit, or the spirit of a demon, what is the spirit **of** man? Or should I say, **in** man?

PROFESSOR: We have long understood that man is comprised of a physical, mental, and spiritual nature!

WILLIAM: So, if man is spiritual, does man 'have' a spirit? Is there a 'spirit' part of man that does not perish as his physical nature does?

PROFESSOR: Or maybe the question should be, Does man have a vacuum?—an unfulfilled aspect in his mental and emotional make-up that will be filled by **a 'spirit'** who then becomes that person's 'spirit'? Let us see what inspiration tells us:

Ye Shall Receive Power, page 91:
"When one is fully emptied of self *[selfishness stems from Satan]*, when every false god is cast out of the soul, **the vacuum** is supplied by the inflowing of the Spirit of Christ *[the Holy Spirit]*.

Ye Shall Receive Power, page 293:
"But in order that Christ may be in the soul *[the "body" with the "breath of life" in it (Gen. 2:7)]*, it must first be emptied of self *[the spirit of Satan]*, then there is a **vacuum** created **that may be supplied** *[filled]* **by the Holy Spirit**."

Ye Shall Receive Power, page 350:
"We must be emptied of self. But this is not all that is required; for when we have renounced our idols *[those things that a demonic spirit incites us to "worship"]*, the **vacuum** must be supplied. If the heart *[mind}* is left desolate, and the **vacuum** not supplied, it will be in the condition of him whose house was 'empty, swept, and garnished' (Matthew 12:44), but **without a guest to occupy it.** The evil spirit took unto himself seven other

spirits more wicked than himself, **and they entered in and dwelt there**; and the last state of that man was worse than the first...."

Writing to Christ's followers, Paul tells us which "Spirit" we are to have:

1 Corinthians 2:12:
"Now **we have received** not the spirit of the world *[Satan is the "god of this world." 2 Corinthians 4:4.]*, but **the spirit which is of God** *[which is the Holy Spirit]*; that we might know the things that are freely given us of God."

I believe that we have only one choice to make in life—we can choose which 'spirit' will fill that vacuum. Man is controlled by either God's Spirit or by one of Satan's. We can choose what spirit will dwell in our body temple to prompt our decisions. If a man opens the door of his heart to Christ, he will receive the Holy Spirit, who will prompt, not coerce, to right choices. Paul, addressing the Corinthian **believers**, said:

1 Corinthians 3:16, 17:
16) "Know ye not that ye are the temple of God, and *that* **the Spirit of God dwelleth in you?**
17)   If any man defile the temple of God, him shall God destroy; for the temple of God is holy, which *temple* ye are".

1 Corinthians 6:19, 20:
19) "What? know ye not that your body is the temple of the Holy Ghost *which is* in you, which ye have of God, and ye are not your own?
20)   For ye are bought with a price: therefore glorify God in your body, **and in your spirit, which are God's."**

By the Holy Spirit, as His Representative, God dwells in the true believer.

2 Corinthians 6:16-7:1:
16) "And what agreement hath the temple of God with idols? for ye are the temple of the living God; as God hath said, **I will dwell in them, and walk in *them;*** and I will be their God, and they shall be my people.

17)   Wherefore come out from among them *[who are controlled by demonic spirits]*, and be ye separate, saith the Lord, and touch not the unclean *thing; and* I will receive you,

18)   And will be a Father unto you, and ye shall be my sons and daughters, saith the Lord Almighty.

7:1)   Having therefore these promises, dearly beloved, let us cleanse ourselves from **all filthiness** of the flesh **and spirit**, perfecting holiness in the fear of God."

Paul also refers to the "filthiness of the flesh and spirit" (2 Corinthians 7:1) which are our corrupted appetites and habits and also the carnal spirit of enmity against God that we are born with, and which must be evicted by our choice and the power of God.   And James warns us:

James 4:15:
"Do ye think that the scripture saith in vain, The **spirit** that dwelleth in us lusteth to envy?"

Such is the carnal spirit with which we are born.   When we accept Jesus as Lord and Saviour, the Holy Spirit takes his rightful place in the body temple and the carnal spirit is evicted.

WILLIAM: What a wonderful awesome privilege we have—that our bodies are temples for God.

PROFESSOR: If man's body and life has received the indwelling presence of the Holy Spirit, he is a temple of the Holy Ghost.   That man is united to Divinity.   The Spirit and Life that was in Christ, the Holy Spirit, is in that man, and his life is hid with Christ in God; that man can never die the "penalty-death" for he has "passed from death unto life" (John 5:24) provided that man remains faithful.   The Spirit that raised up Christ from the dead will raise him up, or translate him, at the last trump (Romans 8:11; 1 Corinthians 15:52).

Colossians 3:3:
"For ye are dead *["I" and the disposition to be selfish, has died and must die daily]***, and your** *[everlasting]* **life is hid with Christ in God."**

John 5:24:

393

"Verily, verily, I say unto you, He that heareth my word, and believeth on him that sent me, hath everlasting life, **and shall not come into condemnation; but is passed from death unto life."**

Romans 8:11:
"But if the Spirit of him that raised up Jesus from the dead dwell in you, he that raised up Christ from the dead shall also **quicken your mortal bodies by his Spirit that dwelleth in you."**

WILLIAM: What happens if a man chooses to turn his back on Christ?

PROFESSOR: If a man does not choose to receive Jesus through the indwelling presence of the Holy Spirit, then demons will assuredly take up residence. If a man is joined unto his idols, he is controlled by the powers of darkness and is "dead in trespasses and sins." He will receive the wrath of God and have his part "in the lake of fire." Also, take note that the Spirit of God is "one" and brings godly unity whereas the spirits of demons are "legion" (Mark 5:9) and bring discord. The Bible warning is plain that we have to continually examine ourselves to see what "spirit" we are of (2 Corinthians 13:5; Luke 9:55):

Matthew 12:43-45:
43) "When the unclean spirit is gone out of a man, he walketh through dry places, seeking rest, and findeth none.

44) Then he saith, I will return into my house from whence I came out; and when he is come, he findeth it **empty,** swept, and garnished.

45) Then goeth he, and taketh with himself seven other spirits more wicked than himself, and they enter in and dwell there: and the last state of that man is worse than the first. Even so shall it be also unto this wicked generation."

But to those who have opened to Christ's knocking, Paul writes:

Ephesians 2:1:
"And you hath he **quickened** *[made alive],* who were dead in trespasses and sins;"

Jesus Himself was filled with the Holy Spirit, and exercised Holy Spirit power. Jesus Himself said:

Matthew 12:28:
"But if I cast out demons by the Spirit of God, then the kingdom of God is come to you."

He came to cast out wrong spirits, and to "renew a right spirit" within us (Psalm 51:10).

<u>Desire of Ages</u>, pages 37, 38:
"Jesus came to restore in man the image of his Maker. None but Christ can fashion anew the character that has been ruined by sin. **He came to expel the demons that had controlled the will.**"

We have to choose Christ or eternal loss:

John: 3:36:
"He that believeth not the Son *[not believing that He can and will save His people from sin and its power]* shall not see life; **but the wrath of God abideth on him.**"

Matthew 25:41:
"Then shall he say also unto them on the left hand, Depart from me, **ye cursed, into everlasting fire, prepared for the devil and his angels:**"

WILLIAM: So every morning, we have one decision to make: Whom will we serve?"

PROFESSOR: Yes, Paul said:

1 Corinthians 15:31:
"I die daily."

Galatians 2:20:
"I am crucified with Christ: nevertheless I live; yet not I, but Christ liveth **in** me *[by His Spirit]*: and the life which I now live in the flesh I live by the faith of the Son of God, who loved me, and gave himself for me."

Paul is here referring to receiving the Holy Spirit administered **"life"** of Christ, which supersedes the probationary life-span "life force" that is the lot of "post fall" mankind, who, (lacking the indwelling Holy Spirit) are spiritually dead in trespass and sin, until they accept Christ's saving grace. Those who follow Christ have now "passed from death to life" and provisionally have "everlasting life"—the "life of Christ." Their "immortality" is secure as long as they retain the indwelling presence of the Holy Spirit—their "seal unto the day of redemption." (Eph. 4:30). Listen to how Jesus describes this transaction:

John 5:24:
"Verily, verily, I say unto you, He that heareth my word, and believeth on him *[the Father]* that sent me, **hath everlasting life**, and shall not come into condemnation *[to eternal death]*; but is passed from death unto life."

This quotation from the Spirit of Prophecy sums it up:

Desire of Ages, page 324:
"When the soul surrenders itself to Christ, a new power takes possession of the new heart *[the "swept clean" chamber]*. A change is wrought which man can never accomplish for himself. It is a supernatural work, bringing a supernatural element into human nature. **The soul that is yielded to Christ becomes His own fortress, which He holds in a revolted world, and He intends that no authority shall be known in it but His own. A soul thus kept in possession by the heavenly agencies is impregnable to the assaults of Satan.**

"But unless we do yield ourselves to the control of Christ, we shall be dominated by the wicked one. **We must inevitably be under the control of the one or the other of the two great powers that are contending for the supremacy of the world.** It is not necessary for us deliberately to choose the service of the kingdom of darkness in order to come under its dominion. **We have only to neglect** to ally ourselves with the kingdom of light. If we do not co-operate with the heavenly agencies, **Satan will take possession of the heart, and will make it his abiding place.**

"The only defense against evil is the indwelling of Christ in the heart through faith in His righteousness. Unless we become vitally connected with God, we can never resist the unhallowed effects of self-love, self-indulgence, and temptation to sin. We may leave off many bad habits, for the time we may part

396

company with Satan *[but leave the chamber empty]*; but without a vital connection with God, **through the surrender of ourselves to Him moment by moment, we shall be overcome.** Without a personal acquaintance with Christ, and a continual communion, we are at the mercy of the enemy, and shall do his bidding in the end."

WILLIAM: So what is the "spirit" that returns unto the Father when a man dies?

PROFESSOR: It is the 'Spirit' spoken of in:

Ecclesiastes 12:7:
"Then shall the dust return to the earth as it was: and the spirit *[Heb. Ruwach, #7303, Strong's Concordance]* shall return unto God who gave it."

In this instance, if we look at:

Genesis 7:22:
"All in whose nostrils was the breath of life, of all that was in the dry land, died."

Here we see that this is referring to "life force" from God, which is administered by the Holy Spirit, who is the Father's agent in upholding the universe.

WILLIAM: I also have one more question. How do you explain these verses?

Romans 8:16:
"**The Spirit itself** beareth witness with **our spirit,** that we are the children **of God."**

Numbers 16:22:
"And they fell upon their faces, and said, **O God, the God of the spirits of all flesh,** shall one man sin, and wilt thou be wroth with all the congregation?"

PROFESSOR: Part of the answer is found in:

Hebrews 1:13, 14:

13) "But to which of the angels said he at any time, Sit on my right hand, until I make thine enemies thy footstool?

14) Are **they not all ministering spirits,** sent forth to minister for them who shall be heirs of salvation?"

Our attending angel will agree with the Holy Spirit that we are children of God. This shows the close relationship the angels have with the Holy Spirit, and their acquaintance with our spiritual condition. However, **there is another aspect to this question** also. We find reference to it in:

Lift Him Up, page 124 (*Review & Herald*, May 12, 1896):
"The Holy Spirit moves upon **the inner self** until it becomes conscious of the divine power of God, and every spiritual faculty is quickened to decided action."

This "inner self" or mental awareness is **also** referred to in Scripture as the "spirit of a man." This is not some "immortal" or separate entity that lives on after man dies; **this is speaking of man's conscious and unconscious perception of self and surrounding influences.**

From what we have just studied, William, you can see that, when a man is filled with the Holy Spirit, he is filled with the Spirit of God and the Spirit of Christ (Romans 8:9) for the Holy Spirit is then also controlling "their inner-self" as they submit to Him who is the "right Spirit" who is now renewed in them (Psalms 51:10). By submission to the control of the Holy Spirit, man's character becomes like Christ's, and Jesus' character is like the Father's. A blessed assimilation takes place, and Jesus' prayer (John 17) is fulfilled, and the followers of Christ become "one" in the same way that the Godhead is "one."

Chapter 32

THE UNKNOWN GOD

PROFESSOR: Particularly, from the 4th century, up until the present, the enemy of souls has sought to obscure the 'Doctrine of God' behind a screen of fabrications that originate in his distorted mind. Insidiously he has insinuated the misrepresentations of paganism and it's icons into the church of God so that, today, the **true knowledge** of God and the Godhead has been almost universally obscured and the true relationship of the "only true God and Jesus Christ whom *[He]* has sent" (John 17:3) is almost unknown.

True knowledge is the only safe foundation for successive doctrines to be predicated upon and the 'doctrine of God' is foundational. As we have seen and demonstrated, a false Trinitarian perception of the Godhead undergirds a host of doctrinal aberrations. God's people need to return to the true understanding and knowledge of God, as He has revealed Himself and His "Fellow" (Zechariah 13:7), in order to have safe footing as, in the future, they are called upon to give a reason for the truths they hold. Today we have practically reverted to the situation Paul encountered in Athens. Let us read:

> **Act 17:22, 23:**
> 22) "Then Paul stood in the midst of Mars' hill, and said, *Ye men of Athens*, I perceive that in all things ye are too superstitious.
> 23) For as I passed by, and beheld your devotions, I found an altar with this inscription, TO THE UNKNOWN GOD. Whom therefore ye ignorantly worship, **him declare I unto you.**"

WILLIAM: The UNKNOWN GOD is almost "unknown" today!

PROFESSOR: Let's read on and we will see Who it was that Paul declared Him to be.

> **Acts 17:24-30:**
> 24) **"God that made the world and all things therein,** seeing that **he is Lord of heaven and earth,** dwelleth not in temples made with hands;

25) Neither is worshipped with men's hands, as though he needed any thing, **seeing he giveth to all life, and breath, and all things;**

26) And hath made of one blood all nations of men for to dwell on all the face of the earth, and hath determined the times before appointed, and the bounds of their habitation;

27) That they should seek the Lord, if haply they might feel after him, and find him, though he be not far from every one of us:

28) For in him we live, and move, and have our being; as certain also of your own poets have said, For we are also his offspring.

29) Forasmuch then as we are the offspring of God, **we ought not to think that the Godhead is like unto gold, or silver, or stone, graven by art and man's device.** *[A false perception or doctrine of God is also a "device" of man.]*

30) And the times of this ignorance God winked at; **but now commandeth all men every where to repent:"**

WILLIAM: Paul identifies the UNKNOWN GOD as the Creator. But Who, ultimately, is the Creator?

PROFESSOR: The Bible clearly identifies the Creator as God the Father with Jesus being His active agent in Creation:

Ephesians 3:9:
And to make all men see what is the fellowship of the mystery, which from the beginning of the world hath been hid in **God, who created all things** <u>by</u> Jesus Christ:

Hebrews 1:1, 2:
1) "God, who at sundry times and in divers manners spake in time past unto the fathers by the prophets,

2) Hath in these last days spoken unto us by his Son, whom he hath appointed heir of all things, **<u>by</u> whom also he made the worlds;"**

The One Who is identified as the Creator in the Scriptures is God the Father. Notice that even Jesus calls the Father, the Creator of the world.

Revelation 10:1, 5, 6:
1) "And I saw another **mighty angel** *[Jesus]* come down from heaven, clothed with a cloud: and a rainbow *was* upon his head, **and his face** *was* **as it were the sun, and his feet as pillars of fire:**

5) And the angel which I saw stand upon the sea and upon the earth lifted up his hand to heaven,

6) <u>**And sware by him** *[the Father]* **that liveth for ever and ever, who created heaven, and the things that therein are, and the earth, and the things that therein are, and the sea, and the things which are therein,**</u> that there should be time no longer:"

God's messenger endorses this understanding:

<u>Testimonies to the Church</u>, Volume 1, page 297:
"He *[Christ]* **was ever directing their minds to God** *[the Father]*, **the Creator of the universe,** as the source of their strength and wisdom."

WILLIAM: God the Father is definitely the Creator spoken of in the Bible.

PROFESSOR: And He is the UNKNOWN GOD. Notice Paul's next statements:

Acts 17:30, 31:
30) **"And the times of this ignorance God winked at; but now commandeth all men every where to repent:**

31) Because **he hath appointed a day, in the which he** *[the Father]* **will judge the world in righteousness <u>by</u>** *that* **man** *[Jesus]* **whom he hath ordained;** *whereof* he hath given assurance unto all *men,* in that he hath raised him from the dead."

WILLIAM: "That man whom he *[the UNKNOWN GOD]* hath ordained" is Jesus Christ. This shows that the Father is the UNKNOWN GOD who ordained Jesus. And that is just what Paul said in another place:

Acts 10:38:
"How **God** *[the Father]* **anointed Jesus of Nazareth** with the Holy Ghost and with power: who went about doing good, and

healing all that were oppressed of the devil; for God was with Him *[by His Spirit]*."

PROFESSOR: Yes, Paul was trying to reveal to the Athenians that God the Father, the Creator of heaven and earth, is the UNKNOWN GOD.

WILLIAM: Then this is the identity of the God we are commanded to worship in the First Angel's message of Revelation 14:

Revelation 14:7:
"Saying with a loud voice, Fear God, and give glory to him; for the hour of his judgment is come: **and worship him that made heaven, and earth, and the sea, and the fountains of waters.**"

PROFESSOR: And this was the same God identified by the SDA pioneers in their 1872 Statement of Principles, published by Battle Creek. This therefore, is the same God worshiped by James and Ellen White all their lives.

1872 SDA Fundamental Principles No. 1 and 2:
"**I.** That **there is one God, a personal, spiritual being,** the **creator of all things,** omnipotent, omniscient, and eternal, infinite in wisdom, holiness, justice, goodness, truth, and mercy; unchangeable, and **everywhere present by his representative, the Holy Spirit.** Ps. 139:7.

"**II.** That there is **one Lord Jesus Christ, the Son of the Eternal Father, the one by whom God created all things,** and by whom they do consist; that he took on him the nature of the seed of Abraham for the redemption of our fallen race; that he dwelt among men full of grace and truth, lived our example, died our sacrifice, was raised for our justification, ascended on high to be our only mediator in the sanctuary in Heaven, where, with his own blood he makes atonement for our sins; which atonement so far from being made on the cross, which was but the offering of the sacrifice, is the very last portion of his work as priest according to the example of the Levitical priesthood, which foreshadowed and prefigured the ministry of our Lord in Heaven. See Lev. 16; Heb. 8:4, 5; 9:6, 7; c."

WILLIAM: Unlike the Trinity doctrine which is now in the 1980 Fundamental SDA Statements of Belief as 'Belief #2', that 1872 statement can be supported by a plain "Thus saith the Lord:"

1 Corinthians 8:6:
"But to us there is but **one God, the Father, of whom are all things,** and we in him; **and one Lord Jesus Christ, by whom are all things,** and we by him."

PROFESSOR: Jesus, Himself, prayed to His Father: such a truth would have no meaning if He was 'consubstantial' with His Father, for that would mean He would be praying to an extension of Himself.

John 14:16:
"And **I will pray the Father**, and he shall give you another Comforter, that he may abide with you for ever;"

Paul also said that God was now commanding "men <u>everywhere</u> to repent" and, thus, to worship the Creator.

Acts 17:30:
"And the times of this ignorance God winked at; but now commandeth all men every where to repent:"

During periods of ignorance God winks at the low level of comprehension concerning Himself and the Godhead.   He expects, however, that men shall search out the truth of God as for hidden treasure, for, ultimately—**as the Holy Spirit of God leads into all truth (John 16:13)—it becomes a salvational issue (see John 17:3); Just as the Sabbath finally becomes a salvational issue at the end of time**.   From then on God no longer winks at either ignorance or at wrong choice.   It finally becomes an issue of eternal life or eternal death.   The Scripture is clear on this point.   Just how salvational this issue is, is highlighted in the verse we have looked at so frequently:

John 17:3:
"And this is life eternal, that they might know thee the only true God, and Jesus Christ, whom thou hast sent."

WILLIAM: Why is the Holy Spirit not mentioned in that verse?

PROFESSOR: It takes divine insight administered by the Holy Spirit to know the only true God and Jesus Christ.

Jesus and the Holy Spirit came to make known the Father and His truth:

Matthew 11:25-27:

25) "At that time Jesus answered and said, I thank thee, **O Father, Lord of heaven and earth,** because <u>thou hast hid these things from the wise and prudent, and hast revealed them unto babes</u>.

26) Even so, Father: for so it seemed good in thy sight.

27) All things are delivered unto me of my Father: and no man knoweth the Son, but the Father; neither knoweth any man the Father, save the Son, **and he to whomsoever the Son will reveal him** *[through the Holy Spirit]*."

Luke 10:22:

"All things are delivered to me of my Father: and **no man knoweth** who the Son is, but the Father; and **who the Father is**, but the Son, and **[he] to whom the Son will reveal [him]**."

1 Corinthians 2:7-12:

7) "But we speak **the wisdom of God in a mystery**, [even] the hidden [wisdom], which God ordained before the world unto our glory:

8) Which none of the princes of this world knew: for had they known [it], they would not have crucified the Lord of glory. *[i.e. If they had understood the truth of the Godhead and Christ's standing viz a viz His Father, they could not have denied His right to call Himself the Son of God, thus claiming to be God. They, however, had driven the Holy Spirit from them and could not understand.]*

9) But as it is written, Eye hath not seen, nor ear heard, neither have entered into the heart of man, the things which God hath prepared for them that love him.

10) But **God hath revealed [them] unto us by his Spirit**: for the Spirit searcheth all things, yea, the deep things of God.

11) For what man knoweth the things of a man, save the spirit of man which is in him? even so **the things of God knoweth no man, but the Spirit of God**.

12)   **Now we have received, not the spirit of the world, but the spirit which is of God; <u>that we might know</u> the things that are freely given to us of God.**"

We are commanded to worship God the Father in the First Angel's Message. This was the God worshiped by the early SDA pioneers. This is the UNKNOWN God that Paul told the Athenians to worship. This is the "only true God" Whom Jesus said was "eternal life" to know. I think one can safely say that this is ultimately a salvational doctrine, and is integral to proclaiming the First Angel's Message fully.

Revelation 14:7:
"Saying with a loud voice, Fear God, and give glory to him; for the hour of his judgment is come: **and worship him that made heaven, and earth, and the sea, and the fountains of waters** *[through Jesus the Son.   It is, therefore, entirely appropriate to worship and honor the Son, but not to the exclusion of worshipping and honoring His Father: the "Most High God"]*."

PROFESSOR: God's messenger has relayed to us the following end-time criterion: namely that we shall be judged not by what we did not know, but by what we could have known if we had taken the trouble to find out.

Last Day Events, pages 217.5 – 218.2:
"None will be condemned for not heeding light and knowledge that they never had, and they could not obtain. But **many refuse to obey the truth that is presented to them by Christ's ambassadors, because <u>they wish to conform to the world's standard</u>,** and the truth that has reached their understanding, the light that has shone in the soul, will condemn them in the judgment
"Those who have an opportunity to hear the truth and yet take no pains to hear or understand it, thinking that if they do not hear they will not be accountable, will be judged guilty before God the same as if they had heard and rejected. There will be no excuse for those who choose to go in error when they might understand what is truth. In His sufferings and death Jesus has made atonement for all sins of ignorance, but there is no provision made for willful blindness

"We shall not be held accountable for the light that has not reached our perception, but for that which we have resisted and refused. A man could not apprehend the truth which had never been presented to him, and therefore could not be condemned for light he had never had."

Chapter 33

WHO ARE WE PRAYING TO?

WILLIAM: This whole discussion about the broad differences between the Trinity and the Godhead, brings to mind the question, which may seem odd, but it is this: Who are we praying to?

PROFESSOR: That is a very important question, which does seem simple, but really, since it deals with the unseen, we can only know the answer by the Word of God, and the records of church history.

WILLIAM: Church history?

PROFESSOR: Yes. For instance, when the Jewish church leadership said to Pilate, the Roman governor of Judea, **"We have no king, but Caesar,"** that declaration was heard by God and recorded in His Word as an official decision by the leadership of the Jewish church-nation: They did not want Jesus to be their king, but would rather have Caesar. So, as a church system, their corporate prayers were basically meaningless because they rejected Jesus, who was not only the Lamb, but is also the High Priest and Mediator for all the human race—the One by Whom our prayers are made acceptable to the Father. Jesus said, "No man cometh unto the Father, but by Me." John 14:6.

WILLIAM: Yet are not prayers still heard in the Jewish synagogues?

PROFESSOR: William, there are times when prayers are heard by men, but not by God. Isaiah said this long ago, and it applies to everyone for all time:

Isaiah 1:10-15:
10) "Hear the word of the LORD, ye rulers of Sodom; give ear unto the law of our God, ye people of Gomorrah.

11) To what purpose [is] the multitude of your sacrifices unto me? saith the LORD: I am full of the burnt offerings of rams, and the fat of fed beasts; and I delight not in the blood of bullocks, or of lambs, or of he goats.

12) When ye come to appear before me, who hath required this at your hand, to tread my courts?

13) Bring no more vain oblations; incense is an abomination unto me; the new moons and sabbaths, the calling of assemblies, I cannot away with; [it is] iniquity, even the solemn meeting.

14) Your new moons and your appointed feasts my soul hateth: they are a trouble unto me; I am weary to bear [them].

15) **And when ye spread forth your hands, I will hide mine eyes from you: yea, when ye make many prayers, I will not hear: your hands are full of blood.**" *[The blood of sacrifice; necessitated by their continuous, willful, sinfulness, and the blood of those lost in consequence of their negative example.]*

1 Samuel 15:22:
"Hath the LORD as great delight in burnt offerings and sacrifices, as in obeying the voice of the LORD?

Sometimes the point is reached when the ear will no longer hear the voice of mercy pleading. In Christ's day, that time came when Jesus left the Jewish temple for the last time and said:

Matthew 23:38:
"Behold, your house is left unto you desolate."

WILLIAM: But the forms of worship and the prayers continued there for another 40 years.

PROFESSOR: When any church system is in corporate rebellion (sin), the prayers of the rebellious only go as high as the ceiling. Rebellion is as the sin of witchcraft (1 Samuel 15:23) and "spiritual formation" **is** open witchcraft—open rebellion and is now entrenched within our ranks!

But to answer your question, let us first think about prayer.

WILLIAM: Yes, so what blocks our prayer from being heard?

PROFESSOR: David says,

Psalm 66:18:
"If I regard iniquity in my heart, the Lord will not hear me:"

408

William, there is only one prayer that you can be sure the Lord will hear when you have sin in your heart, and which He will answer every time. And that prayer is the prayer for deliverance from sin.

WILLIAM: Who inspires that prayer?

PROFESSOR: The Holy Spirit works on our heart and mind to utter a prayer to God. Every sincere prayer of soul hunger is inspired by the Holy Spirit.

Romans 8:26:
"Likewise the Spirit also helpeth our infirmities: for we know not what we should pray for as we ought: but the Spirit itself maketh intercession for us with groanings which cannot be uttered."

Signs of the Times, October 3, 1892:
"The Holy Spirit indites all genuine prayer. I have learned to know that in all my intercessions the Spirit intercedes for me and for all saints; but his intercessions are according to the will of God, never contrary to his will. "The Spirit also helpeth our infirmities;" and the Spirit, being God, knoweth the mind of God; therefore in every prayer of ours for the sick, or for other needs, the will of God is to be regarded. "For what man knoweth the things of a man, save the spirit of man which is in him? even so the things of God knoweth no man, but the Spirit of God." If we are taught of God, we shall pray in conformity to his revealed will, and in submission to his will which we know not. We are to make supplication according to the will of God, relying on the precious word, and believing that Christ not only gave himself for but to his disciples. The record declares, 'He breathed on them, and saith unto them, Receive ye the Holy Ghost.'

"Jesus is waiting to breathe upon all his disciples, and give them the inspiration of his sanctifying spirit, and transfuse the vital influence from himself to his people."

WILLIAM: Then where do our prayers go?

PROFESSOR: Long ago Jacob had a dream:

Genesis 28:12, 13:

12)   "And he dreamed, and behold a ladder set up on the earth, and the top of it reached to heaven: and behold the angels of God ascending and descending on it.

13)   And, behold, the LORD *[the Father]* stood above it."

Jesus commented on this dream in:

John 1:51:
"And he saith unto him, Verily, verily, I say unto you, Hereafter ye shall see heaven open, and the angels of God ascending and descending upon the Son of man."

The ladder is a symbol of Jesus. The angels ascend to God bearing our prayers, and they descend with God's answers to our prayers.

Selected Messages Book 2, pages 439, 440:
"As he *[the earthly father]* bows with his family at the altar of prayer to offer up his grateful thanks to God for His preserving care of himself and loved ones through the day, angels of God hover in the room, and bear the fervent prayers of God-fearing parents to heaven, as sweet incense, which are answered by returning blessings."

The book of Revelation tells us what happens to our prayers in heaven.

Revelation 8:3, 4:
3)   "And another angel came and stood at the altar, having a golden censer; and there was given unto him **much incense, that he should offer it with the prayers of all saints upon the golden altar which was before the throne.**
4)   And the smoke of the incense, which came with the prayers of the saints, ascended up before God out of the angel's hand."

This Angel *[the Greek meaning of the word "Angel" is Messenger]* is Jesus, our great High Priest in the heavenly sanctuary. He is the one who standing by the altar of incense, receives our prayers and mingles them with the incense of His righteousness and then, presents them to God the Father.

WILLIAM: He is the mediator between God and man as Paul says:

410

1 Timothy 2:5:
"For there is one God, and one mediator between God and men, the man Christ Jesus;"

PROFESSOR: It is interesting that in the Bible the incense was renewed on the golden altar in the Holy Place every morning and evening. This was the time for prayer:

Psalm 141:2:
"Let my prayer be set forth before thee as incense; and the lifting up of my hands as the evening sacrifice."

Luke 1:10:
"And the whole multitude of the people were praying without at the time of incense."

WILLIAM: So the Holy Spirit inspires our prayers. The angels bear them up to Jesus our High Priest and mediator, who mingles them with His righteousness, and presents them to God.

PROFESSOR: Yes. Jesus taught us to pray to the Father in the Lord's Prayer:

Matthew 6:9:
"After this manner therefore pray ye: **Our Father** which art in heaven, Hallowed be thy name."

If we sincerely pray for God's will to be done, **He** will hear our prayer.

WILLIAM: Doesn't everybody do this?

PROFESSOR: Things are not as plain as they seem. How many want **their** will to be done and not the Father's will? There are also two entities going by the name of Jesus today, and two entities going by the name of God the Father today.

WILLIAM: And two "Holy Spirits," too—the true and the false.

PROFESSOR: The mainline church systems are praying to a false 'God', through a false 'Christ', inspired by a false 'Holy Spirit'. That's if they are praying to God at all. Some are taught to pray to Mary, or one of the

411

saints—souls that are sleeping in their graves until the resurrection. **Please remember, however, that many are praying to the "UNKNOWN GOD"** (Acts 17:13) **ignorantly,** and the "times of ignorance God winked at" (Acts 17:30). **Religious leaders have again obscured the truths concerning the "only true God and Jesus Christ whom He has sent."** (John 17:3).

WILLIAM: What about the Seventh-day Adventist church?

PROFESSOR: At the 1955-56 Martin and Barnhouse meetings, it was decided that Christ's work in the Most Holy Place was not vital for salvation. Instead, it was postulated that the atonement was all done at the cross, ignoring the High Priestly phase of Christ's work of atonement.

They also agreed with Martin and Barnhouse that they would trade away the Biblical doctrine of Hebrews 2—that Jesus Christ came in the flesh of Abraham: our fallen humanity—and receive the Catholic doctrine that Jesus came in the sinless flesh of Adam before the fall.

The SDA church leaders, in making this decision, **reverted to the conceptual Holy Place** apartment of the sanctuary as required by the evangelicals. Read Letters to the Church, by M. L. Andreason; Questions on Doctrine, put out by the General Conference leadership; The Word Was Made Flesh, by Ralph Larson; The Greatest Conspiracy, by Neil C Livingston; etc.

WILLIAM: Since Jesus is the Light of the world, they lost who the real Jesus is, and where He is. They put themselves in darkness.

By implication they are also saying that the door to the Most Holy Place that Jesus opened is closed, and the door to the Holy Place that He closed is open:

Revelation 3:7, 8:
7) "And to the angel of the church in Philadelphia write; These things saith he that is holy, he that is true, he that hath the key of David, he that openeth, and no man shutteth; and shutteth, and no man openeth;
8) I know thy works: behold, I have set before thee an open door, and no man can shut it: for thou hast a little strength, and hast kept my word, and hast not denied my name."

PROFESSOR: Unfortunately, that is true. Satan hates the sanctuary. It is God's fortress of truth.

412

WILLIAM: Right. Daniel calls it the "sanctuary of strength." Daniel 11:31. And David says:

Psalm 96:6:
"Honour and majesty are before him: strength and beauty are in his sanctuary."

PROFESSOR: Having not followed the true Mediator, **the false 'Christ' has led them to a false ecumenical 'God'.** In 1980, the Trinity doctrine was incorporated as Fundamental Belief #2, thereby making fraternity with the "mainline" and evangelical "churches" possible!

WILLIAM: Which describes the one "God," who is three "Persons," which are really "emanations" or "modalities."

PROFESSOR: Now I am going to read a vision that was given to God's messenger about what is really going on in the religious world in this anti-typical Day of Atonement after 1844:

Broadside 1, *To the Little Remnant Scattered Abroad*, April 6, 1846:
"In February, 1845, I had a vision of events commencing with the Midnight Cry. I saw a throne and on it sat the Father and the Son. I gazed on Jesus' countenance and admired his lovely person. **The Father's person I could not behold,** for a cloud of glorious light covered him. **I asked Jesus if his Father had a form like himself. He said he had,** but I could not behold it, for said he if you should once behold the glory of his person you would cease to exist. Before the throne I saw the Advent people, the church, and the world. I saw a company, bowed down before the throne, deeply interested, while the most of them stood up disinterested and careless. **Those who were bowed before the throne would offer up their prayers and look to Jesus; then he would look to his Father, and appeared to be pleading with Him.** A light would come from the Father to the Son, and from the Son to the praying company. Then I saw an exceeding bright light come from the Father to the Son, and from the Son it waved over the people before the throne. But few would receive this great light; many came out from under it and immediately resisted it; others were careless and did not cherish the light, and it moved off from them; some cherished it, and

413

went and bowed down with the little praying company. This company all received the light, and rejoiced in it, as their countenances shone with its glory. **And I saw the Father rise from the throne, and in a flaming Chariot go into the Holy of Holies, within the veil, and did sit.** There I saw thrones that I had never seen before. <u>Then Jesus rose up from the throne</u>, and the most of those who were bowed down arose with Him; **and I did not see one ray of light pass from Jesus to the careless multitude after he arose, and <u>they were left in perfect darkness.</u>** *[Notice: no more spiritual light to "first apartment" worshippers.]* Those who rose up when Jesus did, kept their eyes fixed on Him as He left the throne and led them out a little way. - Then He raised His right arm and we heard his lovely voice saying, "Wait here-I am going to my Father to receive the Kingdom; keep your garments spotless, and in a little while I will return from the wedding and receive you to myself." And I saw a cloudy chariot, with wheels like flaming fire, and Angels were all around it as it came where Jesus was. **He stepped into the chariot and was borne to the Holiest where the Father sat.** There I beheld Jesus, as He was standing before the Father, a great High Priest. On the hem of His garment was a bell and pomegranate. Then Jesus shew me the difference between faith and feeling. And I saw those who rose up with Jesus send up their faith to Him in the Holiest, **and pray-my Father give us thy Spirit**. Then Jesus would breathe upon them the Holy Ghost. In the breath was light, power, and much love, joy and peace.

"Then I turned to look at the company who were still bowed before the *[empty]* throne; they did not know that Jesus had left it. Satan appeared to be by the throne, trying to carry on the work of God; **I saw them look up to the throne and pray, my Father give us thy Spirit; then Satan would breathe upon them an unholy influence;** in it there was light and much power, but no sweet love, joy and peace. *[Notice where "first apartment" worshippers get their "light."]* Satan's object was to keep them deceived, and to draw back and deceive God's children. **I saw one after another leave the company who were praying to Jesus in the Holiest, and go and join those before the *[empty]* throne, and <u>they at once received the unholy influence of Satan.</u>**"

414

WILLIAM: From what we have just read, since, 1955 and 1980, who have the "deceivers and the deceived" been praying to?

PROFESSOR: In 1955-56, the SDA church corporation joined with Babylon the Great, and her daughters, in the Holy Place.   "Genetic modification" has been taking place and many of God's denominated people are now organized into a structure that is becoming a "sister" to fallen Babylon; incorporating her spiritual DNA (See Manuscript Releases, Volume 21, page 380.1). The mainline SDA church corporation has been praying to the same "God" that those in the Holy Place are praying to—and that god is the TRINITY. Ecumenical involvement is now far advanced.

WILLIAM: From what we have just read, it appears that we can easily be tricked into worshipping Satan. That means that the conceptual god of all the mainline "Christian" churches—the conceptual god of the beast and the false prophet (Roman Catholic Church and fallen Protestant church systems) is Satan.

PROFESSOR: That is just what the Bible teaches:

Revelation 13:4:
"And **they worshipped the dragon** *[SATAN]* which gave power unto the beast: and **they worshipped** *[by obeying]* **the beast,** saying, Who is like unto the beast? who is able to make war with him?"

WILLIAM: That is why God is telling everyone on planet earth through the First Angel's message to "Fear God, and worship Him *[by obeying Him]* who made heaven, and earth, and the sea, and the fountains of waters." Revelation 14:7.

PROFESSOR: Precisely. True worship is much more than prayer, or the verbal extolling of God; His love, power, compassion, justice, mercy, and infinite intelligence. True worship involves loving, faith filled obedience. Jesus said: "If ye love me, keep my commandments" (John 14:15). Jesus' commandments are manifested in such instructions by Him as: "...Love one another, as I have loved you..." (John 13:34); "...Love your enemies, bless them that curse you, do good to them that hate you, and pray for them which despitefully use you, and persecute you" (Matthew 5:44); "...be thou faithful unto death..." (Revelation 2:10), and many more commandments that **all** expand our understanding of the Decalogue of His

415

Father in order to broaden, deepen and elevate our understanding of His Father and His Father's Law. Jesus Himself further opens our understanding on this topic:

John 15:10:
"If ye **keep <u>my</u> commandments**, ye shall abide in my love; **even as I have kept <u>my Father's</u> commandments**, and abide in his love."

To worship Jesus is to obey Him in the same way that He worshipfully obeys His Father. Indeed, to thus worship Jesus is also worshipping the Father "in Spirit and in truth" and that is what the Father seeks:

John 4:23:
"But the hour cometh, and now is, when **the true worshippers shall worship the Father in spirit and in truth: for the Father seeketh such to worship him.**"

To pray to and to worship the "God" of the fallen churches and to fraternize in ecumenical involvement with them (see Appendix G) **is a flagrant violation of Jesus' and His Father's command:**

Testimonies Volume 9, page 17:
"God's word to His people is: "**Come out from among them, and be ye separate**, . . . and <u>touch not</u> the unclean thing; and I will receive you, and will be a Father unto you, and ye shall be My sons and daughters." "Ye are a chosen generation, a royal priesthood, an holy nation, a peculiar people; that ye should show forth the praises of Him who hath called you out of darkness into His marvelous light." 2 Corinthians 6: 17, 18; 1 Peter 2:9. God's people are to be distinguished as a people who serve Him fully, wholeheartedly, taking no honor to themselves, and remembering that by a most solemn covenant they have bound themselves to serve the Lord and Him only."

Chapter 34

TRINITARIANISM DISTORTS THE TRUTH—
PART ONE

WILLIAM: Professor. I have another question.

PROFESSOR: Yes, William. What's on your mind?

(William handed Professor Miller a copy of the September, 2010 edition of *Adventist World,* and asked him to turn to page 40.)

WILLIAM: Do you see the "What If?" column by Angel Manuel Rodriguez and his posted answer to the reader's question: "Had Jesus sinned, what would have happened to Him?"

PROFESSOR: Yes. (The reader may see the actual article by Angel Rodriguez at the end of this chapter.)

WILLIAM: Look at this part of his answer, under the third subsection ("**3. Jesus' Future:**") where he writes:

> Angel Rodriguez, *Adventist World,* September, 2010 edition:
> "Could we postulate that there was an **alternative future** for Jesus in case He sinned? …Let me put it as bluntly as I can: Had Jesus failed, the God we now know would not be our God. In other words, with respect to us, **He *[God]* would have ceased to exist.**"

That doesn't seem right to me. Is this true?

PROFESSOR: William, the consubstantial "God" that Angel "knows" would "have ceased to exist", were such a 'God' a reality. This is a classic example of how Trinitarianism distorts the truth. No, this answer is incorrect, and I dare say it is plain non-sense! Let me explain:

God the Father, who maintains the integrity of the Godhead, would have still remained in "His high and holy place" (Isaiah 57:15; <u>Manuscript Releases</u>, Volume 16, page 292; <u>Ministry of Healing</u>, page 417.2). All mankind would simply have remained carnal: at perpetual enmity with God. Satan's existence would have continued as the "god of this world" (2 Cor. 4:4) for his claims and accusations against God and His law would have been seen as vindicated. The inhabitants of this world would have been condemned to continual servitude to Satan, whose very existence God would "legally" be required to sustain. Sin would have been "immortalized." (SDA Bible Commentary, Volume 1, page 1082 makes clear the possibility for sin to be "immortalized")

WILLIAM: I would like to see that.

PROFESSOR: Yes, I will show you some clear statements from the Spirit of Prophecy. But first, look at what he says here. (Rodriguez continues):

> Angel Rodriguez, *Adventist World,* September, 2010 edition:
> "The failure **of Jesus** would have meant that **God** was unable to overcome the forces of evil…." (Ibid.)

WILLIAM: It seems that Angel Rodriguez believes that Christ and God the Father are of **one substance.**

PROFESSOR: You're right. He does not understand the truth that Jesus came to demonstrate—that **humanity**, united to the divine power of the Holy Spirit, could "overcome every inherited and, "in our case, every "cultivated tendency to evil."

WILLIAM: All the members of the Godhead were separate distinct eternal Beings.

PROFESSOR: Yes! No one was controlling the will of Jesus Christ. Christ had his own autonomous will and, as "the man Christ Jesus," he could place His will in opposition to His Father's will. If Christ had ever done that, however, it would not have negated the Father, neither would the Father seem non-existent to the lost. He would only be disregarded, feared, and hated. Fallen humanity would be at "enmity against God" perpetually. None of this would demonstrate that Satan could overcome God. It would only demonstrate that **fallen humanity, even when united to the Divinity of the Holy Spirit**, had not succeeded in overcoming Satan.

WILLIAM: So God the Father would not have lost and would still have existed.

418

PROFESSOR: William, He would have lost His precious Son and all mankind, and Satan would forever have plagued the universe. But you remember that Revelation 12 tells us that God overcame Satan in heaven and cast him out.

WILLIAM: Yes.

PROFESSOR: Angel Rodriguez is, however, correct in his observation that God's plan of salvation would have been derailed, and that God would have been "forced" "to abandon us." (Ibid.) However, for Angel to state that "Had the human nature of the son of God failed, God Himself would have failed," (Ibid.) is a clear misrepresentation of the facts. **The fall of Lucifer and the loss of a third of the angels, and the fall of man, were not indications that God had failed.** They are all expressions of something God **allowed.** **They are examples of the negative deployment of "choice" inherent in "free will"**—just as the postulated **wrong choice** by Christ would have been. Choices have consequences.

WILLIAM: The bad choices of His creatures are great disappointments to God the Father, but not a failure on His part. He had to allow the beings He created to have freedom to choose.

PROFESSOR: William, I want to show you some sobering statements from God's messenger, Ellen White. She gives us some amazing, but disturbing, insights into what would have followed had Jesus sinned:

> *Signs of the Times,* May 10, 1899:
> "Though Christ humbled Himself to become man, the Godhead was still His own. His **Deity** *[His being a Divine Member of the* Godhead*]* **could not be lost while He stood faithful and true to His loyalty** *[to His Father].*"

As we can see from this statement, Christ could have **lost His Deity!** Mark that point, you will see why shortly. Now look at:

> Desire of Ages, page 49:
> "Into the world where Satan claimed dominion God **permitted** His Son to come, a helpless babe, subject to the weakness of humanity. He **permitted** Him to meet life's peril in common with every human soul, to fight the battle as every child

of humanity must fight it, **at the risk of failure and <u>eternal loss</u>."**

Jesus risked everything in order to save us. The risk was very real, and all depended on Jesus' choices in every circumstance, moment by moment:

<u>The Faith I Live By</u>, page 49:
"Could Satan in the least particular have tempted Christ to sin, he would have bruised the Saviour's head. As it was, he could only touch His heel. Had the head of Christ been touched *[if Satan had been able to bring Christ to mental disloyalty to His Father in any way]*, **the hope of the human race would have perished.** Divine wrath *[from God the Father]* would have come upon Christ as it came upon Adam. **<u>Christ</u> and the church would have been <u>without hope</u>."** (5BC, page 1131).

William, do you realize that **if it were possible that divine wrath could come upon Christ, from His Father, this implies that Christ cannot be an indivisible 'hypostasis' in conjunction with His Father!**
Satan's existence would have been secured as the "god of this world."

<u>Manuscript Releases</u>, Volume 16, pages 119, 120:
"Not merely for this world, but for the universe of heaven and the worlds that God had created, was the controversy to be forever settled. The confederacy of darkness were watching for the semblance of a chance to rise and triumph over the divine and human Substitute and Surety of the human race, that the apostate might shout Victory, **and the world and its inhabitants <u>forever</u> become his kingdom."**

<u>Seventh-day Adventist Bible Commentary</u>, Volume 1, page 1082.6:
"God's only begotten Son volunteered to take the sin of man upon Himself, and to make an atonement for the fallen race. There could have been no pardon for sin had this atonement not been made. Had God pardoned Adam's sin without an atonement, **sin would have been <u>immortalized</u>,** and would have been perpetuated with a boldness that would have been without restraint (RH April 23, 1901)."

WILLIAM: Mercy! Those last three quotations are especially powerful. That is a totally different scenario to that which Angel Rodriguez presented to us from his Trinitarian "speculations."

PROFESSOR: The reality is this: Eternal **separation** from His Father, eternal and infinite loss; eternally perpetuated sin and universal harassment by Satan; eternal non-existence for Christ, and hence infinite loss to Himself and His Father—were all some of the risks Christ was willing to take, to reach us where we are, in the glorious (glory filled demonstration of the love and mercy of God) hope of saving even a remnant. William, look at what God's messenger says about this:

> Manuscript Releases, Volume 10, page 385.1:
> "To the honor and glory of God, His beloved Son--the Surety, the Substitute--was delivered up and descended into the prisonhouse of the grave. The new tomb enclosed Him in its rocky chambers. **If one single sin had tainted His character** *[see comment after quote]* **the stone would never have been rolled away from the door of His rocky chamber**, and the world with its burden of guilt would have perished. But it was only for a little while the divine Vanquisher seemed the vanquished. The serpent had bruised the heel, but Christ could not be holden by death *[because He had triumphed over "sin in the flesh" Christ automatically triumphed over sin's penalty; in full accord with the original covenant "obey and live". Patriarchs and Prophets, page 53.1].* The stone was rolled away. The Lord Jesus walked forth from His prison house a triumphant, majestic conqueror, and proclaimed over the rent sepulcher of Joseph, "I am the resurrection and the life" (John 11:25).—Ms. 81, 1893, page 11. (Diary entry for Sunday, July 2, 1893, Wellington, New Zealand.)"

NOTE: If one sin had tainted Christ's character, He would, as we have seen, lost His Deity (*Sings of the Times,* May 10, 1899). He would not have had His immortal life, which He had laid down at the incarnation, administered to Him again (Romans 8:11) for the Holy Spirit, the mighty third Person of the Godhead, would have separated from Him forever, leaving only the Most High God and the mighty third Person of the Godhead to sustain the universe which, without them, would implode into non-existence.

General Conference Bulletin, December 1, 1895 par. 22:
"Remember that Christ risked all; 'tempted like as we are,' **he staked even his own eternal existence** upon the issue of the conflict. Heaven itself was imperiled for our redemption."

Heaven was "imperiled", in the sense that Satan would have remained, having eternal status as one who had overturned God's plans. If Christ had not triumphed, Satan would not have fallen "as lightening" (Luke 10:18) by being "cast down" (Revelation 12:9, 10); in other words, by being disbarred from harassing the coming and going angels at the gates of heaven. Such access would have continued in perpetuity, a constant threat to the peace of heaven and the universe. God's messenger speaks of this harassment in:

Spirit of Prophecy, Volume 1, page 30.3:
"Satan would invent means to annoy the heavenly angels, and show contempt for his *[God's]* authority. As he could not gain admission within the gates of Heaven, he would wait just at the entrance, to taunt the angels and seek contention with them as they went in and out."

Spirit of Prophecy, Volume 3, page 194.1:
"At the death of Jesus the soldiers had beheld the earth wrapped in profound darkness at midday; but at the resurrection they saw the brightness of the angels illuminate the night, and heard the inhabitants of Heaven singing with great joy and triumph: **Thou hast vanquished Satan and the powers of darkness! Thou hast swallowed up death in victory!** 'And I heard a loud voice saying in Heaven, **Now is come salvation and strength, and the kingdom of our God, and the power of his Christ; for the accuser of our brethren is cast down, who accused them before our God day and night.'"**

And William, take particular note: **for it to be possible that Jesus could lose His eternal existence, that fact makes it impossible for Him to be of the same identical nature, consubstantial with His Father. A Trinitarian Christ could never risk all for us. A Trinitarian Christ could never be in danger of being in the tomb forever.**
The reality is this: Eternal **separation** from His Father; eternal and infinite loss; eternally perpetuated sin and universal harassment by Satan infinite loss to Himself and His Father—were all some of the risks Christ

was willing to take, to reach us where we are, in the glorious hope of saving even a remnant.

WILLIAM: And Moses, Enoch, and Elijah would have had to return from heaven! I can see how belief in a false doctrine distorts our understanding of truth, and takes away a true understanding of the real, mind-blowing risk that Jesus and His Father took to save mankind.

PROFESSOR: Let me show you one more item: Later, in the December, 2010, issue of *Adventist World*, on page 45, a letter from a lay member residing in Lakewood, Washington appeared, responding to Angel Manuel Rodriguez's September, 2010, article on the question, "What if Jesus had sinned?"
 This reader writes:

> "...So the thought came to me, **Could two parts of the Trinity exist without the other?** Then remorse set in, and **I realized that God was willing to give up His existence for me.** Of course we would all have lost. **Nothing can exist without all Three.** Oh, what a Savior we have!"

WILLIAM: Evidently, this misguided member has fully bought into Trinitarian doctrine.

PROFESSOR: His words reveal that his concept of the "Trinity" is that of an indivisible "substance" or "essence" termed "God" which cannot exist if one of its "parts" or "modalities" is missing! Already, in this person's deceived thinking, "God" is a "non-entity"—not a distinct personable Being. And his thinking has been misguided, corroborated, and endorsed by Angel Rodriguez's article. And he was the head of the Bible Research Institute.

WILLIAM: Whose word carries weight and authority with the lay members. I can see how needful it is that we all study God's word for ourselves, and seek for truth as for hidden treasure.

PROFESSOR: I am glad that we don't have to surmise or "postulate" concerning "an alternative future for Jesus in case He sinned." As we have seen, God's messenger, Ellen White, has revealed that "alternative" to His people. Thank God the question is now academic only! Here is Rodriguez's article for you to read:

423

From: www.adventistworld.org/article.php?id=847
Actual article by Angel Rodriguez below. (Emphasis in bold added by
Professor Miller.)

What If?

QUESTION: *Had Jesus sinned, what would have happened to Him?*

By Angel Manuel Rodriguez

This question, phrased in different ways, is often asked. And I'm always reluctant to deal with it because it is an invitation to speculate on matters about which we know nothing. What's surprising is that some take their speculations so seriously that they become dogmatic about them. Humility should be a fundamental characteristic of any Bible student.

In this particular case my reluctance is determined by what we do know. We know that Jesus did not sin. That should be enough. But those interested in the question press the issue: Could He have sinned? Had He sinned, what would have been the consequences of His sin? In order to avoid dealing with this question again, let me make some comments that you may or may not find helpful.

1. *Jesus and Sin:* Could Jesus have sinned? My unambiguous answer: Yes! This is something the Bible supports. Jesus was absolutely human and was subject to temptations such as the ones we confront, as well as to others that we will never have to face (Heb. 4:15). Every day Jesus struggled against sin and was victorious over it. This was a real conflict; not because He had a nature corrupted by sin, but because He, like each one of us, had free will. It is free will that allows us to choose God's side in the cosmic conflict. Rebellion is the rejection of that freedom or, more specifically, giving it up and choosing death.
The typical example of Jesus' potential for sinning is His experience in Gethsemane, when His will would have urged Him to preserve His personal life, while His duty to the Father and the salvation of humanity called Him

424

to self-sacrifice and death (Matt. 26:39). The power and reality of this temptation was predicated on the possibility of not doing God's will. Otherwise the whole struggle would have been a pantomime, a self-deceptive exercise, or an illusion.

2. *Jesus' Uniqueness:* The fact that Jesus overcame every temptation is incomprehensible to us because we are all sinners. The sinlessness of Jesus creates theological problems for those who would make Him very much like us. It is at this point that His uniqueness is manifested with great power. Whether we want it or not—and I personally want it—He is different from all of us! He never committed a sin in any form, type, action, or thought. He is the only and exclusive human being who has ever lived without sinning. It is this uniqueness that seems to prompt people to ask, What if He had sinned? We seem to feel uncomfortable with His sinlessness. But we shouldn't be, because it is the prerequisite for the atonement.

3. *Jesus' Future:* We can also affirm that the future of Jesus and our future are one, because He was victorious over evil and reconciled us to His Father. Could we postulate that there was an alternative future for Jesus in case He sinned?

Here's where the speculation comes in the form of a theological argument. Let me put it as bluntly as I can: **Had Jesus failed, the God we now know would not be our God. In other words, with respect to us, He would have ceased to exist. The failure of Jesus would have meant that God was unable to overcome the forces of evil and that Satan was powerful enough to overcome Him** by derailing His plan of salvation, thus forcing God to abandon us.

As you can see, in my speculations the stakes are very high. The defeat of our biblical God at the moment of His greatest manifestation of power on the cross of Christ is something we can hardly begin to imagine, much less take seriously.

Since the biblical God is by definition unbeatable, our question remains almost unanswered. **Had the human nature of the Son of God failed, God Himself would have failed.** But He did not. Amen!

Angel Manuel Rodríguez was director of the **Biblical Research Institute of the General Conference**.

RESPONSE TO ANGEL RODRIGUEZ'S ARTICLE IN ADVENTIST WORLD, SEPT. 2010:
Found in: *Adventist World-NAD,* December, 2010, page 45:

Oh, How He Loves Me

I read the article "What If" by Angel Manuel Rodriguez (September 2010), and the question "What if Jesus had sinned?" somewhat clarified what would have happened to Him if He had sinned.

I remember Ellen White writing that "Satan with his fierce temptations wrung the heart of Jesus. The Saviour could not see through the portals of the tomb. Hope did not present to Him His coming forth from the grave a conqueror, or tell Him of the Father's acceptance of the sacrifice. He feared that sin was so offensive to God that Their separation was to be eternal. Christ felt the anguish which the sinner will feel when mercy shall no longer plead for the guilty race. It was the sense of sin, bringing the Father's wrath upon Him as man's substitute, that made the cup He drank so bitter, and broke the heart of the Son of God" (The Desire of Ages, page 753).

So the thought came to me, _Could two parts of the Trinity exist without the other?_ Then remorse set in, and I realized that God was willing to give up His existence for me. Of course, we would all have lost. **Nothing can exist without all three.** Oh, what a Savior we have!

R-R-
Lakewood, Washington

Chapter 35

TRINITARIANISM DISTORTS THE TRUTH—PART TWO

WILLIAM: Hi Professor. I wanted to ask how the Trinity doctrine relates to other false doctrines?

PROFESSOR: Well, there is an important link that **has not been perceived by many Adventists.**

WILLIAM: Yes. What is that?

PROFESSOR: **It is the link between the teaching on the consubstantial nature of God, as taught in Trinitarian doctrine, and the false Anti-Christ teaching, which is based, in part, on a wrong interpretation of 1 John 4:1-3 and 2 John 7: namely, that Christ did not come in our fallen human nature**—the "seed of Abraham"-type humanity as described so clearly in Hebrews Ch. 2. William, I want you to pay careful attention to what I am about to tell you. In the autumn of 1895 a campmeeting was held in Armadale, Victoria, Australia. **Ellen White <u>wrote</u> a report on the campmeeting** which was printed in:

> *Review and Herald* of January 7, 1896:
> "In the evening **Professor Prescott** gave a most valuable lesson, precious as gold... **Truth was separated from error**, and made by the divine Spirit to shine like precious jewels. It was shown that perfect obedience to all of the commandments of God is essential for the salvation of souls. **Obedience to the laws of God's kingdom reveals <u>the divine in the human, sanctifying the character.</u>"**

The title of Elder Prescott's sermon to which Sister White referred was **"The Word Became Flesh."** Time does not permit me to present this whole beautiful sermon, but the following quotations will indicate to you the gist of Elder Prescott's message which Sister White so resoundingly endorsed. This complete sermon was printed in:

The Bible Echo, January 6 and 13 of 1896:

"Now to Abraham and his seed were the promises make. He saith not, and to seeds, as of many' but as of one, and to thy seed, which is Christ. Gal 3:16

"Now verily, he helps the seed of Abraham by Himself becoming the seed of Abraham. God, sending His own Son in the likeness of **sinful flesh** *[Strong's 4561: sarx – human nature with its frailties, physical or moral, and passions.]*, and for sin **condemned sin in the flesh;** that the righteousness of the law might be revealed in us, who walk not after the flesh, but after the Spirit.

"So you see that what the Scripture states very plainly is that Jesus Christ **had exactly the same flesh that we bear – <u>flesh of sin</u>,** flesh in which we sin, flesh, however, in which He did not sin, but He **<u>bore our</u>** sins in that flesh of sin. **<u>Do not set this point aside.</u>**

"No matter how you may have looked at it in the past, look at it now as it is in that way, the more reason you will have to thank God that it is so."

"Let us enter into the Experience that God has given Jesus Christ to us **to dwell in our sinful flesh,** to work out **in our sinful flesh** what He worked out when He was here. He came and lived here that we might, through Him, reflect the image of God. **This is the very heart of Christianity**. **<u>Anything contrary to it is not Christianity</u>**. 'Beloved, believe not every spirit but try the spirits whether they are of God: because many false prophets are gone out into the world. **Hereby know ye the Spirit of God: every spirit that confesseth that Jesus Christ is come in the flesh** *[Strong's 4561: Sarx: most commonly translated "sinful flesh"]* **is of God: and every spirit that confesseth not that Jesus Christ is come in the [sinful] flesh [4561: sarx] <u>IS NOT OF GOD</u>."** 1 John 4:1-3

(In verse 4, John goes on to say that to deny that Jesus came in the "sarx" or sinful flesh "is that spirit of anti-Christ".)

Elder Prescott continues:

"Now that cannot mean simply to acknowledge that Jesus Christ was here and lived in the flesh. **The devils make that acknowledgement**. They know that Christ had come in the flesh.

"The faith that comes by the Spirit of God says, "Jesus Christ is come in **my** flesh *[which is clearly sinful]*; I have received Him.""

I also want you to notice, William, how other pioneers were in harmony with Elder Prescott's, and of course Sister White's, views.

E.J. Waggoner, then editor of the Signs, and writing in the *General Conference Bulletin* of 1897, February 17, page 57, wrote:
"The word was made **perfect** flesh **in Adam, but in Christ was the word made fallen flesh**. Christ goes down to the bottom, and there is the Word flesh, **sinful flesh**.""

In the same Bulletin on page 45 col. 2 and page 46, col.1, Waggoner also wrote:

"**God took upon Himself sinful flesh**... *[Christ]* **came in fallen humanity**.""

Uriah Smith, college teacher, General Conference secretary and Review editor wrote in his book Looking Unto Jesus (c1897) page 23, wrote:
"In the likeness of sinful flesh *[some, today, try to make that "unlikeness"]*, **He reached down to the very depths of man's fallen condition**, and became obedient unto death, even the ignominious death of the cross.""

M.C. Wilcox, editor of the Signs, writing in the *Signs of the Times* of January 3, 1900, page 1 col. 2, wrote:
"He was not only "made in the likeness of sinful flesh" Rom 8:3, "but He bore the sinful flesh. The likeness was not merely outward. His flesh was the same as that of all humanity; for He 'was made of the seed of David according to the flesh' (see Acts 2:30 and Romans 1:3).'

"**Every crime in the catalog was manifest among those through whom Jesus received His heritage of the flesh**. God prepared that body in which He would 'in all things' be 'like unto His brethren,' of 'the seed of Abraham,' partaker 'of flesh and blood!' Hebrews 2:14-17. **Have others inherited corrupt tendencies in the flesh? – So did He**. Were the ancestors of others coveting, grasping, adulterous, given to pleasure? So were His. **He was made like us that He might make us like Him.**

"But having the flesh with all its sinful tendencies, He did not sin. Living faith made dominant the Spirit of God over all fleshly tendencies."

'Oh no!' We hear someone exclaim, 'In her letter to Elder Baker (c1895, 1896) Mrs. White clearly states that: "Not for one moment was there in Him an **evil** propensity." Therefore the above given quotation from Elder Wilcox, and others, is error and not truth!'

Well, **let us look at what God's messenger said about propensities**:

Seventh-day Adventist Bible Commentary Volume 5, page 1128 (quoted from the 'Baker letter'):
"Not for one moment was there in Him an **evil propensity**."
She also said:
Review and Herald, April 24, 1900:
"**We** need not **retain one sinful propensity**." – So we who are born with them need not **retain** them!

She stated further:

Review and Herald, February 10, 1885:
"He was made like unto His brethren, with the same **susceptibilities**, mental and physical *[Roget's Thesaurus lists 'susceptibilities' and 'propensities' as synonyms]*.

After reading the three above given quotes some superficial readers might argue that Mrs. White was writing on both sides of an issue; however, the following two quotes, when juxtaposed, will show that she was not confused; and will immediately place the whole polemic in perspective and show the true meaning inherent in her words:

"Our natural propensities must be controlled, or we can never overcome **as Christ overcame."** 4T, page 235	"Not for one moment was there in Him an **evil propensity."** 5 SDA BC, page 1128

Note the distinction between 'natural' propensities and 'evil' propensities. These, to God's messenger, are two separate categories. We should not force Ellen White to contradict herself (which, of course, she never did) by ignoring the fact that she clearly distinguishes between Christ having our "natural" (sinful) propensities and that He avoided sin by controlling them, and our **evil** propensities (which are '**natural**' **propensities which have been permitted, by our carnal will, to bear fruit through indulgence and enactment thereby becoming evil**); which Christians must eliminate from their experience. Christ controlled the natural, inherited propensities – never indulging them in the exercise or enactment of evil.

So to take her statement: "Not for one moment was there in Him an **evil** propensity," and read into it as if she had written 'natural' (sinful) propensity, and then draw from that the conclusion that Ellen White was indicating that Christ took the **unfallen** nature of Adam before the fall, is unwarranted. It should rather be seen as an emphatic affirmation that He did not sin, though "in all points tempted like as we are." (Hebrews 4:15). **The importance of this is that if Christ did not have the same fallen human nature as we have, then he could not, and did not, and does not "reach us where we are", but only reached 'unfallen' humanity, who needed no Saviour.**

In short, if "Jesus" was a consubstantial and inseparable modality of the "one God substance" or "essence," and were to co-inhabit a body of "fallen" human nature, together with the human "soul" (spirit) of such a "fallen human nature"-person, then **that "fallen nature"-body would be instantly consumed by the "presence of God"!!**

Catholics have recognized this and have accordingly and logically, evolved the doctrinal teaching that Christ came with "unfallen or immaculate" human nature. In order to explain how Christ did not inherit fallen human nature from Mary, the doctrine of the "Immaculate Conception" was finally evolved, which teaches that:

Catechism of the Catholic Church, pages 123, 124:
"The most blessed Virgin Mary was, from the first moment of her conception, by a singular grace and privilege of Almighty God and by virtue of the merits of Jesus Christ, Saviour of the human race, **preserved immune from all stain of original sin.**"
Ineffabilis Deus, proclaimed by **Pope Pius IX in 1854**: DS 2803,

431

WILLIAM: I know that the Bible says clearly in Romans 1:3 that God's "Son Jesus Christ our Lord …was made of the seed of David according to the flesh." And also, there are these clear verses in:

Hebrews 2:14, 17:
"Forasmuch then as the children are partakers of flesh and blood, **he also himself likewise took part of the same;** …Wherefore **in all things it behoved him to be made like unto his brethren**."

The Scriptures are very clear that Jesus came in our **fallen humanity**.

PROFESSOR: **And God's messenger also totally refutes this 'immaculate nature' heresy of the Papacy:**

Desire of Ages, page 48.
"It would have been an almost infinite humiliation for the Son of God to take man's nature, even when Adam stood in his innocence in Eden. But Jesus accepted humanity when the race had been weakened by four thousand years of sin. Like every child of Adam **He accepted the results of the working of the great law of heredity. What these results were is shown in the history of His earthly ancestors. He came with such a heredity to share our sorrows and temptations,** and to give us the example of a sinless life" *[despite His having such an inheritance in the flesh. Therefore, Jesus' life on earth "condemns sin in the flesh" of fallen humanity. He demonstrated victory over sin in the same humanity that we share.]*

Desire of Ages, page 117.
"For four thousand years the race had been decreasing in physical strength, in mental power, and in moral worth; and **Christ took upon Him the infirmities of degenerate humanity. Only thus could He rescue man from the lowest depths of his degradation**."

SDA Bible Commentary, Volume 7, page 929. (MS 1, 1892)
"Christ's overcoming and obedience is that of a true human being. In our conclusions, we make many mistakes because of our erroneous views of the human nature of our Lord. **When we**

give to His human nature a power that it is not possible for man *[us]* to have in his conflicts with Satan, we destroy the completeness of His humanity. His imputed grace and power He gives to all who receive Him by faith.

"The obedience of Christ to His Father was the same obedience that is required of *[fallen]* man. Man cannot overcome Satan's temptations without divine power to combine with his instrumentality. So with Jesus Christ; He could lay hold of divine power. He came not to our world to give the obedience of a lesser God to a greater, but as a man to obey God's holy law, and in this way He is our example. The Lord Jesus came to our world, not to reveal what a God could do, but what a man could do, through faith in God's power to help in every emergency. Man is, through faith, to be a partaker in the divine nature, and to overcome every temptation wherewith he is beset.

The Lord now demands that every son and daughter of Adam, through faith in Jesus Christ, serve Him in human nature which we now have. The Lord Jesus has bridged the gulf that sin has made. He has connected earth with heaven, and finite man with the infinite God. Jesus, the world's Redeemer, could only keep the commandments of God in the same way that humanity can keep them."

In these and kindred statements God's messenger plainly opposes Trinitarian teaching.

Regrettably the denominational capitulation to Trinitarianism and the notion that Jesus came to this world in the human nature of Adam before the fall and the further associated notion to down-play the significance of Christ's high priestly ministry, on our behalf, in the Most Holy apartment of the Heavenly Sanctuary, all of which was precipitated at the evangelical/denominational conferences in 1955-1956 with Barnhouse and Martin, which resulted in the publication of the officially endorsed book 'Questions on Doctrine', all contributed to the derailing of God's denominated people from the track of truth, at least on the part of the 'organizational structure'.

WILLIAM: How does this affect General Conference sponsored Seventh-day Adventism?

PROFESSOR: Sadly, as you know William, leading General Conference Adventist theologians teach Trinitarian doctrine **and** teach the accompanying doctrines of 1) Augustinian "original sin" and 2) that the **unfallen** nature of Adam was Christ's earthly humanity. By the sheer pressure of logic these Adventist theologians are going to have to invent a doctrine explaining how Mary did not pass on to her Son—the Son of man—her own humanity!! Or, they will have to adopt the "Immaculate Conception" doctrine of Romanism.

Failing these two options, the prudent step would be to return to the Bible and the Anti-Trinitarian doctrine of the Godhead, as presented in both the Scriptures and the Spirit of Prophecy writings, both of which are indited by God's Holy Spirit through His servant/messengers.

The baleful effects of these aberrant, Trinitarian-based, doctrines—1) "Original Sin" and 2) Christ coming with the unfallen Nature of Adam before the Fall—are seen in the precipitous slide in standards and behavior within the SDA denomination. From the secretive, manipulative, and deceptive practices of leadership with regard to Church financial dealings and the vindictiveness displayed against "whistle blowers" such as M.L. Andreasen; David Dennis; Albert Koppel; John Normile (See Who Watches, Who Cares, page 40); etc., against honest enquirers, against faithful standard bearers, to the bizarre music and worship and dress styles being adopted, and to the pernicious introduction of spiritualistic "Spiritual Exercises" (Spiritual Formation) that place men in direct contract with demons. All these, and a host of other "fruit", bear testimony to the level of intoxication that Rome's wine has already induced among "God's denominated people."

WILLIAM: We truly weep between the porch and the altar. The effect of the wine of Babylon certainly does dull the mind and confuse the senses, so that one cannot discern the holy from the common, the true from the false, etc.

PROFESSOR: The Roman doctrine of **Transubstantiation**—the teaching that through the "hocus pocus" incantations of the priest, when he proclaims "hoc est enim Corpus meum" (*'This is My* [Christ's] *body')*, and **then the little round "wafer" is magically "transformed" into the literal "body of Christ" and "Christ" is "sacrificed again"**—this whole blasphemous ceremony, which according to Romanism makes the priest the creator of his "Creator"—is all **based on the doctrine of the Trinity.**

WILLIAM: How?

PROFESSOR: Since the Divine nature of Christ is, according to this nebulous doctrine, a manifestation or "modality" of the "indivisible" God substance, and which simply returned to "God" at Christ's crucifixion, leaving only His "immaculate" human body as an "appeasement" sacrifice on Calvary's cross; and since, according to this teaching, the Life laid down by Christ was only a human life (the same sort of life which men can invoke through the procreative act)—it is no stretch to a Romanist therefore, to propose that **a "celibate" priest, who is "married" to the "Mother Church" can through mystical ceremonial involvement "reproduce: a "body of Christ" for re-"sacrifice" and so purchase "merit" for the participants of the "mass." The one-in-three Trinity doctrine promotes spiritualism.**

This is all a "mass"-ive hoax that has been "peddled" to the people. It constitutes a significant portion of the "merchandise" (Rev. 18: 3,11, 15, 23) of Rome which, together with "indulgences," "confession," "penance," "Christmas," "Easter," "St. Valentine's Day," "St. Patrick's Day," "Halloween," etc. are "commodities" marketed by Rome, which generate countless millions in revenue, not only for Rome, but for the "merchants of the earth."

WILLIAM: How? How do they make money from false doctrines?

PROFESSOR: **How?** The financial implications of the various 'holy days' are self-evident. Furthermore, by "pilgrimage" tourism and all the accompanying services involved in "servicing" such tourists; by "selling" the idea that "sin" can be absolved by human priestly "mediation" and incantations, so that gambling, racketeering, over-reaching, and any imaginable venal sin, can have the eternal consequence so easily and conveniently removed by the "church;" all of these methods, and a plethora of other ways, all generate "income" so that the "merchants of the earth" wax rich on the abundance of the "delicacies" that Rome peddles: And it all reaches back to a foundational false "doctrine of God"—the Trinity. That is why the "man of sin" is given that Biblical title.

435

Chapter 36

TRINITARIANISM DISTORTS THE TRUTH— PART THREE

LETTER TO DOUG BACHELOR

To: Pastor Doug Bachelor
c/o Amazing Facts
P.O. Box 1058
Roseville, CA 95678—8058

Dear Pastor Doug:

It is not without some concern about how well I am able to express my thoughts that I have put pen to paper. You head a large and much respected ministry and you are, in your own right, highly respected by Adventist across the spectrum of believers. Knowing something of the demands on your time and attention that the scope of your Ministry must make, what am about to bring to your attention may have slipped under the radar.

Among the series of 'comic' books put together by Jim Pincoski under the 'Amazing Facts' label, is one entitled, "What About The Trinity." Throughout this 'comic' are illustrations of yourself and a Pastor Anderson and throughout the two of you 'verbalize' the comics' message explaining the 'Trinity.'

Throughout the 'comic' there are many truthful statements regarding the three mighty Persons of the Godhead. However, on various pages, which propose to discuss, are insinuations/insertions of Catholic Trinitarian error which are given credence by having you associated with the expounding of this error. They are also given credence by being linked with the truth concerning the Godhead.

ITEM ONE

On pages 10 and 11 the reader is introduced to the notion that since the Human Body is comprised of 268 bones and 63 trillion cells, that "Somehow we all have an idea in our heads that each of us is just 'one' person!!"

Right there is a not so subtle intimation of the Catholic Doctrine of "Consubstantiation"—A pivotal component of the Catholic 'Trinity' doctrine. Essentially 'consubstantiation' teaches that God the Father, God the Son, and God the Holy Spirit are three emanations of the same substance, i.e. the Trinity!

The doctrine of the Godhead, on the other hand, teaches that the members of the Godhead are three separate and distinct beings. God's messenger to his church indicates that the members of the Godhead are **ONE** in purpose, in mind, in character, **but not in Person. It is thus that God and Christ are One.**" *Ministry of Healing, 422.*

ITEM TWO

Furthermore on page 11 of the 'comic' it is finally stated—"It shouldn't be too hard to believe that God Could Be Able to Split Himself Into 3 Separate Beings – After all, each 'ONE' of us is split into 63 trillion cells." This teaching certainly sounds like 'consubstantiation' and when coupled with the Catholic term 'Trinity,' that 'consubstantiation' notion is, not so overtly, endorsed.

ITEM THREE

On page 44 of the comic the Nicaean Creed (325 AD) is quoted: "We believe in one God …and in one Lord Jesus Christ, the Son of God, begotten from the father, only begotten, that is **From the Substance of the Father,** God from God light from light, True God from True God, Begotten not made, **Of One Substance With the Father,….**"

This 'Consubstantiality' is a figment of Greek Spiritism; a Platonic ectoplasm that flies in the face of revealed truth. Revealed Truth indicates that there never was a time that Michael/Jesus was not **with** God *Evangelism, 615).* Neither God's word in Scripture or in the revelations and messages given through His messenger to His last day church, ever state that they **share** a common 'Substance.' When Jesus was born of a woman, having the Holy Spirit as his earthly progenitor, a new creature came onto the Universal Stage—a union of Creature and Creator. This new being, Jesus, was not 'spoken' into existence, nor formed of clay to have the breath of life breathed into his nostrils, NO, He Was Born, or 'Begotten.' See Heb. 1:5,6. (When He came forth from the grave with His glorified body, He was, in a sense, born/begotten. Again, see Acts 13:33, 34.)

It is my studied belief that this is why Jesus is referred to as the ONLY BEGOTTEN of the Father. The 'Substance' of the 'man' Christ Jesus was (and is) DEFINITELY NOT the 'Substance' of the Father. Jesus was born with our fallen human nature and then raised with glorified human nature. Jesus remains fully God, but is not of God the Father's substance. The Catholic Doctrine of the 'Trinity,' which the Catholic Church declares is the foundation of all her doctrine (error) is, therefore, diametrically antithetical to the true doctrine of the Godhead.

The question may legitimately be asked, why were the Adventist Pioneers so vociferously anti-trinitarian? There has to be a reason and a good one!

The Handbook for Today's Catholic, page 16, states: "The mystery of **the Trinity is the central doctrine of Catholic faith. Upon it are based ALL other teaching of the church."**

Does this mean that the doctrines of 'original sin,' infant baptism,' and the 'immaculate conception,' etc., are ALL based on this 'central doctrine'—the doctrine of the Trinity? Let us examine this hypothesis. If these doctrines (original sin, etc.) are false doctrines, then the foundational doctrine on which they are predicated must also be false. False doctrine can never be built on pure truth, while at the same time false doctrine must cling to 'some' truth in order to sustain itself from falling like Dagon, flat on its face.

Turning to the Catechism of the Catholic Church, page 54, 55, we read the Trinity Doctrine set out as follows:

Page 54: "The Christian faith confesses that God is one in Nature Substance and Essence."

Page 55: "We firmly believe and confess without reservation that there is only one True God, Eternal, Infinite (Immensus) and Unchangeable, Incomprehensible, Mighty and Ineffable, The Father and the Son and the Holy Spirit; Three Persons indeed, **but one essence, substance or nature** entirely simple." *[The Catholic Church has coined a word to encapsulate this teaching; the word is 'Consubstantiation' which means sharing the same substance or essence.]*

Page 180 of the Catechism of the Catholic Church states: "To believe in the Holy Spirit is to profess that the Holy Spirit is one of the Persons of the Holy Trinity, **consubstantial** with the Father and the Son...."

It follows logically that if the Father, the Son and the Holy Spirit co-share one substance then they are each but different revelations of that one substance and that is indeed how they have portrayed their notion of the Trinity.

Let us examine where such a notion or doctrine will lead us.—
The Roman Catholic 'Trinity' doctrine, the doctrine of Consubstantiality,' demands a **two-nature** Christology. Simply put, it demands that Jesus had a **human** and a **Divine** nature, and that their two natures were separate at all times, with only his human nature dying on the cross. In contrast to this, the Pioneers believed in a **one-nature** Christology, the **human** and the **Divine** being "blended" into one.

Notice what the prophet wrote on **this** issue: "Christ could have done nothing during his earthly ministry in saving fallen man if the Divine had not **blended** with the human. The limited capacity of man cannot define this wonderful mystery—the **blending** of the two natures, the Divine and the human. It can never be explained. Man must wonder and be silent. **And yet man is privileged to be a partaker of the Divine nature,** and in this way he can to some degree enter into the mystery. Divinity took the nature of Humanity, and for what purpose? That through the righteousness of Christ, humanity might partake of the Divine nature." <u>1888 Materials</u>, page 332, *"Doctrine of Righteousness by Faith."*

"When he came to the world for the first time, Divinity and humanity were **blended. This is our only HOPE.** The son of man is fully qualified to be the originator (2nd Adam, see 1 Cor. 15:47) of a humanity that will **blend** with Divinity by partaking of the Divine nature." *Signs of the Times,* March 8, 1899.

Methodists, like other daughters of Rome, have as a denomination accepted Rome's foundational doctrine—the 'Trinity'! Uriah Smith, writing in the *Review and Herald,* March 27, 1888, responded to an article in the *'Free Methodist'* a Chicago church paper, in which the article writer, C.E. Harrow, Jr., put forth the idea that Jesus was not possessed of a dual **(or blended)** nature while here upon the earth. Smith responded—"at the same time he (Harrow) fails to answer the point made by Seventh-Day Adventists, that if his nature can be separated into human and Divine, and only the human part died, then the world is furnished with only a **human sacrifice, not a Divine Sacrifice,** as we contend."

Taking Catholic falsehood to their natural conclusion: 'The Trinitarian view is that the Son of God had three distinct natures at the same time (during his incarnation): namely (1) a human body, (2) a human soul, united with (3) His Divine Nature: The body being mortal, the soul immortal, the divinity co-equal, co-existent, and co-eternal with the everlasting Father (so where did Jesus empty Himself so that He of His own self 'could do nothing'?). Now none of the advocates of the Trinitarian theory claimed that either his Soul or Divinity died /but/ that the body was the only part of this triple being which actually died. *[That is why his 'soul'*

could, according to them, go to hell and preach to the souls there when H
was in the grave!] The death of the cross, hence according to this view
was only the sacrifice of the most inferior part—the human body—of th
Son of God." *Review and Herald,* No. 21, 1854, J.M. Stephenson, author
James White, editor.)

We who know the Sanctuary Doctrine, can also legitimately ask, now
that according to Trinitarian Doctrine, Jesus' mortal human nature died, and
post ascension, his Divinity and Soul have ascended to Heaven, then wha
kind of 'High Priest' is currently interceding in our behalf? Certainly no
the "man" Christ Jesus! Also, if as Trinitarians' postulate, Jesus was
consubstantial representative of the "Divine Trinity" whilst here on eart
then, clearly, he could not be "tempted in all points like as we are" for it i
not possible to tempt God (James 1:13: "For God cannot be tempted wit
evil....")

Writing in the Review and Herald, Nov. 5, 1861, J.N. Loughborough pu
it this way, speaking of the Trinity, he said, "Its origin is pagan an
fabulous. Instead of pointing us to scripture for proof of the Trinity, we ar
pointed to the **trident** of the Persians, with the assertion that 'by this the
design to teach the idea of a Trinity,' and if they had the doctrine of th
trinity, they must have received it by tradition from the people of God."

ITEM FOUR

On page 47 of the comic book, it is stated: "God decided that he woul
need to be 3 separate beings! God had always known the end from th
beginning—and because of his unlimited love, he decided to do it by bein
a Trinity!" On the very next page, page 48, it states 'God is love'...
takes **more than just one being** to show love." Well... if there was ever
'time' when 'God' was just one being, before God "decided that he woul
need to be 3 separate beings," well then, when God was just ONE Being
God could not have been 'love' at that point because the comic just said tha
there has to be more than one person to show love. The absurdity of thes
statements is clear.

ITEM FIVE

On page 53 of the comic book, Mary is discussed and is correctly show
not to be the 4th person of the Godhead, "not a Co-mediatrix and co
redemptrix" as the Catholic Church now canonizes her. However,
Catholic falsehood is propagated on page 53: "Mary was just the earthl
Mother of God; she was **not** the 'creator of God.'" This partial trut
conceals a hidden barb. Jesus, who thought it not robbery to be equal wit
God, made Himself of none-effect and took upon himself the form of

ervant in the body that was prepared for him. **He was already God. Being born of Mary added nothing to his godhood.** Mary was simply the human vehicle whereby Jesus took upon himself our humanity, our flesh. To call Mary the 'Mother of God' is an old heathen blasphemy which harps back to Nimrod, Semiramis and Tammuz. It is a typical Catholic distortion of this truth aimed at justifying the worship of a woman whom we know to be dead. (If Mary, a human being, can be a 'mediatrix,' then why cannot a priest, a human being, be a mediator in Jesus' stead: **Anti-Christ = *in the place of Christ.*)**

ITEM SIX

On page 40 of the comic, one is also introduced to a Trinitarian hymn written in 1826 by Reginald Heber, "Holy, holy, holy, God in three persons, Blessed Trinity." To which a resounding "Amen" is added. This hymn appears as #73 in the 1985 'new' SDA Church Hymnal. This song was put into the 1909 and 1941 SDA Hymnals, but the 'Trinity' wording was changed to "God over all who rules eternity," and, "Perfect in power, in love and purity." This purposeful and deliberate change in the wording was done so as to give no credence to the 'Trinity' notion with its innate connotations on 'consubstantiation.'

WORD-CRAFT

Words convey the meaning harbored by those who coined them. Subtly, Catholic terminology is infiltrating our ranks. Once people become accustomed to them and decide that the term describes or defines what they believe, such persons are more vulnerable to a paradigm shift when the real meaning and intent of the term finally confronts them. (In similar fashion, terms like "Eucharist'—(for "communion," or the "Lord's Supper') also find ingress and sow ecumenical seed that will lead to a baleful harvest in the future.)

In the 1985 SDA Church Hymnal, song #73 has the wording changed back to the original Trinitarian wording. In 1988, the book <u>Seventh-Day Adventists Believe</u> ...27 Fundamental Beliefs, under the heading, 'The Godhead,' we find the terms *Godhead* and *Trinity* are employed interchangeably, as though the one is the equivalent of the other.

Such is not the case! Nowhere in the Scriptures of the King James version, nor anywhere in the communications of God's messenger, is the term 'Trinity' or 'Triune God' (or 'co-equal,' or 'co-eternal') ever used. And with good reason. The 'Godhead' is the correct term and is predicated on an understanding of three Separate and Distinct Divine Persons *["One in purpose, in mind, in character, but not in person. It is thus that God and*

441

Christ are One." Ministry of Healing page 422]. The 'Trinity' is a false god, predicated on the Gnostic, spiritualistic notion of three emanations of one substance.

In the book <u>Issues: the Seventh-Day Adventist Church and Certain Private Ministries</u>, put out by the General Conference in 1980, the following is found on page 39: "For those who would wish to define 'Historic Adventism' in terms of specific doctrinal content, the 1872 date presents a real dilemma…. Would one be willing to accept **all** the content from the earlier era? Are the modern defenders of so-called historical Adventism really prepared to return to a non-Trinitarian position?"

The answer, of course, is a resounding **Yes!** The doctrine of the Godhead comprised of three separate and distinct Divine Persons is the only true doctrine to which God's people can safely subscribe.

In the *Advent Review & Sabbath Herald,* February 7, 1856, Elder White wrote the following:

"The "mystery of iniquity" began to work in the church in Paul's day. It finally crowded out the simplicity of the gospel, **and corrupted the doctrine of Christ**, and the church went into the wilderness. Martin Luther, and other reformers, arose in the strength of God, and with the Word and Spirit, made mighty strides in the Reformation. The greatest fault we can find in the Reformation is, the Reformers stopped reforming. Had they gone on, and onward, till they had left the last vestige of Papacy behind, such **as (1) Natural immortality, (2) Sprinkling, (3) The Trinity and (4) Sunday-keeping,** the church would now be free from her unscriptural errors."

ITEM SEVEN

Finally, on page 56 of the comic is a closing statement. The statement reads as follows: "It is very important to have a proper understanding about all 3 persons of the Godhead. They are not 3 God's, they are **One God in Persons—and The Only Way** for us to be saved is to accept Jesus Christ as your Lord and Savior, **and to Accept the Holy Trinity!"**

As we have seen, the 'Trinity' doctrine is unholy. The Godhead doctrine teaches three separate and distinct persons in **one Godhead, not** one God in 3 persons. Trinitarian doctrine leads to a corruption of true faith and to accept that corruption places God's people in spiritual jeopardy.

Respectfully In His Service,

Professor 'B. Miller'

Dear Reader – regard this whole page as in parenthesis.)

His Message is Our Mission

Amazing Facts, Inc.
P.O. Box 1058
Roseville, CA 95678
916.434.3880
Fax: 916.434.3889
www.amazingfacts.org

ADMINISTRATION

October 23, 2008

Barry Mellor
919 Swafford Rd
Spring City, TN 37381

Dear Barry,

Thank you for your letter. I certainly respect your freedom to disagree with me! I understand what you are saying, and recognize that many of the Adventist pioneers held differing views on the concept of the trinity and the Godhead. I would refer you to www.adventistbiblicalresearch.org for an excellent discussion that follows the learning process within the Adventist church on this topic.

May the Lord guide you as you continue to grow in knowledge and grace!

Warm Christian regards,

Doug Batchelor
President/Speaker

DB/ch

Dear Pastor Doug,

This book is my response to your above letter and the material you sent. I did phone your secretary in April of 2013 and tried to arrange sending you a copy of the manuscript. She told me that you were busy, and that she would relay my message; that you would call me back. I view this material on the Godhead as so vital that I have proceeded to publish as I have not yet received your call. It is now April, 2014.

PROFESSOR: William, the distorted "Trinitarian" perception of "God" is more widely and deeply entrenched than one may think. Take note of the following:

A STATEMENT BY KIM KJAER, from AMAZING FACTS
"A mousetrap is made up of several parts which work together to seize its unsuspecting prey as it happily nibbles on one of his favorite foods. Removing even a single component of the trap, such as the spring, renders its remaining parts completely ineffective. ...God also is a combination of three entities and is manifested as the Father, The Son, and the Holy Spirit. **Were any one Person of the Godhead removed, God would cease to be God.**" Amazing Facts/*Inside Report,* article, "The Trinity, Is it Biblical?"

This perception corresponds exactly with that of Angel Rodriguez, as we saw previously. It is breathtaking to see what depths of misunderstanding Trinitarian doctrine can lead to—as demonstrated by the above quotation!

Firstly, to compare the functions of the members of the Godhead with the operations of the parts of a mousetrap *[a contraption of man's devising]* is... well, bordering on being blasphemous.

Secondly, we know that during His incarnation Christ could have sinned. Both He and His Father took that very real risk. Had Jesus sinned, His separation from His Father would have been eternal. Nevertheless, God would have continued to be God on His throne—despite the crushing and eternally painful loss. The rest of the limitless universe depends on His sustaining power. Without the sustaining power of God, the universe would implode. Even Satan knows that. As a separate and distinct individual, the Father maintained the integrity of the Godhead during the incarnation, while His Son and the Holy Spirit condescended to come into direct contact with our sinful nature in a lost world of sinners. As we have seen, God would not have ceased to exist!

444

Chapter 37

TRINITARIANISM TRENDS TO BAD 'BIRDS'

James White referred to Trinitarianism as an "absurdity". To what lengths of absurdity and corruption can Trinitarianism lead one? The following statements give some indication:

2007 Amazing Facts cartoon book "What About The Trinity?" by Jim Pinkoski with Doug Batchelor and Pastor Anderson, page 46:
"Jesus had to lower himself into human flesh to be able to die for our sins – but "Eternal" Beings cannot die, especially a GOD who pre-existed the creation of the universe! **So how did GOD arrange it so that GOD could die for us? <u>One of HIM decided to lower HIMSELF into human flesh, into a body that could die.</u>**"

This cartoon caricature again emphasizes the Romish delusion that only a "body" died to redeem us, after one of "Him" lowered "Himself" into it, and then, obviously, had to vacate it, so that it could die. Surely, we can see that this concept destroys our perception of the value of the sacrifice made on our behalf. Furthermore, the weight and value of the Law is, likewise, devalued and made of "none effect" and "lightly regarded". Incidentally, we have been taught by God's messenger that it was separation from His Father that caused the death of Jesus; so does the above mean that God only separated from a human body and that is what caused the body to die? How then does that differ from our death, when our breath returns to God who gave it? How can any of the above be an expiation for the sins of the world

Regarding how worshipping an 'idol god' of human devising can negatively affect our moral perceptions. God's messenger has warned us:

Review and Herald, May 17, 1887:
"It is now the duty of God's commandment-keeping people to watch and pray, to search the Scriptures diligently, to hide the word of God in the heart, **lest they sin against Him <u>in idolatrous thoughts</u> and <u>debasing practices</u>, and thus the church of God become demoralized like the fallen churches**

whom prophecy represents as being filled with every <u>unclean and hateful bird</u>."

May the reader decide if there are any 'unclean and hateful birds' evident in the next quotation:

**** *WARNING: THE NEXT QUOTE IS ABSOLUTELY GROSS AND BLASPHEMOUS* ****

I reluctantly include it, but wished to show how far we can degenerate spiritually when we don't know the God we should worship. As abominable as this quote is, parts that were even more detestable were edited out:

Dr. Hyveth Williams, from a sermon delivered at a women's retreat at the Sligo SDA Church in Takoma Park, Maryland on February 2, 2002. (www.sdadefend.com/MINDEX-U-Z/Williams.pdf):

"And so, Naomi said to Ruth, 'When he lies down for sexual intimacy, find out exactly where he's lying down . . Find out where God is lying down. **The God of heaven, <u>holy Trinity</u>; they are lying down on earth**, in the hope that we're going to come and find out where they are, so we can get into some intimate relation with them . . God wants to impregnate you, so it can be said, This holy thing, this thing, this seed that is coming in your stomach is a holy one . . He wants to romance with you. He wants to marry you. He wants to make babies with you . . . So Christ in you can be the hope of glory. He wants you to be intimate with Him. He wants you to uncover His secret places, and say, I'm ready! Let's get it on! God wants that with us. And only us women can understand that, because we cherish this; we yearn for this undiluted intimacy!. . . This is what God wants us to be . . ."

One may justifiably ask: **'What has Hyveth's reprobate rendition of the story of Ruth and Boaz and her blasphemous besmirchment of God got to do with the issue of the Trinity?'** In the quote given below we find the answer to where the wicked ideas of Miss Williams have their roots:

<u>**International Catholic University – Lesson 11: The Holy**</u>

446

Trinity (you can find this on-line at:
http://icuweb.home.comcast.net/~icuweb/c02511.htm):

"When we reflect on our faith it is extremely important to realize that there is **only one God, but that *in* God there are three distinct Persons**. There is a question, then, obviously of both unity and multiplicity in God. We must retain both of them. In order to stress the divine unity **the Fathers of the Church emphasized the mutual or reciprocal penetration and indwelling of the three divine Persons in one another. We note among human lovers the drive toward union. Kisses and embraces are manifestations of this drive. The impulse of love towards mutual penetration which we witness among human beings is a faint reflection of the mutual indwelling of the three divine Persons.**

"The doctrine of mutual penetration or indwelling of the three divine Persons was officially taught by the Council of Florence in the fifteenth century. The Council Fathers declared: "Because of this unity the Father is entirely in the Son and entirely in the Holy Spirit; the Son is entirely in the Father and entirely in the Holy Spirit; the Holy Spirit is entirely in the Father and entirely in the Son" (*Denzinger* 704). In theology this mutual indwelling has been called, since the eighth century, "circumincession" which comes from the Latin *circum-incedere* and means "to move around in."

"I have already mentioned the impulse of love towards union. **In the Trinity each divine Person is irresistibly drawn, by the very constitution of his being, to the other two. Branded *[?]* in the very depths of each one of them is a necessary outward impulse urging him to give himself fully to the other two, to pour himself out into the divine receptacle of the other two.** Here we find an unceasing circulation of life and *[homosexual?]* love. Thus, since each Person is necessarily in the other two, unity is achieved because of this irresistible impulse in each Person, which mightily draws them to one another."

Rome's rendition of the interrelationships of their invention, the Trinity, amply demonstrate the thought processes of the "whore" of Revelation, to whom the Dragon gave his seat, power and authority (Revelation 13:2). Surely the same "spirit" is discernable in the blasphemy broadcast from the lips of Hyveth Williams, a woman who holds high honor in the Adventist denomination: A chair at Andrew's University as professor of homiletics in the Theological Seminary. Surely the 'sentiments' she has flaunted in her sermon demonstrate that Babylon's and her bemusings are "unclean" "birds of a feather". **What does her endorsement by the denomination indicate? Are we becoming a "sister to fallen Babylon"?** God's messenger warned of that danger:

> Testimonies on Sexual Behavior, Adultery, and Divorce, page 188.3:
> "Cleansing of the Camp. We must as a people arouse and cleanse the camp of Israel. Licentiousness, unlawful intimacy, and unholy practices are coming in among us in a large degree; and ministers who are handling sacred things are guilty of sin in this respect. They are coveting their neighbors' wives, and the seventh commandment is broken. **We are in danger of becoming a sister to fallen Babylon, of allowing our churches to become corrupted, and filled with every foul spirit, a cage for every unclean and hateful bird; and will we be clear unless we make decided movements to cure the existing evil?"**

While the above is primarily speaking to physical and mental adultery, etc., **the principle applies equally to the spiritual breaking of the seventh commandment: to spiritual licentiousness and false worship.** May God help His denominated people to wake up and cleanse the camp; each individual beginning with themselves.

Chapter 38

EKRON'S "ELIXIR"

PROFESSOR: Over the last number of decades, and particularly since the 1950's, God's denominated people have largely assumed the terms 'Godhead' and 'Trinity' to be synonymous, and have used the two terms interchangeably. This is often seen in church literature and, of course, is as we have seen, very noticeable in "Fundamental Beliefs". By the grace of God, I trust that what we have studied amply demonstrates that these two terms are diametrically opposite in both implication and connotation; and, therefore, in meaning. However, to this day, most Adventists lay persons, even those who decidedly oppose the spiritualistic notion of one "God essence" manifesting itself in three different ways, happily accept the term 'Trinity', even though they would decidedly reject the underlying concepts that the term represents.

However, such is not the case with most of the 'thought leaders' of the denomination. Adventist theologians fully apprehend and comprehend the full range of implications behind the term 'Trinity', and have, as we shall discover in this study, fully committed their position and talent to purvey and to push Trinitarianism, in all its grotesqueness, into the forefront of the denomination's psyche, while at the same time obscuring the underlying objectionable implications of this philosophical idol. We propose to examine a few bench mark works by some of the foremost Adventist theologians peddling full blown Trinitarianism to the Advent people. In their book:

The Trinity, by Woodrow Whidden, Jerry Moon and John W. Reeve: It is stated on page 219:

"...the evidence is also clear that Ellen White **recognized** at least two major types of Trinitarian belief *[She did?]*, one that she consistently opposed all her life. *[the truth is that God's messenger recognized that two streams of belief concerning the* ***Godhead*** *prevailed among Pioneer Adventists: 1) A two Person Godhead comprised of only the Father and the Son from whom the Holy Spirit was only an emanation of their power, and 2) a three Person Godhead comprised of the Father, the Son and the "Mighty Third Person of the Godhead." The former view, she totally rejected and corrected:* **thereby establishing the <u>truth</u> on** *this issue. The Trinity, on the other hand, was not a part of her belief system. She opposed it as we have demonstrated. The authors of "The Trinity" go on to say:]* The view she eventually came to agree with portrays the three members of the Godhead as tangible, personal individuals *[absolutely correct, except the Holy Spirit can hardly be described as "tangible" in His present form.],* living from eternity **in union of nature**, character, purpose, and love, yet each having an individual identity…"

    Please note the deceptive injection of the phrase "…<u>in union of nature</u>…" into terminology derived from the inspired writings of God's messenger (namely, <u>Ministry of Healing</u> pages 421, 422) which categorically declares that the Members of the Godhead "are **one** in **purpose**, in **mind**, in **character**, but **not** in person." **In the same way** that **Christ and His disciples are one**: a oneness attained between completely separate and distinct individuals. On page 421 of <u>Ministry of Healing</u>, God's messenger plainly states that "the personality of the Father and the Son, **also the unity that exists between them** are represented in the 17th chapter of John, in the prayer of Christ for His disciples: John 17:21, 22 "That they all may be one; as thou, Father, [art] in me, and I in thee, that they also may be one in us: that the world may believe that thou hast sent me. And the glory which thou gavest me I have given them; **that they may be one, even as** *[in the same way]* **we are one**:"

    Nothing could be plainer than that God's messenger, in the above given quotes, was completely overturning the notion of the **consubstantial** nature of Deity as taught in Trinitarianism: she **was NOT stating that Members of the Godhead had a "union OF nature"**. Here we find Whidden, Moon and Reeve displaying how "men of talent and pleasing address… employ their powers to deceive." (<u>Great Controversy</u>, page 608)

    Some will be quick to protest that Whidden, Moon and Reeves' interpretation must be correct and they will point to what God's messenger wrote in <u>Patriarchs and Prophets</u> page 34, which states that: "Christ, the Word, the only begotten of God, was one with the eternal Father--**one in nature**, in character, in purpose --…" etc., which, they feel, seems to imply that Christ and the Father indeed share one nature and that for me to postulate that there was a "deceptive injection" of the phrase "**union of nature**" needs an apology and correction.

    Let me point out once again that for Christ to be "**one in** nature" with His Father was the same as saying that you and I are "one in nature", but we are NOT in **"union OF nature"**, which describes 'consubstantiality'; and that to inject **that phrase** was indeed deceptive.

On page 188 of their book "The Trinity", they purport to "examine the evidence of her *[Ellen White's]* early beliefs about the Godhead." Thus, subtly, the implication is mooted that God's messenger **changed** her **views** on the doctrine of God. **This would serve to call into question whether she was underlined or not**. On pages 204 and 205 of their book they try to equate the changes in her views, on such subjects as meat eating, etc. where God corrected her past habits and introduced in vision the health message, to how her understanding of the Godhead morphed over time. Once again, these men are strongly implying that Ellen White's **"views"** are the "authority" of her writings. In truth the one "view" is a correction of lifestyle; **the other is fundamental Bible doctrine**. The fact that God's messenger came out of a Trinitarian church, the Methodist Church, and yet avoided all usage of Trinitarian terminology; never opposed her husband's vociferous anti-Trinitarianism nor ever corrected him in his views of so important a doctrine, but actually endorsed that God was leading him when she wrote:

> Testimonies to the Church, Volume 3, page 85:
> **"He (God) has also given my husband great light upon Bible subjects, not for himself alone, but for others.** I saw that these things should be written and talked out, and **that new light would continue to shine upon the word** *[This "new light", of course, would not contradict that already established.].***"**

And also that she, herself, penned so many statements, including a whole chapter in Ministry of Healing that totally overthrow Trinitarian teaching, is ample evidence that her "underlined" on **this topic never changed** for she was God's messenger, and on the doctrine of God, He, who "changes not" never inspired his messenger to deviate a hairs breadth from the Biblical doctrine of the Godhead, penned by Holy men of old, to some philosophical idol concocted under the very dubious motivation prevailing at the Council of Nicea in the 4th century (See page 14, 123, 262 of this book).

On pages 204 and 205 of their book this trio of Trinitarians present the following gobbledygook:

> "…that on the basis of interpreting obscure [?] passages by clearer passages , we should view purported **evidence [??] of Trinitarianism in her later writings through the lens of her earlier non-Trinitarian statements…"**

The truth is that some of Sister White's statements only include the Father and the Son (Patriarch & Prophets, page 36: "The Son of God shared the Father's throne, and the glory of the eternal, self-existent One encircled both.... Before the assembled inhabitants of heaven the King declared that none but Christ, the Only Begotten of God, could fully enter into **His purposes,** and to Him it was committed to **execute** the mighty counsels of His will."), which some seized upon to endorse their "two Person Godhead" views. However God's messenger corrected that error by clearly enunciating that the Holy Spirit is the "Mighty **Third Person** of the Godhead". In other words that the Godhead are indeed a "Heavenly Trio": a Three Person Godhead, not a spiritualistic, ectoplasmic Platonic, Aristotelian, "substance" morphing into three "hypostases".

This pro-Trinitarian trio correctly state on page 205 of their book that God's messenger "...did not believe that we had no more truth to discover (Letter 5, 1849, in Manuscript Releases, Volume 5, page 200)." What they omit to present is that God's messenger made it very clear that new truth or light would NOT **contradict** established truth ("Through all these centuries the truth of God has remained the same. That which was truth in the beginning is truth now. Although new and important truths appropriate for succeeding generations have been opened to the understanding, the present revealings **do not contradict those of the past. Every new truth understood only makes more significant the old."** That I May Know Him page 197.2). **The denomination's Bible based beliefs on this topic of the Godhead were established in 1872. They have subsequently been changed.**

On page 206 of their book, in the Chapter entitled "Ellen White's Role in the Trinity Debate", the author of that chapter states: "But I have not found any statement from her pen that criticizes a Biblical view of the Trinity." That is hardly amazing! There is **no "Biblical view"** of the Trinity, simply because the Trinity doctrine is unbiblical, as even acknowledged by Rome herself as well as by her prominent theologians (see pages 19 and 20 of this book). God's messenger, however, totally endorsed the Biblical doctrine of the Godhead, a term **not** synonymous with the pagan inspired 'Trinity' concept.

In Section Two, Chapter 9, of their book "The Trinity", Jerry Moon, who actually authored this section, discloses the sources of all the false and convoluted rationales behind Trinitarian doctrine: The pagan Greco-Roman philosophers: Plato and Aristotle; the Gnostics and the Helenized, so called early church "Fathers" like Marcion, Irenaeus, Sabellius, Origen, Augustine, Athanasius, Basil of Ancyra, Euseius Bomaventure, etc.

From this "cracked cistern" the turbid, clouded waters of 'Trinitarian thought' tap. It is from this "thought stream" that students from worldly universities are taught. Into this troubled tributary Adventist theologians have tapped by seeking for worldly accreditation and worldly recognition.

By seeking worldly approbation and acceptance Adventism has absorbed Augustinian doctrine on the 'nature of Christ'; on Trinitarianism and now on the Jesuit practices on "Spirituality" and "knowing God" called "Spiritual Formation".

Ecumenism is the order of the day and in order to participate each participant must subscribe to a belief in the 'Trinity'. The somnolent "saints" are drinking it all in.

Here is another example of Ekron's 'Elixir':

"1+1+1=One - The keystone of biblical theology" an article by Norman R. Gulley in *Adventist World* of February 2010 pages 30-31:

In his article, Norman Gulley correctly perceives the analogous statements on 'One'ness between man and wife, as recorded in Genesis 2:24, where "they twain" become "one (echad) flesh", and Members of the Godhead being "one (echad) Lord". However, Gulley then goes on to declare that these analogous statements of Scripture suggest "that God *[singular ?]* is united, or more than one Person." This is theological saber-dancing at its worst. Clearly, a man and a woman are separate and distinct individuals of the same nature, **but not consubstantial (homousios) in nature: Yet they become "one" (echad)**. The analogy to Deuteronomy 6:4 is made plain from Jesus' own rendering (Mark 12:29) of the Hebrew 'shemmah' of Deut. 6:4. In the koine Greek of the New Testament, the 'Supreme Authority' (kurios) spoken of by Jesus in Mark 12:29, when quoting the shemmah, is referring to the name Jehovah or Yaweh of Deuteronomy 6:4 where the name is translated into the title "LORD", who is then titled "Our God" (El Oheem: a plural term) who is/are "one" (echad) Lord (Yaweh/Jehovah) or, as Jesus put it, "one Lord" (kurios: Supreme Authority). **If the 'one'ness (echad) of marriage partners is analogous to the 'one'ness (echad) of Members of the Godhead, then that 'one'ness is analogous to that of separate and distinct individuals of the same, but not consubstantial nature, being 'one'**—just as God's messenger described the 'one'ness of the Godhead in Ministry of Healing page 422 (See Chapter 25 of this book and also page 356). And the Scriptures describe their 'one'ness in John 17:21-23 (See Chapter 23 on the Shemmah in this book). Also, remember that the name Jehovah (or Yaweh) is scripturally applied to the Father and to Christ since they both are "self-existent", and, as we have seen, the Holy Spirit is their Spirit. To maintain that Deuteronomy 6:4 and Genesis 2:24 "suggests" a consubstantial Trinity is a fancy dance side step aimed at avoiding the cutting sword blade of truth. All this helps promote Papal error in our ranks.

Norman Gulley observes that **"God could not be love if He was solitary, for whom would He love? It takes more than one to love."** (Reader, please note:) Gulley's thoughts parallel those of a Catholic counterpart, as recorded in:

My Catholic Faith, page 31:

"1. This is the simplest way by which the **distinct origin** of each Divine Person has been explained: God is a spirit, and the first act of a Spirit is to know and understand God, **knowing Himself from all eternity** brings forth the knowledge of Himself, His own image. This was not a mere thought, as our knowledge of ourselves would be, but a Living Person, **of the same substance** and one with the Father. *This is God the Son.* Thus the Father 'begets' the Son, the Divine Word, the Wisdom of the Father....

"2. God the Father, seeing His own Image in the Son, loves the Son; and God the Son loves the Father from all eternity. **Each loves the other**, because each sees in the other the Infinity of the Godhead, the beauty of Divinity, the Supreme Truth of God. The two Persons loving each other do not just have a thought, as human beings would have, but **from Their mutual love is breathed forth, as it were, a Living Person, one with Them, and of Their own substance. This is God the Holy Ghost.** Thus the Holy Ghost, the Spirit of Love, 'proceeds' from the Father and the Son....

"3. But we are *not to suppose* that once God the Father begot the Son and now no longer does so, nor that once the love of the Father and the Son for each other breathed forth the Holy Ghost, but now no longer does. These truths are eternal, everlasting.

"God the Father **eternally knows Himself, and continues to know Himself**, and thus continues to bring forth the Son. **God the Father and God the Son continue to love each other, and their delight in each other continues to bring forth the Spirit of Love, God the Holy Ghost**. In a similar way, fire has light and color. As long as there is fire, it continues to produce light.

454

As long as there is fire with light, there is produced color. But all three exist at one and the same time."

Since we know from inspiration that God the Father, God the Son and God the Holy Spirit are all eternal and "self-existent", this fact precludes them from ever being "solitary" for they have always existed in unison. **Being "self-existent" precludes them from 'bringing forth' each other.** A single "God essence" would, conceptually, have been "single" prior to manifesting itself in different "hypostases", or "modalities", or falsely defined "persons", so how could He have been "love" whilst still single? This whole circular, self-defeating argument of both Gulley and his Catholic counterpart is exploded by their own misconception of the 'one'ness of God. On the other hand, **mutual love is perfectly in tune with the Biblical, inspired presentation of a Heavenly Trio operating as a unit in perfect harmony.**

Under the subtitle "Hints of the Trinity in the Old Testament", Gulley, a research professor in Systematic Theology at Southern University, asserts: **"Scripture often indicates that God is more than one.** Plurality is indicated in the following: In creation "God said [singular], 'Let us [plural] make man in our image'" (Gen 1:26). And he proceeds to quote Gen. 11:7 and Isa. 6:8 which are other verses of scripture where there is internal dialogue between Members of the Godhead. What is amazing is that Gulley recognizes that God, speaking in Gen. 1:26, is 'singular', and that God is speaking to another Member of the Godhead, which immediately indicates that more than one Divine Person is present; in other, words, the Godhead has a plurality of Members who cannot be consubstantial since they are each **"self-existent"**.

What Gulley doesn't tell his readership is that the word for "God" in Gen. 1:26 is 'Elohiym' (#430 in Strong's), which means Gods (plural) in the ordinary sense. Therefore, for Gulley to claim that "God" is singular in Gen. 1:26 and in Gen. 11:7 and Isa. 6:8 is a cause for red flags to rise over his exegesis, especially considering that Trinitarians invariably refer to the Shemmah in Deut. 6:4 "the Lord our God is one Lord," where the central word "God" is also 'Elohiym' and they, the Trinitarians, then claim that the **plural** term, consequently denotes a Trinity; a "Triune God". (See Chapter 23 on the "Shemmah")

In a previous lesson we have plainly demonstrated – from inspiration and not from speculation – that God who said, "Whom shall **I** send? And who will go for **us**?" (Isa. 6:8) was the Father. God's messenger tells us:

The Youth's Instructor, June 21, 1900 par. 2:

455

> "...and when God asked, "Whom shall I send?" he *[Christ]*
> could reply, "Here am I; send me." He could pledge himself to
> become man's surety; ..."

To play fast and loose with the "ordinary sense" plurality of the word
"Elohiym" confuses and confounds the point that Gulley is trying to make.
The truth is that God (Elohiym) the Father, the "Supreme Ruler" of the
universe (#430 in Strong's: "...but spec. used...of **the Supreme God**; ..."
is the 'Sender' who 'sends' Jesus into His incarnational role as our Saviour.
When the Father asks, "...who will go for us?" He is speaking to the Holy
Spirit: the Third Person of the Godhead and to Christ, and so, of course
"us" is plural. **None** of this even begins to imply a one-in-three Trinity but
plainly portrays a three Person Godhead.

"God in Three Persons – Blessed Trinity" an article by Jo Ann Davidson
in *Adventist World*, March 2011, page 28-29

It is noteworthy that Davidson has taken the title for her article from
Hymn #73 of the new 1985 <u>Seventh-day Adventist Hymnal</u> which is
discussed on pages ... of this book. The pioneers also sang "Holy, Holy
Holy", but shied away from Trinitarian Reginald Heber's closing words and
inserted "Perfect in power, in love and purity." The new Adventist hymnal
has undergone a complete about face and has reinserted the words Davidson
has chosen to employ as her title for this article

Davidson states in her article: "Belief in **a God of three Persons** is one
of the most demanding Biblical teachings."

The Bible, however, does not teach any such thing. The Biblical
evidence discloses three separate and distinct Beings, each designated by
the title "God" and all three comprising the Unit Biblically termed the
"Godhead" with one Member of the Godhead being referred to as the "Most
High God": He being the "God" of both His equal Fellows and of all other
lesser "gods" (Ps. 82:1-6 and John 10:34); therefore, He is a "God of gods"
the "One God" of the Bible. We have already discussed at length how this
arrangement, undertaken by the Members of the Godhead, in no way
detracts from Christ's divinity or worship worthiness, for to worship Him is
to worship His Father who sent Jesus to represent Himself to sinners.

**Davidson says (ibid page 29) that: "Paul often speaks of the triune
God**, relating salvation to three Persons of the Trinity (2 Cor. 1:21, 22)."

Firstly, Paul NEVER "speaks of the triune God, ..." Secondly, when
we read 2 Cor. 1:20 through 22 we find Paul discussing how "all the

promises of God" find their "yea" and "amen" in Christ (vs. 20) and Paul proceeds to say:

2 Corinthians 1:21, 22:
    21) "Now he [God the Father] which stablisheth us with you in Christ *[by the unction of His Holy Spirit]*, and hath anointed us *[with His Spirit]*, [is] God;
    22)   Who hath also sealed us, and given the earnest of the Spirit in our hearts."

  From these verses we are informed that the "you" and the "us" of vs. 21 can be established **in** Christ by having the indwelling Holy Spirit who is also Christ's Spirit and the Father's Spirit (Rom. 8:9): making redeemed and sanctified sinners "one" (echad) with the Son and therefore with the Father in that they all share <u>one Spirit</u>. The Scriptures are very clear on this point:

1 Corinthians 6:17:
    "But he that is joined unto the Lord is **one spirit**."

1 Corinthians 12:13:
    "For by **one Spirit** are we all baptized into **one body**, whether [we be] Jews or Gentiles, whether [we be] bond or free; and have been all made to drink into **one Spirit**."

Ephesians 2:18:
    "For through him we both have access by **one Spirit unto the Father**."

Ephesians 4:4:
    "[There is] **one body, and one Spirit**, even as ye are called in one hope of your calling;"

Philippians 1:27:
    "Only let your conversation be as it becometh the gospel of Christ: that whether I come and see you, or else be absent, I may hear of your affairs, that ye stand fast in **one spirit, with one mind** striving together for the faith of the gospel;"

  Sharing one Spirit makes separate and distinct individuals, "one in purpose, intent and character" (<u>Ministry of Healing</u> page 422), and thereby fulfilling Christ's prayer for that 'one'ness (John 17:21, 22). All this is possible because of what Jesus has done for **"us"**. He is therefore the "Yea" and "Amen" of this divine transaction. Praise His name!

"Distinct – But Indivisible" an article by Daniel K. Bediako, in the June 2012 issue of *Adventist World*, pages 22-23:

In his article, Bediako concedes that "In the New Testament the Father the Son, and the Holy Spirit are presented as **distinct persons**" but, as a staunch Trinitarian, he proceeds, further on in the article, to state that:

> "There is a Trinitarian formula, *[in the New Testament (?)]* which presents the Godhead as consisting of three **coequal** and **coeternal** persons who, while distinct, **are an undivided** unity."

In truth, the Members of the Godhead **are equal NOT** "coequal" and **NOT** "coeternal" but are each **ETERNAL**: That fact is what makes them "distinct". Both in his title and in his article Bediako stresses the indivisibility of the Trinity. As we have seen before, and now stress once more, it was **separation from** His Father that caused the propitiatory death of our Saviour. Trinitarianism, and its concomitant "consubstantiality" negates, not only Christ's substitutionary "penalty" death on our behalf, but also totally undermines His High Priestly ministry in the Most Holy Place of the Heavenly Sanctuary. Our pioneers saw, and we reconfirm, that it is absurd for one "hypostasis" of an **indivisible** Trinitarian "substance" to intercede with another "hypostasis" of the same **indivisible** "substance". For confirmation we repeat the pioneer, J. N. Loughborough's concise expression of the early Adventist belief on this issue:

Loughborough, *Review and Herald*, Volume 18, page 184, 1861:

> "To believe that doctrine *[the Trinity doctrine]* when reading the Scriptures, we must believe that God **sent Himself** into the world, died to recover the world to Himself, **raised Himself** from the dead, **ascended to Himself** in Heaven, **pleads before Himself** in heaven to reconcile the world to Himself, and **is the only Mediator between man and Himself...**"

Bediako goes on to quote Matthew 28:19: "Go therefore and make disciples of all nations, baptizing them in the name of the Father and the Son and the Holy Spirit." And he then goes on to expound: "Note that baptism takes place not in the names but in the **name** of the Father, the Son, and the Holy Spirit." He then claims that:

> "This implies *[?]* that while the persons of the Godhead are **distinct**, they are **indissolubly united in essence and nature:** 'Therefore it is evident that **in God's substance** there are **three persons, in which the one God is recognized.**'"

Bediako has just quoted Ekkehardt Mueller, another Adventist theologian, as a confirmation of his view.

It is difficult to understand how theologians, can conceivably be the framers of Adventist beliefs, to the absolute contradiction of those beliefs held and published (1872), after careful, prayerful, study by Adventist founders such as James White and his wife.

The Biblical truth on the other hand, is clear and simple: the "name", given in Scripture, for that Holy Unit comprised of three separate and distinct Beings, whose 'one'ness is described by God's messenger in Ministry of Healing page 422 and in the 17th Chapter of John vs. 21 and 22, is the "Godhead": a term that in **NO WAY** equates to the **consubstantiality**, or, as Bediako calls it, **'indissolubility'** of the 'Trinity'. Always bear in mind that the Godhead was **sundered**. It was **"separation"** from His Father that cost the Divine Life of Jesus; One equal with the Law of the Godhead; One who had never previously, in all eternity, been separated from His Father. Truly, both Jesus, who came to "show us the Father", and the Holy Spirit, who reveals the Father and the Son through the inspired Word and through His personal engagement with the human mind, both reveal to us the "Most High God", the "God of gods", the "only true God" of John 17:3. That was and is their mission: To make known the only true God and Jesus Christ whom He *[the Father]* has sent" because He *[the Father]* "so loved the world".

Bediako goes on to say:

> "Because **God is one in three**, the **terms** Father, Son, and Holy Spirit may best be understood in terms of function *[as in 'modalities' or 'hypostases'?]* as opposed to relation."

The Bible on the other hand, clearly employs the terms – Father and Son to describe a **relationship**, for Jesus is described as "…the only Begotten of the Father" John 1:14. (this whole concept is fully described in Chapter 12 of this book). The Holy Spirit is referred to, in Scripture, as "the Spirit of God" and the "Spirit of Christ": He inhabits both and proceeds from both.

The description is relational. Their **functions** in the plan of salvation are clear from Scripture: The Father is the Sustainer of all things and the One who "so loved the world" and is the 'Sender'; Jesus is our Redeemer and Mediator, our Saviour **through whom the Father is reconciling the world unto Himself**; and the Holy Spirit is the regenerating Agent and Guide, administering divine power and grace and guidance to sinners in search of salvation.

For Bediako to claim that "we worship **one God who reveals Himself in and consists of three distinct persons who participate in one substance** and coexist in unity." is pure consubstantial Trinitarianism at its worst; and then to claim that "this doctrine is Biblical" is a contradiction of all the Biblical, inspired and historical evidence. Rome herself, the formulator of this heresy, acknowledges that there is NO Biblical support for this doctrine formulated at the Council of Nicea AD 325 (4th Century after Christ, see page 14 of this book). The next book we will look at is:

"The God many Christians claim to know is not the God of the Bible. It's time we got reacquainted with OUR AWESOME GOD. A Refresher Course," by Reinder Bruinsma and published by Pacific Press Publishing Association: (page 464)

The Adventist theologian, Reinder Bruinsma declares a powerful truism in the lengthy title to his above mentioned book. Regrettably Bruinsma does not present the "God of the Bible" but, lamentably, that of Rome. He declares on page 91 of his book: "It is a basic *[to the Church of Rome]* Christian *[?]* doctrine that **God is a Trinity of three persons having one substance."**

Bruinsma goes on to say:
"The doctrine of the Trinity tells us that the one and only true Christian God is in some mysterious way **a oneness, but in a three-ness** *[this man is emulating Tertullian in word invention]* of **different ways** in which **He** relates to His creatures. It also tells us that this **three-ness never compromised the basic oneness of His divine being."**

Whew! The cowboys called that 'double talk'!
On page 94 of his book, Bruinsma concedes that:

460

"'The doctrine of the Trinity did not receive its **traditional** shape until the fourth and fifth centuries.'...The **creeds** from the Council of Nicea (325) and the Council of Chalcedon (451) finally formulated the doctrine of Christ that was to be accepted by the vast majority of Christian churches."

What a red flag to any true believer! The foundational doctrine of all of the Church of Rome's doctrinal aberrations was established at Nicea (325). The false teaching on the nature of Christ (now also established in Adventism and popularly known as the 'New Theology') established at Chalcedon (451), incidentally, is based on the preposterous notion that Christ was consubstantial with the Father – implying that Christ's indivisible 'Godhead' nature came to dwell among men in an "immaculate" nature which was quite unlike the "Seed of Abraham" or the "Seed of David" described in the Bible. Of course the term "immaculate" was first only applied to Mary, Christ's mother; for Rome had to invent the doctrine of the "Immaculate Conception" of Mary, in order to account for her not passing on to Christ the "infirmities" of the fallen human condition. Christ's consubstantial indivisibility from the one God "essence" would have instantly consumed both Mary, the recipient of the divine "Seed", and any "fallen" humanity that she could have passed on to Christ, had she not been 'immaculated'.

How, oh how, people of God, can we get so caught in the convoluted coils of such corruption and accept the discordant councils of a corrupt church system. The determinations of the Council of Chalcedon were openly rejected by the ancient eastern churches of Egypt, Syria, Armenia and Assyria – some of them still Sabbath keepers at that time. Apostasy comes principally from the western church. Truer Christianity was longer preserved in the east, until hounded down and subjugated by Rome. (The reader is strongly urged to read Truth Triumphant by B. G. Wilkinson on this history.)

On page 95 of his book, Bruinsma proposes, concerning God's messenger:

"Though apparently still reluctant to actually use the term "trinity", Ellen G. White expressed in 1905 what by then had become accepted Adventist teaching: 'There are three living person's in the heavenly trio... the Father, the Son and the Holy Spirit.'" *[Evangelism, page 615.1]*

461

To imply that God's messenger was 'reluctantly' supporting a concept described by the term 'Trinity' which term she still avoided now that the church (leadership?) had supposedly come to accept the teaching described by that term at that early date, is to really relegate her role to that of following leadership's expounding of 'truth'. What does that imply regarding the Holy Spirit's guidance of her thoughts and expressions? Of course, God's messenger described the "Heavenly Trio", the Godhead. She was demonstrably correcting those leaders and church members who still thought that the Holy Spirit was simply an emanation of power from Christ and from the Father (See Chapter's. 2, 4 and 7 of this book)

Brunsma says on page 97 of his book:

> "…in faith I accept the paradox of the Trinity. God is one. **He** is one in "three persons", yet **He** is one." *[Lower down, on the same page, he says]* "…Father, Son and Holy Spirit – somehow **they** are separate, yet inseparable. Somehow **they** are three, and yet **they** are one." *[This man needs to read what God has revealed concerning the "oneness" of the Godhead in Ministry of Healing page 422 and in the book of John 17:21, 22. What Brunsma has just expressed demonstrates the confusion inherent in Trinitarianism.]*

What he has written is confusion! He goes on to add:

> "…we must remember that we know about God only what He has decided to reveal to us *[How we pray, and would hope, that this man would stay by that which God has "decided to reveal to us" and not what was concocted by an apostate church system in the 4th and 5th centuries after Christ]*. And the truth is that God has, over time, revealed **Himself** to us **as Father, as Son, and as Holy Spirit."** *[The truth is that the Father has revealed Himself to us, from whom sin has brought a separation, **through** His Son and **through** the Holy Spirit who inspired holy men of old to pen and portray the great love of the Father toward us.]*

In his summing up, on page 101 of his book, Bruinsma presents his conclusions as follows:

> "We have not been able to solve the mystery of the Trinity *[no one can! It is confusion, the foundation stone of Babylon!]*. But in faith we can accept its glorious truth *[?]* – God is one.

462

There is no other God beside Him. He comes to us in His magnificent three-ness being – Father, Son, and Holy Spirit. This three-in-one God is all we need."

Oh, that this man would but go and read what the Bible – not an ecumenical council – has to say about what we really need. **Especially as told us in John 17:3 and vs. 20-22.**
God's messenger gives us the guidance:

Great Controversy, page 595.1:
"But God will have a people upon the earth to maintain the Bible, and **the Bible only, as the standard of all doctrines**, and the basis of all reforms. The opinions of learned men, the deductions of science, **the creeds or decisions of ecclesiastical councils**, as numerous and discordant as are the churches which they represent, **the voice of the majority**,-- not one or all of these should be regarded as evidence for or against any point of religious faith. **Before accepting any doctrine or precept, we should demand a plain "Thus saith the Lord" in its support**."

It is not only Conference theologians who subscribe to and propagate Catholic style Trinitarianism. This phenomenon is also to be found among some Historic Adventists. The Standish Brothers, Vance Ferrel, and others have consistently opposed Trinitarianism, while many others do not have clear cut ideas on this topic. Bruce Bivens' book entitled "Are we missing something here? The Godhead, the Holy Spirit, and the 'Eternal Price' paid for our Salvation", opposes Trinitarianism but contains many aberrations which go beyond the scope of this book. However, we propose to examine the work of one 'Historic' Adventist writer who comes out squarely on the side of classic Trinitarianism.
Gordon Anderson has published his eleven page booklet **"The Trinity" in the light of Vance Ferrel's doctrine of 'The Godhead'. "What Do Seventh-day Adventists Believe?"**
In his introduction, Anderson states as follows:

"The Bible does not contain the word 'trinity.' For this reason, those who oppose this teaching say that we must reject the doctrine of the trinity. **It's interesting that the Bible does not contain the word 'millennium' and yet many of the people who reject the Trinity for this reason are happy to use** the word 'millennium' to describe the 1000 years of Revelation 20."

This trite observation by Anderson completely ignores the fact that God's inspired messenger employed the term "millennium" in all of the instances referenced below. However, she, who came out of the Trinitarian Methodist Church, consistently and deliberately avoided ever employing that, God-disparaging term 'Trinity'. On the other hand, the term "millennium" is frequently used in the 'Spirit of Prophecy' books, for example: DA 633; FE 357; GW 92, 166, 279; GC (1888) 321, 379, 384, 588; LDE 136, 237; Life Sketches of James and Ellen White 137, 166, 379; Life Sketches of E.G. White 21, 44; Manuscript Releases: 2 MR 208 and 21 MR 325.

I believe that the above given, inspired usage of the term "millennium" is justification enough for God's denominated people to use that term in good conscience. I believe also, that the careful avoidance of using the term "Trinity" by God's messenger should inspire all to diligently delve into the reasons why God inspired His handmaid to assiduously shun so popular and "acceptable" a term.

On page 3 of his booklet, Anderson poses his following observation regarding the denominational pioneers and their views on the nature of God:

"They were probably aware that there were differences of opinion on the nature of God but they didn't at that time see how one's views on the nature of God affected other things that you believe."

Really? Is that a true or even justifiable observation? As we have already noted in study #2 and elsewhere in this book; the pioneers were **VERY** aware of the implications of a wrong view of the Godhead and the 'nature of God'. The following references should serve to correct any false impression, given by Anderson, that the pioneers were unaware that variant views on the 'nature of God' leave unaffected one's views on other issues of salvation:

The following references can be found quoted on the designated pages of this book.

Page
27   J. S. White, The Day Star, January 24, 1846
21   Joseph Bates, Past and Present Experience pages 187, 188;

1848

28   J. S. White, Review and Herald, September 12, 1854

32   J. M. Stephenson, Review and Herald (editor - J. S. White), November 21, 1854

131   J. S. White, Review and Herald, February 7, 1856

23   Merrit E Cornell, Facts for the Times, page 76; 1858

29   J. S. White, Life Incidents, page 343; 1868

32   J. S. White, "Mutual Obligation", Review and Herald, June 13, 1871

36   J. N. Andrews, Review and Herald, January 27, 1874

29   J. S. White, Review and Herald, November 29, 1877

30   J. S. White, Bible Adventism pages 41, 48, 49

43   J. H. Waggoner, The Atonement in the Light of Nature and Revelation pages 164, 165, 168, 169; 1884

47   Judson Sylvaneous Washburn (1863-1955), Letter written in 1939

And so we must enquire of Brother Anderson, "How readest thou?"

In addition, and also found on page 3 of his pamphlet, Anderson writes concerning Jones and Waggoner and their defense of the 1888 doctrine of Righteousness By Faith, with that doctrine's innate imperative to be predicated on Christ's full divinity:

> "So Jones and Waggoner decided to publish some literature to make this teaching clear.   In 1892 they circulated a tract entitled 'The Bible Doctrine of the Trinity.'"

This article was **borrowed** by Jones and Waggoner from **a non-Adventist theologian**, the Reverend Samuel T. Spear, DD; whose original article was titled "The Subordination of Christ".   The main thrust of the article by Spear was to establish the full divinity of Jesus which is, of course, fundamental to grasping the full authority and foundation of that precious doctrine: "Righteousness by Faith".   This is the doctrine rejected and withstood by the Conference leadership in 1888; especially those swayed by the false "Arian" notion that Christ had a beginning and was, therefore, a "lesser" divine Being than the Father.   Furthermore, the proposition that the Holy Spirit was simply an emanation of God's power also militated against the truth that, as a fully divine Member of the Godhead, He could actually 'dwell' in the body temple of a redeemed sinner and inspire and empower them to reflect Christ fully, while Christ's perfect obedience in humanity and His penalty paying blood could and

465

would cover their former profligacy and sin, and any future, repented of stumbling.

Did Jones and Waggoner have clearly and positively held beliefs on the validity of the Trinity doctrine? I don't think so, for they never penned them. Notice the following statements from Jones in his evaluation of the deliberations at the Council of Nicea:

> The Two Republics, by A. T. Jones, 1891 page 334:
> "...it was an attempt of the finite to measure, to analyze, and even to dissect, the Infinite. It was an attempt to make the human superior to the divine. God is infinite. No finite mind can comprehend him as he actually is. Christ is the Word – the expression of the thought – of God; and none but he knows the depth of the meaning of that Word. 'He had a name written that no man knew but he himself; ... and his name is called The Word of God." Rev. xix, 12, 13. Neither the nature nor the relationship of the Father and the Son can ever be measured by the mind of man. 'No man knoweth the Son but the Father, neither knoweth any man the Father save the Son and he to whomsoever the Son will reveal him." Matt. xi, 27. This revelation of the Father by the Son cannot be complete in this world. It will require the eternal ages for man to understand 'the exceeding riches of his grace in his kindness toward us through Christ Jesus.' Eph. i, 7. Therefore, no man's conception of God can ever be fixed as the true conception of god. God will still be infinitely beyond the broadest comprehension that the mind of man can measure. **The true conception of God can be attained only through 'the Spirit of revelation in the knowledge of Him.'** Eph. i, 17. *[Not by corrupt human Councils]*. Therefore the only thing for men to do to find out the Almighty to perfection, is, by true faith in Jesus Christ, to receive the abiding presence of this Spirit of revelation, and then quietly and joyfully wait for the eternal ages to reveal 'the depth of the riches both of the wisdom and the knowledge of God.'"

However, Jones did correctly perceive the crux of the dispute at Nicea to be over "consubstantiality":

> Ibid, page 334:
> **"Whether the Son of God therefore, is of the same substance or only of like substance, with the Father, was the**

466

question in dispute. The controversy was carried on in Greek, and as expressed in Greek **the whole question turned upon a single letter. The word which expressed Alexander's belief, is Homoousion** *[one indivisible substance]*. **The word which expressed the belief of Arius, is Homoiousion** *[similar substance]*."

Throughout his above mentioned book, Jones records the base motivations and chicanery of the Alexandrian/Athenasian Catholic party and the dubious evolution of the Trinity doctrine that finally prevailed. Scripture possess the question:

Matthew 7:16:
"Ye shall know them by their fruits. Do men gather grapes of thorns, or figs of thistles?"

The answer should be obvious!
In fairness to Anderson, it is true that in Jones' record of the events and the creed evolved at Nicea, the term "Trinity" was employed by both parties to the debate, despite the opposing hypotheses behind each party's doctrines. Even Constantine was confused enough about the issues at stake as to perceive no distinction between the Greek words "Homoousious" (same indivisible substance) "Homoiousious" (like substance):

Ibid, page 350:
"Eusebius of Caesarea, the panegyrist and one of the counselors of Constantine, took a whole day to 'deliberate.' *[On whether to go along with the Nicean creed or not]* In his deliberation **he consulted the emperor, <u>who so explained the term Homoousion that it could be understood as Homoiousion</u>. He 'declared that the word, <u>as he understood it,</u> involved no such material unity of the persons of the God-head as Eusebius feared might be deduced from it.'** -- Stanley.23 In this sense, therefore, Eusebius adopted the test, and subscribed to the creed."

So a presiding 'semi-pagan', and decidedly confused, emperor decided the issues of the day. This is "confusion" otherwise known as "Babylon" Great Controversy page 383.1)
One thing is very clear from the history of this infamous council: God had no part in its ultimate declarations and the concluding connotations that

would, ever after, be appended to the term "Trinity". It is no wonder therefore, that God's messenger so carefully avoided that word to describe the Godhead – under inspiration from God! And so we find that Anderson's deployment of Jones and Waggoner's names to bolster the impression that Trinitarianism is a valid and acceptable concept for God' denominated people to embrace is without foundation. A careful reading of A.T. Jones' "The Two Republics" will confront the reader with a carefully documented history of that turbulent, manipulated, ambition ridden Council of confrontation, which had all the hallmarks of hell.

One may then ask, 'What about E. J. Waggoner? Perhaps he was Trinitarian.' To answer we may allow Waggoner to speak for himself:

> *The Present Truth* (UK) February 6, 1902, page 83.12:
>
> "**You ask what we teach about the Trinity. Inasmuch as we find no such expression in the Scriptures, we do not teach anything about it**. But as to the Being of God, - Divinity as revealed in the Father, the Word (the Son), and the Holy Spirit, **we believe and teach just what the Bible says, and nothing else**. No man can by searching find out God. No creature can understand the Almighty to perfection. The finite mind cannot comprehend infinity. Therefore, in discussions about the Trinity, about **the nature of God** *[describing Him as an 'essence']*, Christ, and the Holy Spirit, are manifestations of gross presumption."

In answer to a direct question from a reader Waggoner answered as follows:

> *The Present Truth* (UK) July 30, 1903, page 483.1 and 2:
>
> "7. Do you believe in the Trinity?
>
> "**If I knew what you meant by the term, I might tell you; but from the days of Athanasius until now all discussion about the Trinity has been an attempt to define the indefinable and the incomprehensible.** Thousands have been put to death for not professing belief in a formula which even its professors could not comprehend, nor state in terms that anybody else could comprehend. The Scriptures reveal "One God and Father of all," our Lord Jesus Christ, who is the brightness of the Father's glory, and "the eternal Spirit" through whom Christ offered Himself and was raised from the dead; and **we do not profess any knowledge of them beyond what the Scriptures**

468

give us. **In teaching and preaching the Gospel <u>we always confine ourselves strictly to Scripture terms and language; those who manufacture terms must be looked to for definitions of them</u>**. It is attest not to presume to define what the Bible has not defined, nor to attempt to explain infinity."

Responding to an article in the Christian Union, comparing, among other things, the Trinity to the Hindu Triad, Waggoner commented as follows:

Signs of the Times, December 14, 1888, page 757.3 and 4:
"...the Christian Union offers the following remarks, **which we heartily indorse, because they are in harmony with the Scriptures**:
""…. have substituted for an **ignorant belief in a Hindu Triad a belief nearly as ignorant in** *[their concept of God as expressed in]* **the Christian Trinity**....""

From the above, the only honest conclusion must be that Waggoner and Jones cannot be presented as endorsement for Trinitarianism.

In a letter to the "Mid America Sisterhood of Churches", Gordon Anderson clarified his own stand and wrote as follows:

"**God has chosen to manifest <u>Himself</u>** *[one indivisible entity]* **to mankind <u>in Three Persons</u>**: our Father in heaven, the Lord Jesus Christ our Saviour, and the Holy Spirit our Comforter."

I perceive no real difference between Anderson's postulation and that of the Papacy: that the modalities of the Father, the Son, and the Holy Spirit are three manifestations of the one indivisible "God" "essence" or "substance". This sounds like classical Trinitarianism to me. This is "speculation beyond what Scripture has revealed." Even Rome acknowledges that the doctrine of the Trinity is not to be found in the Scriptures.

In Israel's time 'some' chose to call God "Baal". That did not make their choice right. God's messenger and her husband **deliberately** chose not to employ a term which has powerful and disparaging connotations against God. Both the terms "Godhead" and "Heavenly Trio" are not synonyms for the word "Trinity". As for the term "Trinity" who's earliest recorded "Christian" usage of that term was by Theophilus of Antioch (died

185 AD). Please refer to the Appendices D and E in the back of this boo which demonstrates, beyond dispute, that the term's concept is rooted in th philosophies of Plato, Aristotle, etc. and was and is a distinctly pagan, non Christian term which, along with a host of other pagan ideas, practices, an dogmas was adopted into "Catholic Christianity." For Anderson t categorically state that "neither the word **nor the concept** was found in an non-Christian religion before Theophilus invented the term," is a patentl false declaration. (See Appendix M)

Anderson is correct, however, in asserting that "provided we remai firmly within the truths revealed in God's Word, we shall be safe."

I know that Anderson is gravely concerned about what appears to him t be the promotion of "Tri-theism". The Bible reveals God the Father, Go the Son, and God the Holy Spirit; and that these three are one. God' messenger clarifies that "one"-ness as being "one in mind, purpose, an intent;" and that we can be "one" with Them even as they "are one." Th "one"-ness is effected by the Holy Spirit. The Holy Spirit who "searche out he deep things of the mind of God; the Holy Spirit who dwells in Chris He is the Spirit of God and the Spirit of Christ. He can dwell in us an make us 'one'.

Psalm 82:6 declare that God's children are "gods" (lower case). Jesu quoted these words in His own defense (John 10:33-36), thereby adding Hi endorsement to the concept. In Psalms 82:1 we are told that "He judget among the gods." So we see from the Scriptures that there are indeed "god many" (1Cor. 8:5). However Jesus distinctly declares His Father to be Hi God and plainly states that His Father is greater than He (John 20:17; 14:28 Selected Messages Book 1, page 263).

The Scriptures also reveal that God the Father is a "God of gods", "God of the living and not of the dead;" therefore not a God over idol which "are no gods" (Jer. 16:20) and have no life, but that He is Christ' God, the Holy Spirit's God, (who worshipfully obeys and carries out Hi bidding) and the God of all His redeemed children whom **He** calls god That is why John 17:3 declares Him to be "**the only true God**" whom w cannot "know" except through Jesus whom He has sent. To love, worshi and obey Christ Jesus is to love, worship and obey His Father, Whom H declares unto us, Whose character He portrays to us and of Whose Perso He is the express image. He shows us the Father. He points us to th Father: the **monotheistic** "one God" of the Scriptures Whom the whol world has wandered away from, as they, and a host of worldly Adventist wander after the beast.

Some may "feel" that this is not an important issue! Such are in dire opposition to John 17:3 "And this is life eternal, that they might know the

470

he only true God, and Jesus Christ, whom thou hast sent." "The times of gnorance God winked at" Acts 17:30, but as we near the end and knowledge (particularly knowledge of God and His Word) shall be ncreased;" "all truth", as revealed by the Holy Spirit, will become alvational for "None but those who have fortified the mind with the **truths f the Bible** will stand through the last great conflict." (Great Controversy, age 593.2)

Chapter 39

WHOM DO WE WORSHIP: THE GOD OF THE FIRST DAY OR THE GOD OF THE SABBATH?

**"It is as easy to make an idol of false doctrines and theories ...
By misrepresenting the attributes of God,
Satan leads men to conceive of Him in a false character."**
Great Controversy, *583*

A NEW GOD?

Could it be that many Seventh-day Adventists are ignorantly worshipping the same God that they are told not to worship in the third angel's message—the god of the beast power? Or are we just calling the true Godhead by the name of a false god? What 'God' are we worshipping today? Could modern Israel, like Israel of old, be worshipping a false god?

> **1 Kings 18:21:**
> **"How long halt ye between two opinions? If the LORD *be* God, follow him: but if Baal, *then* follow him."**

Are these words of Elijah applicable today?

THE GODHEAD

"Godhead" is the term used in the NT that describes the Father, Son and Holy Spirit. The word for **"God"** in the OT Hebrew is "Elohim". It conventionally, means "Gods" in the plural, but can also refer to the **supreme God** (See Chapter 23 of this book). In the Scriptures that follow the Father is speaking with His Fellows and He calls the collective Godhead **"Us"**:

> **Gen. 1:26:**
> **"And God said, Let <u>us</u> make man in our image, after our likeness."**

> **Gen. 11:7:**

"Go to, let <u>us</u> go down, and there confound their language, that they may not understand one another's speech."

Isaiah 6:8:
"Also I heard the voice of the Lord, saying, Whom shall I send, and who will go for <u>us</u>?"

These verses show that the Godhead consists of more than one divine Being. There is a unity in the Godhead. The Father, Son, and Holy Spirit work together for our salvation in perfect harmony.

THE FATHER, SON, AND HOLY SPIRIT ARE EACH ETERNAL

The Bible tells us that the Father, Son, and Holy Spirit are each eternal Beings:

THE FATHER:

Psalms 106:48:
"Blessed be the LORD God of Israel from <u>everlasting to everlasting</u>: and let all the people say, Amen."

1Timothy 1:17:
"Now unto the King <u>eternal</u>, immortal, invisible, the only wise God, be honor and glory for ever and ever. Amen."

These verses tell us that God the Father is Eternal. If He is eternal, then He has no beginning, no end.

THE SON:

Micah 5:2:
"But thou, Bethlehem Ephratah, though thou be little among the thousands of Judah, yet out of thee shall he come forth unto me that is to be ruler in Israel; whose goings forth have been from of old, <u>from everlasting</u>."

John 1:1, 2, 14:
1) "In the beginning was the Word, and the Word was with God, and <u>the Word was God</u>.
2) The same was in the beginning with God.

473

14)   And the Word was made flesh, and dwelt among us, (and we beheld his glory, the glory as of the only begotten of the Father,) full of grace and truth."

Matthew 1:23:
"Behold, a virgin shall be with child, and shall bring forth a son, and they shall call his name Emmanuel, which being interpreted is, <u>God with us</u>."

These Scriptures show us that Jesus is God. Being God Jesus is Eternal. If He is eternal, then He has no beginning, no end.

THE HOLY SPIRIT:

Acts 5:3, 4:
3) "But Peter said, Ananias, why hath Satan filled thine heart to lie <u>to the HolyGhost</u>, and to keep back *part* of the price of the land?
4) ... Why hast thou conceived this thing in thine heart? thou hast ot lied unto men, but <u>unto God</u>."

Hebrews 9:14:
"How much more shall the blood of Christ, who through the <u>eternal Spirit</u> offered himself   without spot   to   God, purge your conscience from dead works to serve the living God?"

These verses tell us that the Holy Spirit is Eternal. If He is eternal, then He has no beginning, no end.

Thus, the Godhead is composed of three distinct eternal (no beginning, no end) Beings: The Father, The Son, and The Holy Spirit.

THE GODHEAD IS COMPOSED OF THREE SEPARATE, DISTINCT, ETERNAL BEINGS

Matthew 3:16, 17:
"And <u>Jesus</u>, when he was baptized, went up straightway out of the water: and, lo, the heavens were opened unto him, and he saw the <u>Spirit of God</u> descending like a dove, and lighting upon him: And lo <u>a voice from heaven</u> (the Father), saying, This is my beloved Son, in whom I am well pleased."

474

Here we see Jesus on the Earth itself, the Holy Spirit in the sky above the earth, and the Father in Heaven above both the earth and sky. The Bible shows us three distinct Beings.

1 Corinthians 12:4-6:
"Now there are diversities of gifts, but the same <u>Spirit</u>. And there are differences of administrations, but the same <u>Lord</u>. And there are diversities of operations, but it is the same <u>God</u> which worketh all in all."

According to their office, the Father does things that the Son does not do, and vice versa. The Holy Spirit does things that neither the Father nor the Son do. Yet all three are in "one accord" and we need all three for our salvation.

Isaiah 48:16:
"Come ye near unto me, hear ye this; I have not spoken in secret from the beginning; from the time that it was, there *am* I: and now the <u>Lord GOD</u>, and his <u>Spirit</u>, hath sent <u>Me</u>."

Here the Heavenly Trio is clearly seen in the Old Testament. But they are more clearly seen in the NT as the next four verses show:

2 Corinthians 13:14:
"The grace of the <u>Lord Jesus Christ</u>, and the love of <u>God</u>, and the communion of the <u>Holy Ghost</u>, be with you all. Amen."

1 Peter 1:2:
"Elect according to the foreknowledge of <u>God the Father</u>, through sanctification of the <u>Spirit</u>, unto obedience and sprinkling of the blood of <u>Jesus Christ</u>: Grace unto you, and peace, be multiplied."

Revelation 1:4, 5:
4) "Grace be unto you, and peace, from <u>him which is, and which was, and which is to come</u> (the Father); and from <u>the seven Spirits</u> (the Holy Spirit) which are before his throne;

5)   And from <u>Jesus Christ</u>, who is the faithful witness, and the first begotten of the dead, and the prince of the kings of the earth."

Matthew 28:19:
"Go ye therefore, and teach all nations, baptizing them in the name of the <u>Father</u>, and of the <u>Son</u>, and of the <u>Holy Ghost</u>."

The Godhead is composed of three separate, DISTINCT, eternal Beings

HEAVENLY TRIO SYMBOLIZED BY LINTEL AND TWO DOORPOSTS AT PASSOVER

Exodus 12:22:
"And ye shall take a bunch of hyssop, and dip it in the blood that is in the bason, **and strike the lintel and the two side posts** with the blood that is in the bason; and none of you shall go out at the door of his house until the morning."

Note: **God the Father, symbolized by the lintel,** maintains th integrity of the Godhead in heaven. He does not come directly in contac with earth, for sinners would be instantly destroyed.

The two side posts represent the Holy Spirit and Michael, the On who is like God, who come down from heaven and come into contac with sinful humanity.

The wooden door represents Christ's humanity after th incarnation. "By a new and living way, which he hath consecrated for us through **the veil, that is to say, his flesh.**" Heb. 10:20. Jesus said, 'I an the door.'" John 10:7, 9.

Note: (See illustration on page 261) The door, representing Christ' humanity, is attached to one of the side posts—not the side post tha represents His divinity, but the side post that represents the Holy Spirit Christ did not rest his weight on his own strength. Christ did not use Hi own divine power whilst on earth. He rested in the power of the Hol Spirit.

THE ONLY TRUE GOD of John 17:3 IS THE FATHER

Exodus 23:20:
"Behold, **I** *[the Father]* **send an Angel** *[Michael]* before thee, to keep thee in the way, and to bring thee into the place which I have prepared." "And this is life eternal, that they might know thee **the only true God, and Jesus Christ whom thou** *[the Father]* **hast sent.**" John 17:3.

476

2 Corinthians 11:31:
"**The God and Father** of our Lord Jesus Christ, which is blessed for evermore..."

Ephesians 1:3:
"Blessed be **the God and Father** of our Lord Jesus Christ, who hath blessed us with all spiritual blessings in heavenly places in Christ."

Ephesians 4:6:
"**One God and Father** of all, who is above all, and through all, and in you all."

1 Peter 1:3:
"Blessed be **the God and Father** of our Lord Jesus Christ..."

1 Timothy 2:5:
"For there is **one God**, and **one mediator between God and men, the man Christ Jesus**."

THE ABOVE IS NOT THE TRINITY

Many will agree with the above statements about the Godhead and think that they are describing the Trinity as well. But, as we have established, the Trinity is a **strangely different concept** about God.

DEFINITION OF THE TRINITY

The term "Trinity" is nowhere found in the Bible. It is an unscriptural term that describes an unscriptural entity. The theological definition of the Trinity was painstakingly arrived at in the creeds formulated by the Roman Catholic Church. The term as defined by the Roman Catholic Church is subscribed to by all Protestant churches who teach the Trinity. Those who developed the term have the sole right to define the term. That is, the SDA Church cannot make the word Trinity mean something different than that which the rest of the world believes it to mean.

The following "correct" definition for the 'Trinity' comes from:

My Catholic Faith, by Bishop Louis Laravoire Morrow, S.T.D., pages 30-33:

(a) God is **One** yet at the same time **He is three Persons.**
*[The word **"Persons" does not mean what we think it means.** See point "c."]*

477

(b)   **One** means one identical nature, essence, or being, which or who **is essentially the Father.** The Oneness is not generic based on likeness, but rather is numeric based on sameness.

(c)   "Three persons" does not mean "persons" as we normally understand the word, but rather, three **expressions, extensions, manifestations,** or **modes** *[otherwise theologically called 'hypostases.']*

(d)   The Father is neither begotten nor does He proceed from anyone else since **He is the Source** from which all else flows.

(e)   **The Person of the Son is begotten from the Father by an eternal generation, a never ending process.**   This is compared to the rays of the sun that are never separated from the sun itself.

(f)   **The Holy Spirit is** not made, nor created, nor begotten, **but proceeds from the Father through the Son.**

(g)   The Three Persons are truly distinct from each other by virtue of **the processes of filiation and spiration,** which however, **does not make them separate Entities with independent self-consciousness.**

(h)   "The whole three Persons are **co-eternal together, and co-equal.**" page31.   **Because the Son and the Spirit are derived from the Father,** the Son and the Holy Spirit are **co-eternal and co-equal** with the Father. *[Notice: these "co"-words are code-words for the Trinity.]*

(i)   "We only say that there are three Persons in one God, that is, three Persons, and one nature or essence." page 33. *[The theological word which explains the Trinity is **consubstantiality** (homoousios), which means more than one person inhabit the **same substance** without division or separation.   God and His nature are synonymous.]*

(j)   "We are **forbidden** by the Catholic Religion to say, there be three Gods or three Lords." page 33. "All are one and the same God." page 32.

This proves the truthfulness of Daniel 11:38 that the Catholic Churc honors a "god of forces"—the Trinity.

ORIGIN OF THE TRINITY CONCEPT

The term and concept of the Trinity, first introduced by theologians i the third century, was catapulted into the limelight at the Council of Nicaea 325 AD. The Emperor Constantine gathered the religious leaders of th

478

world in an effort to achieve unity on the nature of the Godhead. Instead it caused a controversy which has never ceased. We quote now from Truth Triumphant, by SDA theologian Benjamin Wilkinson.

Truth Triumphant, pages 91 and 92:
"Assembling under the sanction of a united church and state, that famous gathering **commanded the submission of believers to new doctrines**.... The burning question of the decades succeeding the Council of Nicaea was how to state the relations of the Three Persons of the Godhead: Father, Son, and Holy Ghost. **The Council had decided, and the papacy had appropriated the decision as its own.** The personalities of the Trinity were not confounded, and the **substance was not divided.** The Roman clergy claimed that Christianity had found in the Greek word *homoousios* (in English, 'consubstantiality') an appropriate term to express this relationship.

"**Then the papal party proceeded to call those who would not subscribe to this teaching, Arians**, while they took to themselves the title of Trinitarians. An **erroneous charge** was circulated that **all** who were called Arians believed that Christ was a created being. This stirred up the indignation of those who were not guilty of the charge.

"It will be interesting ...to examine for a moment this word, this term, which has split many a church and has caused many a sincere Christian to be burned at the stake. In English the word is '**consubstantial,**' connoting that **more than one person inhabit the same substance without division or separation.** The original term in Greek is *homoousios,* from *homos*, meaning '**identical,**' and *ousia*, the word for 'being.'

"However, a great trouble arose, since there are two terms in Greek of historical fame. The first *homos,* meaning '**identical,**' and the second, *homoios,* meaning 'similar' or 'like unto,' had both of them a stormy history. The spelling of these words is much alike. The difference in meaning, when applied to the Godhead, is bewildering to simple-hearted believers. Nevertheless, **those who would think in terms of *homoiousian,* or 'similar,'** instead of *homoousian,* or 'identical,' **were promptly labeled as heretics and Arians by the clergy.**"

The papal view of the Trinity was forced upon the world. The trinity doctrine became the centerpiece of its whole theology. This apostasy occurred during the **Pergamos** church period of Revelation 2—the time of the **"falling away"** that Paul prophesied would come (2 Thess.

2:3)—when the church (Balaam) would join itself with the state (Balac), sell off the truth for worldly fame, power, and riches, and **allow false pagan doctrines to march into the "elevated" church. Thus, the false Trinity concept originated in the very time period that the original great church apostasy was prophesied to take place**.

HOW THE "PERSONS" OF THE TRINITY HAVE DISTINCT "ORIGINS"

Quoting from:

My Catholic Faith, page 31:
"1. This is the simplest way by which the *distinct ORIGIN* of each Divine Person has been explained: God is a spirit, and the first act of a Spirit is to know and understand God, **knowing Himself from all eternity** brings forth the knowledge of Himself, His own image. This was not a mere thought, as our knowledge of ourselves would be, but a Living Person, of the same substance and one with the Father. *This is God the Son.* Thus the Father 'begets' the Son, the Divine Word, the Wisdom of the Father....

"2. God the Father, seeing His own Image in the Son, *loves* the Son; and God the Son loves the Father from all eternity. **Each loves the other**, because each sees in the other the Infinity of the Godhead, the beauty of Divinity, the Supreme Truth of God. The two Persons loving each other do not just have a thought, as human beings would have, but from Their mutual love is breathed forth, as it were, a Living Person, one with Them, and of Their own substance. *This is God the Holy Ghost.* Thus the Holy Ghost, the Spirit of Love, 'proceeds' from the Father and the Son....

"3. But we are *not to suppose* that once God the Father begot the Son and now no longer does so, nor that once the love of the Father and the Son for each other breathed forth the Holy Ghost, but now no longer does. These truths are eternal, everlasting.

"God the Father **eternally knows Himself, and continues to know Himself**, and thus continues to bring forth the Son. **God the Father and God the Son continue to love each other, and their delight in each other continues to bring forth the Spirit of Love, God the Holy Ghost.** In a similar way, fire has light and color. As long as there is fire, it continues to produce light. As long as there is fire with light, there is produced color. But all three exist at one and the same time."

480

This **shocking** description of the origin of the Godhead is even more graphically described in the official Catholic Encyclopedia. Is it any wonder that such a philosophical idol—the Trinity concept—would have the potential to breed so much sexual misconduct within the churches that subscribe to it.

THE TRINITY ILLUSTRATED

The following illustration of the Trinity is taken from _My Catholic Faith,_ by Father Louis LaRavoire Morrow, page 32. It is a very popular catechism among Roman Catholics.

This illustration shows why the concept of the Trinity is false—the Son and Holy Spirit have an "origin". "We speak of three 'Persons' in God because to each belongs something we cannot attribute to any other: His **distinct origin.**" Page 30. Also, since they have the same substance, they are not eternal all by themselves. Instead, they are strangely labeled as "**co-eternal**". "**The whole three persons are co-eternal together.**" page 31.

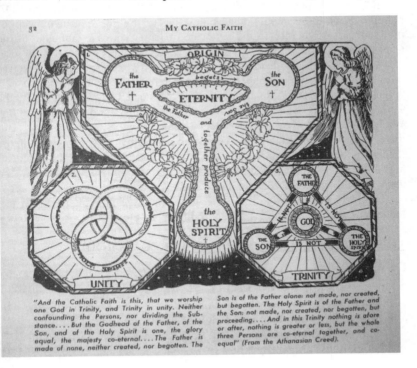

"And the Catholic Faith is this, that we worship one God in Trinity, and Trinity in unity. Neither confounding the Persons, nor dividing the Substance.... But the Godhead of the Father, of the Son, and of the Holy Spirit is one, the glory equal, the majesty co-eternal.... The Father is made of none, neither created, nor begotten. The Son is of the Father alone: not made, nor created, but begotten. The Holy Spirit is of the Father and the Son: not made, nor created, nor begotten, but proceeding.... And in this Trinity nothing is afore or after, nothing is greater or less, but the whole three Persons are co-eternal together, and co-equal" (From the Athanasian Creed).

TRINITY ERRORS

    * Father, Son, and Holy Spirit are all of one substance.

    * The three "Persons" are really not persons, but "manifestations" of one mega-god.

    * The Father, Son, and Holy Spirit are not "united", but "triune."

    * They are not eternal, but "co-eternal".

    * The Son, and Holy Spirit are not "un-derived", and so cannot be described as "self-existent."

    * The one mega-God is a spirit without body or parts, and hence are not entitled to the name Yaweh, which means "self-existent".

LET THERE BE NO CONFUSION

The man-made terms **"Trinity"** and **"triune"** have for long centuries been established to describe a false concept of God. Those who recoil from such a concept should never use the term **"trinity"**, **"triune"**, or **"co-equal,"** or **"co-eternal"** (as is done in point #2 of 28 fundamental SDA beliefs). Such terms should never be used as a label for the true concept of the Godhead—thus mixing the language of Israel with the language of the Canaanites.

When SDA church leaders use these **"Trinity"** code-words to describe the God we worship, Christians from other fallen denominations (see 2nd Angel's message) think that we worship the same God that they do—the Catholic concept. SDA leaders are paid theologians and must know this. We have seen that Gen. Conf. leaders actually do worship the Trinity. But there is confusion among the membership. Many are not aware of the precise theological definition of the "Trinity" and believe that the Godhead and the Trinity are the same concepts. Many strenuously hold onto the term, not knowing that they are unwittingly subscribing to a false God.

The Holy Spirit guided the Bible writers, and Ellen White to never use the terms **"trinity,"** **"triune,"** **"co-equal,"** or **"co-eternal."**

THE GODHEAD IS NOT A ONE-IN-THREE ONE GOD

Hebrews 1:8, 9:

"But unto the Son _he saith_, Thy throne, O God, _is_ for ever and ever: a sceptre of righteousness _is_ the sceptre of thy kingdom. Thou hast loved righteousness, and hated iniquity; therefore God, _even_ thy God, hath anointed thee with the oil of gladness above thy fellows." _[Quoted from Psalm 45:6, 7]._

Here the Father Himself is calling His Son, *"O God."* This passage also declares God the Father to be the God of Jesus Christ as well when it says, *"therefore God, even **thy God**, hath anointed thee with the oil of gladness…"* One God is speaking to the other God, saying that "thy God" has anointed Him, His Son! This passage declares plainly there is more than ONE God in the Godhead thereby disproving the Trinity doctrine.

1 John 5:7:
"For there are three that bear record in heaven, the Father, the Word, and the Holy Ghost: and these three are one."

Does this mean there is one single God, or that they are in one accord, in unity? The next verse makes it plain, but let Jesus clarify:

John 17:20-23:
20) "Neither pray I for these alone, but for them also which shall believe on me through their word;
21) "That they all may be one; as thou, Father, art in me, and I in thee, that they also may be one in us: that the world may believe that thou hast sent me.
22) And the glory which thou gavest me I have given them; that they may be one, even as we are one:
23) I in them, and thou in me, that they may be made perfect in one; and that the world may know that thou hast sent me, and hast loved them, as thou hast loved me."

The God given, definitive statement from God's messenger that we cannot emphasize enough since it makes so clear the "one-ness" of the Godhead is the oft quoted:

Ministry of Healing page 422:
"The unity that exists between Christ and His disciples does not destroy the personality of either. They are one in purpose, in mind, in character, but not in person. It is thus that God and Christ are one."

Deuteronomy 6:4:
"The Lord our God is one Lord."

As we have noted, the word for "God" is "Elohiym." Which means "Gods" plural or 'supreme divinity'. The word for "one" is the Hebrew, "echad," which means a oneness in unity. It is the same unity as is seen in:

Genesis 2:24:
"Therefore shall a man leave his father and his mother, and shall cleave unto his wife: and they shall be <u>one</u> _["echad"]_ flesh."

When the Bible says that the Father, Son, and Holy Spirit are "one", and when Jesus says that **"I and My Father are one,"** it simply means that they are perfectly united—each is willing to give themselves totally to save us from sin. All heaven is poured out in the plan of salvation. They are so like each other in their purpose, character, and love, that Jesus could say, **"He that hath seen Me hath seen the Father." Jn. 14:9**.

GOD THE FATHER IS ABOVE ALL

1 Cor. 15:27, 28:
27) "For he hath put all things under his (Christ's) feet. But when he saith all things are put under _him, it is_ manifest that he is excepted, which did put all things under him.
28) And when all things shall be subdued unto him, then shall the Son also himself be subject unto him that put all things under him, that God may be all in all."

This verse would not make sense if the Father and the Son were of "one essence" or the same indivisible "substance".

Matthew 12:32:
"Whosoever speaketh a word against the Son of man, it shall be forgiven him: but whosoever speaketh against the Holy Ghost, it shall not be forgiven him…."

This would not be true if they were both the same 'God', but they are distinct Beings with different responsibilities in the plan of salvation.

John 14:1:
"Let not your heart be troubled: ye believe in God, believe also in me."

There are two distinct divine Beings to believe in.   Indwelling the believer, the Holy Spirit—the 3rd Person of the Godhead—gives the power of grace to believe.

Matthew 26:39:
"And he went a little farther, and fell on his face, and prayed, saying, O my Father, if it be possible, let this cup pass from me: nevertheless not as I will, but as thou wilt."

In this prayer of Jesus, we see clearly that God has a will, and Jesus has a will. They were two separate distinct Beings.

Matthew 27:46:
"And about the ninth hour Jesus cried with a loud voice, saying, ...My God, my God, why hast thou forsaken me?" If separation between the Father and the Son is impossible as the Trinity doctrine teaches, what happened here?

Philippians 2:6:
"Who, being in the form of God, thought it not robbery to be equal with God."

Does that mean 'equal' to Himself? Obviously not! Jesus was in the form of God, and was equal to God the Father. **The true Godhead wants a spiritual harmony, not merely a physical sameness**.

Phil. 2:5:
"Let this mind be in you, which was also in Christ Jesus."

Romans 15:16:
"That I should be the minister of Jesus Christ to the Gentiles, ministering the gospel of God, that the offering up of the Gentiles might be acceptable, being sanctified by the Holy Ghost."

The **Father**, the **Son**, and the **Holy Spirit** work together to save us.

THE GODHEAD CREATED MAN IN THEIR IMAGE

A question that is posed: **'If God is a three-in-one god,** then man, being created in the image of God, would also be three persons in one,

485

wouldn't he?' Some may ask, "But isn't man a three-fold creature—physical, mental, and spiritual?"

Let SDA pioneer, R.J. Cottrell answer that question:

Review & Herald, November 19, 1857:
"I might say that a tree consists of body, bark and leaves, and no one perhaps would dispute it. But if I should affirm that each tree consists of three trees, the assertion would possibly be doubted by some. But if all admitted that one tree is three trees, I might then affirm that there were ninety trees in my orchard, when no one could count but thirty. I might then proceed and say, I have ninety trees in my orchard, and as each tree consists of three trees, I have two hundred and seventy. So if one man is three men, you may multiply him by three as often as you please. But if it takes body, soul *[he should have said 'mind', for a body with the breadth of God in it is the "soul"]* and spirit to make one perfect, living man; then separate these, and the man is unmade."

THE SDA PIONEERS ADAMANT AGAINST THE TRINITY

The SDA pioneers did not try to explain the exact nature of the Godhead, but they did wholeheartedly reject the Trinity concept.

Joseph Bates wrote:

The Autobiography Of Elder Joseph Bates, page 204:
"Respecting the trinity, I concluded that it was an impossibility for me to believe that the Lord Jesus Christ, the Son of the Father, was also the Almighty God, the Father, one and the same being. I said to my father, 'If you can convince me that we are one in this sense, that you are my father, and I your son; and also that I am your father, and you my son, then I can believe in the trinity.'

R.J. Cottrell wrote:

Review & Herald, July 6, 1869:
"To hold the doctrine of the Trinity is not so much an evidence of evil intention as of **intoxication from that wine of which all the nations have drunk.** The fact that this was one of the leading doctrines, if not the very chief, upon which the

bishop of Rome was exalted to popedom, does not say much in its favor."

Listen now to what James White wrote:

Review & Herald, September 12, 1854.
"As fundamental errors, we might class with this counterfeit Sabbath **other errors** which Protestants have brought away from the Catholic Church, such as sprinkling for baptism, **the trinity**, the consciousness of the dead and eternal life in misery. The mass who have held these fundamental errors, have doubtless done it ignorantly, **but can it be supposed that the church of Christ will carry along with her these errors till the judgment scenes burst upon the world? We think not.**"

Review & Herald, February 7, 1856:
"Martin Luther, and other reformers, arose in the strength of God, and with the Word and Spirit, made mighty strides in the Reformation. The greatest fault we can find in the Reformation is, **the Reformers stopped reforming. Had they gone on, and onward, till they had left the last vestige of Papacy behind**, such as natural immortality, sprinkling, **the trinity**, and Sunday keeping, the church would now be free from her **unscriptural errors**."

James White also wrote in:

<u>Life Incidents</u>, page 343
"Jesus prayed that His disciples might be one as He was one with His Father. This prayer did not contemplate one disciple with twelve heads, but twelve disciples, made one in object and effort in the cause of their Master. Neither are the Father and the Son parts of the three-one God. They are two distinct beings, yet one in the design and accomplishment of redemption." (<u>Defending the Godhead</u>, page 85)

None of the foremost SDA pioneers believed in the Trinity. Because of this fact and because of what has happened in the modern SDA church (as we have seen), General Conference theologian George Knight wrote in:

Ministry, October, 1993:

"Most of the founders of Seventh-day Adventism would **not be able to join the church today** if they had to subscribe to the denomination's Fundamental Beliefs. More specifically, **most would not be able to agree to belief number 2, which deals with the doctrine of the trinity**."

ELLEN WHITE NEVER USES THE TERM "TRINITY."

During the years that span from **1898** (when God's messenger wrote the "Desire of Ages") and 1915 (when she died) Ellen White made many statements referring to the 'Heavenly Trio'; the three 'Powers'; the three eternal Dignitaries'; **showing that there are the three persons in the Godhead.** Nevertheless she never employed the term 'Trinity'. She also never hinted at correcting her husband, James White's, assertive anti Trinitarian stance. Those who claim that such terms as 'Heavenly Trio' prove that she taught a 'Trinity', fail to realize that Ellen White fully understood what the term 'Trinity' meant: **One** 'substance' manifested and functioning as three distinct persons whose 'substance' was indivisible.

On the other hand a 'Trio' connotes three separate and distinct persons (with personalities) functioning harmoniously to effect one common goal. God's messenger was clearly aware that the term 'Trinity' would have misrepresented the Truth. The doctrine of **consubstantiation,** and of eternal generation, which predicates Trinitarianism, in effect teaches that the Son and the Holy Spirit **are not separate from the Father, but are intrinsically a part of the Being called God.** The Son being eternally generated & the 'Spirit' continuously proceeding from both.

In the book:

> The Holy Catholic Faith, Volume 1, page 311, Catholic scholars declare:
> "**All three possess not a similar, but the self-same nature.**... The Divine nature is not divided between the persons: **The Divine nature is not multiplied, but <u>one and indivisible</u>.** . . There are not three omnipotents, infinite and omniscients but only One infinite, One omnipotent, & One omniscient. The Three Divine Persons, possessing the self-same nature, are inseparable though distinct."

As we have clearly seen, such teaching strikes at the heart of the plan of salvation: It was separation from His Father that brought about Jesus death—not the cross. (See Story of Jesus, page 145; TMK page 19; 2

pages 206, 209, 214 etc.) If 'God' is one "indivisible" substance manifested in three different modes (as taught by Trinitarian doctrine) then, how could He cry out, "Why hast Thou forsaken Me?—if indeed the persons of the Godhead are inseparable?

All of the assertions by God's messenger that the members of the Godhead are separate & distinct individual persons clearly correct the false teachings of Trinitarianism & the gross errors that such a false doctrine lead to.

WHAT GOD'S MESSENGER DID SAY

God the Father has spoken to His people through the inspiration of the Holy Spirit on prophets. (Hebrews 1:1; 2 Peter 1:21). Believing that Ellen White fulfills the qualifications of a true prophet, this makes Ellen G. White spokesperson for the Godhead to the church. Let the Holy Spirit speak to us now, through her, concerning the Godhead. Here are some simple and plain statements:

Evangelism, pages 614, 615:
"**There are three living persons of the heavenly trio; in the name of these three great powers—the Father, the Son, and the Holy Spirit**—those who receive Christ by living faith are baptized, and these powers will cooperate with the obedient subjects of heaven in their efforts to live the new life in Christ." *(Special Testimonies, Series B, No. 7, pages 62, 63)*

"The **eternal heavenly dignitaries—God, and Christ, and the Holy Spirit**—arming them [the disciples] with more than mortal energy …would advance with them to the work and convince the world of sin." *(Manuscript 145, 1901)* Ibid. page 616

"In the great closing work we shall meet with perplexities that we know not how to deal with, but let us not forget that the three great powers of heaven are working, that a divine hand is on the wheel, and that God will bring His purposes to pass." *(Manuscript 118, 1902)* Ibid. page 65

Upward Look, page 148:
"The word of salvation is not a small matter, but so vast that the **highest authorities** are taken hold of by the expressed faith of the human agent. The **eternal Godhead—the Father, the**

Son, and the Holy Ghost—is involved in the action required to make assurance to the human agent."

Sons and Daughters of God, page 351:

"When you gave yourself to Christ, you made a pledge in the presence of **the Father, the Son, and the Holy Spirit—the three great personal Dignitaries of heaven.**" *7 Bible Commentary,* page 959

Concerning Jesus:

Review & Herald, April 5, 1906

"The Lord Jesus Christ, the divine Son of God, **existed from eternity, a distinct person,** yet one with the Father." .

Evangelism, page 615:

"He is the Eternal, **self-existent** Son."

Desire of Ages, page 530:

"Jesus declared, 'I am the resurrection, and the life.' In Christ is life, original, **unborrowed, underived....**"

Concerning the Holy Spirit:

Evangelism, page 616:

"We need to realize that the Holy Spirit, **who is as much a Person as God is a Person,** is walking through these grounds." .

Though the term "trinity" had been in use for centuries, the Holy Spirit through Ellen G. White never used the term. It was a term well known to the SDA pioneers and membership. Instead, as we have seen, the Holy Spirit used these terms to represent the truth concerning the Godhead: "The Heavenly Trio," "Three Great Powers," "Three Living Persons," "Three Holy Dignitaries of heaven," and "Three holiest Beings in heaven," "The Eternal Godhead," and "Three great Worthies in heaven." **All these terms describe three separate, distinct, eternal Beings.** It is the concept that most Adventists believe in today—even by many of those who mistakenly use the term "trinity."

MORE QUESTIONS

Because the word "trinity" is being used so much recently by the leadership of the SDA church, we have to ask, "Has the true concept of three separate eternal Beings in the Godhead, been officially changed to the false Trinitarian concept of one 'God' with three continual manifestations all of one substance?"

It is a fact that belief in the Trinity is required for membership in the World Council of Churches. Take note of the significance of the following quotation:

> **So Much In Common, page 107 (1973) Co-authored by B.B. Beach and Dr. Lukas Vischer – Faith and Order Secretariat of the WCC:**
> **"The member churches of the World Council of Churches and Seventh-Day Adventists are in agreement on the fundamental articles of the Christian faith as set forth in the three ancient symbols (Apostolicum, Nicaeno-Constantinopolitum, Athanasium). This agreement finds expression in <u>unqualified acceptance</u> of the <u>doctrine of the Trinity</u> and the Two-Natures."**

Is this new "God" an ecumenical ploy to make our SDA church agreeable to the fallen churches? This is a tremendously serious issue that involves the first and second commandments.

> **1—"Thou shalt have no other gods before me." Ex. 20:3.**
> **2—"Thou shalt not make unto thee any graven image, or any likeness of any thing that is in heaven above, or that is in the earth beneath, or that is in the water under the earth. Thou shalt not bow down thyself to them, nor serve them: for I the LORD thy God am a jealous God, visiting the iniquity of the fathers upon the children unto the third and fourth generation of them that hate me; And shewing mercy unto thousands of them that love me, and keep my commandments." Exodus 20:4-6.**

HOW THE TRINITY DOCTRINE CREPT INTO THE ADVENTIST CHURCH

This is not an exhaustive history of insurgency of the term "trinity" into modern Adventism, but it will give an indication of how it happened.

491

1913: F. M. Wilcox's "Trinity" statement appears in the *Review and Herald*, October 9, 1913, page 21.

1915: Seventh-day Adventist pioneer, prophetess, Ellen G. White, dies.

As God had led the children of Israel out of Egypt by a prophet, so had He led the children of Israel in these days. The words of Moses at his death are prophetic for our time as well: **Deuteronomy 31: 27, 29: "For I know thy rebellion, and thy stiff neck: behold, while I am yet alive with you this day, ye have been rebellious against the LORD; and how much more after my death?**

For I know that after my death ye will utterly corrupt yourselves, and turn aside from the way which I have commanded you; and evil will befall you in the latter days;"

1928-1931: SDA leaders, repeating the apostasy of the Pergamos church period, join with the world and decide to let the church's educational and medical systems be guided by the world's accreditation standards. Thus, SDA teachers must now be trained according to worldly criteria.

1931: The "Statement of Fundamental Beliefs." In 1930 church administrators in Africa requested that the General Conference include a statement in the Yearbook of what Seventh-day Adventists believe. "Such a statement," they said, "would help government officials and others to a better understanding of our work." [General Conference Committee Minutes (December 29, 1930), 195.]

A committee of four (M. E. Kern, E. R. Palmer, C. H. Watson, and **F. M. Wilcox**) was appointed to draft such a statement. They produced a 22-point statement that in 1931 was printed in the Adventist Yearbook:

<u>1931 Seventh-day Adventist Yearbook</u>, page 377.3, 4:

2. "That **the Godhead, or <u>Trinity</u>,** consists of the Eternal Father, a personal, spiritual Being, omnipotent, omnipresent, omniscient, infinite in wisdom and love; the Lord Jesus Christ, the Son of the Eternal Father, through whom all things were created and through whom the salvation of the redeemed hosts will be accomplished; the Holy Spirit, the third person of the Godhead, the great regenerating power in the work of redemption. Matt. 28:19.

3. "That Jesus Christ is very God, **being of the same nature and essence as the Eternal Father**. While retaining His divine nature He took upon Himself the nature of the human family,

lived on the earth as a man, exemplified in His life as our Example the principles of righteousness, attested His relationship to God by many mighty miracles, died for our sins on the cross, was raised from the dead, and ascended to the Father where He ever lives to make intercession for us. John 1:1, 14; Heb. 2:9–18; 8:1, 2; 4:14–16; 7:25."

The first time the term "Trinity" is officially used was in Point No. 2 of he 1931 Statement of Beliefs: This was the first time the word *Trinity* was ver officially used to define Seventh-day Adventist belief. Here we see vord-craft at its best—placing an erroneous term right beside one that is rue. It confuses the mind and makes the false term (Trinity) seem cceptable because the right term is still there. Belief #4 about Christ is ubtly worded to be agreeable to Trinitarian believers—*"Jesus Christ is ery God, being <u>of the same nature and essence</u> as the Eternal Father."*

946: In the book *Evangelism,* editors LeRoy Edwin Froom and Roy llen Anderson compiled E.G. White's statements and <u>inserted</u> the vord <u>"Trinity"</u> in subtitles to advance the Trinity doctrine, even hough she and all the pioneers were anti-Trinitarian.

955, 1956: General Conference leaders privately met with Barnhouse and Martin to discuss SDA theology. Doctrinal changes (including the false aching on the human nature of Christ), still unrepented of, were officially nade.

958: The Trinity is again introduced into the SDA church when the book, *uestions On Doctrine,* is published at the request of evangelicals arnhouse and Martin. (See pages 11, 22 of that book.) Martin was reparing to write the book, *Kingdom of the Cults,* and call the SDA Church "cult," until the SDA Church leaders quickly changed SDA doctrines. his avoided the stigma of being labeled a "cult," as Barnhouse and Martin ould label all anti-Trinitarians.

959: <u>Christian Beliefs</u>, by T. H. Jemison, written for collegiate students, romotes the Trinity concept: "That **there is one God, and the divine ature is not and cannot be divided,** is an outstanding truth of the Old estament. ...Despite the distinctions in personality which the Scriptures ake when speaking of the Godhead, there is only one God. How the ather, Son and the Holy Spirit can be distinguished personally and yet be completely one has not been revealed to man and is beyond comprehension." Ibid, page 74.

1968: The SDA Church connects with the World Council of Churches and National Council of Churches. **(The WCC requires a statement of belief in the Trinity in order to become a member church.)**

1971: LeRoy Froom writes *Movement of Destiny* in which he claims that in 1888 God was trying to bring the doctrine of the Trinity into the Seventh day Adventist Church through E.J. Wagonner and A.T. Jones, but that the church could not go forward because we did not believe in the Trinity. Froom writes: "Wagonner spoke with studied care. He phrased his thoughts with exactness, and in full understanding of their import. He clearly believed in the Trinity of Persons comprising the Godhead. And in such a frame of reference he thus recognized **the component** First, Second, and Third Persons as **coequal and consubstantial**...." *Movement of Destiny,* page 279. (See the whole chapter, pages 269-280 in his book.) In other words, **Froom claims that part of the latter rain that God wants to give to the SDA church is a belief in the Trinity doctrine! Question: Has an acceptance of Trinitarianism heralded an upsurge in godliness among God's denominated people, or has it rather heralded an avalanche of apostasy?**

1980: The SDA Church officially adopts the Trinity as Point #2 of the 27 Statements of Belief in the General Conference at Dallas, TX. It reads: *"There is one God: Father, Son, and Holy Spirit, a unity of three co-eternal persons. God is immortal, all-powerful, all-knowing, above all, and ever present. He is infinite and beyond human comprehension, yet known through His self-revelation. He is forever worthy of worship, adoration, and service by the whole creation."* Notice the word *"co-eternal."* Why was not the word "eternal" used, which would be the normal word to use? It is because *"co-eternal"* is a code word for the Trinity doctrine as we have seen in the Catholic Catechism. It means that they are all eternal together with the **same substance.** Also, the word *"persons"* means **"mode of manifestation."**

In the explanation of Pt. #2 in the following text of the book *Seventh day Adventists Believe,* the word Trinity is openly used. In fact, Pt. #2 is often labeled, "The Trinity." (See SDA Yearbook and Baptismal Certificate.)

1981: *Adventist Review,* March 5, 1981, page 3, quotes General Conference President, Neal C. Wilson: "There is another universal and **truly catholic** organization, the Seventh-day Adventist Church." Somehow, under prevailing trends, the word 'catholic' seems to imply more than simply 'universal".

1985: A new church hymnal is published. In the Contents, a category of hymns is labeled, *TRINITY,* pages 70-73.

One of these hymns, *Holy, Holy, Holy,* was originally written in 1826 by Reginald Heber. In its original form it was a Trinitarian song, which read at the end of the first and fourth stanzas as follows: *"God in three persons, blessed Trinity!"* This song was put into the 1909 and 1941 Seventh-day Adventist Hymnals, but the trinity part was changed to: *"God over all who rules eternity!"* and *"Perfect in power, in love and purity."* This song was purposely changed into a non-trinitarian song by Seventh-day Adventists, reflecting their views on the *Trinity* at the time of the change.

In the new 1985 Adventist Hymnal this song was changed back to its original, reflecting the views of the Adventist Church at this time. Once it was *Non-Trinitarian*, but now has changed into a *Trinitarian* church.

Not only that, but another hymn, was changed in the new hymnal. More new wording appeared. In the hymn *Come, Thou Almighty King,* SDA worshippers are led to sing: *"To Thee, **great One in Three**, eternal praises be."*

At least thirteen hymns to the trinity were added that did not appear in the old hymnal. In *Creator of the Stars of Night,* Adventists are led to sing to a false God with these words: *"To God the Father, God the Son, and God the Spirit, **Three in one.**"* The new hymn, *"Of the Father's Love Begotten"* teaches Adventists that Christ was begotten *"Ere the worlds began to be."*

If that were not enough, there is a responsive reading in the back of the hymnal devoted to God under the title, *"TRINITY."* [**Astoundingly**, of the 225 places where Scripture is used in the new SDA Hymnal, the Catholic versions predominate. For example, the *Jerusalem Bible* is used 38 times, the *NIV* 69 times and the *RSV* 28 times, (60%), while the Protestant *King James Version* is used just 15 times (7%).]

Thus, since 1985, the SDA church officially has an officially selected and approved hymnal from which Adventists worship the god of the beast system. It is a Catholic hymnal.

1993: "Most of the founders of Seventh-day Adventism would **not be able to join the church today** if they had to subscribe to the denomination's

Fundamental Beliefs. More specifically, **most would not be able to agree
to belief number 2, which deals with the doctrine of the trinity.**
George Knight, Ministry, October 1993, page 10.

Question: Since the SDA pioneers would not be able to join the modern
G.C.-sponsored church system, would they continue to worship the true
God separately—apart from the present apostasy?

1994: "Likewise the Trinitarian understanding of God, **now part of our
fundamental beliefs,** was not generally held by the early Adventists. Even
today **a few do not subscribe to it.**" William G. Johnsson, *Adventist
Review,* January 6, 1994, pages 10, 11.

1999: The SDA church in Poland signs an agreement statement with the
Roman Catholic Church in which it says that the SDA church should not be
considered a "sect" because "in its teaching and service **it cultivates the
most important principles of Catholic faith, especially the belief in the
Blessed Trinity.**" (See Appendix: G)

2000: Reinder Bruinsma writes *Our Awesome God*, published by Pacific
Press. The seventh chapter teaches God's people all about the God 'we'
worship—the Trinity concept. After explaining the history of the Trinity
doctrine in the fourth century AD and how "person" means "a mode of
manifestation," he writes: "It is a basic Christian doctrine that God is a
Trinity of three persons **having one substance.** ...It took the Adventist
Church until far into the nineteenth century to agree that **the doctrine of the
Trinity was indeed biblical** and **belonged among the fundamental
Adventist beliefs.**" *Our Awesome God*, page 91. (See in Chapter 38 page
428)

2006: The Adult Sabbath School Quarterly Lesson for **Sunday**, March 26
is entitled, **"The Triune God."** After quoting the second fundamental
belief of the Seventh-day Adventist church, it then states: "In other words
Adventism **along with millions of other Christians**—believe in the **triune**
nature of God; that is, there is one God (Dt. 6:4) who exists as three
Persons."

Question: What god is worshipped by millions of other Christians?
Answer: **The Trinity.** What term describes the church systems that the
millions of other Christians worship in? Answer: **Babylon.** How can we
worship the same God, when they worship their god on another day than the
one our God has told us to worship on?

Let's hear James White again: "As fundamental errors, we might class with this counterfeit Sabbath **other errors which Protestants have brought away from the Catholic church**, such as sprinkling for baptism, **the trinity**, the consciousness of the dead and eternal life in misery. The **mass** who have held these fundamental errors, have doubtless done it ignorantly, **BUT CAN IT BE SUPPOSED THAT THE CHURCH OF CHRIST WILL CARRY ALONG WITH HER THESE ERRORS TILL THE JUDGMENT SCENES BURST UPON THE WORLD? We think not.**" *Review & Herald,* September 12, 1854.

"**The greatest fault** we can find in the Reformation **is, the Reformers stopped reforming.** Had they gone on, and onward, till they had left the last vestige of Papacy behind, such as natural immortality, sprinkling, **the trinity**, and Sunday keeping, the church would now be **free from her unscriptural errors.**" James White, *Review & Herald,* February 7, 1856.

Again, the 2006 Sabbath School quarterly cites two Ellen White quotations where she calls the Father, Son, and Holy Spirit **"the heavenly trio"** and **"these three great powers"** as a support for the trinity doctrine. This is misleading and untrue, as we have seen.

Finally, the 2006 quarterly asks, "What analogies—such as **a triangle or a three-pronged fork**—can help someone understand the idea of how one God can be composed of three equal Persons?"

We answer: The pagan god Neptune (really Satan) holds a 3-pronged spear—a trident. These analogies mix pagan symbols with Scripture which results in the papacy. Why not use the analogy that was given by Ellen White—the **trio**—three separate individuals singing in perfect harmony?

2006: Adventist Theological Society National Conference meets March 30 to April 1. 18 SDA theologians present topics on the Trinity. The final meeting topic? **"The Trinity: A MARK of Seventh-day Adventist identity."** (A "Mark" they got from the "Beast"?)

2006, Nov.: William Johnsson gives presentation to the Presbyterian Church in Ecumenical Dialogue #1 in Nov., 2006, in which he says, "As we look over the 28 statements of Adventist doctrine, we are led to three conclusions: (1) The articles that are first and form the basis for the remainder, **namely** articles dealing with **the Trinity**, the person of Christ, and salvation, **conform to orthodox Christian understanding....**" (See Appendix K)

2008: **"Seventh-Day Adventists agree with many Catholic doctrines including the Trinity."** From Catholic Answers, article *"Seventh-Day Adventism."*

2009: February, 2009, *Ministry* magazine devoted to the topic of **The Trinity. This issue was mailed out to non-SDA pastors, and one article is written by a non-SDA.**

2010: SDA's celebrate the 100th anniversary of the ecumenical movement. **(See Appendix O)**

ARE WE REPEATING HISTORY?

> **Jeremiah 23:26, 27:**
> **"How long shall this be in the heart of the prophets that prophesy lies? Yea, they are prophets of the deceit of their own heart. Which think to cause my people to forget My Name by their dreams which they tell every man to his neighbour, as their fathers have forgotten My name for Baal."**

> **Revelation 2:20:**
> **"Notwithstanding I have a few things against thee, because thou sufferest that woman Jezebel** (papal teachings in the church)**, which calleth herself a prophetess, to teach and to seduce my servants to commit fornication, and to eat things sacrificed unto idols."**

We obviously have a strange new god in the Seventh-day Adventist church—one that our fathers knew not.

This is why most of Israel who left Egypt never made it to the Promised Land. See **Deuteronomy 32:16, 17, 21.**

This is why Israel was later taken captive by Babylon. See **Jeremiah 44:2, 3.**

Other verses could be added, but these two suffice to show us that we are repeating history because we have forgotten how God has led us in the past, and His teachings in our past history (Counsels for the Church, page 359.4).

BAAL WORSHIP TODAY

God says:

Exodus 20:2:
"Thou shalt have no other gods before me."
Let us hear how easy it is to have another 'god'.

<u>Great Controversy</u>, page 583:
"It is as easy to make an idol of false doctrines and theories as to fashion an idol of wood or stone. **By misrepresenting the <u>attributes</u> of God,** Satan leads men to conceive of Him in a false character. With many, **a philosophical idol** is enthroned in the place of Jehovah; **while the living God, as <u>He</u> is revealed <u>in His word</u>, <u>in Christ</u>, and <u>in the works of creation</u>, is worshiped by <u>but few</u>.** Thousands deify nature while they deny the God of nature. Though in a different form, **idolatry exists in the Christian world today** as verily as it existed among ancient Israel in the days of Elijah. <u>**The god** of many professedly wise</u> **men, of philosophers, poets, politicians, journalists—the god of polished fashionable circles, of many colleges and universities, <u>even of some theological institutions—is little better than Baal, the sun-god of Phoenicia</u>.**"

The accepted God of today in the Christian world is the trinity—one mega-God with three manifestations. Yes, there is Baal worship today as verily as it existed in the days of Elijah.

Chapter 40

An Exhortation

EZEKIEL SEES OUR DAY

Ezekiel prophesied (in Chapter 8) that in the last days such a false go as the trinity would be set up by modern Israel just before the sealin (which is recorded in Chapter 9).

In Ezekiel it says that an **image of jealousy, which provoketh t jealousy,** would be set up. Read:

> **Ezekiel 8: 5, 6:**
> **5) "...Then said he unto me, Son of man, lift up thine eyes now the way toward the north. So I lifted up mine eyes the way toward the north, and behold northward at the gate of the altar this image of jealousy in the entry.**
>
> **6) He said furthermore unto me, Son of man, seest thou what they do? Even the great abominations that the house of Israel committeth here, <u>that I should go far off from my sanctuary</u>?"**

God's Spirit doesn't stay around where a false 'god' is set up, especiall by those who should know better.

We are seeing the above prophecy fulfilled in the setting-up of th Catholic Trinity as the **official god of the Seventh-day Adventist churcl** By default, every Seventh-day Adventist worshipper is, knowingly (unknowingly, worshiping where the Trinity is venerated on any give Sabbath in any conference-owned church building, where the consensus i toward Trinitarianism.

This is one reason why many true, awakened; Seventh-day Adventist are following the counsel of 2 Corinthians 6:14-18 and worshipping God i little companies where the truth is being sought out and protected.

God approves of them:

> <u>Testimonies to the Church</u>, Volume 5, pages 209, 210:
> "<u>**At the time when the danger and depression of the church are greatest**</u>, **the LITTLE COMPANY who are standing in the light** will be sighing and crying for the

abominations that are done in the land. **But more especially will their prayers arise in behalf of the church because its members are doing after the manner of the world.**

"The earnest prayers of this FAITHFUL FEW will not be in vain. When the Lord comes forth as an avenger, **He will also come as a protector of all those who have preserved the faith in its purity** and kept themselves unspotted from the world."

ARE YOU TRUE TO YOUR BAPTISMAL VOWS?

We appeal to your sense of loyalty to the Father, Son, and Holy Spirit. At baptism we entered into a solemn covenant with the eternal Godhead, the Heavenly Trio: **Matthew 28:19: "Go ye therefore, and teach all nations, baptizing them in the name of the Father, and of the Son, and of the Holy Ghost." "Self-existent" is the applicable 'name' of each separate and distinct member of the Godhead (Jehovah = self-existent).**

Listen to what the Spirit of Prophecy says about our baptismal vow:

Evangelism, page 615:

(a) "There are **three living persons of the heavenly trio; in the name of these three great powers—the Father, the Son, and the Holy Spirit**—those who receive Christ by living faith are baptized, and these powers will co-operate with **the obedient** subjects of heaven in their efforts to live the new life in Christ." *(Special Testimonies, Series B, No. 7, pages 62, 63; 1905)*

Evangelism, page 307:

(b) "As Christians submit to the solemn rite of baptism, He registers the vow that they make to be true to Him. This vow is their oath of allegiance. They are baptized in the name of the Father and the Son and the Holy Spirit. Thus they are united with **the three great powers of heaven.** They pledge themselves to renounce the world and to observe the laws of the kingdom of God. Henceforth they are to walk in newness of life. No longer are they to follow the traditions of men. No longer are they to follow dishonest methods. They are to obey the statutes of the kingdom of heaven. **They are to seek God's honor**. If they will be true to their vow, they will be furnished with grace and power that will enable them to fulfill all righteousness. '**As many as received Him, to them gave He power to become the sons of God, even to them that believe on His name.'**" *(Letter 129, 1903).*

501

The Father, Son, and Holy Spirit are yearning to see the church in a unity of love. This can only be reached as we worship the true Godhead of love and unity. God has **"given unto us exceeding great and precious promises: that by these ye might be partakers of the divine** [*Godhead*] **nature...." 2 Peter 1:4.**

At baptism, we enter into a solemn covenant with the Father, the Son, and the Holy Spirit to remain faithful to Them.

THE SCRIPTURES, OUR ONLY SAFEGUARD

Just because point #2 has been written by the leaders of our church doesn't mean it is true. It doesn't mean God expects us to believe it.

> Great Controversy, page 595:
> **"God will have a people upon the earth to maintain the Bible, and the Bible only, as the standard of all doctrines and the basis of all reforms.** The opinions of learned men, the deductions of science, **the creeds or decisions of ecclesiastical councils,** as numerous and discordant as are the churches which they represent, the voice of the majority—**not one nor all of these should be regarded as evidence for or against any point of religious faith.** Before accepting any doctrine or precept, we should demand a **plain** 'Thus saith the Lord' in its support."

There is no plain 'Thus saith the Lord' for the Trinity doctrine. Like evolution it is a deception, an illusion, as well as unscriptural.

We are in the midst of a denominational apostasy. We are calling for corporate repentance.

> Early Writings, page 258:
> "I saw a company who stood well guarded and firm, **giving no countenance to those** [*apostates, even in the General Conference*] **who would unsettle the established faith of the body.** God looked upon them with approbation."

BIBLE PREDICTS AN ATTACK ON GOD'S LAST DAY CHURCH

Rev. 12:17:
"And the dragon was wroth with the woman, and went to make war with the remnant of her seed, which keep the commandments of God, and have the testimony of Jesus Christ [*the Spirit of Prophecy*].**"**

Acts 20:29:

"For I know this, that after my departing shall <u>grievous wolves enter in among you</u>, not sparing the flock. Also <u>of your own selves shall men arise</u>, speaking perverse things, to draw away disciples after them."

. G. W. PREDICTS APOSTASY

<u>Selected Messages Book 1</u>, pages 204, 205, by Ellen G. White:

"The enemy of souls has sought to bring in the supposition that a great reformation was to take place among Seventh-day Adventists, and that this **reformation would consist in giving up the doctrines which stand as the pillars of our faith**, and engaging in a process of reorganization. Were this reformation to take place, what would result? **The principles of truth that God in His wisdom has given to the remnant church, would be discarded. <u>Our religion would be changed.</u>** The fundamental principles that have sustained the work for the last fifty years would be **accounted as error. A <u>new organization</u> would be established. Books of a new order would be written. A system of intellectual philosophy** would be introduced. The founders of this system would go into the cities, and do a wonderful work. **The Sabbath of course, would be lightly regarded, as also the God who created it.** Nothing would be allowed to stand in the way of the new movement. The leaders would teach that virtue is better than vice, but **God being removed,** they would place their dependence on human power, which, without God, is worthless. Their foundation would be built on the sand, and **storm and tempest would sweep away the structure.**"

RINITARIANISM LEADS TO SPIRITUALISM

In Revelation, there is a false Trinity—the dragon (Spiritualistic aganism), the beast (Roman Catholicism: a union of church and state), and e false prophet (apostate Protestantism). What god is worshipped in the urches of these entities? <u>The Trinity.</u>

Behind the Trinity is Satan. **Rev. 13:4: "And they worshipped the ragon, which gave power unto the beast: and they worshipped the east,** saying, Who is like unto the beast? Who is able to make war with m?"

503

The trinity concept of one mega-god with three manifestations, all of th same substance, is basically **spiritualism**. Satan can impersonate th trinity. He is the one who can appear in three ways. He can manifes himself as different beings, even as an angel of light, but **he canno duplicate the Heavenly Trio**, for there is no holy harmony in "hell".

The fallen churches that worship the trinity are described as **"th habitation of devils, and the hold of every foul spirit, and a cage o every unclean and hateful bird." Revelation 18:2.** Worship of the trinit leads to a church-cloaked spiritualism. See **Isaiah 28:14, 15.**

Let me explain: Since, according to Trinitarianism, "God" ha manifested 'Himself' in three different ways, and that each manifestation i indivisible/inseparable from 'God', it follows, as we have repeatedly note that "Christ" did not actually die on the cross, only the human body 'He inhabited died. Since the Bible clearly states that He did not ascend to 'Hi Father' until after 'He' had spoken to Mary Magdalene (John 20:17), th Catholic theologians have come up with the doctrine (based on misunderstanding of 1 Peter 3:18, 19) that "Christ" went and preached t the "spirits" (or 'souls') in "prison" (hell). Obviously these "spirits" (c 'souls') were also 'alive', to warrant being preached to. The implication are clear: According to this perception, Satan was telling the truth when h said to Eve that she would not "surely die". This is the foundational li behind spiritualism and makes of this Trinitarian "Christ" a co-conspirat in this heresy.

WHAT WILL HAPPEN?

We have been made aware that Sunday worship is devoted to th Trinity, and that after the Council of Nicea in 325 AD, the Council of **Laodicea** met in 364 AD and outlawed Sabbath keeping. **The Trinity an Sunday worship go together. When the Sunday test comes, what wi happen to those who are worshipping the same 'god' as the bea system, and have compromised their faith and practice by deviatin from the worship of the "only true God"** (John 17:3); **the Creator Go who instituted the seventh day Sabbath?**

The answer is found in:

The Great Controversy, page 608:

"As the storm approaches, **a large class who have professed faith in the third angel's message, but have not been sanctified through obedience to the truth, abandon their position and join the ranks of the opposition. By uniting with the world and PARTAKING OF ITS SPIRIT**, they have

504

come to view matters in nearly the same light; and when the test is brought, they are prepared to choose the easy, popular side. Men of talent and pleasing address, who once rejoiced in the truth, **employ their powers to deceive and mislead souls.** They become the most bitter enemies of their former brethren

DON'T BE SHAKEN OUT OF THE STRUCTURE OF TRUTH

Early Writings, page 50:
"The mighty shaking has commenced and will go on, and all will be shaken out who are not willing to take a **bold and unyielding stand for the truth** *[in ALL its aspects]* and to sacrifice for God and His cause." *[This was written before the General Conference ever existed. Thus, the shaking is not in or out of an organization, but in or out of truth.]*

THE ELIJAH MESSAGE

We are actually living in days parallel to Elijah, and like him we must give a similar message to modern Israel:

1 Kings 18:21:
"How long halt ye between two opinions? If the LORD *be* God, follow him: but if Baal, *then* follow him."

We are dealing especially with a **corporate sin** and apostasy.
This is a call especially for the General Conference, Union Conference, and Conference leaders to repent; and for them to **publicly and clearly state to all, that the SDA church worships the Biblical Godhead—Father, Son, and Holy Spirit—three, distinct, eternal (not co-eternal) beings, and to purge from the denominational books all misleading terms such as "trinity," "triune," "co-equal," and "co-eternal."**
Lead us back to worship the true Godhead of the Bible. Bring back the blueprint educational and medical system. Repent of the agreement made with Martin and Barnhouse in 1955-56. Give us back the Protestant Bible and a true Second Advent (non-catholic) songbook.
This is a call for Seventh-day Adventist churches to repent. Pastors, lead your congregations to officially and **publicly declare** to the General Conference, Union, Conference leaders, and to the local community that your church worships the true Godhead, not the Trinity.
This is a call for Seventh-day Adventist church members to repent. If the leadership does not repent, then you as an individual can still turn and

follow the 'only true God and Jesus Christ, whom He has sent', and worship Him through the power imparted by His Holy Spirit, made possible by Jesus' sacrifice. **Whom do you choose to worship? Follow the example of those who went before us:**

Great Controversy, page 43:
"The foul leaven of idolatry, thus brought into the church, continued its baleful work. **Unsound doctrines**, superstitious rites, and idolatrous ceremonies **were incorporated into her faith and worship.** As the followers of Christ united with idolaters, the Christian religion became corrupted, and the church lost her purity and power. There were some, however, who were not misled by these delusions. **They still maintained their fidelity to the Author of truth and worshiped God alone.**"

Joshua 24:15:
"And if it seem evil unto you to serve the LORD *[Jehovah]*, choose you this day whom ye will serve; whether the gods which your fathers served that *were* on the other side of the flood, or the gods of the Amorites, in whose land ye dwell: but as for me and my house, we will serve the LORD." *[Yahweh = self-existent].*

Jesus pleads:

Rev. 3:20:
"If any man hear my voice...."

GOD'S WARNING

Rev. 14:12:
"If any man worship the beast and his image,** and receive his mark in his forehead, or in his hand, **the same shall drink of the wine of the wrath of God,** which is poured out without mixture into the cup of his indignation."

GOD'S ADMONITION

Jude 1:3-5:
1) "Beloved, when I gave all diligence to write unto you of the common salvation, it was needful for me to write unto you, and exhort you that ye should EARNESTLY

506

CONTEND for the faith which was once delivered unto the saints.

2) _[Why?]_ "**For there are certain men crept in unawares,** who were before of old ordained to this condemnation, ungodly men, turning the grace of our God into lasciviousness, **and denying the only Lord God, and our Lord Jesus Christ.**

3) _[If we don't cling to the truth, what will happen?]_ "**I will therefore put you in remembrance, though ye once knew this, how that the Lord, having saved the people out of the land of Egypt, afterward destroyed them that believed not.**"

GOD'S PROMISE

2 Corinthians 6:14-18; 7:1:

14) "...**what communion hath light with darkness**?

15) **And what concord hath Christ with Belial?** ...

16) **And what agreement hath the temple of God with idols?** ...

17) **Wherefore, come out from among them, and be ye separate,** saith the Lord, and **touch not the unclean thing;** and I will receive you,

18) **And will be a Father unto you, and ye shall be my sons and daughters, saith the Lord Almighty.**"

7:1) "**Having therefore these promises, dearly beloved, let us cleanse ourselves from all filthiness of the flesh and spirit, perfecting holiness in the fear of God.**"

FALSE	TRUE	FALSE
TRINITY	**THE GODHEAD**	**HOLY SPIRIT: AN IMPERSONAL FORCE**
325AD—Council of Nicea—Trinity Established.	From Eternity: 　The Father Eternal. 　The Son Eternal. 　The Holy Spirit Eternal.	The Father: Eternal
One God with three personalities—all of one substance—continually manifested.	The Son and Holy Spirit voluntarily chose submissive roles. God the Father—the Most High God	The Son: Begotten way back in eternity. (Originated from the Father.)
The Father knows Himself: Jesus continually 'begotten' or 'generated'.	Three distinct, Eternal Beings	The Holy Spirit: an impersonal force, power, or influence. (Originated from the Father and Son.)
The Father & the Son 'know' each Other: The Holy Spirit continually proceeding from both.	Life—original, unborrowed, **underived**.	Similar in some ways to the Trinity doctrine, except the Holy Spirit is a force, not a 'person'.
Sabbath keeping outlawed at Council of Laodicea in 364 AD. Sunday worship devoted to Trinity.	Oneness, a unity of love, a harmony of thought, purpose, and character.	
----------------------	---------------------	---------------------
Adherents: Roman Catholicism Fallen Protestantism , Gen. Conf. sponsored-SDA	Adherents: True Seventh-Day Adventists	Adherents: Jehovah Witnesses Smyrna Gospel Church Some SDA Pioneers, like Uriah Smith, who had to be corrected by God's messenger.

Chapter 41

A SYNOPSIS: THE TRUE GOD OF THE BIBLE

WILLIAM: Professor, Why was the Seventh-day Adventist Church raised up?

PROFESSOR: Let me read you this quotation from the pen of Ellen White:

> Testimonies to the Church, Volume .9, page 19:
> **"In a special sense Seventh-day Adventists have been set in the world as watchmen and light bearers.** To them has been entrusted the last warning for a perishing world. **"They have been given a work of the most solemn import—the proclamation of the first, second, and third angels' messages.** "There is no other work of so great importance. **They are to allow nothing else to absorb their attention."**

The only reason for the existence of the Seventh-day Adventist church is to give the Three Angels' messages to a dying world. But today the name given by God to His denominated people has been trademarked by an entity that has lost a true appreciation of the messages, and their duty to proclaim them. Nevertheless, the true Seventh-day Adventist church that is approved of God is composed of people giving the Three Angel's Messages "in verity," teaching the truth about righteousness by faith which teaching has to include the sanctuary message which is, in turn, predicated upon Christ's role as mediator between God and man.   This true teaching is totally undermined by the heresy of consubstantiality.

The first angel's message: the "judgment hour" message of Revelation 14:7, incorporates the 'loud' call to "Fear God, and give glory to Him": that is, to allow Him to demonstrate in, and through our lives, His power to save His people **from their sins** and to reflect His glorious character, as demonstrated to us by example through His precious Son.

This same 'loud' call is **an invitation to worship the Creator God; the Father, who created all things through His Son.** This call presupposes knowing Him "the only true God and Jesus Christ whom [He] hast sent" John 17:3). It is not possible to truly 'know' Him, or His Son, when He is perceived as a spiritualistic "non-entity" of man's devising, as is done in Trinitarianism.   The world, and the worldly churches that worship this philosophical idol, all amply demonstrate, by their 'fruits', just what are their 'roots'. The first angel's message is a call to a return to true worship of the 'only true God and His Son.'

The second and third angel's messages both constitutes a call to 'come out' of Babylon's fraternity: to get as far as possible from her intoxicating goblet filled with false doctrines.

WILLIAM: Those who teach the truth are approved of God. **Those who are giving the true Three Angels' messages are the true Seventh-day Adventist church, whether they are in or out of the organized structure that has trademarked the name**.

PROFESSOR: Correct. Those who are standing on the Three Angels' Messages are on the firm platform that cannot be shaken! Notice the following statement from a chapter entitle, "**A Firm Platform**," in Early Writings:

> Early Writings, pages 258, 259:
> "I saw a company who stood well-guarded and firm, **giving no countenance to those who would unsettle the established faith of the body. God looked upon them with approbation.**
>
> "**I was shown three steps—the first, second, and third angels' messages. Said my accompanying angel, "Woe to him who shall move a block or stir a pin of these messages.** The true understanding of these messages is of vital importance. The destiny of souls hangs upon the manner in which they are received.**"

WILLIAM: Who are those "who would unsettle the established faith of the body"?

PROFESSOR: One tends to think of outside attackers, but we will see that God's messenger warned that those most prominent in apostasy would be in the General Conference of SDA, just as the apostasy was led by the Sanhedrin in the days of Christ. She warns: "We have far more to fear from within that from without.":

> Selected Messages Book 1, page 122:
> "We have far more to fear from within than from without. **The hindrances to strength and success are far greater from the church itself than from the world**. ...How often have the

510

professed advocates of the truth proved the greatest obstacle to its advancement! The unbelief indulged, the doubts expressed, **the darkness cherished, encourage the presence of evil angels, and open the way for the accomplishment of Satan's devices.**"

We need to remember Jesus' words found in:

Matthew 11:25:
"...I thank thee, O Father, Lord of heaven and earth, because thou hast hid these things from the wise *[in their own eyes]* **and prudent** *[in dodging difficult duty]*, **and hast revealed them unto babes.**"

As with ancient Israel at Christ's first coming, so with modern Israel:

Testimonies to the Church, Volume 5, pages 80, 82, 80, 94:
"In the **last solemn work few great men will be engaged.**"
Ibid, page 80

[They] "have trusted to intellect, genius, or talent ...*[and]* **did not keep pace with the light**.... God will work a work **in our day** that but few anticipate. **He will raise up and exalt among us those who are taught rather by the unction of His Spirit than by the outward training of scientific institutions....** God will manifest that He is not dependent on learned, self-important mortals." Ibid. page 82.

[In Jesus' day the people had been led to believe that God's work depended upon the priests and rabbis, just as we] "...have been inclined to think that where there are no faithful ministers there can be no true Christians, but this is not the case. **God has promised that where the shepherds are not true He will take charge of the flock Himself.** God has never made the flock wholly dependent upon human instrumentalities." Ibid, page 80

"The sin of ancient Israel was in disregarding the expressed will of God and following their own way *[today this is seen in degree-oriented education, "celebration" style worship services; competitive sports at our academies, colleges, and universities; dubious curricula; N.L.P.; Spiritual Formation; Ecumenism; "New" theology; and on and on; ad nauseum]* **according to the leadings of unsanctified hearts. Modern Israel are fast following in their footsteps, and the displeasure of the Lord is as surely resting upon them.**" Ibid, page 94.

511

Testimonies to Ministers, pages 468, 469:

"The religion of many among us will be the religion of apostate Israel *[they had a false concept of God and His character and a false concept of the Messiah]*, because they love their own way, and forsake the way of the Lord. ... **I know that a work must be done for the people, or many will not be prepared to receive the light of the *[4ᵗʰ]* angel *[of Rev. 18:1-4]* sent down from heaven to lighten the whole earth with his glory."

Upward Look, page 131:

"The Lord Jesus will always have a chosen people to serve Him. When the Jewish people rejected Christ, the Prince of life, He took from them the kingdom of God and gave it unto the Gentiles. __God will continue to work on this principle with every branch of His work.__ **When __a church__ proves unfaithful to the word of the Lord, __whatever__ their position may be, __however high and sacred their calling__, the Lord can no longer work with them. Others are then chosen to bear important responsibilities.** But, if these in turn do not purify their lives from every wrong action, if they do not establish pure and holy principles in all their borders, then the Lord will grievously afflict and humble them and, unless they repent, will remove them from their place and make them a reproach. . . ."

WILLIAM: The verses that come to my mind are:

Jeremiah 6:16:

"Thus saith the LORD, Stand ye in the ways, and see, and **ask for the old paths, where is the good way, and walk therein, and ye shall find rest for your souls.** But they said, We will not walk therein."

Jude 3, 4:

"Beloved, when I gave all diligence to write unto you of the common salvation, it was needful for me to write unto you, and exhort [you] that **ye should earnestly contend for the faith which was once delivered unto the saints**. For there are certain men crept in unawares...."

I know that in the First Angel's Message we are commanded to:

Revelation 14:7:
> **"Worship Him that made heaven, and earth, and the sea, and the fountains of waters."**

It seems that we have to go back to the old paths of Seventh-day Adventism to be on the right path—and this call to worship the Creator is right in the beginning of the old paths—the faith once delivered to the SDA pioneer saints.

PROFESSOR: This is New Testament authority to worship the Creator on the day that He sanctified and blessed—the seventh-day Sabbath. This command to worship the Creator was obeyed by the Seventh-day Adventist church in its inception. As we have read over and over again, in 1872 the Seventh-day Adventist Publishing Assoc. published a list of 25 Fundamental Principles, as taught and practiced by Seventh-day Adventists.

The first two statements proclaimed:

1872 Statement of Principles of Seventh-day Adventists:
> **"1—That there is one God, <u>a personal, spiritual Being, the Creator of all things</u>,** omnipotent, omniscient, and eternal, infinite in wisdom, holiness, justice, goodness, truth, and mercy, unchangeable, **and everywhere present by His representative, the Holy Spirit.**
>
> **"2--That there is one Lord Jesus Christ, the Son of the Eternal Father, the One <u>by whom He created all things</u>, and by whom they do consist."**

WILLIAM: They obviously saw the Father and the Son as distinctly separate Beings, and they saw the Father as the Creator, accomplishing His purposes through His Son.

PROFESSOR: Paul, in his letter to the Ephesians, gives us the answer:

Ephesians 3:9:
> "And to make all men see what is **<u>the fellowship</u>** of the mystery *[This mysterious fellowship is the fellowship of a shared Spirit who proceeds from the Father and from the Son, Who are one in purpose, character, and intent, and proceeds to execute Their will. "<u>Fellowship</u>" can only exist between separate and distinct beings.]*, which from the beginning of the world hath been hid in **God, who created all things** by Jesus Christ." *[The*

513

*will and power of God, the Father, are intrinsic in the Word
(Christ) as They, by the Mighty Third Person of the Godhead,
execute Their mutual will.]*

The book of Hebrews tells us the same thing:

Hebrews 1:1, 2:
1) "God, …
2) Hath in these last days spoken unto us by his Son, whom
he hath appointed heir of all things, **by whom also He** *[God the
Father]* **made the worlds**."

God the Father is the Creator of all things. He created all things through
Jesus Christ, and the Spirit of Prophecy confirms that God the Father is the
ultimate Creator.

Testimonies to the Church, Volume 1, page 297:
"He *[Jesus]* was ever directing their minds to **God, the
Creator of the universe,** as the source of their strength and
wisdom."

Notice in the quotations above, that Ellen White always refers to the
Father simply as "God."

WILLIAM: Who then is the "God" who speaks in Genesis 1:26: "**And
God said, Let us make man in our image, after our likeness**." Is it God
the Father, or Jesus, the Holy Spirit, or all three? According to the Trinity
doctrine, it should be all three.

PROFESSOR: However the Spirit of Prophecy clarifies this for us.

Early Writings, page 145:
"**But when God said to His Son, 'Let us make man in our
image,' Satan was jealous of Jesus.**"

This plainly explains Genesis 1:26—It was the Father talking to His
Son. So **the Most High God that was officially worshipped in the
Seventh-day Adventist church for the first century of its existence was
God the Father.** Again, **He is the God we are commanded to worship in
the First Angel's message: "Worship Him that made heaven, and
earth, and the sea, and the fountains of waters. Rev. 14:7. This**

command also directs our attention to the end of the week of Creation when the seventh-day Sabbath was blessed, and sanctified by God as the appointed day to worship Him. This is part of the fourth commandment:

Exodus 20:8-11:
 8) "Remember the sabbath day, to keep it holy.
 9) Six days shalt thou labour, and do all thy work:
 10) But the seventh day [is] the sabbath of the LORD thy God: [in it] thou shalt not do any work, thou, nor thy son, nor thy daughter, thy manservant, nor thy maidservant, nor thy cattle, nor thy stranger that [is] within thy gates:
 11) For [in] six days the LORD made heaven and earth, the sea, and all that in them [is], and rested the seventh day: wherefore the LORD blessed the sabbath day, and hallowed it.8) "Remember the sabbath day, to keep it holy. Six days shalt thou labour, and do all thy work: **But the seventh day *is* the sabbath of the LORD thy God:** *in it* thou shalt not do any work, thou, nor thy son, nor thy daughter, thy manservant, nor thy maidservant, nor thy cattle, nor thy stranger that *is* within thy gates: **For *in* six days the LORD made heaven and earth, the sea, and all that in them *is*, and rested the seventh day: wherefore the LORD blessed the sabbath day, and hallowed it.**"

 Notice that the reason for worshiping God is the fact that He is the Creator. Since He created all things through Jesus, before Jesus subordinated Himself, and since Jesus is also titled 'God', God commands all to worship Jesus also (Hebrews 1:6), <u>for to worship the Son is to worshipfully obey the Father</u>. However, our duty to worship the "Most High God" supremely is just what the Spirit of Prophecy says as well:

 <u>Great Controversy</u>, pages 436, 437:
 "**The duty to worship God is based upon the fact that He is the Creator** and that to Him all other beings owe their existence. And wherever, in the Bible, His claim to reverence and worship, above the gods of the heathen, is presented, there is cited the evidence of His creative power. 'All the gods of the nations are idols: but **the Lord made the heavens**.' Psalm 96:5.

"Says the psalmist: 'Know ye that **the Lord He is God: it is He that hath made us,** and not we ourselves.' 'O come, let us worship and bow down: **let us kneel before the Lord our Maker.**' Psalm 100:3; 95:6. And the holy beings who worship God in heaven state, as the reason why their homage is due to Him: 'Thou art worthy, **O Lord,** to receive glory and honor and power: **for Thou hast created all things.**' Revelation 4:11."

We read a moment ago the 1872 statement of beliefs, as held by the pioneers, which underscored the separate and distinct personhood of both the Father and the Son.

WILLIAM: That statement agrees with the Bible, Spirit of Prophecy, and the First Angel's Message.

PROFESSOR: **That definition of God was held by James and Ellen White all through their lives**, and would last till 1980—65 years after the death of Ellen White.

WILLIAM: That doesn't auger well for the denomination today. According to Fundamental Belief #2 of the church's current statement both James and Ellen White, together with almost all of the other pioneers would be unwelcome in the church today as long as they held to their convictions against consubstantiality which is the foundational concept of Trinitarianism.

PROFESSOR: You're right, William. And **the change has a lot to do with the Third Angel's Message, where we find a terrible warning from God not to violate the first commandment. <u>Surely, worshipping the 'God' invented by the beast system is, in effect, to worship the beast</u>:**

Revelation 14: 9, 10:
"If any man **worship the beast and his image,** …The same shall drink of the wine of the wrath of God."

WILLIAM: What is the beast and his image?

PROFESSOR: The beast system is identified in Rev. 13 as the Roman Catholic church/state system. The "image of the beast" is also church/state system that will be formed by the second beast of Rev. 13– identified as fallen-Protestant America.

516

WILLIAM: What is the god that is worshipped in these two entities?

PROFESSOR: It is the false Catholic Trinity concept of God.

WILLIAM: Because all the mainline Christian churches worship the Trinity?

PROFESSOR: Yes. There are many differences in doctrine between the Roman Catholic Church and the various fallen Protestant denominations, but the doctrine of the Trinity is not one of them. Notice how the Catholic Church and the popular Protestant denominations all unitedly proclaim a worship of one Deity, but who is composed of three "persons"—all consisting of the same essence, or substance.

For instance, the **Roman Catholic church**, which established the doctrine in 325 AD at the Council of Nicea, states that "The Church never ceases to proclaim her faith in **one only God**: Father, Son and Holy Spirit. ...The **mystery** of the Most Holy Trinity is the central mystery of the Christian faith and of Christian life."

The **Greek Orthodox Archdiocese of America** states: "The fundamental truth of the Orthodox Church is the faith revealed in the **True God:** the Holy Trinity of the Father, the Son, and the Holy Ghost."

The **Lutheran Church (Missouri Synod)** teaches that "The one true God. is the Father and the Son and the Holy Ghost, three distinct persons, **but of one and the same divine essence,** equal in power, equal in eternity, equal in majesty, because each person possesses the one divine essence."

The **Presbyterian Church (USA)** says, "We trust in the **one triune God.**"

The **Southern Baptist Convention** declares: "The **eternal triune God** reveals **Himself** to us as Father, Son, and Holy Spirit, with distinct personal attributes, but **without division of nature, essence, or being.**"

The **Assemblies of God: "The one true God has revealed Himself** as the eternally self-existent "I AM," the Creator of heaven and earth and the Redeemer of mankind. **He has further revealed <u>Himself</u>** as embodying the principles of relationship and association **as Father, Son and Holy Ghost.**

517

And also, the **United Methodist Church** concurs with all in these words: "There is but **one living and true God,** everlasting, <u>**without body or parts**</u>, of infinite power, wisdom, and goodness; **the maker and preserver of all things,** both visible and invisible. And **in unity of this Godhead there are three persons, of one substance, power, and eternity**—the Father, the Son, and the Holy Ghost.

WILLIAM: I am glad you're done with that list.

PROFESSOR: Not quite, William, there is one more I am not happy to read.

The Seventh-day Adventist church, at the 1980 General Conference in Dallas, TX, voted to adopt the "27 Fundamental Beliefs" and in it the Trinity was made the official 'God' worshipped in every SDA church around the world with these words: **"There is one God: Father, Son, and Holy Spirit, a unity of three <u>co-eternal</u> Persons..."**

WILLIAM: **It seems to me that the Three Angels' Messages goes to every nation and denomination, and brings everyone on planet Earth to a choice: Will you worship the Creator, or the Trinity; the God of the creation Sabbath or the 'God' of the false sabbath?**

PROFESSOR: Yes. In the Three Angels' Messages of Revelation 14:9-12 we must choose between:

a) TWO GODS.
b) TWO MODES OF WORSHIP;
c) TWO DISTINCT SABBATH DAYS that manifest that worship

These facts show us that in these last days, we are living in a world that is confused about which God to worship.

WILLIAM: The times we are living in today are virtually identical to the days of Elijah!

PROFESSOR: Excellent point, William.

1 Kings 18:21:
"And Elijah came unto all the people, and said, **How long halt ye between two opinions? If the LORD** *be* **God, follow**

him: but if Baal, *then* follow him. And the people answered him not a word."

Hosea 4:1, 6:
1) "Hear the word of the LORD, ye children of Israel: for the LORD hath a controversy with the inhabitants of the land, because *there is* no truth, nor mercy, **nor knowledge of God in the land.**
6) My people are destroyed for lack of knowledge."

Now, let us turn our attention to the subject of the "Godhead." Here is a Bible verse that uses the term:

Acts 17:29:
"Forasmuch then as we are the offspring of God, we ought not to think that **the Godhead** is like unto gold, or silver, or stone, graven by art and man's device."

WILLIAM: Is the term "Godhead" the same as the title "God"?

PROFESSOR: Good revision question, William. Many are confused by these terms. Let us see what the Spirit of Prophecy says:

Counsels on Health, page 222:
"**The Godhead** was stirred with pity for the race, and **the Father, the Son, and the Holy Spirit gave Themselves** to the working out of the plan of redemption."

Special Testimonies, Series B, No. 7, pages 62, 63: (Evangelism, page 615.)
"**There are three living persons of the heavenly trio; in the name of these three great powers—the Father, the Son, and the Holy Spirit—**Those who receive Christ by living faith are baptized, and these powers will co-operate with the obedient subjects of heaven in their efforts to live the new life in Christ."

SDA Bible Commentary, Volume 7, page 959.
"When you gave yourself to Christ, you made a pledge in the presence of **the Father, the Son, and the Holy Spirit—the three great personal Dignitaries of heaven.**"

519

Thus, we see that the Godhead is the Heavenly Trio—Father, Son, and Holy Spirit—three distinct eternal Beings. This is what we found in the 1872 statement of principles—the original beliefs of the SDA church:

> **1**—That there is **one God, a personal, spiritual Being, the Creator** of all things, omnipotent, omniscient, and eternal, infinite in wisdom, holiness, justice, goodness, truth, and mercy, unchangeable, and everywhere present by **His representative, the Holy Spirit.**
>
> **2**—That there is **one Lord Jesus Christ, the Son of the Eternal Father,** the One by whom He created all things, and by whom they do consist.

The Godhead is not three manifestations of one God, but is composed of three distinct Eternal Beings.

WILLIAM: We saw that the Bible teaches that each member of the Godhead is eternal.

THE FIRST MEMBER OF THE GODHEAD

PROFESSOR: Yes, William, each is eternal. Let's look at the first Member of the Godhead—God the Father—the Creator of all things:

Isaiah 40:28:
"Hast thou not known? Hast thou not heard, that **the everlasting God, the LORD, the Creator of the ends of the earth,** fainteth not, neither is weary? There is no searching of his understanding *[by us]*."

God's messenger records clear instruction on how to approach and to write or speak of the "Supreme Being", "our Heavenly Father":

God's Amazing Grace, page 94:
"'Our Father which art in heaven, Hallowed be thy name.' Matthew 6:9.
"To hallow the name of the Lord requires that the words in which we speak of the **Supreme Being** *[as in "Most High God"]* be uttered with reverence. 'Holy and reverend is his name' (Ps. 111:9). **We are never in any manner to treat lightly the titles or appellations of the Deity**. In prayer we enter the audience

chamber of the **Most High**; and we should come before Him with holy awe. The angels veil their faces in His presence. The cherubim and the bright and holy seraphim approach His throne with solemn reverence. How much more should we, finite, sinful beings, come in a reverent manner before the Lord, our Maker!

"But to hallow the name of the Lord means much more than this. We may, like the Jews in Christ's day, manifest the greatest outward reverence for God, and yet profane His name continually. 'The name of the Lord" is "merciful and gracious, long-suffering, and abundant in goodness and truth, . . . forgiving iniquity and transgression and sin' (Ex. 34:5-7). Of the church of Christ it is written, 'This is the name wherewith she shall be called, The Lord our Righteousness' (Jer. 33:16). This name is put upon every follower of Christ. It is the heritage of the child of God. **The family are called after the Father** *[Jesus, was called after the Father, the Father Himself said, "Behold, I send an Angel before thee, to keep thee in the way, and to bring thee into the place which I have prepared. 21 Beware of him, and obey his voice, provoke him not; for he will not pardon your transgressions: **for my name [is] in him**." Ex. 23:20, 21, consequently, Jesus is also referred to by the name "Jehovah"].* The prophet Jeremiah, in the time of Israel's sore distress and tribulation, prayed, 'We are called by thy name; *[children of the Most High God: Jehovah]* leave us not' (Jer. 14:9).

"This name is hallowed by the angels of heaven, by the inhabitants of unfallen worlds. When you pray, 'Hallowed be thy name,' you ask that it may be hallowed in this world, hallowed in you. God has acknowledged you before men and angels as His child; pray that you may do no dishonor to the 'worthy name by which ye are called' (James 2:7). God sends you into the world as His representatives. In every act of life you are to make manifest the name of God. This petition calls upon you to possess His character. You cannot hallow His name, you cannot represent Him to the world, unless in life and character you represent the very life and character of God. **This you can do only through the acceptance of the grace and righteousness of Christ.** *["John 14:6 Jesus saith unto him, I am the way, the truth, and the life: **no man cometh unto the Father, but by me**."]*

THE SECOND MEMBER OF THE GODHEAD

WILLIAM: We know that Jesus is eternal, like His Father.

PROFESSOR: That is right, let us see what the Bible and God's messenger says:

> **John 1:1-3:**
> 1) "**In the beginning was the Word, and the Word was with God, and the Word was God.**
> 2) **The same was in the beginning WITH God.**
> 3) All things were made by him; and without him was not any thing made that was made."

Never forget, William, that the term "God" is a title indicating status, like the term "king." Both Christ and the Holy Spirit have this title, as we have seen. But we must never forget that the Father is referred to as a "God of gods" and "the Most High God" to whom both the Holy Spirit and Christ defer. They are as eternal as He, and concerning His Son we read:

> **Micah 5:2:**
> "But thou, Bethlehem Ephratah, though thou be little among the thousands of Judah, **yet out of thee shall he come forth** unto me **that is to be ruler in Israel; whose goings forth have been from of old, from everlasting.**"

Evangelism, page 615.3 (Manuscript 101, 1897):
> "...He is the **ETERNAL, SELF-EXISTENT** Son." *[Not "generated" or "begotten" at some point in pre-history].*

Review & Herald, April 5, 1906:
> "The Lord Jesus Christ, the divine Son of God, **EXISTED FROM ETERNITY**, a distinct person, yet one with the Father."

With that 'one-ness' that we have discussed at length.

THE THIRD MEMBER OF THE GODHEAD

WILLIAM: Without a doubt, Jesus is an eternal Member of the Godhead. What about **the Holy Spirit?** Many have other views about Him. Some do not believe that the Holy Spirit is as much God as is the Father and the Son.

PROFESSOR: As we have already noted the Bible and Spirit of Prophecy is clear. The Holy Spirit is eternal, like the Father and the Son:

Hebrews 9:14:
"How much more shall the blood of Christ, who through **the eternal Spirit** offered himself without spot to God, purge your conscience from dead works to serve the living God?"

He is a distinct Person:

Sermons & Talks, Volume 2, page 137.
"We need to realize that the Holy Spirit, who is as much a person as God is a person, is walking through these grounds, unseen by human eyes."

He is also God:

Acts 5:3, 4:
3) "But Peter said, Ananias, why hath Satan filled thine heart **to lie to the Holy Ghost,** and to keep back part of the price of the land?
4) Whiles it remained, was it not thine own? And after it was sold, was it not in thine own power? Why hast thou conceived this thing in thine heart? **Thou hast not lied unto men, but unto God.**"

Ye Shall Receive Power, page 29:
"'The Spirit also helpeth our infirmities;' **and the Spirit, being God, knoweth the mind of God.**"

But neither the Holy Spirit nor the Son are the "Most High God": the Father is.

WILLIAM: The Father, Son, and Holy Spirit are definitely the Heavenly Trio.

PROFESSOR: And, as we have repeatedly noted, all three are seen in the original 1872 SDA Statement of Principles:

"1—That there is <u>one God</u>, a personal, spiritual Being, <u>the Creator of all things</u>, omnipotent, omniscient, and eternal,

infinite in wisdom, holiness, justice, goodness, truth, and mercy, unchangeable, and everywhere present by <u>His representative, the Holy Spirit</u>.

2--That there is <u>one Lord Jesus Christ</u>, the Son of the Eternal Father, <u>the One by whom He created all things</u>, and by whom they do consist."

THE HEAVENLY TRIO

The Heavenly Trio are seen together in many verses of Scripture that show each fulfilling their distinctive roles in the plan of salvation they formulated. Here are a few:

Matthew 3:16, 17:
16) "And Jesus, when he was baptized, went up straightway out of the water: and, lo, the heavens were opened unto him, and he saw **the Spirit of God** descending like a dove, and lighting upon him:

17) And lo a voice from heaven, saying, This is my beloved Son, in whom I am well pleased."

Matthew 28:19:
"Go ye therefore, and teach all nations, baptizing them in **the name** *[we have discussed this "name", See Chapters 13 and 23 of this book]* **of the Father, and of the Son, and of the Holy Ghost."**

1 Corinthians 12:4-6:

4) "Now there are diversities of gifts, **but the same Spirit.**

5) And there are differences of ad-ministrations, **but the same Lord.**

6) And there are diversities of operations, but it is **the same God which worketh all in all."**

2 Corinthians 13:14:

"The grace of **the Lord Jesus Christ,** and the love of **God,** and the communion of **the Holy Ghost,** *be* with you all. Amen."

Ephesians 4:4-6:

4) "There is one body, and **one Spirit,** even as ye are called in one hope of your calling;

5) One Lord, one faith, one baptism,

6) **One God and Father of all,** who is above all, and through all, and in you all *[by His Spirit, the mighty third Person of the Godhead]."*

All three of the Heavenly Trio participate with us when we pray: **1—** **he indwelling Holy Spirit inspires the prayer.** Angels bear our prayers ⟩ Jesus, our great High Priest in the heavenly sanctuary **2—Jesus mingles is righteousness with our prayer and presents it to the Father. 3— he Father answers our prayer.**

The Heavenly Trio each plays a role in last day events to save us. here are **three** great events that we, living during the close of earth's story, must be ready for, and participate in, to be saved eternally:

1—The Latter Rain
2—The Voice of God
3—The Second Coming

'ILLIAM: I see what you are aiming at!

The first is the coming of the Holy Spirit;
The second is the voice of God the Father;
The third is the coming of Jesus Christ.

ROFESSOR: Each plays a different, but vital role, in the final events of lvation.

HE "ONE GOD" OF THE BIBLE

WILLIAM: For quick revision, since there are three distinct Beings called "God", who then is the "One God" of the Bible?

PROFESSOR: The Bible says there is "one God," William. Let's see again Who the Bible tells us this is:

1 Corinthians 8:6:
"But to us there is but **one God, the Father, of whom** *are* **all things, and we in him;** and one Lord Jesus Christ, by whom *are* all things, and we by him."

Ephesians 4:4-6:
4) "There is one body, and one Spirit, even as ye are called in one hope of your calling;

5) One Lord, one faith, one baptism,

6) One God and Father of all, who is above all, and through all, and in you all."

1Timothy 2:5:
"**For there is one God, and** *[there is]* **one mediator between God and men, the man Christ Jesus.**"

WILLIAM: **God the Father then, is clearly the "one God" of the Bible.**

PROFESSOR: In fact, the God of the Bible **is** the Father. The Father is the God of the Old Testament:

Acts 3:13:
"**The God of Abraham, and of Isaac, and of Jacob, the God of our fathers,** hath glorified his Son Jesus; whom ye delivered up, and denied him in the presence of Pilate, when he was determined to let him go."

He is the God of the New Testament as well:
Romans 3:26, 29:
26) "To declare, I say, at this time His righteousness: that **He** *[God the* Father*]* **might be just, and the justifier of him which believeth in Jesus.**

29) ...**Is He** *[the Father]* **the God of the Jews only? is he not also of the Gentiles? Yes, of the Gentiles also:**"

WILLIAM: I have noticed that all the writers of the New Testament say that God is the Father, too. Paul does this in all his letters. For instance:

Romans 1:7, 8:
7) "Grace to you and peace from <u>God our Father,</u> and the Lord Jesus Christ.
8) First, I thank <u>my God</u> through Jesus Christ for you all...."

2 Corinthians 1:2, 3:
2) "Grace *be* to you and peace from **God our Father,** and *from* the Lord Jesus Christ.
3) **Blessed** *be* **God,** even the Father of our Lord Jesus Christ, the Father of mercies, and <u>the God of all comfort</u>."

Ephesians 1:2:
"Grace *be* to you, and peace, **from** <u>God our Father,</u> and *from* the Lord Jesus Christ."

Titus 1:1:
"Paul, **a servant of God,** and an apostle of Jesus Christ, according to the faith of **God's** elect, and the acknowledging of the truth which is after godliness."

PROFESSOR: And James and Peter and Jude and John each identify the Father as "God" as well:

James 3:9:
"Therewith bless we **God, even the Father.**"

1 Peter 1:2:
"Elect according to the foreknowledge of **God the Father,** through sanctification of the Spirit, unto obedience and sprinkling of the blood of Jesus Christ: Grace unto you, and peace, be multiplied."

Jude 1:
Jude, the servant of Jesus Christ, and brother of James, to them that are sanctified by **God the Father,** and preserved in Jesus Christ, and called:

2 John 1:3

527

Grace be with you, mercy, and peace, from **God the Father**, and from the Lord Jesus Christ, the Son of the Father, in truth and love.

WILLIAM: ONE GOD; THREE DIVINE PERSONS. TELL AGAIN HOW COME ONE HAS THE PRE-EMINENCE?

PROFESSOR: Look at these two inspired statements. They carry the explanation. Before His incarnation, **Jesus was Equal to the Father:**

Great Controversy, page 493:
"By Christ the Father wrought in the creation of all heavenly beings... and to Christ, <u>equally with the Father</u>, all heaven gave allegiance."

Philippians 2:5-7:
5) "Let this mind be in you, which was also in **Christ Jesus:**
6) Who, being in the form of God, thought it not robbery to be equal with God:
7) <u>But made himself of no reputation, and took upon him the form of a servant</u>, and was made in the likeness of men."

As we have seen, in the plan of salvation Jesus volunteered to take subordinate position to the Father.

Isaiah 6:8:
"Also I heard the voice of the Lord, saying, Whom shall I send, and who will go for us? Then said I, Here am I; send me."

We usually think of the volunteer as Isaiah. But a careful reading of the entire chapter reveals that the "volunteer" is to preach to the end of the world. It was really a Divine Being, even Jesus Christ, who volunteered. He volunteered to be the Lamb of God.

The Youth's Instructor, June 21, 1900:
"Christ is equal with God, infinite and omnipotent *[His "equality" does not preclude Him from voluntary submission].* He could pay the ransom for man's freedom. He is the eternal, self-existing Son, on whom no yoke had come; **and when God**

528

asked, **"Whom shall I send?"** he could reply, **"Here am I;
send me."**

This statement is confirmed by the Bible:

Isaiah 48:16:
"Come ye near unto me, hear ye this; I have not spoken in
secret from the beginning; **from the time that it was, there am
I: and now the Lord GOD, and his Spirit, hath sent me."**

Jesus is the 'Sent' of God.

Isaiah 61:1:
"The Spirit of the Lord GOD is upon me; because the
LORD hath anointed me to preach good tidings unto the meek;
He hath sent me to bind up the brokenhearted, to proclaim
liberty to the captives, and the opening of the prison to them that
are bound."

Acts 10: 38:
"How **God** anointed **Jesus of Nazareth** with the **Holy Ghost**
and with power: who went about doing good, and healing all that
were oppressed of the devil; for God was with him.

Great Controversy, pages 502, 503:
"But the death of Christ was an argument in man's behalf that
could not be overthrown. The penalty of the law fell upon **Him
who was equal with God...."**

WILLIAM: If Jesus was eternal and equal with the Father, how did He
become the 'Son' of God?

PROFESSOR: He volunteered in the plan of salvation, and it is recorded
that His Father declared:

Hebrews 1:5:
"For unto which of the angels said he at any time, **Thou art
my Son, this day have I begotten thee?** And again, **I will be to
him a Father, and he shall be to me a Son?"**

Notice the future tense in the last verse. There never was a time when Jesus was not God's "Fellow" (Zech. 13:7), but there was a future time, in the plan of salvation, when Jesus would be "begotten of the Father":

John 1:14
"And the Word was made flesh, and dwelt among us, (and we beheld his glory, the glory as of **the only begotten of the Father**,) full of grace and truth."

WILLIAM: So remind me, when was Jesus begotten?

PROFESSOR: While Jesus was first begotten by the Holy Spirit through Mary into fallen human flesh at his birth in Bethlehem, Jesus was again 'begotten' of God at His resurrection into glorified humanity. He then ascended to the heavenly Zion. The New Testament confirms this:

Acts 13:33:
"God hath fulfilled the same unto us their children, in that **he hath raised up Jesus again;** as it is also written in the second psalm, **Thou art my Son, <u>this day</u> have I begotten thee.**"

WILLIAM: The Holy Spirit is also submitted to the Father in the plan of salvation. He has also submitted Himself to the Son as well.

John 15:26:
"But when **the Comforter** is come, **whom I will send unto you from the Father, even the Spirit of truth, which proceedeth from the Father, he shall testify of me.**"

John 16:13:
"**Howbeit when he, the Spirit of truth, is come,** he will guide you into all truth: **for he shall not speak of himself; but whatsoever he shall hear, that shall he speak: and he will show you things to come.**"

<u>Acts of the Apostles</u>, pages 51, 52:
"**It is not essential for us to be able to define just what the Holy Spirit is.** Christ tells us that the Spirit is the Comforter, 'the Spirit of truth, which proceedeth from the Father.' It is plainly declared regarding the Holy Spirit that, in His work of guiding men into all truth, 'He shall not speak of Himself.' John

15:26; 16:13. **The nature of the Holy Spirit is a mystery. Men cannot explain it, because the Lord has not revealed it to them."**

For a "Person," as the Holy Spirit is, to be formless most of the time, ↑d to be omnipresent, implies a "nature" beyond our ken. The Holy Spirit ⁄en inhabits the mind of God. It is through the Holy Spirit that mind is ↑ked with mind. This is how the Father, and the Son, and Christ's true sciples are all one.

1 Corinthians 2:10-12, 16:
    10) **"But God hath revealed them unto us by his Spirit: for the Spirit searcheth all things, yea, the deep things of God.**
    11) **For what man knoweth the things of a man, save the spirit of man which is in him? Even so the things of God knoweth no man, but the Spirit of God.**
    12) Now **we have received**, not the spirit of the world, but **the spirit which is of God**; that we might know the things that are freely given to us of God.
    16) ...For who hath known the mind of the Lord, that he may instruct him? **But we have the mind of Christ."**

HE GODHEAD SYMBOLIZED IN THE OT.

We have seen the precious symbol, displaying the separate, distinct, operative, personhood, and functions of the Members of that Godly unit ⁈ know as the 'Godhead', is graphically outlined in the following ripture:

Exodus 12:22:
    "And ye shall take a bunch of hyssop, and dip [it] in the blood that [is] in the basin, and **strike the lintel and the two side posts** with the blood that [is] in the basin."

The blood, applied in faith, was applied on **three distinct entities—the tel and the two side posts.** These three entities represent the Heavenly io. (See illustration on page 270 of this book)   All three suffered in the ↑n of salvation.
The lintel, poised above the two side posts, **and never touching the ↑th, symbolizes the Father. He remains in heaven and maintains the**

531

integrity of the Godhead, separate from sin and sinners.   God's Wor says:

> **Ephesians 4:4-6:**
> 4) "[There is] one *[church]* body, and **one Spirit**, even as ye are called in one hope of your calling;
> 5) **One Lord**, one faith, one baptism,
> 6) **One God** and Father of all, who [is] <u>above all</u>, and **through all, and in you all.**" *[By His Spirit].*

The two side posts represent the Holy Spirit and Jesus Christ. The have access to heaven, but have given up aspects of their divinity in order come down from heaven to make contact with sinful humanity.

The door represents Christ's pivotal humanity: the only true entrance the 'fold':

> Our High Calling, page 48:
> "The **humanity** of the Son of God is **everything** to us. It is the golden chain that binds our souls to Christ, and through Christ to God."

> **John 10:7 (See also Hebrews 10:20):**
> **"Then said Jesus unto them again, Verily, verily, I say unto you, I am the door of the sheep."**

The humanity of Christ was powerless. **Jesus said, "I can of mine ov self do nothing." John 5:30.** Christ did not rely on His own divine power work any miracle. The door of Christ's humanity was thus hinged upon t Holy Spirit "Side Post." Christ did every miracle, through faith, by t indwelling Holy Spirit, and resisted temptation in that same power. Thus, I provides an example of how we can overcome. Only through the indwelli of the Holy Spirit in our body temples can we overcome as Jesus overcan Of His own divine power we are told:

> Desire of Ages, page 336:
> "That power He had laid down, and He says, "I can of Mine own self do nothing." John 5:30. **He trusted in the Father's might.** It was in faith—faith in God's love and care—that Jesus rested, and **the power of that word which stilled the storm was the power of God.**"

532

This power of God was manifested in Christ through the Holy Spirit, the representative of the Father.

THE NEW TESTAMENT 'LINTEL AND TWO SIDE POSTS'

1 John 5:7:
"For there are three that bear record in heaven, the Father, the Word, and the Holy Ghost: and these three are one."

The Heavenly Trio bear witness in heaven and are one. This one-ness is not an integral 'one'ness. That is, **the Heavenly Trio are not all the same identical indivisible substance.** This one-ness is described in:

John 17:21, 22:
21) **"That they all may be one; as thou, Father, *art* in me, and I in thee, that they also may be one in us:** that the world may believe that thou hast sent me.
22) And the glory which thou gavest me I have given them; **that they may be one, even as we are one.** I in them, and thou in me, that they may be made perfect in one."

This is a 'one'ness of harmony and agreement as we have repeatedly noted. God's messenger says,

Ministry of Healing, page 422:
"The unity that exists between Christ and His disciples does not destroy the personality of either. They are **one in purpose, in mind, in character, but not in person. It is thus that God and Christ are one.**"

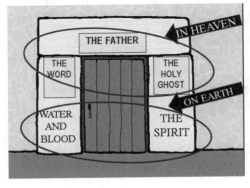

The verses before and after 1 John 5:7 depict the two side posts **Verse 6 and 8 state:**

> **1 John 5:6, 8:**
> 6) **"This is he that came by water and blood, even Jesus Christ; not by water only, but by water and blood.** And it is the Spirit that beareth witness, because the Spirit is truth.
> 8) **"…And there are three that bear witness in earth, the Spirit, and the water, and the blood: and these three <u>agree in one</u>."**

The (1)**Spirit** and the (2)water and the (3)blood bear witness on earth **but the 'water' and the 'blood' are Christ's 'witnesses'**, witnessing t His Messiahship. Thus, **there are two Divine Beings that bear witness o earth, the Spirit and Jesus Christ.**

Again, together with the Father, "these three **agree in one,**" which is th same **"one-ness"** as in verse 7 quoted above.

Thus we have the Father (as represented by the lintel) in heaven; and th Word, and the Holy Ghost—namely Christ and the Holy Spirit (a represented by the two side posts)—reaching from heaven to earth: fro the Father to us.

<u>ANOTHER EXAMPLE</u>

Matthew 5:45:

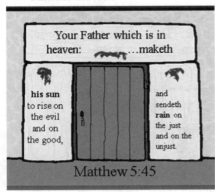

Your Father which is in heaven: …maketh

his sun to rise on the evil and on the good,

and sendeth rain on the just and on the unjust.

Matthew 5:45

"Your **Father which is in heaven** *[the Lintel]*: maketh His **sun** *[Jesus, the Sun of righteousness—one Side Post that comes from heaven to earth]* to rise on the evil and on the good, and sendeth **rain** *[the Holy Spirit, the early and latter rain—the other Side Post that comes from heaven to earth]* on the just and on the unjust."

The Spirit of prophecy confirms this understanding:

Christ's Object Lessons, page 202:
"...men have the power to shut themselves away from **sunshine and shower.** So while the **Sun of Righteous-ness** shines, **and the showers of grace** fall freely for all, we may by separating ourselves from God *[by rejecting the only channels of communication to Himself that God has provided]* still 'inhabit the parched places in the wilderness.'"

'HE TWO SIDE-POSTS: JESUS CHRIST AND THE HOLY SPIRIT

Jesus and the Holy Spirit are often seen together in the Scriptures. For istance, Jesus is the Word of God, and the Holy Spirit inspires holy men to rite the Word.

Revelation 2:8, 11:
8) "And unto the angel of the church in Smyrna write; **These things saith the first and the last, which was dead, and is alive;**

11) ...He that hath an ear, let him hear what **the Spirit saith unto the churches;** He that overcometh shall not be hurt of the second death."

HE FATHER: CALLED THE MOST HIGH GOD IN THE IBLE—REPRESENTED BY THE LINTEL

Mark 5:7:
"And cried with a loud voice, and said, What have I to do with thee, **Jesus, thou Son of the most high God?** I adjure thee by God, that thou torment me not."

Genesis 14:18, 19:
18) "And Melchizedek king of Salem brought forth bread and wine: **and he was the priest of the most high God.**

19) And he blessed him, and said, Blessed be Abram of **the most high God, possessor of heaven and earth."**

Deuteronomy 32:8:
"When **the Most High** divided to the nations their inheritance, when he separated the sons of Adam, he set the bounds of the people according to the number of the children of Israel."

NEBUCHADNEZZAR PERCEIVES THE HEAVENLY TRIO (in his own words!)

Daniel 3:25:
"He answered and said, Lo, I see four men loose, walking in the midst of the fire, and they have no hurt; **and the form of the fourth is like the <u>Son of God</u>.**"

Daniel 3:26:
"Then Nebuchadnezzar came near to the mouth of the burning fiery furnace, and spake, and said, Shadrach, Meshach, and Abednego, **ye servants of the <u>most high God,</u>** come forth, and come hither. Then Shadrach, Meshach, and Abednego, came forth of the midst of the fire."

So, the learned Nebuchadnezzar held the concept of "the Most High God" and recognized that there was more than one divine Person going by the title "God"; and he recognized that they share one "Spirit."

Daniel 4:8:
"But at the last Daniel came in before me, whose name was Belteshazzar, **...and in whom is the spirit of the holy gods.**"

THE FATHER: THE 'ONE GOD' OF JESUS AND THE HOLY SPIRIT

Deuteronomy 10:17:
"**For the LORD your God is God of gods, and Lord of lords, a great God,** a mighty, and a terrible, which regardeth not persons, nor taketh reward."

John 14:28:
"...If ye loved me, ye would rejoice, because I said, I go unto the Father: **for my Father is greater than I.**"

Hebrews 1:8, 9:
8) "**But unto the Son he saith, Thy throne, O God, is for ever and ever:** a sceptre of righteousness is the sceptre of thy kingdom.

536

9) "Thou hast loved righteousness, and hated iniquity; therefore God *[the Father]*, <u>even thy God</u>, hath anointed thee with the oil of gladness above thy fellows."

So Jesus is God (that is a **Title** befitting His station in the Godhead), **but His Father is <u>His God</u>.**

John 20:17:

"Jesus saith unto her, Touch me not; for I am not yet ascended to my Father: but go to my brethren, and say unto them, **I ascend unto my Father, and your Father; <u>and to my God, and your God.</u>**"

Revelation 3:12:

"Him that overcometh will I make a pillar in **the temple of <u>my God,</u>** and he shall go no more out: and I will write upon him **the name of <u>my God,</u>** and the name of **the city of <u>my God,</u>** *which is* new Jerusalem, which cometh down out of heaven from <u>**my God.**</u>"

John 17:3:

"And this is life eternal, that they might know **thee the only true God, and Jesus Christ, whom thou hast sent.**"

1 Corinthians 11:3:

"But I would have you know, that the head of every man is Christ; and the head of the woman is the man; **and the head of Christ is God.**"

1 Corinthians 15: 27, 28:

27) **"For he (*the Father*) hath put all things under his** (*Christ's*) **feet. But when he saith all things are put under *him*** (*Christ*)**, *it is* manifest that he (*the Father*) is excepted, which did put all things under him.**

28) **And when all things shall be subdued unto him** (*the Son*)**, then shall the Son also himself be subject unto him** (the Father) **that put all things under him, that God** (*the Father*) **may be all in all.**"

CHALLENGING SCRIPTURES—ONE

In Isaiah 45 there are a series of verses where the LORD i speaking, and He says that He is the LORD, and there is none els beside Him.

Isaiah 45:5, 6, 18, 21, 22:
5) **"I am the LORD, and there is none else, there is no God beside me:** I girded thee, though thou hast not known me."

6) "That they may know from the rising of the sun, and from the west, that **there is none beside me. I am the LORD, and there is none else.**"

18) **"For thus saith the LORD that created the heavens; God himself that formed the earth and made it;** he hath established it, he created it not in vain, he formed it to be inhabited: **I am the LORD; and there is none else."**

21) "...Who hath declared this from ancient time? Who hath told it from that time? Have not I the LORD? **And there is no God else beside me;** a just God and a Saviour; **there is none beside me.**

22) "Look unto me, and be ye saved, all the ends of the earth: **for I am God, and there is none else."**

Who is the LORD who is talking? **Let the Bible be its ow interpreter.** In fact, Isaiah himself will make clear who is talking. **T next Scripture will show that God the Father is the LORD, the speak in these verses:**
Isaiah 48:16:
"Come ye near unto me, hear ye this; I have not spoken in secret from the beginning; from the time that it was, there am I: **and now the Lord GOD** *[the Father]***, and his Spirit, hath sent me** *[Jesus]*."

There were "none beside" the "Most High" for He holds that uniq status in the plan of salvation.

CHALLENGING SCRIPTURES—TWO

The following verse is akin to the verses in Isaiah. Here is the famo verse from the writings of Moses:

Deuteronomy 6:4, 5:
4) **"Hear, O Israel: The LORD our God is one LORD:**

5)   And thou shalt love the LORD thy God with all thine heart, and with all thy soul, and with all thy might."

Who is the LORD that we are to love with all our heart, soul, and might? Let the Bible interpret itself. Moses himself will explain:

Deuteronomy 18:15:
"The LORD thy God will raise up unto thee a Prophet from the midst of thee, of thy brethren, **like unto me** *[He will lead His people to the "Promised Land"]*; unto him ye shall hearken."

Here the LORD is going to raise up a 'Prophet', which is referring to Jesus. Thus, we see that the LORD of Deut. 6 is God the Father.

CHALLENGING SCRIPTURES—THREE

Exodus 20:3:
"Thou shalt have no other gods before me."

Who is "Me"? This question is answered by asking first: HOW DO THE HEAVENLY TRIO GUIDE US?
- **God guides us through the 10 commandments, which define sin and righteousness; and is the standard of judgment. Revelation 14:12.**
- **Jesus guides us through the Word, which is really a commentary on the Ten Commandments, and the how to keep them by the power of God. John 1:1-3.**
- **The Holy Spirit guides us through our conscience enlightened by the Ten Commandments and the Word. Is. 30:21.**

Notice that the message of the Third Angel of Revelation 14 tells us that the commandments are God the Father's.

Revelation 14:12:
"Here is the patience of the saints; Here are they that keep **the commandments of God,** and have the faith of Jesus."

Thus, the God of the first commandment is God the Father. When we sin, we sin against Him. However, we also sin against Jesus, who relinquished and suffered so much in order to save us from sin; and we sin against the Holy Spirit, who condescends to dwell in, and have dealings with, fallen man. We sin against their sacrificial work to try and bring man back into harmony with God the Father. Sin wounds the Godhead! But since the Father is maintaining the integrity of the Godhead, we sin principally, against Him.

Genesis 39:9:
"How then can I do this great wickedness, **and sin against God**?"

THE ORIGINAL GOD OF THE SECOND ADVENT MOVEMENT IS RIGHT IN THE 3 ANGELS' MESSAGES.

1872 Statement of Principles:
"**1—That there is one God, a personal, spiritual Being, the Creator of all things, omnipotent, omniscient, and eternal, infinite in *[love]*, wisdom, holiness, justice, goodness, truth, and mercy, unchangeable, and everywhere present by His representative, the Holy Spirit.**"

The God defined in the 1872 Statement of Principles is the same God defined in the First Angel's Message.

Revelation 14:7:
"**Worship Him that made heaven, and earth, and the sea, and the fountains of waters *[through* Jesus the Word. John *1:1]*.**"

The 144,000 will worship the Father:

Revelation 14:1:
"And I looked, and, lo, a Lamb stood on the mount Sion, and with him an hundred forty *and* four thousand, **having his Father's name written in their foreheads.**"

CHALLENGING SCRIPTURES—FOUR

1 John 4:8:
"**He that loveth not knoweth not God; for God is love.**"

Who is "God" in this verse? The next verse will tell:

1 John 4:9:
"**In this was manifested the love of God toward us, because that God <u>sent</u> his only begotten Son into the world, that we might live through him.**"

God the Father is love. We can know that for that is how Jesus has revealed Him to us.

CHALLENGING SOP STATMENT

The Signs of the Times, Nov. 27, 1893:
"The Jews had never before heard such words from human lips, and a convicting influence attended them; for it seemed that divinity flashed through humanity as Jesus said, 'I and my Father are one.' The words of Christ were full of deep meaning as he put forth the claim that he and the Father were of **one substance**, possessing **the same** attributes."

This statement from Ellen White seems, to some, to suggest the Trinity doctrine of consubstantiation.   It is true that the Father and the Son were of one substance, meaning the same spiritual nature of Deity. But it is not true that they are of the identical, indivisible substance, as the Trinity doctrine teaches. People are made of one substance, human flesh, all having human nature, but not the same identical, indivisible substance. No, we are distinct and separate beings. The same is true of the Father and the Son, in whose image we are made.

<u>Ministry of Healing</u>, page 422:
"The unity that exists between Christ and His disciples does not destroy the personality of either. They are one in purpose, in mind, in character, **but not in person**. It is **thus that God and Christ are one.**"

At the formulation of the Trinity doctrine at Nicea in 325 AD, if the doctrine was worded as the EGW statement, there would have been agreement among all—both Arians and Catholics. But the Catholic Church forced all to believe it as they did—that the Father, Son, and Holy Spirit were of the same identical, indivisible substance. See <u>Truth Triumphant</u>, pages 85, 86.

DOES IT MATTER?

Whom Do We Worship? The One of Three? Or the Three-in-One God?

Great Controversy, page 583:

"It is as easy to make an idol of false doctrines and theories as to fashion an idol of wood or stone. By misrepresenting the attributes of God, Satan leads men to conceive of Him in a false character. With many, a philosophical idol is enthroned in the place of Jehovah; WHILE THE LIVING GOD, AS HE IS REVEALED IN HIS WORD, IN CHRIST, AND IN THE WORKS OF CREATION, IS WORSHIPED BY BUT FEW."

WHY IS THIS IMPORTANT? THE PRINCIPLE OF THE EXODUS:

Just as God led His people out of Egypt by His Angel (Michael, the pre incarnate Jesus Christ) and brought them to the Promised Land, it will b the same God who leads His people, by Jesus Christ, out of Babylon (from 1844 to the present), and finally brings them into the heavenly Promise Land.

IN THE END, IT WILL LOOK DIFFERENT!

Instead of fire coming down from heaven in answer to the prayer God's true people, **the fire will appear to confirm the teachings of th false prophet.**

Revelation 13:13:

"And he doeth great wonders, so that he maketh fire come down from heaven on the earth in the sight of men."

THE ORIGINAL GOD OF THE SECOND ADVENT MOVEMENT

1872 SDA Statement of Principles

1—That there is one God, a personal, spiritual Being, the Creator of all things, omnipotent, omniscient, and eternal, infinite in wisdom, holiness, justice, goodness, truth, and mercy, unchangeable, and everywhere present by His representative, the Holy Spirit.

542

2—That there is one Lord Jesus Christ, the Son of the Eternal Father, the One by whom He created all things, and by whom they do consist.

Jesus is the One whom the Father and the Holy Spirit sent. Jesus is the One who volunteered to go.

Evangelism, pages 614, 615:
"There are **three living persons** of the **heavenly trio;** in the name of these **three great powers—the Father, the Son, and the Holy Spirit**—those who receive Christ by living faith are baptized, and **these powers** will cooperate with the obedient subjects of heaven in their efforts to live the new life in Christ."

1980—THE NEW FALSE GOD IN THE SDA CHURCH—THE TRINITY

Seventh-day Adventists Believe, page 16:
Belief #2—"There is one God: Father, Son, and Holy Spirit, a unity of three <u>co-eternal</u> Persons."

FACTS ABOUT THE TRINITY

The **"Trinity" doctrine teaches that there is one God with three personalities—all of one identical indivisible substance—continually manifested.**

The **"Trinity" was established in 325AD at the Council of Nicea, in the 4th Century <u>after</u> Christ, during the epitome of apostasy.**

Sunday worship is devoted to the Trinity.

Roman Catholicism and Fallen Protestantism have always worshipped the Trinity and, since 1980, the Seventh-day Adventist Church, now officially worships the Trinity.

FACTS ABOUT THE GODHEAD

There is **One Most High God—the Father—The "one God" of Scripture—a status necessitated by the implementation of the plan of salvation.**

There are **Three distinct Eternal Beings: The Father, Son, and Holy Spirit—Each Individual is Eternal.** Not "Co-eternal."

The Son and Holy Spirit voluntarily chose submissive roles in the implementation of the plan of salvation.

Life—original, unborrowed, underived is the natural possession of each.

Oneness—a unity of love, a harmony of thought, purpose, character, and Spirit.

True Seventh-day Adventists worship the Father (the Most High God), **through the Son** (Jesus Christ), **and by the Holy Spirit—the Three Distinct Eternal Beings of the Heavenly Trio—also termed 'the Godhead.'**

Worship being most appropriately demonstrated by obedience to every word proceeding from the mouth of God and relayed through the Son and the Holy Spirit to us—for example: 7th-day Sabbath worship.

SDA PIONEERS VIEW OF THE TRINITY

James White, *Review & Herald,* September 12, 1854.

"**As fundamental errors, we might class with this counterfeit Sabbath other errors which Protestants have brought away from the Catholic Church, such as** sprinkling for baptism, **the trinity,** the consciousness of the dead and eternal life in misery.

"The mass who have held these fundamental errors, have doubtless done it ignorantly, **but can it be supposed that the church of Christ will carry along with her these errors till the judgment scenes burst upon the world? We think not.**"

James White, *Review & Herald,* February 7, 1856:

"Martin Luther, and other reformers, arose in **the strength of God, and with the Word and Spirit,** made mighty strides in the Reformation.   **The greatest fault we can find in the Reformation is, the Reformers stopped reforming.** Had they gone on, and onward, till they had left the **last vestige of Papacy behind,** such as natural immortality, sprinkling, **the trinity, and** Sunday keeping, **the church would now be free from her unscriptural errors.**"

Joseph Bates, 1868, The Autobiography Of Elder Joseph Bates, page 204:

"Respecting the trinity, I concluded that it was an impossibility for me to believe that the Lord Jesus Christ, the Son

544

of the Father, was also the Almighty God, the Father, one and the same being. I said to my father, 'If you can convince me that we are one in this sense, that you are my father, and I your son; and also that I am your father, and you my son, then I can believe in the trinity.'

R.J. Cottrell, *Review & Herald*, July 6, 1869:
   "**To hold the doctrine of the Trinity** is not so much an evidence of evil intention as of **intoxication from that wine of which all the nations have drunk.** The fact that this was one of the leading doctrines, if not the very chief, upon which the bishop of Rome was exalted to popedom, does not say much in its favor."

Using subtle wording, the worship of **the Catholic concept of the Trinity** is officially incorporated into the 27 Statements of Belief at the 1980 Dallas GC. Thus, 127 YEARS after 1872, the Seventh - day Adventist church chose to adopt this **fundamental error and make it a fundamental belief!** This watershed is noted and highlighted by a prominent Trinitarian Adventist:

George Knight, *Ministry,* Oct., 1993:
   "**Most of the founders of Seventh-day Adventism would not be able to join the church today if they had to subscribe to the denomination's Fundamental Beliefs. More specifically, most would not be able to agree to belief number 2, which deals with the doctrine of the trinity.**"

Even the famous Catholic theologian, Hans Kung, declares that there is no evidence for the Trinity in the Bible: Kung states:

Christianity: Essence, History, and Future, page 95, New York, 1995:
   "In Judaism, indeed throughout the New Testament, while there is belief in God the Father, in Jesus the Son and in God's Holy Spirit, **there is no doctrine of one God in three persons (modes of being), no doctrine of a 'triune God,' a 'Trinity.'**"

MORE EVIDENCES OF THE NEW GOD in the SDA CHURCH

1985—18 new hymns to the Trinity in the new SDA Hymnal—never before in SDA hymnals.

1999—POLISH SDA—CATHOLIC AGREEMENT: After 15 years of dialogue, the Polish SDA could state clearly:

> "The SDA Church ...in its teaching and service, cultivates the most important principles of Catholic faith, <u>especially the belief in the Blessed Trinity</u>."

2000—SDA Leader and Administrator, Reinder Bruinsma, writes the book, <u>Our Awesome God</u>. In it he admits:

> "It is a basic Christian doctrine that God is a Trinity of three persons ('modes of eternal manifestation') having one substance (essence or being). "It took the Adventist Church until far into the 19th century to agree that the doctrine of the Trinity was indeed biblical and belonged among the fundamental Adventist beliefs."

Notice, this illustration from a SDA Bible Study Handbook, which clearly depicts the false Catholic Trinity concept:

2006—Sabbath School Quarterly: "TheTriune God."

> "'There is one God: Father, Son, and Holy Spirit, a unity of three co-eternal Persons.' "In other words, Adventists— along with millions of other Christians—believe in <u>the triune</u>

nature of God; that is, there is one God who exists as three Persons."

"What analogies—such as …a three-pronged fork—can help someone understand the idea of how one God can be composed of three equal Persons?"

The Three-Pronged Fork is the illustration of God that Satan likes. The Hindu 'Shiva' holds the same Trident.

The prophet Jeremiah poses the cogent question:

Jeremiah 2:11-13:
11) "Hath a nation changed *their* gods, which *are* yet no gods? but my people have changed their glory for *that which* doth not profit.

12) Be astonished, O ye heavens, at this, and be horribly afraid, be ye very desolate, saith the LORD.

13) For my people have committed two evils; they have forsaken me the fountain of living waters, *and* hewed them out cisterns, broken cisterns, that can hold no water."

Small wonder that Ellen White never used the word "Trinity"; despite her coming out of a Trinitarian church. This is significant because her writings were inspired by the Holy Spirit. This error blossomed after her death.

Just before Moses died God warned him what would happen after his death.

Deuteronomy 31:16:
"The LORD said unto Moses, Behold, **thou shalt sleep with thy fathers;** and this people will rise up, **and go a whoring after the gods of the strangers of the land,** whither they go *to be*

547

among them, and will forsake me, and break my covenant which I have made with them."

These words, spoken to Moses, could equally have been spoken to Ellen White. The same deviation has occurred, among God's denominated people, since God's messenger has gone to her rest.

WHAT ARE WE TO DO?

As individuals and as a Church Body we are to:

Joshua 24:15:
"Choose you this day whom ye will serve; Whether the gods which your fathers served that *were* on the other side of the flood, or the gods of the Amorites, in whose land ye dwell: But as for me and my house, we will serve the LORD.

Even if your church building is owned by a conference under the General Conference of SDA, declare to the conference and to the General Conference that, as a local church body, you officially worship the Godhead and not the Trinity, and that you are adhering to the 1872 Statement of Principles. Unless this is done, you are officially still worshipping the Trinity, a false God.

Declare that you pray to the Most High God, the Father, through Jesus our Mediator; employing faith filled submissive prayer as indited by the Holy Spirit and that you worship the Godhead through obedience.

WORSHIP WHERE THE PRESENCE OF JESUS IS.

Matthew 18:20:
"For where two or three are gathered together in my name, there am I in the midst of them."

Upward Look, page 315:
"The presence of Christ alone constitutes a church."

DON'T WORSHIP AT THE TRINITY WORSHIP CENTERS

God has "seven thousand" who don't "bow the knee to Baal." It is time to stop worshiping God ignorantly as the Greeks worshipped the "**unknown**

548

God" (see Acts 17). It is time to **know** the "only true God and Jesus Christ" whom He "hast sent". (John 17:3.)

Chapter 42

TRI-THEISM AND THE TRUTH

WILLIAM: Because I believe in the Heavenly Trio, some label me a "tri-theist," and tell me that is heresy!

PROFESSOR: "Tri-theism" is the label applied to those who declare that God the Father, God the Son, and God the Holy Spirit, are three, separate and distinct Eternal Beings, who **are not consubstantial one with the other.** Such labeling stems from spiritual myopia!

WILLIAM: What do you mean?

PROFESSOR: The word of God declares that, "There be gods many." (1 Corinthians 8:5).

Jesus Himself reminded His accusers of Psalm 82:6 when He defended His claim to be the Son of God despite His being a man (John 10:33-36):

John 10:33-36:
33) "The Jews answered him, saying, For a good work we stone thee not; but for blasphemy; and because that thou, being a man, makest thyself God.

34) Jesus answered them, Is it not written in your law, I said, **Ye are gods**? *[Psalms 82:6]*

35) If he *[the Holy Spirit, speaking to man for the* Father*]* called them **gods, unto whom the word of God came,** and the scripture cannot be broken;

36) Say ye of him, **whom the Father hath sanctified**, and **sent** into the world *[see Isaiah 6:8; 48:16; John 17:3]*, Thou blasphemest; because I said, **I am the Son of God?**

You see, William, Jesus was saying that in the Word of God, God the Father calls His followers "gods"!

WILLIAM: Amazing. How can that be?

PROFESSOR: Very simple. Turn to:
2 Peter 1:4:

"Whereby are given unto us **exceeding great and precious promises: that by these ye might be partakers of the <u>divine</u> nature,** having escaped the corruption that is in the world through lust."

You see, if we receive the Holy Spirit imparted Word of God—the "exceeding great and precious promises"—we become "partakers of the divine nature." The Greek word for **"divine"** in this verse is the same word used for "Godhead" in Acts 17:29, Rom. 1:20, and Col. 2:9.

WILLIAM: Oh, I see. We can partake of the "divine nature"—or "Godhead" nature—through the ministration of the Holy Spirit. When we simply believe God's Word, the "exceeding great and precious promises," we receive the Holy Spirit in the Word and through the Word.

PROFESSOR: Yes, Jesus said:

John 6:63:
"It is the spirit that quickeneth; the flesh profiteth nothing: **the words that I speak unto you, they are spirit, and they are life."**

Thus, we see that truly "There be gods many (1 Corinthians 8:5).

WILLIAM: Couldn't this "gods many" mean "idols"?

PROFESSOR: We saw that this **is not** a reference to "idols." The Word of God teaches that "idols" "are no gods." (See 2 Chron. 13:9; Jer. 5:7; Jer. 16:20; Gal. 4:8).

WILLIAM: But Professor, if there be "gods many," then the Scriptures must teach a sort of **"holy polytheism."**

PROFESSOR: But that does not mean that all "gods" are to be worshiped! The Scriptures clarify that **there is "One God" Who rules over all. He is the "God of gods."** (Deut. 10:17; Joshua 22:22; Psalm 136:2). **He is Jesus' God** (John 20:17). **He is the "only True God."** (John 17:3.) **He is "God the Father."** And Jesus said, "No man cometh **unto the Father, but by Me."** (John 14:6). Jesus is the Way (to the Father); the Truth (about the Father); and the Life ("As the living Father hath sent Me, and **I live by the Father: So he that eateth Me, even He shall live by Me."** John 6:57.)

WILLIAM: Does that mean Jesus was a "lesser" God?

PROFESSOR: None of the above denigrates Jesus, nor does it detract from His divinity. All of the above is an illustration of the levels of self abnegation that Christ willingly accepted, indeed chose, in order to reach us where we are; while His Father maintained the integrity of the Godhead "in His high and holy place" (Isaiah 57:15). **Yet God through the Holy Spirit dwells "with him also that is of a contrite and humble Spirit."** Jesus self-sacrifice is part of the "**infinite** sacrifice" paid for man's redemption.

In the Godhead, there are three mighty Beings Whom the Scripture term "God." The Godhead is a unit of three distinct Eternal Persons—God the Father, God the Son, and God the Holy Ghost. They are **not** of "one indivisible substance." **"God"** is not a **name**, it is a **title**. This **"Heavenly Trio"**—these "three great Powers" of heaven may all be referred to by this title. The spiritually myopic think that the term "tri-theism" describes an appalling error. However, when, in the councils of the "Heavenly Trio," two Members voluntarily subordinated Themselves to the remaining Person, and accepted to serve Him as **Their God, what you are now confronted with is "mono-theism"!**

WILLIAM: That would mean that the Father is the "true God" of the Bible

PROFESSOR: Yes, He is the "One"—the "Most High God"; the "God of Gods." (1 Timothy 2:5; Mark 5:7; Deut. 10:17). **Mono-theism is a situation necessitated by sin**. It is because of sin, that the Father has to hold to His "high and holy place," keeping in touch with His Creation through His representative, the Holy Spirit, while His Son mediates between Him and fallen humanity. God the Father—the "Only True God" (of John 17:3), risked losing His "Fellow" (Zech. 13:7), His Son, our Saviour: God the Father risked being the "Only True God" for eternity Read the clear Biblical confirmation:

1 Corinthians 8:6:
"But to us there is but **one God, the Father,** of whom are all things, and we in him; and one Lord Jesus Christ, by whom are all things, and we by him."

Under the present "mono-theistic" dispensation, we approach the "Only True God"—the Father—through Jesus Christ, Whom He has sent. And our **desire** to come to God through the Son is supplied to us through the ministration of the Holy Spirit.

552

WILLIAM: So "spiritual myopia" develops when we don't take into consideration events in the history of the plan of salvation that have affected the status of each Member of the Godhead.

PROFESSOR: What you have just expressed is clearly seen in:

1 Corinthians 11:3:
"But I would have you know, that **the head of every man is Christ; and the head of the woman** *is* **the man; and the head of Christ** *is* **God.**"

As in the Godhead, even so in marriage, subordination of one equal partner to another has been necessitated by the inception of sin (Genesis 3:16 and Phil. 2:6)—the situation where one member of the unit has to "rule." Would that all men would "rule" their family units in Godly love, as the Father does.

553

Chapter 43

WORTHY, WORTHY, IS THE LAMB

PROFESSOR: By those who think along the conventional, customary, superficial lines, the points that we have been discussing these past days will be regarded as putting Jesus down; as making Jesus out to be a "lesser" God. But think about it: **Does the fact that the Scriptures say that in the family "the man is the head of the woman" (1 Corinthians 11:3), imply that a wife is a lesser person? No! They are equal in nature, but not in station!**

WILLIAM: We know what the status of Jesus was before sin entered the universe!

PROFESSOR: Throughout eternity the Father and the Son had always been equal in nature. However, their equality of status, at the commencement of Lucifer's rebellion, had to be clarified by the Father. Before Creation, God the Father established and made known the status of His Son to the heavenly host:

> Lift Him Up, page 18.3 (Spirit of Prophecy, Volume 1, pages 17, 18):
> "Lucifer in heaven, before his rebellion, was a high and exalted angel, next in honor to God's dear Son. His countenance, like those of the other angels, was mild and expressive of happiness. His forehead was high and broad, showing a powerful intellect. His form was perfect; his bearing noble and majestic. A special light beamed in his countenance and shone around him brighter and more beautiful than around the other angels; yet Christ, God's dear Son, had the preeminence over all the angelic host. He was one with the Father before the angels were created. **Lucifer was envious of Christ, and gradually assumed command which devolved on Christ alone.** *[Those who thirst after 'kingly power' attempt to usurp Christ's authority over His people, even today.]*
> "**The great Creator** assembled the heavenly host, that He might in the presence of all the angels confer special honor upon His Son. **The Son was seated on the throne with the Father,**

and the heavenly throng of holy angels was gathered around them. The Father then made known that **it was <u>ordained by Himself</u> that Christ, His Son, should be equal with Himself; so that <u>wherever was the presence of His Son, it was as His own presence.</u>** The word of the Son was to be obeyed as readily as the word of the Father. His Son He had invested with authority to command the heavenly host. Especially was His Son to work in union with Himself in the anticipated creation of the earth and every living thing that should exist upon the earth. His Son would carry out His will and His purposes but would do nothing of Himself alone. The Father's will would be fulfilled in Him."

This profound statement makes it crystal clear that **to worship Jesus is tantamount to worshiping His Father** since "the presence of His Son, ...was as His own Presence." Jesus, the express image of His Father's person and of His character, was as much of a representation of the Father as fallen man could bear without being consumed. Laying aside the panoply of divinity, He came to make known the Father, of Whom Satan had sown such terrible misconception. **(Incidentally, why would Lucifer have been jealous of a consubstantial hypostasis?)**

WILLIAM: But, since Jesus laid aside His divinity, would He still be worthy to be worshipped?

PROFESSOR: Think about it, JESUS, LAYING ASIDE THE POWERS OF DEITY SO UNSELFISHLY, AND WITH SUCH LOVE AND COMPASSION FOR HIS PEOPLE, SHOULD INSPIRE STILL GREATER DEVOTION AND WORSHIP—NOT LESS! Besides, much of that which Jesus, One who was equal with God the Father, had laid aside and risked losing forever (5BC 1131; 1 SM 256), He now receives back:

Revelation 5:1-2, 5-6, 8-10, 12:

1) "And I saw in the right hand of him that sat on the throne a book written within and on the backside, sealed with seven seals.

2) And I saw a strong angel proclaiming with a loud voice, Who is worthy to open the book, and to loose the seals thereof?...

5) And one of the elders saith unto me *[John]*, Weep not: behold, the Lion of the tribe of Juda, the Root of David, hath prevailed to open the book, and to loose the seven seals thereof.

555

6)   And I beheld, and, lo, in the midst of the throne and of the four beasts, and in the midst of the elders, stood a Lamb as it had been slain, having seven horns and seven eyes, which are the seven Spirits of God sent forth into all the earth....

8)   And when he had taken the book, the four beasts and four *and* twenty elders **fell down before the Lamb,** having every one of them harps, and golden vials full of odours, which are the prayers of saints.

9)   And they sung a new song, saying, **Thou art worthy** to take the book, and to open the seals thereof: for thou wast slain, and hast **redeemed us to God** by thy blood out of every kindred, and tongue, and people, and nation;

10)   And hast made **us unto our God** kings and priests: and we shall reign on the earth....

12)   Saying with a loud voice, **Worthy is the Lamb that was slain to <u>receive</u> power, and riches, and wisdom, and strength, and honour, and glory, and blessing."**

All of the above would have been forfeited if Jesus had failed in His mission. The truly awe-inspiring, unparalleled risk that Jesus took when He humbled Himself to become man is alluded to in the following statement by God's messenger:

Signs of the Times, May 10, 1899:
    "Though Christ humbled Himself to become man, the Godhead was still His own *[He was still the Second Person of the Godhead. He was still God].* **His Deity** *[His being a Divine Member of the Godhead]* **could not be lost while He stood faithful and true to His loyalty** *[to His Father]."* (1 SM, page 256)

Notice, He could have lost His Deity! This point is emphasized in the following statement:

The Faith I Live By, page 49:
    Could Satan in the least particular have tempted Christ to sin, he would have bruised the Saviour's head. As it was, he could only touch His heel. Had the head of Christ been touched, the hope of the human race would have perished. Divine wrath *[from God the Father]* would have come upon Christ as it came

556

upon *[the* first*]* Adam. **Christ and the church would have been without hope.**" (5BC, page 1131)

'ILLIAM: How do Jesus and the Holy Spirit relate to each other?

ROFESSOR: On the south side of the **first Sanctuary apartment,** the [enorah, the golden candlestick, with the central stem and the six branches rming seven lamps—this Menorah was a symbolic representation of sus. The central stem, made of solid gold and filled with oil, fitly presented His righteous holiness and obedience to His Father. The oil presenting the Holy Spirit with which He was, and is, filled, and Who, om and through Him, flows out to give light and life to His church—His ːople. The branches of the Menorah represent the Man whose name is he Branch." (Zech. 6:12). Through Him, as represented in these ˙anches, flows the Holy Oil, which empowers the spiritual life of His ːople. His people—"the light of the world" (Matt. 5:14), have their flame ndled by Him who said, "I am the light of the world" (John 8:12) while e was on earth (John 9:5). (Jesus is the "holy fire" which must kindle our vn altars of sacrifice where "self" must "die daily.") Since His ascension e is the channel of light and life, through Whom we have access to the ›ther Comforter" Whom the Father gladly sends at Jesus' request (John ł:15-18) so that, because of the redemption price paid by Jesus, fallen men ıd women may receive, permanently if they so choose, the indwelling ˙esence of the Holy Spirit, who is the Spirit of God and the Spirit of Christ ¿omans 8:9).

Were it not for Jesus' sacrifice, none of this would be possible. ankind would be in outer darkness. He, because of His faith in His ther, as demonstrated on the cross, is our channel of light and life. **He is orthy of our worship, our love, our devotion, our obedience, our yalty.** "WORTHY, WORTHY, IS THE LAMB."

'ILLIAM: Will Jesus reign as King equal with the Father in the kingdom ˙ glory?

¿OFESSOR: When Jesus closes His High Priestly ministry and puts off is High Priestly garments, the Kingdom of Grace, His Father's kingdom, ıters a new phase. At that time, Jesus dons His kingly robes to execute dgment. They are the "garments of vengeance" to the wicked. When He ›mes to take His people home—they who have been the "light of the orld" during His heavenly ministry, He comes as "King of kings" and ›rd of lords." (His people are to be "kings and priests," remember.) The

"Kingdom of Glory" is begun and "all things" are put "under" Christ—i subjection to Him. **All except One!**

Paul expresses this truth in the following words:

> **1 Corinthians 15:27, 28:**
> 27) "For he *[God the Father]* hath put all things under his *[*Christ's*]* feet. But when he saith all things are put under *him [Christ], it is* **manifest that He *[the Father]* is excepted, which did put all things under him** *[Christ]*.
> 28)   And when all things shall be subdued unto him, **then shall the Son also himself be subject unto him** *[God the Father]* **that put all things under him** *[Christ]*, **that God** *[the Father—the Most High God]* **may be all in all."**

God the Father remains "the Most High God." **Father and Son a** **forever equal in Deity, but not in station.** That is what the Scriptur plainly teach, "…and the Scripture cannot be broken." (John 10:35.)

I want you to notice the clear perspective into which God's messeng places Jesus' role in reuniting us lost sinners with God, from whom we ha become separated by sin:

> Manuscript Releases Volume 10, page 389.2:
> "Jesus came from heaven to **reveal God**. He came to **represent the Father**. The time, the strength, the money expended in searching out these old, buried-up inscriptions, will not bring a greater knowledge than that which Christ has brought to our world. **His prayer to His Father is (and I would that you would listen as for your life): 'And this is life eternal, that they might know thee, the only true God, and Jesus Christ, whom He hath sent' (John 17:3). Union with Christ is an union with God through Christ**. There is a life in the soul of everyone who has formed this mystical, spiritual union with Christ that never fades or fails."

The spiritual union with God the Father, which is effected throu Christ, eventually leads the redeemed sinner to actually stand in tl physical presence of Jesus' Father, our Father. Be aware of how God messenger succinctly describes this, yet at the same time warns of tl danger of holding false concepts of God that can lead into "paths of Satan making", thereby derailing and frustrating God's plan for them:

Manuscript Releases Volume 9, page 124.1-3:

"**Christ took with Him to the heavenly courts His glorified humanity.** To those who receive Him, **He gives power to become the sons of God, that at last God may receive them as His, to dwell with Him throughout all eternity. If during this life they are loyal to God, they will at last "see His face, and His name shall be in their foreheads."** And what is the happiness of heaven but to see God? What greater joy could come to the sinner, saved by the grace of Christ, than to look upon the face of God, and know Him as Father? "Now we see through a glass, darkly; but then face to face: now I know in part; but then shall I know even as also I am known" (1 Corinthians 13:12).

"**Some today are coming to hold false ideas of the invisible God** *[See chapter 4, "John Harvey Kellogg and the Trinity" of this book]*, **and are presenting these ideas to others.** Let those who do this know that **their childish portrayal of God is a misconception. They know not God. Before the world, before angels, and before men, they are giving a false representation of Him.**

"To those to whom these fanciful interpretations are presented, I would say, **"Let not these sentiments charm your senses, and lead you into paths of Satan's making. Beware, beware, of spiritualistic** *[SPIRITUALISM, A SYSTEM OF INTERPRETATION THAT SPIRITUALIZES AWAY THE TEACHINGS OF THE SCRIPTURES.]* **ideas of God.** Those who entertain such ideas greatly dishonor Him. Let everyone humble His heart before God."--Manuscript 124, 1903, pages 1-6. ("A Personal God," October 14, 1903)." (See Chapter 4 in this book)

Chapter 44

A TRUE KNOWLEDGE OF GOD
Chapter 35 of <u>Ministry of Healing</u> by Ellen G. White

PROFESSOR: Today we are going to read an important chapter in <u>Ministry of Healing</u> called "A True Knowledge of God." The chapter is an inspired treatise refuting and confounding the deceptive premises of Trinitarianism and cogently outlining the truths of the biblical doctrine of God. Let's begin:

> <u>Ministry of Healing</u>, page 409:
> "Like our **Saviour,** we are in this world to do service for **God.**"

WILLIAM: Wait. That first sentence tells a lot.

PROFESSOR: What do you see?

WILLIAM: Firstly, that the Saviour is Jesus, and God is the Father. Two distinct Beings are mentioned here. Secondly, I see that here, when Ellen White here uses the word "God", she means the Father. And, thirdly, I see that she is pointing to a subordination of the Son to the Father—subordination which we know He voluntarily chose. Jesus was "in this world to do service for God" (His Father) and we should follow His example.

PROFESSOR: Very good. Let's continue:

> <u>Ministry of Healing</u>, page 409:
> "We are here to become like God in character, and by a life of service to reveal Him to the world. In order to be co-workers with God, in order to become like Him and to reveal His character, we must know Him aright. We must know Him as He reveals Himself.
> **"A knowledge of God is the foundation of all true education and of all true service. It is the only real safeguard against temptation.** It is this alone that can make us like God in

character. This is the knowledge needed by all who are working for the uplifting of their fellow men. **Transformation of character, purity of life, efficiency in service, adherence to correct principles, <u>all depend upon a right knowledge of God</u>. THIS knowledge is the essential preparation both for this life and for the life to come.**

"The knowledge of the Holy is understanding." Proverbs 9:10.

Through a knowledge of Him are given unto us "all things that pertain unto life and godliness." 2 Peter 1:3.

"This is life eternal," said Jesus, "that they might know Thee the only true God, and Jesus Christ, whom Thou hast sent." John 17:3.

"Thus saith the Lord, Let not the wise man glory in his wisdom, Neither let the mighty man glory in his might, Let not the rich man glory in his riches: But let him that glorieth glory in this, That he understandeth and knoweth Me, That **I am the Lord** which exercise loving-kindness, Judgment, and righteousness, in the earth: For in these things I delight, saith the Lord." Jeremiah 9:23, 24.

"We need to study the revelations of Himself <u>that God has given</u> [*not those that come from Paganism and Rome. See Appendix F]*

"Acquaint now thyself with Him, And be at peace: Thereby good shall come unto thee. Receive, I pray thee, the law from His mouth, And lay up His words in thy heart.... And the Almighty will be thy treasure....

"Then shalt thou delight thyself in the Almighty, And shalt lift up thy face unto God. Thou shalt make thy prayer unto Him, And He will hear thee; And thou shalt pay thy vows. Thou shalt also decree a thing, And it shall be established unto thee; And light shall shine upon thy ways.

"When they cast thee down, thou shalt say, There is lifting up; And the humble person He will save." Job 22:21-29, A.R.V.

"The invisible things of Him since the creation of the world are clearly seen, being perceived through the things that are made, even His everlasting power and divinity." Romans 1:20, A.R.V.

"The things of nature that we now behold give us but a faint conception of Eden's glory. Sin has marred earth's beauty; on all things may be seen traces of the work of evil. Yet much that is beautiful remains. Nature testifies that **One infinite in power, great in goodness, mercy, and love, created the earth,** and filled it with life and gladness. Even in their blighted state, all things reveal the handiwork of the great Master Artist. Wherever we turn, we may hear the voice of **God,** and see evidences of His goodness.

"From the solemn roll of the deep-toned thunder and old ocean's ceaseless roar, to the glad songs that make the forests vocal with melody, nature's ten thousand voices speak His praise. In earth and sea and sky, with their marvelous tint and color, varying in gorgeous contrast or blended in harmony, we behold His glory. The everlasting hills tell us of His power. The trees that wave their green banners in the sunlight, and the flowers in their delicate beauty, point to their **Creator.** The living green that carpets the brown earth tells of **God's** care for the humblest of His creatures. The caves of the sea and the depths of the earth reveal His treasures. He who placed the pearls in the ocean and the amethyst and chrysolite among the rocks, is a lover of the beautiful. The sun rising in the heavens is a representative of Him who is the life and light of all that He has made. All the brightness and beauty that adorn the earth and light up the heavens, speak of God.

"His glory covered the heavens."

"The earth is full of Thy riches."

"Day unto day uttereth speech, And night unto night showeth knowledge. There is no speech nor language, Without these their voice is heard. Their line is gone out through all the earth, And their words to the end of the world." Habakkuk 3:3; Psalm 104:24; 19:2-4, margin.

"All things tell of His tender, **fatherly** care and of His desire to make His children happy.

"The mighty power that works through all nature and sustains all things is not, as some men of science represent, merely an all-pervading principle, an actuating energy. **God is a Spirit; yet He is a personal Being; for so He has revealed Himself:"**

PROFESSOR: Who is this talking about?

WILLIAM: The Father, the Creator of heaven and earth.

ROFESSOR: Good. Let's continue.

Ministry of Healing, page 413:

"The Lord is the true God, He is the living God, and an everlasting King:... The gods that have not made the heavens and the earth, Even they shall perish from the earth, and from under these heavens."

"The portion of Jacob is not like them: For **He is the former of all things**."

"He hath made the earth by His power, He hath established the world by His wisdom, And hath stretched out the heavens by His discretion." Jeremiah 10:10, 11, 16, 12.

Nature Is Not God

"God's handiwork in nature is not God Himself in nature. The things of nature are an expression of God's character and power; but we are not to regard nature as God. The artistic skill of human beings produces very beautiful workmanship, things that delight the eye, and these things reveal to us something of the thought of the designer; but the thing made is not the maker. It is not the work, but the workman, that is counted worthy of honor. So while nature is an expression of God's thought, it is not nature, but the God of nature, that is to be exalted.

"Let us worship and bow down: Let us kneel before the Lord."

"In His hand are the deep places of the earth; The heights of the mountains are His also. The sea is His, and He made it; And His hands formed the dry land." Psalm 95:6; 95:4, 5, A.R.V.

"Seek Him that maketh the Pleiades and Orion, And turneth the shadow of death into the morning, And maketh the day dark with night;"

"He that formeth the mountains, and createth the wind, And declareth unto man what is His thought;"

"He that buildeth His spheres in the heaven, And hath founded His arch [Noyes's translation] in the earth;"

"He that calleth for the waters of the sea, And poureth them out upon the face of the earth; Jehovah is His name." Amos 5:8, A.R.V.; 4:13, A.R.V.; 9:6, margin; 9:6, A.R.V.

The Creation of the Earth

The work of creation cannot be explained by science. What science can explain the mystery of life?

"Through faith we understand that the worlds were framed by the word of God, so that things which are seen were not made of things which do appear." Hebrews 11:3.

"I form the light, and create darkness:... I the Lord do all these things.... I have made the earth, And created man upon it: I, even My hands, have stretched out the heavens, And all their host have I commanded."

"When I call unto them, they stand up together." Isaiah 45:7-12; 48:13.

In the creation of the earth, God was not indebted to pre-existing matter. "He spake, and it was;... He commanded, and it stood fast." Psalm 33:9. All things, material or spiritual, stood up before the Lord Jehovah at His voice and were created for His own purpose. The heavens and all the host of them, the earth and all things therein, came into existence by the breath of His mouth.

In the creation of man was manifest the agency of **a personal God.** When God had made man in His image, the human form was perfect in all its arrangements, but it was without life. **Then a personal, self-existing God breathed into that form the breath of life,** and man became a living, intelligent being. All parts of the human organism were set in action. The heart, the arteries, the veins, the tongue, the hands, the feet, the senses, the faculties of the mind, all began their work, and all were placed under law. Man became a living soul. **Through Christ the Word, a personal God created man and endowed him with intelligence and power.**

Our substance was not hid from Him when we were made in secret; His eyes saw our substance, yet being imperfect, and in His book all our members were written when as yet there were none of them.

Above all lower orders of being, God designed that man, the crowning work of His creation, should express His thought and reveal His glory. But man is not to exalt himself as God *[as the papacy has]*.

"Make a joyful noise unto the Lord.... Serve the Lord with gladness: Come before His presence with singing. Know ye that

564

the Lord He is God: It is He that hath made us, and His we are; We are His people, and the sheep of His pasture. Enter into His gates with thanksgiving, And into His courts with praise: Be thankful unto Him, and bless His name."

"Exalt the Lord our God, And worship at His holy hill; For the Lord our God is holy." Psalm 100:1-4, margin; 99:9.

God is constantly employed in upholding and using as His servants the things that He has made. He works through the laws of nature, using them as His instruments. They are not self-acting. Nature in her work testifies of the intelligent presence and active agency of a Being who moves in all things according to His will.

"Forever, O Lord, Thy word is settled in heaven. Thy faithfulness is unto all generations: Thou hast established the earth, and it abideth. They continue this day according to Thine ordinances: For all are Thy servants."

"Whatsoever the Lord pleased, that did He In heaven, and in earth, in the seas, and all deep places."

"He commanded, and they were created. He hath also established them for ever and ever: He hath made a decree which shall not pass." Psalm 119:89-91; 135:6; 148:5, 6.

It is not by inherent power that year by year the earth yields its bounties and continues its march around the sun. The hand of the Infinite One is perpetually at work guiding this planet. It is God's power continually exercised that keeps the earth in position in its rotation. It is God who causes the sun to rise in the heavens. He opens the windows of heaven and gives rain.

"He giveth snow like wool: He scattereth the hoarfrost like ashes."

"When He uttereth His voice, there is a multitude of waters in the heavens, And He causeth the vapors to ascend from the ends of the earth; He maketh lightnings with rain, And bringeth forth the wind out of His treasures." Psalm 147:16; Jeremiah 10:13.

It is by His power that vegetation is caused to flourish, that every leaf appears, every flower blooms, every fruit develops.

The mechanism of the human body cannot be fully understood; it presents mysteries that baffle the most intelligent. It is not as the result of a mechanism, which, once set in motion, continues its work, that the pulse beats and breath follows breath. In God we live and move and have our being. The beating heart, the throbbing pulse, every nerve and muscle in the living organism, is kept in order and activity by the power of an ever-present God.

The Bible shows us God in His high and holy place, not in a state of inactivity, not in silence and solitude, but surrounded by ten thousand times ten thousand and thousands of thousands of holy beings, all waiting to do His will. Through these messengers He is in active communication with every part of His dominion. **By His Spirit He is everywhere present. Through the agency of His Spirit and His angels He ministers to the children of men.**

Above the distractions of the earth He sits enthroned; all things are open to His divine survey; and from His great and calm eternity He orders that which His providence sees best.

"The way of man is not in himself: It is not in man that walketh to direct his steps."

"Trust in the Lord with all thine heart.... In all thy ways acknowledge Him, And He shall direct thy paths."

"The eye of the Lord is upon them that fear Him, Upon them that hope in His mercy; To deliver their soul from death, And to keep them alive in famine."

"How precious is Thy loving-kindness, O God!... The children of men take refuge under the shadow of Thy wings."

"Happy is he that hath the God of Jacob for his help, Whose hope is in the Lord his God."

"The earth, O Jehovah, is full of Thy loving-kindness." Thou lovest "righteousness and justice." Thou "art the confidence of all the ends of the earth, And of them that are afar off upon the sea: Who by His strength setteth fast the mountains, Being girded about with might; Who stilleth the roaring of the seas,... And the tumult of the peoples."

"Thou makest the outgoings of the morning and evening to rejoice."

"Thou crownest the year with Thy goodness; And Thy paths drop fatness."

"The Lord upholdeth all that fall, And raiseth up all those that be bowed down. The eyes of all wait upon Thee; And Thou givest them their meat in due season. Thou openest Thine hand, And satisfiest the desire of every living thing." Jeremiah 10:23;

Proverbs 3:5, 6; Psalm 33:18, 19; 36:7, A.R.V.; 146:5; 119:64, A.R.V.; 33:5, A.R.V.; 65:5-7, A.R.V.; 65:8, 11; 145:14-16.

Personality of God Revealed in Christ

"As a **personal** being, God has revealed Himself in His Son. The outshining of the Father's glory, "and the express image of His person," **Jesus, as a personal Saviour, came to the world. As a personal Saviour He ascended on high. As a personal Saviour He intercedes in the heavenly courts. Before the throne of God in our behalf ministers "One like unto the Son of man."** Hebrews 1:3; Revelation 1:13.

Christ, the Light of the world, veiled the dazzling splendor of His divinity and came to live as a man among men, that they might, without being consumed, become acquainted with their Creator. Since sin brought separation between man and his Maker, **no man has seen God** at any time, except as He is manifested through Christ.

"I and My Father are one," Christ declared. "No man knoweth the Son, but the Father; neither knoweth any man the Father, save the Son, and he to whomsoever the Son will reveal Him." John 10:30; Matthew 11:27.

Christ came to teach human beings what God desires them to know. In the heavens above, in the earth, in the broad waters of the ocean, we see the handiwork of God. All created things testify to His power, His wisdom, His love. Yet not from the stars or the ocean or the cataract can we learn of the personality of God as it was revealed in Christ.

God saw that a clearer revelation than nature was needed to portray both His personality and His character. He sent His Son into the world to manifest, so far as could be endured by human sight, the nature and the attributes of the invisible God.

Revealed to the Disciples

"Let us study the words that Christ spoke in the upper chamber on the night before His crucifixion. He was nearing His hour of trial, and He sought to comfort His disciples, who were to be so severely tempted and tried.

567

"Let not your heart be troubled," He said. "Ye believe in God, believe also in Me. In My Father's house are many mansions: if it were not so, I would have told you. I go to prepare a place for you. . . .

"Thomas saith unto Him, Lord, we know not whither Thou goest; and how can we know the way? Jesus saith unto him, **I am the way, the truth, and the life: no man cometh <u>unto the Father</u>, but by Me.** If ye had known Me, ye should have known My Father also: and from henceforth ye know Him, and have seen Him....

"Lord, show us the Father," said Philip, "and it sufficeth us. Jesus saith unto him, Have I been so long time with you, and yet hast thou not known Me, Philip? **he that hath <u>seen Me</u> hath seen <u>the Father</u>;** and how sayest thou then, Show us the Father? Believest thou not that I am in the Father, and the Father in Me? the words that I speak unto you I speak not of Myself: but the Father that dwelleth in Me, He doeth the works." John 14:1-10.

The disciples did not yet understand Christ's words concerning His relation to God. **Much of His teaching was still dark to them. Christ <u>desired them to have a clearer, more distinct knowledge of God</u>.**

"These things have I spoken unto you in parables," He said; "but the time cometh, when I shall no more speak unto you in parables, but I shall show you plainly of the Father." John 16:25, margin.

When, on the Day of Pentecost, the Holy Spirit was poured out on the disciples, they understood more fully the truths that Christ had spoken in parables. Much of the teaching that had been a mystery to them was made clear. But not even then did the disciples receive the complete fulfillment of Christ's promise. They received all the knowledge of God <u>that they could bear</u>, but the complete fulfillment of the promise that Christ would show them <u>plainly of the Father</u> was yet to come. Thus it is today. Our knowledge of God is partial and imperfect. When the conflict is ended, and the Man Christ Jesus acknowledges before the Father His faithful workers, who in a world of sin have borne true witness for Him, they will understand clearly what now are mysteries to them.

Christ took with Him to the heavenly courts His glorified humanity. To those who receive Him He gives power to

become the sons of God, that at last <u>God</u> may receive them as His, to dwell with Him throughout eternity. If during this life they are <u>loyal to God</u>, they will at last "see His face; and His name shall be in their foreheads." Revelation 22:4. And what is the happiness of heaven <u>but to see God</u>? What greater joy could come to the sinner saved by the grace of Christ than to look upon the face of God and know Him as Father?

The Scriptures clearly indicate the relation between God and Christ, and they bring to view as clearly <u>the personality</u> and <u>individuality</u> of <u>each</u>.

"God, who at sundry times and in divers manners spake in time past unto the fathers by the prophets, hath in these last days spoken unto us by His Son; . . . who being the brightness of His glory, and the express image of His person, and upholding all things by the word of His power, when He had by Himself purged our sins, sat down on the right hand of the Majesty on high; being made so much better than the angels, as He hath by inheritance obtained a more excellent name than they. For unto which of the angels said He at any time.

"Thou art My Son, This day have I begotten Thee?

And again, I will be to Him a Father, And He shall be to Me a Son?" Hebrews 1:1-5.

The personality of the Father and the Son, also the unity that exists between Them, are presented in the seventeenth chapter of John, in the prayer of Christ for His disciples:

"Neither pray I for these alone, but for them also which shall believe on Me through their word; **that they all may be one;** as **Thou, Father, art in Me, and I in Thee, that they also may be one in Us:** that the world may believe that Thou hast sent Me." John 17:20, 21.

The unity that exists between Christ and His disciples does not destroy <u>the personality</u> *[or individual 'personhood']* of either. They are one in purpose, in mind, in character, <u>but not in person</u>. IT IS <u>THUS</u> *[i.e. this is the way]* THAT GOD AND CHRIST ARE ONE.

Character of God Revealed in Christ

Taking humanity upon Him, Christ came to be <u>one</u> with humanity, and at the same time to reveal <u>our heavenly Father</u> to sinful human beings. He who had been in the

569

presence of the Father from the beginning, He who was the express image of the invisible God, **was alone able to reveal the character of the Deity to mankind.** He was in all things made like unto His brethren. He became flesh even as we are. He was hungry and thirsty and weary. He was sustained by food and refreshed by sleep. He shared the lot of men; yet He was the blameless Son of God. He was a stranger and sojourner on the earth—in the world, but not of the world; tempted and tried as men and women today are tempted and tried, yet living a life free from sin. Tender, compassionate, sympathetic, ever considerate of others, He represented the character of God, and was constantly engaged in service for God and man.

"Jehovah hath anointed Me," He said, "To preach good tidings unto the poor; He hath sent Me to bind up the brokenhearted, To proclaim liberty to the captives,"

"And recovering of sight to the blind;"

"To proclaim the year of Jehovah's favor;... To comfort all that mourn." Isaiah 61:1, A.R.V., margin; Luke 4:18; Isaiah 61:2, A.R.V.

"Love your enemies," He bids us; "bless them that curse you, do good to them that hate you, and pray for them which despitefully use you, and persecute you; that ye may be the children of your Father which is in heaven;" "for He is kind unto the unthankful and to the evil." "He maketh His sun to rise on the evil and on the good, and sendeth rain on the just and on the unjust." "Be ye therefore merciful, as your Father also is merciful." Matthew 5:44, 45; Luke 6:35; Matthew 5:45; Luke 6:36.

"Through the tender mercy of our God;... The Dayspring from on high hath visited us, To give light to them that sit in darkness and in the shadow of death, To guide our feet into the way of peace." Luke 1:78, 79.

The Glory of the Cross

The revelation of God's love to man centers in the cross. Its full significance tongue cannot utter, pen cannot portray, the mind of man cannot comprehend. Looking upon the cross of

Calvary, we can only say, "**God** so loved the world, that He gave His only-begotten Son, that whosoever believeth in Him should not perish, but have everlasting life." John 3:16.

Christ crucified for our sins, Christ risen from the dead, Christ ascended on high, is the science of salvation that we are to learn and to teach.

Was Christ

"Who, existing in the <u>form</u> of God, counted not the being on an <u>equality</u> with God a thing to be grasped, but emptied Himself, taking the form of a servant, being made in the likeness of men; and being found in fashion as a man, He humbled Himself, becoming obedient even unto death, yea, the death of the cross." Philippians 2:6-8, A.R.V.

"It is Christ that **died**, yea rather, that is risen again, who is even **at the right hand <u>of God</u>**." "**Wherefore He is able also to save them to the uttermost that come <u>unto God</u> by Him, seeing He ever liveth to make intercession for them.**" Romans 8:34; Hebrews 7:25.

"We have not a high priest that cannot be touched with the feeling of our infirmities; but One that hath been in all points tempted like as we are, yet without sin." Hebrews 4:15, A.R.V.

It is through the gift of Christ that we receive every blessing. Through that gift there comes to us day by day the unfailing flow of Jehovah's goodness. Every flower, with its delicate tints and its fragrance, is given for our enjoyment through that one Gift. The sun and the moon were made by Him. There is not a star which beautifies the heavens that He did not make. Every drop of rain that falls, every ray of light shed upon our unthankful world, testifies to the love of God in Christ. Everything is supplied to us through the one unspeakable Gift, God's only-begotten Son. He was nailed to the cross that all these bounties might flow to God's workmanship.

"Behold, what manner of love the Father hath bestowed upon us, that we should be called the sons of God." 1 John 3:1.

"Men have not heard, nor perceived by the ear, Neither hath the eye seen a God besides Thee, Who worketh for him that waiteth for Him." Isaiah 64:4, A.R.V.

The Knowledge That Works Transformation

The knowledge of God as revealed in Christ is the knowledge that all who are saved must have. It is the knowledge that works transformation of character. This knowledge, received, will re-create the soul **in the image of God.** It will impart to the whole being a spiritual power that is divine.

"We all, with open face beholding as in a glass the glory of the Lord, are changed into the same image from glory to glory." 2 Corinthians 3:18.

Of His own life the Saviour said, "I have kept My Father's commandments." John 15:10. "The Father hath not left Me alone; for I do always those things that please Him." John 8:29. **As Jesus was in human nature, so God means His followers to be.** In His strength we are to live the life of purity and nobility which the Saviour lived.

"For this cause," Paul says, **"I bow my knees unto the Father of our Lord Jesus Christ, of whom the whole family in heaven and earth is named,** that He would grant you, according to the riches of His glory, to be strengthened with might **by His Spirit in the inner man;** that Christ may dwell in your hearts by faith; that ye, being rooted and grounded in love, may be able to comprehend with all saints what is the breadth, and length, and depth, and height; and to know the love of Christ, which passeth knowledge, that ye might be filled with all the fullness of God." Ephesians 3:14-19.

We "do not cease to pray for you, and to desire that ye might be filled with the knowledge of His will in all wisdom and spiritual understanding; that ye might walk worthy of the Lord unto all pleasing, being fruitful in every good work, **and increasing** in the **knowledge of God;** strengthened with all might, according to His glorious power, unto all patience and long-suffering with joyfulness." Colossians 1:9-11."

PROFESSOR: William, I want you to take careful note of what God messenger now says about what we have just read, in her next words s affirms:

"THIS is the knowledge which God is inviting us to receive, and BESIDE WHICH ALL ELSE IS VANITY AND NOTHINGNESS."

Many today are worshipping in a state of vague mental confusion in their concept of God. Look at the warning given by God's messenger about why false concepts of God are generated and spread abroad:

Notebook Leaflets Volume 1, page 123.6, 7; 124.5-7:
"Be careful what you teach. Those who are learners of Christ will teach the same things that He taught. {1NL 123.6}

"The religious bodies all over Christendom will become more and more closely united in sentiment *[binding themselves together in ecumenical agreement]*. **THEY WILL MAKE OF GOD A PECULIAR SOMETHING in order to escape from** *[obedient]* **loyalty to Him who is pure, holy, and undefiled, and who denounces all sin as a production of the apostate** *[who from the beginning has taught that one can disobey and still "not surely die" that is, one can continue in sin and be saved]*. ..." {1NL 123.7}

[God's messenger now quotes from John 17:21 and goes on to clarify:] "...that they all may be one; as Thou, Father, art in Me, and I in Thee, that they also may be one in us." {1NL 124.5}

"These words *[which, in the context of John 17:21, are only referring to the Father and Christ]* **present God and Christ as two distinct personalities.** {1NL 124.6}

"Christ prays that a pure, holy love *[imparted by the indwelling Holy Spirit]* may bind His followers to Himself, and to the Father, that **this close fellowship** may be a sign that God loves as His own Son those *[clearly separate and distinct persons]* who believe in Him. {1NL 124.7}

Our Father calls on us all:

John 4:23:
"But the hour cometh, <u>and now is</u>, when the <u>true worshippers shall worship the **Father** in spirit and in TRUTH</u>: for the **Father** seeketh such to worship him."

Let's heed His call!

APPENDICES

WIKIPEDIA ENCYCLOPEDIA ON THE "TRINITY":

"Tertullian, a Latin theologian who wrote in the early 3rd century, i
credited as being the first to use the Latin words "Trinity", "person" an
"substance" to explain that the Father, Son, and Holy Spirit are "one i
essence—not one in Person."

THEOPHILUS USE OF THE WORD "TRINITY" – 181 AD

CHAPTER XV.—OF THE FOURTH DAY:

"On the fourth day the luminaries were made; because God, wh
possesses foreknowledge, knew the follies of the vain philosophers, tha
they were going to say, that the things which grow on the earth ar
produced form the heavenly bodies, so as to exclude God.   In orde
therefore, that the truth might be obvious, the plants and seeds wer
produced prior to the heavenly bodies, for what is posterior cannot produc
that which is prior.   And these contain the pattern and type of a grea
mystery.   For the sun is a type of God, and the moon of man.   And as th
sun far surpasses the moon in power and glory, so far does God surpas
man.   And as the sun remains ever full, never becoming less, so does Go
always abide perfect, being full of all power, and understanding, an
wisdom, and immortality, and all good.   But the moon wanes monthly, an
in a manner dies, being a type of man; then it is born again, and is crescen
for a pattern of the future resurrection.   In like manner also the three day
which were before **the luminaries, are types of the Trinity, of God, an
His Word, and His wisdom**.   And the fourth is they type of a man, wh
needs light, that so there may be God, the Word, wisdom, man.   Wherefo
also on the fourth day the lights were made.   The disposition of the star
too, contains a type of the arrangement and order of the righteous and piou
and of those who keep the law and commandments of God.   For the brillia
and bright stars are an imitation of the prophets, and therefore they rema
fixed, not declining, nor passing from place to place.   And those which ho

he second place in brightness, are types of the people of the righteous. And hose, again, which change their position, and flee from place to place, which also are cared planets, they too are a type of the men who have wandered from God, abandoning His law and commandments."

My note: It is clear, when reading Theophilus' complete work, that he was very conversant with Greek and Roman philosophy, and also that his use of the word Trinity was not employed to describe the Godhead.]

APPENDIX C

THEOPHILUS ON THE TRINITY" FROM WIKIPEDIA ENCYCLOPEDIA:

Trinity

"It is most notable for being the earliest extant **Christian** work to use the word "Trinity" (Greek: trias) but not to refer to the Father, Son and Holy Spirit. Theophilus himself puts it as "God, his Word (Logos) and his Wisdom (Sophia)."[22] It is possible that the word may have been used before this time as many Greek Christian works before Theophilus were lost [???].[23] The context for his use of the word Trinity is commentary on the successive work of the creation weeks (Genesis chapters 1-3). According to Theophilus, the sun is the image of God; the moon of man, whose death and resurrection are prefigured by the monthly changes of that luminary. The first three days before the creation of the heavenly bodies are types of the Trinity.

Theophilus explains the Trinity as follows:

'In like manner also the three days which were before the luminaries, are types of the Trinity, of God, and His Word, and His wisdom. And the fourth is the type of man, who needs light, that so there may be God, the Word, wisdom, man.' -- Theophilus[24]

Alternatively, the references to the references to the Logos and Sophia (wisdom) may be ideas taken from Greek philosophy or Hellenistic Judaism. The concept of intermediate divine beings was common to Platonism and heretical Jewish sects. In Proverbs 8 Wisdom (as feminine consort) is described as God's Counsellor and Workmistress, who dwelt beside Him before the creation of the world."

APPENDIX D:

http://basildon.adventistchurch.org.uk/what-we-believe

Basildon District Seventh-day Adventist church

a Christian faith community preparing the world for the return of Jesus Christ

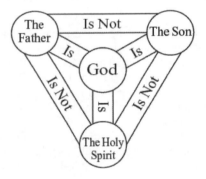

The Trinity

There is one God, the Father, Son, and Holy Spirit, a unity of three co-eternal Persons usually called the Trinity. God the Father is the Creator, Source, Sustainer, and Sovereign of all creation. God the eternal Son became incarnate in Jesus Christ, through Whom all things were created; the character of God is revealed; the salvation of humanity is accomplished; and the world is judged. God the Holy Spirit draws men and women to Himself [?] and gives spiritual gifts to the Church.

APPENDIX E:

THE FIFTEEN TRINITY HYMNS

Never before in any SDA Hymnal were there songs dedicated to the Trinity. This latest SDA hymnal has at least FIFTEEN, which designates it as 'acceptable' in the view of the Roman Catholic Church and the World Council of Churches. The inclusion of these hymns makes the Trinity, by default, the "God" of every hymn of this book, even if the remaining hymns are correctly worded. The "lump" has been "leavened":

1. Hymn No. 2 (*All Creatures of Our God and King*): This hymn is written in 1225 AD (at the height of the Dark Ages) by one of the most popular of Catholic "saints"—Francis of Assisi. In this Catholic hymn, not found in any previous SDA hymnal, Adventists worship the Catholic concept of God with these words: *"Oh, Praise the Father, praise the Son, and Praise the Spirit, **Three in One**."*

2. Hymn 27 (*Rejoice, Ye Pure in Heart!*): Verse 5 was taken out of the old hymnal and replaced with: *"Praise Him who reigns on high, The Lord whom we adore, The Father, Son, and Holy Ghost, **One God** forevermore."*

3. Hymn 30 (*Holy God, We Praise Your Name*): This is bold Trinitarian teaching out in the open. No subtlety here. *"Three we name You; **While in essence only one. Undivided** God we claim you."* In the "trinity" concept all three "manifestations" of God are of one identical substance. The Bible and Spirit of Prophecy clearly teach the Three as being three separate, equal, divine, eternal Persons.

4. Hymn No. 42 (*Now That Daylight Fills the Sky*): This is another Latin hymn from the 7th or 8th century that was translated and given to us by John Neale of the Oxford Movement. Use by permission of the Lutheran church, it teaches SDA's that God is three persons.

5. Hymn No. 47 (*God, Who Made the Earth and Heaven*): In this new hymn (not in any earlier SDA hymnal), Adventists sing, "Blest Three in One."

6. Hymn No. 71 (*Come, Thou Almighty King*): Again, the wording of this hymn was changed in the new hymnal! In *Come, Thou Almighty King*, SDA worshippers are led to worship the Catholic Trinity concept of God: *"To Thee, **great One in Three**, eternal praises be."* Old SDA hymnals did not have this wording in this hymn.

7. Hymn No. 72 (*Creator of the Stars of Night*): This hymn written in the 800's in Latin was another Trinity hymn given to us by John Neale of the infamous Oxford Movement. Adventists are again led to sing to a false

God with these words: *"To God the Father, God the Son, and God the Spirit, **Three in one.***

8. Hymn No. 73 (*Holy, Holy, and Holy*): This hymn was originally written in 1826 by Reginald Heber. In its original form it was a Trinitarian song which read at the end of the first and fourth stanzas as follows: *"God in three persons, blessed Trinity!"* This song was put into the 1909 and 1941 Seventh-day Adventist Hymnals, but the trinity part was purposely changed to: *"God over all who rules eternity!"* and *"Perfect in power, in love and purity."* This reflected the long-held anti-Trinitarian view held by the SDA church since 1872. In the 1985 Adventist Hymnal this song was changed back to its original wording, praising the Catholic three-in-one God. I reflects the new, unscriptural views of the Adventist Church. Unless there is a public repentance, we can only conclude that it has now changed into a *Trinitarian* church. In other words, the SDA Corporation now worships the same god as the Catholic Church system.

9. Hymn No. 116 (*Of the Father's Love Begotten*): This new hymn teaches Adventists that Christ was begotten *"Of the Father's love begotten Ere the worlds began to be."* This is a Trinitarian concept. Seventh-day Adventists believe that Jesus had life original, unborrowed, and underived. He was 'begotten' at Bethlehem. Acts 13:33 teaches that he was 'begotten' at His resurrection.

10. Hymn No. 148 (*O Love, How Deep, How Broad*): Written in the Dark Ages by Thomas a Kempis (1380-1471). Another Roman Catholic monk has given the SDA hymnal yet another hymn devoted to *"the Trinity whom we adore forever and forevermore."*

11. Hymn No. 228 (*A Hymn of Glory Let us Sing*): Written by the Venerable Bede, a Benedictine monk in the 8th century. Now Adventists can sing about Jesus, who is "with Father and with Spirit, one"—another hymn devoted to the Trinity that Bede believed in.

12. Hymn No. 235 (*Christ is Made the Sure Foundation*): This was a "Latin hymn" of the 7th century, which was popularized by John Neale, the hymn writer of the Oxford Movement. It appeared in an earlier SDA hymnal but the Catholic teaching was left out. In the current SDA Hymnal however, it was brought back to the light, and through it Seventh-day Adventists worship the Catholic Trinity concept of God: *"Praise and honor to the Father, Praise and honor to the Son, Praise and honor to the Spirit, **Ever three and ever one.***" The oneness meant is a physical oneness for in the Trinity, all are composed of the same identical substance.

13. Hymn No. 234 (*Christ Is the World's Light*): This hymn teaches Adventists to pray to the Catholic Trinity concept of the three-in-one God

*"Give God the glory, **God and none other.** Give God the glory, Spirit, Son, and Father; Give God the glory."*

4, 15. Hymns Nos. 694 and 695 (*Praise God, From Whom All Blessings*): This is a classic hymn that is devoted to the Trinity God. In it SDA's *"Praise **Him**… Praise Father, Son, and Holy Ghost."*

APPENDIX F:

http://test2.lutheranworld.org/What_We_Do/OEA/Bilateral_Relations/OEA-Lutheran-Seventh_day_Adventist.html

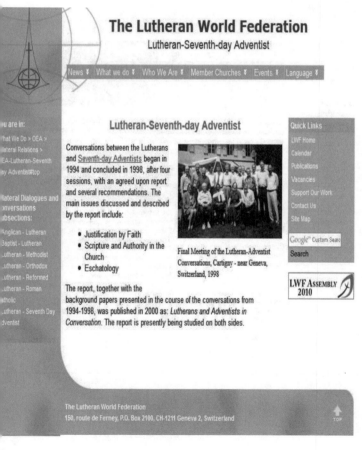

The Lutheran World Federation
Lutheran-Seventh-day Adventist

News ▾ | What we do ▾ | Who We Are ▾ | Member Churches ▾ | Events ▾ | Language ▾

you are in:
What We Do > OEA >
Bilateral Relations >
OEA-Lutheran-Seventh
day Adventist#top

Bilateral Dialogues and
Conversations
subsections:

Anglican - Lutheran
Baptist - Lutheran
Lutheran - Methodist
Lutheran - Orthodox
Lutheran - Reformed
Lutheran - Roman
Catholic
Lutheran - Seventh Day
Adventist

Lutheran-Seventh-day Adventist

Conversations between the Lutherans and Seventh-day Adventists began in 1994 and concluded in 1998, after four sessions, with an agreed upon report and several recommendations. The main issues discussed and described by the report include:

- Justification by Faith
- Scripture and Authority in the Church
- Eschatology

The report, together with the background papers presented in the course of the conversations from 1994-1998, was published in 2000 as: *Lutherans and Adventists in Conversation*. The report is presently being studied on both sides.

Final Meeting of the Lutheran-Adventist Conversations, Cartigny - near Geneva, Switzerland, 1998

Quick Links

LWF Home
Calendar
Publications
Vacancies
Support Our Work
Contact Us
Site Map

Google™ Custom Search
Search

LWF ASSEMBLY 2010

The Lutheran World Federation
150, route de Ferney, P.O. Box 2100, CH-1211 Geneva 2, Switzerland

TOP

APPENDIX G:

http://test2.lutheranworld.org/What_We_Do/OEA/Bilateral_Relations/OEA-Lutheran-Roman_Catholic.html

The Lutheran World Federation
Lutheran-Roman Catholic

I I I I I I

You are in:

What We Do > OEA
> Bilateral Relations
> OEA-Lutheran-
Roman Catholic

**Bilateral
Dialogues and
Conversations
Subsections:**

- Anglican - Lutheran
- Baptist - Lutheran
- Lutheran -
Methodist
- Lutheran -
Orthodox
- Lutheran -
Reformed
- Lutheran - Roman
Catholic
- Lutheran - Seventh
Day Adventist

Lutheran-Roman Catholic

Contacts established between the LWF and Roman Catholic Church during the Second Vatican Council led to the formation of a Lutheran-Roman Catholic Working Group which met in 1965 and 1966. It was officially authorized by both parties to discuss possible contacts, conversations, and forms of cooperation. The Working Group agreed that it was important to enter into comprehensive dialogue about the basic issues that separate and unite the two churches.

Lutheran-Roman Catholic Commission on Unity, Würzburg, Germany, 2002

Lutheran - Roman Catholic Commission on Unity, Opole, Poland, 1998

Following the official endorsement of the Working Group's recommendation by the LWF and Roman Catholic Church, the Joint Lutheran-Roman Catholic Study Commission met for the first time in 1967. After five sessions it submitted a report titled "The Gospel and the Church" in 1972. This report, known as the Malta Report, remains a significant ecumenical attempt to consider various aspects of the church in a broad theological perspective.

Subsequent Lutheran-Roman Catholic dialogue has gone deeper into specific areas only partially addressed in the Malta Report. The following reports of the international Lutheran-Roman Catholic dialogue have been published:

- The Eucharist (1978)

- Ways to Community (1980)
- The Ministry in the Church (1981)
- Facing Unity (1984)
- Church and Justification (1994)

The present Lutheran-Roman Catholic Commission on Unity is studying "The Apostolicity of the Church." A report on its outcome is expected in 2004.

The Joint Declaration on the Doctrine of Justification

Global Lutheran-Roman Catholic relations have been positively affected by the Joint Declaration on the Doctrine of Justification (JDDJ) and its celebration in Augsburg, Germany on 31 October 1999. Please click Joint Declaration on the Doctrine of Justification for more information on this important ecumenical development.

The JDDJ is the result of various dialogue phases between Lutherans and Roman Catholics, both regionally and internationally. A comprehensive study program to follow-up the JDDJ is now being implemented. Please click for more information on the Follow-up of the Joint Declaration on the Doctrine of Justification.

Regional Level

Significant regional relations between Lutherans and Roman Catholics exist in different parts of the world.

In Germany, dialogue between the Protestant Church in Germany (EKD) and the German Bishops' Conference of the Roman Catholic Church has focused on a number of central theological themes. A major study was undertaken on the doctrinal condemnations of the Reformation era regarding justification, ministry and the sacraments, and whether they still apply.

In the USA, Lutheran-Roman Catholic dialogue has also focused on theological areas central to the common faith - justification by faith, for example - as well as traditionally controversial issues such as the status of Mary, the saints, and the Petrine ministry. Both of these regional dialogues have contributed substantially to the Joint Declaration on the Doctrine of Justification.

The Lutheran World Federation
150, route de Ferney, P.O. Box 2100, CH-1211 Geneva 2, Switzerland

APPENDIX H:

ADVENTISTS AND PAPACY SIGN PACT–December 14, 1999

updated 1/6/2008

Part One of this appendix is a February 15, 2000 article from Adventist News Network that revealed to the world the fact of a Seventh-day Adventist–Roman Catholic Agreement.

Part Two is Our response to the world showing why this is a betrayal of sacred trust.

Part Three Shows THE ACTUAL DOCUMENT

*** PART ONE ***

ADVENTISTS AND PAPACY SIGN PACT

Adventist Church Cannot be Treated as a Sect, Warsaw, Poland .. [ANN **Feb 15, 2000**]

"*The Seventh-day Adventist Church cannot be treated either as a 'new religious movement,' or as a sect*," declares **a joint statement** drawn by the Roman Catholic Church and the Adventist Church in Poland. Recognizing each other's autonomy and independence, the document was issued following **15 years of dialogue** aimed at better understanding of the teachings and practice of the Catholic and the Adventist Churches, as well as **improving relations** without compromising each other's identity. The document cites the fact that "*relations between Catholics and Adventists have not been best in the past.*"

The statement was signed by representatives of the Churches, including **Pastor Wladyslaw Polok, president of the Adventist Church in Poland** and **Archbishop Alfons Nossol, chairman of the Polish Episcopate's Commission for Ecumenical Affairs.** "*With regret we recognize cases when the different religious and civic circles have denied the ecclesiastical status of the Seventh-day Adventist Church, even referring to it as 'sect.' Such an approach is unacceptable and, we believe, it is highly detrimental for the mutual relations*," the document states. "*This document affirms religious liberty. We are regarding it as an important development*

582

ot only for our Church in Poland. Religious minorities are too often
egarded as less than what they are," said Pastor Polok.

he statement recognizes that though the Churches can refer to similarities,
ey also see difference between each other's "doctrine, practice and church
olicies." **However, both sides affirm a need to cultivate respect for
ach other and learn to understand each other**. The dialogue was
conducted *on the basis of partnership, care to uphold a full identity of
oth sides, as well as their autonomy and independence, in the spirit of
utual respect and Christian love, and in recognition of the ideals of
lerance and religious freedom."*

This is an important turn of events for our Church," says Prof.
achariasz Lyko, who for many years was responsible for the Polish
dventist Church's public affairs. *"This development is not a result of
iticism, public attacks or confrontation, but Christian kindness toward
ch other and respect for dignity of a human person."*

*Many of us can recall how we have been labeled with different names. We
ve been misunderstood and often ridiculed. As for us, we wanted to sit
own together and recognize that **Christian love requires a different kind
f relation in the society we are a part of**. As Seventh-day Adventists we
ek to take a positive approach to other faiths. **We have stated this
ublicly and this document affirms our attitude** [sic],"* he added.

he document does not deal with doctrinal and theological issues. During
e years of meetings, both sides presented their theological views and
octrinal positions in the interest of better understanding between both
onfessions. *"Our Church recognizes that such dialogue cannot be a
alogue of compromise, but one of cooperative spirit and common
derstanding,"* Lyko explained. *"**We are doing nothing different except
hat the early pioneers of our Church supported and advocated**. It is
ways better to engage in a respectful conversation than in a confrontation
at often prevents achieving desired changes,"* he said.

yko commented that *"**as a Church, our side was not interested in
mpromising any of our fundamental beliefs**."*

*"Over the years, however, as the exchange of information between us
ok place, we noted many confessional similarities but also differences.
he Catholic side recognizes in the document the Christocentric character
f our beliefs, and ESPECIALLY OUR BELIEF IN THE TRINITY, as
ell as ecclesiological identity of the Church, a status affirmed by an act of
e Polish Parliament. On our part, we spoke of a need to change attitudes
ward our denomination and recognized the openness of the Catholic
hurch, especially in recent times, toward the Bible,"* Lyko explained.

583

Appendices

***

Below is an excellent response to the article.

*** PART TWO ***

ADVENTISTS SIGN DOCUMENT WITH *"ANTICHRIST"*

Report After Fifteen Year Dialogue
By Neil C. Livingston

[ADVENTIST NEWS NETWORK]: This Week's News: **Feb. 1**
2000 Warsaw, Poland. "Adventist Church Cannot Be Treated As
Sect," Say Adventists and Catholics In Poland.
"The Seventh-day Adventist Church cannot be treated either as a new
religious movement, or as a sect," declares a joint statement drawn by the
Roman Catholic Church and the [Seventh-day] Adventist Church
in Poland. [From Adventist Headquarters in Warsaw Poland.]
"Recognizing each other's autonomy and independence, the document
was issued following 15 years of dialogue aimed at better understanding of
the teachings and practice of the Catholic and the Adventist Churches, as
well as improving relations without compromising each other's identity."
Comment. "This first paragraph reveals two important facts;. (1)
Seventh-day Adventist Church leadership had been dialoging with the
Roman Catholic Church for "15 years." (2) The result of this dialogue is
"document" of joint agreement. Rather than comment on this obvious
breach of trust, we will let the inspired messenger to the Seventh-day
Adventist Church comment: "Romanism is now regarded by Protestant
[Adventists also?] with far greater favor than in former years," Ellen White
wrote.
"**In those countries where Catholicism is not in the ascendancy**
and the papists are taking a conciliatory course in order to gain
influence, there is an increasing indifference concerning the doctrines that
separate the reformed churches from the papal hierarchy; the opinion is
gaining ground that, after all, **we do not differ so widely upon vital points**
as has been supposed, and that a little concession on our part *will bring*
***us into a better understanding with Rome.*"** (Ellen G. White, *The Great*
Controversy, page 563, emphasis supplied).

584

"The time was when Protestants *[including Adventists]* placed a high
alue upon the liberty of conscience which had been so dearly purchased,"
llen concluded. "They taught their children to abhor popery *and held that
) seek harmony with Rome would be disloyalty to God*. But how widely
lfferent are the sentiments now expressed!" (*ibid.*, GC, page 563, emphasis
1pplied).

Adventist News Network Continued.: "The document cites the fact
1at "relations between Catholics and Adventists have not been best in the
1st." The statement was signed by representatives of the Churches,
1cluding Pastor Wladyslaw Polok, president of the *[Seventh-day]*
dventist Church in Poland, and Archbishop Alfons Nossol, chairman of
1e Polish Episcopate's Commission for Ecumenical Affairs.

Comment.: The statement that "relations between Catholics and
dventists have not been best in the past" proves that this signed
1ocument" is a new Seventh-day Adventist position on the papacy. Notice
so that the "statement was signed by representatives of the
1urches." Seventh-day Adventist leadership, **beyond the knowledge of
1e laity**, signs an agreement with Rome - With the Antichrist? **They
1port the signing after the fact.** Most Adventists are fast asleep and will
2ver know the difference. But what does the messenger of the Lord say?

"The papacy is just what prophecy declared that she would be, **the
1ostasy of the latter times**," Ellen White warned. (2 Thessalonians 2:3,
quoted). "It is a part of her policy to assume the character which will
1st accomplish her purpose; **but beneath the variable appearance of the
1ameleon she conceals the invariable venom of the serpent**." (*ibid.,
1e Great Controversy*, page 571, emphasis supplied).

"The defenders of the papacy declare that the church has been
aligned, and the Protestant *[Adventist also?]* world are inclined to accept
1e statement," Ellen White stated. "Many urge that it is unjust to judge the
1urch of today by the abominations and absurdities that marked her reign
1ring the centuries of ignorance and darkness. They excuse her horrible
1uelty as the result of the barbarism of the times **and plead that the
1fluence of modern civilization has changed her sentiments**." (*ibid.,
2C, page 563, emphasis supplied).

Adventist News Network Continued.: "With regret we recognize
1ses when the different religious and civic circles have denied the
1clesiastical status of the Seventh-day Adventist Church, even referring to
2as a sect. Such an approach is unacceptable and, we believe, it is highly
1trimental for the mutual relations," the document states.

Comment.: Should we be concerned about what the papacy and other
1urches of Babylon think of us. **Does Adventist leadership still believe

585

that the papacy is still the great Antichrist? Evidently not! Then th
statement says that "it is highly detrimental for the mutual relations." Wha
mutual relations? Are we to now have "relations" with the great Antichris
of Revelation 13? "Be ye not unequally yoked together wit
unbelievers: for what fellowship hath righteousness with unrighteousness
the apostle Paul wrote, "and what communion hath light with darkness? ('
Corinthians 6:14).

"Have these *[Adventist]* persons forgotten the claim of infallibility pu
forth for eight hundred years by this haughty power?" Ellen White ask
"...how can she renounce the principles which governed her course in pas
ages?" (*ibid.*, GC, page 564, emphasis supplied.

Adventist News Network Continued.: "This document affirm
religious liberty. We are regarding it as an important development not onl
for our Church in Poland. Religious minorities are too often regarded a
less than what they are," said Pastor Polok.

Comment.: "The document affirms religious liberty." You must b
kidding! Since when did the papacy ever care about religious liberty?
pastor Polak, and Adventist leadership, totally ignorant of the chapte
"Liberty of Conscience Threatened," in the book, *The Grea
Controversy*? The sub-title alone, "Aims of the Papacy," exposes the tru
motives of the Antichrist! "The papal church will never relinquish h
claim to infallibility," Ellen White warned.

"All that she has done in her persecution of those who reject h
dogmas she holds to be right; and **would she not repeat the same act
should the opportunity be presented**?" (*ibid.*, GC, page 564, emphas
supplied).

"Let the restraints now imposed by secular governments be remove
and Rome be reinstated in her former power," Ellen White warned, "an
there would speedily be a revival of her tyranny and persecution.
(*ibid.*, GC, page 564, emphasis supplied).

Adventist News Network Continued.: "The statement recognizes tha
though the Churches can refer to similarities, they also see differenc
between each other's 'doctrine, practice and church policies.'" Howeve
both sides affirm a need to cultivate respect for each other and learn t
understand each other. The dialogue was "conducted on the basis c
partnership, care to uphold a full identity of both sides, as well as the
autonomy and independence, in the spirit of mutual respect and Christia
love, and in recognition of the ideals of tolerance and religious freedom."

Comment.: "The dialogue was "conducted on the basis c
partnership... independence ...mutual respect and Christian lov
..recognition of the ideals of tolerance and religiou

586

reedom?" Astounding! It is almost unbelievable that anyone calling hemselves a Seventh-day Adventist, let alone those in leadership, could be o ignorant, or even worse disregard, the history of the papacy during the lark ages and the Reformation. Are Seventh-day Adventists still 'rotestant? Evidently not, for they point out that, "The statement ecognizes that... the Churches can refer to similarities," between the ieventh-day Adventist Church, and the Roman Catholic Church. (See, Bert 3. Beach and Lukas Vischer, <u>So Much In Common</u>, Between the Seventh-lay Adventist Church, and the World Council of Churches, Geneva, iwitzerland, 1973). (Note: A copy of *So Much In Common* may be obtained rom: *Adventist Laymen's Foundation*, PAGE O. Box 69, Ozone, AR '2854).

"But Romanism as a system is no more in harmony with the gospel of Christ now than at any former period in her history," Ellen White wrote. **'The Protestant** *[and now Adventist?]* **churches are in great darkness, or hey would discern the signs of the times."** (*ibid.*, GC, page 565, emphasis upplied).

"The Roman Church is far-reaching in her plans and modes of peration," Ellen White continued. "She is employing every device to xtend her influence and increase her power in preparation for a fierce and letermined conflict to regain control of the world, to re-establish ersecution, **and to undo all that Protestantism has done."** (*ibid.*, GC, age 565, emphasis supplied).

"Catholicism is gaining ground upon every side. See the increasing umber of her churches and chapels in Protestant countries. **Look at the opularity of her colleges and seminaries in America, so widely atronized by Protestants.**

"Look at the growth of ritualism in England and the frequent lefections to the ranks of the Catholics. These things should awaken the nxiety of all who prize the pure principles of the gospel." Ellen G. White, *The Great Controversy*, pages 565, 566. (emphasis supplied.)

Adventist News Network Continued.: "This is an important turn of vents for **our Church**," says Prof. Zachariasz Lyko, who for many years was responsible for the Polish Adventist Church's public affairs. "This levelopment is not a result of criticism, public attacks or confrontation, but Christian kindness toward each other and respect for dignity of a human erson."

Comment.: "Christian kindness toward each other" and "respect for lignity of a human person." Christian kindness and dignity for what human erson? The pope? Please! The dark history of nearly 2,000 years testifies o the "Christian kindness" of the papacy toward other faiths "Protestants

[Adventists] have tampered with and patronized popery; **they have made compromises and concessions which papists themselves are surprised to see and fail to understand,"** Ellen White stated. "Men are closing their eyes to the real character of Romanism and the dangers to be apprehended from her supremacy." (*ibid.*, GC, page 565, emphasis supplied). "The people need to be aroused to resist the advances of this most dangerous foe to civil and religious liberty," Ellen White added further. (*ibid.*, GC, page 566, emphasis supplied). Yet the report stated that, "Prof. Zachariasz Lyko who for many years was responsible for the Polish Adventist Church' public affairs," which is part of the Seventh-day Adventist "Religious Liberty" department. **Indeed, the leadership of the SDA Church "need to be aroused to resist the advances of this most dangerous foe to civil and religious liberty."** *Adventist News Network Continued.:* "Many of us can recall how we have been labeled with different names. We have been misunderstood and often ridiculed. As for us, we wanted to sit down together and recognize that Christian love requires a different kind of relation in the society we are a part of. As Seventh-day Adventists we seek to take a positive approach to other faiths*[Roman Catholic].* We have stated this publicly and this document affirms our attitude," he added. *Comment.:* "for us, we wanted to sit down together *[with papists]* and recognize that Christian love requires a different kind of relation *in the society we are a part of.*" We will let the Spirit of Prophecy address this one: "They *[Protestants/Adventists]* excuse her horrible cruelty as the result of the barbarism of the times," Ellen White stated, **"and plead that the influence of modern civilization has changed her sentiments."** (*ibid.*, GC, page 563, emphasis supplied)."We wanted to sit down together," with papists? The report stated that the Adventist wished to "recognize that Christian love requires a different kind of relation." What kind of a relationship can there be with the great Antichrist of the last days? "As Seventh-day Adventists we seek." That is the problem. **Leadership "seeks" and decisions are made in the name of Seventh-day Adventists - and laity knows nothing about what leadership is seeking and signing! Leadership then reports to laity fifteen years after the fact.** "A prayerful study of the Bible would show Protestants *[Adventists]* the real character of the papacy and would cause them to **abhor and to shun it;"** Ellen White observed, "but many are so wise in their own conceit that they feel no need of humbly seeking God that they may be led into the truth." (*ibid.*, GC, page 572, emphasis supplied).*Adventist News Network Continued.:* "The document does not deal with doctrinal and theological issues. During the years of meetings both sides presented their theological views and doctrinal positions in the

terest of better understanding between both confessions.
omment.: "During the years of meetings *[fifteen years to be exact]*, both
des *[Seventh-day Adventist and Roman Catholic]* presented their
eological views and doctrinal positions in the interest of better
iderstanding between both confessions." Does anyone really believe that
e papacy cares a whit what Seventh-day Adventists believe and teach -
cept for pioneer Adventist views that the papacy is the great Ant-Christ!

"As the Protestants *[and now Adventist]* churches have been seeking
e favor of the world, false charity has blinded their eyes," Ellen White
rote. "They do not see but that it is right to believe good of all evil, **and as
le inevitable result they will finally believe evil of all good.**" (*ibid.*, GC,
ige 571, emphasis supplied). "Instead of standing in defense of the faith
ice delivered to the saints," Ellen White stated, "they are now, as it were,
**ologizing to Rome for their uncharitable opinion of her, begging
irdon for their bigotry.**" (*ibid.*, GC, pages 571, 572, emphasis supplied).

Adventist News Network Continued.: Our Church recognizes that
ich dialogue cannot be a dialogue of compromise, but one of cooperative
irit and common understanding," Lyko explained.

Comment.: "Church recognizes": "Leadership is always ready and
illing to tell the world, or even the papacy, what "our Church recognizes"
what Seventh-day Adventists believe. In the same breath, leadership
lks of a "common understanding" with the papacy. How blind are the
aders of the contemporary Seventh-day Adventist Church? "It is not
ithout reason that the claim has been put forth in Protestant countries that
atholicism differs less widely from Protestantism than in former times,"
len White stated. "There has been a change; but the change is not in the
pacy. Catholicism indeed resembles much of the Protestantism *[and now
iventism]* that now exists, **because Protestantism** *[Adventism]* **has so
eatly degenerated since the days of the Reformers** *[and since our
oneers]*." (*ibid.*, GC, page 571, emphasis supplied).

Adventist News Network Continued.: "We are doing nothing
fferent except what the early pioneers of our Church supported and
vocated. It is always better to engage in a respectful conversation than in
:onfrontation that often prevents achieving desired changes," he said.

Comment.: "What the early pioneers of our Church supported and
vocated???" What history is contemporary Adventist leadership
ading? Surely not Seventh-day Adventist history! One only need observe
e works of Waggoner and Jones, Uriah Smith, Andrews and James White
see that this is a totally false statement. "If we desire to understand the
termined cruelty of Satan, manifested for hundreds of years, not among
ose who never heard of God, but in the very heart and throughout the

extent of Christendom, we have only to look at the history of Romanism, Ellen White wrote. "Through this mammoth system of deception the princ of evil achieves his purpose of bringing dishonor to God and wretchednes to man." (*ibid.*, GC, page 570, emphasis supplied.)

Adventist News Network Continued.: Lyko commented that "as Church, our side was not interested in compromising any of ou fundamental beliefs."

Comment.: **Seventh-day Adventist leadership had alread compromised the "Fundamental Beliefs" in the Evangelic Conferences of 1955-56!** (See, Neil C. Livingston, *The Greate Conspiracy*, Chapter 12, "The Ultimate Betrayal www.adventist4truth.com).

Adventist News Network Conclusion: "Over the years, however, a the exchange of information between us took place, we noted man confessional similarities but also differences. The Catholic side recogniz in the document the Christocentric character of our beliefs, and especiall our belief in the Trinity, as well as ecclesiological identity of the Church, status affirmed by an act of the Polish Parliament. On our part, we spoke a need to change attitudes toward our denomination and recognized th openness of the Catholic Church, especially in recent times, toward th Bible," Lyko explained. [Ray Dabrowski]

Our Conclusion.: **"The Catholic** side recognizes in the document th Christocentric character of our beliefs, and ESPECIALLY OUR BELIE IN THE TRINITY?" **There was no** [*official*] **statement in Adventi theology on the "Trinity" until fifteen years after the death of Elle White**, when the "new" Statements of Fundamental Belief, and a offici *Church Manual* were published in 1931. (See, Neil C. Livingston, *Th Greatest Conspiracy*, Chapter 7, "Creed and Church Manual."). *[Se Chapter 8 of this book on the 1913 Wilcox statement.]*

The doctrine of the "Trinity" must be stated to be accepted by th National and World Council of Churches. In the same sentence it is state that "The Catholic side recognizes in the document… our belief in. ecclesiological identity of the Church." What Church? The Rom Catholic Church, or the Seventh-day Adventist Church. Does it real matter! Both Catholic and Adventist Churches now wield "ecclesiologic authority" over their members. Both systems excommunica (disfellowship) members for the dastardly crime of not recognizing th **ecclesiological authority** of the Church. "Over the years . . . as th exchange of information between us took place?" Adventist laymen a always in the dark about what leadership is up to. Again, this report com to light fifteen years after the fact! "We noted many **confession**

590

milarities?" Does that statement make you uneasy dear Adventist
other and sister?

"There is as great a difference in our faith and that of nominal
ofessors as the heavens are higher than the earth," Ellen White observed.
piritual Gifts, Volume 2, page 300). This statement would be doubly
pplicable to the Roman Catholic Church, would it not? Yet SDA
adership states, "We noted many confessional similarities" between the
achings of the Seventh-day Adventist Church and the Roman Catholic
hurch. Either the leadership of the Seventh-day Adventist Church have
one completely bonkers, **or Satan has taken the helm of the ship.** Which
these two (or both) scenarios is true is difficult to discern. Ellen White's
'arning About the Papacy: "The Roman Church now presents a fair front
the world, covering with apologies her record of horrible cruelties," Ellen
'hite warned. "She has clothed herself in Christlike garments; but she is
ichanged." (*The Great Controversy*, page 571, emphasis supplied). "Every
inciple of the papacy that existed in past ages exists today," Ellen White
ontinued. "The doctrines devised in the darkest ages are still held. **Let
ne deceive themselves.**" (*ibid., The Great Controversy*, page 571,
nphasis supplied). "The papacy that Protestants *[and now Adventists]* are
ow so ready to honor **is the same that ruled the world in the days of the
eformation**," Ellen White stated, "**when men of God stood up, at the
ril of their lives, to expose her iniquity.**" (*ibid., The Great Controversy*,
ge 571, emphasis supplied)."She possesses the same pride and arrogant
sumption that lorded it over kings and princes, and claimed the
erogatives of God," Ellen White concluded. . ."Her spirit is no less cruel
id despotic now *than when she crushed out human liberty and slew the
ints of the Most High.*" (*ibid., The Great Controversy*, page 571, emphasis
pplied). Oh, dear reader, the deceptions of Satan in these last hours of
rth's history are very clever. Pray, as you have never prayed before, dear
other! Pray for your family and your children, dear sister! Seek ye the
ord, all ye meek of the earth... seek righteousness, seek meekness: it may
ye shall be hid in the day of the Lord's anger. (Zephaniah 2:3). **How can
e Adventist church identify the papacy as the beast if it is partners
ith them? The conference is not spreading the three angel's messages
the world. They would rather follow the papacy than do their duty to
od.**

591

*** PART THREE ***

THE ACTUAL DOCUMENT OF THE AGREEMENT

S T A T E M E N T of the Commission of the Episcopate for Ecumenica Matters of the Catholic Church in Poland and the Superior Authority of th Seventh-day Adventist Church in Poland to celebrate the 15th anniversar of inter-denominational dialogue:

On 14th December 1999 in the primatial hall at 19 Miodow Street in Warsaw, a solemn Anniversary Meeting of the Commission c the Episcopate for Ecumenical Matters and the Superior Authority c the Seventh-day Adventist Church was held to celebrate the 15t anniversary of inter-denominational Catholic-Adventist dialogu conducted within the framework of the Bilateral Dialogue Unit, wher members from the **Adventist side** were **the priests**: Professor Assistan Professor Zachariasz Lyko, Andrzej Sicilski, MA and Assistant-Professc Bernard Koziróg; while from the Catholic side where the priests: Professc Assistant-Professor Lucjan Balter, Professor Assistant-Professor Micha Czajkowski and Doctor Marcin Wojtowicz.

Apart from the above mentioned members of the Unit, th Anniversary Meeting was also attended by the priests: Archbisho Professor Assistant-Professor Alfons Nossol (President of the Commissio of the Episcopate for Ecumenical Matters), Bishop Doctor Seni Wladyslaw Miziolek (vice-president of the Commission), Bishop Professc Assistant-Professor Jan Bernard Szlaga (member of the Commission Professor Assistant-Professor Piotr Jaskola (secretary of the Commission Doctor Wojciech Hanc (member of the Commission) and Doctor Krzyszt(Rozanski (member of the Commission on the Catholic side), **Wladysla Polok, MA (president of the Seventh-day Adventist Church) and Ja Krysta, BA (president of the South Diocese of the Seventh-da Adventist Church on the Adventist side)** and the following statement w accepted in the course of the Meeting:

1. The inter-denominational Catholic dialogue, started in 1984, has bee conducted according to the principles of brotherhood, concern for tot identity of both Parties as well as their autonomy and independence, in th spirit of mutual respect and Christian love and observance of ideals (tolerance and religious freedom.

We consider the **fifteen years** of Christian dialogue between the presentatives of our Churches to be a very positive experience and a ance to get to know not only the differences which divide our Churches it also the **numerous similarities** that - without breaking the professed inciples of faith – enable us to maintain friendly, good neighbourly lations, create opportunities for discussions, meetings and visits as well as utual cooperation in interchurch areas, morality and charity, education and ience and the dissemination of the Bible, including also common prayer.

The Adventist side, in approving the terms mentions the open attitude of e Catholic Church towards the Bible, whereas the Catholic side stresses provingly the Christ-centred teachings cultivated in the Adventist Church.

However, regrettably, it happens that various religious and secular books fuse to acknowledge the ecclesial status of the Seventh-day Adventist hurch and the Church is referred to as a "sect". Such an attitude is acceptable and we consider it highly detrimental to our mutual relations well as the inter-denominational dialogue that has been successfully nducted for so many years.

It is neither possible to treat the Seventh-day Adventist Church like a ew religious movement" because it has been in existence in Polish Lands r over 110 years, nor like a "sect", because firstly–it has a specific ctrine, organization and cultic rites, **secondly–in its teaching and service cultivates the most important principles of Catholic faith, especially e belief in the Blessed Trinity,** and thirdly–no traits characteristic for cts described in the Vatican paper "On new religious movements and cts" dated 1986 can be attributed to it.

ιe Seventh-day Adventist Church, which belongs to the Church of Jesus ιrist, in Poland has a statutory form for the regulation of its legal status, ntributes positive religious and moral values to the life of our society and ats the Catholic Church as well as other Christian Churches and religious d social communities with respect and in the spirit of the gospel, human ιhts and the principles of freedom of religion and belief.

Despite the fact that Catholic-Adventist relations in the past were not vays positive, and that apart from **many similarities** there are also ctrinal, structural and cultic differences, we are convinced that the ιristian dialogue conducted between our Churches is advisable and neficial in every respect because it helps, as experience shows, not only improve and develop the inter-denominational relations between urches** but also to disseminate the gospel, good, social peace and the ιry of God.

Taking into consideration all positive achievements of the past fifteen ars of our Roman Catholic - Adventist inter-denominational dialogue, we

593

would like to thank the Superior Authorities of both Churches for a examples of benevolence and ask for further support for the Christia dialogue in the name of love and truth. **We are also especially grateful the Only One God in the BLESSED TRINITY for the privilege of brotherly dialogue and common Christian prayer for the gift of unity i Christ.**

Co-presidents of the Anniversary Meeting

Priest Archbishop Prof. Assistant Prof. Alfons Nossol, President of the Commission of the Episcopate for Ecumenical Matters

Priest Wladyslaw Polok, MA, President of the Seventh-day Adventist Church in the Republic of Poland

Participants:

From the Catholic side:	From the Adventist side:
Priest Bishop Dr. Senior Wladyslaw Miziolek Vice-President of the Commission of the Episcopate for Ecumenical Matters	Priest Jan Krysta, BA President of the South Dioces of the Seventh-day Adventis Church in Krakow
Priest Bishop Prof. Assistant Prof. Jan Bernard Szlaga Member of the Commission of the Episcopate	Priest Andrzej Sicinski, MA Secretary of the Adventist Church- Member of the Bilateral Dialogue Unit for Ecumenical Matters
Priest Prof. Assistant Prof. Lucjan Balter Co-president of the Bilateral Dialogue Unit	Priest Prof. Assistant Prof. Zachariasz Lyko, Co-president of the Bilateral Dialogue Unit
Priest Prof. Asst. Prof. Michal Czajkowski Member of the Bilateral Dialogue Unit	Priest Assistant Prof. Bernard Koziróg Member of the Bilateral Dialogue Unit
Priest Dr. Marcin Wojtowicz	

Member of the Bilateral Dialogue Unit

Priest Prof. Assistant Prof. Piotr Jaskola
Secretary of the Commission of the Episcopate for Ecumenical Matters

Priest Dr. Wojciech Hanc
Member of the Episcopate for Ecumenical Matters

Priest Dr. Krzysztof Rozanski
Member of the Episcopate for Ecumenical Matters

The Protestants *[and now Adventists, it seems,]* of the United States will be foremost in stretching their hands across the gulf... to clasp hands with the Roman power; ... this country will follow in the steps of Rome in trampling on the rights of conscience."
***Last Day Events*, page 144.**

**We call on the General Conference
to repent of this agreement with Rome,
AND
the belief in the "Blessed Holy Trinity Doctrine".**

APPENDIX I:

DOCTOR OF MINISTRY   DISCIPLESHIP & SPIRITUAL FORMATION

Andrews University

WHAT IS IT?

The new Doctor of Ministry concentration in Discipleship and Spiritual Formation will provide a theological framework and theoretical understanding of discipleship and spiritual formation. It will integrate the leader's personal spiritual transformation with the skills involved in 'one on one' spiritual mentoring. Strategies and resources will be developed to enable the pastor to cultivate a congregation that will value and nurture discipleship, spiritual growth and caring outreach to the wider community.

The course will foster a learning atmosphere that will provide a practical model of reflection upon and engagement with those devotional practices and patterns of life that shape and define who we are as disciples of Jesus.

WHEN DOES IT BEGIN?

The teaching intensive for the first module will be February 14–26, 2010.

WHERE WILL THE INTENSIVES BE HELD?

The first year's intensives will be in Orlando, Florida. The second year's intensives will be held on the campus of Andrews University (see chart opposite).

HOW IS THE PROGRAM ORGANIZED?

Each of the four modules includes a teaching intensive, one each year over the next four years 2010 – 2013 (see chart opposite).

During the program you will also participate in regional work groups, build a professional portfolio, read and reflect on the best literature in discipleship and spiritual formation, as well as develop and evaluate a professional project within the context of your own congregation or leadership responsibilities.

■ Embrace and carry out a biblically and theologically faithful praxis of discipleship and spiritual formation both individually and corporately.

■ Discern truth from counterfeit as a means of both personal and corporate protection in light of the growing number of non-biblical "spiritualities".

FACULTY

You will interact with professors and pastoral practitioners in the area of discipleship and spiritual formation like these:

Jon Dybdahl, PhD
Professor of World Missions,
Seventh-day Adventist Theological Seminary

Ben Maxson, DMin
Senior Pastor, Paradise Seventh-day Adventist Church,
California

OUTCOMES — WHAT WILL THE PROGRAM ENABLE YOU TO DO?

Upon completing this program, the participants will be able to:

■ Articulate a Seventh-day Adventist perspective on discipleship and spiritual formation.

■ Understand and integrate the 'devotional habits' (spiritual disciplines) into one's own life and ministry.

■ Demonstrate continuing growth in spiritual leadership and ministry.

■ Through spiritual mentoring, assist church members who are struggling for consistency and depth in their journey with God

■ Train spiritually mature and relationally gifted people as spiritual mentors.

■ Cultivate a congregation that nurtures discipleship and spiritual growth.

■ Shape the church into an 'authentic community' involved in a life of evangelism through loving and nurturing relationships.

Joe Kidder, DMin
Associate Professor of Christian Ministry,
Seventh-day Adventist Theological Seminary

A. Allan Martin, PhD, CFLE
Associate Professor of Discipleship & Family Ministry,
Seventh-day Adventist Theological Seminary

Allan Walshe, DMin
Associate Professor of Christian Ministry,
Seventh-day Adventist Theological Seminary

Jane Thayer, PhD
Associate Professor Emerita of Religious Education,
Seventh-day Adventist Theological Seminary

Richard Davidson, PhD
Professor of Old Testament Interpretation,
Seventh-day Adventist Theological Seminary

Bill Knott, PhD
Editor & Executive Publisher, Adventist Review

Monte Sahlin, MDiv
Director of Research and Special Projects,
Ohio Conference of Seventh-day Adventists

AND OTHERS

For more information:

Contact Rita Pusey
269-471-3318, walshe@andrews.edu

The concentration coordinator is
Dr. Allan Walshe
269-471-3318, walshe@andrews.edu

Enrollment is limited to 25. Reserve your place now! Application deadline Dec. 1, 2009

Module Descriptions	2010	2011	2012	2013
Biblical & Historical Perspective GSEM796 (2 credits) Allan Walshe Jon Dybdahl	February 14-22 Orlando, FL			
Self-Reflection for Ministry GSEM796 (2 credits) Jane Thayer	February 23-26 Orlando, FL			
The Personal Practice of Devotion GSEM797 (4 credits) Allan Walshe		May 3-12 Andrews University		
Disciple-Making in the Local Church GSEM798 (4 credits) Bill Knott and/or Barry Gane		May 16-20 Andrews University		
Maturing the Discipleship & Congregational Caring GSEM799 (4 credits) Ben Maxson			February 13-21 Lake Union University	
DMin Project GSEM796D (6 credits)				
Community and Spiritual Maturity for Discipleship & Spiritual Formation GSEM798 (4 credits) Ben Maxson				
DMin Project GSEM796D (6 credits)				Modules 11-16 Andrews University

Act Now to Reserve Your Place   Call 888-717-6244

Adventists Join Planning Committee for the World Council of Churches

Recently, on June 8, 2006, Adventist News Network published an article entitled "Adventist Missiologist Joins Edinburgh 2010 Planning Group" written by Kristi Spurgeon. We have included part of this article below:

"The World Council of Churches is now planning for Edinburgh 2010 and Jon Dybdahl, retiring Walla Walla College president, is the sole Seventh-day Adventist representative on the planning committee. The world church appointed Dybdahl after a request was made for Adventist Church participation in the event."

"I'm excited that I've been invited to be a part of this," says Dybdahl. "I'm curious to see what will happen and how it will all work out this time." "I think it's an amazing thing to ask an Adventist to be part of the planning, which is beginning even now," Dybdahl told Adventist News Network in a telephone interview." Adventist News Network, June 8, 2006, Kristi

Spurgeon/ANN Staff.
Source:
http://news.adventist.org/data/2006/05/1149800560/index.html.en
(See also: HTTP://NEWS.ADVENTIST.ORG/ALL-
NEWS/NEWS/GO/2006-06-07/WORLD-CHURCH-
ADVENTIST-MISSIOLOGIST-JOINS-EDINBURGH-2010-
PLANNING-GROUP/)

(NOTE: This sort of ecumenical involvement is predicated upon the denominationa acceptance of the Trinity doctrine.)

PPENDIX K:

A Profile of Seventh-day Adventists
By William G. Johnsson, Ph.D.

Prepared for the Presbyterian Church (U.S.A.) – Seventh-day Adventist
iurch dialogue, November 1, 2006, Silver Spring, Maryland)

The Heart of Seventh-day Adventism

Every Christian denomination has certain passages of Scripture which,
ediated through her tradition, express her *raison d'être*. For the Seventh-
y Adventist Church, probably no word from the Lord is more significant
has played a greater role in her history than Revelation 14:6, 7: "Then I
w another angel flying in midair, and he had the eternal gospel to
oclaim to those who live on the earth—to every nation, tribe, language
d people. He said in a loud voice, 'Fear God and give him glory, because
e hour of his judgment has come. Worship him who made the heavens,
e earth, the sea and the springs of water'" –Rev. 14, 6:7 (N.I.V.).

First, it is an apocalyptic message. The Book of Revelation, along with
niel, has played a significant role in Adventism. The focus of
ocalyptic, the end of all things in the second coming of Jesus, has been
shrined in the very name Seventh-day *Adventist*. Adventists are a people
apocalyptic, with all the New Testament ethos, expectation, possibilities,
d potential for problems that apocalyptic brings.

Yet the *heart* of Revelation 14:6, 7 is the "eternal gospel." Adventists
ld to the orthodox doctrines of the Trinity, the deity of Christ, and
vation only through His merits. If apocalyptic shapes the presentation of
e Adventist message, the heart of that message is the good news common
mainline Christian bodies.

The passage calls men and women to put God first. It proclaims Him
eator of heaven and earth, Lord of all. It sets Him forth as the Judge of
living and the dead. It calls for a life lived, as John Milton put it, "as
er in my great taskmaster's eye." And these ideas are precious to
venth-day Adventists. Adventists are a people of high ethical concerns.
ctrine is important for them, but practice even more so. They set forth
d and His character, and uphold His Ten Commandment law. Out of that
ncern—to make God and His claims first in the life—arises their most
tinctive practice and the other part of their name, *Seventh-day* Adventist.

Finally, Revelation 14:6, 7 sets forth a mission. Its vision is the world for
rist—the world with all its races and peoples and languages and
rvelous human diversity bowing before His throne, a world where the

599

ancient hostilities and alienations of race, color, language, sex, statu‍ profession, and innate prejudices have been abolished by the Cross ‍ Christ. So, while the Seventh-day Adventist Church is still comparative‍ small with about 15 million baptized members (all those who associa‍ themselves with the church probably number 25-30 million), she ‍ extraordinary in her worldwide thrust. She is the most widespre‍ Protestant denomination: she is rooted in more than 200 countries. And al‍ one of the fastest growing, adding about 1 million members each year.

In capsule form, then, Revelation 14:6, 7 captures the spirit of Adventis‍ But whence came this movement? What are her roots, in history a‍ Christian thought? What are her distinctive...

The relatively short history of the Seventh-day Adventist Chur‍ shows significant development in the understanding and articulation ‍ doctrine. Among the early Adventists the term "present truth" (deriv‍ from 2 Peter 1:12) enshrined a key idea—that this movement would seek ‍ be led by the Holy Spirit and be open to embrace new understandings as ‍ might direct.

Adventist understanding of doctrine today is encapsulated in t‍ Fundamental Beliefs, which number 28. We should notice the preamb‍ to this statement of beliefs and also the first article. In the preamble we s‍ enshrined the concern that Adventists shall remain open to ongoi‍ understandings of Scripture as the Spirit may lead. And the very first artic‍ sets forth the Scriptures as the basis for Adventist teachings:

> "Seventh-day Adventists accept the Bible as their only creed and hold certain fundamental beliefs to be the teaching of the Holy Scriptures. These beliefs, as set forth here, constitute the church's understanding and expression of the teaching of Scripture. Revision of these statements may be expected at a General Conference session when the church is led by the Holy Spirit to a fuller understanding of Bible truth or finds better language in which to express the teachings of God's Holy Word.

> The Holy Scriptures

> The Holy Scriptures, Old and New Testaments, are the written Word of God, given by divine inspiration through holy men of God who spoke and wrote as they were moved by the Holy Spirit. In this Word, God has committed to man the knowledge necessary for salvation. The Holy Scriptures are the infallible

revelation of His will. They are the standard of character, the test of experience, the authoritative revealer of doctrines, and the trustworthy record of God's acts in history (2 Peters 1:20, 21; 2 Tim. 3:16, 17; Ps. 119:105; Prov. 30:5, 6; Isa. 8:20; John 17:17; I Thess. 2:13; Heb. 4:12).

The doctrines addressed in the 28 Fundamental Beliefs are as follows:

1. The Holy Scriptures
2. The Trinity
3. The Father
4. The Son
5. The Holy Spirit
6. Creation
7. The Nature of Man
8. The Great Controversy between Christ and Satan
9. The Life, Death, and Resurrection of Christ
10. The Experience of Salvation
11. Growing in Christ
12. The Church
13. The Remnant and its Mission
14. Unity in the Body of Christ
15. Baptism
16. The Lord's Supper
17. Spiritual Gifts and Ministries
18. The Gift of Prophecy
19. The Law of God
20. The Sabbath
21. Stewardship
22. Christian Behavior
23. Marriage and the Family
24. Christ's Ministry in the Heavenly Sanctuary
25. The Second Coming of Christ
26. Death and Resurrection
27. The Millennium and the End of Sin
28. The New Earth

These articles can be changed only at a world conference/council of the church, which convenes only every five years. At the last council, in 2005, a new belief was added—"Growing in Christ." This article, which sets forth Jesus' victory over demonic forces and meaninglessness, arose out of mission needs of the global church.

As we look over the 28 statements of Adventist doctrine, we are led to three conclusions: (1) **The articles that are first and form the basis for the reminder, namely articles dealing with the Trinity, the person of Christ, and salvation, conform to ORTHODOX Christian understanding.** (2) Not one of the articles is absolutely unique to the Seventh-day Adventist Church. Even fundamental belief such as no. 24, dealing with the ministry of Christ in the heavenly sanctuary and the pre-Advent judgment, clearly belongs in traditions setting forth the heavenly work of Christ and the final judgment. (3) If we are to speak of uniqueness concerning Adventist doctrine, then, it is in the *configuration* of doctrine rather than in individual beliefs.... So the Adventists leadership believes i and prootes the 'orthodox' (+Catholic) concept of the Trinity.

APPENDIX L:

POPE STYLES HIMSELF GOD ON EARTH:

Quoted in the Great Controversy 1911, page 679 under Appendix, 'General Notes':

"PAGE 50. TITLES.--IN A PASSAGE WHICH IS INCLUDED IN TH ROMAN CATHOLIC CANON LAW, OR CORPUS JURIS CANONIC POPE INNOCENT III DECLARES THAT THE ROMAN PONTIFF I "THE VICEGERENT UPON EARTH, NOT OF A MERE MAN, BUT O VERY GOD;" AND IN A GLOSS ON THE PASSAGE IT I EXPLAINED THAT THIS IS BECAUSE HE IS THE VICEGERENT O CHRIST, WHO IS "VERY GOD AND VERY MAN." SE DECRETALES DOMINI GREGORII PAPAE IX (DECRETALS OF TH LORD POPE GREGORY IX), LIBER 1, DE TRANSLATION EPISCOPORUM, (ON THE TRANSFERENCE OF BISHOPS), TITLE ' CH. 3; CORPUS JURIS CANONICI (2D LEIPZIG ED., 1881), COL. 9' (PARIS, 1612), TOM. 2, DECRETALES, COL. 205. THE DOCUMENT WHICH FORMED THE DECRETALS WERE GATHERED B GRATIAN, WHO WAS TEACHING AT THE UNIVERSITY O BOLOGNA ABOUT THE YEAR 1140. HIS WORK WAS ADDED T AND RE-EDITED BY POPE GREGORY IX IN AN EDITION ISSUE IN 1234. OTHER DOCUMENTS APPEARED IN SUCCEEDING YEAR FROM TIME TO TIME INCLUDING THE EXTRAVAGANTE! ADDED TOWARD THE CLOSE OF THE FIFTEENTH CENTURY, AL OF THESE, WITH GRATIAN'S DECRETUM, WERE PUBLISHED A THE CORPUS JURIS CANONICI IN 1582. POPE PIUS AUTHORIZED THE CODIFICATION IN CANON LAW IN 1904, AN THE RESULTING CODE BECAME EFFECTIVE IN 1918. {GC 679.1}

FOR THE TITLE "LORD GOD THE POPE" SEE A GLOSS ON TH EXTRAVAGANTES OF POPE JOHN XXII, TITLE 14, CH. DECLARAMUS. IN AN ANTWERP EDITION OF TH EXTRAVAGANTES, DATED 1584, THE WORDS "DOMINUM DEU! NOSTRUM PAPAM" ("OUR LORD GOD THE POPE") OCCUR I

OLUMN 153. IN A PARIS EDITION, DATED 1612, THEY OCCUR IN
OLUMN 140. IN SEVERAL EDITIONS PUBLISHED SINCE 1612 THE
/ORD "DEUM" ("GOD") HAS BEEN OMITTED. {GC 679.2}

PAGE 50. INFALLIBILITY.--ON THE DOCTRINE OF
NFALLIBILITY AS SET FORTH AT THE VATICAN COUNCIL OF
370-71, SEE PHILIP SCHAFF, THE CREEDS OF CHRISTENDOM,
OLUME 2, DOGMATIC DECREES OF THE VATICAN COUNCIL,
AGE 234-271, WHERE BOTH THE LATIN AND THE ENGLISH
EXTS ARE GIVEN. FOR DISCUSSION SEE, FOR THE ROMAN
ATHOLIC VIEW, THE CATHOLIC ENCYCLOPEDIA, VOLUME 7,
RT. "INFALLIBILITY," BY PATRICK J. TONER, PAGE 790 FF.;
AMES CARDINAL GIBBONS, THE FAITH OF OUR FATHERS
BALTIMORE: JOHN MURPHY COMPANY, 110TH ED., 1917), CHS.
11. FOR ROMAN CATHOLIC OPPOSITION TO THE DOCTRINE OF
APAL INFALLIBILITY, SEE JOHANN JOSEPH IGNAZ VON
OLLINGER (PSEUDONYM "JANUS") THE POPE AND THE
OUNCIL (NEW YORK: CHARLES SCRIBNER'S SONS, 1869); AND
'.J. SPARROW SIMPSON, ROMAN CATHOLIC OPPOSITION TO
APAL INFALLIBILITY (LONDON: JOHN MURRAY, 1909). FOR THE
ON-ROMAN VIEW, SEE GEORGE SALMON, INFALLIBILITY OF
HE CHURCH (LONDON: JOHN MURRAY, REV. ED., 1914)."

Found in the Registers of Boniface VIII in the Vatican Archives: "Reg.
atic", LFol. 387, The Catholic Encyclopedia, 1913 by the Encyclopedia
·ess, Inc.:

In the Papal Bull 'Sanctum' put out by Pope Boniface Viii
(Benedetto Gaetani) on November 18, 1302, he declared:

"The Roman Pontiff judges all men, but is judged by no
one.

"We declare, assert, define and pronounce: to be subject to
the Roman Pontiff is to every human creature altogether
necessary for salvation...

"That which was spoken of Christ...

"Thou hast subdued all things under His feet, may well
seem verified in me. I have authority of the King of kings.

"I am all in all and above all, so that God, Himself and I,
the Vicar of God, have but one consistory, and I am able to do
almost all that God can do.

"What therefore, can you make of me but God?"

U.S. Roman Catholic Church And Protestant Denominations Agree To Recognize Each Other's Baptism

Posted: 01/29/2013 3:37 pm EST | Updated: 01/29/2013 5:17 pm EST
(http://www.huffingtonpost.com/2013/01/29/catholic-protestant-baptism-
recognize_n_2575915.html)

Follow:
Catholic Church, Christian Reformed Church In North America, Commo
Agreement On Mutual Recognition Of Baptism, Presbyterian Church
(USA), Ecumenical Relations, Reformed Church In America, United
Church Of Christ, Religion News

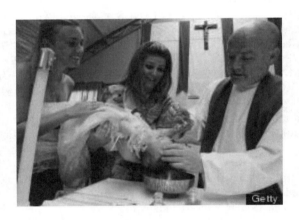

The Rev. Cuthbert O'Connell baptizes baby Trish Cucurullo as moth
Sheena Cucurullo (L) and godmother Shannon Ball assist following Sund
Mass at Saint Clare Catholic Church's on August 19, 2007 in Wavelan
Mississippi.

In a monumental occasion for ecumenical relations, the U.S. Rom
Catholic church and a group of Protestant denominations plan to sign
document on Tuesday evening to formally agree to recognize each othe
baptisms.

Catholic leaders will join representatives from the Presbyterian Chur
(U.S.A.), Christian Reformed Church in North America, Reformed Chur
in America and United Church of Christ at the ceremony in Austin, Texa
to sign the agreement, which is called the "Common Agreement on Mutu

ecognition of Baptism." The event coincides with the national meeting of
hristian Churches Together in the U.S.A.

Currently, the Protestant churches recognize Roman Catholic baptisms,
it the Catholic church does not always recognize theirs. The mutual
greement on baptisms, a key sacrament in the churches, has been discussed
etween denominational leadership for seven years **and hinges in part on
voking trinity of the "Father, Son and Holy Spirit" during the
aptism.**

In a report in the <u>Austin American-Statesman</u>, Bishop Joe Vasquez of the
iocese Austin told the newspaper that the effort "is part of our response to
sus' prayer that 'we all be one.'"

The Roman Catholic church as a whole has generally recognized the
ptisms of most mainstream Christian denominations since the Second
atican Council, a series of historic church meetings from 1962 to 1965,
it the formal baptism agreement is the first of its kind for the U.S. church.

According to a <u>prior statement from the U.S. Conference of Catholic
shops</u>, which was released in 2010 when bishops were deliberating the
reement, the understanding between the churches "affirms that both
itholic and Reformed Christians hold that baptism is the sacramental bond
unity for the Body of Christ, which is to be performed only once, by an
thorized minister, with flowing water, using the Scriptural Trinitarian
rmula of 'Father, Son and Holy Spirit.' The agreement encourages all local
iristian communities to keep baptismal records."

**The Austin newspaper reported that Tuesday's agreement says that
or our baptisms to be mutually recognized, water and the scriptural
initarian formula 'Father, Son, and Holy Spirit' (Matthew 28: 19-20)
ust be used in the baptismal rite."**

The earlier bishops' statement explained the origins of the agreement:
n 2002, concerns over certain practices (such as baptism by sprinkling)
d spoken formulas (such as baptism in the name of the Creator, Redeemer
d Sanctifier) used by some Christians led the Pontifical Council for the
omotion of Christian Unity to urge national bishops' conferences to study
eir mutual understanding of baptism with other Christians. These
estions were examined and resolved by Round Seven of the Reformed-
oman Catholic Dialogue-USA, which produced the Common Agreement,
well as a study entitled "These Living Waters."

The agreement was first approved in 2008 by the General Assembly of the
esbyterian Church (U.S.A.). American Catholic leaders voted on the it in
10 and the agreement was later approved by the governing bodies of the
iristian Reformed Church in North America, Reformed Church in
nerica and United Church of Christ.

APPENDIX N:

STANFORD ENCYCLOPEDIA OF PHILOSOPHY -- SUPPLEMENT TO TRINITY:

History of Trinitarian Doctrines

"Sometimes popular antitrinitarian literature paints the doctrine strongly influenced by, or even illicitly poached from some non-Christia religious or philosophical tradition. Divine threesomes abound in th religious writings and art of ancient Europe, Egypt, and the near east, not mention Hinduism and Mahayana Buddhism. These include vario threesomes of male deities, of female deities, of Father-Mother-Son group or of one body with three heads, or three faces on one head (Griffiths 1996 However, similarity alone doesn't prove Christian copying or indire influence, and many of these examples are because of their time and pla less likely to have influenced the development of the Christian doctrine the Trinity.

"There is, however, arguably a direct influence on early Christia theology by Platonist Jewish philosopher and theologian Philo Alexandria (a.k.a. Philo Judaeus) (ca. 20 BCE - ca. 50 CE). Inspired by th *Timaeus* of Plato, Philo read various Jewish scriptures as teaching that Go created the cosmos by his Word (*logos*) or creative power, and that subsequently governs the cosmos through the seemingly personal agency the Word together with that of God's royal power (Philo *Works*; Morga 1853, 63-148; Norton 1859, 332-74; Wolfson 1973, 60-97).

"Another striking parallel, which has been cited by friends and foes Trinity doctrines, is found in Plotinus' (204–70 CE) triad of the On Intellect, and Soul, in which the latter two mysteriously emanate from th One, and "are the One and not the One; they are the one because they a from it; they are not the One, because it endowed them with what they ha while remaining by itself" (Plotinus *Enneads*, 85).

"Many thinkers influential in the development of trinitarian doctrin were steeped in the thought not only of Middle Platonism a Neoplatonism, but also the Stoics, Aristotle, and other currents in Gre philosophy (Hanson 1988, 856–869). Whether one sees this background a providentially supplied and useful tool, or as an unavoidably distorti influence, those developing the doctrine saw themselves as trying to build

stematic Christian theology on the Bible while remaining faithful to
rlier post-biblical tradition. Many also had the aim of showing
hristianity to be consistent with the best of Greek philosophy. But even if
e doctrine had a non-Christian origin, it would would not follow that it is
lse or unjustified; it could be, that through Philo (or whomever), God
vealed the doctrine to the Christian church. Still, it is contested issue
nether or not the doctrine can be deduced or otherwise inferred from the
hristian Bible, so we must turn to it…

"No trinitarian doctrine is explicitly taught in the Old Testament.
initarians normally grant this, holding that the doctrine was revealed by
od only later, in New Testament times (c.50–c.100) and/or in the Patristic
a (c. 100–800)…."

PENDIX O:

ROM: HTTP://SUSPICIOUSBEREAN.BLOGSPOT.COM
010/06/EDINBURGH-2010-ECUMENICAL-
OVEMENT.HTML

JESDAY, JUNE 15, 2010

linburgh 2010: The ecumenical movement
serves its 100th anniversary

d even things without life giving sound, whether pipe or harp, except
y give a distinction in the sounds, how shall it be known what is piped or
ped?

r if the trumpet give an uncertain sound, who shall prepare himself to the
tle?

likewise ye, except ye utter by the tongue words easy to be understood,
w shall it be known what is spoken? for ye shall speak into the air. I
rinthians 14:7-9

conference to mark the centenary of the World Missionary Conference
s held in Edinburgh from June 2-6, 2010. The conference
anizers acknowledge that the 1910 Edinburgh Conference is considered
starting point of the contemporary ecumenical movement, due to its

607

insistence on the importance of unity and cooperation in worldwi‹ mission.

The participants in 1910 were Protestant churches and missiona‹ organizations, but the 2010 conference includes Pentecostals, Rom‹ Catholics, Orthodox churches, **and even Seventh-Day Adventists**, whi‹ may lead one to wonder what gospel will be proclaimed. Pope Bened‹ XVI sent a formal greeting:
'I send my greetings to those gathered during these days in Scotland for t‹ centennial of the first Edinburgh Missionary Conference, which is n‹ acknowledged to have given birth to the modern ecumenical moveme‹ May we all renew our commitment to work humbly and patiently, under t‹ guidance of the Holy Spirit, to live again together our common aposto‹ heritage.'
Those interested in the liberal slant of Edinburgh 2010 should go to t‹ conference's website and click on the various links. I'll quote a f‹ paragraphs from their Common Call, issued on June 6:

1. Trusting in the triune God and with a renewed sense of urgency, we ‹ called to incarnate and proclaim the good news of salvation, of forgiven‹ of sin, of life in abundance, and of liberation for all poor and oppressed. V‹ are challenged to witness and evangelism in such a way that we are a livi‹ demonstration of the love, righteousness and justice that God intends for t‹ whole world.

2. Remembering Christ's sacrifice on the Cross and his resurrection for t‹ world's salvation, and empowered by the Holy Spirit, we are called ‹ authentic dialogue, respectful engagement and humble witness amo‹ people of other faiths--and no faith--to the uniqueness of Christ. C‹ approach is marked with bold confidence in the gospel message; it bui‹ friendship, seeks reconciliation and practices hospitality.

3. Knowing the Holy Spirit who blows over the world at will, reconnecti‹ creation and bringing authentic life, we are called to become communit‹ of compassion and healing, where young people are actively participating‹ mission, and women and men share power and responsibilities fairly, wh‹ there is a zeal for justice, peace and the protection of the environment, a‹ renewed liturgy reflecting the beauties of the Creator and creation.

4. Disturbed by the asymmetries and imbalances of power that divide a‹ trouble us in church and world, we are called to repentance, to criti‹

flection on systems of power, and to accountable use of power structures. e are called to find practical ways to live as members of One Body in full vareness that God resists the proud, Christ welcomes and empowers the or and afflicted, and the power of the Holy Spirit is manifested in our lnerability.

Recognizing the need to shape a new generation of leaders with thenticity for mission in a world of diversities in the twenty-first century, e are called to work together in new forms of theological education. ecause we are all made in the image of God, these will draw on one other's unique charisms, challenge each other to grow in faith and derstanding, share resources equitably worldwide, involve the entire man being and the whole family of God, and respect the wisdom of our ders while also fostering the participation of children.

BIBLIOGRAPHY:

A Redemptorist Pastoral Publication. *Handbook for Today's Catholic.* Liguori, MC
    Liguori Publications, 1994.

Andrews, J. N. "Immortality Through Christ." *Review and Herald*, January 27,
    1874.

—. "Melchisedec." *Review and Herald*, September 7, 1869.

Andrews, J.N. *The Three Angels Messages.* Cedar Lake, MI: Waymark Books,
    2011.

B. B. Beach; Dr. Lukas Vischer. *So Much in Common.* Geneva: World Council of
    CHurches, 1973.

Barnhouse, Dr. Donald. *Eternity*, September 1956.

Bates, Joseph. "Past and Present Experience." (Letter written to William Miller),
    1848.

—. *The Autobiography Of Elder Joseph Bates.* Battle Creek, MI: Steam Press of th
    Seventh-day Adventist Publishing Assoc., 1868.

Bediako, Daniel K. "Distinct, But Indivisible." *Adventist World*, June 2012.

Bruinsma, Reinder. *Our Awesome God.* Pacific Press Publishing Assoc., 2000.

Butler, G. I. "Letter to J. H. Kellogg." April 5, 1904.

Cardinal Newman; Bishop Challoner; Bishop of Nottingham; Right Rev. Mgr. John
    S. Vaughan; Mgr De Segur; Rev. A. J. Saxton; Rev. R. F. Clarke, S.J.;
    Saint Augustine; Mother Mary Loyola; Father Jerome Savonarola, O.P.;
    and many other renowned Catholic wrtrs. *The Holy Catholic Faith or The
    Lamp of Truth in the Catholic Home Volume 1.* Patrick L. Baine Publishe
    n.d.

Cornell, Merritt E. *Facts for the Times.* Battle Creek, MI: Merritt E. Cornell, 1858.

Cottrell, R. J. "The Trinity." *Review and Herald*, July 6, 1869.

Daniels, A. G. "Letter to W. C. White." October 29, 1903.

Davidson, Jo Ann. "God in Three Persons, Blessed Trinity." *Adventist World*, Marc
    2011.

Dederen, Raoul. "The Mistry of the Trinity - God as Father, Son, and Holy Spirit."
    Adventist Review, August 20, 1993: 8.

Froom, Leroy E. *Movement of Destiny.* Washington D.C. : Review and Herald
    Publishing Assoc., 1928.

—. *Seventh-day Adventist Bible Commentary Volume 7A.* Review and Herald
    Publishing Assoc., 1970.

General Conference of SDA. "Glimpses of Our God." *Sabbath School Quarterly, 1
    Quarter.* 2012. 7.

—. "Growing in Christ." *Sabbath School Quarterly, 4th Quarter.* 2012. 17.

—. "The Holy Spirit." *Sabbath School Quarterly, 2nd Quarter.* 2006.

Gibbons, Edward. *History of Christianity.* 1891.

Gulley, Norman R. "1+1+1=1 - The Keystone of Biblical Theology." *Adventist
    World*, February 2010.

Guy, Fritz. "Uncovering the Origins of the Twenty-seven Fundamental Beliefs."
    Being Adventist in 21st Century Australia, September 2002.

Bibliography

askell, Stephen N. *The Story of the Seer of Patmos*. South Lancaster, MA: South Lancaster Printing Company, 1905.

olt, Russell. *The Doctrine of the Trinity in the Seventh-day Adventist Dnomination: Its Rejection and Acceptance*. Berrien Springs, MI: (Term Paper, Seventh-day Adventish Theological Seminary), 1969.

ull, D. W. "Bible Doctrine of the Divinity of Christ." *Review and Herald*, November 10, 1859.

urdon, John A. "Catholic Doctrine on the Holy Trinity." *The Catholic Faith*, May/June 2001.

m Pinkoski; Doug Batchelor; Pastor Anderson. *What About the Trinity?* Amazing Facts, 2007.

ohnsson, William. *Review and Herald*, January 6, 1994.

ones, A. T. *The Two Republics*. Battle Creek, MI: Review and Herald, 1891.

ellogg, J. H. "Letter to G. I. Butler." October 28, 1903.

—. "Letter to G. I. Butler." February 21, 1904.

ellogg, John Harvey. *The Living Temple*. Battle Creek, Mi: Good Health Publishing Company, 1903.

night, George. "Adventists and Change." *Ministry Magazine*, October 1993.

ung, Hans. *Christianity: Essence, History, and Future*. New York: John Bowden, 1995.

ibreria Editrice Vaticana. *Catechism of the Catholic Church*. Liguori, MO: Liguori Publications, 1994.

imborch, Phillipus. *The History of the Inquisition*. London: London: Sold by J. Gray, 1731.

oughborough, John N. "Guidance of Nature." *Review and Herald*, November 5, 1861.

—. "Questions for Brother Loughborough." *Review and Herald Volume 18*, November 5, 1861.

inisterial Association. *Seventh-day Adventists Believe...A Biblical Exposition of 27 Fundamental Doctrines*. Ministerial Association of the General Conference of SDA, 1988.

orrow, Bishop Louis Laravoire. *My Catholic Faith*. Kenosha, WI: My Mission House, n.d.

orth American Division Officers and Union Presidents. *Issues: The Seventh-day Adventist Church and Certian Private Ministries*. North American Division, 1992.

rescott, W. W. "The Word Became Flesh." *The Bible Echo*, January 6 and 13, 1896.

.R. "Response to Angel Rodriguez's Article in Sept. 2010." *Adventist World*, December 2010.

odriquez, Angel. "Question: Had Jesus sinned, what would have happened to Him?" *Adventist World*, September 2010.

eventh-day Adventists. *A Declaration of the Fundamental Principles Taught and Practiced by Seventh-day Adventists*. Declaration, Battle Creek, MI: Steam Press of the Seventh-day Adventist Publishing Assoc., 1872.

611

Bibliography

Sir William Smith and Henry Wace London. *A Dictionary of Christian Biography Volume 1.* 1877.

Smith, Uriah. "The Spirit of Prophecy and Our Relation to It - Sermon given on March 14, 1891." *General Conference Daily Bulletin, Volume 4*, March 18, 1891.

—. *Looking Unto Jesus.* Chicago: Review and Herald, 1898.

—. *Looking Unto Jesus.* Chicago, IL: Review and Herald , 1898.

—. "S. D. Adventist not Orthodox." *Review and Herald*, March 27, 1888.

—. *Thoughts on the Book of Daniel and the Revelation.* Nashville, TN: Southern Publishing Assoc., 1897.

Spephenson, J. M. "The Atonement." *Review and Herald*, November 21, 1854.

Steinweg, Virginia. *Without Fear for Favor.* Review and Herald, 1979.

Stephenson, J. M. "The Atonement." *Review and Herald*, November 21, 1854.

Stump, Allen. *The Foundation of our Faith.* Welch, VA: Smyrna Gospel Ministries, 2000.

The Catholic Answers. On-Line, 2004.

The Century Distionary and Cyclopedia Volume 1. New York: The Century Company, 1880.

The Concise Oxford Dictionary. Oxford at the Clarendon Press, 1963.

The Encyclopaedia Britannica. Enclycopaedia Britannica, Inc, 1976.

Tuberville, Dr. Henry. *Douay Catechism.* New York: P.J. Kenedy, Excelsior Catholic Publishing House, 1649.

Waggoner, E. J. "Studies in the Book of Hebrews." *General Conference Bulletin*, February 17, 1897.

—. "Sensuous Religion." *Signs of the Times*, December 14, 1888.

—. "The Editor's Private Corner. Do You Believe? (Continued.)." *The Present Truth (UK)*, July 30, 1903.

—. "The Editor's Private Corner. The Spirit that Witnesses." *The Present Truth (UK)*, February 6, 1902.

Waggoner, Joseph H. *The Atonement in the Light of Nature and Revelation.* Oakland, CA: Pacific Press Publishing Company, 1884.

Washburn, Judson Sylvaneous. (Letter written by Washburn in 1939), 1939.

White, Ellen G. *1888 Materials.* Silver Springs, MD: Ellen G. White Estate, 1987.

—. *Acts of the Apostles.* Mountain View, CA: Pacific Press Publishing Assoc., 1911.

—. "The Sabbath of the Bible." *Bible Echo*, October 12, 1896.

—. "To the Little Rremnant Scattered Abroad." *Broadside 1, To the Little Remnant Scattered Abroad*, April 6, 1846.

—. *Christ Object Lessons.* Washington DC: Review and Herald Publishing Assoc., 1900.

—. *Christ Triumphant.* Hagerstown, MD: Review and Herald Publishing Assoc., 1999.

—. *Conflict and Courage.* Hagerstown, MD: Review and Herald Publishing Assoc., 1970.

—. *Counsels for the Church.* Mountain View, CA: Pacific Press Publishing Assoc., 1991.

—. *Counsels on Health.* Mountain View, CA: Pacific Press Publishing Assoc., 1923.

Bibliography

–. *Desire of Ages*. Mountain View, CA: Pacific Press Publishing Assoc., 1898.

–. *Early Writings*. Hagerstown, MD: Review and Herald Publishing Assoc., 1882.

–. *Education*. Mountain View, CA: Pacific Press Publishing Assoc., 1903.

–. *Evangelism*. Washington D.C.: Review and Herald, 1946.

–. *Faith I Live By*. Hagerstown, MD: Review and Herald Publishing Assoc., 1958.

–. "Abiding in Christ." *General Conference Bulletin*, May 17, 1909.

–. "Seeking the Lost." *General Conference bulletin*, December 1, 1895.

–. *God's Amazing Grace*. Washington DC: Review and Herald Publishing Assoc., 1973.

–. *In Heavenly Places*. Washington DC: Review and Herald Publishing Assoc., 1967.

–. *Last Day Events*. Boise, ID: Pacific Press Publishing Assoc., 1992.

–. *Lift Him Up*. Hagerstown, MD: Review and Herald Publishing Assoc., 1988.

–. "Manuscript 101." Ellen G. White Estate, 1897.

–. "Manuscript Release Number 760." Ellen G. White Estate, 1980-1981.

–. *Manuscript Releases Volume 10*. Silver Springs, MD: Ellen G. White Estate, 1990.

–. *Manuscript Releases Volume 11*. Silver Springs, MD: Ellen G. White Estate, 1990.

–. *Manuscript Releases Volume 12*. Silver Spings, MD: Ellen G. White Estate, 1990.

–. *Manuscript Releases Volume 13*. Silver Springs, MD: Ellen G. White Estate, 1990.

–. *Manuscript Releases Volume 14*. Silver Springs, MD: Ellen G. White Estate, 1990.

–. *Manuscript Releases Volume 16*. Silver Springs, MD: Ellen G. White Estate, 1990.

–. *Manuscript Releases Volume 2*. Silver Springs, MD: Ellen G. White Estate, 1987.

–. *Manuscript Releases Volume 4*. Silver Springs, MD: Ellen G. White Estate, 1990.

–. *Manuscript Releases Volume 9*. Silver Springs, MD: Ellen G. White Estate, 1990.

–. *Manuscript Releases, Volume 20*. Silver Springs, MD: Ellen G. White Estate, 1993.

–. *Mind, Character, and Personality Volume 1*. Nashville, TN: Southern Publishing Assoc., 1977.

–. *Mind, Character, and Personality Volume 2*. Nashville, TN: Southern Publishing Assoc., 1977.

. *Ministry of Healing*. Mountain View, CA: Pacific Press Publishing Assoc., 1905.

. *My Life Today*. Hagerstown, MD: Review and Herald Publishing Assoc., 1952.

. *Our Father Cares*. Washington DC: Review and Herald Publishing Assoc., 1991.

. *Our High Calling*. Washington DC: Review and Herald Publishing Assoc., 1961.

Bibliography

—. *Patriachs & Prophets*. Mountain View, CA: Pacific Press Publishing Assoc., 1890.

—. *Peter's Counsel to Parents*. Washington DC: Review and Herald Publishing Assoc., 1981.

—. *Reflecting Christ*. Washington DC: Review and Herald Publishing Assoc., 1985

—. "A Message to Parents." *Review and Herald*, February 1, 1912.

—. "Christ Man's Example." *Review and Herald*, July 5, 1887.

—. "Christian Perfection." *Review and Herald*, April 24, 1900.

—. "How to Meet a Controverted Point of Doctrine." *Review and Herald*, February 18, 1890.

—. "Lessons From the Second Chapter of Philippians." *Review and Herald*, June 1. 1905.

—. "Notes of Travel - Meetings in Chicago." *Review and Herald*, February 10, 1885.

—. "Teach the Word." *Review and Herald*, October 22, 1903.

—. "The Australian Camp Meeting." *Review and Herald*, January 7, 1896.

—. "The Promise of the Spirit." *Review and Herald*, May 19, 1904.

—. "The Remission of Sins." *Review and Herald*, June 13, 1899.

—. "The Sin of Licentiousness." *Review and Herald*, May 17, 1887.

—. "The Word Made Flesh." *Review and Herald*, April 5, 1906.

—. "The Work in Washington." *Review and Herald*, June 1, 1905.

—. "Ye Shall Receive Power." *Sabbath School Worker*, December 1, 1909.

—. *SDA Bible Commentary Volume 1*. Washington DC: Review and Herald Publishing Assoc., 1953.

—. *SDA Bible Commentary Volume 5*. Washington DC: Review and Herald Publishing Assoc., 1956.

—. *SDA Bible Commentary Volume 6*. Washington DC: Review and Herald Publishing Assoc., 1956.

—. *SDA Bible Commentary Volume 7*. Washington DC: Review and Herald Publishing Assoc., 1957.

—. *SDA Bible Commentary Volume 7A*. Washington DC: Review and Herald Publishing Assoc., 1970.

—. *Selected Messages Book 1*. Washington DC: Review and Herald Publishing Assoc., 1958.

—. *Selected Messages Book 2*. Washington DC: Review and Herald Publishing Assoc., 1958.

—. *Selected Messages Book 3*. Washington DC: Review and Herald Publishing Assoc., 1980.

—. *Sermons and Talks Volume 1*. Silver Springs, MD: Ellen G. White Estates, 199

—. "Christ Glorified." *Signs of the Times*, May 10, 1899.

—. "Christ Our Complete Salvation." *Signs of the Times*, May 30, 1895.

—. "Christ the Lawgiver." *Signs of the Times*, April 8, 1897.

—. "Continue in the Son and in the Father." *Signs of the Times*, July 4, 1895.

—. "Faith Brings Light." *Signs of the Times*, October 3, 1892.

—. "Parable of the Householder." *Signs of the Times*, March 8, 1899.

—. "Prompt and Cheerful Obedience." *Signs of the Times*, July 22, 1886.

Bibliography

–. "Resistance to Light #3." *Signs of the Times*, August 29, 1900.

–. "Sin Condemned in the Flesh." *Signs of the Times*, January 16, 1896.

–. "The True Sheep Respond to the Voice of." *Signs of the Times*, November 27, 1893.

–. "The Word Made Flesh." *Signs of the Times*, May 3, 1899.

–. "To Abide in Christ the Will Must Be Surrendered." *Signs of the Times*, October 29, 1894.

–. *Sons and Daughters of God.* Washington DC: Review and Herald Publishing Assoc., 1955.

–. *Special Testimonies, Volume B, Number 2.* Review and Herald, 1903.

–. *Special Testimonies, Volume B, Number 7.* Review and Herald, 1906.

–. *Special Testimonies, Volume B, Number 9.* Review and Herald Publishing Assoc., 1907.

–. *Spirit of Prophecy Volume 1.* Battle Creek, ME: SDA Publishing Assoc., 1870.

–. *Spirit of Prophecy Volume 2.* Battle Creek, MI: SDA Publishing Assoc., 1877.

–. *Spirit of Prophecy Volume 3.* Battle Creek, MI: SDA Publishing Assoc., 1878.

–. *Spirit of Prophecy Volume 4.* Battle Creek, MI: SDA Publishing Assoc., 1884.

–. *Spiritual Gifts Volume 2.* Washington DC: Review and Herald Publishing Assoc., 1860.

–. *Testimonies on Sexual Behavior, Adultery, and Divorce.* Silver Springs, MD: Ellen G. White Estates, 1989.

–. *Testimonies to Ministers.* Boise, ID: Pacific Press Publishing Assoc., 1923.

–. *Testimonies to the Church Volume 1.* Mountain View, CA: Pacific Press Publishing Assoc., 1855-1868.

–. *Testimonies to the Church Volume 2.* Mountain View, CA: Pacific Press Publishing Assoc., 1868-1871.

–. *Testimonies to the Church Volume 3.* Mountain View, CA: Pacific Press Publishing Assoc., 1875.

–. *Testimonies to the Church Volume 4.* Mountain View, CA: Pacific Press Publishing Assoc., 1881.

–. *Testimonies to the Church Volume 5.* Mountain View, CA: Pacific Press Publishing Assoc., 1882-1889.

–. *Testimonies to the Church Volume 8,.* Mountain View, CA: Pacific Press Publishing Assoc., 1904.

–. *The Great Controversy.* Mountain View, CA: Pacific Press Publishing Assoc., 1888.

. "Respond to Divine Love." *The Home Missionary*, December 1, 1894.

. "Against Principalities and Powers." *The Youth's Instructor*, October 26, 1899.

. "Child Life of Jesus." *The Youth's Instructor*, November 21, 1895.

. "Sacrificed For Us." *The Youth's Instructor*, July 20, 1899.

. "The Lord is Risen." *The Youth's Instructor*, May 2, 1901.

. "The Price of our Redemption." *The Youth's Instructor*, June 21, 1900.

. *This Day With God.* Washington DC: Review and Herald Publishing Assoc., 1979.

. *Thoughts from the Mount of Blessings.* Mountain View, CA: Pacific Press Publishing Assoc., 1896.

Bibliography

—. *Upward Look.* Hagerstown, MD: Review and Herald Publishing Assoc., 1982.

White, James S. *Bible Adventism.* Battle Creek, MI: Seventh-day Adventist Publishing Assoc., n.d.

—. *Life Incidents.* Battle Creek, MI: Seventh-day Adventist Publishing Assoc., 1868.

—. "Christ Equal With God." *Review and Herald*, November 29, 1877.

—. "Mutual Obligation." *review and Herald*, June 13, 1871.

—. "The Position of the Remnant." *Review and Herald*, September 12, 1854: 36.

—. "The Word." *Review and Herald*, February 7, 1856 : 148.

—. "The Day Star." *The Day Star*, January 24, 1846.

Wilkenson, B. G. *Truth Triumphant.* Teach Services, 1994.

Woodrow Whidden, Jerry Moon, John W. Reeve. *The Trinity.* Hagerstown, MD: Review and Herald Publishing Assoc., 2002.

Workers from various Unions of the Seventh-day Adventists. *SDA Yearbook.* Battle Creek, MI: Review and Herald Publishing Assoc., 1889.

—. *SDA Yearbook.* Washington D.C.: Review and Herald Publishing Assoc., 1981.